The Essentials of Family Therapy

Third Edition

Michael P. Nichols

Virginia Consortium Program in Clinical Psychology
College of William and Mary

with

Richard C. Schwartz

Director, The Center for Self Leadership, Oak Park, Illinois

Boston ● New York ● San Francisco
Mexico City ● Montreal ● Toronto ● London ● Madrid ● Munich ● Paris
Hong Kong ● Singapore ● Tokyo ● Cape Town ● Sydney

Senior Series Editor: Patricia Quinlin
Series Editorial Assistant: Sara Holliday
Marketing Manager: Laura Lee Manley
Editorial Production Service: Omegatype Typography, Inc.
Composition Buyer: Linda Cox
Manufacturing Buyer: JoAnne Sweeney
Electronic Composition: Omegatype Typography, Inc.
Cover Administrator: Kristina Mose-Libon

For related titles and support materials, visit our online catalog at www.ablongman.com.

Between the time website information is gathered and then published, it is not unusual for some sites to have closed. Also, the transcription of URLs can result in typographical errors. The publisher would appreciate notification where these errors occur so that they may be corrected in subsequent editions.

Library of Congress Cataloging-in-Publication Data

Nichols, Michael P.
    The essentials of family therapy / Michael P. Nichols with Richard C. Schwartz. — 3rd ed.
        p.   cm.
    Brief ed. of: Family therapy : concepts and methods / Michael P. Nichols with Richard
    C. Schwartz. Boston : Pearson / Allyn & Bacon, 2006.
    Includes bibliographical references and index.
    ISBN 0-205-49615-6
    1. Family psychotherapy.   I. Schwartz, Richard C.   II. Title.

RC488.5.N528 2007
616.89'156—dc22

                                                                        2006043232

Printed in the United States of America

10   9   8   7   6   5   4   3   2   1   RRD-VA   11   10   09   08   07   06

Credits appear on page 377, which constitutes an extension of this copyright page.

Contents

PART I   ●   The Context of Family Therapy

---

1   The Foundations of Family Therapy   1

2   The Evolution of Family Therapy   7

PART II ● The Classic Schools of Family Therapy

5 Bowen Family Systems Therapy   81

6 Strategic Family Therapy   102

7   Structural Family Therapy   126

8   Experiential Family Therapy   147

9 Psychoanalytic Family Therapy   167

10 Cognitive-Behavior Family Therapy   189

PART III   ● Recent Developments in Family Therapy

11 Family Therapy in the Twenty-First Century   212

PART IV   ●   The Evaluation of Family Therapy

16 Family Therapy Research: Empirical Foundations and Practice Implications   311

Cynthia Rowe, Ligia Gómez, and Howard Liddle

Foreword

Students of family therapy owe a tremendous debt to Michael Nichols and Richard Schwartz. The theoretical and clinical insights of the revolutionary field of family therapy are scattered through many sources. They thus are often difficult to find and sometimes hard to understand. These authors have done a magnificent job of searching out and reporting both theoretical concepts and clinical techniques. In this third edition, they have strengthened and updated what is surely the best textbook in family therapy.

Because family therapy is now clearly established and embodied in so many different approaches, it's difficult for anyone writing a foreword to say anything new. I'll try to offer some general comments and some of my own experiences.

In the 1960s I was editing *Family Process* and searching the field for new ideas. As I went about trying to get papers for the journal, I became a therapist-watcher visiting different groups. It was interesting to see how people defined family therapy and how often therapists changed the name but not the game as they continued in their usual way of doing therapy while calling it *family therapy*.

Now, a half-century later, one can look back and remember the tremendous outpouring of ideas as well as the passion and excitement of the pioneers. They had discovered something very new, something they had not been trained to understand. I can recall running a meeting in the late 1960s to honor Don Jackson who had recently died. Approximately forty-five therapists attended, almost all of the family therapists in the country at that time. At that meeting, these therapists realized that their views were very different from each other's, and yet it was all family therapy. No one at that time could imagine a textbook encompassing all of this diversity.

It is interesting to be an author who has had his work summarized in a textbook. My various projects included ten years with Gregory Bateson, an unorthodox anthropologist; ten years with John Weakland, a chemical engineer; equal time with William Fry, a student of humor; five years at the Mental Research Institute with Don Jackson, a uniquely innovative psychiatrist; and three years with Virginia Satir, a gifted social worker. I spent ten years in Philadelphia with Salvador Minuchin, who was doing serious work with the poor when others were not, and seventeen years consulting with Milton Erickson, who was a psychiatrist different from all others. I spent ten years in private practice, doing brief therapy and consulting with Erickson.

Those therapists who were willing to be unorthodox brought about change. The defense of orthodoxy—long-term therapy and psychodynamic theory—was everywhere, and change was difficult. Perhaps unorthodox people are necessary to get beyond an orthodox therapy.

The authors of this textbook did well in describing our group as well as other groups I observed over the years. The remarkable thing was how therapists shifted in a decade or so from a passive individual therapy that was financially rewarding, to a social, active therapy, in which the ideas and techniques and philosophy were exactly the opposite.

This text reminds me of the controversies and disagreements that therapists enjoyed in that time of change. I recall that a group of psychiatric residents in San Francisco invited me to teach them a seminar in family therapy. They asked to see me at night and to keep it a secret. It became necessary to train therapists in private institutes and workshops because academicians were still hanging on to the past.

Those days are gone, as this textbook shows. The teachers of the past had to revise their fundamental beliefs as times changed and their students were taking up interactional family views. It was hard on some teachers, usually the better ones, because they had learned their traditional ideas so well and had great investments in them. Now, for better or worse, interpersonal ideas have become established in the field, and this change affects research, diagnosis, and definitions of therapy. Thanks to Mike Nichols and Dick Schwartz, we have a splendid summary of family therapy's past and an indispensable guide to its future.

Jay Haley

Preface

One thing that tends to get lost in academic discussions of family therapy is the feeling of accomplishment that comes from sitting down with an unhappy family and being able to help them. Beginning therapists are understandably anxious about how to proceed. ("How do you get *all of them* to come in?") Veterans often speak in abstractions. They have opinions and discuss big issues—postmodernism, managed care, second-order cybernetics. Although it is tempting to use this space to say Important Things, I prefer to be a little more personal. Treating troubled families has given me the greatest satisfaction imaginable, and I hope that the same is, or will be, true for you.

In this third edition of *The Essentials of Family Therapy*, we try to describe the full scope of family therapy—its rich history, the classic schools, the latest developments—but with more emphasis on clinical practice than history and theory. There are lots of changes in this version: quite a few more case studies; practical suggestions for treating single-parent families, African American families, and gay and lesbian families; more up-to-date descriptions of the latest models; new sections on ethics, home-based care, and research; a richer description of the contemporary influences on the field; and a more thorough and consistent emphasis on clinical techniques throughout.

When you read about therapy, it can be hard to see past the jargon and political packaging to the essential ideas and practices. So, in preparing this volume, we traveled widely to visit and observe the actual sessions of the leading practitioners. The result is a more pragmatic, clinical focus. We hope you like it.

So many people have contributed to my development as a family therapist and to the writing of this book that it is impossible to thank them all. But I would like to single out a few. To the people who taught me family therapy—Lyman Wynne, Murray Bowen, and Salvador Minuchin—thank you.

Some of the people who went out of their way to help us prepare this book were Frank Dattilio, Insoo Berg, Cheryl Rampage, Kathy Weingarten, Leslie Greenberg, Vicki Dickerson, Jeff Zimmerman, Cloe Madanes, Jay Haley, and Salvador Minuchin. To paraphrase John, Paul, George, and Ringo, we get by with *a lot* of help from our friends—and we thank them one and all. We are especially grateful to Patricia Quinlin and Sara Holliday at Allyn and Bacon for making a hard job easier.

Finally, I would like to thank my postgraduate instructors in family life: my wife, Melody, and my children, Sandy and Paul. In the brief span of thirty-nine years, Melody has seen me grow from a shy young man, totally ignorant of how to be a husband and father, to a shy middle-aged man, still bewildered and still trying. Sandy and Paul never cease to amaze me. If in my wildest dreams as a young man I had imagined children to love and be proud of, I wouldn't even have come close to any as fine as Sandy and Paul.

Michael P. Nichols

Major Events in the History of Family Therapy

	Social and Political Context	Development of Family Therapy
1945	F.D.R. dies, Truman becomes president World War II ends in Europe (May 8) and the Pacific (August 14)	Bertalanffy presents general systems theory
1946	Juan Perón elected president of Argentina	Bowen at Menninger Clinic Whitaker at Emory Macy Conference
1947	India partitioned into India and Pakistan	
1948	Truman reelected U.S. president State of Israel established	Whitaker begins conferences on schizophrenia
1949	Communist People's Republic of China established	Bowlby: "The Study and Reduction of Group Tensions in the Family"
1950	N. Korea invades S. Korea	Bateson begins work at Palo Alto V.A.
1951	Julius and Ethel Rosenberg sentenced to death for espionage Sen. Estes Kefauver led Senate probe into organized crime	Ruesch & Bateson: *Communication: The Social Matrix of Society* Bowen residential treatment of mothers and children Lidz at Yale
1952	Eisenhower elected U.S. president	Bateson receives Rockefeller grant to study communication in Palo Alto Wynne at NIMH
1953	Joseph Stalin dies	Whitaker & Malone: *The Roots of Psychotherapy*
1954	Supreme Court rules school segregation unconstitutional	Bateson project research on schizophrenic communication Bowen at NIMH

	Social and Political Context	Development of Family Therapy
1955	Rosa Parks refuses to move to the back of the bus; Martin Luther King, Jr. leads boycott in Montgomery, Ala.	Whitaker in private practice, Altanta, Ga.
1956	Nasser elected president of Egypt Soviet troops crush anti-Communist rebellion in Hungary	Bateson, Jackson, Haley, & Weakland: "Toward a Theory of Schizophrenia"
1957	Russians launch *Sputnik I* Eisenhower sends troops to Little Rock, Ark. to protect school integration	Jackson: "The Question of Family Homeostasis" Ackerman opens the Family Mental Health Clinic of Jewish Family Services in New York Boszormenyi-Nagy opens Family Therapy Department at EPPI in Philadelphia
1958	European Common Market established Charles De Gaulle becomes French premier	Ackerman: *The Psychodynamics of Family Life*
1959	Castro becomes premier of Cuba	MRI founded by Don Jackson
1960	Kennedy elected U.S. president	Family Institute founded by Nathan Ackerman (renamed the Ackerman Institute in 1971) Minuchin and colleagues begin doing family therapy at Wiltwyck
1961	Berlin Wall erected	Bell: *Family Group Therapy* *Family Process* founded by Ackerman and Jackson
1962	Cuban Missile Crisis	Bateson's Palo Alto project ends Haley at MRI
1963	Kennedy assassinated	Haley: *Strategies of Psychotherapy*
1964	Johnson elected U.S. president Nobel Peace Prize awarded to Martin Luther King, Jr.	Satir: *Conjoint Family Therapy* Norbert Wiener dies (b. 1894)
1965	Passage of Medicare Malcolm X assassinated	Minuchin becomes director of Philadelphia Child Guidance Clinic Whitaker at University of Wisconsin

	Social and Political Context	*Development of Family Therapy*
1966	Red Guards demonstrate in China Indira Gandhi becomes prime minister of India	Brief Therapy Center at MRI begun under directorship of Richard Fisch Ackerman: *Treating the Troubled Family*
1967	Six-Day War between Israel and Arab states Urban riots in Cleveland, Newark, and Detroit	Watzlawick, Beavin, & Jackson: *Pragmatics of Human Communication* Dicks: *Marital Tensions*
1968	Nixon elected U.S. president Robert Kennedy and Martin Luther King, Jr. assassinated	Don Jackson dies (b. 1920)
1969	Widespread demonstrations against war in Vietnam	Bandura: *Principles of Behavior Modification* Wolpe: *The Practice of Behavior Therapy*
1970	Student protests against Vietnam War result in killing of four students at Kent State	Masters & Johnson: *Human Sexual Inadequacy* Laing & Esterson: *Sanity, Madness and the Family*
1971	Twenty-Sixth Amendment grants right to vote to eighteen-year-olds	Nathan Ackerman dies (b. 1908)
1972	Nixon reelected U.S. president	Bateson: *Steps to an Ecology of Mind* Wynne at University of Rochester
1973	Supreme Court rules that states may not prohibit abortion Energy crisis created by oil shortages	Center for Family Learning founded by Phil Guerin Boszormenyi-Nagy & Spark: *Invisible Loyalties*
1974	Nixon resigns	Minuchin: *Families and Family Therapy* Watzlawick, Weakland, & Fisch: *Change*
1975	Vietnam War ends	Mahler, Pine, & Bergman: *The Psychological Birth of the Human Infant* Stuart: "Behavioral Remedies for Marital Ills"
1976	Carter elected U.S. president	Haley: *Problem-Solving Therapy* Haley to Washington, D.C.
1977	President Carter pardons most Vietnam War draft evaders	Family Institute of Westchester founded by Betty Carter
1978	Camp David Accords between Egypt and Israel	Hare-Mustin: "A Feminist Approach to Family Therapy" Selvini Palazzoli et al.: *Paradox and Counterparadox*

Social and Political Context	Development of Family Therapy
1979 England's Margaret Thatcher becomes West's first woman prime minister Iranian militants seize U.S. Embassy in Tehran and hold hostages	Founding of Brief Therapy Center in Milwaukee Bateson: *Mind and Nature*
1980 Reagan elected U.S. president U.S. boycotts summer Olympics in Moscow	Haley: *Leaving Home* Milton Erickson dies (b. 1901) Gregory Bateson dies (b. 1904)
1981 Sandra Day O'Connor first woman justice of Supreme Court	Hoffman: *The Foundations of Family Therapy* Madanes: *Strategic Family Therapy* Minuchin & Fishman: *Family Therapy Techniques*
1982 Equal Rights Amendment fails ratification Falklands war	Gilligan: *In a Different Voice* Fisch, Weakland, & Segal: *Tactics of Change* *The Family Therapy Networker* founded by Richard Simon
1983 U.S. invades Grenada Terrorist bombing of Marine headquarters in Beirut	Doherty & Baird: *Family Therapy and Family Medicine* Keeney: *Aesthetics of Change*
1984 Reagan reelected U.S. president U.S.S.R. boycotts summer Olympics in Los Angeles	Watzlawick: *The Invented Reality* Madanes: *Behind the One-Way Mirror*
1985 Gorbachev becomes leader of U.S.S.R.	de Shazer: *Keys to Solution in Brief Therapy* Gergen: "The Social Constructionist Movement in Modern Psychology"
1986 Space shuttle *Challenger* explodes	Anderson et al.: *Schizophrenia and the Family* Selvini Palazzoli: "Towards a General Model of Psychotic Family Games"
1987 Congress investigates Iran-Contra affair	Tom Andersen: "The Reflecting Team" Guerin et al.: *The Evaluation and Treatment of Marital Conflict* Scharff & Scharff: *Object Relations Family Therapy*
1988 George Bush elected U.S. president	Kerr & Bowen: *Family Evaluation* Virginia Satir dies (b. 1916)
1989 The Berlin Wall comes down	Boyd-Franklin: *Black Families in Therapy*

	Social and Political Context	Development of Family Therapy
1990	Iraq invades Kuwait	Murray Bowen dies (b. 1913) White & Epston: *Narrative Means to Therapeutic Ends*
1991	Persian Gulf War against Iraq	Harold Goolishian dies (b. 1924)
1992	Clinton elected U.S. president	Family Institute of New Jersey founded by Monica McGoldrick
1993	Ethnic cleansing in Bosnia Los Angeles police officers convicted in Rodney King beating	Israel Zwerling dies (b. 1917) Minuchin & Nichols: *Family Healing*
1994	Republicans win majority in Congress Nelson Mandela elected president of South Africa	David and Jill Scharff leave Washington School of Psychiatry to begin the International Institute of Object Relations Therapy
1995	Oklahoma City federal building bombed	Carl Whitaker dies (b. 1912) John Weakland dies (b. 1919) Salvador Minuchin retires Family Studies Inc. renamed The Minuchin Center
1996	Clinton reelected U.S. president	Edwin Friedman dies (b. 1932) Eron & Lund: *Narrative Solutions in Brief Therapy* Freedman & Combs: *Narrative Therapy*
1997	Princess Diana dies in auto accident Hong Kong reverts to China	Michael Goldstein dies (b. 1930)
1998	President Clinton impeached by House of Representatives	Minuchin, Colapinto, & Minuchin: *Working with Families of the Poor*
1999	President Clinton acquitted in impeachment trial	Neil Jacobson dies (b. 1949) John Elderkin Bell dies (b. 1913) Mara Selvini Palazzoli dies (b. 1916)
2000	George W. Bush elected U.S. president	Millennium Conference, Toronto, Canada
2001	September 11 terrorist attacks	James Framo dies (b. 1922)

	Social and Political Context	Development of Family Therapy
2002	Sex abuse scandal in Catholic Church Corporate corruption at Enron	Lipchik: *Beyond Techniques in Solution-Focused Therapy*
2003	U.S. invades Iraq	Greenan & Tunnell: *Couple Therapy with Gay Men*
2004	George W. Bush reelected U.S. president	Gianfranco Cecchin dies (b. 1932)

The Foundations of Family Therapy

There wasn't much information on the intake sheet. Just a name, Holly Roberts, the fact that she was a senior in college, and her presenting complaint: "trouble making decisions."

The first thing Holly said when she sat down was, "I'm not sure I need to be here. You probably have a lot of people who need help more than I do." Then she started to cry.

It was springtime. The tulips were up; the trees were turning light, leafy green; and purple clumps of lilacs perfumed the air. Life and all its possibilities stretched out before her, but Holly was naggingly, unaccountably depressed.

The decision Holly was having trouble making was what to do after graduation. The more she tried to figure it out, the less able she was to concentrate. She started sleeping late, missing classes. Finally, her roommate talked her into going to the Health Service. "I wouldn't have come," Holly said. "I can take care of my own problems."

I was into cathartic therapy back then. Most people have stories to tell and tears to shed. Some of the stories, I suspected, were dramatized for sympathy and attention. Most people seem to give themselves permission to cry only with some very acceptable excuse. Of all the human emotions we're ashamed of, feeling sorry for ourselves tops the list.

I didn't know what was behind Holly's depression, but I was sure I could help. I felt comfortable with depressed people. Ever since my senior year in high school, when my friend Alex died, I'd been a little depressed myself.

●

After Alex died, the rest of the summer was a dark blur. I cried a lot. And I got mad whenever anyone suggested that life goes on. Alex's minister said that his death wasn't a real tragedy, because now "Alex was with God in heaven." I wanted to scream; but I numbed myself instead. In the fall I went off to college, and, even though it seemed somehow disloyal to Alex, life did go on. I still cried from time to time, but with the tears came a painful discovery. Not all of my grief was for Alex. Yes, I loved him. Yes, I missed him. But his death also provided me with the justification to cry about the everyday sorrows in my own life. Maybe grief is always like that. At the time, though, it struck me as a betrayal. I was using Alex's death to feel sorry for myself.

●

What, I wondered was making Holly so sad? In fact, Holly didn't have a dramatic story. Her feelings weren't focused. After those first few minutes in my office, she rarely cried. When she did, it was more an involuntary leakage than a sobbing release. She talked about the future

1

and about not knowing what she wanted to do with her life. She talked about not having a boyfriend—in fact, she rarely had any dates. She never said much about her family. If the truth be told, I wasn't terribly interested. Back then I thought home was the place you had to leave in order to grow up.

Holly was vulnerable and needed someone to lean on, but something made her hold back, as though she didn't feel safe, didn't quite trust me. It was frustrating. I wanted to help her.

A month went by and Holly's depression only got worse. I started seeing her three times a week, but we weren't really getting anywhere. One Friday afternoon Holly was feeling so despondent that I didn't think she should go back to her dorm alone. I asked her instead to lie down on the couch in my office and, with her permission, I called her parents.

Mrs. Roberts answered the phone. I told her that I thought she and her husband should come to Rochester and meet with me and Holly to discuss the advisability of Holly taking a medical leave of absence and going home. Unsure as I was of my authority back then, I steeled myself for an argument. Mrs. Roberts surprised me by agreeing to come at once.

The first thing that struck me about Holly's parents was the disparity in their ages. Lena Roberts looked like a slightly older version of Holly; she couldn't have been much over thirty-five. Her husband looked sixty. It turned out that he was Holly's stepfather. They had married when Holly was sixteen.

Looking back, I don't remember much being said in that first meeting. Both parents were very concerned about Holly. "We'll do whatever you think best," Mrs. Roberts said. Mr. Morgan (Holly's stepfather) said they could arrange for a good psychiatrist "to help Holly over this crisis." But Holly said she didn't want to go home, and she said this with more energy than I'd heard from her in a long time. That was on Saturday. I suggested that there was no need to rush into a decision, so we arranged to meet again on Monday.

When Holly and her parents sat down in my office on Monday morning, it was obvious that something had happened. Mrs. Roberts's eyes were red from crying. Holly glowered at her and looked away, her mouth tight and grim. Mr. Morgan turned to me. "We've been fighting all weekend. Holly heaps abuse on me, and when I try to respond, Lena takes her side. That's the way it's been since day one of this marriage."

The story that came out was one of those sad tales of jealousy and resentment that turns ordinary love into bitter, injured feelings and, all too often, tears families apart. Lena Roberts was thirty-four when she met Tom Morgan. He was a robust fifty-six. The second obvious difference between them was money. He was a successful stockbroker who'd retired to run a horse farm. She was waitressing to support herself and her daughter. It was a second marriage for both of them.

Lena looked to Tom to be the missing father figure in Holly's life. Unfortunately, she couldn't accept all the rules Tom felt invited to enforce. And so Tom became the wicked stepfather. He made the mistake of trying to take over, and, when the predictable arguments ensued, Lena sided with her daughter. Things got bad, and then worse. There were tears and midnight shouting matches. Twice Holly ran away to a friend's house for a few days. The triangle nearly proved Lena and Tom's undoing, but things calmed down when Holly went off to college.

Holly expected to leave home and not look back. She would make new friends. She would study hard and choose a career. She would *never* depend on a man to support her. Unfortunately, she left home with unfinished business. She hated Tom for the way he picked on her and for the way he treated her mother. He was always demanding to know where her mother was going, who she was going with, and when she would be back. If her mother was the least little bit late, there would be a scene. Why did her mother put up with it?

Blaming Tom was simple and satisfying. But another set of feelings, harder to face, was eating at Holly. She hated her mother for marrying Tom and letting him be so mean to her. What had her mother seen in him in the first place?

Had she sold out for a big house and a fancy car? Holly didn't have answers to these questions; she didn't even dare allow them into full awareness. Unfortunately, repression doesn't work like locking something in a closet and forgetting about it. It takes a lot of energy to keep unwelcome emotions at bay.

Holly found excuses not to go home much during college. It didn't even feel like home anymore. She buried herself in her studies. But rage and bitterness gnawed at her until, in her senior year, facing an uncertain future, knowing only that she couldn't go home again, she gave in to hopelessness. No wonder she was depressed.

I found the whole story sad. Not knowing much about family dynamics and never having lived in a stepfamily, I wondered why they couldn't just try to get along. The worst of it was that they had so little sympathy for each other. Why couldn't Holly accept her mother's right to find love a second time around? Why couldn't Tom respect the priority of his wife's relationship with her daughter? And why couldn't Lena listen to her daughter's adolescent anger without getting so defensive?

That session with Holly and her parents was my first lesson in family therapy. Family members in therapy talk, not about actual experiences, but about reconstructed memories that resemble the original experiences only in certain ways. Holly's memories resembled her mother's memories very little, and her step father's not at all. In the gaps between their truths was little room for reason and no desire to pursue it.

Although that meeting may not have been terribly productive, it certainly put Holly's unhappiness in perspective. No longer did I think of her as a tragic young woman, all alone in the world. She was that, of course, but she was also a daughter torn between running away from a home she no longer felt part of and being afraid to leave her mother alone with a man she didn't trust. I think that's when I became a family therapist.

To say that I didn't know much about families, much less about techniques for helping them, would be an understatement. But family therapy isn't just a new set of techniques; it's a whole new approach to understanding human behavior—as fundamentally shaped by its social context.

The Myth of the Hero

Ours is a culture that celebrates the uniqueness of the individual and the search for an autonomous self. Holly's story could be told as a coming of age drama: a young person's struggle to break away from childhood and provincialism, to take hold of adulthood and promise and the future. If she fails, we're tempted to look inside the young adult, the failed hero.

Although the unbounded individualism of the hero may be encouraged more for men than for women, as a cultural ideal it casts its shadow on us all. Even if Holly cares about connection as much as autonomy, she may be judged by the prevailing image of accomplishment.

We were raised on the myth of the hero: the Lone Ranger, Robin Hood, Wonder Woman. When we got older we searched out real-life heroes: Eleanor Roosevelt, Martin Luther King, Nelson Mandela. These were men and women who stood for something. If only we could be a little more like these larger-than-life individuals who seemed to rise above their circumstances.

Only later did we begin to realize that the "circumstances" we wanted to rise above were part of the human condition—our inescapable connection to our families. The romantic image of the hero is based on the illusion that authentic selfhood can be achieved as an autonomous individual. We do many things alone, including some of our most heroic acts, but we are defined and sustained by a network of human relationships. Our need to worship heroes is partly a need to rise above inadequacy and self-doubt, but perhaps equally a product of imagining a life unfettered by all those pesky relationships that somehow never quite go as we wish.

When we do think about families, it's often in negative terms—as forces of dependency holding us back, or as destructive elements in the lives of our patients. What catches our attention in families are differences and discord. The harmonies of family life—loyalty, tolerance, mutual aid and assistance—often slide by unnoticed, part of the taken-for-granted background of life. If we would be heroes, then we must have villains.

There's a lot of talk these days about "dysfunctional families." Unfortunately, much of this amounts to little more than parent bashing. We suffer because of what *they* did: our mother's drinking, our father's unreasonable expectations—these are the causes of our unhappiness. Perhaps this is an advance on stewing in guilt and shame, but it's a long way from understanding what really goes on in families.

One reason for blaming family sorrows on the personal failings of parents is that it's hard for the average person to see past individual personalities to the structural patterns that make them a family—a system of interconnected lives governed by strict but unspoken rules.

People feel controlled and helpless not because they are victims of parental folly and deceit, but because they don't understand the forces that hurl husbands and wives and parents and children together. Plagued by anxiety and depression, or merely troubled and uncertain, some people turn to psychotherapy for help and consolation. In the process, they turn away from the irritants that propel them into therapy. Chief among these are unhappy relationships—with friends and lovers, *and* with the family. Our disorders are private ailments. When we retreat to the safety of a synthetic relationship, the last thing we want is to take our families with us. Is it any wonder, then, that when Freud ventured to explore the dark forces of the mind, he locked the family outside the consulting room?

Psychotherapeutic Sanctuary

It's tempting to look back on the days before family therapy and see those who insisted on segregating patients from their families as naive exponents of a fossilized view of mental disorder, according to which psychiatric maladies were firmly embedded in the heads of individuals. Considering that clinicians didn't begin treating

Freud excluded the family from psychoanalysis to help patients feel safe to explore the full range of their thoughts and feelings.

whole families together until the mid 1950s, it's tempting to ask, "What took them so long?" In fact, there are good reasons for conducting therapy in private.

The two most influential approaches to psychotherapy in the twentieth century, Freud's psychoanalysis and Rogers's client-centered therapy, were both predicated on the assumption that psychological problems arise from unhealthy interactions with others and can best be alleviated in a private relationship between therapist and patient. Freud wasn't interested in the living family; he was interested in the family-as-remembered. By conducting treatment in private, Freud safeguarded patients' trust in the sanctity of the therapeutic relationship and thus maximized the likelihood that they would repeat, in relation to the analyst, the understandings and misunderstandings of childhood.

The therapy Carl Rogers developed was designed to help patients uncover their real feelings. Unhappily, said Rogers, our innate tendency toward *self-actualization* gets subverted by our craving for approval. We learn to do what we think others want, even though it may not be what's best for us.

Gradually, this conflict between self-fulfillment and need for approval leads to denial and distortion of our inner promptings—and even of the feelings that signal them. We swallow our anger, stifle our exuberance, and bury our lives under a mountain of expectations.

The Rogerian therapist listens sympathetically, offering understanding, warmth, and respect. In the presence of such an accepting listener, patients gradually get in touch with their own feelings and inner promptings.

Like the psychoanalyst, the client-centered therapist maintains absolute privacy in the therapeutic relationship to avoid any possibility that patients' feelings might be subverted to win approval. Only an objective outsider could be counted on to provide the unconditional acceptance to help patients rediscover their real selves. That's why family members had no place in the work of client-centered therapy.

Family versus Individual Therapy

As you can see, there are valid reasons for conducting psychotherapy in private. But although there is a strong claim to be made for individual psychotherapy, there are equally strong claims to be made for family therapy.

Keep in mind that individual therapy and family therapy each offers an approach to treatment—and a way of understanding human behavior. As approaches to treatment, both have their virtues. Individual therapy can provide the concentrated focus to help people face their fears and learn to become more fully themselves. Individual therapists have always recognized the importance of family life in shaping personality, but they assume that these influences are internalized and that intrapsychic dynamics become the dominant forces controlling behavior. Treatment can and should, therefore, be directed at the person and his or her personal makeup. Family therapists, on the other hand, believe that the dominant forces in our lives are located externally, in the family. Therapy based on this framework is directed at changing the structure of the family. When family organization is transformed, the life of every family member is altered accordingly.

This last point—that changing a family changes the life of each of its members—is important enough to elaborate. Family therapy influences the entire family; therefore, improve-

ment can be lasting because each and every family member is changed *and* continues to exert synchronous change on each other.

Almost any sort of human difficulty can be treated with either individual or family therapy. But certain problems are especially suited to a family approach, among them problems with children (who must, regardless of what happens in therapy, return home to their parents), complaints about a marriage or other intimate relationship, family feuds, and symptoms that develop at the time of a major family transition.

If problems that arise around family transitions make a therapist think first about the role of the family, individual therapy may be especially useful when people identify something about themselves that they've tried in vain to change *and* their social environment seems to be stable. Thus, if a woman gets depressed during her first year at college, a therapist might wonder if her sadness is related to leaving home, and to leaving her parents alone with each other. But if the same woman were to get depressed in her thirties, say, during a long period of stability in her life, we might wonder if there's something about the way she approaches life, something about the way she hasn't fulfilled herself, that's responsible for her unhappiness. Examining her life in private—away from troubled relationships—doesn't mean, however, that she should believe that she can fulfill herself in isolation from the other people in her life.

The view of persons as separate entities, with families acting on them, is consistent with the way we experience ourselves. We recognize the influence of intimates—especially as obligation and constraint—but it's hard to see that we are embedded in a network of relationships, that we are part of something larger than ourselves.

The Power of Family Therapy

The power of family therapy derives from bringing men and women, parents and children together to transform their interactions. Instead of isolating individuals from the emotional origins of their conflict, problems are addressed at their source.

What keeps people stuck is their great difficulty in seeing their own participation in the problems that plague them. With eyes fixed firmly on what those recalcitrant others are doing, it's hard for most people to see the patterns that bind them together. The family therapist's job is to give them a wake-up call. When a husband complains that his wife nags, and the therapist asks him how he contributes to her doing that, the therapist is challenging the husband to see the hyphenated him-and-her of their interactions.

When Bob and Shirley came for help with marital problems, her complaint was that he never shared his feelings; his was that she always criticized him. This, of course, is a classic trading of complaints that keeps couples stuck as long as they fail to see the reciprocal pattern in which each partner provokes in the other precisely the behavior he or she cannot stand. So the therapist said to Bob, "If you were a frog, what would you be like if Shirley changed you into a prince?" When Bob countered that one reason he doesn't talk with her is because she's so critical, it seemed to the couple like the same old argument. But the therapist saw this as the beginning of a change—Bob speaking up more. One way to create an opening for change in rigid

families is to support the blamed person and help bring him back into the fray.

When Shirley criticized Bob for complaining, he tried to retreat, but the therapist said, "No, continue. You are still a frog."

Bob tried to shift responsibility back to Shirley. "Doesn't she have to kiss me first?" But the therapist said, "No, in real life that comes afterward. You have to earn it."

In the opening of *Anna Karenina*, Tolstoy wrote: "All happy families resemble one another; each unhappy family is unhappy in its own way." Every family may be unhappy in its own way, but they all stumble over the same familiar challenges of family life. It's no secret what these challenges are—learning to live together, dealing with difficult relatives, chasing after children, coping with adolescence, and so on. What not everyone realizes, however, is that a relatively small number of systems dynamics, once understood, illuminate these challenges and enable families to move successfully through the predictable dilemmas of life. Like all healers, family therapists sometimes deal with bizarre and baffling cases, but much of their work is with ordinary human beings learning life's painful lessons. Their stories, and the stories of the men and women of family therapy who have undertaken to help them, are the inspiration for this book.

—Questions to Consider——————————————

1. What would be some good reasons for recommending individual therapy rather than family therapy in certain cases?
2. While it's possible to address both the psychology of individuals and their interactions, what are some of the trade-offs of

focusing on the system or focusing on individuals in a family therapy case?
3. How could you teach a course on psychopathology that recognized the influence of the family on various "mental illnesses"?

—Recommended Readings——————————————

Lasch, C. 1977. *The culture of narcissism.* New York: Norton.

Nichols, M. P. 1987. *The self in the system.* New York: Brunner/Mazel.

Nichols, M. P. 1999. *Inside family therapy.* Boston: Allyn and Bacon.

The Evolution of Family Therapy

In this chapter we explore the antecedents and early years of family therapy. One finds two fascinating stories here: one of personalities, one of ideas. The first story revolves around the pioneers, the iconoclasts, and great originals who somehow broke the mold of seeing life and its problems as a function of individuals and their psychology. Make no mistake: The shift from an individual to a systemic perspective was a revolutionary one, providing those who grasped it with a powerful tool for understanding and resolving human problems.

The second story in the evolution of family therapy is one of ideas. The restless curiosity of the first family therapists led them to a variety of ingenious ways to conceptualize the joys and sorrows of family life.

As you read this history, stay open to surprises. Be ready to reexamine easy assumptions—including the assumption that family therapy began as a benevolent effort to support the institution of the family. The truth is, therapists first encountered the family system as an adversary.

The Undeclared War

Although we came to think of asylums as places of cruelty and detention, they were originally built to rescue the insane from persecution by their relatives, from being locked away and tormented in the family attic. Accordingly except for purposes of footing the bill, hospital psychiatrists have kept families at arm's length. In the 1950s, however, two puzzling developments forced therapists to recognize the family's power to alter the course of treatment.

Therapists began to notice that often when a patient got better, someone else in the family got worse, almost as though the family *needed* a symptomatic member. As in the game of hide-and-seek, it didn't seem to matter who was "it" as long as someone played the part. In one case, Don Jackson (1954) was treating a woman for depression. When she began to improve, her husband complained that she was getting worse When she continued to improve, her husband lost his job. Eventually, when the woman was completely well, her husband killed himself. Was this man's stability predicated on having a sick wife?

In another of Jackson's cases, a husband urged his wife to seek treatment for "frigidity." When, after several months of therapy, she grew sexually responsive, he became impotent.

The other strange story of shifting disturbance was that patients frequently improved in the hospital only to get worse when they went home. In a bizarre case of Oedipus revisited,

Salvador Minuchin treated a young man hospitalized multiple times for trying to scratch out his own eyes. The man functioned normally in Bellevue but returned to self-mutilation each time he went home. He could be sane, it seemed, only in an insane world.

It turned out that the young man was extremely close to his mother, a bond that grew even tighter during the seven years of his father's mysterious absence. The father was a compulsive gambler who disappeared shortly after being declared legally incompetent. The rumor was that the Mafia had kidnapped him. When, just as mysteriously, the father returned, his son began his bizarre attempts at self-mutilation. Perhaps he wanted to blind himself so as not to see his obsession with his mother and hatred of his father.

But this family was neither ancient nor Greek, and Minuchin was more pragmatist than poet. So he challenged the father to protect his son by beginning to deal directly with his wife, and then challenged the man's demeaning attitude toward her, which had made her feel all the more need for her son's proximity and protection. The therapy was a challenge to the family's structure and, in Bellevue, working with the psychiatric staff toward easing the young man back into the family, into harm's way.

Minuchin confronted the father, saying, "As a father of a child in danger, what you're doing isn't enough."

"What *should* I do?" asked the man.

"I don't know," Minuchin replied. "Ask your son." Then, for the first time in years, father and son began talking to each other. Just as they were about to run out of things to say, Dr. Minuchin commented to both parents: "In a strange way, he's telling you that he prefers to be treated like a young child. When he was in the hospital he was twenty-three. Now that he's returned home, he's six."

What this case dramatizes is how parents sometimes use their children—as a buffer to protect them from intimacy. To the would-be Oedipus, Minuchin said, "You're scratching your eyes for your mother, so that she'll have something to worry about. You're a good boy. Good children sacrifice themselves for their parents."

What these cases demonstrated was that families are made of strange glue—they stretch but never let go. Few blamed the family for outright malevolence, yet there was an invidious undercurrent to these observations. The official story of family therapy is one of respect for the institution of the family, but maybe none of us ever quite gets over the adolescent idea that families are the enemy of freedom.

The impact of a patient's improvement on the family isn't always negative. Fisher and Mendell (1958) reported a spread of positive changes from patients to other family members. Whether the influence patients and their families have on each other is malignant or benign isn't the point. The point is, change in one person changes the system.

Small Group Dynamics

Those who first sought to understand and treat families found a ready parallel in small groups. **Group dynamics** are relevant to family therapy because group life is a complex blend of individual personalities and superordinate properties of the group.

In 1920, the pioneering social psychologist William McDougall published *The Group Mind* in which he described how a group's continuity depends on the group being an important idea in the minds of its members; on the need for boundaries and structures in which differentiation of function could occur; and on the importance of customs and habits, so that relationships could be fixed and defined. A more scientific approach to group dynamics was ushered in during the 1940s by Kurt Lewin, whose *field theory* (Lewin, 1951) guided a generation of researchers, industrial psychologists, group therapists, and agents of social change.

Drawing on the Gestalt school of perceptual psychology, Lewin developed the notion that the group is more than the sum of its parts. This transcendent property of groups has obvious relevance to family therapists, who must work not only with individuals but also with family systems—and their famous resistance to change.

Analyzing what he called *quasi-stationary social equilibrium*, Lewin pointed out that changing group behavior first requires "unfreezing." Only after something shakes up a group's beliefs are its members likely to accept change. In individual therapy this process is initiated by the disquieting experiences that lead people to seek help. Once an individual accepts the status of patient, that person has already begun to unfreeze old habits. When families come for treatment, it's a different story.

Many family members aren't sufficiently unsettled by the symptomatic member's predicament to think about changing their own ways. Furthermore, family members bring their primary reference group with them, with all its traditions and habits. Consequently, more effort is required to unfreeze, or shake up, families before real change can take place. The need for unfreezing foreshadowed early family therapists' concerns about disrupting family **homeostasis,** a notion that dominated family therapy for decades.

Wilfred Bion was another major student of group dynamics who emphasized the group as a whole, with its own dynamics and structure. According to Bion (1948), most groups become distracted from their primary tasks by engaging in patterns of *fight-flight, dependency,* or *pairing.* Bion's "basic assumptions" are easily extrapolated to family therapy: Some families skirt around hot issues like a cat circling a snake. Others use therapy to bicker endlessly, never really contemplating compromise, much less change. Dependency masquerades as therapy when families allow therapists to subvert their autonomy in the name of problem solving. Pairing is seen in families when one parent colludes with the children to undermine the other parent.

The **process/content** distinction in group dynamics likewise had a major impact on family treatment. Experienced therapists learn to attend as much to *how* families talk as to the content of their discussions. For example, a mother might tell her daughter that she shouldn't play with Barbie dolls because she shouldn't aspire to an image of bubble-headed beauty. The *content* of the mother's message is: Respect yourself as a person, not as an ornament. But if the mother expresses her point of view by disparaging the daughter's feelings, then the *process* of her message would be: Your feelings don't count

Unfortunately, the content of some discussions is so compelling that therapists get sidetracked from the process. Suppose, for example, that a therapist invites a teenage boy to talk with his mother about wanting to drop out of school. Say that the boy mumbles something about school being stupid, and his mother responds with a lecture about the need for an education. A therapist who gets drawn in to support the mother's position may be making a mistake. In terms of content, the mother might be right: A high school diploma does come in handy. But maybe it's more important at the moment to help the boy learn to speak up for himself—and for his mother to learn to listen.

Role theory, explored in the literature of psychoanalysis and group dynamics, had particularly important applications to the study of families. The expectations that roles carry bring regularity to complex social situations.

Roles tend to be stereotyped in most groups. Virginia Satir (1972) described family roles such as "the placator" or "the disagreeable one" in her book *Peoplemaking.* If you think about it, you may have played a fairly predictable role in your family. Perhaps you were "the good child," "the moody one," "the rebel," or "the successful child." The trouble is, such roles can be hard to put aside.

One thing that makes role theory so useful in understanding families is that roles tend to be reciprocal and complementary. Say, for example, that a woman is slightly more anxious to spend time together with her boyfriend than he is. Maybe, left to his own devices, he'd call twice a week. But if she calls three times a week, he may never get around to picking up the phone. If their relationship progresses and this pattern is played out, she may always play the role of the pursuer and he, the distancer. Or take the case of two parents, both of whom want their children to behave at the dinner table. But let's say that the father has a slightly shorter fuse—he tells them to quiet down five seconds after they start getting rowdy, whereas his wife would wait half a minute. If he always speaks up first, she'll never get a chance. Eventually these parents may become polarized into complementary roles of strictness and leniency. What makes such reciprocity resistant to change is that the roles reinforce each other—and each person waits for the other to change.

It was a short step from observing a patient's reactions to other members of a group—some of whom might be similar to siblings or parents—to observing interactions in real families. Given the diverse techniques for exploring interpersonal relationships developed by group therapists, it was natural that some family therapists would apply a group treatment model to working with families. After all, what are families but collective groups with various subgroups?

From a technical viewpoint, group and family therapies are similar: Both are complex and amorphous, more like everyday social reality than individual therapy. In groups and families each patient must react to a number of people, not just the therapist, and therapeutic use of this interaction is the definitive mechanism of change in both settings. Consequently, many group and family therapists endeavor to remain relatively decentralized so that patients in the room will relate to each other.

On closer examination, however, we can see that the differences between families and groups are so significant that group therapy has only limited applicability to family treatment. Family members have a long history and, more importantly, a future together. Revealing yourself to strangers is safer than exposing yourself to members of your own family. In fact, serious harm can be done by therapists who are so naive as to push family members to always "be completely honest and open" with each other. There's no taking back rash disclosures that might better have re-

mained private—the affair long since over or the admission that a woman *does* care more about her career than her children. Continuity, commitment, and shared distortions all make family therapy different from group therapy.

Therapy groups are designed to provide an atmosphere of warmth and support. This feeling of safety among sympathetic strangers cannot be part of family therapy, because, instead of separating treatment from a stressful environment, the stressful environment is brought into treatment. Furthermore, in group therapy, patients can have equal power and status, whereas democratic equality isn't appropriate in families. Someone has to be in charge. Furthermore, the official patient in the family is likely to feel isolated and stigmatized. After all, he or she is "the problem." The sense of protection in being part of a compassionate group of strangers, who won't have to be faced across the dinner table, doesn't exist in family therapy.

The Child Guidance Movement

It was Freud who introduced the idea that psychological disorders were the consequence of unsolved problems of childhood. Alfred Adler was the first of Freud's followers to pursue the implication that treating the growing child might be the most effective way to prevent adult neuroses. To that end, Adler organized child guidance clinics in Vienna, where not only children but also families and teachers were counseled. Adler's approach was to offer encouragement and support in an atmosphere of optimism and confidence. His technique helped alleviate children's feelings of inferiority so they could work out a healthy life style, achieving competence and success through social usefulness.

Although child guidance clinics remained few in number until after World War II, they now exist in every city in the United States, providing for the study and treatment of childhood problems and the complex social and family forces contributing to them. Gradually, child guidance workers concluded that the real problem wasn't the obvious one, the child's symptoms, but rather the tensions in the family that were the source of those symptoms. At first, the tendency was to blame the parents, especially the mother.

The chief cause of childhood psychological problems, according to David Levy (1943), was *maternal overprotectiveness.* Mothers who had themselves been deprived of love while growing up became overprotective of their children. Some were domineering, others overindulgent. Children of domineering mothers were submissive at home but had difficulty making friends; children with indulgent mothers were disobedient at home but well behaved at school.

During this period, Frieda Fromm-Reichmann (1948) coined one of the most damning terms in the history of psychiatry, the **schizophreno-genic mother.** These domineering, aggressive, and rejecting women, especially when they were married to passive men, were thought to provide the pathologic parenting that produced schizophrenia.

The tendency to blame parents, especially mothers, for problems in the family was an evolutionary misdirection that continues to haunt the field. Nevertheless, by paying attention to what went on between parents and children, Levy and Fromm-Reichmann helped pave the way for family therapy.

Although the importance of the family was recognized, mothers and children were still treated separately, and discussion between therapists was discouraged on the grounds that it might compromise the individual therapeutic relationships. The usual arrangement was for a psychiatrist to treat the child while a social worker saw the mother. Counseling the mother was secondary to treating the child. In this model, the family was viewed as an extension of the child rather than the other way around.

The emphasis in the child guidance movement eventually changed from seeing parents as the problem to seeing problems in the relationship among patients, parents, and significant others. This shift had profound consequences. No longer was psychopathology located within individuals; no longer were parents villains and

patients victims. Now their interaction was seen as the problem.

John Bowlby's work at the Tavistock Clinic exemplified the transition to a family approach. Bowlby (1949) was treating a child and making slow progress. Feeling frustrated, he decided to see the child and his parents together for a session. During the first half of this two-hour session, the child and parents took turns complaining, each blaming the other. During the second half of the session, Bowlby interpreted to each of them what he thought their contributions to the problem were. Eventually, by working together, all three members of the family developed some sympathy for each other's point of view.

Although he was impressed with the usefulness of this conjoint interview, Bowlby remained wedded to the one-to-one format. Family meetings might be a useful catalyst but only as an adjunct to the *real* treatment, individual psychoanalytic therapy.

What Bowlby tried as an experiment, Nathan Ackerman saw to fruition—family therapy as the primary form of treatment. As early as 1938, Ackerman went on record as suggesting the value of viewing the family as a unit when dealing with disturbance in any of its members (Ackerman, 1938). Subsequently he recommended studying the family as a means of understanding the child—instead of the other way around (Ackerman & Sobel, 1950). Once he saw the need to understand the family in order to diagnose problems, Ackerman soon took the next step—family treatment. Before we get to that, however, let us examine parallel developments in social work and research on schizophrenia that led to the birth of family therapy.

The Influence of Social Work

No history of family therapy would be complete without mentioning the enormous contribution of social workers and their tradition of public service. Since the beginning of the profession, social workers have been concerned with the family, both as the critical social unit and as the focus of intervention (Ackerman, Beatman, & Sherman, 1961). Indeed, the core paradigm of social work—treating the person-in-the-environment—anticipated family therapy's ecological approach long before systems theory was introduced.

The field of social work grew out of the charity movements in Great Britain and the United States in the late nineteenth century. Then, as now, social workers were dedicated to improving the condition of society's poor and underprivileged. In addition to ministering to clients' basic needs for food, clothing, and shelter, social workers sought to relieve emotional distress and to redress the social forces responsible for extremes of poverty and privilege.

The *friendly visitor* was a caseworker who visited families in their homes to assess their needs and offer help. By bringing helpers into the homes of their clients, these visits broke down the artificiality of the doctor–patient model. (Family therapists these days are rediscovering the value of getting out of the office and meeting clients where they live.)

These turn-of-the-century caseworkers were well aware of something it took psychiatry fifty more years to discover—that families must be considered as units. Mary Richmond (1917), in her classic text, *Social Diagnosis*, prescribed treatment of "the whole family" and warned against isolating family members from their natural context. Richmond's concept of *family cohesion* had a strikingly modern ring, anticipating as it did later work on role theory, group dynamics, and, of course, structural family therapy. According to Richmond, the degree of emotional bonding between family members was critical to their ability to survive and flourish.

Richmond anticipated developments that family therapy became concerned with in the 1980s by viewing families as systems within systems. As Bardhill and Saunders pointed out (1988, p. 319),

She recognized that families are not isolated wholes (closed systems), but exist in a particular social context, which interactively influences and is influenced by their functioning (i.e., they are open). She graphically depicted this situation using a set of concentric circles to represent various systemic levels from the individual to the cultural. Her approach to practice was to consider the potential effect of all interventions on every systemic level, and to understand and to use the reciprocal interaction of the systemic hierarchy for therapeutic purposes. She truly took a systemic view of human distress.

When the family therapy movement was launched, social workers were among the most important contributors. Among the leaders who came into family therapy through social work training were Virginia Satir, Ray Bardhill, Peggy Papp, Lynn Hoffman, Froma Walsh, Insoo Berg, Jay Lappin, Richard Stuart, Harry Aponte, Michael White, Doug Breunlin, Olga Silverstein, Lois Braverman, Steve de Shazer, Peggy Penn, Betty Carter, Braulio Montalvo, and Monica McGoldrick. (Incidentally, even starting such a list is difficult because unless it went on for pages it would have to omit a host of important names.)

Research on Family Dynamics and the Etiology of Schizophrenia

Gregory Bateson—Palo Alto

One of the groups with the strongest claim to originating family therapy was Gregory Bateson's schizophrenia project in Palo Alto, California. The Palo Alto project began in the fall of 1952 when Bateson received a grant from the Rockefeller Foundation to study the nature of communication. All communications, Bateson had written (Bateson, 1951), have two different levels or functions—*report* and *command*. Every message has a stated content, as, for instance, "Wash your hands, it's time for dinner"; but in addition, the message carries how it is to be taken. In this case the second message is that the speaker is in charge. This second message—**metacommunication**—is covert and often unnoticed. If a wife scolds her husband for running the dishwasher when it's only half full, and he says OK but turns around and does exactly the same thing two days later, she may be annoyed that he doesn't listen to her. She means the message. But maybe he didn't like the metamessage. Maybe he doesn't like her telling him what to do as though she were his mother.

Bateson was joined in 1953 by Jay Haley and John Weakland. In 1954, Bateson received a two-year grant from the Macy Foundation to study schizophrenic communication. Shortly thereafter the group was joined by Don Jackson, a brilliant psychiatrist who served as clinical consultant.

The group's interests turned to developing a communication theory that might explain the origin and nature of schizophrenia, particularly in the context of families. Worth noting, however, is that in the early days of the project none of them thought of actually observing schizophrenics and their families. Once they agreed that schizophrenic communication might be a product of what was learned inside the family, the group looked for circumstances that could lead to such confused and confusing patterns of speech.

In 1956 Bateson and his colleagues published their famous report, "Toward a Theory of Schizophrenia," in which they introduced the concept of the **double bind.** They assumed that psychotic behavior might make sense in the context of pathologic family communication. Patients weren't crazy in some meaningless way; they were an extension of a crazy family environment. Consider someone in an important relationship where escape isn't feasible and response is necessary; when he or she receives two related but contradictory messages on different levels, but finds it difficult to detect or comment on the inconsistency (Bateson, Jackson, Haley, & Weakland, 1956), that person is in a double bind.

Because this difficult concept is often misused as a synonym for paradox or simply contradictory messages, it's worth reviewing each feature of the double bind as the authors listed them:

1. Two or more persons in an important relationship;
2. Repeated experience;
3. A primary negative injunction, such as "Don't do X or I will punish you";
4. A second injunction at a more abstract level conflicting with the first, also enforced by punishment or perceived threat;
5. A tertiary negative injunction prohibiting escape and demanding a response. Without this restriction the "victim" won't feel bound;
6. Finally, the complete set of ingredients is no longer necessary once the victim is conditioned to perceive the world in terms of double binds; any part of the sequence becomes sufficient to trigger panic or rage.

Most examples of double binds in the literature are inadequate because they don't include all of the critical features. Robin Skynner, for instance, cited (1976): "Boys must stand up for themselves and not be sissies"—but "Don't be rough . . . don't be rude to your mother." Confusing? Yes. Conflict? Maybe. But these two messages don't constitute a double bind; they're merely a contradiction. Faced with two such statements, a child is free to obey either one, alternate, or even complain about the contradiction. This and many similar examples neglect the specification that the two messages are conveyed on different levels.

A better example is the one given in the original article by Bateson, Jackson, Haley, and Weakland (1956). A young man recovering in the hospital from a schizophrenic episode was visited by his mother. When he put his arm around her, she stiffened. But when he withdrew, she asked, "Don't you love me anymore?" He blushed, and she said, "Dear, you must not be so easily embarrassed and afraid of your feelings." Following this exchange, the patient assaulted an aide and had to be put in seclusion.

Notice that all six features of the double bind were present in this exchange, and also that the young man was obviously caught. There is no bind if the subject is not bound. The concept is interactional.

Another example of a double bind is a teacher who urges his students to participate in class but gets impatient if one of them actually interrupts with a question or comment. Then a baffling thing happens. For some strange reason that scientists have yet to decipher, students tend not to speak up in classes in which their comments are disparaged. When the professor finally does get around to asking for questions and no one responds, he gets angry. ("Students are so passive!") If any of the students has the temerity to comment on the professor's lack of receptivity, he'll probably get even angrier. Thus the students will be punished for accurately perceiving that the teacher really wants only his own ideas to be heard and admired. (This example is, of course, purely hypothetical.)

We're all caught in occasional double binds, but the schizophrenic has to deal with them continually—and the effect is maddening. Unable to comment on the dilemma, the schizophrenic responds defensively, perhaps by being concrete and literal, perhaps by speaking in metaphors. Eventually the schizophrenic may come to assume that behind every statement lies a concealed meaning.

The discovery that schizophrenic symptoms made sense in the context of some families may have been a scientific advance, but it had moral and political overtones. Not only did these investigators see themselves as avenging knights bent on rescuing **identified patients** by slaying family dragons, but they were also crusaders in a holy war against the psychiatric establishment. Outnumbered and surrounded by hostile critics, the champions of family therapy challenged the orthodox assumption that schizophrenia was a biological disease. Psychological healers everywhere cheered. Unfortunately, they were wrong.

The observation that schizophrenic behavior seems to *fit* in some families doesn't mean that families *cause* schizophrenia. In logic, this kind of inference is called "Jumping to Conclusions." Sadly, as we shall see, families of schizophrenic members suffered for years under the implication that they were to blame for the tragedy of their children's psychoses.

Theodore Lidz—Yale

Theodore Lidz challenged the then-current belief that maternal rejection was the major distinguishing feature of schizophrenic families and observed that frequently the more destructive influence was that of the fathers (Lidz, Cornelison, Fleck, & Terry, 1957). After describing some of the pathologic characteristics of fathers in schizophrenic families, Lidz turned his attention to defects in the marital relationship. The theme underlying his findings was an absence of *role reciprocity*. In a successful relationship, it's not enough to fulfill your own role, that is, to be an effective person; it's also necessary to balance your role with your partner's, that is, to be an effective pair.

In focusing on the failure to arrive at reciprocal, cooperative roles, Lidz identified two general types of marital discord. In the first, **marital schism,** husbands and wives chronically undercut each other's worth and competed openly for their children's affection. Their marriages were combat zones. The second pattern, **marital skew,** involves serious psychopathology in one partner who dominates the other. Thus, one parent becomes passive and dependent whereas the other appears to be a strong parent figure, but is, in fact, a pathologic bully. In all these families, unhappy children were torn by conflicting loyalties and weighted down with the pressure to balance their parents' precarious marriages.

Lyman Wynne—National Institute of Mental Health

Lyman Wynne's studies of schizophrenic families began in 1954 when he started seeing the parents of his hospitalized patients in twice-weekly therapy sessions. What struck Wynne about these disturbed families were the strangely unreal qualities of both positive and negative emotions, which he labeled **pseudomutual-**

Lyman Wynne's studies linked communication deviance in families to thought disorder in schizophrenic patients.

ity and **pseudohostility** and the nature of the boundaries around them—**rubber fences**—apparently yielding but actually impervious to outside influence (especially from therapists).

Pseudomutuality (Wynne, Ryckoff, Day, & Hirsch, 1958) is a facade of togetherness that masks conflict and blocks intimacy. Such families are so preoccupied with fitting together that there's no room for separate identities. The surface togetherness of pseudomutual families masks the fact that they can't tolerate either deeper, more honest relationships or independence.

Pseudohostility is a different guise for a similar collusion to obscure *alignments* and *splits* (Wynne, 1961). Although noisy and intense, it signals only a superficial split. Pseudohostility is more like the bickering of a situation-comedy family than real animosity. Like pseudomutuality, it blurs intimacy and affection as well as deeper conflicts; and, like pseudomutuality, pseudohostility distorts communication and impairs rational thinking about relationships.

The **rubber fence** is an invisible barrier that stretches to permit obligatory extrafamilial involvement, such as going to school, but springs back if that involvement goes too far. The family's rigid role structure is thus protected by social isolation. The most damaging feature of the rubber fence is that those who most need outside contact to correct family distortions are the ones allowed it least. Instead of being a subsystem of society (Parsons & Bales, 1955), the schizophrenic family becomes a sick little society unto itself.

Wynne linked the new concept of *communication deviance* with the older notion of *thought disorder*. He saw communication as the vehicle for transmitting thought disorder, the defining characteristic of schizophrenia. Communication deviance is a more interactional concept than thought disorder and more readily observable than double binds. By 1978 Wynne had studied more than 600 families and gathered incontrovertible evidence that disordered styles of communication are a distinguishing feature of families with young adult schizophrenics. Similar disorders also appear in families of borderlines, neurotics, and normals, but are progressively less severe (Singer, Wynne, & Toohey, 1978). This observation—that communication deviance isn't confined solely to schizophrenic families but exists on a continuum (greater deviance with more severe pathology)—is consistent with other studies that describe a "spectrum of schizophrenic disorders."

Role Theorists

The founders of family therapy gained momentum for their fledgling discipline by concentrating narrowly on verbal communication. Doing so may have been adaptive at the time, but focusing exclusively on this one aspect of family life neglected both individual intersubjectivity and broader social influences.

Role theorists, like John Spiegel, described how individuals were differentiated into social roles within family systems. This important fact was obscured by oversimplified versions of systems theory, according to which individuals were treated like cogs in a machine. As early as 1954, Spiegel pointed out that the system in therapy includes the therapist as well as the family (an idea reintroduced later as **second-order cybernetics**). He also made a valuable distinction between *interactions* and *transactions*. Billiard balls *interact*—they collide and alter each other's course but remain essentially unchanged. People *transact*—they come together in ways that not only alter each other's course but also affect internal changes.

R. D. Laing's analysis of family dynamics was often more polemical than scholarly, but his observations helped popularize the family's role in psychopathology. Laing (1965) borrowed Marx's concept of **mystification** (class exploitation) and applied it to the "politics of families." Mystification refers to distorting children's experience by denying or relabeling it. One example of this is a parent telling a child who's feeling sad, "You must be tired" (*Go to bed and leave me alone*). Similarly, the idea that "good" children are always quiet breeds compliant, but spiritless, children.

The prime function of mystification is to maintain the status quo. Mystification contradicts perceptions and feelings and, more ominously, reality. When parents mystify a child's experience, the child's existence becomes inauthentic. Because their feelings aren't accepted, these children project a *false self* and keep the *real self* private. In mild instances, this produces a lack of authenticity, but if the real self/false self split is carried to extremes, the result is madness (Laing, 1960).

Marriage Counseling

For many years there was no apparent need for a separate profession of marriage counselors. People with marital problems were more likely to discuss them with their doctors, clergy, lawyers, and teachers than to seek out mental health professionals. The first professional centers for marriage counseling were established in about 1930. Paul Popenoe opened the American Institute of Family Relations in Los Angeles, and Abraham and Hannah Stone opened a similar clinic in New York. A third center was the Marriage Council of Philadelphia, begun in 1932 by Emily Hartshorne Mudd (Broderick & Schrader, 1991). At the same time these developments were taking place, a parallel trend among some psychoanalysts led to conjoint marital therapy. Although the majority of analysts have always followed Freud's prohibition against contact with the patient's family, a few broke the rules and experimented with therapy for married partners.

The first report on the psychoanalysis of married couples was made by Clarence Oberndorf at the American Psychiatric Association's 1931 convention (Oberndorf, 1938). Oberndorf advanced the theory that married couples have interlocking neuroses that are best treated in concert. This view was to be the underlying point of agreement among those analysts who became interested in treating couples. "Because of the continuous and intimate nature of marriage, every neurosis in a married person is strongly anchored in the marital relationship. It is a useful and at times indispensable therapeutic measure to concentrate the analytic discussions on the complementary patterns and, if necessary, to have both mates treated" (Mittleman, 1944, p. 491).

In 1948, Bela Mittleman of the New York Psychoanalytic Institute became the first to publish an account of concurrent marital therapy in the United States. Mittleman suggested that husbands and wives could be treated by the same analyst and that by seeing both it was possible to reexamine their irrational perceptions of each other (Mittleman, 1948). This was a revolutionary point of view from an analyst: that the reality of object relationships may be at least as important as their intrapsychic representations.

Meanwhile in Great Britain, where object relations were the central concern of psychoanalysts, Henry Dicks and his associates at the Tavistock Clinic established a Family Psychiatric Unit. Here couples referred by the divorce courts were helped to reconcile their differences (Dicks, 1964). Subsequently, the Balints affiliated their Family Discussion Bureau with the Tavistock Clinic, adding the clinic's prestige to their marital casework agency and, indirectly, to the field of marriage counseling.

In 1956, Mittleman wrote a more extensive description of his views on marital disorders and their treatment. He described a number of complementary marital patterns, including aggressive/submissive and detached/demanding. These odd matches are made, according to Mittleman, because courting couples distort each other's personalities through the eyes of their illusions: She sees his independence as strength; he sees her dependency as admiration. Mittleman also pointed out that the couple's reactions to each other may be shaped by their relationships with their parents. Without insight, unconscious motivation may dominate marital behavior, leading to reciprocal neurotic actions and reactions. For treatment, Mittleman believed that 20 percent of the time one therapist could handle all members of the family but that in other cases separate therapists for the members may be better.

At about this time Don Jackson and Jay Haley were also writing about marital therapy within the framework of communications analysis. As their ideas gained prominence among marital therapists, the field of marital therapy was absorbed into the larger family therapy movement.

Many writers don't distinguish between marital and family therapy. Therapy for couples, according to this way of thinking, is just family therapy applied to a particular family subsystem. We tend to agree with this perspective and, therefore, you will find our description of various approaches to couples and their problems embedded in the discussions of the models considered in this book. There is, however, a case to be made for considering couples therapy a distinct enterprise (Gurman & Jacobson, 2002).

Historically, many of the influential approaches to couples therapy came before their family therapy counterparts. Among these are cognitive-behavioral marital therapy, object relations marital therapy, emotionally focused couples therapy, and many of the integrative approaches considered in Chapter 14. Beyond the question of which came first, couples therapy differs in practice from family therapy in allowing for more in-depth focus on the psychology and experience of individuals. Sessions with the whole family tend to be noisy affairs. While it's possible in this context to spend time talking with family members about their feelings, wishes, and fears, it isn't possible to spend much time exploring the psychology of any one individual—much less two. Doing therapy with couples, on the

other hand, permits a much closer focus on both dyadic exchanges and on the underlying experience of intimate relationships.

From Research to Treatment: The Pioneers of Family Therapy

We have seen how family therapy was anticipated by developments in hospital psychiatry, group dynamics, interpersonal psychiatry, the child guidance movement, and research on schizophrenia. But who actually started family therapy? Although there are rival claims to this honor, the distinction should probably be shared by John Elderkin Bell, Don Jackson, Nathan Ackerman, and Murray Bowen. In addition to these founders of family therapy, Jay Haley, Virginia Satir, Carl Whitaker, Lyman Wynne, Ivan Boszormenyi-Nagy, and Salvador Minuchin were also significant pioneers.

John Elderkin Bell

John Elderkin Bell, a psychologist at Clark University in Worcester, Massachusetts, who began treating families in 1951, occupies a unique position in the history of family therapy. Although he may have been the first family therapist, he is mentioned only tangentially in two of the most important historical accounts of the movement (Guerin, 1976; Kaslow, 1980). The reason for this is that although he began seeing families in the 1950s, he didn't publish his ideas until a decade later. Moreover, unlike the other parents of family therapy, he had few offspring. He didn't establish a clinic, develop a training program, or train well-known students.

Bell's approach (Bell, 1961, 1962) was taken directly from group therapy. *Family group therapy* relied primarily on stimulating open discussion to help families solve their problems. Like a group therapist, Bell intervened to encourage silent participants to speak up, and he interpreted the reasons for their defensiveness.

Bell believed that family group therapy goes through predictable phases just as do groups

John Elderkin Bell

One of the first family therapists was John Elderkin Bell, who began treating families in the early 1950s. Bell's ingenious approach to family therapy involved a step-by-step plan of attack to treat family problems in stages. Bell's treatment model was an outgrowth of group therapy and was aptly named "family group therapy." Bell believed that the treatment of families should follow a series of stages designed to encourage communication among family members and to solve family problems.

of strangers. In his early work (Bell, 1961), he structured treatment in a series of stages, each of which concentrated on a particular segment of the family. Later, he became less directive and allowed families to evolve through a naturally unfolding sequence.

Palo Alto

The Bateson group stumbled onto family therapy more or less by accident. Once they began to interview schizophrenic families in 1954, hoping to decipher their patterns of communication, project members found themselves drawn into helping roles by the pain of these unhappy people (Jackson & Weakland, 1961). Although Bateson was the undisputed scientific leader of the group, Don Jackson and Jay Haley were most influential in developing family therapy.

Jackson rejected the psychoanalytic concepts he learned in training and focused instead on the dynamics of interchange between persons. Analysis of communication was his primary instrument. By 1954 Jackson had developed a rudimentary family interactional therapy, which he reported in a paper, "The Question of Family Homeostasis," delivered to the American Psychiatric Association convention in St. Louis. Borrowing from biology and systems theory, Jackson described families as homeostatic units.

Jackson's concept of **family homeostasis**—families as units that resist change—was to become the defining metaphor of family therapy's

early years. In hindsight, we can say that the focus on homeostasis overemphasized the conservative properties of families. At the time, however, the recognition that families resist change was enormously productive for understanding what keeps people stuck.

In "Schizophrenic Symptoms and Family Interaction" (Jackson & Weakland, 1959), Jackson illustrated how patients' symptoms preserve stability in their families. In one case a young woman diagnosed as a catatonic schizophrenic had as her most prominent symptom a profound indecisiveness. When she did behave decisively, however, her parents fell apart. Her mother became helpless and dependent; her father became, literally, impotent. In one family meeting, her parents failed to notice when the patient made a simple decision. Only after listening to a taped replay of the session *three times* did the parents finally hear their daughter's statement. The patient's indecision was neither crazy nor senseless; rather it protected her parents from facing their own difficulties. This case is one of the earliest published examples of how even psychotic symptoms can be meaningful in the family context. This paper also contains the shrewd observation that children's symptoms are often an exaggerated version of their parents' problems.

Another construct important to Jackson's thinking was the dichotomy between **symmetrical** and **complementary** relationships. (Like so many of the seminal ideas of family therapy, this one was first articulated by Bateson).

Don Jackson

The vibrant and creative talent of Don Jackson led to his prominent place among the founders of family therapy. A graduate of Stanford University School of Medicine, Jackson rejected the psychoanalytic concepts of his training in favor of cybernetics and communication theory, which he used to develop a pragmatic, problem-solving model of therapy.

Jackson's particular genius was in describing how patterns of communication reflect unspoken rules that govern relationships. According to Jackson, the early stage of a relationship is a kind of bargaining game in which the partners work out the rules that will subsequently govern the nature of their relationship. These "marital quid pro quos" are the basis on which the marriage contract will be written. Jackson died in 1968.

Complementary relationships are those in which partners are different in ways that fit together, like interlocking pieces of a jigsaw puzzle: If one is logical, the other is emotional; if one is weak, the other is strong. *Symmetrical* relationships are based on equality and similarity. Marriages between two partners who both have careers and share housekeeping chores are symmetrical. (Incidentally, if you actually find a couple who both have careers and share housekeeping equally, you'll know you're not in Kansas, Dorothy!)

Jackson's **family rules** hypothesis was simply a means of summarizing the observation that within any committed unit (dyad, triad, or larger group) there were redundant behavior patterns. Rules (as any student of philosophy learns when studying determinism) can describe regularity rather than regulation. A second part of the rules hypothesis was that family members use only some of the full range of behavior available to them. This seemingly innocent fact is what makes family therapy so useful.

Families who come to therapy can be seen as stuck in a narrow range of options, or unnecessarily rigid rules. Because the rules in families aren't spelled out, no one ratifies them, and they're hard to change. The therapist, however, as an outsider can help families see—and reexamine—the rules they live by.

Jackson's therapeutic strategies were based on the premise that psychiatric problems resulted from the way people behave with each other in a given context. Human problems were interactional *and* situational. To resolve problems, Jackson sought first to distinguish interactions (*redundant behavior patterns*) that were functional from those that were dysfunctional (*problem-maintaining*). To do so, he observed when problems occurred and in what context, who was present, and how people responded to the problem. Given the assumption that symptoms are homeostatic mechanisms, Jackson would wonder out loud how a family might be worse off if the problem got better. An individual may want to get better, but the family might need someone to play the sick role. Even positive change can be a threat to the defensive order of things.

A father's drinking, for example, might keep him from making demands on his wife or enforcing discipline over his children. Unfortunately, following Jackson, some family therapists jumped from the observation that symptoms *may* serve a purpose to the assumption that some families *need* a sick member, which, in turn, led to a view of parents victimizing **scapegoated** children. Despite the fancy language, this approach was part of the time-honored tradition of blaming parents for the failings of their children. If a six-year-old misbehaves around the house, perhaps we should look to his parents. But a husband's drinking isn't necessarily his family's fault, and certainly it wasn't fair to imply that families were responsible for the psychotic behavior of their schizophrenic members.

Looking back, we can see how the **cybernetic metaphor** of the family as a machine led to a view of the therapist as more mechanic than healer. In their zeal to rescue family "scapegoats" from the clutches of their "pathological families," early family therapists may have provoked some of the resistance they complained of.

The great discovery of the Bateson group was that there is no such thing as a simple communication; every message is qualified by another message on a higher level. In *Strategies of Psychotherapy*, Jay Haley explored how covert messages are used in the struggle for control that characterizes many relationships. Symptoms, he argued, represent an incongruence between levels of communication. The symptomatic person does something, such as touching a doorknob six times before turning it, while at the same time denying that he's *really* doing it. He can't help it; it's his condition. Meanwhile, the person's symptoms—over which he has no control—have consequences. A person with a "compulsion" of such proportions can hardly be expected to get himself out of the house in the morning, can he?

Since symptomatic behavior wasn't "reasonable," Haley didn't rely on reasoning with patients to help them. Instead, therapy became a strategic game of cat-and-mouse.

Haley (1963) defined therapy as a directive form of treatment and acknowledged his debt to Milton Erickson, with whom he studied hypnosis from 1954 to 1960. In what he called "brief therapy," Haley zeroed in on the context and possible function of the patient's symptoms. His first moves were designed to gain control of the therapeutic relationship. Haley cited Erickson's device of advising patients that in the first interview they may be willing to say some things and they'll want to withhold others, and that the latter, of course, should be withheld. Here, of course, the therapist is directing patients to do what they would do anyway and thus subtly gaining the upper hand.

The decisive technique in brief therapy was the use of *directives.* As Haley put it, it isn't enough to explain problems to patients; what counts is getting them to *do* something about them.

One of Haley's patients was a freelance photographer who compulsively made silly blunders that ruined every picture. Eventually he became so preoccupied with avoiding mistakes that he was too nervous to take pictures at all. Haley instructed the man to go out and take three pictures, making one deliberate error in each. The paradox here is that you can't accidentally make a mistake if you are doing so deliberately.

In another case, Haley told an insomniac that if he woke up in the middle of the night he should get out of bed and wax the kitchen floor. Instant cure! The cybernetic principle here is: People will do anything to get out of housework.

Most of the ideas that came out of the Palo Alto group—double bind, complementarity, quid pro quo—focused on dyads, but Haley also became interested in triads or, as he called them, **coalitions.** Coalitions should be distinguished from alliances, cooperative arrangements between two parties, not formed at the expense of a third. In symptomatic families, Haley observed, most coalitions were *cross-generational*, one parent ganging up with a child against the other parent.

In "Toward a Theory of Pathological Systems," Haley described what he called *perverse triangles*, which may lead to violence, psychopathology, or the breakup of a system. A perverse triangle is a hidden coalition that undermines generational hierarchies. Examples include a child running to his grandmother every time his mother tries to punish him, or one parent complaining about the other to the children. Perverse triangles also occur in organizations when, for example, a supervisor joins with one subordinate against another, or when a professor complains to his students about the department chair. In looking beyond cybernetics and dyads to triads and hierarchies, Haley was to become an important bridge between strategic and structural approaches to family therapy.

Another member of the Palo Alto group who played a leading role in family therapy's first decade was Virginia Satir, one of the great charismatic healers. Known more for her clinical artistry than for theoretical contributions, Satir's impact was most vivid to those lucky enough to see her in action. Like her confreres, Satir was interested in communication, but she added an emotional dimension that helped counterbalance what was otherwise a relatively cool and cerebral approach.

Satir saw troubled family members as trapped in narrow family roles, like *victim, placator, defiant one*, or *rescuer*, that constrained relationships and sapped self-esteem. Her concern with freeing family members from the grip of such life-constricting roles was consistent with her major focus, which was always on the individual. Thus, Satir was a humanizing force in the early days of family therapy, when many were so enamored of the systems metaphor that they neglected the emotional life of families.

Satir concentrated on clarifying communication, expressing feelings, and fostering a climate of mutual acceptance and warmth. Her great strength was to connect with families—not in terms of conflict and bickering but in terms of hopes and fears, yearnings and disappointments. One of the things for which Satir was justly famous was her ability to turn negatives into positives.

In one case, cited by Lynn Hoffman (1981), Satir interviewed the family of an adolescent boy, son of the local minister, who had gotten two of his classmates pregnant. On one side of the room sat the boy's parents and siblings. The boy sat in the opposite corner with his head down. Satir introduced herself and said to the boy, "Well, your father has told me a lot about the situation on the phone, and I just want to say before we begin that we know one thing for sure: We know you have good seed." The boy looked up in amazement as Satir turned to the boy's mother and asked brightly, "Could you start by telling us your perception?"

The 1964 publication of Satir's book *Conjoint Family Therapy* did much to popularize the family therapy movement. This book, along with *Pragmatics of Human Communication* (Watzlawick, Beavin, & Jackson, 1957), helped make the Palo Alto group's brand of systemic thinking the leading model of the 1960s.

Murray Bowen

Like many of the founders of family therapy, Murray Bowen was a psychiatrist who specialized in schizophrenia. Unlike others, however, he emphasized theory in his work, and to this day Bowen's theory is the most fertile system of ideas that family therapy has produced.

Bowen began his clinical work at the Menninger Clinic in 1946, where he studied mothers and their schizophrenic children. His major interest at the time was mother–child symbiosis, which led to his concept of **differentiation of self** (autonomy from others and separation of thought from feeling). From Menninger, Bowen moved to the National Institute of Mental Health (NIMH), where he developed a project to hospitalize whole families with schizophrenic members. It was this project that expanded the concept of mother–child symbiosis to include the role of fathers, and led to the concept of *triangles* (diverting conflict between two people by involving a third). In 1959, Bowen left NIMH for Georgetown Medical School where he was a professor of psychiatry and director of his own training program until his death in the fall of 1990.

Beginning in 1955, when Bowen started bringing family members together to discuss their problems, he was struck by their **emotional reactivity.** Feelings overwhelmed thinking and drowned out individuality in the chaos of the group. Bowen felt the family's tendency to pull him into the center of this **undifferentiated family ego mass,** and he had to make a concerted effort to remain objective (Bowen, 1961). The ability to remain neutral and attentive to the process, rather than the content, of family discussions is what distinguishes a therapist from a participant in a family's drama.

To control the level of emotion, Bowen encouraged family members to talk to him, not to each other. He found that it was easier for people to listen without becoming reactive when other family members spoke to the therapist instead of to each other.

Bowen also discovered that therapists weren't immune from being sucked into family conflicts. This awareness led to his greatest insight. Whenever two people are struggling with conflict they can't resolve, there is an automatic tendency to draw in a third party. In fact, as Bowen came to believe, the **triangle** is the smallest stable unit of relationship.

A husband who can't stand his wife's habitual lateness, but who also can't stand up and tell her so, may start complaining about her to one of his children. His complaining may release some tension, but the very process of complaining to a third party makes him less likely to address the problem at its source. We all complain about other people from time to time, but what Bowen realized was that this "triangling" process is destructive when it becomes a regular feature of a relationship.

Another thing Bowen discovered about triangles is that they spread out. In the following case, a family had become entangled in a whole labyrinth of triangles.

One Sunday morning "Mrs. McNeil," who was anxious to get the family to church on time, yelled at her nine-year-old son to hurry up. When he told her to "quit bitching," she slapped him. At that point her fourteen-year-old daughter, Megan, grabbed her, and the two of them started wrestling. Then Megan ran next door to her friend's house. When the friend's parents noticed that she had a cut lip and Megan told them what had happened, they called the police. One thing led to another, and by the time the family came to therapy the following triangles were in place: Mrs. McNeil, who'd been ordered out of the house by the family court judge, was allied with her lawyer against the judge; she also had an individual therapist who joined her in thinking she was being hounded unfairly by the child protective workers. The nine-year-old was still mad at his mother, and his father supported him in blaming her for flying off the handle. Mr. McNeil, who was a recovering alcoholic, formed an alliance with his sponsor, who felt that Mr. McNeil was on his way to a breakdown unless his wife started being more supportive. Meanwhile Megan had formed a triangle with the neighbors, who thought her parents shouldn't be allowed to have children. In short, everyone had an advocate—everyone, that is, except the family unit.

In 1966, an emotional crisis occurred in Bowen's family that led him to initiate a personal voyage of discovery that turned out to be as significant for Bowen's theory as Freud's self-analysis was for psychoanalysis.

As an adult, Bowen, the oldest of five children from a tightly knit rural family, kept his distance from his parents and the rest of his extended family. Like many of us, he mistook avoidance for emancipation. But as he later realized, unfinished emotional business stays with us, making us vulnerable to repeat conflicts we never got around to working out with our families.

Bowen's most important achievement was detriangling himself from his parents, who'd been accustomed to complaining to him about each other. Most of us are flattered to receive such confidences, but Bowen came to recognize this triangulation for what it was. When his mother complained about his father, he told his father: "Your wife told me a story about you; I wonder why she told me instead of you." Naturally, his father discussed this with his mother and, naturally, she was annoyed.

Although his efforts generated the kind of emotional upheaval that comes of breaking family rules, Bowen's maneuver was effective in keeping his parents from trying to get him to take sides—and made it harder for them to avoid discussing things between themselves. Repeating what someone says to you about someone else is one way to stop triangling in its tracks.

Through his efforts in his own family Bowen discovered that differentiation of self is best accomplished by developing an individual, person-to-person relationship with each parent and with as many members of the extended family as possible. If visiting is difficult, letters and phone calls can help reestablish relationships, particularly if they're personal and intimate. Differentiating one's self from the family is completed when these relationships are maintained without becoming emotionally reactive or taking part in triangles.

Nathan Ackerman

Nathan Ackerman was a child psychiatrist whose pioneering work with families remained faithful to his psychoanalytic roots. Although his interest in intrapsychic conflict may have seemed less innovative than the Palo Alto group's focus on communication as feedback, he had a keen sense of the overall organization of families. Families, Ackerman said, may give the appearance of unity, but underneath they are split into competing factions. This you may recognize as similar to the psychoanalytic model of individuals who, despite apparent unity of personality, are actually minds in conflict, driven by warring drives and defenses.

Ackerman joined the staff of the Menninger Clinic and in 1937 became chief psychiatrist of the Child Guidance Clinic. At first he followed the child guidance model, having a psychiatrist treat the child and a social worker see the mother. By the mid-1940s, he began to experiment with the same therapist seeing both. Unlike Bowlby, Ackerman did more than use these conjoint sessions as a temporary expedient; instead, he began to see the family as the basic unit of treatment.

In 1955 Ackerman organized the first session on family diagnosis at a meeting of the American Orthopsychiatric Association. At that meeting, Jackson, Bowen, Wynne, and Ackerman learned about each other's work and joined in a

---

Nathan Ackerman

Nathan Ackerman's astute ability to understand families enabled him to look beyond behavioral interactions and into the hearts and minds of each family member. He used his forceful personality to uncover the family's defenses and allow their feelings, hopes, and desires to surface. Ackerman's psychoanalytic training is evident in his contributions and theoretical approach to family therapy. Ackerman proposed that underneath the apparent unity of families there existed a layer of intrapsychic conflict that divided family members into factions.

Together with Don Jackson, Ackerman founded the first family therapy journal, *Family Process*, which is still the leading journal of ideas in the field. In 1957 Ackerman established the Family Mental Health Clinic in New York City and began teaching at Columbia University. He opened the Family Institute in 1960, which was renamed the Ackerman Institute after his death in 1971.

sense of common purpose. Two years later Ackerman opened the Family Mental Health Clinic of Jewish Family Services in New York City and began teaching at Columbia University. In 1960 he founded the Family Institute, which was renamed the Ackerman Institute following his death in 1971.

Although other family therapists downplayed the psychology of individuals, Ackerman was as concerned with what goes on inside people as with what goes on between them. He never lost sight of feelings, hopes, and desires. In fact, Ackerman's model of the family was like the psychoanalytic model of an individual writ large; instead of conscious and unconscious issues, Ackerman talked about how families confront some issues while avoiding others, particularly those involving sex and aggression. He saw his job as a therapist as one of stirring things up, bringing family secrets out into the open. He was an *agent provocateur*, prompting revelations and confrontations with his wit and willingness to stick his nose into personal family issues.

To promote honest emotional interchange, Ackerman "tickled the defenses" of family members—his phrase for provoking people to open up and say what's really on their minds. What are thought to be family secrets, Ackerman said, generally turn out to be common knowledge but simply not talked about. However, as long as a family trusts their therapist, they feel freer to speak about matters they usually avoid.

To encourage families to relax their emotional restraint, Ackerman himself was unrestrained. He freely sided first with one part of the family and then with another. He didn't think it was necessary—or possible—always to be neutral; instead, he believed that balance was achieved in the long run by moving back and forth, giving support now to one, later to another family member. At times he was unabashedly blunt. If he thought someone was lying, he said so. To critics who suggested this directness might generate too much anxiety, Ackerman replied that people get more reassurance from honesty than from false politeness.

Ackerman urged therapists to become emotionally engaged with families and to bring dormant conflicts into the open. How does a therapist encourage candid disclosures? Ackerman did it by challenging avoidance and emotional dishonesty ("tickling the defenses"). Perhaps his most enduring contribution was his consistent respect for individual persons *and* whole families; he never lost sight of the self in the system.

Carl Whitaker

Even among the unorthodox founders of family therapy, Carl Whitaker stood out as the most irreverent. His view of psychologically troubled people was that they were alienated from feeling and frozen into devitalized routines (Whitaker & Malone, 1953). Whitaker turned up the emotional temperature. His "Psychotherapy of the Absurd" (Whitaker, 1975) was a blend of warm support and unpredictable emotional goading, designed to loosen people up and help them get in touch with their experience in a deeper, more personal way.

Given his bold and inventive approach to individual therapy, it isn't surprising that Whitaker became one of the first to break with psychiatric tradition and experiment with family treatment. In 1943, he and John Warkentin, working in Oakridge, Tennessee, began including spouses and eventually children in treatment. Whitaker also pioneered the use of cotherapy, in the belief that a supportive partner helped free therapists to react without fear of countertransference.

Whitaker created tension by teasing and confronting families because he believed that stress is necessary for change. He never seemed to have an obvious strategy nor did he use predictable techniques, preferring, as he said, to let his unconscious run the therapy (Whitaker, 1976). Although his work seemed totally unthought-out, even outrageous at times, it had a consistent theme. All of his interventions had the effect of promoting flexibility. He didn't so much push families to change in a particular direction as he challenged them to open up—to become more fully themselves and more fully together.

In 1946, Whitaker became chairman of the Department of Psychiatry at Emory University, where he continued to experiment with family treatment with a special interest in schizophrenics and their families. During this period Whitaker organized a series of conferences that eventually led to the first major meeting of the family therapy movement. Beginning in 1946, Whitaker and his colleagues began twice-yearly conferences during which they observed and discussed each other's work with families. The group found these sessions enormously helpful, and mutual observation, using one-way vision screens, has since become one of the hallmarks of family therapy.

Whitaker resigned from Emory in 1955 and entered private practice, where he and his partners at the Atlanta Psychiatric Clinic developed an "experiential" form of psychotherapy, using a number of highly provocative techniques in the treatment of families, individuals, groups, and couples (Whitaker, 1958).

During the late 1970s Whitaker seemed to mellow and also to add a greater understanding of family dynamics to his shoot-from-the-hip interventions. In the process, the former wild man of family therapy became one of its elder statesmen. Whitaker's death in April 1995 left the field with a piece of its heart missing.

Ivan Boszormenyi-Nagy

Ivan Boszormenyi-Nagy, who came to family therapy from psychoanalysis, has been one of the seminal thinkers in the movement since its earliest days. In 1957 he founded the Eastern Pennsylvania Psychiatric Institute in Philadelphia, where he attracted a host of highly talented colleagues and students. Among these were James Framo, one of the few psychologists in the early family therapy movement, and Geraldine Spark, a social worker who worked with Boszormenyi-Nagy as cotherapist and coauthor of *Invisible Loyalties* (Boszormenyi-Nagy & Spark, 1973).

This group was joined by Ross Speck, who did his psychiatric residency in the early 1960s and developed, along with Carolyn Attneave, **network therapy,** which broadened the context of treatment far beyond the nuclear family. In this approach, as many people as possible who are connected to the patient are invited to attend therapy sessions. Often as many as fifty people, including extended family, friends, neighbors, and teachers, are brought together to discuss ways to support and help the patient change (Speck & Attneave, 1973).

Boszormenyi-Nagy describes himself as a therapist who went from being an analyst, prizing secrecy and confidentiality, to a family therapist, fighting the forces of pathology on an open battlefield. One of his most important contributions was to add ethical accountability to the usual therapeutic goals and techniques. According to Boszormenyi-Nagy, neither pleasure nor expediency is a sufficient guide to human behavior. Instead, he believes that family members have to base their relationships on trust and loyalty, and that they must balance the ledger of entitlement and indebtedness.

Salvador Minuchin

When Minuchin first burst onto the scene, it was the drama of his brilliant clinical demonstrations that people found captivating. This compelling man with an elegant Latin accent would seduce, provoke, bully, or bewilder families into changing—as the situation required. But even Minuchin's legendary flair didn't have the same galvanizing impact of the practical simplicity of his structural model.

Minuchin began his career as a family therapist in the early 1960s when he discovered two patterns common to troubled families: Some are *enmeshed*—chaotic and tightly interconnected; others are *disengaged*—isolated and seemingly unrelated. Both types lack clear lines of authority. Enmeshed parents are too entangled with their children to exercise leadership; disengaged parents are too distant to provide effective support.

Family problems are tenacious and resistant to change because they're embedded in powerful but unseen structures. Take, for example, a mother futilely remonstrating with a willful child. The mother can scold, punish, reward with gold stars, or try leniency; but as long as she's enmeshed (overly involved) with the child, her efforts lack force because she lacks authority. Moreover, because the behavior of one family member is always related to that of others, the mother will have trouble stepping back as long as her husband remains disengaged.

Once a social system such as a family becomes structured, attempts to change the rules constitute what family therapists call **first-order change**—change within a system that itself remains invariant. For the mother in the previous example to start practicing stricter discipline would be an example of first-order change. The enmeshed mother is caught in an illusion of alternatives. She can be strict or lenient; the result is the same because she remains trapped in a triangle. What's needed is **second-order change**—a change in the system itself.

Minuchin first worked out his ideas while struggling with the problems of juvenile delinquency at the Wiltwyck School for Boys in New York. Family therapy with urban slum families was a new development, and publication of his ideas (Minuchin, Montalvo, Guerney, Rosman, & Schumer, 1967) led to his being invited to become the director of the Philadelphia Child Guidance Clinic in 1965. Minuchin brought Braulio Montalvo and Bernice Rosman with him, and they were joined in 1967 by Jay Haley. Together they transformed a traditional child guidance clinic into one of the great centers of the family therapy movement.

The techniques of *structural family therapy* fall into two general strategies. First the therapist must accommodate to the family in order to "join" them. To begin by challenging a family's preferred mode of relating is almost guaranteed to provoke resistance. If, instead, the therapist starts by trying to understand and accept the family, they'll be more likely to accept treatment. (No one is eager to accept advice from someone they feel doesn't understand them.) Once this initial joining is accomplished, the structural family therapist begins to use *restructuring* tech-

niques. These are active maneuvers designed to disrupt dysfunctional structures by strengthening diffuse boundaries and loosening rigid ones (Minuchin & Fishman, 1981).

In 1981 Minuchin moved to New York and established what is now known as the Minuchin Center for the Family, where he pursued his dedication to teaching family therapists from all over the world and his commitment to social justice by working with the foster care system. He also continued to turn out a steady stream of the most influential books in the field. His 1974 *Families and Family Therapy* is deservedly the most popular book in the history of family therapy, and his 1993 *Family Healing* contains some of the most moving descriptions of family therapy ever written.

Other Early Centers of Family Therapy

In New York, Israel Zwerling and Marilyn Mendelsohn organized the Family Studies Section at Albert Einstein College of Medicine. Andrew Ferber was named director in 1964, and later Philip Guerin, a protégé of Murray Bowen, joined the section. Nathan Ackerman served as a consultant, and the group assembled an impressive array of family therapists with diverse orientations. These included Chris Beels, Betty Carter, Monica McGoldrick, Peggy Papp, and Thomas Fogarty.

Philip Guerin became Director of Training in 1970 and shortly thereafter, in 1973, he founded the Center for Family Learning in Westchester, where he and Thomas Fogarty developed one of the finest family therapy training programs in the nation.

In Galveston, Texas, Robert MacGregor and his colleagues developed *multiple impact therapy* (MacGregor, 1967). It was a case of necessity being the mother of invention. MacGregor's clinic served a large population scattered widely over southeastern Texas, and many of his clients had to travel hundreds of miles. Because they had to come such distances, most of these people were unable to return for weekly sessions. Therefore, to have maximum impact in a short time, Mac-

Gregor assembled a team of professionals who worked intensively with the families for two full days. Although few family therapists have used such marathon sessions, the team approach continues to be one of the hallmarks of the field.

In Boston the two most significant early contributions to family therapy were both in the experiential wing of the movement. Norman Paul developed an "operational mourning" approach designed to resolve impacted grief, and Fred and Bunny Duhl set up the Boston Family Institute, where they developed "integrative family therapy."

In Chicago, the Family Institute of Chicago and the Institute for Juvenile Research were important centers of the early scene in family therapy. At the Family Institute, Charles and Jan Kramer developed a clinical training program that was later affiliated with Northwestern University Medical School. The Institute for Juvenile Research also mounted a training program under the leadership of Irv Borstein, with the consultation of Carl Whitaker.

The work of Nathan Epstein and his colleagues, first formulated in the department of psychiatry at McMaster University in Hamilton, Ontario, was a problem-centered approach (Epstein, Bishop, & Baldarin, 1981). The "McMaster Model" goes step by step—elucidating the problem, gathering data, considering alternative resolutions, and assessing the learning process—to help families understand their interactions and build on their newly acquired coping skills. Epstein later relocated to Brown University in Providence, Rhode Island.

Important developments in family therapy also occurred outside the United States: Robin Skynner (1976) introduced psychodynamic family therapy at the Institute of Family Therapy in London. British psychiatrist John Howells (1971) developed a system of family diagnosis as a necessary step for planning therapeutic intervention. West German Helm Stierlin (1972) integrated psychodynamic and systemic ideas for treating troubled adolescents. In Rome, Maurizio Andolfi worked with families early in the 1970s and founded, in 1974, the Italian Society for Family Therapy; Mara Selvini Palazzoli and her colleagues founded the Institute for Family Studies in Milan in 1967.

●

Now that you've seen how family therapy emerged in several different places at once, we hope you haven't lost sight of one thing: There is a tremendous satisfaction in seeing how people's behavior makes sense in the context of their families. Meeting with a family for the first time is like turning on a light in a dark room.

The Golden Age of Family Therapy

In their first decade family therapists had all the enthusiasm and bravado of new kids on the block. "Look at this!" Haley and Jackson and Bowen seemed to say when they discovered the extent to which the whole family was implicated in the symptoms of individual patients. These new-style healers were pioneers, busy opening up new territory and staking their claim against unfriendly elements in the psychiatric establishment.

While they were struggling for legitimacy, family clinicians emphasized their common beliefs and downplayed their differences. Troubles, they agreed, came in families. But if the watchword of the 1960s was "Look at this!"—emphasizing the leap of understanding made possible by seeing whole families together—the rallying cry of the 1970s was "Look what I can do!" as the new kids flexed their muscles and carved out their own turf.

The period from 1970 to 1985 saw the flowering of the famous schools of family therapy when the pioneers established training centers and worked out the implications of their models. The leading approach in the 1960s was the *communications model* developed in Palo Alto. The book of the decade was *Pragmatics of Human Communication*, the text that introduced the systemic version of family therapy (and led some people to believe that reading it would make them family therapists). The model of the 1980s was *strategic therapy,* and the books of the decade described its three most vital approaches: *Change* by Watzlawick, Weakland, and Fisch[1]; *Problem-Solving Therapy* by Jay Haley; and *Paradox and Counterparadox* by Mara Selvini Palazzoli and her Milan associates. The 1970s belonged to Salvador Minuchin. His *Families and Family Therapy* and the simple yet compelling model of *structural family therapy* it described dominated the decade.

Structural theory seemed to offer just what family therapists were looking for: a simple way of describing family organization and a set of easy-to-follow steps to treatment. So persuasive were the ideas described in *Families and Family Therapy* that for a while it seemed that all you had to do to transform families was to join them, map their structure, and then do what Salvador Minuchin did to unbalance them. That was the rub.

In hindsight, we might ask whether the impressive power of Minuchin's approach was a product of the method or the man. (The answer is, probably a little of both.) In the 1970s, however, the widely shared belief that structural family therapy could be easily learned drew people from all over the world to what was for a decade the epicenter of the family therapy movement: the Philadelphia Child Guidance Clinic.

The strategic therapy that flourished in the 1980s was centered in three unique and creative groups: The Palo Alto Mental Research Institute's brief-therapy group, including John Weakland, Paul Watzlawick, and Richard Fisch; Jay Haley and Cloe Madanes, codirectors of the Family Therapy Institute of Washington, D.C.; and Mara Selvini Palazzoli and her colleagues in Milan. But the leading influence in the decade of strategic therapy was exerted by Milton Erickson, albeit from beyond the grave.

Erickson's genius was much admired and much imitated. Family therapists came to idolize Erickson the way we as children idolized Cap-

tain Marvel. We'd come home from Saturday matinees all pumped up, get out our toy swords, put on our magic capes—and presto! *We* were superheroes. We were just kids and so we didn't bother translating our heroes' mythic powers into our own terms. Unfortunately, many of those who were starstruck by Erickson's legendary therapeutic tales did the same thing. Instead of grasping the principles on which they were predicated, many therapists just tried to imitate his "uncommon techniques." To be any kind of competent therapist you must keep your psychological distance from the supreme artists—the Minuchins, the Milton Ericksons, the Michael Whites. Otherwise you end up aping the magic of their style rather than grasping the substance of their ideas.

Part of what made Jay Haley's strategic directives so attractive was that they were a wonderful way to gain power and control over people—for their own good—without the usual frustration of trying to convince them to do the right thing. (Most people already know what's good for them. The hard part is getting them to *do* it.) So, for example, in the case of a person who is bulimic, a strategic directive might be for the patient's family to set out a mess of fried chicken, french fries, cookies, and ice cream. Then, with the family watching, the patient would mash up all the food with her hands, symbolizing what goes on in her stomach. After the food was reduced to a soggy mess, she would stuff it into the toilet. Then when the toilet clogged, she would have to ask the family member she resented most to unclog it. This task would symbolize not only what the person with bulimia does to herself but also what she puts the family through (Madanes, 1981).

What the strategic camp added to Erickson's creative problem solving was a simple framework for understanding how families get stuck in their problems. According to the MRI model, problems develop and persist from mismanagement of ordinary life difficulties. The original difficulty becomes a problem when mishandling leads people to get stuck in more-of-the-same solutions. It was a perverse twist on the old adage, "If at first you don't succeed, try, try again."

---

1. Although actually published in 1974, this book and its sequel, *The Tactics of Change,* were most widely read and taught in the 1980s.

The Milan group built on the ideas pioneered at MRI, especially the use of the therapeutic double bind, or what they referred to as *counterparadox*. Here's an example from *Paradox and Counterparadox* (Selvini Palazzoli, Boscolo, Cecchin, & Prata, 1978). The authors describe using a counterparadoxical approach with a six-year-old boy and his family. At the end of the session, young Bruno was praised for acting crazy to protect his father. By occupying his mother's time with fights and tantrums, the boy generously allowed his father more time for work and relaxation. Bruno was encouraged to continue doing what he was already doing, lest this comfortable arrangement be disrupted.

The appeal of the strategic approach was pragmatism. Making good use of the cybernetic metaphor, strategic therapists zeroed in on how family systems were regulated by negative feedback. They achieved remarkable results simply by disrupting the interactions that maintained symptoms. What eventually turned therapists off to these approaches was their gamesmanship. Their interventions were transparently manipulative. The result was like watching a clumsy magician—you could see him stacking the deck.

Meanwhile, as structural and strategic approaches rose and fell in popularity, four other models of family therapy flourished quietly. Though they never took center stage, *experiential, psychoanalytic, behavioral,* and *Bowenian* models grew and prospered. Although these schools never achieved the cachet of family therapy's latest fads, each of them produced solid clinical approaches, which will be examined at length in subsequent chapters.

Looking back from soberer times, it's difficult to convey the excitement and optimism that energized family therapy in its golden age. Training centers sprouted up all over the country, workshops were packed, and the leaders of the movement were celebrated like rock stars. Active and forceful interveners, their self-assurance was infectious. Minuchin, Whitaker, Haley, Madanes, and Selvini Palazzoli seemed to rise above the limitations of ordinary talk therapy. Young therapists needed inspiration, and they found it. They learned from the masters, and they idolized them.

Somewhere in the mid-1980s a reaction set in. Despite optimistic assumptions, these activist approaches didn't always work. So the field took revenge on those they'd idealized by cutting them down to size. Maybe it was Haley's manipulativeness that turned them off, or that Minuchin sometimes seemed more bossy than brilliant. Family therapists had marveled at their creativity and tried to copy it, but creativity can't be copied.

By the end of the 1980s, the leaders of the major schools were growing older and their influence was waning. What once seemed heroic now seemed aggressive and overbearing. A series of challenges—feminist and postmodern critiques, the reemergence of analytic and biological models, the magic bullet Prozac, the success of recovery programs like Alcoholics Anonymous, the ugly facts of wife beating and child abuse that challenged the notion that domestic problems were always a product of relationship—shook our confidence in the models we knew to be true, knew would work. We'll take a closer look at these challenges in subsequent chapters.

—Summary—

1. Family therapy has a short history but a long past. For many years therapists resisted the idea of seeing a patient's relatives in order to safeguard the privacy of the patient–therapist relationship. Freudians excluded the real family to uncover the unconscious, introjected family; Rogerians kept relatives away to provide unconditional positive regard; and hospital psychiatrists discouraged family visits because they might disrupt the benign milieu of the hospital.

2. Several converging developments in the 1950s led to a new view, namely, that the family was a living system, an organic whole. Hospital psychiatrists noticed that often when patients improved, someone else in the family got worse. Thus it became clear that change in any one person changes the whole system. Eventually it became apparent that changing the family might be the most effective way to change the individual.

3. Although practicing clinicians in hospitals and child guidance clinics prepared the way for family therapy, the most important breakthroughs were achieved in the 1950s by workers who were scientists first, healers second. In Palo Alto, Gregory Bateson, Jay Haley, Don Jackson, and John Weakland, studying communication, discovered that schizophrenia made sense in the context of *pathologic family communication*. Schizophrenics weren't crazy in some meaningless way; their apparently illogical behavior was understandable in the context of their families. At Yale, Theodore Lidz found a striking pattern of instability and conflict in the families of schizophrenics. *Marital schism* (open conflict) and *marital skew* (pathologic balance) had profound effects on the development of children. Murray Bowen's observation of how mothers and their schizophrenic offspring go through cycles of closeness and distance was the forerunner of the *pursuer–distancer* dynamic. By hospitalizing whole families for observation and treatment, Bowen implicitly located the problem of schizophrenia in an *undifferentiated family ego mass* and even extended it beyond the nuclear family to three generations. Lyman Wynne linked schizophrenia to the family by demonstrating how *communication deviance* contributes to thought disorder.

4. These observations launched the family therapy movement, but the excitement they generated blurred the distinction between what researchers observed and what they concluded. What they observed was that the behavior of schizophrenics *fit* with their families; what they concluded was that the family must be the *cause*

of schizophrenia. A second conclusion was even more influential. Family dynamics—double binds, pseudomutuality, undifferentiated family ego mass—began to be seen as products of a "system" rather than as features of persons who share certain qualities because they live together. Thus was born a new creature, the *family system*.

5. Who was the first to practice family therapy? This turns out to be a difficult question. As in every field, there were visionaries who anticipated the development of family therapy. Freud, for example, treated "Little Hans" by working with his father as early as 1908. Such experiments, however, weren't sufficient to challenge the hegemony of individual therapy until the climate of the times was receptive. In the early 1950s, family therapy was begun independently in four different places: by John Bell at Clark University, Murray Bowen at NIMH, Nathan Ackerman in New York, and Don Jackson and Jay Haley in Palo Alto.

6. These pioneers had distinctly different backgrounds and clinical orientations. Not surprisingly, therefore, the approaches they developed were also quite different. This diversity still characterizes the field today. Had family therapy been started by a single person, as was psychoanalysis, it's unlikely that there would have been so much creative competition so soon.

7. In addition to those just mentioned, others who made significant contributions to the founding of family therapy were Lyman Wynne, Theodore Lidz, Virginia Satir, Carl Whitaker, Ivan Boszormenyi-Nagy, Robert MacGregor, and Salvador Minuchin.

8. What we've called family therapy's golden age—the flowering of the schools in the 1970s and 1980s—was the high-water mark of our self-confidence. Armed with Haley's or Minuchin's latest text, therapists pledged allegiance to one school or another and set off with a sense of mission. What drew them to activist approaches was certainty and charisma. What soured them was hubris. To some, structural family therapy—at least as they had seen it

demonstrated at workshops—began to seem like bullying. Others saw the shrewdness of the strategic approach as manipulative. The tactics were clever but cold. Families were described as stubborn; they couldn't be reasoned with. You don't tell a cybernetic machine what you really believe. Therapists got tired of that way of thinking.

9. In the early years, family therapists were animated by a tremendous sense of enthusiasm and conviction. Today, in the wake of postmodern critiques, managed care, and a resurgence of biological psychiatry, we're less sure of ourselves. In subsequent chapters we'll see how today's family therapists have managed to synthesize creative new ideas with some of the best of the earlier models. But as we explore each of the famous models in depth, we'll also see how some good ideas have been unwisely neglected.

10. All the complexity of the family therapy field should not, however, obscure its basic premise: The family is the context of human problems. Like all human groups, the family has emergent properties—the whole is greater than the sum of its parts. Moreover, no matter how many and varied the explanations of these emergent properties, they all fall into two categories: *structure* and *process*. The structure of families includes *triangles*, *subsystems*, and *boundaries*. Among the processes that describe family interaction—*emotional reactivity*, *dysfunctional communication*, and so on—the central concept is circularity. Rather than worrying about who started what, family therapists understand and treat human problems as a series of moves and countermoves, in repeating cycles.

—Questions to Consider—

1. Which of the early concepts of family therapy—complementarity, differentiation of self, homeostasis, resistance—are inherently sexist? Which could be used to support sexist assumptions?
2. Which of Bion's three basic assumptions (fight–flight, pairing, dependency) best describe how you and your classmates behave in your least favorite classes?
3. Which of family therapy's early concepts and methods might tend to foster an adversarial relationship with families? What in your own background might predispose you to approach certain family members as adversaries (e.g., controlling mothers, distant fathers, etc.)?

—Key Concepts—

coalition   An alliance between two persons or social units against a third.

communications theory   The study of relationships in terms of the exchange of verbal and nonverbal messages.

complementary relationship   Relationship based on differences that fit together in which qualities of one make up for lacks in the other.

cybernetics   The study of self-controlling processes in systems, especially the analysis of positive and negative feedback loops.

differentiation of self   Psychological separation of intellect and emotions and in dependence of self from others; opposite of fusion.

double bind   A conflict created when a person receives contradictory messages on different levels of abstraction in an important relationship and cannot leave or comment.

emotional reactivity   The tendency to respond in a knee-jerk emotional fashion, rather than calmly and objectively.

family homeostasis Tendency of families to resist change in order to maintain a steady state.

family rules A descriptive term for redundant behavioral patterns.

family system The family conceived as a collective whole entity made up of individual parts plus the way they function together.

first-order change Superficial change in a system that itself stays invariant.

group dynamics Interactions among group members that emerge as a result of properties of the group rather than merely of their individual personalities.

homeostasis A balanced steady state of equilibrium.

identified patient The symptom-bearer or official patient as identified by the family.

marital schism Lidz's term for pathologic overt marital conflict.

marital skew Lidz's term for a pathologic marriage in which one spouse dominates the other.

metacommunication Every message has two levels, report and command; metacommunication is the implied command or qualifying message.

mystification Laing's concept that many families distort their children's experience by denying or relabeling it.

network therapy A treatment devised by Ross Speck in which a large number of family and friends are assembled to help resolve a patient's problems.

process/content Distinction between how members of a family or group relate (process) and what they talk about (content).

pseudohostility Wynne's term for superficial bickering that masks pathologic alignments in schizophrenic families.

pseudomutuality Wynne's term for the facade of family harmony that characterizes many schizophrenic families.

rubber fence Wynne's term for the rigid boundary surrounding many schizophrenic families, which allows only minimal contact with the surrounding community.

scapegoat A member of the family, usually the identified patient, who is the object of displaced conflict or criticism.

schizophrenogenic mother Fromm-Reichmann's term for aggressive, domineering mothers thought to precipitate schizophrenia in their offspring.

second-order change Basic change in the structure and functioning of a system.

second-order cybernetics The idea that anyone attempting to observe and change a system is therefore part of that system.

symmetrical relationship In relationships, equality or parallel form.

triangle A three-person system; according to Bowen, the smallest stable unit of human relations.

undifferentiated family ego mass Bowen's early term for emotional "stuck-togetherness" or fusion in the family, especially prominent in schizophrenic families.

—Recommended Readings—

Ackerman, N. W. 1958. *The psychodynamics of family life*. New York: Basic Books.

Bowen, M. 1960. A family concept of schizophrenia. In *The etiology of schizophrenia*, D. D. Jackson, ed. New York: Basic Books.

Greenberg, G. S. 1977. The family interactional perspective: A study and examination of the work of Don D. Jackson. *Family Process. 16:* 385–412.

Haley, J., and Hoffman, L., eds. 1968. *Techniques of family therapy*. New York: Basic Books.

Jackson, D. D. 1957. The question of family homeostasis. *The Psychiatric Quarterly Supplement. 31:* 79–90.

Jackson, D. D. 1965. Family rules: Marital quid pro quo. *Archives of General Psychiatry. 12:* 589–594.

Lidz, T., Cornelison, A., Fleck, S., and Terry, D. 1957. Intrafamilial environment of schizophrenic patients. II: Marital schism and marital skew. *American Journal of Psychiatry. 20:* 241–248.

Weakland, J. H. 1960. The "double-bind" hypothesis of schizophrenia and three-party interaction. In *The etiology of schizophrenia*, D. D. Jackson, ed. New York: Basic Books.

Wynne, L. C., Ryckoff, I., Day, J., and Hirsch, S. I. 1958. Pseudo-mutuality in the family relationships of schizophrenics. *Psychiatry*. 21: 205–220.

References

Ackerman, N. W. 1938. The unity of the family. *Archives of Pediatrics*. 55: 51–62.

Ackerman, N. W. 1961. A dynamic frame for the clinical approach to family conflict. In *Exploring the base for family therapy*, N. W. Ackerman, F. L. Beatman, and S. N. Sherman, eds. New York: Family Services Association of America.

Ackerman, N. W., Beatman, F., and Sherman, S. N., eds. 1961. *Exploring the base for family therapy*. New York: Family Services Association of America.

Ackerman, N. W., and Sobel, R. 1950. Family diagnosis: An approach to the preschool child. *American Journal of Orthopsychiatry*. 20: 744–753.

Bardhill, D. R., and Saunders, B. E. 1988. In *Handbook of family therapy training and supervision*, H. A. Liddle, D.C. Brennlin, and R. C. Schwartz, eds. New York: Guilford Press.

Bateson, G. 1951. Information and codification: A philosophical approach. In *Communication: The social matrix of psychiatry*, J. Ruesch and G. Bateson, eds. New York: Norton.

Bateson, G., Jackson, D. D., Haley, J., and Weakland, J. 1956. Toward a theory of schizophrenia. *Behavioral Sciences*. 1: 251–264.

Bell, J. E. 1961. *Family Group Therapy*. Public Health Monograph #64. Washington, DC: U.S. Government Printing Office.

Bell, J. E. 1962. Recent advances in family group therapy. *Journal of Child Psychology and Psychiatry*. 3: 1–15.

Bion, W. R. 1948. Experience in groups. *Human Relations*. 1: 314–329.

Boszormenyi-Nagy, I., and Spark, G. L. 1973. Invisible loyalties: *Reciprocity in intergenerational family therapy*. New York: Harper & Row.

Bowen, M. 1961. Family psychotherapy. *American Journal of Orthopsychiatry*. 31: 40–60.

Bowlby, J. P. 1949. The study and reduction of group tensions in the family. *Human Relations*. 2: 123–138.

Broderick, C. B., and Schrader, S. S. 1991. The history of professional marriage and family therapy. In *Handbook of Family Therapy*, Vol. II, A. S. Gurman and D. P. Kniskern, eds. New York: Brunner/Mazel.

Dicks, H. V. 1964. Concepts of marital diagnosis and therapy as developed at the Tavistock Family Psychiatric Clinic, London, England. In *Marriage counseling in medical practice*, E. M. Nash, L. Jessner, and D. W. Abse, eds. Chapel Hill: University of North Carolina Press.

Epstein, N. B., Bishop, D. S., and Baldarin, L. M. 1981. McMaster model of family functioning. In *Normal family problems*, F. Walsh, ed. New York: Guilford Press.

Fisher, S., and Mendell, D. 1958. The spread of psychotherapeutic effects from the patient to his family group. *Psychiatry*. 21: 133–140.

Fromm-Reichmann, F. 1948. Notes on the development of treatment of schizophrenics by psychoanalytic psychotherapy. *Psychiatry*. 11: 263–274.

Guerin, P. J. 1976. Family therapy: The first twenty-five years. In *Family therapy: Theory and practice*, P. J. Guerin, ed. New York: Gardner Press.

Gurman, A. S., and Jacobson, N. S. 2002. *Clinical Handbook of Couple Therapy*, 3rd ed. New York: Guilford Press.

Haley, J. 1963. *Strategies of psychotherapy*. New York: Grune & Stratton.

Hoffman, L. 1981. *Foundations of family therapy*. New York: Basic Books.

Howells, J. G. 1971. *Theory and practice of family psychiatry*. New York: Brunner/Mazel.

Jackson, D. D. 1954. Suicide. *Scientific American*. 191: 88–96.

Jackson, D. D., and Weakland, J. H. 1959. Schizophrenic symptoms and family interaction. *Archives of General Psychiatry*. 1: 618–621.

Jackson, D. D., and Weakland, J. H. 1961. Conjoint family therapy, some considerations on theory, technique, and results. *Psychiatry*. 24: 30–45.

Kaslow, F. W. 1980. History of family therapy in the United States: A kaleidoscopic overview. *Marriage and Family Review*. 3: 77–111.

Laing, R. D. 1960. *The divided self*. London: Tavistock Publications.

Laing, R. D. 1965. Mystification, confusion and conflict. In *Intensive family therapy*, I. Boszormenyi-Nagy and J. L. Framo, eds. New York: Harper & Row.

Levy, D. 1943. *Maternal overprotection*. New York: Columbia University Press.

Lewin, K. 1951. *Field theory in social science*. New York: Harper.

Lidz, T., Cornelison, A., Fleck, S., and Terry, D. 1957. Intrafamilial environment of the schizophrenic patient. I: The father. *Psychiatry. 20:* 329–342.

MacGregor, R. 1967. Progress in multiple impact theory. In *Expanding theory and practice in family therapy*, N. W. Ackerman, F. L. Bateman, and S. N. Sherman, eds. New York: Family Services Association.

Madanes, C. 1981. *Strategic family therapy*. San Francisco: Jossey-Bass.

Minuchin, S. 1974. *Families and family therapy*. Cambridge, MA: Harvard University Press.

Minuchin, S., and Fishman, H. C. 1981. *Family therapy techniques*. Cambridge, MA: Harvard University Press.

Minuchin, S., Montalvo, B., Guerney, B. G., Rosman, B. L., and Schumer, F. 1967. *Families of the slums*. New York: Basic Books.

Minuchin, S., and Nichols, M. P. 1993. *Family healing*. New York: The Free Press.

Mittleman, B. 1944. Complementary neurotic reactions in intimate relationships. *Psychoanalytic Quarterly. 13:* 474–491.

Mittleman, B. 1948. The concurrent analysis of married couples. *Psychoanalytic Quarterly. 17:* 182–197.

Mittleman, B. 1956. Analysis of reciprocal neurotic patterns in family relationships. In *Neurotic interaction in marriage*, V. W. Eisenstein, ed. New York: Basic Books.

Oberndorf, C. P. 1938. Psychoanalysis of married people. *Psychoanalytic Review. 25:* 453–475.

Parsons, T., and Bales, R. F. 1955. *Family, socialization and interaction process:* Glencoe, IL: Free Press.

Richmond, M. E. 1917. *Social diagnosis*. New York: Russell Sage.

Satir, V. 1964. *Conjoint family therapy*. Palo Alto, CA: Science and Behavior Books.

Satir, V. 1972. *Peoplemaking*. Palo Alto, CA: Science and Behavior Books.

Selvini Palazzoli, M., Boscolo, L., Cecchin, G., and Prata, G. 1978. *Paradox and counterparadox*. New York: Jason Aronson.

Singer, M. T., Wynne, L. C., and Toohey, M. L. 1978. Communication disorders and the families of schizophrenics. In *The nature of schizophrenia*, L. C. Wynne, R. L. Cromwell, and S. Matthysse, eds. New York: Wiley.

Skynner, R. 1976. *Systems of family and marital psychotherapy*. New York: Brunner/Mazel.

Speck, R., and Attneave, C. 1973. *Family networks: Rehabilitation and healing*. New York: Pantheon.

Spiegel, J. P. 1954. New perspectives in the study of the family. *Marriage and Family Living. 16:* 4–12.

Stierlin, H. 1972. *Separating parents and adolescents*. New York: Quadrangle/New York Times Books.

Watzlawick, P. A., Beavin, J. H., and Jackson, D. D. 1967. *Pragmatics of human communication*. New York: Norton.

Whitaker, C. A. 1958. Psychotherapy with couples. *American Journal of Psychotherapy. 12:* 18–23.

Whitaker, C. A. 1975. Psychotherapy of the absurd: With a special emphasis on the psychotherapy of aggression. *Family Process. 14:* 1–16.

Whitaker, C. A. 1976. A family is a four-dimensional relationship. In *Family therapy: Theory and practice*, P. J. Guerin, ed. New York: Gardner Press.

Whitaker, C. A., and Malone, T. P. 1953. *The roots of psychotherapy*. New York: Balkiston.

Wynne, L. C. 1961. The study of intrafamilial alignments and splits in exploratory family therapy. *In Exploring the base for family therapy*, N. W. Ackerman, F. L. Beatman, and S. N. Sherman, eds. New York: Family Services Association.

Wynne, L. C., Ryckoff, I., Day, J., and Hirsch, S. I. 1958. Pseudomutuality in the family relationships of schizophrenics. *Psychiatry. 21:* 205–220.

Getting Started in Family Therapy: Basic Techniques

The challenge of describing the basic techniques of family therapy is that there are many legitimately different ways of doing things. The techniques of solution-focused therapy, for example, are very different from those of Bowen systems therapy. In fact, there are alternative approaches to almost every aspect of treatment, from whom to invite, to when and how to terminate. Nevertheless, there are widely shared principles of family therapy, and we offer the following guidelines as a beginning framework for clinical practice. We hope you will find these suggestions helpful, but we trust that you will pick and choose from among them only those you find useful.

Following our guide to the stages of family therapy are sections on assessment, working with special problems and populations, and negotiating with managed care. The reason we chose to consider assessment after the general guidelines to treatment is that assessment is a complex subject, deserving of more consideration than it usually gets.

The Stages of Family Therapy

The Initial Telephone Call

The goal of the initial contact is to get a general overview of the presenting problem and arrange for the family to come for a consultation. Listen to the caller's description of the problem and then identify all members of the household as well as others who might be involved (including the referral source and other agencies). Then schedule the first interview, specifying who will attend (usually everyone in the household).

Although there are things you can learn to say to convert requests for individual therapy into family cases, the most important consideration is attitudinal. First, understand and respect that the worried mother who wants you to treat her child individually or the unhappy husband who wants to talk to you alone has a perfectly legitimate point of view, even if it doesn't happen to coincide with your own. But if you expect to meet with the whole family, a matter-of-fact statement that that's how you work, at least for the initial assessment, will get most families to agree to a consultation.

When a caller presents the problem as limited to one person, a useful way to broaden the focus is to ask how it affects other members of the family. If the caller balks at the idea of bringing in the family or says that a particular member won't attend, say that you'll need to hear from everyone, at least initially, in order to get as much information as possible. Most people accept the need to give their point of view; what they resist is the implication that they're to blame.

When a child is the identified patient, parents may be reluctant to bring siblings whom they don't see as part of the problem. Like the uninvolved husband who is "too busy" to attend, nonsymptomatic brothers and sisters may be important to help broaden the focus from the identified patient's failings to relationship issues in the family.

Broadening the focus does not, however, mean broadening the blame. Family members can often acknowledge a role in family problems if they sense that the therapist isn't looking to assign blame. It isn't necessary to suggest that everyone is involved in the problem. What is important is getting everyone to work together toward a solution.[1]

Finally, because *most* families are reluctant to sit down and face their conflicts, a reminder call before the first session helps cut down on the no-show rate.

The First Interview

The goal of the first interview is to build an alliance with the family and develop a hypothesis about what's maintaining the presenting problem. It's a good idea to come up with a tentative hypothesis (in technical terms, a "hunch") after the initial phone call, and then test it in the first interview. (To avoid imposing pet theories on families, recreating them in the image of one's own bias, it's important to remain open to refuting, not just confirming, your initial hypothesis.) The point isn't to jump to conclusions but to start actively thinking.

The primary objectives of a consultation are to establish rapport and gather information. Introduce yourself to the contact person and then to other adults in the household. Ask parents to introduce their children. Shake hands and greet everyone. Orient the family to the room (observation mirrors, videotaping, toys for children) and to the format of the session (length and purpose). Repeat briefly what the caller told you over the phone (so as not to leave others wondering) and then ask for elaboration. Once you've heard and acknowledged that person's point of view ("So what you're saying is . . . ?"), ask each succeeding member of the family for their viewpoint.

While much of the session will be taken up with a discussion of the major problem, this problem-centered focus can have a disheartening effect. Therefore, spending some time exploring family members' interests and accomplishments is never wasted and sometimes changes the emotional energy of sessions dramatically.

In gathering information, some therapists find it useful to take a family history, and many use **genograms** to diagram the extended family network (see Chapter 5). Others believe that whatever facts are essential will emerge in the natural course of events and prefer to concentrate on the family's presenting concerns and the circumstances surrounding them.

Family therapists develop hypotheses about how family members might be involved in the presenting problem by asking what they've done to try to solve it, and by watching how they interact. Ideas are as important as actions, so it's useful to notice unhelpful explanations of problems as well as unproductive interactions.

Two kinds of information (*content*) that are particularly important are *solutions that don't work* and *transitions in the life cycle.* If whatever the family has been doing to resolve their difficulties hasn't worked, it may be that those attempts are part of the problem. A typical example would be over involved parents trying to help a shy child make friends by coaxing and criticizing her. Sometimes family members say they've "tried everything" to solve their problems. Their problem may be inconsistency. They give up too quickly.

---

1. Not all therapists routinely meet with the entire family. Some find they have more room to maneuver by meeting with individuals or subgroups and then gradually involving others. Others work with the "problem-determined system," only those people directly involved. Still others try to determine who are the "customers"—namely, those people who seem most concerned. If a therapist suspects violence or abuse, individual sessions may enable family members to reveal what they might not discuss in front of the whole family. The point to remember is that family therapy is more a way of looking at things than a technique based on always seeing the whole family together.

Despite the natural tendency to focus on problems and what causes them, it is a family's strengths, not their weaknesses, that are most important in successful therapy. Therefore the therapist should search for resilience (Walsh, 1998). What have these people done well? How have they successfully handled difficulties in the past? What would a hopeful future look like? Even the most discouraged families have had times where they were successful, even though those positive episodes may be obscured by the frustration they feel over their current difficulties.

Although it isn't always apparent (especially to them), most families seek treatment because they have failed to adjust to changing circumstances. If a husband or a wife develops problems within the first few months after a baby's birth, it may be because they haven't shifted effectively from being a unit of two to a unit of three. A new mother may be depressed because she doesn't have enough support. A new father may be jealous of the attention his wife now lavishes on the baby and hurt that she seems too tired to want to do anything with him.

Although the strain of having a baby seems obvious, you'd be amazed at how often depressed young mothers are treated as though there were something wrong with them—"unresolved dependency needs," perhaps, or maybe a Prozac deficiency. The same is true when families develop problems around the time a child enters school or reaches adolescence or with any other developmental shift: The transitional demands on the family are obvious, *if* you think about them.

Novice family therapists may have no experience with some of the transitions their clients are struggling with. When this is the case, it underscores the need for the therapist to remain curious and respectful of a family's predicament rather than jump to conclusions. For example, as a young single man one of us couldn't understand why so many parents with young children rarely went out as a couple anymore. He assumed that they were avoiding being alone together. Subsequent events taught him differently. With small children of his own, he began to wonder how those couples got out so often!

Family therapists explore the **process** of family interaction by asking how family members relate to each other and by inviting them to discuss their problems with one another in the session. The first strategy, asking "process" or "circular" questions, is favored by Bowenians; the second, by structural therapists. In either case, the key question is: What's keeping the family stuck? What forces are keeping them from adapting to the pressures of development and change?

Once they've met with the family, learned about the problem that brings them to treatment, made an effort to understand the family's context, and formulated a conjecture about what needs to be done to resolve the problem, therapists should make a recommendation to the family. This recommendation might include consulting another professional (a learning disability expert, a physician, a lawyer) or even suggesting that the family doesn't need—or doesn't seem ready for—treatment. Often, however, the recommendation will be for a course of family therapy. Although most therapists try to make their recommendation at the end of the first interview, this may be hasty. If it takes two sessions to form a bond with the family, understand their situation, and find out if you can work with them, then take two sessions.

If you think you can help the family with their problem, offer them a **treatment contract.** Acknowledge why they came in, say that it was a good idea, and say that you think you can help. Then negotiate a meeting time, the frequency and length of sessions, who will attend, the presence of observers or use of videotape, the fee, and how insurance is handled. Remember that resistance doesn't magically disappear after the first (or fourteenth) session: So stress the importance of keeping appointments and the need for everyone to attend. Finally, don't forget to emphasize the family's goals and the strengths you've observed in them to meet them.

First Session Checklist

1. Make contact with each member of the family and acknowledge his or her point of view about the problem and feelings about coming to therapy.

2. Establish leadership by controlling the structure and pace of the interview.

3. Develop a working alliance with the family by balancing warmth and professionalism.

4. Compliment clients on positive actions and family strengths.

5. Maintain empathy with individuals and respect for the family's way of doing things.

6. Focus on specific problems and attempted solutions.

7. Develop hypotheses about unhelpful interactions around the presenting problem. Be curious about why these have persisted.

8. Don't overlook the possible involvement of family members, friends, or helpers who aren't present.

9. Negotiate a treatment contract that acknowledges the family's goals and specifies the therapist's framework for structuring treatment.

10. Invite questions.

The Early Phase of Treatment

The early phase of treatment is devoted to refining the therapist's hypothesis into a **formulation** about what's maintaining the problem and beginning to work on resolving it. Now the strategy shifts from alliance building to challenging actions and assumptions. Most therapists are able to figure out what needs to change; what sets good therapists apart is their willingness to push for those changes.

"Pushing for change" may suggest a confrontational style. But what is required to help people risk change isn't any one particular way of working; rather, it is a relentless commitment to helping make things better. This commitment is evident in Michael White's dogged questioning of problem-saturated stories, Phil Guerin's calm insistence that family members stop blaming each other and start looking at themselves, and Virginia Goldner's determined insistence that violent men take responsibility for their behavior.

Regardless of what model they follow, effective therapists are persistent in their pursuit of change. This doesn't just mean sticking with families. It means being willing to intervene, at times energetically. Some therapists prefer to avoid confrontation and find it more effective to use gentle but firm persistence. However, regardless of whether they work directly (and at times use confrontation) or indirectly (and avoid it), good therapists are finishers. Strategies and techniques may vary, but what sets the best therapists apart is their commitment to doing what it takes to see families through to successful resolution of their problems.

Effective family therapy addresses interpersonal conflict, and the first step is to bring it into the consulting room. Often this is not a problem. Couples in conflict or parents feuding with their children usually speak right up about their disagreements. If the family only came because someone sent them (the court, the school, the Department of Protective Services), begin by addressing the family's problem with these outside agencies. How must the family change so as to resolve their conflict with these agencies? How must the family change so that its members won't be in trouble?

When one person is presented as the problem, the therapist challenges **linearity** by asking how others are involved (or affected). What was their role in creating (or managing) the problem? How have they responded to it?

For example: "The problem is Malik. He's disobedient." "How does he get away with that?" Or, "How do you respond when he's disobedient?"

Less confrontive therapists might ask: "When do you notice this?" "What does he do that seems disobedient?" "How does this disobedience affect you?"

Or: "It's me, I'm depressed." "Who in the family is contributing to your depression?" "No one." "Then who's helping you get over it?"

These challenges can be blunt or gentle, depending on the therapist's style and assessment of the family. The point, incidentally, is not to switch from blaming one person (the disobedient child, say) to another (a parent who doesn't discipline effectively) but to broaden the problem to an interactional one. Maybe mother is too lenient with Malik because she finds father too strict, and moreover she may be over invested in the boy because of emotional distance in the marriage.

The best way to challenge unhelpful interactions is to point out patterns that are keeping people stuck. A useful formula for this is: "The more you do X, the more he does Y—and the more you do Y, the more she does X." (For X and Y, try substituting *nag* and *withdraw*, or *punish* and *indulge*.) Incidentally, when you point out what people are doing that isn't working, it's a tactical error to then tell them what they *should* do. Once you shift from pointing out something to giving advice, the family's attention shifts from their own behavior to you and your advice.

> *Therapist:* "When you ignore your wife's complaints, she feels hurt and angry. You may have trouble accepting the anger, but she doesn't feel supported."
> *Client:* "What should I do?"
> *Therapist:* "I don't know. Ask your wife."

Refusing to make suggestions, especially when asked, creates tension that encourages family members to discover their own resources. A solution-focused alternative to challenging unhelpful actions is to ask about successful efforts and then to encourage more of these.

Even though family therapists sometimes challenge assumptions or actions, they continue to listen to people's feelings and points of view. Family members don't listen to each other for long without becoming defensive and reactive. Unfortunately, therapists don't always listen, either—especially when they're eager to jump in to disagree or give advice. But remember that people aren't likely to reconsider their assumptions until they've been heard and understood.

Homework can be used to test flexibility (simply seeing if it is carried out measures willingness to change), to make family members more aware of their role in problems (telling people just to notice something, without necessarily trying to change it, is very instructive), and to suggest new ways of relating.

Typical homework assignments include suggesting that overinvolved parents hire a babysitter and go out together, having argumentative partners take turns talking about their feelings while the other just listens without saying anything (but noticing tendencies to become reactive), and having dependent family members practice spending time alone (or with someone outside the family) and doing more things for themselves. Homework assignments that are likely to generate conflict, such as negotiating house rules with teenagers, should be avoided. Difficult discussions should be saved for when the therapist can act as referee.

Early Phase Checklist

1. Identify major conflicts and bring them into the consulting room.

2. Develop a hypothesis and refine it into a formulation about what the family is doing to perpetuate (or fail to solve) the presenting problem. Formulations should consider process and structure, family rules, triangles, and boundaries.

3. Keep the focus of treatment on primary problems and the interpersonal conditions supporting them.

4. Use homework assignments to address problems and the underlying conditions supporting them.

5. Challenge family members to see their own roles in the problems that plague them.

6. Push for change, in the session and between sessions at home.

7. Make use of supervision to test the validity of formulations and effectiveness of interventions.

The Middle Phase of Treatment

When therapy is anything other than brief and problem-focused, much of the middle phase is devoted to helping family members express themselves and achieve mutual understanding. If a therapist plays too active a role in this process—filtering all conversation through himself or herself—family members won't learn to deal with each other and will continue to manage only as long as they remain in therapy. For this reason, in the middle phase, the therapist takes a less active role and encourages family members to interact more with each other. As they do so, the therapist steps back and observes the process. When dialogue bogs down, the therapist either points out what went wrong or simply encourages them to keep talking—but with less interruption and criticism.

When family members address their conflicts directly, they tend to become anxious and reactive. Anxiety is the enemy of listening. Some therapists (Bowenians, for example) control anxiety by having family members talk only to the therapist. Others prefer to let family members deal with their anxiety by helping them learn to talk with each other less defensively (by saying how they feel and listening to and acknowledging what the other one says). However, even therapists who work primarily with family dialogue need to interrupt when anxiety escalates and conversations become destructive.

Thus in the middle phase of treatment the therapist takes a less directive role and encourages family members to begin to rely on their own resources. The level of anxiety is regulated by alternating between having family members talk among themselves or with the therapist. In either case, the therapist encourages family members to get beyond blaming to talking about what they feel and what they want—and to learn to see their own part in unproductive interactions.

Middle Phase Checklist

1. Use intensity to challenge family members (and ingenuity to get around resistance, and empathy to get underneath defensiveness).

2. Avoid being so directive that the family doesn't learn to improve their own ways of relating to each other.

3. Foster individual responsibility and mutual understanding.

4. Make certain that efforts to improve relationships are having a positive effect on the presenting complaint.

5. If you meet with subgroups, don't lose sight of the whole family picture, and don't neglect any individuals or relationships—especially those difficult ones that are so tempting to avoid.

6. Is therapy stuck on a plateau? Have sessions taken on a sameness and predictability? Does the therapist assume too active a role in choosing what to talk about? Have therapist and family developed a social relationship that has become more important than addressing conflicts? Has the therapist assumed a regular role in the family (an empathic listener to the spouses or a firm parent figure to the children), substituting for a missing function in the family? When therapists find themselves drawn to taking an active response to family members' needs, they should ask themselves who in the family should be taking that role and then encourage that person to do so.

Termination

Termination comes for brief therapists as soon as the presenting problem is resolved. For psychoanalytic therapists, therapy is a long-term learning process and may continue for years. For most therapists, termination comes somewhere between these two extremes and has to do both with the family feeling that they've gotten what they came for and the therapist's sense that treatment has reached a point of diminishing returns. One clue that it may be time to terminate is when the family comes in with nothing but small talk (assuming, of course, that they aren't avoiding conflict).

In individual therapy, where the relationship to the therapist is often the primary vehicle of change, termination focuses on reviewing the relationship and saying goodbye. In family therapy, the focus is more on what the family has learned.

Although some strategic therapists are content to manipulate change without concern that the family understands it, most family therapy has a kind of teaching function, and termination is the time to make sure the family has learned something about how to get along.

It can be helpful to ask the family to anticipate upcoming challenges that might cause setbacks and to discuss with them how they will handle those difficulties. The question "How will you know when things are heading backward and what will you do?" is useful in this regard. Families can be reminded that their present harmony can't be maintained indefinitely and that people have a tendency to overreact to the first sign of relapse, which can trigger a vicious cycle. To paraphrase Zorba the Greek: Life *is* trouble. To be alive is to face difficulties. The real test is how you handle them.

Finally, although in the business of therapy, no news is usually good news, it might be a good idea to check in with the family to see how they're doing a few weeks after termination. This can be done with a letter, phone call, or brief follow-up session. The family will appreciate the therapist's interest, and the therapist will feel a greater sense of closure. A therapeutic relationship is, of necessity, somewhat artificial or at least constrained. But there is no reason to make it less than human—or to forget about families once you terminate with them.

Termination Checklist

1. Has the presenting problem improved?

2. Is the family satisfied that they have gotten what they came for, or are they interested in continuing to learn about themselves and improve their relationships?

3. Does the family have an understanding of what they were doing that wasn't working, and how to avoid the recurrence of similar problems in the future?

4. Do minor recurrences of problems reflect lack of resolution of some underlying dynamic or merely that the family has to readjust to functioning without the therapist?

5. Have family members developed and improved relationships outside the immediate family context as well as within it?

Family Assessment

Family therapists vary widely in the extent to which they make formal assessments. Bowenian therapists complete three-generational genograms before beginning treatment, psychoanalysts take thorough personal histories, and behavioral therapists use a variety of questionnaires and checklists. At the other extreme, structural, solution-focused, and narrative therapists do little in the way of formal evaluation. But regardless of their approach's official posture on assessment, most therapists don't spend enough time making careful evaluations before launching into treatment.

Rather than attempt an exhaustive comparison of assessment procedures, we will instead describe some of the dimensions of family and individual functioning that therapists should consider before embarking on a course of treatment. This summary is designed to be illustrative rather than exhaustive; therefore, you are likely to think of at least one or two important issues we've neglected to mention.

The Presenting Problem

It may seem obvious that the first consideration should be the presenting complaint. Nevertheless, it's worth emphasizing that inquiry into the presenting problem should be detailed and empathic. The minute some therapists hear that a family's problem is, say, misbehavior or poor communication, they're ready to jump into action. Their training has prepared them to deal with misbehaving children or communication problems, and they're raring to go. They know what needs to be done. Before they get started, however, they should realize that they're *not* dealing with "misbehaving children" or "communication problems"; they're dealing with a particular instance of one of these difficulties.

Exploring the presenting problem begins with hearing the family's account, in their own words. Every member of the family should have a chance to express their perspective—and both their descriptions and their feelings should be acknowledged. This open-ended inquiry should be followed by specific, detailed questions to find out more about the precise nature of the problem. If a child misbehaves, what exactly does he do? How often? Under what circumstances? Does he misbehave at school or at home, or both?

The next thing to explore is the family's attempts to deal with the problem. What have they tried? What's been helpful? What hasn't? Has anyone other than those present been involved in trying to help (or hinder) the family with their difficulties?

Understanding the Referral Route

It's important to understand who referred your clients and why. What were their expectations? What assumptions did they communicate to the family?

In many cases the referral process is routine and of no major import. However, it is important to know whether a family's participation is voluntary or coerced, whether all or only some of them recognize the need for treatment, and whether other agencies will have some kind of continuing involvement with the case.

When individual therapists make a family referral, they often have a particular agenda in mind. A college student's counselor once referred him and his family for treatment. It turned out that the young man had uncovered a repressed memory of sexual abuse and assumed that it must have been his father. The family therapist was somehow supposed to mediate between the young man, who couldn't imagine who else might have been responsible for this vaguely remembered incident, and his parents, who absolutely denied that any such thing ever happened. Did the individual therapist expect confrontation, confession, and atonement? Some sort of negotiated agreement? It's best to find out.

It's also important to find out if clients have been in treatment elsewhere. If so, what happened? What expectations or sources of resistance did previous therapy generate? It's even more important to find out if anyone in the family is currently in treatment. Few things are more likely to stalemate progress than two therapists pulling in different directions.

Identifying the Systemic Context

Regardless of who the therapist elects to work with, it's imperative to have a clear understanding of the interpersonal context of the problem. Who all is in the family? Are important figures in the life of the problem not present? A live-in boyfriend? A grandparent who lives next door? Are other social agencies involved? What is the nature of their input? Does the family see them as helpful?

Remember that family therapy is an approach to people in context. The most relevant context may be the immediate family. But families don't exist in a vacuum. The system also includes the extrafamilial context. It may be useful to meet with the teachers and counselors of a child who misbehaves at school to find out what's going on. There are even times when the nuclear family may not be the most important context. Sometimes, for example, a college student's depression has more to do with what's going on in the classroom or dormitory than with what's happening back home.

Stage of the Life Cycle

A family's context has temporal as well as interpersonal dimensions. Most families come to treatment not because something is inherently wrong with them but because they've gotten stuck in life-cycle transitions (Chapter 4). Sometimes this is apparent. Parents may complain, for example, that they don't know what's gotten into Janey. She used to be such a good girl, but now that she's fourteen, she's become sullen and argumentative. (One reason parenting remains an amateur sport is that just when you think you've got the hang of it, the children get a little older and throw you a whole new set of curves.) Adolescence is that stage in the **family life cycle** when young parents have to grow up and relax their grip on their children.

Sometimes it isn't obvious that a family is having trouble adjusting to a new stage in the life cycle. Couples who marry after living together for years may not anticipate that matrimony can stir up unconscious expectations about what it means to be family. More than one couple has been surprised to discover a sharp falling off in their love life after tying the knot. At other times, significant life-cycle changes occur in the parents' generation, and you won't always learn of these influences unless you ask.

Family Structure

The simplest systemic context for a problem is an interactional dynamic between two parties. She nags and he withdraws; restrictive parental control provokes adolescent rebellion and vice versa. Sometimes, though, a dyadic perspective doesn't take in the whole picture.

Family problems become entrenched because they're embedded in powerful but unseen structures. Regardless of what approach a therapist takes, it's wise to understand something about the family's **structure.** What are the **subsystems** and what is the nature of the **boundaries** between them? What is the nature of the boundary around the couple or the family? What triangles are present?

Who plays what roles in the family? Are these individuals and subsystems protected by boundaries that allow them to operate without undue interference—but with access to affection and support?

Here, too, there is a temporal dimension. If a wife goes back to work after years of staying home with the children, the parental subsystem is challenged to shift from a complementary to a symmetrical form. Whether or not family members complain directly about these strains,

they're likely to be relevant to wherever their distress happens to be focused.

Communication

Although some couples do come to therapy saying they have "communication problems" (usually meaning that one partner won't do what the other one wants), working on communication has become a cliché in family therapy. Because communication is the vehicle of relationship, all therapists deal with communication. But clarifying communication is rarely sufficient to solve family problems.

Although conflict doesn't magically disappear when family members start to listen to each other, it's unlikely that conflicts will get solved *before* people start to listen to each other (Nichols, 1995). If, after a session or two and the therapist's "encouragement," family members still seem unable to listen to each other, talk therapy is going to be an uphill battle.

One other point to be made about listening falls under the category of "what's good for the goose is good for the gander." Therapists who encourage family members to listen to each other don't always practice what they preach. A family member will start to protest or explain and the therapist cuts that person off to direct him or her to listen to someone else's point of view. The person who gets cut off may grudgingly listen, but most people aren't really interested in hearing what anyone else has to say until they feel heard and understood themselves.

Family members who learn to listen with understanding often discover that they don't need to change each other (Jacobson & Christensen, 1996). Many problems can be solved, but the problem of living with other people who don't always see things the way you do isn't one of them.

Drug and Alcohol Abuse

Although it may not be necessary to ask every client about drug and alcohol consumption, it's critical to inquire carefully if there is any suspicion that this may be a problem. Don't be too polite. Ask straightforward and specific questions. If a member of a family who's seeking couples or family therapy seems to be abusing drugs or alcohol, think twice about assuming that talk therapy will be the answer to the family's problems.

Domestic Violence and Sexual Abuse

If there is any hint of domestic violence or sexual abuse, the clinician should look into it. The process of questioning can start with the family present, but when there is a strong suspicion of abuse or neglect, it may be wise to meet with family members individually to allow them to talk more openly. Although there is room for disagreement about the advisability of a conjoint approach in cases of minor domestic violence, such as slapping or pushing, it's imperative to consider whether the inevitable stress of seeing a couple together will expose a woman to greater danger from retaliation by her disgruntled partner.

Most states require professionals to report any suspicion of child abuse. Any clinician who considers not reporting suspected child abuse based on his or her own clinical judgment should also consider the consequences of this failure to report becoming known if someone else reports it. It's called losing your license.

Extramarital Involvements

The discovery of an affair is a crisis that will strike many if not most couples some time in their relationship. Infidelity is common, but it's still a crisis. It can destroy a marriage. Extramarital involvements that don't involve sexual intimacy, although less obvious, can sabotage treatment if one or both partners regularly turn to third parties to deal with issues that belong in the couple. (One clue that a relationship is part of a triangle is that it isn't openly talked about.) Would-be-helpful third parties may include family members, friends, and therapists.

A couple once came to therapy complaining that the intimacy had gone out of their relationship. It wasn't so much a matter of conflict, it was just that they never seemed to spend any time together anymore. After a few weeks of slow progress, the wife revealed that she'd been seeing an individual therapist. When the couple's therapist asked why, she replied that she needed to have someone to talk to.

Gender

Unrecognized gender inequalities contribute to family problems in a variety of ways. A wife's dissatisfaction may have deeper roots than the family's focal problems. A husband's reluctance to become more involved in the family may be as much a product of cultural expectations as of any flaw in his character.

Every therapist must work out for himself or herself how to balance between the extremes of naively ignoring the existence of gender inequality and imposing one's personal point of view on clients. It is, however, not reasonable to assume that both partners enter marriage with equal power or that complementarity between spouses is the only dynamic operating in their relationship.

Conflict over gender expectations, whether talked about directly or not, is especially common given the enormous shifts in cultural expectations over the last few decades. Is it still considered a woman's duty to follow her husband's career, moving whenever necessary for his advancement? Is it still true that women are expected to be the primary (which often turns out to be a euphemism for *only*) caregivers for infants and young children?

Regardless of the therapist's values, do the gender roles established in a couple seem to work for them? Or do unresolved differences, conflict, or confusion appear to be sources of stress? Perhaps the single most useful question to ask about gender inequality is, "How does each of the partners experience the fairness of give-and-take in their relationship?"

Cultural Factors[2]

In assessing families for treatment, a therapist should consider the unique subculture a family is from (McGoldrick, Giordano, & Pearce, 1996) as well as the effect of unquestioned assumptions from the larger culture that may have an impact on their problems (Doherty, 1991).

In working with minority families, it may be more important to develop *cultural competence* than to have cultural syntonicity. That is, families may come to trust a therapist who has taken the time to learn about their particular culture as much as one who happens to be of the same race or nationality. One way to develop cultural competence is to make connections after working hours—for example, if you happen to be white, by attending black church services in the community where your clients live or by attending a Latino dance or hanging out in an Asian community center. Such experiences certainly don't make you an expert, but they may help client families feel that you care enough to respect their ways. It's also important to take a one-down position in regard to cultural and ethnic diversity—that is, to ask your clients to teach you about their experiences and traditions.

The challenge for the practitioner is twofold: learning to respect diversity and developing sensitivity to some of the issues faced by members of other cultures and ethnic groups. A host of books are now available describing the characteristics and values of different ethnic groups, many of which are listed in the section on multiculturalism in Chapter 11 of this book. In addition to these academic books, novels—such as *Love in the Time of Cholera, Beloved, The Scent of Green Papaya, The Mambo Kings Play Songs of Love,* and so on—often bring other cultures more vividly to life.

In working with clients from other cultures, it's probably more important to be respectful of differences and curious about other ways of doing things than to attempt to become an expert on ethnicity. However, while it is important to respect other people's differences, it can be a problem to accept uncritically statements to the effect that "We do these (counterproductive) things because of our culture." Unfortunately, it's difficult for a therapist from another culture to assess the validity of such claims. Perhaps the best advice is to be curious; stay open but ask questions.

Even when working with clients from your own culture, it's important to consider the impact of cultural assumptions. How do cultural expectations and aspirations affect the family you're planning to work with? One patient recently complained that his wife expected family life to be like *The Brady Bunch.* His wife's reply was: "It doesn't always have to be *The Jerry Springer Show,* either."

Among common cultural assumptions you may want to be alert for are that getting married means living happily ever after, that sexual satisfaction is something that just comes naturally, that adolescence is always a time of turmoil, and that teenagers only want freedom and no longer need their parents' love and understanding.

The Ethical Dimension

Most therapists are aware of the ethical responsibilities of their profession: Therapy should be for the client's benefit, not to work out unresolved issues for the therapist. Clients are entitled to confidentiality, so limits on privacy imposed by requirements to report to probation officers, parents, or managed care companies should be made clear from the outset. Therapists avoid exploiting the trust and dependency of their clients (and students) and therefore must make every effort to avoid dual relationships. Professionals are obligated to provide the best possible treatment; if they aren't qualified to meet the needs of a particular client, they should refer the case to someone else.

---

2. Issues of culture, as well as race, ethnicity, and social class, will be examined throughout the course of this book. Here we merely wish to offer some preliminary considerations to help novice therapists get through their first few family sessions.

Although most therapists are aware of their own responsibilities, many think less than they might about the ethical dimensions of their clients' behavior. This is an area with no hard and fast rules. However, a complete and conscientious assessment of every family should include some consideration of family members' entitlements and obligations. What loyalty obligations do members of the family have? Are invisible loyalties (Boszormenyi-Nagy & Spark, 1973) constraining their behavior? If so, are these equitable? What is the nature of the partners' commitment to each other? Are these commitments clear? Balanced? What obligations do family members have with regard to fidelity and trustworthiness? Are these obligations being met? A good place to start understanding your ethical responsibilities is by studying the guidelines of your profession. The Ethics Code of the American Psychological Association, for example, outlines such principles as:

- Psychologists offer services only within the areas of their competence, based on education, training, supervision, or professional experience.
- Where there is evidence that an understanding of age, gender, race, ethnicity, culture, national origin, religion, sexual orientation, disability, language, or socioeconomic status is essential for effective implementation of services, psychologists have or seek out training and supervision in these areas—or they make appropriate referrals.
- When psychologists become aware of personal problems that might interfere with their professional duties, they take appropriate measures, such as obtaining professional assistance, and determine whether they should limit, suspend, or terminate their work-related duties.

The Code of Ethics for the National Association of Social Workers (NASW) mandates that:

- Social workers should not engage in dual relationships with clients or former clients.

- Social workers should not solicit private information from clients unless it is essential to providing services.
- Social workers should not disclose confidential information to third-party payers unless clients have authorized such disclosure.
- Social workers should terminate services to clients when such services are no longer required.

While some of these principles may seem obvious, they provide fairly strict guidelines within which practitioners should operate. When it comes to working with couples and families, however, complications arise that create a host of unique ethical dilemmas. When, for example, should a family therapist share with parents information learned in sessions with a child? If a twelve-year-old starts drinking, does the therapist tell her parents?

Recently, professional codes of conduct have added guidelines for treating couples and families. For example, the American Psychological Association (APA) specifies that:

- When psychologists provide services to several people who have a relationship (such as spouses or parents and children), they clarify at the outset which individuals are clients and the relationship the psychologist will have with each person.
- If it becomes apparent that psychologists may be called on to perform potentially conflicting roles (such as family therapist and then witness for one party in divorce proceedings), they attempt to clarify and modify, or withdraw from, roles appropriately.

The National Association of Social Workers states that:

- When social workers provide services to couples or family members, they should clarify with all parties the nature of their professional obligations to the various individuals receiving services.

- When social workers provide counseling to families, they should seek agreement among the parties concerning each individual's right to confidentiality.

The American Association of Marriage and Family Therapy (AAMFT, 1991) publishes its own code of ethics, which covers much of the same ground as those of the APA and NASW. The AAMFT does, however, directly address complications with respect to confidentiality when a therapist sees more than one person in a family:

- Without a written waiver, a family therapist should not disclose information received from any family member—including, presumably, to other family members.

Still, as with many things, it may be easier to expound ethical principles than to apply them in clinical practice, especially in situations that engage powerful emotions.

—Case Study——————

It's clear that therapists must protect their clients' right to confidentiality. But what if a wife reveals that she's having an affair and isn't sure whether to end it? When she goes on to say that her marriage has been stale for years, the therapist recommends a course of couples therapy to see if the marriage can be improved. The woman agrees. But when the therapist suggests that she either break off the affair or tell her husband about it, the woman adamantly refuses. What should the therapist do?

One way to resolve ambiguous ethical dilemmas is to use your own best judgment. In the case of the woman who wanted to work on her marriage but wasn't willing to end her affair or inform her husband, a therapist might decline to offer therapy under circumstances that would make it unlikely to be effective. In that case, the

therapist is obligated to refer the client to another therapist.

Subprinciple 1.6 of the *AAMFT Code of Ethical Principles* states:

- Marriage and family therapists assist persons in obtaining other therapeutic services if a marriage and family therapist is unable or unwilling, for appropriate reasons, to see a person who has requested professional help.

And Subprinciple 1.7 states:

- Marriage and family therapists do not abandon or neglect clients in treatment without making reasonable arrangements for the continuation of such treatment.

Given the same set of circumstances, another therapist might decide that treating the couple even though the woman refused to end her affair might make it possible for the woman to break off the affair later or talk to her husband about it. In this scenario the therapist would be bound by the principle of confidentiality not to reveal—directly or indirectly—what the woman discussed in private.

While the outlines of ethical professional conduct are clear, the pressures on a practitioner are often powerful and subtle. When dealing with clients who are having affairs or considering divorce—or marriage, for that matter—therapists may be influenced by their own unconscious attitudes as well as the clients' projections. What would you assume, for example, about a therapist whose depressed, married clients all tended to get divorced after their individual therapy? What might you speculate about the level of satisfaction in that therapist's own marriage?

The risk of trusting your own judgment in ambiguous ethical situations is imposing your own values on what should be a professional decision. The principles of sound ethical practice are wider, and may be stricter, than our own private morality and good intentions. When in doubt, we recommend that clinicians ask themselves two questions: First, what would happen if the client or important other found out about your actions? Thus, for example, "strategically" telling two siblings in separate conversations that only he or she is mature enough to end the fighting between them, violates the "what if" principle, because it's entirely possible that one or both of them might brag to the other about what the therapist said. (Trust us!)

The second question to ask in order to do the right thing is, can you talk to someone you respect about what you're doing (or considering)? If you're afraid to discuss with a supervisor or a colleague that you are treating two couples in which the wife of one is having an affair with the husband of the other, or that you're considering lending a client money, you may be guilty of the arrogance of assuming that you are above the rules that govern your profession. Feeling compelled to keep something secret suggests that it may be wrong. Otherwise, why not talk about it? The road to hell is paved with the assumption that this situation is special, this client is special, or that you are special.

The following red flags signal potential unethical practices:

- Specialness—something about this situation is special and the ordinary rules don't apply.
- Attraction—intense attraction of any kind, not only romantic but also being impressed with the status of the client.
- Alterations in the therapeutic frame—longer or more frequent sessions, excessive self-disclosure, being unable to say no to the client, and so on, may signal a potential violation of professional boundaries.
- Violating clinical norms—not referring someone in a troubled marriage for couples therapy, accepting personal counseling from a supervisor, and so on.
- Professional isolation—not being willing to discuss your decisions with colleagues.

In reading over our topics for family assessment, you may have noticed that there was no section on individual dynamics. This was deliberate. The distinction between individual and systemic levels of experience is useful but artificial. Regardless of whether you're treating individuals or family groups, competent therapists should always keep in mind that all human experience entails both interactional and personal dimensions (Nichols, 1987). An individual therapist who fails to consider the impact of the therapeutic relationship (as well as relationships outside the office) on a patient's material is missing a most important contribution. Therapists are never blank screens.

By the same token, a family therapist who fails to consider the psychological aspects of a family member's behavior is dealing with only half a deck. Families were never black boxes. Sometimes when family interactions get stuck, it's important to consider the contributions of psychopathology, psychodynamics, or just plain failures of resolve.

Family Therapy with Specific Presenting Problems

Once it was customary for family therapists to assume that their approach could be applied to almost any clinical problem. Today, this one-size-fits-all notion is no longer considered valid, and it has become increasingly common to develop specific techniques for particular populations and problems.

The following are samples of special treatment considerations for two frequently encountered clinical problems, marital violence and sexual abuse of children. Although we hope that these suggestions will provide some ideas for dealing with these difficult situations, remember that responsible therapists recognize the limits of their expertise and refer cases they aren't equipped to handle to more experienced practitioners.

Marital Violence

The question of how to treat marital violence polarizes the field like no other. The prevailing paradigm is to separate couples and assign the offender to an anger-management program while his partner is treated in a battered women's support group (Edelson & Tolman, 1992; Gondolf, 1995). Traditional couples therapy is seen as dangerous and often inappropriate because placing a violent man and his abused partner in close quarters and inviting them to address contentious issues puts the woman at risk and provides the offender with a platform for self-justification (Avis, 1992; Bograd, 1984, 1992; Hansen, 1993). Treating the partners together implies that they share responsibility for the violence and confers a sense of legitimacy on a relationship that may be malignant.

The argument for seeing violent couples together is that violence is the outcome of mutual provocation, an escalation, albeit unacceptable, of the emotionally destructive behavior that characterizes many relationships (Goldner, 1992; Minuchin & Nichols, 1993). When couples are treated together, violent men can learn to recognize the emotional triggers that set them off and to take responsibility for controlling their actions. Their partners can learn to recognize the same danger signals and to take responsibility for ensuring their own safety.

Because few systemic therapists advocate treating couples together when the violence has gone beyond pushing and shoving, some of the debate between advocates of a systemic versus an offender-and-victim model is between apples and oranges. Nevertheless, many feminist thinkers remain opposed to couples therapy with any form of domestic violence (Avis, 1992; Bograd, 1984; Hansen, 1993).

In the absence of empirical evidence showing gender-specific group treatment to be safer or more effective than couples therapy (Brown & O'Leary, 1995; Feldman & Ridley, 1995), clinicians continue to be split into two camps when it comes to the treatment of marital violence. Rather than choose between attempting to resolve the relationship issues that lead to violence or concentrating on providing safety and protection for the women who are victims of violence, it is possible to combine elements of both

approaches—not, however, by doing traditional couples therapy.[3]

In working with violent couples, there must be no ambiguity on the issue of safety. Relationship issues can properly be construed as mutual, but for the crime of violence the perpetrator must be held responsible.

In the initial consultation with couples in whom one suspects violence, it's useful to meet with the partners together and then separately. Seeing the couple together permits you to see them in action, whereas speaking with the woman privately allows you to inquire whether she has left out or minimized information about the level of violence or intimidation to which she has been subjected.

Violent men and battered women trigger strong reactions in anyone who tries to help them. When such couples seek therapy they are often polarized between love and hate, blaming and feeling ashamed, wanting to escape and remaining obsessed with each other. Thus it's not surprising that professional helpers tend to react in extremes: siding with one partner against the other, refusing ever to take sides, exaggerating or minimizing danger, treating the partners like children, or like monsters. To form an alliance with both partners, it's important to convey respect for them as persons, even if you cannot condone some of their actions.

To assess the level of violence, it's necessary to ask direct questions "How often do conflicts between the two of you end in some kind of violence?" "When did this happen most recently?" "What's the worst thing that's ever happened?" It's important to find out if any incidents have resulted in injuries, if weapons have been used, and if the woman is currently afraid.

If the woman has been violent as well as the man, the therapist can make it clear that violence in any form is unacceptable. But it is useful to point out that unless a woman uses a weapon, her aggression is not as dangerous because she

---

3. The following guidelines draw heavily from the work of Virginia Goldner and Gillian Walker, codirectors of the Gender and Violence Project at the Ackerman Institute.

is not as physically powerful. This point can be emphasized by asking the man if he actually feels physically afraid of his partner during an argument (which is her experience of him). The answer is almost always "no."

The more that violence is used as a strategy of intimidation and the more there is a pattern of violence, the more dangerous the man. This is especially true of violence outside the home. A man who gets into fights with other men is far more explosive than a man who is only violent toward someone who can't really fight back. It's also important to inquire about drinking and drug use, which loosen inhibitions, and therapy must emphasize restraint.

In addition to assessing the level of violence, the therapist must also evaluate the partners' ability to work constructively in therapy. Is the man willing to accept responsibility for his behavior? Is the woman willing to take responsibility for her own protection, making her physical safety the first priority? Is the couple able to talk together and to take turns, or are they so emotionally reactive that the therapist must constantly interrupt and control them?

If a therapist decides to risk treating the couple together, it's important to establish zero tolerance for violence. One way of doing this is to make therapy contingent on no further episodes of physical aggression. Virginia Goldner and Gillian Walker define the first couple of sessions as a consultation to determine whether it is possible to create a "therapeutic safety zone" where issues can be confronted without putting the woman in harm's way. They use these initial sessions to focus on the question of safety, while reserving the right to terminate the consultation and propose other treatment alternatives if they feel the case is too dangerous for couples therapy (Goldner, 1998).

With most couples it's useful to encourage dialogue as a way of exploring how the partners communicate. Violent couples, however, tend to be emotionally reactive and, when that is the case, it's better to have them take turns talking to the therapist. In the early stages of work with such couples, therapists should do everything possible to slow them down and make them think.

One of the best antidotes to emotionality is to ask for specific, concrete details. A good place to start is with the most recent violent incident. Ask each of them for a detailed, moment-to-moment description of exactly what happened. Be alert for linguistic evasions of responsibility. A violent man may describe his actions as the result of his partner's "provocation" or of "built-up tensions and pressures." Thus it is not he who hits his wife; it is the pressures that are the culprit. A subtler form of evasion is for the violent partner to describe the problem as his impulsivity. When arguments escalate, he starts to "lose it." In this formulation, the man's impulsive actions are not a choice he makes but an unavoidable consequence of his emotions.

Once both partners have begun to own responsibility for their actions—he for choosing to control his violent impulses, she for taking steps to ensure her safety—it becomes possible to explore the relationship issues that lead to escalating emotional reactivity (Holtzworth-Munroe, Meehan, Rehman, & Marshall, 2002). This does *not*, however, mean that at a certain point violent couples can be treated just like any other couple. Exploring the interactional processes in which both partners participate should never be allowed to imply that both are mutually *responsible* for acts of violence.

When the couple is ready to explore relationship issues, it should be possible to begin to encourage dialogue, so that the therapist and couple can understand what transpires when they try to talk with each other. This brings the couple's relationship into the consulting room. It's one thing to tell a man that he should leave before he gets too angry. It's another thing to actually observe the beginnings of emotional escalation and ask him if he's aware that he's started to get upset and interrupt his partner. It then becomes possible to say, "*This* is the moment when you should leave." At this same point, his partner can be asked if she has begun to feel the first signs of tension and fear.

Taking time out is an almost universally used strategy in marital violence programs. Recognizing the cues of escalating anger (racing heart, feeling tense, standing up, pacing) and removing oneself from the situation before violence occurs is encouraged as a way to head off destructive actions that the partners will later regret. Saying "I'm feeling angry (or scared), and I'm going to take a time-out" helps distinguish this safety device from simply refusing to talk. It must be emphasized that each person is responsible for his or her own time-outs. Telling the other person to take a time-out is not allowed, nor is trying to stop the other from leaving.

Although eliminating escalating aggressive interactions must be the first priority, couples must also learn more constructive methods of addressing their differences. Here is a paradox. Violent men must learn to control their behavior, but it is counterproductive to stifle their complaints. In fact, it is precisely this kind of suppression that leads to the emotional build-ups that result in violent explosions. Moreover, a man who resorts to violence with his partner is often a weak man—weak in the sense of not knowing how to articulate his feelings in a way that his partner can hear. Thus in helping couples learn to negotiate their differences, it is essential to ensure that both partners learn to speak up, and to listen to each other.

Sexual Abuse of Children

When treating families in which a child has been sexually abused, the primary goals are, first, assuring that the abuse does not recur, and, second, reducing the long-term effects of the trauma (Trepper & Barrett, 1989). As with marital violence, treatment of sexual abuse tends to fall into one of two categories: a child protective approach, which can undermine the integrity of the family, or a family systems approach, which can fail to protect the child. We recommend supporting the family while at the same time protecting the child. When these goals seem incompatible—for example, when a father has raped his daughter—protection of the child takes precedence.

Assessment of sexual abuse is often complicated by divergent stories about what happened (Herman, 1992). A father may say that touching his daughter's labia was an accidental occurrence, whereas the daughter reports that this happened more than once and that she experiences it as abusive. A grandfather may claim that his caressing of his grandson is perfectly innocent, whereas the district attorney is filing charges of indecent assault. A child protective worker may believe that a mother is tacitly supporting her husband's abuse of her child, whereas a family therapist may see a mother who is doing her best to save her marriage. Such discrepancies must be resolved by social and legal control agencies.

The first priority is restricting unsupervised access to children for the offender. Next, a careful assessment should be conducted to uncover other possible incidents of abuse or patterns of inappropriate sexual expression (Furniss, 1991). The offender must take responsibility for his or her behavior and receive appropriate treatment for his or her actions (which may include legal punishment). Often these measures will have already been taken by a child protective agency before a family is referred for therapy.

One of the goals of family therapy should be to establish a support system to break through the isolation that facilitates sexual abuse and inhibits disclosure. For this reason, many programs favor a multimodal approach that includes individual, group, and family sessions (Bentovim, Elton, Hildebrand, Tranter, & Vizard, 1988; Trepper & Barrett, 1989). Family sessions should be geared toward increasing support for the victimized child, which may entail supporting and strengthening the parental unit.

When a child is the victim of sexual abuse, social control agents may have to step in to protect the child, which can involve taking over what might be considered parental responsibilities. In the long run, however, it is the family who will be responsible for the child. Therefore, supporting the parents rather than taking over from them, is in the best interests of the child.

In cases where a father or stepfather is sent to jail for sexual crimes against his children, part of a therapist's job is to help the family draw and adjust to a rigid boundary that excludes the guilty person. The same is true if the children are taken out of the home and sent to live with relatives or foster parents. Subsequently, however, if reunion is planned, therapy involves gradually reopening this boundary through visits and other contact, which give the family and therapist the opportunity to work together to improve the family's functioning.

One of the keys to helping resolve the trauma of abuse is to give the child a safe forum to explore her[4] complex and often ambivalent feelings about what happened. In addition to feeling violated and angry, she may feel guilty about having gotten an adult in trouble. Often a child secretly blames the nonoffending parent for not preventing the abuse. Finally, the child may fear that the mother's dependence on the abuser might result in his return, leaving the child once again vulnerable to abuse.

A combination of individual and conjoint sessions helps make it safe to talk about feelings. Meeting first with the nonoffending parent (or parents) allows the mother (or parents) to describe what happened and to express feelings about the abuse without having to edit what she says because the child is present. Among the mother's complex feelings will surely be rage and a sense of betrayal. But a part of her may still love the abuser and miss him if he's incarcerated. She may also feel guilty for not having protected her daughter. It's important to make it safe for her to share all of these feelings.

When first meeting with a mother and abused daughter, it's reassuring to say that, although they would eventually probably want to talk about the abuse, it's up to them to choose where to start. It's also helpful to give parents and children the choice of how much to talk about the abuse and whether to do so first in an individual session or conjointly. If children opt to discuss their feelings privately, they should be reassured that it's up to them to decide what they subsequently want to share with their parents.

When meeting with abused children, it's helpful to explain that the more they talk about what happened, the less troubling their feelings are likely to be. However, it's important to let them decide when and how much to open up. Remember that abused children need to recover a sense of control over their own lives (Sheinberg, True, & Fraenkel, 1994). When family members begin to talk about their feelings, it's wise to keep in mind that feelings don't come in either/or categories. One way to help make it safe for them to talk about complex or even contradictory emotions is to use the metaphor of parts (Schwartz, 1995). Thus, an abused child might be asked, "Does part of you think your mother should have figured out what was happening?" Likewise, the mother might be asked, "Does part of you miss him?"

One problem with meeting privately with a child is that doing so creates secrets. At the end of such sessions, it's helpful to ask the child what she wants to share with her family and how she wants to do so. Some children ask the therapist to take the lead in opening up some of what they want their mothers to understand but find it hard to talk about. Finally, although it is important to help children voice any feelings they may have about feeling guilty for what happened, after exploring these feelings, abused children need to hear over and over that what happened was not their fault.

Working with Managed Care

Rarely has a profession undergone such upheaval as mental health providers have experienced with the advent of managed care. Practitioners, used to making decisions based on their own clinical judgment, are now told by the **managed care** industry which patients they can see, which treatments are preferred, what they can charge, and how many sessions they should offer. Professionals taught to maintain confidentiality in their dealings with patients now find themselves negotiating treatment arrangements over the telephone with anonymous strangers.

---

4. For the sake of simplicity, the following discussion assumes the common instance of a stepfather as abuser and a mother and her abused daughter as clients.

The managed care industry itself has been slow to get its act together. Some of the horror stories we've all heard about care being disallowed or abruptly terminated stem from the early days of managed care when the industry tended to manage by fiat rather than mediation. When asked to approve any but the most limited forms of treatment, the industry's first impulse was to just say no.

Now twenty years into its existence, the managed care industry is coming to terms with two important facts: (1) Although their mandate is still to contain costs, their ultimate responsibility is to see that patients receive effective treatment; (2) although there seems to be a built-in adversarial relationship to practitioners, industry case managers are discovering something that clinicians should also come to terms with—that both sides profit when they begin to work in partnership.[5]

The key to succeeding in a managed care environment is learning to get over the sense that the case manager at the other end of the line is the enemy. Actually, for those who learn to collaborate effectively with managed care, case managers can be the best source of referrals.

For students, learning to work with managed care should begin as early as planning their education. Most managed care companies accept licensed practitioners with graduate degrees in nursing, social work, psychology, and psychiatry. Some, but by no means most, accept other degrees—though not usually on their preferred provider lists. So, just as it's prudent to take state licensing requirements into account when planning postgraduate education, it's also wise to consider the requirements of managed care companies. Moreover, because most companies require at least three years of post-degree experience, it's a good idea to plan on beginning your career in a supervised agency.

In areas with a high concentration of mental health providers, it may be necessary to market your skills to be selected as a managed care provider. Case managers are always looking for competent professionals who can make their jobs easier. Willingness to accept crisis referrals and to work with difficult cases (e.g., borderline, chronic, and multiproblem clients), accessibility, and having specialized expertise help make therapists attractive to managed care companies.

Once you have the opportunity to become a provider, remember to work *with* case managers, not *against* them. You may find the paperwork frustrating, but you should keep in mind that case managers have feelings too—and they have memories. They're just trying to do the job they were hired to do. The biggest mistake a practitioner can make is to become oppositional with case managers.

Case managers appreciate succinct and informative reports. When challenged, many therapists fall back on justifying their requests by saying, "It's my clinical opinion." Being asked to justify their conclusions makes some practitioners angry. They feel they are doing the best they can for their patients. They are practicing efficiently. But they are not used to someone looking over their shoulder. Get used to it. If you use sound clinical judgment, you should be able to provide reasons for your recommendations.

If you can't reach agreement with a case manager, don't lose your temper. If you can't be friendly, don't be hostile. Follow the grievance procedure. Do the required paperwork and submit it on time. Write concise, well-defined treatment plans. Return phone calls promptly. Make arrangements to provide back-up if you're out of town or unable to accept a referral.

In addition to maintaining a positive attitude, being successful in the current health care climate means developing a results-oriented mindset. If you're trained in solution-focused therapy, by all means say so, but don't try to pass yourself off as something you're not. Calling yourself "eclectic" is more likely to sound fuzzy than flexible. The important point is to get a reputation for working within established time limits and getting results.

---

5. Increased competition among managed care companies has increased pressure to build trust and loyalty among providers and to reduce internal costs by spending less administrative time managing providers.

—Questions to Consider—

1. What is lost and what is gained by agreeing to meet with less than the whole family for an initial consultation?
2. What are some things that were suggested in this chapter for practicing family therapy that you disagree with? Why?
3. What are some of the practices in clinics where you have worked or observed that you think unnecessarily violate clients' confidentiality?
4. Should a therapist keep the confidences of a thirteen-year-old child from his or her parents? When not?

—Key Concepts—

boundaries   Emotional barriers that protect and enhance the integrity of individuals, subsystems, and families.

family life cycle   Stages in a family's life, from separating from parents through getting married, having children, retirement, and so on, that generally require modifications in the family's structure.

formulation   A therapeutic hypothesis about what is responsible for creating and maintaining a client's presenting problem.

genogram   A schematic diagram of a family system, using squares to represent males, circles for females, horizontal lines for marriages, and vertical lines for children.

linearity   The notion that one event is a cause and the other is its effect; in behavior, the idea that one behavior is a stimulus and the other a response; as opposed to circular thinking, in which events are thought to be related in a series of interacting loops.

managed care   A system in which third-party companies manage insurance costs by regulating the terms of treatment. Managed care companies select providers, set fees, and control who receives treatment and how many sessions they are allowed.

process/content   Distinction between how members of a family or group relate (process) and what they talk about (content).

structure   Recurrent patterns of interaction that define and stabilize the shape of relationships.

subsystems   Smaller units in families, determined by generation, sex, or function.

treatment contract   An explicit agreement between client(s) and therapist that specifies the terms of therapy, including things like frequency and length of sessions, who is to attend, and fees.

—Recommended Readings—

Anderson, C., and Stewart, S. 1983. *Mastering resistance: A practical guide to family therapy.* New York: Guilford Press.

Minuchin, S., and Fishman, H. C. 1981. *Family therapy techniques.* Cambridge, MA: Harvard University Press.

Patterson, J. E., Williams, L., Grauf-Grounds, C., and Chamow, L. 1998. *Essential skills in family therapy.* New York: Guilford Press.

Sheinberg, M., True, F., and Fraenkel, P. 1994. Treating the sexually abused child: A recursive, multimodel program. *Family Process. 33:* 263–276.

Simon, G. M. 2003. *Beyond technique in family therapy: Finding your therapeutic voice.* Boston: Allyn & Bacon.

Taibbi, R. 1996. *Doing family therapy: Craft and creativity in clinical practice.* New York: Guilford Press.

Trepper, T. S., and Barrett, M. J. 1989. *Systemic treatment of incest: A therapeutic handbook.* New York: Brunner/Mazel.

Walsh, F. 1998. *Strengthening family resilience.* New York: Guilford Press.

—References

AAMFT Code of Ethics. 1991. Washington, DC: American Association for Marriage and Family Therapy.

Avis, J. M. 1992. Where are all the family therapists? Abuse and violence within families and family therapy's response. *Journal of Marital and Family Therapy. 18:* 223–233.

Bentovim, A., Elton, A., Hildebrand, J., Tranter, M., and Vizard, E., eds., 1988. *Child sexual abuse within the family.* London: Wright.

Bograd, M. 1984. Family systems approaches to wife battering: A feminist critique. *American Journal of Orthopsychiatry. 54:* 558–568.

Bograd, M. 1992. Values in conflict: Challenges to family therapists' thinking. *Journal of Marital and Family Therapy. 18:* 243–257.

Boszormenyi-Nagy, I., and Spark, G. 1973. *Invisible loyalties: Reciprocity in intergenerational family therapy.* New York: Harper & Row.

Brown, P. D., and O'Leary, K. D. July. 1995. Marital treatment for wife abuse: A review and evaluation. Paper presented at the 4th International Family Violence Research Conference, Durham, NC.

Doherty, W. 1991. Family therapy goes postmodern. *Family Therapy Networker. 15 (5):* 36–42.

Edelson, E., and Tolman, R. 1992. *Intervention for men who batter.* Newbury Park, CA: Sage Publications.

Feldman, C. M., and Ridley, C. A. 1995. The etiology and treatment of domestic violence between adult partners. *Clinical Psychology: Science and Practice. 2:* 317–348.

Furniss, T. 1991. *The multiprofessional handbook of child sexual abuse: Integrated management, therapy, and legal intervention.* London: Routledge.

Goldner, V. 1992. Making room for both/and. *The Family Therapy Networker. 16 (2):* 55–61.

Goldner, V. 1998. The treatment of violence and victimization in intimate relationships. *Family Process. 37:* 263–286.

Gondolf, E. W. 1995. Gains and process in state batterer programs and standards. *Family Violence and Sexual Assault Bulletin. 11:* 27–28.

Hansen, M. 1993. Feminism and family therapy: A review of feminist critiques of approaches to family violence (pp. 69–82). In *Battering and family therapy: A feminist perspective,* M. Hansen and M. Harway (eds.), Newbury Park, CA: Sage Publications.

Herman, J. L. 1992. *Trauma and recovery.* New York: Basic Books.

Holtzworth-Munroe, A., Meehan, J. C., Eehman, U., and Marshall, A. D. 2002. Intimate partner violence: An introduction for couple therapists. In *Clinical handbook of couple therapy.* 3rd ed., A. Gurman and N. Jacobson, eds. New York: Guilford Press.

Jacobson, N. S., and Christensen, A. 1996. *Integrative couple therapy.* New York: Guilford Press.

McGoldrick, M., Giordano, J., and Pearce, J 1996. *Ethnicity and family therapy,* 2nd ed. New York: Guilford Press.

Minuchin, S., and Nichols. M. P. 1993. *Family healing: Tales of hope and renewal from family therapy.* New York: Free Press.

Nichols, M. P. 1987. *The self in the system.* New York: Brunner/Mazel.

Nichols, M. P. 1995. *The lost art of listening.* New York: Guilford Press.

Schwartz, R. C. 1995. *Internal family systems therapy.* New York: Guilford Press.

Sheinberg, M., True, F., and Fraenkel, P. 1994. Treating the sexually abused child: A recursive, multimodal program. *Family Process. 33:* 263–276.

Trepper, T. S., and Barrett, M. J. 1989. *Systemic treatment of incest: A therapeutic handbook.* New York: Brunner/Mazel.

Walsh, F. 1998. *Strengthening family resilience.* New York: Guilford Press.

The Fundamental Concepts
of Family Therapy

Family therapy is often misunderstood as just another variation of psychotherapy, one in which the whole family is brought into treatment. It is that, of course, but it also involves a whole new way of thinking about human behavior; that is, as fundamentally organized by interpersonal context.

Prior to the advent of family therapy the individual was regarded as the locus of psychological problems and the target for treatment. If a mother called to complain that her fifteen-year-old son was depressed, a clinician would meet with the boy to find out what was wrong. A Rogerian might look for low self-esteem, a Freudian for repressed anger, a behaviorist for a lack of reinforcing activities; but all would assume that the primary forces shaping the boy's mood were located within him and that therapy, therefore, required only the presence of the patient and a therapist.

Family therapy changed all that. Today, if a mother were to seek help for a depressed teenager, most therapists would meet with the boy and his parents together. If a fifteen-year-old is depressed, it's not unreasonable to assume that something might be going on in the family. Perhaps the boy's parents don't get along and he's worried that they might get divorced. Maybe he's having a hard time living up to the expectations created by a successful older sister.

Suppose further that you are the therapist. You meet with the boy and his family and discover that he's *not* worried about his parents or jealous of his sister. In fact, everything "is fine" at home. He's just depressed. Now what?

That *now-what* feeling is a common experience when you start seeing families. Even when there *is* something obviously wrong—the boy is worried about his parents or everybody seems to be shouting and no one is listening—it's often hard to know where to start. You could start by trying to solve the family's problems for them. But then you wouldn't be helping them deal with *why* they are having problems.

To address what's making it hard for a family to cope with their problems, you have to know where to look. For that, you need some way of understanding what makes families tick. You need a theory.

When they first began to observe families discussing their problems, therapists could see immediately that everyone was involved. In the clamor of noisy quarrels, however, it's hard to get beyond the impact of personalities—the sullen adolescent, the controlling mother, the distant father—to see the patterns that connect them. Instead of concentrating on individuals and their personalities, family therapists consider how problems may be, at least in part, a product of the relationships surrounding them. How to understand those relationships is the subject of this chapter.

Cybernetics

The first and perhaps most influential model of how families operate was **cybernetics,** the study of feedback mechanisms in self-regulating systems. What the family shares with other cybernetic systems is a tendency to maintain stability by using information about its performance as feedback.

At the core of cybernetics is the **feedback** loop, the process by which a system gets the information necessary to maintain a steady course. This feedback includes information about the system's performance relative to its external environment as well as the relationship among the system's parts. Feedback loops can be *negative* or *positive.* This distinction refers to the effect they have on deviations from a homeostatic state, not to whether they are beneficial. **Negative feedback** indicates how far off the mark a system is straying and the corrections needed to get it back on course. It signals the system to restore the status quo. Thus, negative feedback is not such a negative thing at all. Its vital, error-correcting information gives order and self-control to automatic machines, to the body and the brain, and to people in their daily lives. **Positive feedback** is information that confirms and reinforces the direction a system is taking.

A familiar example of negative feedback occurs in the home heating system. When the temperature drops below a certain point, the thermostat triggers the furnace to heat the house back to the pre-established range. It is this self-correcting feedback loop that makes the system cybernetic, and it is the system's response to change as a signal to restore its previous state that illustrates negative feedback.

Figure 4.1 shows the basic circularity involved in a feedback loop. Each element has an effect on the next, until the last element "feeds back" the

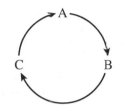

FIGURE 4.1 Circular Causality of a Feedback Loop

cumulative effect into the first part of the cycle. Thus **A** affects **B,** which in turn affects **C,** which feeds back to affect **A,** and so on.

In the example of a home heating system, **A** might be the room temperature; **B,** the thermostat; and **C,** the furnace. Figure 4.2 shows a similar cybernetic feedback loop in a couple. In this case, Jan's housecleaning efforts (output) affect how much housework gets done, which subsequently affects how much housecleaning Billie has to do, which then feeds back (input) to how much housecleaning Jan thinks still needs to be done, and so on.

The cybernetic system turned out to be an apt metaphor for describing how families maintain their stability (Jackson, 1959). Sometimes stability is a good thing, as, for example, when a family continues to function as a cohesive unit despite being threatened by conflict or stress.

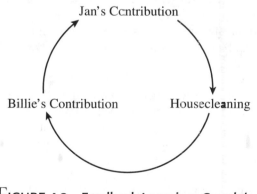

FIGURE 4.2 Feedback Loop in a Couple's Housecleaning Efforts

Sometimes, however, resisting change is not such a good thing, as when a family fails to accommodate to the growth of one of its members. More about this later.

Like negative feedback, positive feedback can have desirable or undesirable consequences. If left unchecked, the reinforcing effects of positive feedback tend to compound a system's errors, leading to runaway processes. The hapless driver on an icy road who sends positive feedback to his automobile engine by stepping on the accelerator can spiral out of control because his brakes are useless to provide the negative feedback to stop the car. Similarly, malignant worry, phobic avoidance, and other forms of neurotic behavior may start out with a relatively trivial concern and build into an out-of-control, destructive process.

Consider, for example, that a panic attack may begin as a relatively harmless instance of being out of breath, but a panicky response to breathlessness may spiral into a terrifying experience. Or, for a more complex example, take the workings of the federal government. Presidents generally surround themselves with advisers who share their viewpoint and who, because they are eager to maintain access, tend to support whatever position the president takes. Their positive feedback can result in the president's taking a bad policy and running with it—like Lyndon Johnson's escalation of the Vietnam War. Fortunately, however, the checks and balances provided by the legislative and judicial branches usually provide the negative feedback to keep administrations from going too far in one direction. To survive and adapt to the world around them, all communication systems—including families—need a healthy balance of positive and negative feedback. As we shall see, however, early family therapists tended to overemphasize negative feedback and resistance to change.

Cybernetics was the brainchild of MIT mathematician Norbert Wiener (1948), who developed what was to become the first model of family dynamics in an extremely unlikely setting. During World War II, Wiener was asked to design a better way to correct and control

the targeting of antiaircraft artillery (Conway & Siegelman, 2005). The German bombers blackening the skies over Europe flew at speeds exceeding 300 miles per hour, and at altitudes as high as 30,000 feet. The flight of an artillery shell to that height could take as long as twenty seconds, and firing that shot accurately—nearly two miles downrange—was no simple task. Wiener's solution was to incorporate a system of internal feedback which enabled antiaircraft guns to automatically regulate their own operations. The signal used to control the artillery was a self-regulating "servomechanism"—the technical term for the first automated machines.

To capture the essence of the new science of communication and control by feedback, Wiener chose the name *cybernetics,* from the Greek for "steersman." He distinguished the two major modes of information, discrete or continuous—digital or analog—and their diverse applications in communication, electronic computing, and automatic control systems. Moreover, he pointed out that the new technical methods of control by information feedback were, in essence, the same universal processes that nature long ago selected as its basic operating system for human beings and all living things (Wiener, 1948). He even suggested that cybernetic theory could be used to explain mental illnesses as self-reinforcing patterns of behavior—as the brain gets stuck in a bad biochemical rut.

Gregory Bateson came into contact with cybernetics at a remarkable series of interdisciplinary meetings called the Macy conferences, beginning in 1942 (Heims, 1991). Bateson and Wiener immediately hit it off at these meetings, and their dialogues were to have a profound impact on Bateson's application of systems theory to family therapy.

Because cybernetics emerged from the study of machines, where positive feedback loops led to destructive "runaways," causing the machinery to break down, the emphasis was on negative feedback and the maintenance of homeostasis. The system's environment would change—the temperature would go up or down—and this change would trigger negative feedback mechanisms to bring the system back to homeostasis—the heat would go on or off. Negative feedback loops control everything from endocrine systems to ecosystems. Animal species are balanced by starvation and predators when they overpopulate and by increases in birth rates when their numbers are depleted. Blood sugar levels are balanced by increases in insulin output when they get too high and increases in appetite when they get too low.

As applied to families, cybernetics focused attention on several phenomena: (1) **family rules,** which govern the range of behavior a family system can tolerate (the family's homeostatic range); (2) **negative feedback** mechanisms that families use to enforce those rules (guilt, punishment, symptoms); (3) **sequences of family interaction** around a problem that characterize a system's reaction to it (feedback loops); and (4) what happens when a system's accustomed negative feedback is ineffective, triggering **positive feedback loops.**

Examples of positive feedback loops are those pesky "vicious cycles" in which the actions taken only make things worse. The well-known "self-fulfilling prophecy" is one such positive feedback loop; one's apprehensions lead to actions that precipitate the feared situation, which in turn justifies one's fears, and so on. Another example of positive feedback is the "bandwagon effect"—the tendency of a cause to gain support simply because of its growing number of adherents. You can probably think of some fads and more than a few pop music groups that owe much of their popularity to the bandwagon effect.

As an example of a self-fulfilling prophecy, consider a young therapist who expects men to be uninvolved in family life. She believes that fathers *should* play an active role in the lives of their children, but her own experience has taught her not to expect much. Suppose she's trying to arrange for a family consultation, and the mother says that her husband won't be able to attend. How is our hypothetical therapist likely to respond? She might accept the mother's statement at face value and, thus, collude to ensure just what she expected. Alternatively, she might

challenge the mother's statement aggressively, thereby displacing her attitude toward men into her relationship with the mother—or push the mother into an oppositional stance with her husband.

To shift to a family example, in a family with a low threshold for the expression of anger, Marcus, the adolescent son, blows up at his parents over their insistence that he not stay out past midnight. Mother is shocked by his outburst and begins to cry. Father responds by grounding Marcus for a month. Rather than reducing Marcus's deviation—bringing his anger back within homeostatic limits—this feedback produces the opposite effect: Marcus explodes and challenges their authority. The parents respond with more crying and punishing, which further increases Marcus's anger, and so on. In this way, the intended negative feedback (crying and punishing) becomes positive feedback. It amplifies rather than diminishes Marcus's deviation. The family is caught in a positive feedback **runaway,** otherwise known as a vicious cycle, which escalates until Marcus runs away from home.

Later, cyberneticians like Walter Buckley and Ross Ashby recognized that positive feedback loops aren't always bad; if they don't get out of hand, they can help systems adjust to changed circumstances. Marcus's family might need to recalibrate their rules for anger to accommodate an adolescent's increased assertiveness. The crisis that this positive feedback loop produced could lead to a reexamination of the family's rules—if the family could step out of the loop long enough to get some perspective. In so doing they would be using **metacommunication,** communicating about their ways of communicating, a process that can lead to a change in a system's rules (Bateson, 1956).

As should now be clear, family cyberneticians focused on the feedback loops within families, otherwise known as patterns of communication, as the fundamental source of family dysfunction. Hence the family theorists most influenced by cybernetics came to be known as the *communications school* (see Chapter 6). Faulty or unclear communication results in inaccurate or incomplete feedback, so the system cannot self-correct (change its rules) and, consequently, overreacts or underreacts to change.

Systems Theory

The greatest challenge facing anyone who treats families is to see past personalities to the patterns of influence that shape family members' behavior. We're so used to seeing what happens in families as a product of individual qualities, like selfishness, tolerance, rebelliousness, submissiveness, and so on, that learning to see patterns of relationship requires a radical shift in perspective.

Experience teaches that what shows up as one person's behavior may be a product of relationship. The same individual may be submissive in one relationship, dominant in another. Like so many qualities we attribute to individuals, submissiveness is only half of a two-part equation. In fact, family therapists use a host of concepts to describe how two people in a relationship contribute to what goes on between them, including *pursuer–distancer, overfunctioning– underfunctioning, control-and-rebel cycles,* and so on. The advantage of such concepts is that either party to the relationship can change his or her part in the pattern. But while it's relatively easy to discover themes in two-person relationships, it's more difficult to see patterns of interaction in larger groups like whole families. That's why family therapists have found systems theory so useful.

Systems theory had its origins in the 1940s, when theoreticians began to construct models of the structure and functioning of organized mechanical and biological units. What these theorists discovered was that things as diverse as simple machines, jet engines, amoebas, and the human brain all share the attributes of a system—that is, an organized assemblage of parts forming a complex whole. Bateson and his colleagues found systems theory to be a perfect vehicle for illuminating the ways in which families functioned as organized units.

According to systems theory, the essential properties of an organism, or living system, are properties of the whole, which none of the parts have. They arise from the relationships among the parts. These properties are destroyed when the system is reduced, either physically or theoretically, to isolated elements. The whole is always greater than the sum of its parts. Thus, from a systems perspective, it would make little sense to try to understand a child's behavior by interviewing him without the rest of his family.

Although some therapists use terms like *systemic* and *systems theory* to mean little more than considering families as units, systems actually have a number of more specific and interesting properties. To begin with, the shift from looking at individuals to considering the family as a system means shifting the focus to patterns of relationship.

Let's take a simple example. If a mother scolds her son, and his father tells her not to be so harsh, and the boy continues to misbehave, a systemic analysis would concentrate on this sequence. For it is this *observable interaction* that reveals how the system functions. To focus on inputs and outputs, a systems analysis deliberately avoids speculating about individuals or asking *why* they do what they do. The most radical expression of this systemic perspective was the **black box metaphor:**

> The impossibility of seeing the mind "at work" has in recent years led to the adoption of the Black Box concept . . . applied to the fact that electronic hardware is by now so complex that it is sometimes more expedient to disregard the internal structure of a device and concentrate on the study of its specific input–output relations. . . . This concept, if applied to psychological and psychiatric problems, has the heuristic advantage that no ultimately unverifiable intrapsychic hypotheses need be invoked, and that one can limit oneself to observable input–output relations, that is, to communication. (Watzlawick, Beavin, & Jackson, 1967, pp. 43–44)

Viewing people as black boxes may seem like the ultimate expression of mechanistic thinking, but this metaphor had the advantage of simplifying the field of study by eliminating speculation about the mind in order to concentrate on people's input and output (communication, behavior).

Among the features of systems seized on by early family therapists, few were more influential—or later more controversial—than **homeostasis,** the self-regulation that allows systems to maintain themselves in a state of dynamic balance. Don Jackson's notion of family homeostasis emphasized that dysfunctional families' tendency to resist change went a long way toward explaining why, despite heroic efforts to improve, so many patients remain stuck (Jackson, 1959). Today we look back on this emphasis on homeostasis as shortchanging families by exaggerating their conservative properties and underestimating their resourcefulness.

Thus, although many of the cybernetic concepts used to describe machines could be extended by analogy to human systems like the family, living systems, it turns out, cannot be adequately described by the same principles as mechanical systems.

General Systems Theory

In the 1940s an Austrian biologist, Ludwig von Bertalanffy, attempted to combine concepts from systems thinking and biology into a universal theory of living systems—from the human mind to the global ecosphere. Starting with investigations of the endocrine system, he began extrapolating to more complex social systems and developed a model that came to be called **general systems theory.**

Mark Davidson, in his fascinating biography, *Uncommon Sense* (1983), summarized Bertalanffy's definition of a system as:

any entity maintained by the mutual interaction of its parts, from atom to cosmos, and including such mundane examples as telephone, postal, and rapid transit systems. A Bertalanffian system can be physical like a television set, biological like a cocker spaniel, psychological like a personality, sociological like a labor union, or symbolic like a set of laws. . . . A system can be composed of smaller systems and can also be part of a larger system, just as a state or province is composed of smaller jurisdictions and also is part of a nation. (p. 26)

The last point is important. Every system is a subsystem of larger systems. But when they adopted the systems perspective, family therapists tended to forget about this spreading network of influence. They treated the family as a system while ignoring the larger systems of community, culture, and politics in which families are embedded.

Bertalanffy pioneered the idea that a system is more than the sum of its parts, in the same sense that a watch is more than a collection of cogs and springs. There's nothing mystical about this, just that when things are organized into a system, something new emerges, the way water comes from the interaction of hydrogen and oxygen. Applied to family therapy, these ideas—that a family system should be seen as more than just a collection of people, and that therapists should focus on interactions rather than on personalities—became central tenets of the field.

Bertalanffy used the metaphor of an organism for social groups, but an organism that was an **open system,** continuously interacting with its environment. Open systems, as opposed to **closed systems** (e.g., machines), sustain themselves by continuously exchanging resources with their surroundings—for example, taking in oxygen and expelling carbon dioxide. Another property of living systems that mechanists forgot was that they don't just react to stimuli, they actively initiate efforts to flourish.

Bertalanffy was a life-long crusader against the mechanistic view of living systems, particularly those living systems called people. He believed that, unlike machines, living organisms demonstrate **equifinality,** the ability to reach a final goal in a variety of ways. (In mechanical systems, the final state and the means to that state are fixed.) He and other biologists used that term to identify the organism's inner-directed ability to protect or restore its wholeness as in the human body's mobilization of antibodies and its ability to repair skin and bone (von Bertalanffy, 1950).

Thus, living organisms are active and creative. They work to sustain their organization, but they aren't motivated solely to preserve the status quo. Family therapists picked up on the concept of homeostasis but, according to Bertalanffy, an over emphasis on this conservative aspect of the organism reduced it to the level of a machine: "If [this] principle of homeostatic maintenance is taken as a rule of behavior, the so-called well-adjusted individual will be [defined as] a well-oiled robot . . ." (quoted in Davidson, 1983, p. 104).

Although homeostasis remains an important concept in family therapy, its limited ability to account for human creativity has been repeatedly emphasized by family therapists in ways that echo Bertalanffy's concerns (Dell, 1982; Hoffman, 1981; Speer, 1970). Cyberneticians had to propose impressive-sounding concepts like **morphogenesis** (Speer, 1970) to account for what Bertalanffy believed was simply a natural property of organisms—to seek, in addition to resisting, change.

To summarize, Bertalanffy brought up many of the issues that have shaped and still are shaping family therapy:

- A system as more than the sum of its parts
- Emphasis on interaction within and among systems versus reductionism
- Human systems as ecologic organisms versus mechanism
- Concept of equifinality
- Homeostatic reactivity versus spontaneous activity

Many of these issues reappear in the ensuing discussion and throughout the book.

Social Constructionism

Systems theory taught us to see how people's lives are shaped by their interchanges with those around them. In focusing on patterns of interaction, however, systems theory left something out. Actually, two things: how family members' beliefs affect their actions and how cultural forces shape those beliefs.

Constructivism

Constructivism captured the imagination of family therapists in the 1980s when studies of brain function showed that we can never know the world as it exists "out there"; all we can know is our subjective experience of it. Research on neural nets (Foerster, 1981) and experiments on the vision of the frog (Maturana & Varela, 1980) indicated that the brain doesn't process images literally, like a camera, but rather registers experience in patterns organized by the nervous system of the observer.[1] Nothing is perceived directly. Everything is filtered through the mind of the observer.

When this new perspective on knowing was reported to the family field by Paul Watzlawick (1984), Paul Dell (1985), and Lynn Hoffman (1988), the effect was a wake-up call—alerting us to the importance of cognition in family life and jolting therapists out of the assumption that they could be objective experts.

Constructivism is the modern expression of a philosophical tradition that goes back at least as far as the eighteenth century. Immanuel Kant (1724–1804), one of the pillars of Western intellectual tradition, regarded knowledge as a product of the way our imaginations are organized. The outside world doesn't simply impress itself onto the *tabula rasa* (blank slate) of our minds, as British Empiricist John Locke (1632–1704) believed. In fact, as Kant argued, our minds are anything but blank. They are highly active filters through which we process, categorize, and interpret the world.

Constructivism first found its way into psychotherapy in the *personal construct theory* of George

---

1. The eye of the frog, for example, doesn't register much but lateral movement—which may be all you really need to know if your main interest in life is catching flies with your tongue.

Kelly (1955). According to Kelly, we make sense of the world by creating our own constructs of the environment. We interpret and organize events, and we make predictions that guide our actions on the basis of these constructs. You might compare this interpreting of experience to seeing the world through a pair of eyeglasses. Because we may need to adjust constructs, therapy became a matter of revising old constructs and developing new ones—trying on different lenses to see which ones enabled a person to navigate the world in more satisfying ways.

The first example of constructivism in family therapy was the strategic technique of **reframing**—relabeling behavior to shift how family members respond to it. Clients respond very differently to a child seen as "hyperactive" than to one who is perceived as "misbehaving." Likewise, the dispirited parents of a rebellious ten-year-old will feel better about themselves if they become convinced that, rather than being "ineffectual disciplinarians," they have an "oppositional child." The first diagnosis suggests that the parents should get tough, but also that they probably won't succeed. The second suggests that coping with a difficult child may require strategizing. The point isn't that one description is better than the other, but rather that if whatever label a family applies to its problems leads to ineffective coping strategies, then perhaps a new label will alter their viewpoint and lead to a more effective response.

When constructivism took hold of family therapy in the mid-1980s, it triggered a fundamental shift in emphasis. Systems metaphors focused on behavior and interaction; constructivism shifted the focus toward exploring the assumptions that people have about their problems. Meaning itself became the target. The goal of therapy shifted from interrupting problematic patterns of behavior to helping clients find new perspectives in their lives through the liberating process of dialogue.

In the vanguard of this movement were Harry Goolishian and Harlene Anderson, whose "collaborative language-based systems approach" was defined less by what therapists do than by what they *don't do*. In this model, therapists *don't*

assume the role of expert, *don't* assume that they know how families should change, and *don't* push them in any particular direction. The role of the therapist isn't to change people but to open doors for them to explore new meanings in their lives.

> The therapist does not control the interview by influencing the conversation toward a particular direction in the sense of content or outcome, nor is the therapist responsible for the direction of change. The therapist is only responsible for creating a space in which dialogical conversation can occur. (Anderson & Goolishian, 1988, p. 385)

Constructivism teaches us to look beyond behavior to the ways we perceive, interpret, and construct our experience. Moreover, in a world where all truth is relative, the perspective of the therapist began to be seen as having no more claim to objectivity than that of the clients. Thus, constructivism undermined the status of the therapist as an objective authority with privileged knowledge of cause and cure.

Acknowledging that how we perceive reality is a construction doesn't mean that there is nothing real out there to perceive and understand. Sticks and stones *can* break bones. Moreover, even the most ardent constructivists (e.g., Efran, Lukens, & Lukens, 1990) remind us that some constructions are more useful than others.

Others have challenged the opposite implication of constructivism—namely, that a therapist without the status of expert is a therapist without influence. In her thoughtful analysis of postmodern therapy, *Back to Reality*, Barbara Held (1995) points out that: ". . . surely there is a contradiction to be faced by these authors when they attempt to deny or minimize the expertise that they also apparently want themselves to have—that therapists must indeed have to legitimate their activity as a profession/discipline" (p. 244).

One of us (M.P.N.) felt strongly enough about what he perceived as the abdication of leadership to remind therapists:

> Are therapists and clients partners in a joint undertaking? Are they equals? No. Clients are, to

paraphrase George Orwell, "more equal" when it comes to whose point of view ultimately counts. Therapists are, or should be, more equal when it comes to training, expertise, and objectivity—*and* taking the lead in what happens during the therapy hour. It's fine to criticize power—if what's meant by that is domination and control; it's not so fine to abdicate leadership. (Nichols, 1993, p. 165)

And further:

If arranging and hosting conversations were all that a therapist did, that person should be called a mediator, or the opposite of a talk-show host (whose aim is to arrange conversations that are nasty and abusive). The therapist as host neglects the role of teacher—a much maligned but essential aspect of any transformative therapy. Therapists teach not by telling people how to run their lives, but by helping them learn something about themselves. (p. 164)

But "telling people how to run their lives" is exactly what Anderson and Goolishian (1988) were concerned about. Constructivism was a revolt against an authoritarian model of therapy, against the image of the therapist as bully.

Anderson and Goolishian favored what they called an attitude of "not-knowing" in which they make room for their clients' ideas to come forward. Instead of approaching families with preconceived notions, they brought only curiosity. It's probably well to remember that even our most cherished metaphors for family life—"system," "enmeshment," "triangles," and so on—are just that: metaphors. They don't exist in some objective reality; they are constructions, some more useful than others.

The construction favored by Anderson and Goolishian was that language creates rather than reflects reality. There is, of course, nothing new in describing therapy ("the talking cure") as dialogue. What was new was the elevation of personal narrative to the pinnacle of interest in family therapy—a field born from discovery of how the personal is shaped by the interpersonal context.

In emphasizing the idiosyncratic perspective of the individual, constructivists were accused by some (e.g.. Minuchin, 1991) of ignoring the social context. Once that solipsistic streak was pointed out, leading constructivists clarified their position: When they said that reality is constructed, they meant *socially* constructed.

The Social Construction of Reality

Social constructionism expands on constructivism much as family therapy expanded on individual psychology. Constructivism says that we relate to the world on the basis of our own interpretations. **Social constructionism** points out that those interpretations are shaped by our context.

If a fourteen-year-old consistently disobeys his parents, a constructivist might point out that the boy may think they don't deserve his respect. In other words, the boy's actions are not simply a product of the parents' disciplinary efforts but also of the boy's construction of their authority. A social constructionist would add that an adolescent's attitudes about parental authority are shaped not only by what goes on in the family but also by messages transmitted from the culture at large.

At school or work, at lunch, in phone conversations, at the movies, and from television, we absorb attitudes and opinions that we carry into our families. Television, to pick one extremely potent influence on the average fourteen-year-old, has made today's children more sophisticated and more cynical. As communications scholar Joshua Meyrowitz (1985) argues in *No Sense of Place,* today's children are exposed to the "back stage" of the adult world, to otherwise hidden doubts and conflicts, foolishness and failures of adult types they see on television. This demystification undermines adolescent confidence in traditional authority structures. It's hard to respect adult wisdom when your image of a parent figure is Homer Simpson.

Both constructivism and social constructionism focus on interpretation of experience as a mediator of behavior. But while constructivists emphasized the subjective mind of the individual, social constructionists place more emphasis on the intersubjective influence of language and culture. According to constructivism, people have problems not merely because of the objective conditions of their lives but also because of their interpretation of those conditions. What social constructionism adds is a recognition of how such meanings emerge in the process of talking with other people.

Therapy then becomes a process of deconstruction—of freeing clients from the tyranny of entrenched beliefs. How this plays out in practice is illustrated in the two most influential recent versions of family therapy: the solution-focused model and narrative therapy.

Inherent in most forms of therapy is the idea that before you can solve a problem, you must figure out what's wrong. This notion seems almost self-evident, but it is a construction—only one way of looking at things. **Solution-focused therapy** turns this assumption on its head, using a totally different construction—namely, that the best way to solve problems is to discover what people do when they're *not* having the problem.

Suppose, for example, that a woman's complaint is that her husband never talks to her. Instead of trying to figure out what's wrong, a solution-focused therapist might ask the woman if she can remember *exceptions* to this complaint. Perhaps she and her husband do have reasonably good conversations when they go for walks or out to dinner. In that case, the therapist might simply suggest that they do more of that. We'll see how solution-focused therapy builds on the insights of constructivism in Chapter 12.

Like their solution-focused colleagues, **narrative** therapists create a shift in their clients' experience by helping them reexamine how they look at things. But whereas solution-focused therapy shifts attention from current failures to past successes in order to mobilize behavioral solutions, narrative therapy's aim is broader and more attitudinal. The decisive technique in this approach—*externalization*—involves the truly radical reconstruction of defining problems not as properties of the persons who suffer them but as alien oppressors. Thus, for example, while the parents of a boy who doesn't keep up with his homework might define him as lazy or as a procrastinator, a narrative therapist would talk instead about times when "Procrastination" gets the better of him—and times when "it" doesn't.

Notice how the former construction—the boy is a procrastinator—is relatively deterministic, where as the latter—Procrastination sometimes gets the better of him—frees the boy from a negative identity, and turns therapy into a struggle for liberation. We'll talk more about narrative therapy and the process of externalization in Chapter 13.

Both solution-focused and narrative therapy are founded on the premise that we build up our ideas about the world in conversation with other people (Gergen, 1985). Moreover, if some of those ideas bog us down in our problems, then new and more productive perspectives can usefully evolve within a cradle of narrative reconstruction. If problems are stories that people have learned to tell themselves, then deconstructing those stories can be an effective way to help people master their problems.

Critics, ourselves among them (Nichols & Schwartz, 2001), have pointed out that by emphasizing the cognitive dimension of individuals and their experience, social constructionists have turned their backs on some of the defining insights of family therapy—namely, that families operate as complex units and that psychological symptoms are often the result of conflicts within the family. Our experience and our identities are partly linguistic constructions, but only partly. If social constructionists have tended to ignore the insights of systems theory and to downplay family conflict, there is nothing inherent in social constructionism that makes this necessary. The kinds of polarized interactions that Bateson, Jackson, and Haley first described fifty years ago—in terms like *complementary* and *symmetrical*—can be understood as reflecting both behavioral interactions *and* social constructions, rather than either one or the other.

Italian psychiatrist Valeria Ugazio (1999) describes how family members differentiate themselves not merely by their actions but by the way they talk about themselves in semantic polarities.

Thus, for example, in a family whose talk about themselves and others can be characterized by the polarity dependence/independence, conversations will tend to be organized around fear and courage, the need for protection and the desire for exploration. As a result of these conversations, members of such a family will grow to define themselves as shy and cautious or bold and adventurous.

Attachment Theory

As the field matured, family therapists showed a renewed interest in the inner life of the individuals who make up the family. Now, in addition to theories about the broad, systemic influences on family members' behavior, **attachment theory** has emerged as a leading tool for describing the deeper roots of close relationships. By destigmatizing dependency in adults (Bowlby, 1988), attachment theory has elevated connectedness to equal status with autonomy.

Attachment theory has been especially fruitful in couples therapy (e.g., Johnson, 2002) where it helps explain how even healthy adults need to depend on each other. In the early years of family therapy, couples treatment was a therapy without a theory. With few exceptions, therapists treated couples with models designed for families (e.g., Bowen, 1978; Haley, 1976; Minuchin, 1974). The exception was behaviorists, who implied that intimacy was a product of reinforcement. Nobody talked much about trust or love or longing. Dependency might be okay for children, but in adults, we were told, it was a sign of "enmeshment."

In emotionally focused couples therapy, Susan Johnson uses attachment theory to deconstruct the familiar dynamic in which one partner criticizes and complains while the other gets defensive and withdraws. What attachment theory suggests is that the criticism and complaining are a protest against disruption of the attachment bond—in other words, the nagging partner may be more insecure than angry.

The notion that how couples deal with each other reflects their attachment history can be traced to the pioneering studies of John Bowlby and Mary Ainsworth.

When Bowlby graduated from Cambridge in the 1940s, it was assumed that infants became attached to their mothers as a consequence of being fed. But Konrad Lorenz (1935) showed that baby geese become attached to parents who don't feed them, and Harry Harlow (1958) found that, under stress, infant monkeys prefer the cloth-covered "mothers" that provided contact comfort to the wire-mesh "mothers" that provided food. Human babies, too, become attached to people who do not feed them (Ainsworth, 1967).

In the 1940s and 1950s, a number of studies found that young children who were separated from their mothers go through a series of reactions that can be described as "protest," "despair," and, finally, "detachment" (e.g., Burlingham & Freud, 1944; Robertson, 1953). In attempting to understand these reactions, Bowlby (1958) concluded that the bond between infants and their parents was based on a biological drive for proximity that evolved through the process of natural selection. When danger threatens, infants who stay close to their parents are less likely to be killed by predators.

Attachment means seeking closeness in the face of stress. Attachment can be seen in cuddling up to mother's soft, warm body and being cuddled in return; looking into her eyes and being gazed at fondly; and holding on to her and being held. These experiences are profoundly comforting.

According to Mary Ainsworth (1967), infants use their attachment figures (usually mothers) as a *secure base* for exploration. When an infant feels threatened, he or she will turn to the caregiver for protection and comfort. Variations in this pattern are evident in two insecure strategies of attachment. In the *avoidant* strategy, the infant inhibits attachment behavior; in the *resistant* strategy, the infant clings to mother and avoids exploration.

Security in the relationship with an attachment figure indicates that an infant is able to rely on that person as a source of comfort and protection. When threats arise, infants in secure relationships are able to direct "attachment behavior" (approaching, crying, reaching out) to their caregivers and take comfort in their reassurance. Infants with secure attachments are confident in the availability of their caregivers and, consequently, confident in their interactions in the world.

This confidence is not evident in infants with anxious attachment relationships. Bids for attention may have been met with indifference or rebuff (Bowlby, 1973). As a result, such infants remain insecure about the availability of caregivers. Moreover, Bowlby argued that because attachment relationships are internalized, these early experiences shape expectations for later relationships of friendship, parenting, and romantic love.

One of the things that distinguishes attachment theory is that it has been extensively studied. What is clear is that it is a stable and influential trait throughout childhood. The type of attachment shown at twelve months predicts: (1) type of attachment at eighteen months (Waters, 1978); (2) frustratability, persistence, cooperativeness, and task enthusiasm at eighteen months (Matas, Arend, & Sroufe, 1978); (3) social competence of preschoolers (Lieberman, 1977); and (4) self-esteem, empathy, and classroom deportment (Sroufe, 1979). The quality of relationship at one year is an excellent predictor of quality of relating up through five years, with the advantage to the securely attached infant compared with the resistantly or avoidantly attached infant.

What is less clearly supported by research is the proposition that styles of attachment in childhood are correlated with attachment styles in intimate adult relationships. Nevertheless, the idea that romantic love can be conceptualized as an attachment process (Hazan & Shaver, 1987) remains a compelling, if as yet unproven, proposition. What the research has established

is that individuals who are anxious over relationships report more relationship conflict, suggesting that some of this conflict is driven by basic insecurities over love, loss, and abandonment. Those who are anxious about their relationships often engage in coercive and distrusting ways of dealing with conflict, which are likely to bring about the very outcomes they fear most (Feeney, 1995).

Attachment theory is applied to clinical treatment by linking symptomatic expressions of fear and anger to disturbances in attachment relationships. Parents can be helped to understand some of their children's disruptive behavior as stemming from the child's anxiety about the parents' availability and responsiveness. Couples can be helped to understand the attachment fears and vulnerabilities behind angry and defensive interactions (Gottman, 1994).

Therapists can use attachment theory to illuminate current relationships by showing how a child's misbehavior might reflect an insecure attachment, or how a husband's avoidance might be due to ambivalent attachment, or how a wife's animosity may be an expression of anxious attachment. When therapists feel drawn into a family's script, they can avoid taking over a role that's missing in the family by using attachment theory to point out family members' needs for being securely cared for. Instead of being recruited to soothe an anxious child or comfort a distressed mate, the therapist can hand back responsibility to the parents or the partner and encourage them to become less defensive and more supportive.

●

After reading this chronology of how theories in family therapy have evolved, the reader may feel overwhelmed at the number of paradigm shifts within the field. It may help to point out a pattern in this apparent discontinuity. The focus of therapy has continually expanded toward ever-wider levels of context. This process started when therapists looked beyond individuals to their families. Suddenly, unexplainable behavior began to make sense. Early family therapists concentrated on assessing and altering sequences of behavioral interaction surrounding problems. Next, it was recognized that those sequences were manifestations of the family's underlying structure, and structure became the target of change. Then a family's structure was seen to be a product of a long-term, multigenerational process that was governed by belief systems, and therapists aimed their interventions at these underlying beliefs. More recently it dawned on therapists that these belief systems did not arise in a vacuum, hence the current interest in cultural influences.

Family therapists, naturalists on the human scene, discovered how individual behavior is shaped by transactions we don't always see. Systems concepts—feedback, circularity, and so on—were useful devices that helped make complex interactions predictable. In keeping with our emphasis on how ideas are actually applied in clinical practice, we now consider the fundamental working concepts of family therapy.

The Working Concepts of Family Therapy

Interpersonal Context

The fundamental premise of family therapy is that people are products of their **context.** Because few people are closer to us than our parents and partners, this notion can be translated into saying that a person's behavior is powerfully influenced by interactions with other family members. Thus, the importance of context can be reduced to the importance of family. It can be, but it shouldn't be.

Although the immediate family is often the most relevant context for understanding behavior, it isn't always. A depressed college student, for example, might be more unhappy about what's going on in the dormitory than about what's happening at home. Furthermore, although the context that family therapists first focused on was behavioral, the interpersonal environment also includes cognitive dimensions such as expectations and assumptions as well as influences from outside the family, at school, at work, with friends, and from the surrounding culture.

The clinical significance of context is that attempts to treat individuals by talking to them once a week for fifty minutes may have less influence than their interactions with other people during the remaining 167 hours of the week. Or to put this positively: Often the most effective way to help people resolve their problems is to meet with them *and* important others in their lives.

Complementarity

Complementarity refers to the reciprocity that is the defining feature of every relationship. In any relationship, one person's behavior is yoked to the other's. Remember the symbol for yin and yang, the masculine and feminine forces in the universe?

Notice how the two parts are complementary and occupy one space. Relationships are like that. If one person changes, the relationship changes. If John starts doing more grocery shopping, Mary likely does less.

Family therapists should think of complementarity whenever they hear one person complaining about another. Take, for example, a husband who says that his wife nags. "She's always after me about something; she's always complaining." From the perspective of complementarity, a family therapist would assume that a wife's complaining is only half of a pattern of mutual influence. Whenever a person is perceived as nagging, it probably means that she hasn't received a fair hearing for her concerns. Not being listened to makes her feel angry and unsupported. No wonder she comes across as nagging.

If, instead of waiting for her to complain, John starts asking her how she feels, Mary will feel more like he cares about her. Or at least she's likely to feel that way. Complementarity doesn't mean that people in relationships control each other; it means that they influence each other.

A therapist can help family members get past blaming—and the powerlessness that goes with it—by pointing out the complementarity of their actions.

"The more you nag, the more he ignores you. *And* the more you ignore her, the more she nags."

Circular Causality

Before the advent of family therapy, explanations of psychopathology were based on linear models: medical, psychodynamic, or behavioral. Etiology was conceived in terms of prior events—disease, emotional conflict, or learning history—that caused symptoms in the present. Using the concept of *circularity*, Bateson helped change the way we think about psychopathology, from something caused by events in the past to something that is part of ongoing, circular feedback loops.

The notion of **linear causality** is based on the Newtonian model, in which the universe is like a billiard table where the balls act unidirectionally on each other. Bateson believed that, although linear causality is useful for describing the world of objects, it is a poor model for the world of living things, because it neglects to account for communication and relationships.

To illustrate this difference, Bateson (1979) used the example of a man kicking a stone. The effect of kicking a stone can be precisely predicted by measuring the force and angle of the kick and the weight of the stone. If the man kicks a dog, on the other hand, the effect will be less predictable. The dog might respond to a kick in any number of ways—cringing, running away, biting, or trying to play—depending on the temperament of the dog and how it interpreted the kick. In response to the dog's reaction, the man

might modify his behavior, and so on, so that the number of possible outcomes is unlimited.

The dog's actions (biting, for example) loop back and affect the man's next move (taking the Lord's name in vain, for example), which in turn affects the dog, and so on. The original action prompts a circular sequence in which each subsequent action recursively affects the other. Linear cause and effect is lost in a circle of mutual influence.

This idea of mutual or **circular causality** is enormously useful for therapists because so many families come in looking to find "the cause" of their problems and determine who is responsible. Instead of joining the family in a logical but unproductive search for who started what, circular causality suggests that problems are sustained by an ongoing series of actions and reactions. Who started it? It rarely matters.

Triangles

Most clients express their concerns in linear terms. It might be a four-year-old who is "unmanageable," or perhaps an ex-wife who "refuses to cooperate" about visitation rights. Even though such complaints suggest that the problem resides in a single individual, most therapists would think to look for relationship issues. "Unmanageable" four-year-olds often turn out to have parents who are ineffective disciplinarians, and ex-wives who are "unreasonable" probably have their own sides of those stories. So a therapist, certainly a family therapist, would probably want to see the four-year-old together with her parents and to meet with both the angry father and his ex-wife.

Let's suppose that the therapist who meets with the four-year-old and her parents sees that indeed the real problem is a lack of discipline. The mother complains that the girl never does what she's told, the father nods in agreement, and the child runs around the room ignoring her mother's requests to sit still. Maybe the parents could use some advice about setting limits. Perhaps. Experience teaches, however, that a child who misbehaves is often standing on one parent's shoulders. When young children are disobedient, it usually means that their parents are in conflict about the rules or how to enforce them.

Perhaps the father is a strict disciplinarian. If so, his wife might feel that she needs to protect her daughter against her husband's harshness, so she becomes more of a friend and ally to her child than a parent-in-charge. Some parents are so angry with each other that their disagreements are plain to see. But many are less open. Their conflicts are painful, so they keep them private. Maybe they think that their personal relationship is none of the therapist's business, or perhaps the father has decided that if his wife doesn't like how he does things, "Then she can damn well do them herself!" The point is this: Relationship problems often turn out to be triangular (Bowen, 1978), even though it may not always be apparent.

A less obvious example of triangular complications often occurs in the case of divorced parents who fight over visitation rights. Most divorces generate enough hurt and anger to make a certain amount of animosity inevitable. Add to that a healthy dose of parental guilt (felt and projected), and you would seem to have a formula for arguments about who gets the kids for holidays, whose turn it is to buy new sneakers, and who was late picking up or dropping them off last weekend. Meeting with the embattled exes is likely to do little to disconfirm the assumption that the problem is between the two of them. Yet even two people who are very angry at each other will eventually find a way to work things out—unless third parties mix in.

What do you suppose happens when a divorced father complains to his new girlfriend about his ex's "unreasonableness"? The same thing that usually happens when one person complains about another. The girlfriend sympathizes with him and, often as not, urges him to get tough with his ex-wife. Meanwhile, the children's mother is equally likely to have a friend encouraging her to become more aggressive. Thus, instead of two people left to work things out between them, one or both of them is egged on to escalate the conflict.

Do *all* relationship problems involve third parties? No, but most do.

Process/Content

Focusing on the **process** of communication, or *how* people talk, rather than on its **content,** or *what* they talk about, may be the most productive conceptual shift a family therapist can make. Imagine, for example, that a therapist encourages a moody freshman to talk to her parents. Imagine further that the young woman rarely expresses herself in words but rather in passive-aggressive protest, and that her parents are, in contrast, all too good at putting their opinions into words. Suppose that the young woman finally begins to express her feeling that college is a waste of time, and her parents counter with an argument about the importance of staying in school. A therapist made anxious by the idea that the young woman might actually drop out of college who intervenes to support the *content* of the parents' position misses an important opportunity to support the *process* whereby the young woman learns to put her feelings into words rather than into self-destructive actions.

Families who come for treatment are usually focused on content issues. A husband wants a divorce, a child refuses to go to school, a wife is depressed. The family therapist talks with the family about the content of their problems but thinks about the process by which they try to resolve them. While the family discusses what to do about the child's refusal to go to school, the therapist notices whether the parents seem to be in charge and whether they support each other. A therapist who tells the parents how to solve the problem (by making the child go to school) is working with content, not process. The child may start going to school, but the parents won't have improved their decision-making process.

Sometimes, of course, content *is* important. If a wife is drinking to drown her worries or a husband is molesting his stepdaughter, something needs to be done about it. But to the extent that therapists focus exclusively on content, they're unlikely to help families become better functioning systems.

Family Structure

Family interactions are predictable—some might say stubborn—because they are embedded in powerful but unseen structures. Dynamic patterns, like pursuer–distancer, describe the *process* of interaction; **family structure** defines the organization within which those interactions take place. Originally, interactions shape structure; but once established, structure shapes interactions.

Families, like other groups, have many options for relating. Soon, however, interactions that were initially free to vary become regular and predictable. Once these patterns are established, family members use only a small fraction of the full range of behavior available to them (Minuchin & Nichols, 1993). Families are structured in **subsystems**—determined by generation, gender, common interests, and function—which are demarcated by interpersonal **boundaries,** invisible barriers that regulate the amount of contact with others (Minuchin, 1974).

Like the membranes of living cells, boundaries safeguard the separateness and autonomy of the family and its subsystems. By spending time alone together and excluding friends and family from some of their activities, a couple establishes a boundary that protects their relationship from intrusion. Later, if they marry and have children, that boundary is preserved by making time to be alone together as a couple without the children. If, on the other hand, the couple includes their children in all of their activities, the boundary separating the generations wears thin and the couple's relationship is sacrificed to parenting. Children won't develop autonomy or initiative if their parents are involved in all of their activities.

Psychoanalytic theory also emphasizes the need for interpersonal boundaries. Beginning with "the psychological birth of the human infant" (Mahler, Pine, & Bergman, 1975), psycho-analysts describe the progressive separation and individuation that culminates in the resolution of oedipal attachments and, eventually, in leaving home. But this is a one-sided emphasis on poorly defined boundaries. Psychoanalysts pay insufficient attention to the problems of emotional isolation stemming from rigid boundaries. This belief in separation as the model and measure of maturity may be an example of male psychology overgeneralized and unquestioned. The danger that people will lose themselves in relationships is no more real than the danger that they will isolate themselves from intimacy.

What family therapists have discovered is that problems result when boundaries are either too rigid or too diffuse. Rigid boundaries are overly restrictive and permit little contact with outside systems, resulting in **disengagement.** Disengagement leaves individuals and subsystems independent but isolated; it fosters autonomy but limits affection and nurture. **Enmeshed** subsystems have diffuse boundaries: They offer heightened feelings of support, but at the expense of independence and autonomy. Enmeshed parents are loving and attentive; however, their children tend to be dependent and may have trouble relating to people outside their family. Enmeshed parents respond too quickly to their children; disengaged parents respond too slowly.

Another important point about boundaries is that they are reciprocal. A mother's enmeshment with her children is directly related to the emotional distance between her and her husband. The less she gets from her husband, the more she needs from her children—and the more preoccupied she is with her children, the less time and energy she has for her husband.

It should not go unnoticed that these arrangements are gendered. This doesn't make them any more right or wrong. It should, however, make us cautious about blaming mothers for cultural expectations and arrangements that perpetuate their role as primary caretakers of children (Luepnitz, 1988). A therapist who recognizes the normative nature of the enmeshed-mother/disengaged-father syndrome but puts the burden on the mother to let go, should ask himself why it doesn't occur to him to challenge the father to take hold.

The Meaning (Function) of Symptoms

When family therapists discovered that an identified patient's symptoms often had a stabilizing influence on the family, they spoke of this homeostatic influence as the **function of the symptom** (Jackson, 1957). In a seminal paper, "The Emotionally Disturbed Child as a Family Scapegoat," Ezra Vogel and Norman Bell (1960) observed that emotionally disturbed children are almost invariably involved in the tensions between their parents. By detouring their conflicts onto one of their children, the parents are able to maintain a stable relationship, though the cost to the child may be great.

According to Vogel and Bell, some chance characteristic of a child is singled out for anxious attention in a process that casts the child as the family's deviant member. Meanwhile, as long as the parents focus their concern on the child, their own conflicts can be ignored.

The idea that a family member's symptoms may serve a homeostatic function alerted therapists to look beyond presenting complaints for latent conflicts that might lie behind them. If a child is a behavior problem, for example, it is often the case that his parents are in conflict about how to deal with him. However, this is not the same thing as saying that the child's misbehavior *benefits* the family. The parents' conflicts may be a result rather than the cause of the child's problems. Notice, incidentally, that the term **scapegoat** is judgmental and one-sided.

The worst consequence of assuming that symptoms serve the family's purposes was setting up an adversarial relationship between families and therapists. This antagonism is often fueled by a tendency to sympathize with children and see parents as oppressors. (Isn't that how a lot of us felt growing up?) It's hard being a parent. Having a difficult child doesn't make it any easier. If parents have to deal with a therapist who assumes that they somehow profit from their child's problems, who could blame them for resisting?

The idea that symptoms serve a function has been largely discredited, and most schools of therapy now call for a collaborative relationship with clients. However, while it's a mistake to assume that symptoms necessarily serve a homeostatic function, it is worth considering the possibility that in some cases a mother's depression or a child's refusal to attend school *might* serve a protective function for the family.

Family Life Cycle

When we think of the life cycle, we tend to think of individuals maturing, mastering the challenges of one age, then moving on to the next. The cycle of human life may be orderly, but it's not a steady, continuous process. We progress in stages, with plateaus and developmental hurdles that demand change. Periods of growth and change are followed by periods of relative stability during which changes are consolidated.

The idea of a **family life cycle** adds two things to our understanding of individual development: When a son or daughter heads off to kindergarten or reaches puberty, not only must the child learn to cope with a new set of circumstances, but the whole family must readjust. Moreover, the developmental transitions that affect children aren't merely their own but their parents' as well. In some cases, even their grandparents'. The strain on a fourteen-year-old's relationship with his parents may be due as much to his father's midlife crisis or his mother's worrying about her own father's retirement as anything the boy himself is going through.

Changes in one generation complicate adjustments in another. A middle-aged father may become disenchanted with his career and decide to become more involved with his family just as his children are growing up and pulling away. His wish to get closer may frustrate their need to be on their own. Or to cite another example becoming more and more familiar, just as a man and woman begin to do more for themselves after launching their children, they may find their children back in the house (after dropping out of school, unable to afford housing, or recovering from an early divorce), and are therefore faced with an awkward version of second parenthood.

One property that families share with other complex systems is that they don't change in a smooth, gradual process, but rather in discontinuous leaps. Falling in love and political revolutions are examples of such leaps. Having a baby is like falling in love and undergoing a revolution at the same time.

Sociologists Evelyn Duvall and Reuben Hill applied a developmental framework to families in the 1940s by dividing family life into discrete stages with tasks to be performed at each stage (Duvall, 1957; Hill & Rodgers, 1964). Family therapists Betty Carter and Monica McGoldrick (1980, 1999) enriched this framework by adding a *multigenerational* point of view, recognizing culturally diverse patterns, and considering stages of divorce and remarriage (Table 4.1).

It's important to recognize that there is no standard version of the family life cycle. Not only do families come in a variety of forms—single-parent families, same-sexed couples, stepfamilies—but various religious, cultural, and ethnic groups may have different norms for various stages. The real value of the life-cycle concept isn't so much learning what's normal or expected at particular stages but recognizing that families often develop problems at transitions in the life cycle.

Problems develop when a family encounters a challenge—environmental or developmental—and is unable to accommodate to the changed circumstances. Thus, problems are usually assumed to be a sign not of a dysfunctional family but simply of one that's having trouble adjusting to one of life's turning points.

Family Narratives

The first family therapists looked beyond individuals to their family relationships to explain how problems were perpetuated. Actions, it turned out, were embedded in interactions—and, of course, the most obvious interactions are behavioral. Double binds, problem-maintaining sequences, aversive control, triangles, enmeshment and disengagement—these concepts all focused on behavior. But in addition to being actors in each other's lives, family members are also storytellers.

By reconstructing the events of their lives in coherent narratives, family members are able to make sense of their experience (White & Epston, 1990). Thus, it is not only actions and interactions that shape families' lives but also the stories they construct and tell. The parents of a two-year-old who tell themselves that he's "oppositional" will respond very differently from parents who tell themselves that their little one is "spunky."

Family narratives organize and make sense of experience. They emphasize events that reinforce the plot line and screen out events that don't fit. The parents who see their two-year-old as oppositional are more likely to notice and remember the times she said no than the times she said yes. A family's interactions and their narrative of events are related in circular fashion: Behavioral events are perceived and organized in narrative form, and this narrative in turn shapes expectations that influence future behavior, and so on.

*M*onica McGoldrick's work reminds therapists that families often have trouble coping with changes in the family life cycle.

TABLE 4.1   The Stages of the Family Life Cycle

Family Life Cycle Stage	Emotional Process of Transition: Key Principles	Second-Order Changes in Family Status Required to Proceed Developmentally
Leaving home: single young adults	Accepting emotional and financial responsibility for self	a. Differentiation of self in relation to family of origin b. Development of intimate peer relationships c. Establishment of self in respect to work and financial independence
The joining of families through marriage: the new couple	Commitment to new system	a. Formation of marital system b. Realignment of relationships with extended families and friends to include spouse
Families with young children	Accepting new members into the system	a. Adjusting marital system to make space for children b. Joining in child rearing, financial, and household tasks c. Realignment of relationships with extended family to include parenting and grandparenting roles
Families with adolescents	Increasing flexibility of family boundaries to permit children's independence and grandparents' frailties	a. Shifting of parent/child relationships to permit adolescent to move into and out of system b. Refocus on midlife marital and career issues c. Beginning shift toward caring for older generation
Launching children and moving on	Accepting a multitude of exits from and entries into the family system	a. Renegotiation of marital system as a dyad b. Development of adult-to-adult relationships between grown children and their parents c. Realignment of relationships to include in-laws and grandchildren d. Dealing with disabilities and death of parents (grandparents)
Families in later life	Accepting the shifting generational roles	a. Maintaining own and/or couple functioning and interests in face of physiological decline: exploration of new familial and social role options b. Support for more central role of middle generation c. Making room in the system for the wisdom and experience of the elderly, supporting the older generation without overfunctioning for them d. Dealing with loss of spouse, siblings, and other peers and preparation for death

Interest in family narrative has become identified with one particular school, Michael White's **narrative therapy,** which emphasizes the fact that families with problems come to therapy with pessimistic narratives that tend to keep them from acting effectively. But a sensitivity to the importance of personal narrative is a useful part of any therapist's work. Therapy is conducted as a dialogue. However much a family therapist may be interested in the process of interaction or the structure of family relationships, he or she must also learn to respect the influence of how they experience events—including the therapist's input.

Gender

When family therapists first applied the systems metaphor—an organization of parts plus the way they function together—they paid more attention to the way families functioned than to their parts. Families were understood in terms of abstractions like "boundaries," "triangles," and "parental subsystems," while family members were often treated as cogs in a machine. The "parts" of a family system never cease being individual human beings; but the preoccupation with the way families were organized tended to obscure the personhood of the individuals who made up the family, including their psychodynamics, psychopathology, personal responsibility—and gender.

Common sense tells us that gender is a fact of life. (Though no one should underestimate social scientists' ability to transcend common sense.) As long as society expects the primary parenting to be done by mothers, girls will shape their identities in relation to someone they expect to be like, whereas boys will respond to their difference as a motive for separating from their mothers. The result is what Nancy Chodorow (1978) aptly called "the reproduction of mothering." Traditionally, women have been raised to have more permeable psychological boundaries, to develop their identities in terms of connection, to cultivate their capacity for empathy, and to be at greater risk for losing themselves in relationships. Men, on the other hand, emerge with more rigid psychological boundaries, disown their dependency needs and fear being engulfed, and often have greater difficulty empathizing with others. We all know men who are nurturing and women who are not, but these are the exceptions that prove the rule.

Awareness of gender and gender inequity has long since penetrated not only family therapy but our entire culture. Translating this awareness into clinical practice, however, is complicated and controversial.

There is room for disagreement between those who strive to maintain clinical neutrality and those who believe that failing to raise gender issues in treatment—money, power, child care, fairness, and so on—runs the risk of reinforcing traditional roles and social arrangements (Walters, Carter, Papp, & Silverstein, 1988). It is not possible, however, to be a fair and effective therapist without being sensitive to how gender issues pervade the life of the family. A therapist who ignores gender may inadvertently show less interest in a woman's career; assume that a child's problems, and child rearing in general, are primarily the mother's responsibility; have a double standard for extramarital affairs; and expect—or at least tolerate—a father's nonparticipation in the family's treatment.

If patriarchy begins at home, a gender-sensitive therapist must recognize the enduring influence of early experience and of unconscious fantasies. How children respond to their parents has significance not only for how they get along but also for the men and women they will become. When a girl speaks derisively about her "bitchy" mother she may unknowingly be disparaging the female in herself. In addition to identification with the same-sex parent, the child's relationship with the other parent is part of what programs future experience with the opposite sex.

A gender-sensitive therapist must also avoid potential inequities in some of the basic assumptions and principles of family therapy. The notion of *circular causality*, for example, which points to mutually reinforcing patterns of behavior, when applied to problems such as battering, incest, or alcoholism, tends to bypass questions of responsibility and makes it hard to consider influences external to the interaction, such as cultural beliefs about appropriate gender behavior. The concept of *neutrality* suggests that all parts of the system contribute equally to its problems and thus renders invisible the differences between family members in power and influence. The same is true of *complementarity*, which suggests that in traditional relationships between men and women the roles are equal though different.

Reconciling these contradictions is not always easy, but ignoring them isn't the answer.

Culture

Among the influences shaping family behavior, few are more powerful than the cultural context. A family from Puerto Rico, for example, may have very different expectations of loyalty and obligation from their adult children than, say, a white middle-class family from Minnesota. One reason for therapists to be sensitive to cultural diversity is to avoid imposing majority values and assumptions on minority groups. There are now a host of excellent books and articles designed to familiarize therapists with families from a variety of backgrounds, including African American (Boyd-Franklin, 1989), Latino (Falicov, 1998), Haitian (Bibb & Casimir, 1996), Asian American (Lee, 1996), and urban poverty (Minuchin, Colapinto, & Minuchin, 1998), to mention just a few. These texts serve as guides for therapists who are about to venture into relatively unknown territory. Although the best way to develop an understanding of people from other cultures may be to spend time with them.

Some students are unsure of the difference between culture and ethnicity. **Culture** refers to common patterns of behavior and experience derived from the settings in which people live. **Ethnicity** refers to the common ancestry through which individuals have evolved shared values and customs—especially among groups that are not white Anglo-Saxon Protestants. *Culture* is the more generic term, and we have chosen it here to emphasize that cultural context is always an issue, even with families who come from backgrounds similar to that of the therapist.

Although cultural influences may be most obvious with families from foreign backgrounds, it is a mistake to assume that members of the same culture necessarily share values and assumptions. A young Jewish therapist might, for example, be surprised at the unsympathetic attitudes of a middle-aged Jewish couple about their children's decision to adopt a black baby.

Appreciating the cultural context of families is complicated by the fact that most families are influenced by multiple contexts, which makes generalization difficult. For example, as noted by Nancy Boyd-Franklin (1989), middle-class African American families stand astride three cultures and are exposed to cultural elements that may be traced to African roots, those that are part of the dominant American culture, and finally the adaptations that people of color make to racism in the dominant culture. Moreover, the cultural context may vary among family members. In immigrant families, for example, it's not uncommon to see conflicts between parents who retain a strong sense of ethnic identity and children who are more eager to adopt the ways of the host country. First-generation parents may blame their children for abandoning the old ways and dishonoring the family, whereas the children may accuse their parents of being stuck in the past. Later, the children's children may develop a renewed appreciation for their cultural roots.

The first mistake a therapist can make in working with clients from different backgrounds is to treat cultural differences as deviant. Although a lack of boundaries between a family and their neighbors and kin might seem problematic to a middle-class white therapist, such more inclusive family networks are not atypical for African American families. The second mistake is to think that a therapist's job is to become an expert on the various cultures he or she works with. While it may be useful for therapists to familiarize themselves with the language, customs, and values of the major groups in their catchment area, an attitude of respect and curiosity about other people's cultures may be more useful than imposing ethnic stereotypes or assuming an understanding of other people. It's important to acknowledge what you do not know.

The third mistake therapists make in working with families from other cultures is to accept everything assumed to be a cultural norm as functional. An effective therapist must be respectful of other people's ways of doing things without giving up the right to question patterns that appear to be counterproductive. Although fluid boundaries may be typical among urban poor families, that doesn't mean it's inevitable for poor families to be dependent on various social services or for agency staff to presume that a family's need entitles workers to enter, unannounced and uninvited, into the family's space, physically and psychologically (Minuchin, Lee, & Simon, 1996).

—Questions to Consider

1. What are some common practices in various forms of therapy that violate the principles of general systems theory?
2. What might be some advantages and disadvantages to a family therapist's learning more about psychoanalytic theory?
3. Does attachment theory offer anything to the practicing family therapist other than suggesting that people have deep needs to be connected?
4. How might your own attitudes about gender make it hard for you to be objective in working with certain families or individuals?

—Key Concepts

attachment theory The study of the innate tendency to seek out closeness to caretakers in the face of stress.

black box metaphor The idea that because the mind is so complex, it is better to study people's input and output (behavior, communication) than to speculate about what goes on in their minds.

boundary Emotional and physical barriers that protect and enhance the integrity of individuals, subsystems, and families.

circular causality The idea that actions are related through a series of recursive loops or repeating cycles.

complementary Relationships based on differences that fit together, where qualities of one make up for lacks in the other.

constructivism A relativistic point of view that emphasizes the subjective construction of reality; implies that what we see in families may be based as much on our preconceptions as on what is actually going on.

context The interpersonal milieu which surrounds and influences the behavior of individuals, families, and larger groups.

culture Common patterns of behavior and experience derived from the settings in which people live.

cybernetics The study of control processes in systems, especially analysis of the flow of information in closed systems.

disengagement Psychological isolation that results from overly rigid boundaries around individuals and subsystems in a family.

enmeshment Loss of autonomy due to a blurring of psychological boundaries.

equifinality The ability of complex systems to reach a given final goal in a variety of different ways.

ethnicity The common ancestry through which groups of people evolve shared values and customs.

family life cycle Stages of family life from separation from one's parents to marriage, having children, growing older, retirement, and, finally, death.

family rules A descriptive term for redundant behavioral patterns, norms, and expectations.

family structure   The functional organization of families that influences how family members interact.

feedback   The return of a portion of the output of a system, especially when used to maintain the output within predetermined limits (negative feedback) or to signal a need to modify the system (positive feedback).

function of the symptom   The idea that symptoms are often ways to distract or otherwise protect family members from threatening conflicts.

general systems theory   A biological model of living systems as whole entities that maintain themselves through continuous input and output from the environment; developed by Ludwig von Bertalanffy.

homeostasis   A balanced steady state of equilibrium.

linear causality   The idea that one event is the cause and another is the effect; in behavior, the idea that one behavior is a stimulus and the other a response.

metacommunication   Every message has two levels, report and command; metacommunication is the implied command or qualifying message.

morphogenesis   The process by which a system changes its structure to adapt to new contexts.

narrative therapy   An approach to treatment that emphasizes the role of the stories people construct about their experience.

negative feedback   See **feedback.**

open system   A system that exchanges information or material with its environment, as opposed to a closed system that does not. Living systems are, by definition, open systems.

positive feedback   See **feedback.**

process/content   Distinction between how members of a family or group relate and what they talk about.

reframing   Relabeling a family's description of behavior to make it more amenable to therapeutic change; for example, describing someone as "discouraged" rather than "depressed."

runaway   Unchecked positive feedback that causes a family or system to get out of control.

scapegoat   A member of the family, usually the identified patient, who is the object of displaced conflict or criticism.

sequences of family interaction   The recurrent patterns of interpersonal interaction that surround and help explain various problems and behaviors.

social constructionism   Like constructivism, challenges the notion of an objective basis for knowledge. Knowledge and meaning are shaped by culturally shared assumptions.

solution-focused therapy   Steve de Shazer's term for a style of therapy that emphasizes the solutions that families have already developed for their problems.

subsystem   Smaller units in families, determined by generation, gender, or function.

symmetrical   In relationships, equality or parallel form.

system, closed   A functionally related group of elements regarded as forming a collective entity that does not interact with the surrounding environment.

system, open   A set of interrelated elements that exchange information, energy, and material with the surrounding environment.

systems theory   A generic term for studying a group of related elements that interact as a whole entity; encompasses general systems theory and cybernetics.

triangle   A three-person system; according to Bowen, the smallest stable unit of human relations.

─Recommended Readings─

Bateson, G. 1971. *Steps to an ecology of mind.* New York: Ballantine.

Bateson, G. 1979. *Mind and nature.* New York: E. P. Dutton.

Bowlby, J. 1988. *A secure base: Clinical application of attachment theory.* London: Routledge.

Carter, E., and McGoldrick, M., eds. 1999. *The expanded family life cycle: A framework for family therapy,* 3rd ed. Boston: Allyn and Bacon.

Davidson, M. 1983. *Uncommon sense: The life and thought of Ludwig von Bertalanffy.* Los Angeles: J. P. Tarcher.

Dell, P. F. 1982. Beyond homeostasis: Toward a concept of coherence. *Family Process. 21:* 21–42.

Haley, J. 1985. Conversations with Erickson. *Family Therapy Networker. 9*(2): 30–43.

Hoffman, L. 1981. *Foundations of family therapy.* New York: Basic Books.

von Bertalanffy, L. 1950. An outline of General System Theory. *British Journal of the Philosophy of Science. 1:* 134–165.

von Bertalanffy, L. 1967. *Robots, men and minds.* New York: George Braziller.

Wiener, N. 1948. *Cybernetics: Or control and communication in the animal and the machine.* Cambridge, MA: Technology Press.

References

Ainsworth, M. D. 1967. *Infancy in Uganda: Infant care and growth of attachment.* Baltimore: Johns Hopkins University Press.

Anderson, H., and Goolishian, H. A. 1988. Human systems as linguistic systems: Evolving ideas about the implications of theory and practice. *Family Process. 27:* 371–393.

Bateson, G. 1956. *Naven.* Stanford, CA: Stanford University Press.

Bateson, G. 1979. *Mind and nature.* New York: E. P. Dutton.

Bibb, A., and Casimir, G. J. 1996. Haitian families. In *Ethnicity and family therapy.* McGoldrick, M., Giordano, J., and Pearce, J. K., eds. New York: Guilford Press.

Bowen, M. 1978. *Family therapy in clinical practice.* New York: Jason Aronson.

Bowlby, J. 1958. The nature of the child's tie to his mother. *International Journal of Psycho-Analysis. 41:* 350–373.

Bowlby, J. 1973. *Attachment and loss: Vol. 2. Separation.* New York: Basic Books.

Bowlby, J. 1979. *The making and breaking of affectional bonds.* London: Tavistock.

Bowlby, J. 1988. *A secure base: Clinical application of attachment theory.* London: Routledge.

Boyd-Franklin, N. 1989. *Black families in therapy: A multisystems approach.* New York: Guilford Press.

Burlingham, D., and Freud, A. 1944. *Infants without families.* London: Allen & Unwin.

Carter, E., and McGoldrick, M., eds. 1980. *The family life cycle: A framework for family therapy.* New York: Gardner Press.

Carter, E., and McGoldrick, M., eds. 1999. *The expanded family life cycle,* 3rd ed. Boston: Allyn and Bacon.

Chodorow, N. 1978. *The reproduction of mothering.* Berkeley, CA: University of California Press.

Conway, F., and Siegelman, J. 2005. *Dark hero of the information age: In search of Norbert Wiener, the father of cybernetics.* New York: Basic Books.

Davidson, M. 1983. *Uncommon sense.* Los Angeles: J. P. Tarcher.

Dell, P. F. 1982. Beyond homeostasis: Toward a concept of coherence. *Family Process. 21*(1): 21–42.

Dell, P. F. 1985. Understanding Bateson and Maturana: Toward a biological foundation for the social sciences. *Journal of Marital and Family Therapy. 11:* 1–20.

Duvall, E. 1957. *Family development.* Philadelphia: Lippincott.

Efran, J. S., Lukens, M. D., and Lukens, R. J. 1990. *Language, structure and change: Frameworks of meaning in psychotherapy.* New York: Norton.

Falicov, C. J. 1998. *Latino families in therapy.* New York: Guilford Press.

Feeney, J. A. 1995. Adult attachment and emotional control. *Personal Relationships. 2:* 143–159

Foerster, H. von. 1981. *Observing systems.* Seaside, CA: Intersystems.

Gergen, K. J. 1985. The social constructionist movement in modern psychology. *American Psychologist. 40:* 266–275.

Gottman, J. 1994. *What predicts divorce.* Hillsdale, NJ: Erlbaum.

Haley, J. 1976. *Problem-solving therapy.* San Francisco: Jossey-Bass.

Harlow, H. 1958. The nature of love. *American Psychologist. 13:* 673–685.

Hazan, C., and Shaver, P. R. 1987. Romantic love conceptualized as an attachment process. *Journal of Personality and Social Psychology. 52:* 511–524.

Heims, S. 1991. *The cybernetics group.* Cambridge, MA: MIT Press.

Held, B. S. 1995. *Back to reality: A critique of postmodern theory in psychotherapy.* New York: Norton.

Hill, R., and Rodgers, R. 1964. The developmental approach. In *Handbook of marriage and the family,* H. T. Christiansen, ed. Chicago: Rand McNally.

Hoffman, L. 1981. *Foundations of family therapy.* New York: Basic Books.

Hoffman, L. 1988. A constructivist position for family therapy. *The Irish Journal of Psychology.* 9: 110–129.

Jackson, D. D. 1957. The question of family homeostasis. *Psychiatric Quarterly Supplement. 31:* 79–90.

Jackson, D. D. 1959. Family interaction, family homeostasis, and some implications for conjoint family therapy. In *Individual and family dynamics,* J. Masserman, ed. New York: Grune & Stratton.

Johnson, S. 2002. *Emotionally focused couple therapy with trauma survivors: Strengthening attachment bonds.* New York: Guilford Press.

Kelly, G. A. 1955. *The psychology of personal constructs.* New York: Norton.

Lee, E. 1996. Asian American families: An overview. In *Ethnicity and family therapy,* McGoldrick, M., Giordano, J., and Pearce, J. K., eds. New York: Guilford Press.

Lieberman, A. F. 1977. Preschoolers' competence with a peer: Relations with attachment and peer experience. *Child Development. 48:* 1277–1287.

Lorenz, K. E. 1935. Der kumpan in der umvelt des vogels. In *Instinctive behavior,* C. H. Schiller, ed. New York: International Universities Press.

Luepnitz, D. A. 1988. *The family interpreted: Feminist theory in clinical practice.* New York: Basic Books.

Mahler, M., Pine F., and Bergman, A. 1975. *The psychological birth of the human infant.* New York: Basic Books.

Matas, L., Arendt, R., and Sroufe, L. A. 1978. Continuity of adaptation in the second year: The relationship between quality of attachment and later competence. *Child Development. 49:* 547–556.

Maturana, H. R., and Varela, F. J., eds. 1980. *Autopoiesis and cognition: The realization of the living.* Boston: Reidel.

Meyrowitz, J. 1985. *No sense of place.* New York: Oxford University Press.

Minuchin, S. 1974. *Families and family therapy.* Cambridge, MA: Harvard University Press.

Minuchin, S. 1991. The seductions of constructivism. *Family Therapy Networker.* 15(5): 47–50.

Minuchin, P., Colapinto, J., and Minuchin, S. 1998. *Working with families of the poor.* New York: Guilford Press.

Minuchin, S., Lee, W-Y., and Simon, G. M. 1996. *Mastering family therapy: Journeys of growth and transformation.* New York: Wiley.

Minuchin, S., and Nichols, M. P. 1993. *Family healing: Tales of hope and renewal from family therapy.* New York: The Free Press.

Nichols, M. P. 1993. The therapist as authority figure. *Family Process. 32:* 163–165.

Nichols, M. P., and Schwartz, R. C. 2001. *Family therapy: Concepts and methods,* 5th ed. Boston: Allyn and Bacon.

Robertson, J. 1953. *A two-year-old goes to hospital.* [Film]. London: Tavistock Child Development Research Unit.

Speer, D.C. 1970. Family systems: Morphostasis and morphogenesis, or "Is homeostasis enough?" *Family Process.* 9(3): 259–278.

Sroufe, L. A. 1979. The coherence of individual development: Early care, attachment and subsequent developmental issues. *American Psychologist. 34:* 834–841.

Ugazio, V. 1999. *Storie permesses, storie proibite: Polarita semantiche familiari e psicopatologie.* Turin: Bollati Boringhieri.

Vogel, E. F., and Bell, N. W. 1960. The emotionally disturbed child as a family scapegoat. In *The family,* N. W. Bell and E. F. Vogel, eds. Glencoe, IL: The Free Press.

von Bertalanffy, L. 1950. An outline of general systems theory. *British Journal of Philosophy of Science.* 1: 39–164.

Walters, M., Carter, B., Papp, P., and Silverstein, O. 1988. *The invisible web: Gender patterns in family relationships.* New York: Guilford Press.

Waters, E. 1978. The reliability and stability of individual differences in infant–mother attachment. *Child Development. 49:* 483–494.

Watzlawick, P., ed. 1984. *The invented reality.* New York: Norton.

Watzlawick, P., Beavin, J. H., and Jackson, D. D. 1967. *Pragmatics of human communication.* New York: Norton.

White, M., and Epston, D. 1990. *Narrative means to therapeutic ends.* New York: Norton.

Wiener, N. 1948. *Cybernetics or control and communication in the animal and the machine.* Cambridge, MA: MIT Press.

Bowen Family Systems Therapy

The pioneers of family therapy recognized that people are products of their social context, but they limited the focus to the nuclear family. Yes, actions are influenced by what goes on in our families. But what are the forces, past and present, that mold those influences? What makes a husband distance himself from family life? What makes a wife neglect her own development to manage her children's lives? Murray Bowen sought answers—and solutions—to such questions in the larger network of family relationships.

According to Bowen, human relationships are driven by two counterbalancing life forces: *individuality* and *togetherness.* Each of us needs companionship and a degree of independence. What makes life interesting—and frustrating—is the tendency for our needs to polarize us. When one partner presses for more connection, the other may feel crowded and pull away. As time goes by, the pursuit of one and withdrawal of the other drives the pair through cycles of closeness and distance.

How successfully people reconcile these two polarities of human nature depends on the extent to which they have learned to manage emotionality, or to use Bowen's term, their *differentiation of self.* More about this later.

Although no one doubts the formative influence of the family, many people imagine that once they leave home they are grown up: independent adults, free at last of their parents' influence. Some people prize individuality and take it as a sign of growth to separate from their parents. Others wish they could be closer to their families but find visits too painful, so they stay away to protect themselves from disappointment and hurt. Once out of range of the immediate conflict, they forget and deny the discord. As Bowen discovered, however, the family remains with us wherever we go. As we shall see, unresolved emotional reactivity to our parents is the most important unfinished business of our lives.

Evolution of the Model

Murray Bowen's professional interest in the family began when he was a psychiatrist at the Menninger Clinic in the late 1940s. Turning his attention to the enigma of schizophrenia, Bowen was struck by the exquisite emotional sensitivity between patients and their mothers. Others had called this reactivity *symbiosis,* as though it were some kind of parasitic mutation. Bowen saw it

Murray Bowen

Among the pioneers of family therapy, Murray Bowen's emphasis on theory as opposed to technique distinguishes his work from the more behaviorally oriented family therapists. Bowen's therapy was an outgrowth of psychoanalytic theory and offers the most comprehensive view of human behavior of any approach to family therapy. The goal in the Bowenian model is *differentiation of self,* namely, the ability to remain oneself in the face of external influences, especially the pressures of family life. The Bowenian model considers the thoughts and feelings of each family member as well as the larger network of family relationships that shapes the life of the family.

simply as an exaggeration of a natural process, a more intense version of the tendency to react emotionally to one another that exists in all relationships.

In 1954 Bowen moved to the National Institute of Mental Health (NIMH), where he initiated a project of hospitalizing entire families containing a schizophrenic member. What he found was that the volatile bond between mothers and their emotionally disturbed offspring inevitably involved the whole family. At the heart of the problem was "anxious attachment," a pathological form of closeness driven by anxiety. In these troubled families, people were emotional prisoners of the way the others behaved. The hallmark of these emotionally stuck-together, or *fused,* relationships was a lack of personal autonomy.

When the NIMH project ended in 1959 and Bowen moved to Georgetown University, he began working with families whose problems were less severe. What he discovered, to his surprise, were many of the same mechanisms he had observed in psychotic families. This convinced him that there is no discontinuity between normal and disturbed families, but that all families vary along a continuum from emotional fusion to differentiation.

During his thirty-one years at Georgetown, Bowen developed a comprehensive theory of family therapy, inspired an entire generation of students, and became an internationally renowned leader of the family therapy movement. He died after a long illness in October 1990.

Among the most prominent of Bowen's students are Philip Guerin and Thomas Fogarty, who joined in 1973 to form the Center for Family Learning in New Rochelle, New York. Under Guerin's leadership, the Center for Family Learning became one of the major centers of family therapy training. Guerin is a laid-back, virtuoso therapist and teacher, and two of his books, *The Evaluation and Treatment of Marital Conflict* and *Working with Relationship Triangles*, are among the most useful in all the family therapy literature.

Betty Carter and Monica McGoldrick are best known for their exposition of the family life cycle (Carter & McGoldrick, 1999) and for championing feminism in family therapy. Michael Kerr was a longtime student and colleague of Bowen's, and since 1977 has been the director of training at the Georgetown Family Center. Kerr is perhaps the most faithful advocate of all Bowen's students, as his brilliant account of Bowen theory

Philip Guerin

As a student of Murray Bowen, Philip Guerin's own innovative ideas led to his developing a sophisticated clinical approach to treating problems of children and adolescents, couples, and individual adults. Guerin's highly articulated model outlines several therapeutic goals, which emphasize the multigenerational context of families, working to calm the emotional level of family members, and defining specific patterns of relationships within families. Guerin's family systems approach is designed to measure the severity of conflict and identify specific areas in need of improvement.

in the book *Family Evaluation* (Kerr & Bowen, 1988) richly demonstrates.

The Basic Model

Most of family therapy's pioneers were pragmatists, more concerned with action than insight, more interested in technique than theory. Bowen was the exception. He was always more committed to systems theory as a way of thinking than as a set of interventions.

According to Bowen, we have less autonomy in our emotional lives than we assume. Most of us are more dependent and reactive to one another than we like to think. Bowen's theory describes how the family, as a multigenerational network of relationships, shapes the interplay of individuality and togetherness using six interlocking concepts (Bowen, 1966, 1976): *differentiation of self, triangles, nuclear family emotional process, multigenerational transmission process, emotional cutoff,* and *societal emotional process.*

Differentiation of Self

The cornerstone of Bowen's theory is both an intrapsychic and an interpersonal concept. Roughly analogous to *ego strength,* **differentia-**

tion of self is the capacity to think and reflect, to not respond automatically to emotional pressures, internal or external (Kerr & Bowen, 1988). It is the ability to be flexible and act wisely, even in the face of anxiety.

Undifferentiated people are easily moved to emotionality. Their lives are driven by reactivity to those around them. The differentiated person is able to balance thinking and feeling: capable of strong emotion and spontaneity but also possessing the self-restraint that comes with the ability to resist the pull of emotional impulses.

In contrast, undifferentiated people tend to react impetuously—with submissiveness or defiance—toward other people. They find it difficult to maintain their own autonomy, especially around anxious issues. Asked what they think, they say what they feel; asked what they believe, they echo what they've heard. They agree with whatever you say, or argue with everything. In contrast, differentiated people are able to take stands on issues because they're able to think things through, decide what they believe, and then act on those beliefs.

Emotional Triangles

Take a minute to think about the most troublesome current relationship in your life. That relationship almost certainly involves one or more third persons. Virtually all relationships are shadowed by third parties—relatives, friends, even memories.

The major influence on the activity of **triangles** is anxiety (Guerin, Fogarty, Fay, & Kautto, 1996). As anxiety increases, people experience a greater need for emotional closeness—or, in reaction to pressure from others, a greater need for distance. The more people are driven by anxiety, the less tolerant they are of one another and the more they are polarized by differences.

When two people have problems they've been unable to work out, they get to the point where it's hard to talk about certain things. Why go through all that aggravation when it only leads to hurt feelings? Eventually one or both partners will turn to someone else for sympathy. Or the conflict will draw in a third person to try to fix it. If the third party's involvement is only temporary or pushes the two people to work out their differences, the triangle doesn't become fixed. But if, as often happens, the third person stays involved, the triangle become a part of the relationship.

The involvement of a third person decreases anxiety in the twosome by spreading it through three relationships. Thus, for example, a wife upset with her husband's distance may increase her involvement with one of the children. What makes this a triangle is diverting energy that might otherwise go into the marriage. The wife's spending time with her daughter may take pressure off her husband to do things he doesn't care to. However, it also decreases the likelihood that husband and wife will develop interests they can share—and it undermines the daughter's independence.

A group of three isn't necessarily a triangle. In a viable threesome, each twosome can interact one-on-one; each person has options for his or her behavior; and each can take "I-positions" without trying to change the other two. In a triangle, on the other hand, each twosome's interaction is tied to the behavior of the third person; each person is driven by reactive forms of behavior, none of them can take a personal position without feeling the need to change the other two; and each person gets involved in the relationship between the other two. Picture a rubber band around three people who cannot allow it to drop. It constrains their movement such that if two people get closer the third must move farther away.

Some triangles seem so innocent that we hardly notice their destructiveness. Most parents can't resist complaining to their children once in a while about their mates. "Your mother's *always* late!" "Your father *never* lets anyone else drive!" These interchanges seem harmless enough. What makes triangles problematic is that they have a tendency to become habitual.

Triangulation lets off steam but freezes conflict in place. It isn't so much that complaining or seeking solace is wrong, but rather that triangles become chronic diversions that undermine relationships.

Nuclear Family Emotional Process

This concept deals with the emotional forces in families that operate over the years in recurrent patterns. Bowen originally used the term **undifferentiated family ego mass** to describe an excess of emotional reactivity or *fusion* in families. If you know someone who rarely seems to hear what you're trying to say because he or she blurts out some criticism or advice, then you know how frustrating it can be to deal with emotionally reactive people.

Lack of differentiation in the family of origin may lead to an *emotional cutoff* from parents, which in turn leads to fusion in marriage—because people with limited emotional resources typically project all their needs onto each other. Because this new fusion is unstable, it tends to produce one or more of the following: (1) reactive emotional distance between the partners; (2) physical or emotional dysfunction in one partner; (3) marital conflict; or (4) projection of the problem onto one or more children. The intensity of these problems is related to the degree of undifferentiation, extent of emotional cutoff from **families of origin,** and level of stress in the system.

A common case is when a husband, who is cut off from his parents and siblings, relates in an extremely distant way to his wife. This predisposes her to focus on the children. Kept at arm's length by her husband, she becomes anxiously attached to the children, usually with greatest intensity toward one particular child. This may be the oldest son or daughter, the youngest, or perhaps the child with traits like one of the parents. This attachment is different from caring concern; it's anxious, enmeshed concern. Because it relieves his own anxiety, the husband accepts his wife's over involvement with the children, which in turn reinforces their entanglement and his distance.

The more the mother focuses her anxiety on a child, the more that child's functioning is stunted. This underdevelopment encourages the mother to hover over the child, distracting her from her own anxieties but crippling the child emotionally.

Multigenerational Transmission Process

This concept describes the transmission of anxiety from generation to generation. In every generation the child most involved in the family's fusion moves toward a lower level of differentiation of self (and chronic anxiety), while the least involved child moves toward a higher level of differentiation (and less anxiety).

Parents who anxiously intrude their concerns on their children leave them little choice but to conform or rebel. Instead of learning to think for themselves, such children function in reaction to others. When these children leave home, they expect to become authors of their own lives. *They're not going to turn out like their parents!* Unfortunately, although we may fight against our inheritance, it usually catches up with us.

Emotional Cutoff

Emotional cutoff describes the way people manage anxiety between generations. The greater the emotional fusion between parents and children, the greater the likelihood of cutoff. Some people seek distance by moving away; others do so emotionally, by avoiding personal conversations or insulating themselves with the presence of third parties.

Michael Nichols (1986) describes how some people mistake emotional cutoff for maturity:

> We take it as a sign of growth to separate from our parents, and we measure our maturity by independence of family ties. Yet many of us still respond to our families as though they were radioactive. Only one thing robs Superman of his extraordinary power: kryptonite, a piece of his home planet. A surprising number of adult men and women are similarly rendered helpless by even a brief visit from their parents. (p. 190)

Societal Emotional Process

Bowen anticipated the contemporary concern about social influence on how families function. Kerr and Bowen (1988) cite the example of the high crime rate in communities with highly stressful environments. Bowen recognized sexism and class and ethnic prejudice as examples of toxic social emotional processes, but he believed that individuals and families with higher levels of differentiation were better able to resist these destructive social influences.

To the theoretical concerns of Bowenian therapists, Monica McGoldrick and Betty Carter added gender and ethnicity. These feminist Bowenians believe that it isn't possible to ignore gender inequalities without ignoring some of the primary forces that keep men and women trapped in inflexible roles. Moreover, they might point out that the previous sentence is inaccurate in implying that men and women alike are victims of gender bias. Women live with constraining social conditions *and* with men who perpetuate them—men who may not feel powerful with their wives and mothers, but who take for granted social conditions that make it easier for men to get ahead in the world.

McGoldrick has also been a leader in calling attention to ethnic differences among families.

Her book *Ethnicity and Family Therapy* (McGoldrick, Pearce, & Giordano, 1982) was a landmark in family therapy's developing sensitivity to this issue. Without understanding how cultural values differ from one ethnic group to the next, there is a danger of therapists imposing their own ways of looking at things on families whose perspectives aren't "dysfunctional" but legitimately different.

Normal Family Development

Optimal development is thought to take place when family members are differentiated, anxiety is low, and partners are in good emotional contact with their own families. Most people leave home in the midst of transforming relationships with their parents from an adolescent to an adult basis. Thus the transformation is usually incomplete, and most of us, even as adults, continue to react with adolescent sensitivity to our parents—or anyone else who pushes the same buttons.

Normally, but not optimally, people reduce contact with their parents and siblings to avoid the anxiety of dealing with them. Once out of the house and on their own, people tend to assume that they've put the old difficulties behind them. However, we all carry unfinished business in the form of unresolved sensitivities that flare up in intense relationships wherever we go. Having learned to ignore their role in family conflicts, most people are unable to prevent recurrences in new relationships.

Another heritage from the past is that the emotional attachment between intimate partners comes to resemble that which each had in their families of origin. People from undifferentiated families continue to be undifferentiated when they form new families. Those who handled anxiety by distance and withdrawal tend to do the same in their marriages. Therefore Bowen was convinced that differentiation of autonomous personalities, accomplished primarily in the family of origin, was both a description of normal development and a prescription for therapeutic improvement.

Betty Carter and Monica McGoldrick (1999) describe the **family life cycle** as a process of expansion, contraction, and realignment of the relationship system to support the entry, exit, and development of family members.

In the *leaving-home stage*, the primary task for young adults is to separate from their families without cutting off or fleeing to an emotional substitute. This is the time to develop an autonomous self before pairing off to form a new union.

In the *joining of families through marriage stage*, the primary task is commitment to the new couple. This is not simply a joining of two individuals; it is a transformation of two entire systems. Although problems in this stage may seem to be primarily between the partners, they may reflect a failure to separate from families of origin or cutoffs that put too much pressure on a couple. The formation of an intimate partnership requires the partners to shift their primary emotional attachment from their parents and friends to the relationship with their mates. Making wedding plans, choosing a place to live, buying a car, the birth of a baby, and choosing a school are all times when this struggle may become explicit.

Families with young children must adjust to make space for the new additions, cooperate in child rearing, keep the marriage from being submerged in parenting, and realign relationships with the extended family. Young mothers and fathers must fulfill their children's needs for nurture and control, and work together as a team. This is an extremely stressful time, especially for new mothers, and it is the life-cycle stage with the highest divorce rate.

The reward for parents who survive the preceding stages is to have their children turn into adolescents. *Adolescence* is a time when children no longer want to be like Mommy and Daddy; they want to be themselves. They struggle to become autonomous individuals and to open family boundaries—and they struggle however hard they must. Parents with satisfying lives of their own welcome (or at least tolerate) the fresh air that blows through the house at this time. Those who insist on controlling their teenagers,

Betty Carter

An ardent and articulate feminist Betty Carter was instrumental in popularizing the concept of the family life cycle and its value in assessing families. Carter emphasized the importance of historical antecedents of family problems and the multigenerational aspects of the life cycle that extended beyond the nuclear family. She expanded the family life cycle concept by considering the stages of divorce and remarriage. Carter served as Codirector of the Women's Project in Family Therapy with Peggy Papp, Olga Silverstein, and Marianne Walters, and has been an outspoken leader about the gender and ethnic inequalities that serve to keep women in inflexible family roles.

as though they were still little ones, may provoke painful escalations of the rebelliousness that's normal for this period.

In the *launching of children and moving on stage*, parents must let their children go and take hold of their own lives. This can be liberating, or it can be a time of *midlife crisis* (Nichols, 1986). Parents must deal not only with changes in their children's and their own lives, but also with changes in their relationships with aging parents, who may need increasing support, or at least don't want to act like parents anymore.

Families in later life must adjust to retirement, which not only means a loss of vocation but also a sudden increase in proximity for the couple. With both partners home all day, the house may seem a lot smaller. Later in life families must cope with declining health, illness, and then death, the great equalizer.

One variation in the life cycle that can no longer be considered abnormal is *divorce*. With the divorce rate at 50 percent and the rate of redivorce at 61 percent (Kreider & Fields, 2002), divorce now strikes the majority of American families. The primary tasks of a divorcing couple are to end the marriage but maintain coopera-

tion as parents. Some postdivorce families become single-parent families—consisting in the main of mothers and children, and in the majority of those cases staggering under the weight of financial strain. The alternative is remarriage and the formation of stepfamilies, in which, often, loneliness is swapped for conflict.

Development of Behavior Disorders

Symptoms result from stress that exceeds a person's ability to manage it. The ability to handle stress is a function of differentiation: The more well differentiated the person, the more resilient he or she will be and the more flexible and sustaining his or her relationships. The less well differentiated the person, the less stress it takes to produce symptoms.

If "differentiation" were reduced to "maturity," the Bowenian formula wouldn't add much to the familiar diathesis–stress model, which says that disease develops when an individual's vulnerability is taxed. The difference is that differentiation isn't just a quality of individuals but also of relationships. A person's basic level of differentiation is largely determined by the degree of autonomy achieved in his or her family, but the *functional level of differentiation* is influenced by the quality of current relationships. Thus, a somewhat immature person who manages to develop healthy relationships is at less risk than an equally immature person who's alone or in unhealthy relationships. Symptoms develop when the level of anxiety exceeds the *system's* ability to handle it.

According to Bowen, the underlying factor in the genesis of psychological problems is emotional fusion, passed down from one generation to the next. The greater the fusion, the more one is programmed by primitive emotional forces and the more vulnerable to the emotionality of others. Although it isn't always apparent, people tend to choose mates with equivalent levels of undifferentiation.

Emotional fusion is based on anxious attachment, which may be manifest either as dependency or isolation. Both the overly dependent and the emotionally isolated person respond with emotional reactivity to stress. What follows is marital conflict, dysfunction in one of the spouses, overconcern with one of the children, or various combinations of all three. When families come for help, they may present with any one of these problems. Whatever the presenting problem, however, the dynamics are similar: Undifferentiation in families of origin is transmitted to marital problems, which are in turn projected onto a symptomatic spouse or child. Thus are problems of the past visited on the future.

How Therapy Works

Bowenians don't try to change people; nor are they much interested in solving problems. They see therapy as an opportunity for people to learn more about themselves and their relationships, so that they can assume responsibility for their own problems. This is not to say, however, that therapists sit back and allow families to sort out their own issues. On the contrary, Bowenian therapy is a process of active inquiry, in which the therapist, guided by the most comprehensive theory in family therapy, helps family members

get past blaming in order to explore their own roles in family problems.

Tracing the pattern of family problems means paying attention to *process* and *structure.* Process refers to patterns of emotional reactivity; structure, to the interlocking network of triangles.

To change a system, modification must take place in the most important triangle in the family—the one involving the marital couple. To accomplish this, the therapist creates a new triangle, a therapeutic one. If the therapist stays in contact with the partners while remaining emotionally neutral, they can begin the process of detriangulation and differentiation that will profoundly and permanently change the entire family system.

The clinical methodology tied to this formulation calls for (1) increasing parents' ability to manage their own anxiety, and thereby becoming better able to handle their children's behavior; and (2) fortifying the couple's emotional functioning by increasing their ability to operate with less anxiety in their families of origin.

Understanding, not action, is the vehicle of cure. Therefore, two of the most important elements in Bowenian therapy may not be apparent to anyone who thinks primarily about techniques. The atmosphere of sessions and the therapist's stance are both designed to minimize emotionality. Therapists ask questions to foster self-reflection and direct them at individuals one at a time, rather than encouraging family dialogues—which have an unfortunate tendency to get overheated. Because clients aren't the only ones to respond emotionally to family dramas, Bowenian therapists strive to control their own reactivity and avoid triangulation. This, of course, is easier said than done. The keys to staying detriangled are to avoid taking sides and to nudge each party toward accepting more responsibility for making things better.

Therapy

Increasing the ability to distinguish between thinking and feeling and learning to use that ability to resolve relationship problems are the guiding principles of Bowenian therapy. Lowering anxiety and increasing *self-focus*—the ability to see one's own role in interpersonal processes—is the primary mechanism of change.

Assessment

Assessment begins with a history of the presenting problem. Exact dates are noted and later checked for their relationship to events in the extended family life cycle. Next comes a history of the nuclear family, including information about when the parents met, their courtship, their marriage, and child rearing. Particular attention is paid to where the family lived and when they moved, especially in relation to the location of the extended family. The next part of the evaluation is devoted to the history of both spouses' births, sibling positions, and significant facts about their childhoods and about the past and current functioning of their parents. All of this information is recorded on a *genogram*, covering at least three generations.

Genograms are schematic diagrams listing family members and their relationships. Included are ages, dates of marriage, deaths, and geographic locations. Men are represented by squares and women by circles, with their ages inside the figures. Horizontal lines indicate marriages, with the date of the marriage on the line; vertical lines connect parents and children (Figure 5.1).[1]

What makes a genogram more than a static portrait of a family's history is the inclusion of relationship conflicts, cutoffs, and triangles. The fact that Uncle Fred was an alcoholic or that Great Grandmother Sophie migrated from Russia is relatively meaningless without some understanding of the patterns of emotional reactivity passed down through the generations.

Certain triangles occur most commonly in different developmental stages. In early marriage in-law triangles are common—raising issues of primacy of attachment and influence.

_____
1. For more detailed suggestions, see McGoldrick & Gerson, 1985.

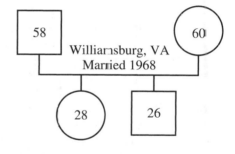

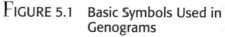

FIGURE 5.1   Basic Symbols Used in Genograms

When children are born and when they reach adolescence, parent–child triangles are so common as to be the norm.

—Case Study——————

Janet and Warren Langdon requested help for their fifteen-year-old son Martin after Mrs. Langdon found marijuana in a plastic bag in his underwear drawer. Mr. and Mrs. Langdon didn't object when the therapist said she'd like to meet with the three of them. It turned out that the discovery of marijuana was just the latest incident in a series of battles between Mrs. Langdon and her son. Lots of fifteen-year-olds experiment with marijuana; not all of them leave the evidence around for their mothers to find it.

After meeting with the family and then talking with the boy and his parents separately, the therapist concluded that Martin didn't appear to have a serious drug problem. Of greater concern, however, were the intensity of his shouting matches with his mother and his poor social adjustment at school. What she told the family was that she was concerned not only about the marijuana but also about these other signs of unhappy adjustment and that she'd like to extend the evaluation by having a couple of additional meetings with Martin and his parents separately. Mr. and Mrs. Langdon agreed, though without much enthusiasm. Martin didn't protest as much as might have been expected.

After his father died, Mr. Langdon and his older sister were raised by their mother. They were all she had left, and she increasingly devoted all her energy to shaping their lives. She was demanding and critical, and resentful of anything they wanted to do outside the family. By late adolescence, Warren could no longer tolerate his mother's domineering. His sister was never able to break free; she remained single and lived at home with her mother. Warren, however, was determined to become independent. Finally, in his mid-twenties, he left home and turned his back on his mother.

Janet Langdon came from a close-knit family. She and her four sisters were very attached to each other and remained best friends. After graduating from high school, Janet announced that she wanted to go to college. This violation of the family norm that daughters stay home and prepare to be wives and mothers provoked a major battle between Janet and her parents. They were struggling to hold on, and she was struggling to break free. Finally Janet left for college, but she was ever after estranged from her parents.

Janet and Warren were immediately drawn to one another. Both were lonely and cut off from their families. After a brief, passionate courtship, they married. The honeymoon didn't last long.

Never having really differentiated himself from his dictatorial mother, Warren was exquisitely sensitive to any hint of criticism or control. He became furious at Janet's slightest attempt to change his habits. Janet, on the other hand, sought to reestablish in her marriage the closeness she'd had in her family. To be close, though, she and Warren would have to share interests and activities. When she moved toward him, suggesting they do something together, Warren got angry and resentful, feeling his individuality impinged upon. After several months of conflict, the two settled into a period of relative equilibrium. Warren put most of his energy into his work, leaving Janet to adjust to the distance between them. A year later Martin was born.

Both of them were delighted to have a baby, but what was for Warren a pleasant addition to the family was for Janet the answer to a desperate need for closeness. The baby meant every-

thing to her. While he was an infant she was the perfect mother, loving him extravagantly and caring for his every need. When Warren tried to become involved with his infant son, Janet hovered about making sure he didn't do anything wrong. This infuriated Warren, and after several bitter blowups, he left Martin to his wife's care.

As he learned to walk and talk, Martin got into mischief, as all children do. He grabbed things, refused to stay in his playpen, and fussed when he didn't get his way. His crying was unbearable to Janet, and she found herself unable to set limits on her precious child.

Martin grew up with a doting mother, thinking he was the center of the universe. Whenever he didn't get what he wanted, he threw a tantrum. Bad as things got, at least the family existed in a kind of equilibrium. Warren was cut off from his wife and son, but he had his work. Janet was alienated from her husband, but she had her baby.

Martin's difficulties began when he started school. Used to getting his own way, he found it impossible to get along with other children. His tantrums did nothing to endear him to his schoolmates. Other children avoided him, and he grew up having few friends. With teachers he acted out his father's battle against any effort to control him. When Janet heard complaints about Martin's behavior, she sided with her son. "Those people don't know how to deal with a creative child!"

Martin grew up with a terrible pattern of adjustment to school and friends but retained his extremely close relationship with his mother. The crisis came with adolescence. Like his father before him, Martin tried to develop independent interests outside the home. However, he was far less capable of separating than his father had been, and his mother was incapable of letting go. The result was the beginning of chronic conflicts between Martin and his mother. Even as they argued and fought, they remained centered on each other. Martin spent more time battling his mother than doing anything else with his life.

Dates of important events, such as deaths, marriages, and divorces, deserve careful study.

These events send emotional shock waves through the family, which may open lines of communication, or these issues may get buried and family members progressively more cut off. Another significant piece of information on the genogram is the location of various segments of the family. Dates, relationships, and localities are the framework for exploring emotional boundaries, fusion, cutoffs, critical conflicts, amount of openness, and the number of current and potential relationships in the family. Figure 5.2 shows symbols that can be used in describing the relationship dynamics among family members.

If three parallel lines are used to indicate overly close (or fused) relationships; a zigzag line, conflict; a dotted line, emotional distance; and a broken line estrangement (or cutoff); triangular patterns across three generations often become vividly clear—as shown in an abbreviated diagram of Sigmund Freud's family (Figure 5.3).

History taking expands the focus from the symptomatic person to the relationship network. In the case of the Langdons, this meant talking with Martin about his relationships at school and with friends as well as those with his parents. With his parents, it meant putting their problems with Martin in context of the story of their relationship.

The history of the nuclear family begins with the meeting and courtship of the parents: "What attracted them to each other?" "What was the early period of their relationship like?" "Were there any serious problems during that period?" "When were the children born, and how did the parents adapt to the new additions?"

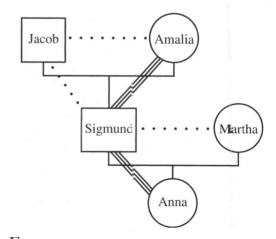

FIGURE 5.3   Genogram of Sigmund Freud's Family

If a therapist fails to take a careful history, associations that can help people gain perspective on their problems may be overlooked. Things like moves and important events, such as a husband's cancer surgery two years earlier, may not even be mentioned, unless a therapist asks. One woman who had been seeing an individual therapist didn't consider it important enough to mention. "What does my seeing a therapist have to do with my daughter's problems?" she said.

Of particular interest are the stresses the family has endured and how they have adapted. This information helps the therapist to evaluate the intensity of chronic anxiety in the family and whether it is linked more to an overload of difficult life events or to a low degree of adaptiveness in the family.

As Figure 5.4 shows, the bare facts of a family genogram only provide a skeleton upon which to flesh out information about the Langdon family.

The decision to extend the assessment beyond the nuclear family depends on the extent of crisis and degree of anxiety the family feels. In the case of the Langdons, both parents seemed eager to discuss their family backgrounds.

Martin's history illustrates Bowen's theory of behavior disorder. As Betty Carter explains (personal communication), symptoms break out

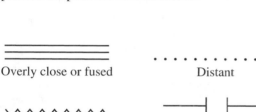

FIGURE 5.2   Genogram Symbols for Relationship Dynamics

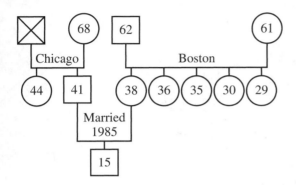

FIGURE 5.4   Langdon Family Genogram

when the "vertical" problems of anxiety and toxic family issues that come down through the generations intersect with the "horizontal" stresses that come at transition points in the life cycle. Thus Martin's greatest vulnerability came when the unresolved fusion he inherited from his mother converged with the stress of his adolescent urge for independence.

In gathering information about extended families, a therapist should ascertain which members of the clan are most involved with the family being evaluated, for it is the nature of ongoing ties to the extended family that has a great impact on both parents and their role in the nuclear family. Of equal importance, however, is finding out who is *not* involved, because people with whom contact has been cut off can be an even greater source of anxiety than the people with whom contact has been maintained.

Therapeutic Techniques

Bowenian therapists believe that understanding how family systems operate is more important than this or that technique. Bowen himself spoke of "technique" with disdain, and he was distressed to see therapists relying on formulaic interventions.

If there were a magic bullet in Bowenian therapy—one essential technique—it would be the **process question.** Process questions are designed to slow people down, diminish anxiety,

and start them thinking—not just about how others are upsetting them, but about how they participate in interpersonal problems.

Process questions are queries designed to explore what's going on inside people and between them: "When your boyfriend insults you, how do you deal with it?" "When your daughter goes on dates, what goes on inside you?"

Notice how in the case study, through a series of questions, the therapist attempts to explore the process of the couple's relationship, asking both partners to think about what's going on between them, increase their awareness of their own contributions, and consider what they're planning to do to take responsibility to make things better.

–Case Study–––––

In interviewing a couple in which the husband was a recovering alcoholic with a history of abuse, the therapist asked: "Where are you with the thoughts about the damage you've done to your wife and kids with your alcoholism?"

When the man acknowledged responsibility for his abusive behavior and seemed genuinely remorseful, the therapist asked about his progress toward recovery, using process questions to focus on rational planning and personal responsibility. For example:

Therapist: "What makes that step so hard?"
Husband: "Pride."
Therapist: "How does that manifest itself?"
Husband: "I get nasty."

Notice how this line of questioning explores not only the man's personal progress, but also how his problems affect others. Relationships take place in a systemic web of connections, but individuals are responsible for their own behavior.

Then the therapist shifted to open a discussion of the wife's role in the couple's difficulties. "So, you're getting better at taking responsibility for the drinking and the behavior connected with it? Do you think your wife appreciates what you're doing and the progress you're making?" And then a few minutes later: "Has your wife ever been able to talk to you about the things she's contributed to the relationship going sour?"

When the therapist asked the wife about her thinking, she reiterated all the annoying things her husband was doing—pressuring her to forgive him and get back together. Although he would eventually like her to consider her own role in the process, the therapist tried to empathize with her upset. "So, he's just bugging you by trying to get you to change your mind?" Then after a few minutes, the therapist tried to shift the wife to thinking more and feeling less. "Can you give me a summary of your thinking—how you came to that conclusion?" When the wife again got angry and blamed her husband, the therapist just listened. A moment later he asked, "What do you do in the face of that abuse?"

> *Wife:* "I get upset."
> *Therapist:* "Do you understand what it is about you that sets him off?"
> *Wife:* "No."
> *Therapist:* "Has he ever been able to tell you?"

Those who followed Bowen also ask questions but move in occasionally to challenge, confront, and explain. Betty Carter, for example, asks questions designed to help couples understand their situation, but she tries to move things along by explaining what works or doesn't work and by assigning tasks. Most of the tasks she assigns are calculated to move people out of triangles. She might, for example, encourage a wife to visit her mother-in-law, or a husband to begin calling his own mother on the phone. Another favorite device of Carter's is to encourage people to write letters, addressing unresolved issues in the family. One way to prevent such letter writing from degenerating into telling people off is to help clients edit out the anger and emotional reactivity.

The second major technique in Bowenian therapy is the "relationship experiment." Process questions are designed to help family mem-

bers realize that it isn't just what other people do, but how they respond to what other people do that perpetuates their problems. Relationship experiments are designed to help clients experience what it's like to act counter to their usual automatic emotionally driven responses. Some of these experiments may help clients resolve their problems, but their primary purpose is to help people discover their ability to move against the ways their emotions are driving them.

—Case Study——————

The Kennedys came to therapy because sixteen-year-old David was doing badly in school. David was on the verge of flunking out of an exclusive private school partly because he was a poor student and partly because his evenings with friends included heavy drinking and marijuana smoking. His father had gotten after him to study harder and had suspended his driving privileges after he came home one school night quite drunk. Unfortunately, these efforts hadn't been very effective, because David didn't respect his father, who was an alcoholic and frequently falling-down drunk around the house. David's stepmother, who'd been living with them for only two years, had little ability to control him, and she knew enough not to try.

I told the parents that I wouldn't see them in family therapy because David didn't respect the father who was drunk every night and who, I added, didn't show any signs of being ready to do anything about his drinking. I did agree, however, to see David to try to help him finish the school year with passing grades.

David was able to pass the eleventh grade, and I continued to see him into the following year, not entirely comfortable in my role as substitute father figure. Although I maintained my resolve not to do therapy with a family that included a member who was actively abusing alcohol, I did meet with the family during three or four crises. The first three crises occurred when Mr. Kennedy's drinking (and, it turned out, cocaine abuse) got way out of control and his father and wife insisted that he reenter treatment.

The most prominent triangle in this case was that Mr. Kennedy's wife and father got together to pressure him to quit drinking. He had gone to rehab several times; but even the few times he'd actually finished a program, he had soon returned to drinking. The only reason he ever sought help was as a result of ultimatums from his wife and father. His wife threatened to leave him, and his father threatened to cut him off from the family estate. This case would go nowhere until this triangle could be modified.

I encouraged Mr. Kennedy's wife and father to work on being less reactive while separating from each other around the issue of Mr. Kennedy's drinking. Mr. Kennedy needed to take a stand for himself, rather than being compliant to his wife's and his father's wishes. In fact, I wondered aloud with him if taking an honest stance with his family wouldn't mean telling them that he didn't intend to quit drinking. What he decided to tell them was that while he was willing to work on controlling his drinking and use of cocaine, he didn't intend to quit.

I encouraged Mr. Kennedy's father to back off and let the other two battle it out. Reluctantly, he agreed to do so. I then got Mrs. Kennedy to make a clear statement about how she felt about her husband's drinking but to discontinue her fruitless efforts to make him stop. I encouraged her to maintain her connection with her father-in-law but without talking about her husband all the time. Two months later, Mr. Kennedy decided to stop drinking and using cocaine.

This time he successfully completed a twenty-eight-day rehab program and entered A.A. and N.A. Six weeks later he once again relapsed. Over the following eight months, Mr. Kennedy's drinking and cocaine abuse got much, much worse. Finally, after a serious altercation with a Jamaican drug dealer, Mr. Kennedy made a serious decision to get sober. This time, instead of going to the respected local rehabilitation center that his father had recommended, he did some research on his own and decided to enter a fa-

mous drug treatment center in California. As of this writing, Mr. Kennedy has been sober for six years.

Bowenian Therapy with Couples.   The essence of couples therapy is to stay connected with both partners without letting them triangle you. In practice, Bowen would connect with each person, one at a time, often beginning with the overfunctioning or more motivated partner. He would ask nonconfrontational questions, verify facts, and hear feelings. But he would frame each question to stimulate cognition rather than encourage expression of feelings. His objective was to elicit and hear out the perceptions and opinions of each partner, without siding emotionally with either one. It's taking sides that keeps people from learning to deal with each other.

When things are calm, feelings can be dealt with more objectively and partners can talk rationally with each other. But when emotion outruns thinking, it's best to ask questions that get couples to think more and feel less—and to talk to the therapist rather than to each other.

Couples who've argued for years about the same old issues are often amazed to discover that the first time they really hear each other is when they listen to their partners talking to a therapist. It's easier to hear when you aren't busy planning your own response. If all else fails to cool things down, Fogarty (1976) recommends seeing spouses in separate sessions.

As partners talk, the therapist concentrates on the *process* of their interaction, not the details under discussion. Focusing on content is a sign that the therapist is emotionally entangled. It may be hard to avoid being drawn in by hot topics like money, sex, or discipline of children, but a therapist's job isn't to settle disputes, it's to help couples do so. The aim is to get clients to express thoughts and opinions to the therapist in the presence of their partners. Should one break down in tears, the therapist remains calm and inquires about the thoughts that touched off the tears. If a couple begins arguing, the therapist becomes more active, calmly questioning one, then the other, and focusing on their respective thoughts. Asking for detailed descriptions of events is one of the best ways to cool overheated emotion and make room for reason.

Metaphors of complementarity help to highlight the process of interactions. Fogarty (1976), for example, described the *pursuer–distancer* dynamic. The more one presses for communication and togetherness, the more the other distances— watches television, works late, or goes off with the children. Frequently, partners pursue and distance in different areas. Men commonly distance themselves emotionally but pursue sexually. The trick, according to Fogarty, is, "Never pursue a distancer." Instead, help the pursuer explore his or her own inner emptiness. "What's in your life besides the other person?"

To underscore the need for objectivity, Bowen spoke of the therapist as a "coach" or "consultant." He didn't mean to imply disinterest but rather to emphasize the neutrality required to avoid triangulation. In traditional terms, this is known as "managing countertransference." Just as analysts are analyzed themselves so they can recognize countertransference, so Bowen considered differentiating a self in one's own family the best way to avoid being emotionally triangled by couples.

To help partners define differentiated identities, it's useful for a therapist to take **I-positions** (Guerin, 1971)—that is, to make nonreactive observations and statements of opinion. The more a therapist takes an autonomous position in relation to the family by refusing to take sides or take over, the easier it is for family members to define themselves to each other. Gradually, family members learn to state their own beliefs and to act on them, without attacking others or becoming overly upset by their responses.

After sufficient harmony had been won with progress toward self-differentiation, Bowen taught couples how emotional systems operate and encouraged them to explore those webs of relationship in their own families (Bowen,

1971). For example, a woman locked into the role of emotional pursuer might be asked to describe her relationship with her father and then compare it with her current relationships. If lessening her preoccupation with her husband and children seemed advisable, the therapist might encourage her to connect with the most emotionally distant member of her family, often her father. The idea wouldn't be to shift her attachment from one set of relationships to another but to help her understand that the intensity of her need is due in part to unfinished business.

Kerr (1971) suggests that when relationships in the nuclear family are being discussed, therapists should ask occasional questions about the family of origin. If family members see that they are repeating earlier patterns, they're more likely to recognize their own emotional reactivity. Recently, Nichols saw a couple unable to decide what to do with their mentally ill teenage daughter. Although the daughter was virtually uncontrollable, her mother found it difficult to consider hospitalization. When asked what her own mother would have done, without hesitating she replied that her long-suffering mother would have been too guilt-ridden even to consider placement—"no matter how much she and the rest of the family might suffer." Little more needed to be said.

Bowenian Therapy with One Person. Bowen's own success at differentiation within his family convinced him that a single highly motivated individual can be the fulcrum for changing an entire family system (Anonymous, 1972). The goal of working with individuals is the same as with larger units: developing person-to-person relationships, seeing family members as people rather than emotionally charged images, learning to recognize triangles, and, finally, detriangling oneself (Bowen, 1974).

The actual process of change is begun by learning more about the larger family—who made up the family, where they lived, what they did, and what they were like. Sometimes a "good relationship" turns out to be one in which tension is managed by distancing tactics, such as infrequent contact, superficial conversation, or gossiping about other family members. Therefore it's useful to ask for descriptions rather than conclusions. Not, "Do you have a good relationship with your parents?" but, "Where do your parents live? How often do you see them? What do you and your mother talk about when you're alone together? Do you ever go out to lunch, just you and your dad?"

Gathering information about the family is an excellent vehicle for the second step toward differentiation, establishing person-to-person relationships with as many family members as possible. This means getting in touch and speaking personally with them, not about other people or impersonal topics. If this sounds easy, try it. Few of us can spend more than a few minutes talking personally with certain family members without getting anxious. When this happens, we're tempted to withdraw, or triangle in another person. Gradually extending the time of personal conversation improves the relationship and helps differentiate a self.

Ultimately, differentiating yourself requires ceasing to participate in interpersonal triangles. The goal is to relate to people without gossiping or taking sides and without counterattacking or defending yourself.

Suppose, for example, that every time you talk to your mother she starts complaining about your father. Maybe it feels good to be confided in. Maybe you have fantasies about rescuing your parents—or at least your mother. In fact, the triangling is destructive to all three relationships: you and Dad, Dad and Mom, and, yes, you and Mom. In triangles, one pair is close and two are distant (Figure 5.5). Sympathizing with Mom alienates Dad. It also makes it less likely that she'll work out her complaints with him.

Once you recognize a triangle for what it is, you can plan to stop participating in it. The idea is to do something to get the other two people to work out their own relationship. The most direct approach is simply to suggest that they do so. In the example just given you could suggest that your mother discuss her concerns with your fa-

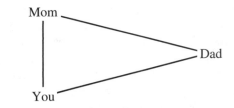

FIGURE 5.5   **Cross-Generational Triangle**

ther *and* refuse to listen to more complaints. Less direct, but more powerful, is to tell Dad that his wife has been complaining about him and you don't know why she doesn't tell him about it. She'll be annoyed, but not forever. A more devious ploy is to over agree with Mom's complaints. When she says he's messy, you say he's a complete slob; when she says he's not very thoughtful, you say he's an ogre. Pretty soon she'll begin to defend him. Maybe she'll decide to work out her complaints with him, or maybe she won't. Either way, you'll have removed yourself from the triangle.

Once you look for them, you'll find triangles everywhere. Common examples include griping about the boss; telling someone that your partner doesn't understand you; undercutting your spouse with the children; and watching television to avoid talking to someone. Breaking free of triangles may not be easy, but the rewards are great. The payoff comes not only from enriching those relationships but also from enhancing your ability to relate to anyone—friends, colleagues, clients, and your spouse and children. Furthermore, if you can remain in emotional contact but change the part you play in the family—and maintain the change despite pressures to change back—the family will have to accommodate to your change.

Useful guidelines to resisting the family's attempts to get you to change back to unproductive but familiar patterns of the past have been enumerated by Carter and Orfanidis (1976), Guerin and Fogarty (1972), and Herz (1991). You can also read about how to work on family tensions by resolving your own emotional sensitivities in two marvelous books by Harriet Lerner: *The*

Dance of Anger (Lerner, 1985) and *The Dance of Intimacy* (Lerner, 1989).

Current Status of the Model

What makes Bowen's theory so useful is that it describes the emotional forces that regulate how we relate to other people. The single greatest impediment to understanding one another is our tendency to become emotionally reactive. Like all things about relationships, emotionality is a two-way street: Some people express themselves with such emotionalism that others react to that pressure rather than hearing what the person is trying to say. Bowenian theory describes this reactivity, traces its origins to the lack of differentiation of self, and explains how to contain emotionalism and move toward self-control—by cultivating relationships widely in the family and learning to listen without becoming defensive or untrue to one's own beliefs.

In Bowenian theory, *anxiety* is the all-purpose explanation (for why people are dependent or avoidant and why they become emotionally reactive), reminiscent of Freudian conflict theory (which explains all symptoms as the result of conflicts about sex and aggression). The second pivotal concept in the Bowenian system is, of course, *differentiation*. Because differentiation is roughly synonymous with maturity, students might ask to what extent is the proposition that more differentiated people function better a circular argument. In respect to the Bowenian tradition of asking questions rather than imposing opinions, we'll let this stand as an open question for your consideration.

A possible shortcoming of the Bowenian approach is that in concentrating on individuals and their extended family relationships, it may neglect the power of working directly with the nuclear family. In many cases the most direct way to resolve family problems is to bring together everyone in the same household and encourage them to face each other and talk about their conflicts. These discussions may turn heated and contentious, but a therapist can help family members realize what they're doing and guide them toward understanding.

Families are occasionally so hostile that their dialogues should be interrupted to help individuals get beyond defensiveness to the hurt feelings underneath. At such times, it is useful, perhaps imperative, to block family members from arguing. But an approach, such as Bowen's, that encourages therapists to always speak to individual family members one at a time, may neglect the power of working with families in action.

The status of extended family systems theory rests not on empirical research but on the elegance of Murray Bowen's conceptual framework, clinical reports of successful treatment, and the personal benefit of those who have worked at differentiating themselves in their families of origin. Bowen's original research with schizophrenic families was more clinical observation than controlled experimentation. In fact, Bowen was decidedly cool to empirical research (Bowen, 1976), preferring instead to refine and integrate theory and practice. Like psychoanalysis, Bowen systems theory is probably best judged not as true or false, but as useful or not useful. On balance, it seems eminently useful.

Phil Guerin and Tom Fogarty have made notable contributions, not only in promulgating Bowenian theory, but also in refining techniques of therapy. Both are master therapists. Betty Carter and Monica McGoldrick have made more of a contribution in studying how families work: the normal family life cycle, ethnic diversity, and the destructive impact of gender inequality. Because they are students of the family as well as therapists, some of their interventions have a decidedly educational flavor. In working with stepfamilies, for example, Betty Carter teaches stepparents not to try to assume an equal position with the biological parents. Stepparents have to earn moral authority; meanwhile what works best is supporting the role of the biological parent. Just as Bowen's approach is influenced by his personal experience, it seems that both Carter and McGoldrick infuse their work as family therapists with their own experience as career women and their convictions about the price of inequality.

—Summary

1. Bowen's conceptual lens was wider than most family therapists, although his unit of treatment was often smaller. But even when he met with just individuals or couples, his concern was always with the multigenerational family system. According to Bowen, the major problem in families is *emotional fusion;* the major goal is *differentiation.*

2. Emotional fusion grows out of an instinctual need for others but is an unhealthy distortion of this need, based on anxious attachment. Some people manifest fusion directly in an excessive need for togetherness; others mask it with a facade of independence. In either case, contagious anxiety drives automatic responses in close relationships that limit the autonomous functioning of both members of the dyad.

3. In addition to extending his analysis of family problems deeper into the anxieties of individuals, Bowen also extended the focus wider, making the triangle the universal unit of analysis—in principle and in practice. When people can't settle their differences, the automatic tendency to involve third parties stabilizes relationships but freezes conflict in place. Bowen's recognition that the majority of family problems have triangular complications was one of his most important contributions and one of the seminal ideas in family therapy.

4. Bowen discouraged therapists from trying to fix relationships and instead encouraged them to remain neutral while exploring the emotional processes in conflictual relationships with process questions. Bowenian therapists rarely give advice. They just keep asking questions. The goal isn't to solve people's problems but to help them learn to see their own role in how their family system operates. This self-discovery isn't merely a matter of introspection, because understanding is seen as a tool for repairing relationships and enhancing one's own autonomous functioning.

Six techniques are prominent in the practice of Bowen family systems therapy:

1. *Genogram.* In addition to recording biographic data, the genogram is used to trace relationship conflicts, cutoffs, and key triangles. This process of collecting information is sometimes therapeutic in and of itself: Family members often say, "It never occurred to me how all those events fit together." The most comprehensive guide to working with genograms is *Genograms in Family Assessment* (McGoldrick & Gerson, 1985).

2. *The Therapy Triangle.* If a therapist can remain free of the emotional reactivity families bring to therapy, clients are better able to reduce their own emotionality and begin to think more clearly about their problems. The danger is that the same process of emotional triangulation families use to stabilize their conflicts will engulf the therapist. If so, therapy will be stalemated. On the other hand, if the therapist can remain free of reactive emotional entanglements—in other words, stay detriangled—the family system and its members will calm down to the point where they can begin to work out their dilemmas.

3. *Process Questions.* Each family member is asked a series of questions aimed at toning down emotion and fostering objective reflection. Process questions are also used to help manage and neutralize triangles, including the potential triangle(s) that may develop between the therapist and various family members. The process question is aimed at calming anxiety and gaining access to information on how the family perceives the problem and how the mechanisms driving the problem operate. If process questions decrease anxiety, people are better able to think clearly.

This clarity allows them to discover more potential options for managing their problems.

4. *Relationship Experiments.* Relationship experiments are carried out around structural alterations in key triangles. The goal is to help family members become aware of systems processes and learn to recognize their own role in them. Perhaps the best illustrations of such experiments are those developed by Fogarty for use with emotional pursuers and distancers. Pursuers are encouraged to restrain their pursuit, stop making demands, decrease pressure for emotional connection, and to see what happens, in themselves and in the relationship. This exercise isn't designed to be a magic cure (as some people hope) but to help clarify the emotional processes involved. Distancers are encouraged to move toward their partners and communicate personal thoughts and feelings—in other words, to find an alternative to avoiding or capitulating to the other person's demands.

5. *Coaching.* Coaching is the Bowenian alternative to the more emotionally involved role common to other forms of therapy. By acting as a coach, the Bowenian therapist hopes to avoid taking over for clients or becoming embroiled in family triangles. Coaching doesn't mean telling people what to do. It means asking questions designed to help people figure out family emotional processes and their role in them.

6. *The "I-Position.'* An "I-position" is a calm and clear statement of personal opinion. In situations of increased tension, it often has a stabilizing effect for one person to be able to detach from the emotionality and adopt an "I-position." Taking a personal stance—saying what you feel instead of what others are "doing"—is one of the most direct ways to break cycles of emotional reactivity. It's the difference between saying "You're lazy" and "I wish you would help me more"; or between "You're always spoiling the children" and "I think we should be stricter with them." It's a big difference.

5. Bowenian therapists not only encourage clients to take I-positions, they also do so themselves. For example, after a family session the mother pulls the therapist aside and confides that her husband has terminal cancer but she doesn't want the children to know. What to do? Take an I-position: Say to the mother: "I believe your children have a right to know about this." What she does, of course, is up to her.

6. Finally, although students of family therapy are likely to evaluate different approaches according to how much sense they make and how useful they promise to be, Bowen himself considered his most important contribution to be showing the way to make human behavior a science. Far more important than developing methods and techniques of family therapy, Murray Bowen made profound contributions to our understanding of how we function as individuals, how we get along with our families, and how these are related.

Questions to Consider

1. In what kinds of cases might a Bowenian approach be useful in treating individual college students in a counseling center?
2. How is the Bowenian emphasis on self-focus unique in family therapy?
3. To what extent is reducing anxiety—in the therapist and clients—essential to any kind of exploratory therapy? What can a therapist do to reduce his or her own anxiety?

4. What are some advantages and disadvantages to speaking to family members one at a time, rather than encouraging them to talk with each other?

5. Are there any members of your extended family from whom you are cut off, and if so is this situation part of a triangle?

Key Concepts

detriangulation   The process by which an individual removes himself or herself from the emotional field of two others.

differentiation of self   Psychological separation of intellect and emotions, and independence of self from others; opposite of fusion.

emotional cutoff   Bowen's term for flight from an unresolved emotional attachment.

family life cycle   Stages of family life from separation from one's parents to marriage, having children, growing older, retirement, and, finally, death.

family of origin   A person's parents and siblings; usually refers to the original nuclear family of an adult.

fusion   A blurring of psychological boundaries between self and others, and a contamination of emotional and intellectual functioning; opposite of differentiation.

genogram   A schematic diagram of the family system, using squares to represent male family members, circles to indicate female family members, horizontal lines for marriages, and vertical lines to indicate children.

I-position   Statements that acknowledge one's personal opinions rather than blaming others ("You never . . .") or moralizing ("Children should always . . .").

multigenerational transmission process   Murray Bowen's concept for the projection of varying degrees of immaturity to different children in the same family; the child who is most involved in the family emotional process emerges with the lowest level of differentiation and passes problems on to succeeding generations.

process questions   Questions designed to help family members think about their own reactions to what others are doing.

relationship experiments   Suggestions for trying new ways of responding to family stresses, designed more to help family members understand how emotional processes work than to solve problems.

triangle   A three-person system; according to Bowen, the smallest stable unit of human relations.

triangulation   Detouring conflict between two people by involving a third person, stabilizing the relationship between the original pair.

undifferentiated family ego mass   Bowen's early term for emotional "stuck-togetherness" or fusion in the family, especially prominent in schizophrenic families.

Recommended Readings

Anonymous. 1972. Differentiation of self in one's family. In *Family interaction*, J. Framo, ed. New York: Springer.

Bowen, M. 1978. *Family therapy in clinical practice.* New York: Jason Aronson.

Carter, E., and Orfanidis, M. M. 1976. Family therapy with one person and the family therapist's own family. In *Family therapy: Theory and practice*, P. J. Guerin, ed. New York: Gardner Press.

Fogarty, T. F. 1976. Systems concepts and the dimensions of self. In *Family therapy: Theory and practice*, P. J. Guerin, ed. New York: Gardner Press.

Fogarty, T. F. 1976. Marital crisis. In *Family therapy: Theory and practice*, P. J. Guerin, ed. New York: Gardner Press.

Guerin, P. J., Fay, L., Burden, S., and Kautto, J. 1987. *The evaluation and treatment of marital conflict: A four-stage approach.* New York: Basic Books.

Guerin, P. J., Fogarty, T. F., Fay, L. F., and Kautto, J. G. 1996. *Working with relationship triangles: The one-two-three of psychotherapy.* New York: Guilford Press.

Guerin, P. J., and Pendagast, E. G. 1976. Evaluation of family system and genogram. In *Family therapy: Theory and practice.* P. J. Guerin, ed. New York: Gardner Press.

Kerr, M. E., and Bowen, M. 1988. *Family evaluation.* New York: Norton.

—References—

Anonymous. 1972. Differentiation of self in one's family. In *Family interaction,* J. Framo, ed. New York: Springer.

Bowen, M. 1966. The use of family theory in clinical practice. *Comprehensive Psychiatry. 7:* 345–374.

Bowen, M. 1971. Family therapy and family group therapy. In *Comprehensive group psychotherapy,* H. Kaplan and B. Sadock, eds. Baltimore: Williams & Wilkins.

Bowen, M. 1974. Toward the differentiation of self in one's family of origin. In *Georgetown Family Symposium,* vol. 1, F. Andres and J. Lorio, eds. Washington, DC: Department of Psychiatry, Georgetown University Medical Center.

Bowen, M. 1976. Theory in the practice of psychotherapy. In *Family therapy: Theory and practice,* P. J. Guerin, ed. New York: Gardner Press.

Carter, B., and McGoldrick, M., eds. 1999. *The expanded family life cycle,* 3rd ed. Boston: Allyn and Bacon.

Carter, E., and Orfanidis, M. M. 1976. Family therapy with one person and the family therapist's own family. In *Family therapy: Theory and practice,* P. J. Guerin, ed. New York: Gardner Press.

Fogarty, T. F. 1976. Marital crisis. In *Family therapy: Theory and practice,* P. J. Guerin, ed. New York: Gardner Press.

Guerin, P. J. 1971. A family affair. *Georgetown Family Symposium,* vol. 1, Washington, DC.

Guerin, P. J., and Fogarty, T. F. 1972. Study your own family. In *The book of family therapy,* A. Ferber, M.

Mendelsohn, and A. Napier, eds. New York: Science House.

Guerin, P. J., Fogarty, T. F., Fay, L. F., and Kautto, J. G. 1996. *Working with relationship triangles: The one-two-three of psychotherapy.* New York: Guilford Press.

Herz, F., ed. 1991. *Reweaving the family tapestry.* New York: Norton.

Kerr, M. 1971. The importance of the extended family. *Georgetown Family Symposium,* vol. 1, Washington, DC.

Kerr, M., and Bowen, M. 1988. *Family evaluation.* New York: Norton.

Kreider, R. and Fields, J. 2002. *Number, timing and duration of marriages and divorces.* Washington, DC: Current Population Reports, U.S. Census Bureau.

Lerner, H. G. 1985. *The dance of anger: A woman's guide to changing patterns of intimate relationships.* New York: Harper & Row.

Lerner, H. G. 1989. *The dance of intimacy: A woman's guide to courageous acts of change in key relationships.* New York: Harper & Row.

McGoldrick, M., and Gerson, R. 1985. *Genograms in family assessment.* New York: Norton.

McGoldrick, M., Pearce, J., and Giordano, J. 1982. *Ethnicity in family therapy.* New York: Guilford Press.

Nichols, M. P. 1986. *Turning forty in the eighties.* New York: Norton.

6

Strategic Family Therapy

With their compelling application of cybernetics and systems theory, strategic approaches captivated family therapy from the mid-1970s to the mid-1980s. Part of the appeal was their pragmatic, problem-solving focus, but there was also a fascination with strategies that could outwit resistance and provoke families into changing, with or without their cooperation. It was this manipulative aspect that eventually turned family therapists against strategic therapy.

The dominant approaches of the 1990s elevated cognition over behavior and encouraged therapists to be collaborative rather than manipulative. Instead of trying to solve problems and provoke change, therapists began to reinforce solutions and inspire change. As a consequence, the once celebrated voices of strategic therapy—Jay Haley, John Weakland, Mara Selvini Palazzoli—have been virtually forgotten. Too bad, because their strategic approaches introduced two of the most powerful insights in all of family therapy: that families often perpetuate problems by their own actions and that directives tailored to the needs of a particular family can sometimes bring about sudden and decisive change.

Evolution of the Model

Strategic therapy grew out of the **communications theory** developed in Bateson's schizophrenia project, which evolved into three distinct models: *MRI's brief therapy model, Haley and Madanes's strategic therapy,* and the *Milan systemic model.* The birthplace of all three was the Mental Research Institute (MRI), where strategic therapy was inspired by Gregory Bateson and Milton Erickson, the anthropologist and the alienist.

In 1952, funded by a Rockefeller Foundation grant to study paradox in communication, Bateson invited Jay Haley, John Weakland, Don Jackson, and William Fry to join him in Palo Alto. Their seminal project, which can be considered the intellectual birthplace of family therapy, led to the conclusion that the exchange of multilayered messages between people defined their relationships.

Under Bateson's influence, the orientation was anthropological. Their goal was to observe families; they stumbled into family therapy more or less by accident. Given Bateson's disinclination to manipulate people, it's ironic that it was he who introduced project members to Milton Erickson. At a time when therapy was considered a laborious, long-term proposition, Erickson's experience as a hypnotherapist convinced him that people could change suddenly, and he made therapy as brief as possible.

Many of what have been called **paradoxical techniques** came out of Erickson's application of hypnotic principles to turn resistance to advantage (Haley, 1981). For example, to induce trance, a hypnotist learns not to point out that a person is fighting going under but, instead, might tell the person to keep his or her eyes open, "until they become unbearably heavy."

Don Jackson founded the Mental Research Institute in 1958 and assembled an energetic and creative staff including Jules Riskin, Virginia Satir, Jay Haley, John Weakland, Paul Watzlawick, Arthur Bodin, and Janet Beavin. After a few years, several of the staff became fascinated with the pragmatic, problem-solving approach of Milton Erickson. This interest led Jackson to establish the Brief Therapy Project under the direction of Richard Fisch. The original group included Arthur Bodin, Jay Haley, Paul Watzlawick, and John Weakland. What emerged was an elegantly brief approach based on identifying and interrupting vicious cycles that occur when attempts to solve problems only perpetuate the problems or make them worse. However, unlike today's therapies, which are brief by default, the Palo Alto approach was brief by design. This approach, known as the MRI model, was described by Watzlawick, Weakland, and Fisch (1974) in *Change: Principles of Problem Formation and Problem Resolution,* and in

a follow-up volume, *The Tactics of Change: Doing Therapy Briefly* (Fisch, Weakland, & Segal, 1982), which remains the most comprehensive statement of the MRI model.

When Jackson died tragically in 1968 at the age of 48, he left a legacy of seminal papers, the leading journal in the field, *Family Process* (which he co-founded with Nathan Ackerman in 1962), and a great sadness at the passing of such a creative talent. The MRI group and the whole field suffered another painful loss in 1995 when John Weakland died of Lou Gehrig's disease.

Jay Haley was always something of an outsider. He entered the field without clinical credentials and established his reputation as a gadfly and critic. His initial impact came from his writing, in which he infused sarcasm with incisive analysis. In "The Art of Psychoanalysis" (Haley, 1963), Haley redefined psychoanalysis as a game of one-upmanship:

> By placing the patient on a couch, the analyst gives the patient the feeling of having his feet up in the air and the knowledge that the analyst has both feet on the ground. Not only is the patient disconcerted by having to lie down while talking, but he finds himself literally below the analyst and so his one-down position is geographically emphasized. In addition, the analyst seats himself behind the couch where he can watch the patient but the patient cannot watch him. This gives the patient the kind of disconcerted feeling a person has when sparring with an opponent while blindfolded. Unable to see what response his ploys provoke, he is unsure when he is one-up and when one-down. Some patients try to solve this problem by saying something like, "I slept with my sister last night," and then whirling around to see how the analyst is responding. These "shocker" ploys usually fail in their effect. The analyst may twitch, but he has time to recover before the patient can whirl fully around and see him. Most analysts have developed ways of handling the whirling patient. As the patient turns, they are gazing off into space, or doodling with a pencil, or braiding belts, or staring at tropical fish. It is essential that the rare patient who gets an

*M*ilton Erickson *is the guiding genius behind the strategic approach to therapy.*

Jay Haley

A brilliant strategist and incisive critic, Jay Haley was a leading figure in developing the Palo Alto Group's communications model and strategic family therapy, which became popular in the 1970s. He studied with three of the most influential pioneers in the evolution of family therapy—Gregory Bateson, Milton Erickson, and Salvador Minuchin, and combined ideas from each of these innovative thinkers to form his own unique brand of family therapy. Haley developed a brief therapy model that focused on the context and possible function of the patient's symptoms and used directives to instruct patients to act in ways that were contrary to their maladaptive behavior. Haley believed that it was more important to get patients to actively do something about their problems rather than help them to understand why they had these problems.

opportunity to observe the analyst see only an impassive demeanor. (pp. 193–194)

After the Bateson project disbanded in 1962, Haley moved to MRI until 1967 when he joined Salvador Minuchin at the Philadelphia Child Guidance Clinic. It was there that Haley became interested in training and supervision, areas in which he made his greatest contribution (Haley, 1996). In 1976 Haley moved to Washington, D.C., where with Cloe Madanes he founded the Family Therapy Institute. Madanes, known as one of the most creative therapists in the field, had previously worked at both MRI and the Philadelphia Child Guidance Clinic. In 1995 Haley left the Family Therapy Institute of Washington, D.C. and moved to San Diego, where he teaches, gives workshops, and continues to make some of the most creative training films in the field of family therapy.

Haley and Madanes are such towering figures that their names often overshadow those who follow in their footsteps. James Keim in Colorado, who developed an innovative way of working with oppositional children, is ably carrying on the Haley–Madanes tradition. Other prominent practitioners of this model include Jerome Price in Michigan, who specializes in difficult adolescents, and Pat Dorgan, who combines strategic therapy with a community mental health model in Gloucester, Virginia.

The MRI model had a major impact on the Milan Associates, Mara Selvini Palazzoli, Luigi Boscolo, Gianfranco Cecchin, and Guiliana Prata. Selvini Palazzoli was a prominent Italian psychoanalyst, specializing in eating disorders, when, out of frustration with the psychoanalytic model (Selvini Palazzoli, 1981), she began to develop her own approach to families. In 1967 she led a group of eight psychiatrists who turned to the ideas of Bateson, Haley, and Watzlawick, which, in 1971, led them to form the Center for the Study of the Family in Milan, where they developed the *Milan systemic model.*

The Basic Model

In *Pragmatics of Human Communication,* Watzlawick, Beavin, and Jackson (1967) sought to develop a calculus of human communication, which they stated in a series of axioms. The first of these axioms is that *people are always communicating.* Because all behavior is communicative, and because one cannot *not* behave, it follows that one cannot *not* communicate. Consider the following example.

Mrs. Rodriguez began by saying, "I just don't know what to do with Ramon anymore. He's not doing well in school, and he doesn't help out around the house. All he wants to do is hang with those awful friends of his. But the worst thing is that he refuses to communicate with us."

At this point, the therapist turned to Ramon and said, "Well, what do you have to say about all of this?" Ramon said nothing. Instead he continued to sit slouched in the corner, with an angry, sullen look on his face.

Ramon isn't "*not* communicating." He's communicating that he's angry and doesn't want to talk about it. Communication also takes place when it isn't intentional, conscious, or successful—that is, in the absence of mutual understanding. (Oh, you've noticed?)

The second axiom is that all messages have *report* and *command* functions (Ruesch & Bateson, 1951). The report (or content) of a message conveys information, whereas the command is a statement about the relationship. For example, the statement, "Mommy, Sandy hit me!" conveys information but also implies a command—*Do something about it.* Notice, however, that the implicit command is ambiguous. The reason for this is that the printed word omits facial and contextual clues. This statement shrieked by a child in tears would have very different implications than if it were uttered by a giggling child.

In families, command messages are patterned as *rules* (Jackson, 1965) which can be deduced from observed redundancies in interaction. Jackson used the term **family rules** as a description of regularity, not regulation. Nobody lays down the rules. In fact, families are generally unaware of them.

The rules, or regularities, of family interaction operate to preserve **family homeostasis** (Jackson, 1965, 1967). Homeostatic mecha-

nisms bring families back to equilibrium in the face of any disruption, and thus serve to resist change. Jackson's notion of family homeostasis describes the conservative aspect of family systems and is similar to the cybernetic concept of **negative feedback.** According to communications analysis, families operate as goal-directed, rule-governed systems.

Communications theorists didn't look for underlying motives; instead, they assumed **circular causality** and analyzed patterns of communications linked together in additive chains of stimulus and response as **feedback loops.** When the response to a family member's problematic behavior exacerbates the problem, that chain is seen as a **positive feedback loop.** The advantage of this formulation is that it focuses on interactions that perpetuate problems, which can be changed, instead of inferring underlying causes, which are often not subject to change.

Strategic therapists took the concept of the *positive feedback loop* and made it the centerpiece of their models. For the MRI group, this translated into a simple yet powerful principle of problem formation: Families encounter many difficulties over the course of their lives; whether a difficulty becomes a "problem" (needing intervention) depends on how family members respond to it (Watzlawick, Weakland, & Fisch, 1974). That is, families often make commonsensical but misguided attempts to solve their difficulties and, on finding that the problem persists, apply more-of-the-same attempted solutions. This only produces an escalation of the problem, which provokes more of the same, and so on—in a vicious cycle.

For example, if Jamal feels threatened by the arrival of a baby sister, he may become temperamental. If so, his father might think he's being defiant and try to get him to act his age by punishing him. But his father's harshness only confirms Jamal's belief that his parents love his sister more than they love him, and so he becomes even more temperamental. Father, in turn, becomes more punitive, and Jamal becomes increasingly alienated. This is an escalating positive feedback loop: The family system is reacting to a deviation in the behavior of one of its members with feedback designed to dampen that deviation (*negative feedback*), but it has the effect of amplifying the deviation (*positive feedback*).

What's needed is for father to reverse his solution. If he could comfort rather than criticize Jamal and help him see that he isn't being displaced, then Jamal might calm down. The system is governed, however, by unspoken rules that allow only one interpretation of Jamal's behavior—as disrespectful. For father to alter his solution, this rule would have to change.

In most families, unspoken rules govern all sorts of behavior. Where a rule promotes the kind of rigid attempted solutions described previously, it isn't just the behavior but the rule that needs to change. When only a specific behavior within a system changes, this is **first-order change,** as opposed to **second-order change,** which occurs when the rules of the system change (Watzlawick, Weakland, & Fisch, 1974). How does one change the rules? One way is by **reframing**—that is, changing father's interpretation of Jamal's behavior from disrespect to fear of displacement, from bad to sad.

Thus, the MRI approach to problems is elegantly simple: First, identify the positive feedback loops that maintain problems; second, determine the rules in order to interrupt the problem-maintaining behavior (or frames) that support those interactions; and third, find a way to change the rules in order to interrupt the problem-maintaining behavior.

Jay Haley added a functionalist emphasis to the cybernetic interpretation, with his interest in the interpersonal payoff of behavior. Later, he incorporated structural concepts picked up in the years he spent working with Minuchin in Philadelphia. For example, Haley might notice that whenever Jamal and his father quarrel, Jamal's mother protects him by criticizing father for being so harsh. Haley might also see Jamal becoming more agitated when mother criticizes father, trying to get his parents' attention off their conflicts and onto him.

Haley believes that the rules around the **hierarchical structure** in the family are crucial

and finds inadequate parental hierarchies lurking behind most problems. Indeed, Haley (1976) suggests that, "an individual is more disturbed in direct proportion to the number of malfunctioning hierarchies in which he is embedded" (p. 117).

To counter a problem's payoff, Haley borrowed Erickson's technique of prescribing **ordeals,** so that the price for keeping a symptom outweighed that of giving it up. To illustrate, consider Erickson's famous maneuver of prescribing that an insomniac set his alarm every night to wake up and wax the kitchen floor. Haley tried to explain all therapy as based on ordeals, suggesting that many people will change just to avoid the ordeals inherent in being a client (Haley, 1984).

Cloe Madanes (1981, 1984) also emphasized the functional aspect of problems, particularly the rescuing operations involved when children use their symptoms to engage their parents. For example, when a daughter sees her mother looking depressed, the daughter can provoke a fight which prods the mother into taking charge. Much of Madanes's approach involves finding ways for children to help their parents openly, so that they won't have to resort to symptoms as sacrificial offerings.

Like Haley, Mara Selvini Palazzoli and her associates (1978b) focused on the power-game aspect of family interactions and, similarly, on the protective function symptoms served for the whole family. They interviewed families about their history, sometimes over several generations, searching for evidence to confirm their hypotheses about how the children's symptoms came to be necessary. These hypotheses often involved elaborate networks of family alliances and coalitions. They usually concluded that the patient developed symptoms to protect one or more family members so as to maintain the delicate network of extended family alliances.

Normal Family Development

According to **general systems theory,** normal families, like all living systems, depend on two vital processes (Maruyama, 1968). First, they maintain integrity in the face of environmental challenges through *negative feedback.* No living system can survive without a coherent structure. On the other hand, too rigid a structure leaves a system ill equipped to adapt to changing circumstances. That's why normal families also have mechanisms of *positive feedback.* Negative feedback resists disruptions to maintain a steady state; positive feedback amplifies innovations to accommodate to altered circumstances. Recognizing that the channel for positive feedback is communication makes it possible to state the case more plainly: Healthy families are able to change because they communicate clearly and are adaptable.

The MRI group resolutely opposed standards of normality: "As therapists, we do not regard any particular way of functioning, relating, or living as a problem if the client is not expressing discontent with it" (Fisch, 1978). Thus, by limiting their task to eliminating problems presented to them, the MRI group avoided taking any position regarding how families *should* behave.

The Milan Associates strove to maintain an attitude of "neutrality" (Selvini Palazzoli et al., 1980). They didn't apply preconceived goals or normative models. Instead, by raising questions that helped families examine themselves and that exposed hidden power games, they trusted that families would reorganize on their own.

In contrast to the relativism of these two approaches, Haley's assessments *were* based on assumptions about sound family functioning. His therapy was designed to help families reorganize into more functional structures, with clear boundaries and generational hierarchy (Haley, 1976).

Development of Behavior Disorders

According to communications theory, the essential **function of symptoms** is to maintain the homeostatic equilibrium of family systems.[1]

Symptomatic families were considered to be trapped in dysfunctional, homeostatic patterns of interaction (Jackson & Weakland 1961). These families cling to their rigid ways and respond to signs of change as negative feedback. That is, change is treated not as an opportunity for growth but as a threat, as the following example illustrates.

> Laban was a quiet boy, the only child of Orthodox Jewish parents from Eastern Europe. His parents left their small farming community to come to the United States where they both found factory work in a large city. Although they were now safe from religious persecution, the couple felt alien and out of synch with their new neighbors. They kept to themselves and took pleasure in raising Laban.
>
> Laban was a frail child with a number of peculiar mannerisms, but to his parents he was perfect. Then he started school. Laban began to make friends with other children and, eager to be accepted, picked up a number of American habits. He chewed gum, watched cartoons, and rode his bicycle all over the neighborhood. His parents were annoyed by the gum chewing and by Laban's fondness for television, but they were genuinely distressed by his eagerness to play with gentile children. They may have come to America to escape persecution, but not to embrace pluralism, much less assimilation. As far as they were concerned, Laban was rejecting their values—"Something must be wrong with him." By the time they called the child guidance clinic, they were convinced that Laban was disturbed, and they asked for help to "make Laban normal again."

Symptoms were seen as messages: "It is not I who does not (or does) want to do this, it is something outside my control—my nerves, my illness, my anxiety, my bad eyes, alcohol, my upbringing, the Communists, or my wife" (Watzlawick, Beavin, & Jackson, 1967, p 80). As the Palo Alto group became more sophisticated, they tried to get past blaming parents for victimizing their children. Symptoms were no longer considered *caused* by communication problems; they were seen as embedded in a pathologic context, within which they might

---

1. The notion of symptoms as functional—implying that families *need* their problems—was to become controversial.

be the only available option. Among the forms of pathologic communication identified were denying that one is communicating, disqualifying the other person's message, confusing levels of communication, discrepant punctuation of communication sequences, symmetrical escalation to competitiveness, rigid complementarity, and paradoxical messages.

A **paradox** is a contradiction that follows correct deduction from logical premises. In family communications, paradoxes usually take the form of **paradoxical injunctions.** A common example is to demand some behavior that by its very nature can only be spontaneous—"You should have more self-confidence." "Tell me you love me." "Be spontaneous!" A person exposed to such paradoxical injunctions is caught in an untenable position. To comply—to act in a spontaneous or self-confident manner—means to be self-consciously deliberate or eager to please. The only way to escape the dilemma is to step outside the context and comment on it, but such **metacommunication** rarely occurs in families. (It's hard to communicate about communication.)

Paradoxical communications are harmless in small doses, but when they take the form of **double binds,** the consequences can be malignant. In a double bind, the two contradictory messages are on different levels of abstraction, and there is an implicit injunction against commenting on the discrepancy. A familiar example is the person who criticizes others for not expressing their feelings but then attacks them when they do.

Continual exposure to paradoxical communication is like the dilemma of a dreamer caught in a nightmare. Nothing the dreamer tries to do in the dream works. The only solution is to step outside the context by waking up. Unfortunately, when you live in a nightmare, it isn't always easy to wake up.

●

In strategic models, there are three basic explanations of how problems develop. The first is cybernetic: Difficulties are turned into chronic problems by misguided solutions, forming *positive-feedback escalations.* The second is struc-

tural: Problems are the result of *incongruous hierarchies.* The third is functional: Problems result when people try to protect or control one another covertly, so that their *symptoms serve a function for the system.* The MRI group limited itself to the first explanation, whereas Haley and the Milan associates embraced all three.

To clarify these differences, consider the following example: Sixteen-year-old Juwan recently began refusing to leave the house. An MRI therapist might ask his parents how they had tried to get him to venture out. The focus would be on the parents' attempted solution, on the assumption that this was likely to be maintaining Juwan's refusal, and on their explanation or "frame" for Juwan's behavior, believing that their framing of the problem might be driving their false solution.

A Haley-style therapist might be interested in the parents' attempted solutions but would also inquire about their marriage, the ways in which Juwan was involved in struggles between them or other family members, and the possible protective nature of Juwan's problem. This therapist would be acting on the assumption that Juwan's behavior might be part of a dysfunctional triangle. The therapist might further assume that this triangular pattern was fueled by unresolved conflicts between the parents. Madanes would also be interested in this triangle but, in addition, would be curious about how Juwan's behavior might be protecting his parents from having to face some threatening issue.

A Milan systemic therapist wouldn't focus so much on attempted solutions but, instead, would ask about past and present relationships in the family. In so doing, the therapist would be trying to uncover a network of power alliances, often running across generations, that constituted the family's "game." Some such game left Juwan in the position of having to use his symptoms to protect other family members. The family might reveal, for example, that if Juwan were to grow up and leave home, his mother would be drawn back into a power struggle between her parents, which she had avoided by having a symptomatic child. Also, by not succeeding in life, Juwan might be protecting his father from the shame of having a child who exceeded him in accomplishment.

How Therapy Works

In the early days of family therapy, the goal was simply to improve communication. Later, the goal was refined to altering specific patterns of communication that maintained problems: "We see the resolution of problems as primarily requiring a substitution of behavior patterns so as to interrupt the vicious, positive feedback circles" (Weakland, Fisch, Watzlawick, & Bodin, 1974, p. 149).

A therapist can either point out problematic sequences or simply block them to effect therapeutic change. The first strategy relies on the power of insight and depends on a willingness to change. The second does not; it is an attempt to beat families at their own games.

Jackson and Haley's work was influenced by the hypnotherapy they learned from Milton Erickson. The hypnotist works by giving instructions whose purpose is often obscure. Haley (1961) recommended asking uncooperative patients to do something in order to provoke a rebellious response, which served to make them concede that they were relating to the therapist. He mentions, as an example, directing a schizophrenic patient to hear voices. If the patient hears voices, then he is complying with the therapist's request; if he doesn't hear voices, he can no longer claim to be crazy.

Haley's (1961) direction to hear voices illustrates the technique of **prescribing the symptom.** By instructing a patient to enact symptomatic behavior, the therapist is demanding that something "involuntary" be done voluntarily. This paradoxical injunction forces one of two outcomes. Either the patient performs the symptom and thus proves it isn't involuntary, or the patient gives up the symptom.

●

For the MRI school, the way to resolve problems is to change the behavior that's been maintaining them. It's believed that through seeing the

results of altering rigid behavioral responses, clients will become more flexible in their problem-solving strategies. When this happens, clients achieve a second-order change—a change in the rules governing their response to problems.

For example, Maria argues with her father about her curfew and her father grounds her. She then runs away and stays with a friend. A first-order intervention at this point might be to help Maria's father find a more effective punishment to tame this out-of-control child. A second-order strategic intervention might be to direct the father to act disappointed and sad around his daughter, implying that he has given up trying to control her. This shifts Maria from feeling trapped by father to feeling concerned about him, and she becomes more reasonable. Her father learns that when attempted solutions aren't working, he needs to try something different. This change is second order in that it is a change in the rules governing the way father and daughter interact.

Haley (1976) believed that telling people what they're doing wrong only mobilizes resistance. He believed that changes in behavior alter perceptions, rather than the other way around. Madanes (1980) said "if a problem can be solved without the family's knowing how or why, that is satisfactory" (p. 79).

The Milan group turned this behaviorism on its head. They were more interested in getting families to see things differently (through a reframing technique called "positive connotation," to be discussed later) than in getting them to *behave* differently. This shift from behavior to cognition set the stage for the constructivist and narrative movements (see Chapters 4 and 13).

Therapy

Assessment

The goals of an MRI assessment are to (1) define a resolvable complaint, (2) identify attempted solutions that maintain the complaint, and (3) understand the clients' unique language for describing the problem. The first two goals show where to intervene, while the third is relevant to how.

The first step is to get a very specific, behavioral picture of the complaint, who sees it as a problem, and why it's a problem now. When a therapist asks, "What is the problem that brings you here today?" many clients reply ambiguously: "We don't communicate," "We think our 14-year-old is depressed," or "Clarence seems to be hyperactive." The MRI therapist inquires about exactly what these complaints mean. "We don't communicate" might mean "My son argues with everything I say," or "My husband hides behind the newspaper and never talks to me." "Depressed" might mean sad and withdrawn or sullen and disagreeable; "hyperactive" might mean disobedient or unable to concentrate. A useful device is to ask, "If we had a videotape of this, what would it look like?"

Once the problem has been defined, the therapist tries to determine who has tried to solve it and how. Sometimes the attempted solution seems obviously to have made things worse. For example, the wife who nags her husband to spend more time with her is likely to succeed only in driving him further away. Likewise the parents who punish their son for fighting with his sister may convince him that they do favor her. Or the husband who does everything his wife asks in order to keep the peace may become so resentful that he starts to hate her.

From this inquiry emerges a formulation of the problem-solution loop and the specific behavior that will be the focus of intervention. Typically, the strategic objective will be a 180-degree reversal of what the clients have been doing. Although interventions typically involve prescribing some alternative behavior, the key is to stop the performance of the problem-maintaining solution (Weakland & Fisch, 1992).

Grasping the clients' unique language and ways of seeing their dilemmas is important to framing suggestions in ways they will accept. For example, a devoutly religious wife might be amenable to the suggestion that she pray for her husband to become more involved with the family rather than continue to criticize his failings. In another case, cited by Shoham and Rohrbaugh (2002), a young woman was seen as perpetuating her boyfriend's jealous accusations by trying to reassure him. Unfortunately, these efforts to reason with the boyfriend only ended up in arguments, which were painful enough to threaten the relationship. Because the woman was a devotee of "mindfulness meditation," the therapist suggested that the next time the boyfriend asked a jealous question and she felt like defending herself, the woman should instead tell him that she was feeling stressed and needed to meditate.

Haley's assessment begins with a careful definition of the problem, expressed from the point of view of every member of the family. Unlike the MRI group, however, Haley also explores the possibility that structural arrangements in the family may be contributing to their problems—especially pathologic triangles or "cross-generational coalitions."

In addition to structural problems, Haley and Madanes also consider the interpersonal payoff of problem behavior. According to Haley, the apparent helplessness of a patient often turns out to be a source of power in relation to others whose lives are dominated by the demands and fears of the symptomatic person. A schizophrenic who refuses to take his medication might, for example, be trying to avoid having to go to work. Although it's not necessary to decide what is or isn't a real illness, Haley tends to assume that all symptomatic behavior is voluntary. Sometimes this distinction is crucial—as, for example, in cases of drug addiction or "losing one's temper."

In the Milan model, assessment begins with a preliminary hypothesis, which is then confirmed or disconfirmed in the initial session. These hypotheses are generally based on the assumption that the **identified patient's** problems were serving a homeostatic or protective function for the family. Therefore assessment of the presenting problem and the family's response to it is based on questions designed to explore the family as a set of interconnected relationships. For example, the reply to a question like, "Who has been more worried about this problem, you or your wife?" suggests a hypothesis about the closeness and distance of family members. The ultimate goal of assessment is to achieve a systemic perspective on the problem.

Therapeutic Techniques

Most of the techniques of communications therapy consisted of teaching rules of communication and manipulating interactions through a variety of strategic maneuvers. The progression of these strategies from straightforward to strategic reflected a growing awareness of how families resist change.

After their opening remarks, therapists asked family members, usually one at a time, to discuss their problems. The therapist listened but concentrated on the process, rather than the content, of communication. When someone spoke in a confused or confusing way, the therapist would insist on rules of clear communication. Satir (1964) was the most straightforward teacher. When someone said something that was unclear, she would clarify the message, and as she did, she impressed on the family basic guidelines for clear speaking.

One rule is that people should always speak in the first person singular when saying what they think. For example:

Husband: We always liked Celia's boyfriends.

Therapist: I'd like you to speak for yourself; later your wife can say what she thinks.

Husband: Yes, but we've always agreed on these things.

Therapist: Perhaps, but you are the expert on how you feel. Speak for yourself, and let her speak for herself.

A similar rule is that opinions should be acknowledged as that, not passed off as facts. Owning personal perspectives, as such, is a necessary step to discussing them in a way that permits legitimate differences of opinion.

Wife: People shouldn't want to do things without their children.

Therapist: So you like to bring the kids along when you and your husband go out?

Wife: Well yes, doesn't everybody?

Husband: I don't. I'd like just the two of us to go out once in a while.

Another rule is that people should speak directly to, not about, each other. This approach avoids ignoring or disqualifying family members and prevents the establishment of destructive coalitions. For example:

Teenager: (To therapist) My mother always has to be right. Isn't that so, Dad?

Therapist: Would you say that to her?

Teenager: I have, but she doesn't listen.

Therapist: Tell her again.

Teenager: (To therapist) Oh, okay. (To mother) Sometimes I get the feeling . . . (Shifts back to therapist) Oh, what's the use!

Therapist: I can see how hard it is, and I guess you've decided that it's no use trying to talk to your mom if she isn't going to listen. But in here, I hope we can learn to speak more directly to each other, so that no one will give up on having his or her say.

As this exchange illustrates, it's difficult to teach people to communicate just by telling them how. It seemed like a good idea, but it didn't work very well. In recognizing that families don't always respond well to direct advice, Jay Haley began to focus more on the family patterns underlying communication problems and to use more indirect means of influence.

In *Strategies of Psychotherapy*, Haley (1963) described the marital relationship in terms of conflicting *levels* of communication. Conflicts occur not only over what rules a couple will follow, but also over who sets the rules.[2] One of Haley's strategies was to spell out the implicit rules that govern family relationships. Dysfunctional rules made explicit become more difficult to follow.

---

2. Recognizing the cybernetic principle in a home heating system may be easier than agreeing on who gets to set the temperature.

For example, some people berate their partners for not expressing themselves, but they talk so much and criticize so loudly that the partners hardly have a chance to speak. If the therapist points this out, it becomes more difficult to follow the implicit rule that one person should only say what the other one wants to hear.

Some of Haley's directives were for changes that seemed so small that the full ramifications weren't immediately apparent. In one couple, for example, in which the husband seemed to have his way most of the time, the wife was asked to say "no" on some minor issue once during the week. This may seem trivial, but it accomplished two things: It made the wife practice speaking up, and it made the husband aware that he was domineering.

Haley's use of directives to manipulate changes in the way families were organized was a pivotal step in the evolution of communications therapy into strategic therapy. Although strategic therapists shared a belief in the need for indirect methods to induce change in families, they developed distinctly different techniques for doing so, which we will therefore examine separately.

The MRI Approach.   The MRI model follows a six-step treatment procedure:

1. Introducing the treatment setup;
2. Inquiring about and defining the problem;
3. Estimating the behavior that is maintaining the problem;
4. Setting goals for treatment;
5. Selecting and making behavioral interventions;
6. Terminating therapy.

Once the preliminaries are concluded, the therapist asks for a clear definition of the primary problem. If a problem is stated in vague terms, such as "We just don't get along," or in terms of presumptive causes, such as "Dad's job is making him depressed," the therapist helps translate it into a clear and concrete goal, asking questions like "What will be the first small sign that things are getting better?"

Once the problem and goal are defined, MRI therapists inquire about attempted solutions that might be maintaining the problem. In general, solutions that tend to perpetuate problems fall into one of three categories:

1. The solution is to deny that a problem exists; action is necessary but not taken. For instance, parents do nothing despite growing evidence that their teenage son is using drugs.

2. The solution is an effort to solve something that isn't really a problem; action is taken when it shouldn't be. For example, parents punish a child for masturbating.

3. The solution is an effort to solve a problem within a framework that makes a solution impossible; action is taken but at the wrong level. For instance, a husband buys increasingly expensive gifts for his wife, when what she wants is affection.

Once the therapist conceives a strategy for altering the problem-maintaining sequence, clients must be convinced to follow this strategy. To sell their directives, MRI therapists *reframe* problems to increase the likelihood of compliance. Thus a therapist might tell an angry teenager that when his father punishes him, it's the only way his father knows how to show his love.

To interrupt problem-maintaining sequences, strategic therapists may try to get family members to do something that runs counter to common sense. Such counterintuitive techniques have been called *paradoxical interventions* (Haley, 1973; Watzlawick, Weakland, & Fisch, 1974).

For example, Watzlawick and colleagues (1974) described a young couple who were bothered by their parents' tendency to treat them like children by doing everything for them. Despite the husband's adequate salary, the parents continued to send money and lavish gifts on them, refused to let them pay even part of a restaurant check, and so on. The strategic team helped the couple solve their difficulty with their doting parents by having them become *less* rather than more competent. Instead of trying to show the parents that they didn't need help, the couple was told to act helpless and dependent, so much so that the parents got disgusted and finally backed off.

The techniques most commonly thought of as paradoxical are symptom prescriptions in which a family is told to continue or embellish the behavior they complain about. In some contexts, such a prescription might be made with the hope that the family will try to comply with it and thereby be forced to reverse their attempted solutions. If Jorge, who is sad, is told to try to become depressed several times a day and his family is asked to encourage him to be sad, then they will no longer try ineffectively to cheer him up and he won't feel guilty for not being happy.

At other times, a therapist might prescribe the symptom while secretly hoping that the clients will rebel against this directive. The therapist might encourage Jorge to continue to be depressed because, in doing so, he's helping his brother (with whom Jorge is competitive) feel superior.

Sometimes a therapist might *prescribe the symptom* with the hope that in doing so the network of relationships that maintain the problem will be exposed. The therapist says that Jorge should remain depressed because that way he can continue to get his mother's attention, which will keep her from looking to father for affection, since father is still overinvolved with his own mother, and so on.

To prevent power struggles, MRI therapists avoid assuming an authoritarian position. Their one-down stance implies equality and invites clients to reduce anxiety and resistance. Although some strategists adopt a one-down position disingenuously, this modest stance was consistent with the late John Weakland's own unassuming character. While sitting clouded in the smoke of his pipe, Weakland discouraged families from trying to change too fast, warning them to go slowly and worrying out loud about the possibility of relapse when improvements did occur. This **restraining** technique reinforced the therapist's one-down position.

The Haley and Madanes Approach. Jay Haley's approach is harder to describe because it's tailored to address the unique requirements of each case. If "strategic" implies systematic, as in the MRI approach, it also implies artful, which is especially true of Haley's therapy. As with other strategic approaches, the definitive technique is the use of **directives**. But Haley's directives aren't simply ploys to outwit families or reverse what they're doing. Rather, they are thoughtful suggestions targeted to the specific requirements of the case.

Haley (1976) believes that if therapy is to end well, it must begin properly. Therefore, he devotes a good deal of attention to the opening moves of treatment. Regardless of who is presented as the official patient, Haley begins by interviewing the entire family. His approach to this initial interview follows four stages: a *social stage*, a *problem stage*, an *interaction stage*, and finally a *goal-setting stage*.

Families are often defensive when they come to therapy. Family members may not know what to expect, and they may be afraid that the therapist will blame them for the problem. Therefore, Haley uses the initial minutes of a first session to help everyone relax. He makes a point of greeting each family member and trying to make sure they're all comfortable. Like a good host, he wants his guests to feel welcome.

After the *social stage*, Haley gets down to business in the *problem stage*, asking each person for his or her perspective. Because mothers are usually more central than fathers, Haley recommends speaking first to the father to increase his involvement. This suggestion illustrates Haley's strategic maneuvering, which begins with the first contact and characterizes all subsequent meetings.

Haley listens carefully to the way each family member describes the problem, making sure that no one interrupts until each has had a turn. During this phase, Haley looks for clues about triangles and hierarchy, but he avoids making any comments about these observations because this might make the family defensive.

Once everyone has had a chance to speak, Haley encourages them to discuss their points of view among themselves. In this, the *interactional stage*, the therapist can observe, rather than just hear about, the interchanges that surround the problem. As they talk, Haley looks for coalitions between family members against others. How functional is the hierarchy? Do the parents work together, or do they undercut each other? During this stage, the therapist is like an anthropologist, trying to discover patterns in the family's actions.

Sometimes Haley ends the first session by giving the family a task. In subsequent sessions, directives play a central role. Effective directives don't usually take the form of simple advice, which is rarely helpful because problems usually persist for a reason.

The following two tasks are taken from Haley's *Problem-Solving Therapy.* One couple, who were out of the habit of being affectionate with each other, were told to behave affectionately "to teach their child how to show affection." In another case, a mother who was unable to control her twelve-year-old son had decided to send him away to military school. Haley suggested that, because the boy had no idea how tough life would be at military school, it would be a good idea for the mother to help prepare him. They both agreed. Haley directed her to teach the boy how to stand at attention, be polite, and wake up early every morning to make his bed. The two of them followed these instructions as if playing a game, with mother as sergeant and son as private. After two weeks the son was behaving so well that his mother no longer felt it necessary to send him away.

James Keim and Jay Lappin (2002) describe a strategic approach to a case with a nagging wife and withdrawing husband. First they reframe the problem as a "breakdown in the negotiation process." A negotiation, the couple is told, is a conversation in which one party makes a request and the other names a price. This reframing allows the wife to make requests without thinking of herself as a nag—and the husband to see himself as having something to gain in negotiations, rather than as a browbeaten husband who is asked to give in to his wife.

Keim and Lappin recommend introducing couples to the negotiation process as experimenting with a "fun exercise" designed to get them back on track with reaching agreements. Then the couple is given a handout with elaborate instructions for negotiating in a constructive fashion and asked to progress from negotiating easy issues in the session to doing so at home and then tackling more difficult issues, first in the session and then at home. Finally, couples are cautioned that even after negotiating some exchanges, they may choose not to accept the quid pro quo terms. Sometimes it is preferable to endure certain problems than to pay the price of trying to change them.

Madanes (1981) used the observation that people will often do something they wouldn't ordinarily do if it's framed as play to develop a whole range of **pretend techniques.** One such strategy is to ask a symptomatic child to pretend to have the symptom and encourage the parents to pretend to help. The child can give up the actual symptom now that pretending to have it is serving the same family function. The following two cases summarized from Madanes (1981) illustrate the pretend technique.

In the first case, a mother sought therapy because her ten-year-old son had night terrors. Madanes suspected that the boy was concerned about his mother, who was poor, spoke little English, and had lost two husbands. Because the boy had night terrors, the therapist asked all the

Cloe Madanes's "pretend techniques" are a clever way to help break control-and-rebel cycles.

members of the family to describe their dreams. Only the mother and the son had nightmares. In the mother's nightmare, someone was breaking into the house. In the boy's, he was being attacked by a witch. When Madanes asked what the mother did when the boy had nightmares, she said that she took him into her bed and told him to pray to God. She thought his nightmares were the work of the devil.

Madanes's conjecture was that the boy's night terrors were both a metaphorical expression of the mother's fears and an attempt to help her. As long as the boy was afraid, his mother had to be strong. Unfortunately, while trying to protect him, she frightened him further by talking about God and the devil. Thus, both mother and child were helping each other in unproductive ways.

The family members were told to pretend that they were home and mother was afraid that someone might break in. The son was asked to protect his mother. In this way the mother had to pretend to need the child's help instead of really needing it. At first the family had difficulty playing the scene because the mother would attack the make-believe thief before the son could help. Thus she communicated that she was capable of taking care of herself and didn't need the son's protection. After the scene was performed correctly, with the son attacking the thief, they discussed the performance. The mother explained that it was difficult to play her part because she was a competent person who could defend herself. Madanes sent the family home with the task of repeating this dramatization every evening for a week. If the son started screaming during his sleep, his mother was to wake him up and replay the scene. They were told that this was important to do no matter how late it was or how tired they were. The son's night terrors soon disappeared.

In the second case, a mother sought treatment for her five-year-old because he had uncontrollable temper tantrums. After talking with the family for a few minutes, Madanes asked the boy to show her what his tantrums were like by pretending to have one. "Okay," he said, "I'm the Incredible Hulk!" He puffed out his chest, flexed his muscles, made a monster face, and started screaming and kicking the furniture. Madanes asked the mother to do what she usually did in such circumstances. The mother responded by telling her son, in a weak and ineffective way, to calm down. She pretended to send him to another room as she tried to do at home. Next, Madanes asked the mother if the boy was doing a good job of pretending. She said he was.

Madanes asked the boy to repeat the scene. This time he was Frankenstein and his tantrum was performed with a rigid posture and a grimacing face. Then Madanes talked with the boy about the Incredible Hulk and Frankenstein and congratulated the mother for raising such an imaginative child.

Following this discussion, mother and son were told to pretend that he was having a tantrum while she was walking him to his room. The boy was told to act like the Incredible Hulk and to make lots of noise. Then they were told to pretend to close the door and hug and kiss. Next Madanes instructed the mother to pretend that *she* was having a tantrum, and the boy was to hug and kiss her. Madanes instructed mother and son to perform both scenes every morning before school and every afternoon when the boy came home. After every performance, the mother was to give the boy milk and cookies if he did a good job. Thus the mother was moved from a helpless position to one of authority in which she was in charge of rewarding her son's make-believe performance. The next week the mother called to say that they didn't need to come for therapy because the boy was behaving very well and his tantrums had ceased.

Haley (1984) returned to his Ericksonian roots in a book called *Ordeal Therapy*, a collection of case studies in which ordeals were prescribed to make symptoms more trouble than they're worth. "If one makes it more difficult for a person to have a symptom than to give it up, the person will give up the symptom" (p. 5). For example, a standard ordeal is for a client to have to get up in the middle of the night and exercise strenuously whenever he or she had symptoms during that day. Another example might be for the client to have to give a present to someone with whom he or she has a poor relationship—for example, a mother-in-law or ex-spouse—each time the symptoms occur.

Haley also used ordeals to restructure families. For example, a sixteen-year-old boy put a variety of items up his behind and then expelled them, leaving his stepmother to clean up the mess. Haley (1984) arranged that, after each such episode, the father had to take his son to their backyard and have the boy dig a hole three feet deep and three feet wide, in which he was to bury all the things he was putting up his rear end. After a few weeks of this, Haley reported that the symptom stopped, the father became more involved with his son, and the stepmother became closer to the father.

The current form of Haley/Madanes therapy, called *strategic humanism*, still involves giving directives, but the directives are now more oriented toward increasing family members' abilities to soothe and love than to gain control over one another. This represents a major shift and is in sync with family therapy's shift away from the power elements of hierarchy and toward finding ways to increase harmony.

An excellent example of strategic humanism's blend of compassion and cleverness is James Keim's work with oppositional children (Keim, 1998). Keim begins by reassuring anxious parents that they aren't to blame for their children's oppositionalism. Next he explains that there are two sides of parental authority—discipline and nurture. To reinforce the parents' authority while avoiding power struggles, Keim encourages them to concentrate on being sympathetic and supportive for a while. The parent who soothes a child with the forgotten language of understanding is every bit as much in charge as one who tries to tell the child what to do. After progress has been made in calming the child down—especially in breaking the pattern by which oppositional children control the mood in the family by arguing with everything their parents say—Keim coaches the parents to post

rules and enforce consequences. This strategy puts parents back in charge of unruly children without the high-intensity melodrama that usually attends work with this population.

The Milan Model.   The original Milan model was highly scripted. Families were treated by male-female cotherapists and observed by other members of a therapy team. The standard format had five parts: *presession, session, intersession, intervention,* and *postsession discussion.* As Boscolo, Cecchin, Hoffman, and Penn (1987) describe:

> During the presession the team came up with an initial hypothesis about the family's presenting problem. . . . During the session itself, the team members would validate, modify, or change the hypothesis. After about forty minutes, the entire team would meet alone to discuss the hypothesis and arrive at an intervention. The treating therapists would then go back to deliver the intervention to the family, either by positively connoting the problem situation or by a ritual to be done by the family that commented on the problem situation and was designed to introduce change. . . . Finally, the team would meet for a postsession discussion to analyze the family's reactions and to plan for the next session. (p. 4)

As indicated in this description, the primary intervention was either a *ritual* or a *positive connotation.*

The **positive connotation** was the most distinctive innovation to emerge from the Milan model. Derived from the MRI technique of reframing symptoms as serving a protective function—for example, Carlo needs to continue to be depressed to distract his parents from their marital issues—the positive connotation avoided the implication that family members benefited from the patient's symptoms. This implication made for resistance that the Milan team found could be circumvented if the patient's behavior was construed not as protecting specific people but as preserving the family's overall harmony. Indeed, every family member's behavior was often connoted in this system-serving way.

The treatment team would hypothesize about how the patient's symptoms fit into the family system and, after a mid-session break, the therapists would deliver this hypothesis to the family, along with the injunction that they should not try to change. Carlo should continue to sacrifice himself by remaining depressed as a way to reassure the family that he will not become an abusive man like his grandfather. Mother should maintain her over involvement with Carlo as a way to make him feel valued while he sacrifices himself. Father should continue to criticize mother and Carlo's relationship so that mother will not be tempted to abandon Carlo and become a wife to her husband.

Rituals were used to engage families in a series of actions that ran counter to, or exaggerated, rigid family rules and myths. For example, one family, which was enmeshed with their large extended family, was told to hold family discussions behind locked doors every other night after dinner, during which each family member was to speak for fifteen minutes about the family. Meanwhile they were to redouble their courtesy to the other members of the clan. By exaggerating the family's loyalty to the extended family while simultaneously breaking that loyalty's rule by meeting apart from the clan and talking about it, the family could examine and break the rule that perpetuated their dysfunctional system.

Rituals were also used to dramatize positive connotations. For example, each family member might have to express his or her gratitude each night to the patient for having the problem (Boscolo et al., 1987). The Milan group also devised a set of rituals based on an "odd and even days" format (Selvini Palazzoli et al., 1978a). For example, a family in which the parents were deadlocked over parental control might be told that on even days of the week father should be in charge of the patient's behavior and mother should act as if she weren't there. On odd days, mother's in charge and father is to stay out of the way. Here, again, the family's rigid sequences are interrupted, and they must react differently to each other.

Positive connotations and rituals were powerful and provocative interventions. To keep families engaged while using such methods, the therapist–family relationship became crucial. Unfortunately, the Milan team originally portrayed therapy as a power struggle between therapists and families. Their main advice to therapists was to remain neutral in the sense of avoiding the appearance of taking sides. This **neutrality** was often manifest as distance, so that therapists delivered their dramatic pronouncements while acting aloof; not surprisingly, families often got angry and didn't return.

In the early 1980s, the original Milan team split around the nature of therapy. Selvini Palazzoli maintained the model's strategic and adversarial bent, although she stopped using paradoxical interventions. Instead she and Guiliana Prata experimented with a ritual called the **invariant prescription,** which they assigned to every family they treated.

Selvini Palazzoli (1986) believed that psychotic and anorexic patients are caught up in a "dirty game," a power struggle originally between their parents that these patients are pulled into. Ultimately, they wind up using their symptoms in an attempt to defeat one parent for the sake of the other. In the invariant prescription, parents were directed to tell their children that they had a secret. They were to go out together for varying periods of time and to do so mysteriously, without warning other family members. Therapy continued this way until the patient's symptoms abated.

In the early 1990s, Selvini Palazzoli reinvented her therapy once more, this time abandoning short-term, strategic therapy (invariant prescription included) for long-term therapy with patients and their families (Selvini, 1993). Thus, she came full circle, beginning with a psychodynamic approach, then focusing on family patterns, and finally returning to long-term therapy that emphasizes insight and focuses on the individual. This new therapy revolves around understanding the denial of family secrets and suffering over generations. In this way, it is linked conceptually, if not technically, to her former models.

Boscolo and Cecchin also moved away from strategic intervening but toward a collaborative style of therapy. This approach grew from their conclusion that the value in the Milan model wasn't so much in the directives (positive connotations and rituals), which had been the model's centerpiece, but in the interview process itself. Their therapy came to center around **circular questioning,** a clinical translation of Bateson's notion of double description. Circular questions are designed to decenter clients by orienting them toward seeing themselves in a relational context and seeing that context from the perspectives of other family members. For example, a therapist might ask, "How might your father have characterized your mother's relationship with your sister, if he had felt free to speak with you about it?" Such questions are structured so that one has to give a relational description in answer.

By asking about relationship patterns like this, the circular nature of problems becomes apparent. Circular questions have been further refined and cataloged by Peggy Penn (1982, 1985) and Karl Tomm (1987a, 1987b). Boscolo (Boscolo & Bertrando, 1992) remains intrigued with their potential. As an example, let's return to Carlo's family and imagine the following conversation (adapted from Hoffman, 1983):

Q: Who is most upset by Carlo's depression?

A: Mother.

Q: How does mother try to help Carlo?

A: She talks to him for hours and tries to do things for him.

Q: Who agrees most with mother's way of trying to help Carlo?

A: The psychiatrist who prescribes his medication.

Q: Who disagrees?

A: Father. He thinks Carlo shouldn't be allowed to do what he wants.

Q: Who agrees with Father?

A: We all think Carlo is babied too much. And Grandma too. Grandpa would probably agree with Mother but he died.

Q: Did Carlo start to get depressed before or after Grandfather's death?

A: Not long after, I guess.

Q: If Grandfather hadn't died, how would the family be different now?

A: Well, Mother and Grandma probably wouldn't fight so much because Grandma wouldn't be living with us. And Mother wouldn't be so sad all the time.

Q: If Mother and Grandma didn't fight so much and Mother wasn't so sad, how do you think Carlo would be?

A: Well, I guess he might be happier too. But then he'd probably be fighting with Father again.

By asking circular questions, the frame for Carlo's problem gradually shifts from a psychiatric one to being symptomatic of changes in the family structure.

Boscolo and Cecchin became aware that the spirit in which these questions were asked determined their usefulness. If a therapist maintains a strategic mind-set—uses the questioning process to strive for a particular outcome—the responses of family members are constrained by their sense that the therapist is after something. If, on the other hand, the therapist asks circular questions out of genuine *curiosity* (Cecchin, 1987), as if joining the family in a research expedition regarding their problem, an atmosphere can be created in which the family can arrive at new understandings of their predicament.

Other Contributions. Strategic therapists pioneered the *team approach* to therapy. Originally, the MRI group used teams behind one-way mirrors to help brainstorm strategies, as did the Milan group. Peggy Papp (1980) and her colleagues at the Ackerman Institute brought the team directly into the therapy process by turning the observers into a "Greek chorus" who reacted to events in the session. For example, the team might, for strategic purposes, disagree with the therapist. In witnessing debates between the team and their therapist over what a family should do, family members might feel that both sides of their ambivalence were being represented. Having the team interact openly with the therapist or even with the family during sessions paved the way for later approaches in which the team might enter the treatment room and discuss the family while the family watched (Andersen, 1987).

Jim Alexander was a behaviorist who, out of frustration with the limits of his behavioral orientation, incorporated strategic ideas. The result was *functional family therapy* (Alexander & Parsons, 1982), which, as the name implies, is concerned with the function that family behavior is designed to achieve (see also Chapter 10). Functional family therapists assume that most family behaviors are attempts to become more or less intimate. Through "relabeling" (another word for reframing), they help family members see each other's actions in that benign light. They also help family members set up contingency management programs to help them achieve the kind of intimacy they want. Functional family therapy represents an interesting blend of strategic and behavioral therapies and, unlike other strategic models, retains the behaviorist ethic of basing interventions on sound research.

Current Status of the Model

Communications family therapy was no mere application of individual psychotherapy to families; it was a radically new conceptualization that altered the very nature of imagination. What was new was the focus on *process*, the form and impact of communication, rather than *content*. Communication was described

as feedback, as a tactic in interpersonal power struggles, and as symptoms. In fact, all behavior is communicative.

When communication takes place in a closed system—an individual's fantasies or a family's private conversations—there's little opportunity for adjusting the system. Only when someone outside the system provides input can correction occur. Because the rules of family functioning are largely unknown to the family, the best way to examine them is to consult an expert in communication. Today the theories of communications therapy have been absorbed into the mainstream of family therapy, and its symptom-focused interventions have become the basis of the strategic and solution-focused models.

Strategic therapies reached the height of their popularity in the early 1980s. They were clever, prescriptive, and systematic—qualities appreciated by therapists who often felt overwhelmed by the emotionality of families in treatment. Then a backlash set in, and people began criticizing strategic therapy's manipulative aspects. Unfortunately, when communications and strategic therapists were confounded by the anxious inflexibility of some families, they may have exaggerated the irrational power of the family system.

In the 1990s the strategic approaches described in this chapter were replaced on family therapy's center stage by more collaborative approaches. But even as the field moves away from an overreliance on technique and manipulation, we shouldn't lose sight of valuable aspects of strategic therapy. These include having a clear therapeutic goal, anticipating how families will react to interventions, understanding and tracking sequences of interaction, and the creative use of directives.

Most of the meager research on the effectiveness of strategic therapy isn't rigorous. More than with any other model in this book, information about strategic therapy is exchanged through the case report format. Nearly all of the articles and books on strategic therapy include at least one description of a successful technique or therapy outcome. Thus strategic therapy appears to have a great deal of anecdotal support for its efficacy (although people tend not to write about their failed cases).

Some strategic groups have tracked their outcomes a little more systematically. In the book *Change,* which launched the MRI model, Watzlawick and colleagues (1974) conducted follow-up phone interviews with ninety-seven consecutive cases three months after treatment and found that 40 percent reported complete relief; 32 percent reported considerable relief; and 28 percent reported no change. Haley (1980) reported on the outcome of his "leaving home" model with schizophrenic young adults and found that, between two and four years after terminating, three of the fourteen had been rehospitalized, while another patient had committed suicide.

Some early studies of the outcome of family therapies based on strategic therapy helped fuel its popularity. In their classic study, Langsley, Machotka, and Flomenhaft (1971) found that family crisis therapy, with similarities to the MRI and Haley models, drastically reduced the need for hospitalization. Alexander and Parsons found their functional family therapy to be more effective in treating a group of delinquents than a client-centered family approach, an eclectic-dynamic approach, or a no-treatment control (Parsons & Alexander, 1973). Stanton and Todd (1982) demonstrated the effectiveness of combining structural and strategic therapies for treating heroin addicts. The results were impressive because family therapy resulted in twice as many days of abstinence from heroin as a methadone maintenance program.

In the early 1980s the Milan associates offered anecdotal reports of amazing outcomes with anorexia nervosa, schizophrenia, and delinquency (Selvini Palazzoli, Boscolo, Cecchin, & Prata, 1978b, 1980). Later, however, members of the original team expressed reservations about the model and implied that it wasn't as effective

as originally suggested (Selvini Palazzoli, 1986; Selvini Palazzoli & Viaro, 1988; Boscolo, 1983). Some who have studied the Milan model more systematically concur with these less enthusiastic impressions (Machal, Feldman, & Sigal, 1989). In discussing their disappointing results with the Milan model, the authors cited clients' negative reactions. Families frequently felt that the therapists were distant and impersonal. Apparently the attitude of adversarial strategizing recommended in *Paradox and Counterparadox* showed through the therapists' attempts to positively connote family behavior. It seems that people have trouble changing if they don't feel cared about.

Although the original Milan model appears to have gone the way of the dinosaurs, two thriving strategic camps currently exist: the MRI group on the West Coast and the Washington School, started by Haley and Madanes on the East Coast.

What people came to rebel against was the gimmickry of formulaic techniques. But gimmickry wasn't inherent in the strategic models. For example, the MRI's emphasis on reversing attempted solutions that don't work is a sound idea. People *do* stay stuck in ruts as long as they pursue self-defeating strategies. If, in some hands, blocking more-of-the-same solutions resulted in a rote application of reverse psychology, that's not the fault of the cybernetic metaphor but of the way it was applied.

Strategic therapists are currently integrating new ideas and keeping up with the postmodern spirit of the twenty-first century. Haley published a book in which the evolution of his thinking is apparent (Haley, 1996), and another book on the influence of the MRI on the field was released (Weakland & Ray, 1995). In addition, some authors have integrated MRI strategic concepts with narrative approaches (Eron & Lund, 1993, 1996). It's good to see that strategic thinking is evolving, because even in this era of the nonexpert therapist, there is still room for thoughtful problem-solving strategies and therapeutic direction.

—Summary——

1. Communications therapy was one of the first and most influential forms of family treatment. Its theoretical development was based on general systems theory, and the therapy that emerged was a systems approach *par excellence*. Communication was the detectable input and output therapists used to analyze the black box of interpersonal systems.

2. Another of the significant ideas of communications therapy was that families are rule-governed systems, maintained by homeostatic feedback mechanisms. Negative feedback accounts for the stability of healthy families and the inflexibility of dysfunctional ones. Because such families don't have adequate positive feedback mechanisms, they're unable to adjust to changing circumstances.

3. Although there were major differences among the therapeutic strategies of Haley, Jackson, Satir, and Watzlawick, they were all committed to altering destructive patterns of communication. They pursued this goal by direct and indirect means. The direct approach, favored by Satir, sought to make family rules explicit and teach clear communication. This approach could be described as establishing ground rules, or metacommunication principles, and included such tactics as telling people to speak for themselves and pointing out nonverbal and multilevel channels of communication.

4. The trouble is, as Haley noted, "One of the difficulties involved in telling patients to do something is the fact that psychiatric patients are noted for their hesitation about doing what they are told." For this reason, communications therapists began to rely on more indirect strategies, designed to provoke change rather than foster awareness. Telling family members to speak for themselves, for example, may challenge a family rule and therefore meet with resistance. With this realization, communications therapy evolved into a treatment of resistance.

5. Resistance and symptoms were treated with a variety of paradoxical directives, known loosely as "therapeutic double binds." Milton Erickson's technique of prescribing resistance was used as a lever to gain control, as, for example, when a therapist tells family members not to reveal everything in the first session. The same ploy was used to prescribe symptoms, an action that made covert rules explicit, implied that such behavior was voluntary, and put the therapist in control.

6. Strategic therapy, derived from Eriksonian hypnotherapy and Batesonian cybernetics, developed a body of powerful procedures for treating psychological problems. Strategic approaches vary in the specifics of theory and technique but share a problem-centered, pragmatic focus on changing behavioral sequences, in which therapists take responsibility for the outcome of therapy. Insight and understanding are eschewed in favor of directives designed to change the way family members interact.

7. The MRI model tries to remain strictly interactional—observing and intervening into sequences of interaction surrounding a problem rather than speculating about the intentions of the interactants. Haley and Madanes, on the other hand, are interested in motives: Haley mainly in the desire to control others and Madanes in the desire to love and be loved. Unlike the MRI group, Haley and Madanes believe that successful treatment often requires structural change, with an emphasis on improving family hierarchy.

8. Like Haley, the Milan Associates originally saw power in the motives of family members. They tried to understand the elaborate multigenerational games that surrounded symptoms. They designed powerful interventions—positive connotation and rituals—to expose these games and change the meaning of the problem. Later, the original group split, with Selvini Palazzoli

going through several transformations until her current long-term approach based on family secrets. Cecchin and Boscolo moved away from formulaic interventions, became more interested in the questioning process as a way to help families to new understandings, and in so doing paved the way for family therapy's current interest in conversation and narrative.

—Questions to Consider———

1. What are some strategic concepts and techniques that could usefully be adopted by practitioners of other approaches?
2. While strategic therapists tend to strategize to manipulate clients, to what extent might it be possible to strategize with clients in a collaborative effort to reverse problem-maintaining solutions? In what kinds of cases might this be more and less feasible?
3. Would an MRI approach be more useful with families who are cooperative or who are resistant?
4. How would you phrase a series of circular questions that would get at the process of communication that occurs in your family therapy class?
5. Are paradoxical interventions necessarily distancing and manipulative?

—Key Concepts———

circular causality   The idea that events are related through a series of interacting loops or repeating cycles.

circular questioning   A method of interviewing developed by the Milan Associates in which questions are asked that highlight differences among family members.

communications theory   The study of relationships in terms of the exchange of verbal and nonverbal messages.

cybernetics   The study of control processes in systems, especially analysis of the flow of information in closed systems.

directives   Homework assignments designed to help families interrupt homeostatic patterns of problem-maintaining behavior.

double bind   A conflict created when a person receives contradictory messages on different levels of abstraction in an important relationship and cannot leave or comment.

family homeostasis   Tendency of families to resist change to maintain a steady state.

family ritual   Technique used by Selvini Palazzoli and her Milan Associates that prescribes a set of actions designed to change a family system's rules.

family rules   A descriptive term for redundant behavioral patterns.

feedback loops   The return of a portion of the output of a system, especially when used to maintain the output within predetermined limits (negative feedback) or to signal a need to modify the system (positive feedback).

first-order change   Superficial change in a system that stays invariant.

function of the symptom   The idea that symptoms are often ways to distract or protect family members from threatening conflicts.

general systems theory   A biological model of living systems as whole entities that maintain themselves through continuous input and output from the environment; developed by Ludwig von Bertalanffy.

hierarchical structure   Family functioning based on clear generational boundaries, whereby the parents maintain control and authority.

homeostasis   A balanced, steady state of equilibrium.

identified patient The symptom-bearer or official patient.

invariant prescription A technique developed by Mara Selvini Palazzoli in which parents are directed to mysteriously sneak away together.

metacommunication Every message has two levels, report and command; metacommunication is the implied command or qualifying message.

negative feedback See **feedback loops.**

neutrality Selvini Palazzoli's term for balanced acceptance of family members.

ordeals A paradoxical intervention in which the client is directed to do something that is more of a hardship than the symptom.

paradox A self-contradictory statement based on a valid deduction from acceptable premises.

paradoxical injunction A technique used in strategic therapy whereby the therapist directs family members to continue their symptomatic behavior. If they conform, they admit control and expose secondary gain; if they rebel, they give up their symptoms.

positive connotation Selvini Palazzoli's technique of ascribing positive motives to family behavior to promote family cohesion and avoid resistance to therapy.

positive feedback loop See **feedback loops.**

prescribing the symptom A paradoxical technique that forces a patient either to give up a symptom or to admit that it is under voluntary control.

pretend techniques Madanes's playful paradoxical intervention in which family members are asked to pretend to engage in symptomatic behavior. The paradox is if they are pretending to have a symptom, the symptom cannot be real.

reframing Relabeling a family's description of behavior to make it more amenable to therapeutic change; for example, describing someone as "lazy" rather than "depressed."

restraining A strategic technique for overcoming resistance by suggesting that a family not change.

rituals See **family ritual.**

second-order change Basic change in the structure of a system.

—Recommended Readings—

Cecchin, G. 1987. Hypothesizing, circularity and neutrality revisited. *Family Process.* 26: 405–413.

Fisch, R., Weakland, J. H., and Segal, L. 1982. *The tactics of change: Doing therapy briefly.* San Francisco: Jossey-Bass.

Haley, J. 1976. *Problem-solving therapy.* San Francisco: Jossey-Bass.

Haley, J. 1980. *Leaving home.* New York: McGraw-Hill.

Jackson, D. D. 1961. Interactional psychotherapy. In *Contemporary psychotherapies,* M. T. Stein, ed. New York: Free Press of Glencoe.

Jackson, D. D. 1967. *Therapy, communication and change.* Palo Alto, CA: Science and Behavior Books.

Keim, J. 1998. Strategic therapy. In *Case studies in couple and family therapy,* F. Dattilio, ed. New York: Guilford Press.

Lederer, W., and Jackson, D. D. 1968. *Mirages of marriage.* New York: Norton.

Madanes, C. 1981. *Strategic family therapy.* San Francisco: Jossey-Bass.

Madanes, C. 1984. *Behind the one-way mirror.* San Francisco: Jossey-Bass.

Price, J. 1996. *Power and compassion: Working with difficult adolescents and abused parents.* New York: Guilford Press.

Rabkin, R. 1972. *Strategic psychotherapy.* New York: Basic Books.

Selvini Palazzoli, M., Boscolo, L., Cecchin, G., and Prata, G. 1978. *Paradox and counterparadox.* New York: Jason Aronson.

Tomm, K. 1987. Interventive interviewing: Part 1. Strategizing as a fourth guideline for the therapists. *Family Process.* 26: 3–14.

Watzlawick, P., Beavin, J. H., and Jackson, D. D. 1967. *Pragmatics of human communication.* New York: Norton.

Watzlawick, P., Weakland, J., and Fisch, R. 1974. *Change: Principles of problem formation and problem resolution.* New York: Norton.

—References—

Alexander, J., and Parsons, B. 1982. *Functional family therapy.* Monterey, CA: Brooks Cole.

Andersen, T. 1987. The reflecting team: Dialogue and meta-dialogue in clinical work. *Family Process. 26:* 415–417.

Boscolo, L. 1983. Final discussion. In *Psychosocial intervention in schizophrenia: An international view,* H. Stierlin, L. Wynne, and M. Wirsching, eds. Berlin: Springer-Verlag.

Boscolo, L., and Bertrando, P. 1992. The reflexive loop of past, present, and future in systemic therapy and consultation. *Family Process. 31:* 119–133.

Boscolo, L., Cecchin, G., Hoffman, L., and Penn, P. 1987. *Milan systemic family therapy.* New York: Basic Books.

Cecchin, G. 1987. Hypothesizing, circularity and neutrality revisited: An invitation to curiosity. *Family Process. 26:* 405–413.

Eron, J., and Lund, T. 1993. An approach to how problems evolve and dissolve: Integrating narrative and strategic concepts. *Family Process. 32:* 291–309.

Eron, J., and Lund, T. 1996. *Narrative solutions in brief therapy.* New York: Guilford Press.

Fisch, R. 1978. Review of problem-solving therapy, by Jay Haley. *Family Process. 17:* 107–110.

Fisch, R., Weakland, J., and Segal, L. 1982. *The tactics of change.* San Francisco: Jossey-Bass.

Haley, J. 1961. Control in psychotherapy with schizophrenics. *Archives of General Psychiatry. 5:* 340–353.

Haley, J. 1963. *Strategies of psychotherapy.* New York: Grune & Stratton.

Haley, J. 1973. *Uncommon therapy.* New York: Norton.

Haley, J. 1976. *Problem-solving therapy.* San Francisco: Jossey-Bass.

Haley, J. 1980. *Leaving home: The therapy of disturbed young people.* New York: McGraw-Hill.

Haley, J. 1981. *Reflections on therapy.* Chevy Chase, MD: The Family Therapy Institute of Washington, DC.

Haley, J. 1984. *Ordeal therapy.* San Francisco: Jossey-Bass.

Haley, J. 1996. *Learning and teaching therapy.* New York: Guilford Press.

Hoffman, L. 1983. A co-evolutionary framework for systemic family therapy. In *Diagnosis and assessment in family therapy,* J. Hansen and B. Keeney, eds. Rockville, MD: Aspen Systems.

Jackson, D. D. 1965. Family rules: The marital quid pro quo. *Archives of General Psychiatry. 12:* 589–594.

Jackson, D. D. 1967. Aspects of conjoint family therapy. In *Family therapy and disturbed families,* G. H. Zuk and I. Boszormenyi-Nagy, eds. Palo Alto: Science and Behavior Books.

Jackson, D. D., and Weakland, J. H. 1961. Conjoint family therapy: Some consideration on theory, technique, and results. *Psychiatry. 24:* 30–45.

Keim, J. 1998. Strategic family therapy. In *Case studies in couple and family therapy,* F. Dattilio, ed. New York: Guilford Press.

Keim, J., and Lappin, J. 2002. Structural-strategic marital therapy. In *Clinical handbook of couple therapy,* A. S. Gurman and N. S. Jacobson, eds. New York: Guilford Press.

Langsley, D., Machotka, P., and Flomenhaft, K. 1971. Avoiding mental hospital admission: A follow-up study. *American Journal of Psychiatry. 127:* 1391–1394.

Machal, M., Feldman, R., and Sigal, J., 1989. The unraveling of a treatment program: A follow-up study of the Milan approach to family therapy. *Family Process. 28:* 457–470.

Madanes, C. 1980. Protection, paradox and pretending. *Family Process. 19:* 73–85.

Madanes, C. 1981. *Strategic family therapy.* San Francisco: Jossey-Bass.

Madanes, C. 1984. *Behind the one-way mirror.* San Francisco: Jossey-Bass.

Marayuma, M. 1968. The second cybernetics: Deviation-amplifying mutual causal processes. In *Modern systems research for the behavioral scientist,* W. Buckley, ed. Chicago: Aldine.

Papp, P. 1980. The Greek chorus and other techniques of paradoxical therapy. *Family Process. 19:* 45–57.

Parsons, B., and Alexander, J. 1973. Short term family intervention: A therapy outcome study. *Journal of Consulting and Clinical Psychology. 41:* 95–201.

Penn, P. 1982. Circular questioning. *Family Process. 21:* 267–280.

Penn, P. 1985. Feed-forward: Further questioning, future maps. *Family Process. 24:* 299–310.

Ruesch, J., and Bateson, G. 1951. *Communication: The social matrix of psychiatry.* New York: Norton.

Satir, V. 1964. *Conjoint family therapy.* Palo Alto, CA: Science and Behavior Books.

Selvini, M. 1993. Major mental disorders. distorted reality and family secrets. Unpublished manuscript.

Selvini Palazzoli, M. 1981. *Self-starvation: From the intrapsychic to the transpersonal approach to anorexia nervosa.* New York: Jason Aronson.

Selvini Palazzoli, M. 1986. Towards a general model of psychotic games. *Journal of Marital and Family Therapy. 12:* 339–349.

Selvini Palazzoli, M., Boscolo, L., Cecchin G., and Prata, G. 1978a. A ritualized prescription in family therapy: Odd days and even days. *Journal of Marriage and Family Counseling. 4:* 3–9.

Selvini Palazzoli, M., Boscolo, L., Cecchin, G., and Prata, G. 1978b. *Paradox and counterparadox.* New York: Jason Aronson.

Selvini Palazzoli, M., Boscolo, L., Cecchin, G., and Prata, G. 1980. Hypothesizing—circularity—neutrality: Three guidelines for the conductor of the session. *Family Process. 19:* 3–12.

Selvini Palazzoli, M., and Viaro, M. 1988. The anorectic process in the family: A six-stage model as a guide for individual therapy. *Family Process. 27:* 129–148.

Shoham, V., and Rohrbaugh, M. J. 2002. Brief strategic couple therapy In *Clinical handbook of couple therapy,* A. S. Gurman and N. S. Jacobson, eds. New York: Guilford Press.

Stanton, D., Todd, T., and Associates. 1982. *The family therapy of drug abuse and addiction.* New York: Guilford Press.

Tomm, K. 1987a. Interventive interviewing: Part I. Strategizing as a fourth guideline for the therapist. *Family Process. 26:* 3–13.

Tomm, K. 1987b. Interventive interviewing: Part II. Reflexive questioning as a means to enable self-healing. *Family Process. 26:* 167–184.

Watzlawick, P. A. 1966. A structured family interview. *Family Process. 5:* 256–271.

Watzlawick, P., Beavin J., and Jackson, D. 1967. *Pragmatics of human communication.* New York: Norton.

Watzlawick, P., Weakland, J., and Fisch, R. 1974. *Change: Principles of problem formation and problem resolution.* New York: Norton.

Weakland, J., and Fisch, R. 1992. Brief therapy—MRI Style. In *The first session in brief therapy,* S. H. Budman, N. F. Hoyt, and S. Friedman, eds. New York: Guilford Press.

Weakland, J., Fisch, R., Watzlawick, P., and Bodin, A. 1974. Brief therapy: Focused problem resolution. *Family Process. 13:* 141–168.

Weakland, J., and Ray, W., eds. 1995. *Propagations: Thirty years of influence from the Mental Research Institute.* Binghamton, NY: Haworth Press.

Structural Family Therapy

One of the reasons family therapy can be difficult is that families often appear as collections of individuals who affect each other in powerful but unpredictable ways. Structural family therapy offers a framework that brings order and meaning to those transactions. The consistent patterns of family behavior are what allow us to consider that they have a **structure,** although, of course, only in a functional sense. The emotional boundaries and coalitions that make up a family's structure are abstractions; nevertheless, using the concept of family structure enables therapists to intervene in a systematic and organized way.

Families who seek help are usually concerned about a specific problem. It might be a child who misbehaves or a couple who doesn't get along. Family therapists typically look beyond the specifics of those problems to the family's attempts to solve them. This leads to the dynamics of interaction. The misbehaving child might have parents who scold but never reward him. The couple may be caught up in a pursuer–distancer dynamic, or they might be unable to talk without arguing.

What structural family therapy adds to the equation is a recognition of the overall organization that supports and maintains those interactions. The "parents who scold" might turn out to be two partners who undermine each other because one is wrapped up in the child while the other is an angry outsider. If so, attempts to encourage effective discipline are likely to fail unless the structural problem is addressed and the parents develop a real partnership. Similarly a couple who don't get along may not be able to improve their relationship until they create a boundary between themselves and intrusive children or in-laws.

The discovery that families are organized into **subsystems** with **boundaries** regulating the contact family members have with each other turned out to be one of the defining insights of family therapy. Perhaps equally important, though, was the introduction of the technique of **enactment,** in which family members are encouraged to deal directly with each other in sessions, permitting the therapist to observe and modify their interactions.

Evolution of the Model

When he first burst onto the scene, Salvador Minuchin's galvanizing impact was as a master of technique. His most lasting contribution, however, was a theory of family structure and set of guidelines to organize therapeutic techniques. This structural approach was so successful that it captivated the field in the 1970s, and Minuchin built the Philadelphia Child Guidance

Salvador Minuchin

Born and raised in Argentina, Salvador Minuchin began his career as a family therapist in the early 1960s when he discovered two patterns common to troubled families: Some are "enmeshed," chaotic and tightly interconnected, while others are "disengaged," isolated and seemingly unrelated. In his classic text, *Families and Family Therapy*, Minuchin (1974) taught therapists to see family relationships and patterns more clearly. In 1965 Minuchin became the director of the Philadelphia Child Guidance Clinic, which eventually became the world's leading center for family therapy.

In 1969, Minuchin, Haley, Braulio Montalvo, and Bernice Rosman developed a highly successful training program that emphasized hands-on experience, on-line supervision, and the use of videotapes to learn and apply the techniques of structural family therapy. In 1981, Minuchin established a center for the practice and training of structural family therapy in New York, which after his retirement in 1996 was renamed the Minuchin Center for the Family.

Clinic into a world-famous complex, where thousands of family therapists have been trained in structural family therapy.

Minuchin was born and raised in Argentina. He served as a physician in the Israeli army, then came to the United States, where he studied child psychiatry with Nathan Ackerman. After completing his training, Minuchin returned to Israel in 1952 to work with displaced children. He moved back to the United States in 1954 to begin psychoanalytic training at the William Alanson White Institute, where he studied the interpersonal psychiatry of Harry Stack Sullivan. After leaving the White Institute, Minuchin took a job at the Wiltwyck School for delinquent boys, where he suggested to his staff that they start seeing families.

At Wiltwyck, Minuchin and his colleagues—Dick Auerswald, Charlie King, Braulio Montalvo, and Clara Rabinowitz—taught themselves family therapy, inventing it as they went along. To do so, they built a one-way mirror and took turns observing each other work. In 1962 Minuchin made a hajj to what was then the Mecca of family therapy, Palo Alto. There he met Jay Haley and began a friendship that blossomed into an extraordinarily fertile collaboration.

The success of Minuchin's work with families at Wiltwyck led to a groundbreaking book, *Families of the Slums* (Minuchin, Montalvo, Guerney, Rosman, & Schumer, 1967). Minuchin's reputation as a virtuoso therapist grew, and he was invited to become the director of the Philadelphia Child Guidance Clinic in 1965. The clinic then consisted of fewer than a dozen staff members. From this modest beginning, Minuchin created one of the largest and most prestigious child guidance clinics in the world.

Among Minuchin's colleagues in Philadelphia were Braulio Montalvo, Jay Haley, Bernice

Rosman, Harry Aponte, Carter Umbarger, Marianne Walters, Charles Fishman, Cloe Madanes, and Stephen Greenstein, all of whom had a role in shaping structural family therapy. By the 1970s, structural family therapy had become the most widely practiced of all systems of family therapy.

After leaving Philadelphia in 1981, Minuchin started his own center in New York, where he continued to practice and teach until 1996, when he retired and moved to Boston. Although he retired (again) and moved to Boca Raton, Florida in 2005, Dr. Minuchin still travels and teaches throughout the world.

Like players on a team with a superstar, some of Minuchin's colleagues are not as well known as they might be. Foremost among these is Braulio Montalvo, one of the underrated geniuses of family therapy. Born and raised in Puerto Rico, Montalvo, like Minuchin, has always been committed to treating poor and minority families. Like Minuchin, he is also a brilliant therapist, though he favors a gentler, more supportive approach.

Following Minuchin's retirement, the center in New York was renamed the Minuchin Center for the Family, and the torch has been passed to a new generation. Among Minuchin's prominent students are Jorge Colapinto, now at the Ackerman Institute in New York; Jay Lappin, who works with child welfare for the state of Delaware; Michael Nichols, who teaches at the College of William and Mary; and Charles Fishman, in private practice in Philadelphia.

The Basic Model

Beginners tend to get bogged down in the content of family problems because they don't have a blueprint to help them see the patterns of family dynamics. Structural family therapy offers such a blueprint and provides a basis for organizing strategies of treatment. Three constructs are the essential components of structural family theory: *structure, subsystems,* and *boundaries.*

Family structure is built up from the repetitive sequences of a family's interactions.

Once patterns are established, family members use only a fraction of the full range of behavior available to them. The first time the baby cries or a teenager misses the school bus, it's not clear who will do what. Will the load be shared? Will a quarrel ensue? Will one person get stuck with most of the work? Soon, however, patterns are set, roles assigned, and things take on a sameness and predictability. "Who's going to . . . ?" becomes "She'll probably . . ." and then "She always. . . ."

Family structure is reinforced by the expectations that establish rules in the family. For example, a rule such as "family members should always protect one another" will be manifest in various ways. If a boy gets into a fight with another boy in the neighborhood, his mother will go to the neighbors to complain. If a teenager has to get up early for school, mother wakes her. If a husband is too hung over to go to work in the morning, his wife calls in to say he has the flu. If the parents have an argument, their children interrupt. The parents are so preoccupied with the doings of their children that it keeps them from spending time alone together. These sequences are *isomorphic:* They're structured. Changing any of them may not alter the basic structure, but modifying the underlying structure will have ripple effects on all family transactions.

Family structure is shaped partly by universal and partly by idiosyncratic constraints. For example, all families have some kind of **hierarchical structure,** with adults and children having different amounts of authority. Family members also tend to have reciprocal and complementary functions. Often these become so ingrained that their origins are forgotten and they are presumed necessary rather than optional. If a young mother, overwhelmed by the demands of her infant, gets upset and complains to her husband, he may respond in various ways. Perhaps he'll move closer and share the burdens of childrearing. This creates a united parental team. If, on the other hand, he decides that his wife is "depressed," she may end up in psychotherapy for the emotional support she needs. This creates a structure in which the mother remains distant from her husband and learns to turn outside the family for sympathy. Whatever the pattern, it tends to be self-perpetuating. Although alternatives are available, families are unlikely to consider them until changing circumstances produce stress in the system.

Families don't walk in and hand you their structural patterns as if they were bringing an apple to the teacher. What they bring is chaos and confusion. You have to uncover the subtext—and you have to be careful that it's accurate—not imposed but discovered. Two things are necessary: a theoretical system that explains structure, and seeing the family in action. Knowing that a family is a single-parent family, or that parents are having trouble with their middle child doesn't tell you what their structure is. Structure becomes evident only when you observe actual interactions among family members.

Consider the following: A mother calls to complain of misbehavior in her seventeen-year-old son. She is asked to bring her husband, son, and the three younger children to the first session. When they arrive, the mother describes a series of minor ways in which the son is disobedient. He interrupts to say that she's always on his case, he never gets a break from his mother. This spontaneous bickering between mother and son reveals a preoccupation with each other—a preoccupation no less intense simply because it's conflictual. This sequence doesn't, however, tell the whole story. It doesn't include the father or the other children. They must be engaged to observe their roles in the family structure. If the father sides with his wife but seems unconcerned, then it may be that the mother's preoccupation with her son is related to her husband's neglect. If the three younger children side with their mother and describe their brother as bad, then it becomes clear that all the children are close to

their mother—close and obedient up to a point, then close and disobedient.

Families are differentiated into *subsystems*—based on generation, gender, and function—which are demarcated by interpersonal boundaries, invisible barriers that regulate contact with others. A rule forbidding phone calls at dinnertime establishes a boundary that shields the family from intrusion. Subsystems that aren't adequately protected by boundaries limit the development of relationship skills. If children are permitted to interrupt their parents' conversations, the boundary separating the generations is eroded and the couple's relationship is subverted to parenting. If parents always step in to settle arguments between their children, the children won't learn to fight their own battles.

Interpersonal boundaries vary from rigid to diffuse (Figure 7.1). Rigid boundaries are restrictive and permit little contact with outside subsystems, resulting in **disengagement.** Disengaged subsystems are independent but isolated. On the plus side, this fosters autonomy. On the other hand, disengagement limits affection and support. Disengaged families must come under extreme stress before they mobilize assistance. **Enmeshed** subsystems offer closeness and support but at the expense of independent competence. Too much closeness cripples initiative.

Although "structure" suggests a static condition, Minuchin (1974) also described developmental aspects of family organization. Families begin when two people in love decide to share their lives together, but a period of often difficult adjustment is required before they complete the transition from courtship to a functional partnership. They must learn to **accommodate** to each other's needs and styles of interaction. He learns to accommodate to her wish to be kissed hello and good-bye. She learns to leave

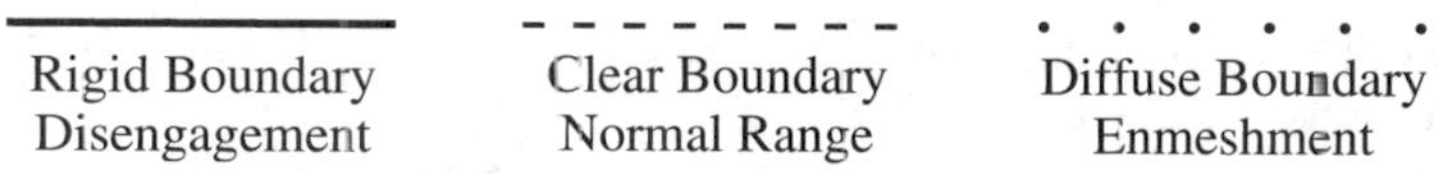

| Rigid Boundary | Clear Boundary | Diffuse Boundary |
| Disengagement | Normal Range | Enmeshment |

FIGURE 7.1 Interpersonal Boundaries

him alone with his paper and morning coffee. These little arrangements, multiplied a thousand times, may be accomplished easily or only after intense struggle. Whatever the case, this process of accommodation cements the couple into a unit.

The spouse subsystem must also develop a boundary that separates it from parents, children, and other outsiders. All too often, husband and wife give up the space they need for mutual support when children are born. Too rigid a boundary around the couple can deprive the children of care and attention, but in our child-centered culture the boundary between parents and children is often ambiguous at best.

In *Institutionalizing Madness* (Elizur & Minuchin, 1989), Minuchin makes a compelling case for a structural view of emotional problems that extends beyond the family itself to encompass the entire community. As Minuchin points out, unless therapists learn to look beyond the limited slice of ecology in which they work to the larger social structures within which their work is embedded, their efforts may amount to little more than spinning wheels.

Normal Family Development

What distinguishes a normal family isn't an absence of problems, but a functional structure for dealing with them. All couples must learn to adjust to each other, raise their children, deal with their parents, cope with their jobs, and fit into their communities. The nature of these struggles changes with developmental stages and situational crises.

When two people join to form a couple, the structural requirements for the new union are *accommodation* and *boundary making*. The first priority is mutual accommodation to manage the myriad details of everyday living. Each partner tries to organize the relationship along familiar lines and pressures the other to comply. They must agree on major issues, such as where to live and if and when to have children. Less obvious, but equally important, they must coordinate daily rituals, like what to watch on television,

what to eat for supper, when to go to bed, and what to do there.

In accommodating to each other, a couple must negotiate the boundary between them as well as the boundary protecting them from the outside. Each partner tends to be more comfortable with the level of closeness that existed in his or her own family. Because these expectations differ, a struggle ensues that may be the most difficult aspect of a new union. He wants to play poker with the boys; she feels deserted. She wants to talk; he wants to watch ESPN. His focus is on his career; her focus is on the relationship. Each thinks the other unreasonable, and terribly hurtful.

Couples must also define a boundary separating them from their original families. Rather suddenly the families they grew up in must take second place to the new marriage. This, too, can be a difficult adjustment, both for newlyweds and for their parents.

The birth of a child instantly transforms the family structure; the pattern of interaction between the *parental subsystem* and *child subsystem* must be worked out and later modified to fit changing circumstances. A clear boundary enables the children to interact with their parents but excludes them from the spouse subsystem. Parents and children may eat together, play together, and share much of each others' lives. But there are some things that need not be shared. Husband and wife are sustained as a loving couple, and enhanced as parents, if they make time to be alone together—to talk, to go out to dinner occasionally, to fight, and to make love. Unhappily, the clamorous demands of children often make parents lose sight of their need to maintain the integrity of their relationship.

In addition to maintaining privacy for the couple, a clear generational boundary establishes a hierarchical structure and allows parents to exercise a position of leadership. All too often this hierarchy is subverted by a child-centered ethos, which affects helping professionals as well as parents. Parents enmeshed with their children tend to argue with them about who's in charge and to misguidedly share—or shirk—

responsibility for making parental decisions. Offering a child a choice in picking out clothes or choosing friends encourages self-reliance. Asking children whether they want to go to school or trying to convince a toddler that it's dangerous to play in the street simply blurs the line of authority.

Minuchin (1974) warns therapists not to mistake growing pains for pathology. The normal family experiences anxiety and disruption as its members grow and change. Many families seek help at transitional stages, and therapists should keep in mind that family members may simply be in the process of modifying their structure to adjust to new circumstances.

Development of Behavior Disorders

Modifications in structure are required when the family or one of its members encounters external pressures (a parent is laid off, the family moves) and when developmental transitions are reached (a child reaches adolescence, parents retire). Healthy families accommodate to changed circumstances; less adaptive families increase the rigidity of structures that are no longer functional.

In disengaged families, boundaries are rigid and the family fails to mobilize support when it's needed. Disengaged parents may be unaware that a child is depressed or experiencing difficulties at school until the problem is advanced.

A single mother recently brought her twelve-year-old son to the clinic after discovering that he had missed two weeks of school. *Two weeks!* thought the therapist, that's a long time not to know your child has been skipping school. A structural perspective would make two important points. First, the obvious disengagement between this mother and child is no more significant than the disengagement between the mother and school authorities. Second, a structural analysis might help to get past blaming this woman for failing to know what was going on in her son's life. If she's disengaged from her son, what is occupying her elsewhere? Maybe the financial burden of single parenthood is simply

overwhelming. Maybe she's still grief-stricken over the death of her husband. The point to remember is that if someone is disengaged in one relationship, he or she is likely to be preoccupied elsewhere.

In enmeshed families, boundaries are diffuse and family members become dependent on one another. Intrusive parents create difficulties by stunting the development of their children and interfering with their ability to solve their own problems.

Although we may refer to enmeshed and disengaged families, it's more accurate to think of particular subsystems as being enmeshed or disengaged. In fact enmeshment and disengagement tend to be reciprocal, so that, for example, a father who's overly involved with his work is likely to neglect his family. A frequently encountered pattern is the enmeshed-mother/disengaged-father syndrome—"the signature arrangement of the troubled middle-class family" (Minuchin & Nichols, 1993, p. 121)

Feminists have criticized the notion of an enmeshed-mother/disengaged-father syndrome because they worry about blaming mothers for an arrangement that is culturally sanctioned. This concern is valid. But prejudice and blaming are due to insensitive application of these ideas, not inherent in the ideas themselves. Skewed relationships, whatever the reason for them, can be problematic, though naturally no single family member should be blamed or expected to unilaterally redress imbalances.

Structural therapists use a few simple symbols to diagram structural problems, and these diagrams usually suggest what changes are required. Figure 7.2 shows some of the symbols used to diagram family structure.

One problem often seen by family therapists arises when parents who are unable to resolve conflicts between themselves divert the focus of concern onto a child. Instead of worrying about each other, they worry about the child (see Figure 7.3). Although this reduces the strain on father (F) and mother (M), it victimizes the child (C).

An equally common pattern is when "conflicts between the spouses are played out in the

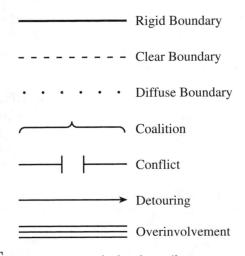

FIGURE 7.2   **Symbols of Family Structure**

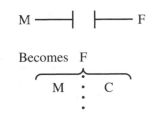

FIGURE 7.4   **Mother–Child Coalition**

parenting battlefield—and as they pull in different directions, the confused children become casualties" (Minuchin & Nichols, 1993, p. 149). Father says mother is too permissive; she says he's too strict. He may withdraw, causing her to criticize his lack of involvement, which in turn causes further withdrawal. The enmeshed mother responds to the child's needs with excessive concern. The disengaged father tends not to respond at all. Both may be critical of the other's way, but they perpetuate each other's behavior with their own. The result is a **cross-generational coalition** between mother and child (Figure 7.4).

Some families function well when the children are young but are unable to adjust to a growing child's need for discipline and control. Young children in enmeshed families (Figure 7.5) re-

ceive wonderful care: Their parents give them lots of attention. Although such parents may be too tired to have much time for each other, the system may be moderately successful.

If, however, these doting parents don't teach their children to obey rules and respect authority, the children may be unprepared to negotiate their entrance into school. Used to getting their own way, they may be unruly and disruptive. Several possible consequences may bring the family into treatment. The children may be reluctant to go to school, and their fears may be reinforced by "understanding" parents who permit them to stay home (Figure 7.6). Such a case may be labeled as school phobia and may become entrenched if parents permit their children to remain at home for more than a few days.

Alternatively, the children of such a family may go to school but, because they haven't learned to accommodate to others, they may be rejected by their schoolmates. Such children often become depressed and withdrawn. In other cases, children enmeshed with their parents become discipline problems, in which case school authorities may initiate counseling.

A major upheaval that requires structural adjustment occurs when divorced partners remarry. Such "blended families" either readjust

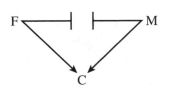

FIGURE 7.3   **Scapegoating as a Means of Detouring Conflict**

F • • • • • M
• • • • • •
Children

FIGURE 7.5   **Parents Enmeshed with Children**

FIGURE 7.6 School Phobia

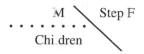

FIGURE 7.8 Failure to Accept a Stepparent

their boundaries or soon experience transitional conflicts. When a woman divorces, she and her children must learn to readjust to a structure that establishes a clear boundary separating the divorced spouses but still permits contact between father and children; then if she remarries, the family must readjust to functioning with a new husband and stepfather (Figure 7.7).

Sometimes it's hard for a mother and children to allow a stepfather to participate in the parental subsystem. Mother and children have long since established transactional rules and learned to accommodate to each other. The new parent may be treated as an outsider who's supposed to learn the "right" way of doing things, rather than as a new partner who will give as well as receive ideas about childrearing (Figure 7.8).

The more mother and children insist on maintaining their familiar patterns without in-

cluding the stepfather, the more frustrated and angry he'll become. The result may lead to child abuse or chronic arguing between the parents. The sooner such families enter treatment, the easier it is to help them adjust to the transition.

An important aspect of structural problems is that symptoms in one family member reflect not only that person's connections, but also other relationships in the family. If Johnny, age sixteen, is depressed, it's helpful to know that he's enmeshed with his mother. Discovering that she demands absolute obedience and refuses to accept independent thinking or outside relationships helps to explain his depression (Figure 7.9). But that's only a partial view of the family system.

Why is the mother enmeshed with her son? Perhaps she's disengaged from her husband. Perhaps she's a widow who hasn't found new friends, a job, or other interests. Helping Johnny resolve his depression may best be accomplished by helping his mother satisfy her own needs for closeness with other adults in her life.

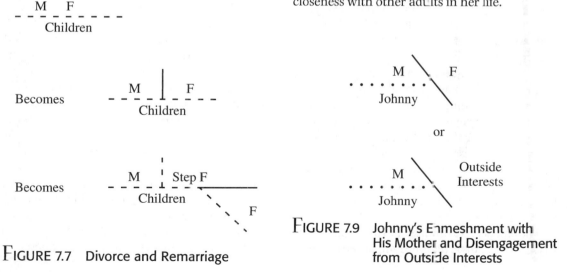

FIGURE 7.7 Divorce and Remarriage

FIGURE 7.9 Johnny's Enmeshment with His Mother and Disengagement from Outside Interests

How Therapy Works

Structural treatment is designed to alter the organization of the family so that its members can better deal with their own problems. The goal of therapy is structural change; problem solving is a byproduct.

By adjusting boundaries and realigning subsystems, the therapist changes the behavior and experience of each of the family members and thus opens alternative patterns of interaction that can modify family structure. Far from seeing families as inherently flawed, structural therapists see their work as activating latent adaptive patterns that are already in client families' repertoires (Simon, 1995). It's not a matter of creating new structures but of activating dormant ones.

Although every family is unique, families have common structural goals. Most important is the creation of an effective hierarchy. Parents are expected to be in charge, not to relate as equals to their children. With enmeshed families, the goal is to differentiate individuals and subsystems by strengthening the boundaries around them. With disengaged families, the goal is to increase interaction by making boundaries more permeable.

The therapist produces change by joining the family, probing for areas of flexibility, and then activating dormant structural alternatives. **Joining** gets the therapist into the family; *accommodating* to their style gives him leverage; and *restructuring* maneuvers transform the family structure.

To join a family, the therapist conveys acceptance of family members and respect for their ways of doing things. If parents come for help with a child's problems, the therapist doesn't begin by asking for the child's opinion. This would convey lack of respect for the parents. Only after successfully joining with a family is it fruitful to attempt restructuring—the often dramatic confrontations that challenge families and encourage them to change.

The first task is to understand the family's view of their problems. This is accomplished by tracking their perspectives, in the content they use to explain them and in the process with which they demonstrate them. The family therapist then **reframes** these formulations into one based on an understanding of family structure.

What makes structural family therapy unique is that it uses *enactments* within therapy sessions to bring about the reframing. This is the *sine qua non* of structural family therapy: observing and modifying family transactions in the immediate context of the session. Structural therapists work with what they *see*, not with what family members describe.

Therapy

Assessment

Because problems are a function of the entire family structure, it's important to include the whole group for assessment. For example, if a father complains of a child's misbehavior, seeing the child alone won't help the father to state rules clearly or enforce them effectively. Nor will seeing the father and child together stop the stepmother from undercutting the father's authority. Only by seeing the whole family interacting is it possible to get a complete picture of their structure.

Sometimes even the whole family isn't enough, because the family may not always be the complete or even most relevant context. A mother's depression might be due to problems at work. A son's difficulties at school might be due more to the situation at school than to the one in the family. In such instances, structural therapists work with the most relevant context.

Finally, some problems may be treated as problems of the individual. As Minuchin (1974) has written, "Pathology may be inside the patient, in his social context, or in the feedback between them" (p. 9). Elsewhere Minuchin (Minuchin, Rosman, & Baker, 1978) referred to the danger of "denying the individual while enthroning the system" (p. 91). While interviewing a family to see how the parents deal with their children, a careful observer might notice that one child has a neurological problem or a learning disability. Such problems need to be identified and appropriate referrals made. Usually when a child has trouble in school, there's a problem in the family or school context. Usually, but not always.

Dr. Minuchin and his colleagues have recently written a book in which the process of assessment is organized in four steps (Minuchin, Nichols, & Lee, 2007). The first step is to ask questions about the presenting complaint until family members begin to see that the problem goes beyond the symptom bearer to include the whole family. The second step is to help family members see how their interactions may inadvertently be perpetuating the presenting problem. The third step is a brief exploration of the past, focusing on how the adults in the family came to develop the perspectives that now influence their problematic interactions. The fourth step is to explore options that family members can take to interact in more productive ways that will create a shift in the family structure and help resolve the presenting complaint.

Therapeutic Techniques

In *Families and Family Therapy*, Minuchin (1974) listed three overlapping stages in structural family therapy. The therapist (1) joins the family in a position of leadership, (2) maps the family's underlying structure, and (3) intervenes to transform this structure. This program is simple, in the sense that it follows a clear plan, but complicated because of the endless variety of family patterns.

If they are to be effective, a therapist's moves cannot be preplanned or rehearsed. Good therapists are more than technicians. The strategy of therapy, on the other hand, must be organized. In general, structural family therapy follows these steps:

1. Joining and accommodating;
2. Enactment;
3. Structural mapping;
4. Highlighting and modifying interactions;
5. Boundary making;
6. Unbalancing;
7. Challenging unproductive assumptions.

Joining and Accommodating. Individual patients generally enter therapy already predisposed to accept the therapist's authority. By seeking treatment, an individual tacitly acknowledges suffering, need for help, and willingness to trust the therapist. Not so with families.

The family therapist is an unwelcome outsider. After all, why did she insist on seeing the whole family? Family members expect to be told that they're doing something wrong, and they're prepared to defend themselves.

The therapist must first disarm defenses and ease anxiety. This is done by building an alliance of understanding with each member of the family.

Everyone has a story to tell, and in unhappy families almost everyone feels misunderstood. The first step in breaking the cycle of misunderstanding is to offer the empathy family members may be temporarily unable to provide each other. Hearing, understanding, and acknowledging each person's account of the family's sorrows provides information—and begins to release family members from the resentment of unheard feelings. Joining, as this empathic connection is called, opens the way for family members to begin listening to each other and establishes a bond with the therapist that enables them to accept the challenges to come.

These initial conversations convey respect, not only for the individuals in the family but also for the family's structure and organization. The therapist shows respect for parents by honoring their authority. They, not their children, are asked first to describe the problems. If a family elects one person to speak for the others, the therapist notes this but does not initially challenge it.

Children also have special concerns and capacities. They should be greeted gently and asked simple, concrete questions, "Hi, I'm so-and-so; what's your name? Oh, Laura, that's a nice name. Where do you go to school, Laura?" Avoid the usual grown-up questions ("And what do *you* want to be when you grow up?"). Try something a little fresher ("What do you hate most about school?"). Those who wish to remain silent should be "allowed" to do so. They will anyway. "And what's your view of the problem?" (Grim silence.) "I see, you don't feel like saying anything right now? That's fine; perhaps you'll have something to say later."

It's particularly important to join powerful family members as well as angry ones. Special pains must be taken to accept the point of view of the father who thinks therapy is hooey or of the embittered teenager who feels like an accused criminal. It's also important to reconnect with such people at frequent intervals, particularly when things begin to heat up.

Enactment.   Family structure is manifest in the way family members interact. It can't always be inferred from their descriptions. Therefore, asking questions such as "Who's in charge?" or "Do you two agree?" tends to be unproductive. Families generally describe themselves more as they think they should be than as they are.

Getting family members to talk with each other runs counter to their expectations. They expect to present their case to an expert and then be told what to do. If asked to discuss something in the session, they'll say: "We've already talked about this"; or "It won't do any good, he (or she) doesn't listen"; or "But *you're* supposed to be the expert."

If the therapist begins by giving each person a chance to speak, usually one will say something about another that can be a springboard for an **enactment.** When, for example, one parent says that the other is too strict, the therapist can initiate an enactment by saying: "She says you're too strict; can you answer her?" Picking a specific issue for response is more effective than vague requests, such as "Why don't you talk this over?"

Enactments require three operations. First, the therapist notices a problematic sequence. Perhaps, for example, when mother talks to her daughter they relate like peers, and little brother gets left out. Second, the therapist initiates an enactment. For example, the therapist might say

to the mother, "Talk this over with your kids." Third, and most important, the therapist must guide the family to modify the enactment. If mother talks to her children in such a way that she doesn't take responsibility for major decisions, the therapist encourages her to do so as the family continues the enactment.

Once an enactment breaks down, the therapist intervenes in one of two ways: commenting on what went wrong or simply pushing them to keep going. For example, if a father responds to the suggestion to talk with his ten-year-old daughter about how she's feeling by berating her, the therapist could say to the father: "Congratulations." *Father:* "What do you mean?" *Therapist:* "Congratulations; you win, she loses." Or the therapist could simply nudge the transaction by saying to the father: "Good, keep talking, but help her express her feelings more. She's still a little girl; she needs your help."

Once an enactment is begun, the therapist can discover many things about a family's structure. How long can two people talk without being interrupted—that is, how clear is the boundary around their relationship? Does one attack, the other defend? Who is central, who peripheral? Do parents bring children into their discussions—that is, are they enmeshed?

Families demonstrate enmeshment by frequent interruptions, speaking for each other, doing things for children that they can do for themselves, or constantly arguing. In disengaged families one may see a husband sitting impassively while his wife cries; a total absence of conflict; a surprising ignorance of important information about the children; or a lack of concern for each other's interests.

If, as soon as the first session starts, the children begin running around the room while their parents protest ineffectually, the therapist doesn't need to hear what goes on at home to see the executive incompetence. If a mother and daughter rant and rave at each other while the father sits silently in the corner, it isn't necessary to ask how involved he is at home. In fact, asking may yield a less accurate picture than the one revealed spontaneously.

Structural Mapping. Preliminary assessments are based on interactions in the first session. In later sessions these formulations are refined and revised. Although there is some danger of bending families to fit categories when they're applied early, the greater danger is waiting too long. Families quickly *induct* therapists into their culture. A family that initially appears to be chaotic and enmeshed soon comes to be just the familiar Jones family. For this reason, it's critical to develop provisional hypotheses relatively early in the process.

Suppose, for example, that you're about to see a mother, her sixteen-year-old daughter, and the stepfather. The mother called to complain about her daughter's misbehavior. What do you imagine the structure might be? How would you test your hypothesis? A good guess might be that mother and daughter are enmeshed, excluding the stepfather. This can be tested in the session by seeing if mother and daughter talk mostly about each other— whether positively or negatively. The stepfather's disengagement would be confirmed if he and his wife were unable to converse without the daughter's intrusion.

Structural assessments take into account both the problem the family presents and the structural dynamics they display. And they include all family members. In this instance, knowing that the mother and daughter are enmeshed isn't enough; you also have to know what role the stepfather plays. If he's close with his wife but distant from the daughter, finding mutually enjoyable activities for stepfather and stepdaughter will help increase the girl's independence from her mother. On the other hand, if the mother's proximity to her daughter appears to be a function of her distance from her husband, then the marital pair might be the most productive focus.

Highlighting and Modifying Interactions. Once families begin to interact, problematic transactions emerge. Recognizing their structural implications requires focusing on process, not content.

Perhaps a wife complains, "We have a communication problem. My husband won't talk to me; he never expresses his feelings." The therapist then initiates an enactment to see what actually does happen. "Your wife says it's a communication problem; can you respond to that? Talk with her." If, when they talk, the wife becomes domineering and critical while the husband grows increasingly silent, then the therapist sees what's wrong: The problem isn't that he doesn't talk (which is a linear explanation). Nor is the problem simply that she nags (also a linear explanation). The problem is that the more she nags, the more he withdraws, and the more he withdraws, the more she nags.

The trick is to modify this pattern. This may require forceful intervening, or what structural therapists call **intensity.**

Structural therapists achieve intensity by selective regulation of affect, repetition, and duration. Tone, volume, pacing, and choice of words can be used to raise affective intensity. It helps if you know what you want to say. Here's an example of a limp statement: "People are always concerned with themselves, kind of seeing themselves as the center of attention and just looking for whatever they can get. Wouldn't it be nice, for a change, if everybody started thinking about what they could do for others?" Compare that with, "Ask not what your country can do for you—ask what you can do for your country." John Kennedy's words had impact because they were brief and to the point. Therapists don't need to make speeches, but they do occasionally have to speak forcefully to get the point across.

Affective intensity isn't simply a matter of clever phrasing. You have to know how and when to be provocative. For example, Mike Nichols was recently working with a family in which a twenty-nine-year-old woman with anorexia nervosa was the identified patient. Although the family maintained a facade of togetherness, it was rigidly structured; the mother and her anorexic daughter were enmeshed, while the father was excluded. In this family, the father was the only one to express anger openly, and this was part of the official rationale for why he was excluded. His daughter was afraid of his anger, which she freely admitted. What was less clear, however, was that the mother had covertly taught the daughter to avoid her father, because she herself couldn't deal with him. Consequently, the daughter grew up afraid of her father, and of men in general.

> At one point the father, describing how isolated he felt from his daughter, said he thought it was because she feared his anger. The daughter agreed, "It's his fault, all right." The therapist asked the mother what she thought, and she replied, "It isn't *his* fault."
>
> The therapist said, "You're right."
>
> The mother went on, denying her real feelings to avoid conflict, "It's no one's fault."
>
> The therapist answered in a way that got her attention, "That's not true."
>
> Startled, she asked what he meant.
>
> "It's *your* fault," he said.

This level of intensity was necessary to interrupt a rigid pattern of conflict–avoidance that sustained a destructive **coalition** between mother and daughter. The content—who really is afraid of anger—was less important than the structural goal: freeing the daughter from her over-involvement with her mother.

Intensity can also be achieved by extending the duration of a sequence beyond the point where homeostasis sets back in. A common example is the management of tantrums. Temper tantrums are maintained by parents who give in. They *try* not to give in; they just don't try long enough. Recently a four-year-old girl began to scream bloody murder when her sister left the room. She wanted to go with her sister. Her screaming was almost unbearable, and the parents were ready to back down. However, the therapist urged that they not allow themselves to be defeated and suggested that they hold her until she calmed down. She screamed for thirty minutes! Everyone in the room was frazzled. But the little girl finally realized that she was not going to get her way, and so she calmed down. Subsequently, the parents were able to use the same intensity of duration to break her of this destructive habit.

Sometimes intensity requires repetition of a theme in a variety of contexts. Infantilizing parents may have to be told not to hang up their child's coat, not to speak for her, not to take her to the bathroom, and not to do many other things that she's able to do for herself.

What we're calling "intensity" may strike some as overly aggressive. Although there's no denying that Minuchin and his followers tend to be interventionists, the point of intensity is not to bully people but to push them past the point where they give up on getting through to each other. An alternative strategy is the use of **empathy** to help family members get beneath the surface of their defensive wrangling.

If, for example, the parents of a disobedient child are locked in a cycle of unproductive quarreling in which the mother attacks the father for not being involved and he responds with excuses, a therapist could use intensity to push them to come up with a plan for dealing with their child's behavior. Or, the therapist could interrupt their squabbling and, using empathy, talk to them one at a time about what they're feeling. The wife who shows only anger might be covering up the hurt and longing she feels. The husband who neither gets involved nor fights back when he feels attacked might be too annoyed at his wife's anger to see that she needs him. Once these more genuine kinds of emotions are articulated, they can serve as a basis for clients reconnecting with each other in a less defensive manner.

Shaping competence is another method of modifying interactions, and it's a hallmark of structural family therapy. Intensity is used to block the stream of interactions. Shaping competence is like altering the direction of flow. By reinforcing positives, structural therapists help family members use functional alternatives that are already in their repertoire.

Even when people make a lot of mistakes, it's usually possible to pick out something they're doing successfully. A sense of timing helps. For example, in a large chaotic family the parents were extremely ineffective at controlling their children. At one point the therapist turned to the mother and said, "It's too noisy in here; would you quiet the kids?" Knowing how much difficulty the woman had with discipline, the therapist was poised to comment on any step in the direction of effective management. The mother had to yell "Quiet!" a couple of times before the children momentarily stopped what they were doing. Quickly—before the children resumed their misbehavior—the therapist complimented her for "loving her kids enough to be firm with them." Thus the message was "You're a competent person, you know how to be firm." If the therapist had waited until the chaos resumed before telling the mother she should be firmer, the message would be "You're incompetent."

Boundary Making. In enmeshed families, interventions are designed to strengthen boundaries. Family members are urged to speak for themselves, interruptions are blocked, and dyads are helped to finish conversations without intrusion. A therapist who wishes to support the sibling system and protect it from unnecessary parental intrusion might say, "Susie and Sean, talk this over, and everyone else will listen carefully." If children interrupt their parents, a therapist might challenge the parents to strengthen the hierarchical boundary by saying, "Why don't you get them to butt out so that you two grownups can settle this."

Although structural therapy is begun with the whole family, subsequent sessions may be held with individuals or subgroups to strengthen their boundaries. An overprotected teenager is supported as an independent person with individual needs by participating in some individual sessions. Parents so enmeshed with their children that they never have private conversations may begin to learn how if they meet separately with the therapist.

When a forty-year-old woman called the clinic for help with depression, she was asked to come in with the rest of her family. It soon became apparent that this woman was overburdened by her four children and received little support from her husband, either as a mate or a father. The therapist's strategy was to strengthen the boundary between the mother

and children and help the parents move closer together. This was done in stages. First the therapist joined the oldest child, a sixteen-year-old girl, and supported her competence as a potential helper for her mother. Once this was done, the girl was able to assume a good deal of responsibility for her younger siblings, both in sessions and at home.

Freed from their preoccupation with the children, the parents now had the opportunity to talk more with each other. They had little to say, however. This wasn't the result of hidden conflict but instead reflected a marriage of two relatively nonverbal people. After several sessions of trying to get the pair talking, the therapist realized that, although talking may be fun for some people, it might not be for others. So, to support the bond between the couple, the therapist asked them to plan a special trip together. They chose a boat ride on a nearby lake. When they returned for the next session, they were beaming. They had a wonderful time. Subsequently, they decided to spend a little time out together each week.

Unbalancing. In boundary making, the therapist aims to realign relationships *between* subsystems. In unbalancing, the goal is to change relationships *within* a subsystem. What often keeps families stuck in stalemate is that members in conflict are balanced in opposition and, as a result, remain frozen in inaction. In unbalancing, the therapist joins and supports one individual or subsystem.

Taking sides—let's call it what it is—seems like a violation of therapy's sacred cannon of neutrality. However, the therapist takes sides to unbalance and realign the system, not because she is the arbiter of right and wrong. Ultimately, balance and fairness are achieved because the therapist sides in turn with various members of the family.

For example, when the MacLean family sought help for an "unmanageable" child, a terror who'd been expelled from two schools, Dr. Minuchin uncovered a covert split between the parents, held in balance by not being talked about. The ten-year-old's misbehavior was dramatically visible; his father had to drag him kicking and screaming into the consulting room. Meanwhile, his little brother sat quietly, smiling engagingly. The good boy.

To broaden the focus from an "impossible child" to issues of parental control and cooperation, Minuchin asked about seven-year-old Kevin, who misbehaved invisibly. He peed on the floor in the bathroom. According to his father, Kevin's peeing on the floor was due to "inattentiveness." The mother laughed when Minuchin said "nobody could have such poor aim."

Minuchin talked with the boy about how wolves mark their territory and suggested that he expand his territory by peeing in all four corners of the family room.

Minuchin: "Do you have a dog?"
Kevin: "No."
Minuchin: "Oh, so you're the family dog?"

In the process of discussing the boy who peed—and his parents' response—Minuchin dramatized how the parents polarized and undercut each other.

Minuchin: "Why would he do such a thing?"
Father: "I don't know if he did it on purpose."
Minuchin: "Maybe he was in a trance?"
Father: "No, I think it was carelessness."
Minuchin: "His aim must be terrible."

The father described the boy's behavior as accidental; the mother considered it defiant. One reason parents fall under the control of their young children is that they avoid confronting their differences. Differences are normal, but they become detrimental when one parent undercuts the other's handling of the children. (It's cowardly revenge for unaddressed grievances.)

Minuchin's gentle but insistent pressure on the couple to talk about how they respond, without switching to how the children behave, led to their bringing up long-held but seldom-voiced resentments.

Mother: "Bob makes excuses for the children's behavior because he doesn't want to get in there and help me find a solution for the problem."
Father: "Yes, but when I did try to help, you'd always criticize me. So after a while I gave up."

Like a photographic print in a developing tray, the spouses' conflict had become visible. Minuchin protected the parents from embarrassment (and the children from being burdened) by asking the children to leave the room. Without the preoccupation of parenting, the spouses could face each other, man and woman—and talk about their hurts and grievances. It turned out to be a sad story of lonely disengagement.

Minuchin: "Do you two have areas of agreement?"

He said yes; she said no. He was a minimizer; she was a critic.

Minuchin: "When did you divorce Bob and marry the children?"

She turned quiet; he looked off into space. She said, softly: "Probably ten years ago."

What followed was a painful but familiar story of how a marriage can drown in parenting. The conflict was never resolved because it never surfaced. So the rift never healed.

With Minuchin's help, the couple took turns talking about their pain—and learning to listen. By unbalancing, Minuchin brought pressure to bear to help this couple break through their differences, open up to each other, fight for what they want, and, finally, begin to come together—as husband and wife and as parents.

Unbalancing is part of a struggle for change that sometimes takes on the appearance of combat. When a therapist says to a father that he's not doing enough or to a mother that she's excluding her husband, it may seem that the combat is between the therapist and the family, that he or she is attacking them. But the real combat is between them and fear—fear of change.

Challenging Unproductive Assumptions.
Although structural family therapy is not primarily a cognitive approach, its practitioners sometimes challenge the way clients see things. Changing the way family members relate to each other offers alternative views of their situation. The converse is also true: Changing the way family members view their situation enables them to change the way they relate to each other.

When six-year-old Cassie's parents complain about her behavior, they say she's "hyper," "sensitive," a "nervous child." Such constructions have tremendous power. Is a child's behavior "misbehavior," or is it a symptom of "nervousness?" Is it "naughty," or is it a "cry for help"? Is the child mad or bad, and who is in charge? What's in a name? Plenty.

Sometimes a therapist acts as a teacher, offering information and advice, often about structural matters. Doing so is likely to be a restructuring maneuver and must be done in a way that minimizes resistance. A therapist does this by delivering a "stroke and kick." If the therapist were dealing with a family in which the mother speaks for her children, he might say to her, "You are very helpful" (stroke). But to the child, "Mommy takes away your voice. Can you speak for yourself?" (kick). Thus mother is defined as helpful but intrusive (a stroke and a kick).

Current Status of the Model

In *Families and Family Therapy*, Minuchin (1974) taught family therapists to see what they were looking at. Through the prism of structural family theory, previously puzzling interactions suddenly swam into focus. Where others saw only chaos and cruelty, Minuchin saw structure: families organized into subsystems with boundaries. This enormously successful book not only taught us to see *enmeshment* and *disengagement*,

but also let us hope that changing them was just a matter of *joining, enactment,* and *unbalancing.* Minuchin made changing families look simple.

Anyone who watched Minuchin at work ten or twenty years after the publication of *Families and Family Therapy* would see a creative therapist still evolving, not someone frozen in time. One would still see the patented confrontations ("Who's the sheriff in this family?") but fewer enactments, less stage-directed dialogue. One would also hear bits and pieces borrowed from Carl Whitaker ("When did you divorce your wife and marry your job?") and others. Minuchin combines many things in his work. To those familiar with his earlier work, all of this raises the question: Is Minuchin still a structural family therapist? The question is, of course, absurd; we raise it to make a point: Structural family therapy isn't a set of techniques; it's a way of looking at families.

Minuchin recently wrote a new book that describes his latest thinking about therapeutic techniques (Minuchin, Nichols, & Lee, 2007). In this book, the authors describe a three-stage process of creating a framework for systemic family therapy. The first step ("Is the Customer Always Right?") is to challenge the family certainty that the primary problem is located in the internal machinery of the identified patient, in a process of probing but respectful questioning. The second step ("The Supporting Cast") is to explore what family members may be doing to perpetuate the presenting problem. The third step ("The Origin of the Specious") is to explore past experiences that may organize and distort family members' perceptions of the identified patient and thus perpetuate the presenting problem. The authors continue to emphasize the need for structural assessment, the use of enactments, and working with experiential intensity ("How to Lose Friends and Influence People"), but as you can see from this description the structural model has evolved to include a somewhat greater emphasis on cognition and insight.

In *Families of the Slums*, Minuchin and colleagues (1967) described the structural characteristics of low socioeconomic families and demonstrated the effectiveness of family therapy with this population. Prior to treatment, mothers in client families were found to be either over- or undercontrolling; either way their children were more disruptive than those in nonclient families. After treatment, mothers used less coercive control yet were clearer and firmer. In this study, seven of eleven families were judged to be improved after six months to a year of family therapy. Although no control group was used, the authors compared their results favorably with the usual 50 percent success rate at Wiltwyck.

Some of the strongest empirical support for structural family therapy comes from a series of studies with psychosomatic children and young adult drug addicts. Studies demonstrating the effectiveness of therapy with psychosomatic children are convincing because of the physiological measures used and dramatic because of the life-threatening nature of the problems. Minuchin, Rosman, and Baker (1978) reported one study that demonstrated how family conflict can precipitate ketoacidosis crises in psychosomatic-type diabetic children. In baseline interviews, parents discussed family problems with their children absent. Normal spouses showed the highest levels of confrontation, whereas psychosomatic spouses exhibited a wide range of conflict-avoidance maneuvers. Next, the therapist pressed the parents to increase the level of their conflict while their children observed behind a one-way mirror. As the parents argued, only the psychosomatic children seemed really upset. Moreover, these children's manifest distress was accompanied by dramatic increases in free fatty acid levels of the blood, a measure related to ketoacidosis. In the third stage of these interviews, the patients joined their parents. Normal and behavior-disorder parents continued as before, but the psychosomatic parents detoured their conflict, either by drawing their children into their discussions or by switching the subject from themselves to the children. When this happened, the free fatty acid levels of the parents fell, whereas the children's levels continued to rise.

This study provided strong confirmation of the clinical observation that psychosomatic children are involved in the regulation of stress between their parents.

Minuchin, Rosman, and Baker (1978) summarized the results of treating fifty-three cases of anorexia nervosa with structural family therapy. After a course of treatment that included hospitalization followed by family therapy on an outpatient basis, forty-three anorexic children were "greatly improved," two were "improved," three showed "no change," two were "worse," and three had dropped out. Although ethical considerations precluded a control treatment with these seriously ill children, the 90 percent improvement rate is impressive, especially compared with the 30 percent mortality rate for this disorder.

Duke Stanton showed that structural family therapy can be an effective form of treatment for drug addicts and their families. In a well-controlled study, Stanton and Todd (1979) compared family therapy with a family placebo condition and individual therapy. Symptom reduction was significant with structural family therapy; the level of positive change was more than double that achieved in the other conditions, and these positive effects persisted at follow-up of six and twelve months.

More recently, structural family therapy has been successfully applied to establish more adaptive parenting roles in heroin addicts (Grief & Dreschler, 1993) and as a means to reduce the likelihood that African American and Latino youths would initiate drug use (Santiseban et al., 1997). Other studies indicate that structural family therapy is equal in effectiveness to communication training and behavioral management training in reducing negative communication, conflicts, and expressed anger between adolescents diagnosed with ADHD and their parents (Barkley, Guevremont, Anastopoulos, & Fletcher, 1992). Structural family therapy has also been found to be effective for treating adolescent disorders, such as conduct disorders (Szapocznik et al., 1989; Chamberlain & Rosicky,

1995) and anorexia nervosa (Campbell & Patterson, 1995).

Although structural family therapy is so closely identified with Salvador Minuchin that they were once synonymous, it may be a good idea to differentiate the man from the model. When we think of structural family therapy, we tend to remember the approach as described in *Families and Family Therapy*, published in 1974. That book remains a good introduction to structural theory but emphasizes only the techniques Minuchin favored at the time. Minuchin himself has evolved considerably in the last thirty years, from an often blunt young therapist, always ready to challenge families, to a more seasoned clinician, still challenging but far gentler in his approach. If some of the examples in this chapter strike you as overly aggressive, you may be right. Some of these vignettes were taken from the 1970s, when family therapists tended to favor a confrontational style. While the confrontational style may have characterized some practitioners

of structural family therapy, it was never an essential feature of this approach.

Minuchin has evolved conceptually as well, from an almost exclusive focus on interpersonal interactions to consider the cognitive perspectives guiding those interactions and the past roots of those perspectives (Minuchin, Nichols, & Lee, 2007). But the structural approach he created also exists independently of his work, and is embodied in the definitive literature on this model (e.g., Minuchin, 1974; Minuchin & Fishman, 1981; Colapinto, 1991; Minuchin & Nichols, 1993) as well as in the ongoing work of his students and colleagues. The structural model directs clinicians to look beyond the content of problems, and even beyond the dynamics of interaction, to the underlying family organization that supports and constrains those interactions. Much has changed since 1974, but the structural model still stands; and it continues to be the most widely used way of understanding what goes on in the nuclear family.

Summary

1. Minuchin may be best known for the artistry of his clinical technique, yet his structural theory has become the most widely used conceptual model in the field. The reason structural theory is so popular is that it's simple, inclusive, and practical. The basic concepts—boundaries, subsystems, alignments, and complementarity—are easily grasped and applied. They take into account the individual, family, and social context; and they provide a clear organizing framework for understanding and treating families.

2. The most important tenet of this approach is that every family has a structure, and this structure is revealed only when the family is in action. According to this view, therapists who fail to consider the entire family's structure and intervene in only one subsystem are unlikely to effect lasting change. If a mother's overinvolvement with her son is part of a structure that in-

cludes distance from her husband, no amount of therapy for the mother and son is likely to bring about basic change in the family.

3. Subsystems are units of the family based on function. If the leadership of a family is taken over by a father and daughter, then they, not the husband and wife, are the executive subsystem. Subsystems are circumscribed and regulated by interpersonal boundaries. In healthy families, boundaries are clear enough to protect independence and autonomy, and permeable enough to allow mutual support and affection. Enmeshed families are characterized by diffuse boundaries, disengaged families by rigid boundaries.

4. Once they've gained a family's trust, therapists promote family interaction while assuming a decentralized role. From this position, they can watch what goes on in the family and make a structural assessment, which includes

the problem and the organization that supports it. These assessments are framed in terms of boundaries and subsystems, easily conceptualized as two-dimensional maps used to suggest avenues for change.

5. Once they have successfully joined and assessed a family, structural therapists proceed to activate dormant structures using techniques that alter alignments and shift power within and between subsystems. These restructuring techniques are concrete, forceful, and sometimes dramatic. However, their success depends as much on the joining and assessment as on the power of the techniques themselves.

Questions to Consider

1. What might be lost and what might be gained by exploring past experiences that helped shape how family members currently interact to form a family's structure?
2. How would you diagram the structure of your own family? At what point, if any, did you begin to think of your family's structure as anything other than the natural way families operate?
3. To what extent is the enmeshed-mother/disengaged-father syndrome embedded in social and cultural arrangements that families have little ability to change?
4. Can you think of clinical situations you've encountered in your training that ignored a family's (or other system's) structure, possibly with unfortunate consequences?

Key Concepts

accommodation   Elements of a system automatically adjust to coordinate their functioning; people may have to work at it.

boundary   A concept used in structural family therapy to describe emotional barriers that protect and enhance the integrity of individuals, subsystems, and families.

coalition   An alliance between two persons or social units against a third.

cross-generational coalition   An inappropriate alliance between a parent and child, who side together against a third member of the family.

disengagement   Minuchin's term for psychological isolation that results from overly rigid boundaries around individuals and subsystems in a family.

empathy   Understanding and acknowledging what someone is really feeling; in structural family therapy empathy is used to help clients stop bickering and talk about their feelings.

enactment   An interaction stimulated in structural family therapy to observe and then change transactions that make up family structure.

enmeshment   Minuchin's term for loss of autonomy due to a blurring of psychological boundaries.

family structure   The functional organization of families that determines how family members interact.

hierarchical structure   Family functioning based on clear generational boundaries, where the parents maintain control and authority.

intensity   Minuchin's term for changing maladaptive transactions by using strong affect, repeated intervention, or prolonged pressure.

joining   A structural family therapy term for accepting and accommodating to families to win their confidence and circumvent resistance.

reframing Relabeling a family's description of behavior to make it more amenable to therapeutic change; for example, describing someone as "discouraged" rather than "depressed."

shaping competence Reinforcing positives rather than confronting deficiences.

structure Recurrent patterns of interaction that define and stabilize the shape of relationships.

subsystem Smaller units in families, determined by generation, sex, or function.

—Recommended Readings

Colapinto J. 1991. Structural family therapy. In *Handbook of family therapy*, vol. II, A. S. Gurman and D. P. Kniskern, eds. New York: Brunner/Mazel.

Minuchin, S. 1974. *Families and family therapy*. Cambridge, MA: Harvard University Press.

Minuchin, S., and Fishman, H. C. 1981. *Family therapy techniques*. Cambridge, MA: Harvard University Press.

Minuchin, S., Lee, W-Y., and Simon, G. M. 1996. *Mastering family therapy: Journeys of growth and transformation*. New York: Wiley.

Minuchin, S., and Nichols, M. P. 1993. *Family healing: Tales of hope and renewal from family therapy*. New York: The Free Press.

Minuchin, S., and Nichols, M. P. 1998. Structural family therapy. In *Case studies in couple and family therapy*, F. M. Dattilio, ed. New York: Guilford Press.

Minuchin, S., Nichols, M. P., and Lee, W-Y. 2007. *Assessing couples and families: From symptom to system*. Boston: Allyn & Bacon.

Nichols, M. P. 1999. *Inside family therapy*. Boston: Allyn & Bacon.

Nichols, M. P., and Minuchin, S. 1999. Short-term structural family therapy with couples. In *Short-term couple therapy*, J. M. Donovan, ed. New York: Guilford Press.

—References

Barkely, R., Guevremont, D., Anastopoulos, A., and Fletcher, K. 1992. A comparison of three family therapy programs for treating family conflicts in adolescents with attention-deficit hyperactivity disorder. *Journal of Consulting and Clinical Psychology*. 60: 450–463.

Campbell, T., and Patterson, J. 1995. The effectiveness of family interventions in the treatment of physical illness. *Journal of Marital and Family Therapy*. 21: 545–584.

Chamberlain, P., and Rosicky, J. 1995. The effectiveness of family therapy in the treatment of adolescents with conduct disorders and delinquency. *Journal of Marital and Family Therapy*. 21: 441–459.

Elizur, J., and Minuchin, S. 1989. *Institutionalizing madness: Families, therapy, and society*. New York: Basic Books.

Grief, G., and Dreschler, L. 1993. Common issues for parents in a methadone maintenance group. *Journal of Substance Abuse Treatment*. 10: 335–339.

Minuchin, S. 1974. *Families and family therapy*. Cambridge, MA: Harvard University Press.

Minuchin, S., Montalvo, E., Guerney, B., Rosman, B., and Schumer, F. 1967. *Families of the slums*. New York: Basic Books.

Minuchin, S., and Nichols, M. P. 1993. *Family healing: Tales of hope and renewal from family therapy*. New York: The Free Press.

Minuchin, S., Nichols, M. P., and Lee, W-Y. 2007. *Assessing couples and families: From symptom to system*. Boston: Allyn & Bacon.

Minuchin, S., Rosman, B., and Baker, L. 1978. *Psychosomatic families: Anorexia nervosa in context*. Cambridge, MA: Harvard University Press.

Santiseban, D., Coatsworth, J., Perez-Vidal, A., Mitrani, V., Jean-Gilles, M., and Szapocznik, J. 1997. Brief structural/strategic family therapy with African American and Hispanic high-risk youth. *Journal of Community Psychology*. 25: 453–471.

Simon, G. M. 1995. A revisionist rendering of structural family therapy. *Journal of Marital and Family Therapy.* 21: 17–26.

Stanton, M. D., and Todd, T. C. 1979. Structural family therapy with drug addicts. In *The family therapy of drug and alcohol abuse,* E. Kaufman and P. Kaufmann, eds. New York: Gardner Press.

Szapocznik, J., Rio, A., Murray, E., Cohen, R., Scopetta, M., Rivas-Vasquez, A., Hervis, O., Posada, V., and Kurtines, W. 1989. Structural family therapy versus psychodynamic child therapy for problematic Hispanic boys. *Journal of Consulting and Clinical Psychology.* 57: 571–578.

Experiential Family Therapy

8

An experiential branch of family therapy emerged from the humanistic wing of psychology that, like the expressive therapies that inspired it, emphasized immediate, here-and-now experience. Experiential therapy was most popular when family therapy was young, when therapists talked about systems but borrowed their techniques from individual and group therapies. From Gestalt therapy and encounter groups came evocative techniques like *role-playing* and *emotional confrontation*, while other expressive methods such as *sculpting* and *family drawing* bore the influence of the arts and of psychodrama.

In focusing more on emotional experience than on the dynamics of interaction, experiential therapists seemed out of step with the rest of family therapy. Indeed, by emphasizing individuals and their feelings, experiential treatment may never have been as well suited to family therapy as were approaches that dealt with systems and action. With the passing of the inspirational leaders of this tradition, Virginia Satir and Carl Whitaker, the methods they popularized began to seem dated, more a product of the sixties than of today's world.

Recently, however, experiential approaches have been enjoying a revival. As we shall see, two of the newer models, Greenberg and Johnson's

(1985) *emotionally focused couples therapy* and Schwartz's (1995) *internal family systems model*, have combined the emotional impact of an experiential focus on the individual with a more sophisticated understanding of family systems.

As the first great cathartic therapist, Sigmund Freud, discovered, getting in touch with painful feelings is not, by itself, a sufficient model of psychotherapy. On the other hand, ignoring or rationalizing unhappy emotions may cheat clients out of the opportunity to get to the heart of their problems. Thus the experiential emphasis on emotional expression continues to be a useful counterweight to the reductionistic emphasis on behavior and cognition common to today's problem-solving approaches.

Evolution of the Model

Two giants stand out in the development of experiential family therapy: Carl Whitaker and Virginia Satir. Whitaker was the leading exponent of a freewheeling, intuitive approach aimed at puncturing pretense and liberating family members to be themselves. He was among the first to do psychotherapy with families and, although he was once considered a maverick, he eventually became one of the most admired therapists in

Carl Whitaker

Carl Whitaker's unconventional thinking formed the basis of a bold and inventive approach to family therapy. He believed that active personal involvement was the best way to bring about changes in families and promote flexibility among family members. He relied on his own personality and wisdom rather than any fixed techniques to stir things up in families and to help family members open up and be more fully themselves.

the field. Iconoclastic, even outrageous at times, Whitaker nevertheless retained the respect of the family therapy establishment. He may have been their Puck, but he was one of them.

Whitaker grew up on a dairy farm in upstate New York. Rural isolation bred a certain shyness but also conditioned him to be less bound by social convention. After medical school and a residency in obstetrics and gynecology, Whitaker went into psychiatry, where he became fascinated by the psychotic mind. Unfortunately—or fortunately—back in the 1940s, Whitaker couldn't rely on neuroleptic drugs to blunt the hallucinatory imaginings of his patients; instead he listened and learned to understand thoughts, crazy but human, thoughts most of us usually keep buried.

After working at the University of Louisville College of Medicine and the Oakridge Hospital, Whitaker accepted the chair of Emory University's Department of Psychiatry, where he remained from 1946 to 1955, when, in the face of mounting pressure to make the department more psychoanalytic, Whitaker and his entire faculty, including Thomas Malone, John Warkentin, and Richard Felder, resigned to establish the Atlanta Psychiatric Clinic. Experiential psychotherapy was born of this union, and

the group produced a number of provocative and challenging papers (Whitaker & Malone, 1953). In 1965 Whitaker moved to the University of Wisconsin Medical School. After his retirement in the 1980s, he traveled widely to share his wisdom and experience at conventions and workshops. His death in 1995 was a great loss. Among Whitaker's best-known associates are Augustus Napier, now in private practice in Atlanta, and David Keith, at the State University of New York in Syracuse.

The other towering figure among experiential family therapists was Virginia Satir. As an early member of the Mental Research Institute (MRI), Satir emphasized communication (see Chapter 6) as well as emotional experiencing.

Satir began seeing families in private practice in Chicago in 1951. In 1955 she was invited to set up a training program for residents at the Illinois State Psychiatric Institute (where one of her students was Ivan Boszormenyi-Nagy). In 1959 Don Jackson invited her to join him at MRI, where Satir became the first director of training and remained until 1966, when she left to become the director of the Esalen Institute in Big Sur, California.

Satir was the archetypal nurturing therapist in a field enamored with abstract concepts and

Virginia Satir

Virginia Satir believed that a healthy family life involved open and reciprocal sharing of affection, feelings, and love. Satir began treating families in 1951 and established a training program for psychiatric residents at the Illinois State Psychiatric Institute in 1955. Satir served as the director of training at the Mental Research Institute in Palo Alto from 1959 to 1966 and at the Esalen Institute in Big Sur beginning in 1966. She described family roles, such as "the rescuer" or "the placator," that function to constrain relationships in families. Satir's warmth and caring were evident in her incorporation of feeling and compassion in the therapeutic relationship.

strategic maneuvers. Her warmth and genuineness gave her tremendous appeal as she traveled the country giving demonstrations and workshops. Her ability to move audiences made her family therapy's most celebrated humanist. Satir died of pancreatic cancer in 1988.

Among the most recent experiential approaches is the **emotionally focused couples therapy** of Leslie Greenberg and Susan Johnson, which draws on Perls, Satir, and the MRI group (Greenberg & Johnson, 1985, 1986, 1988). Another specialized approach to the inner emotional life of families is Richard Schwartz's (1995) **internal family systems therapy,** in which clients' conflicting inner voices are personified as "parts" and then reintegrated using a variety of psychodramatic techniques.

The Basic Model

Experiential family therapy is founded on the premise that the root cause of family problems is emotional suppression. Although children must learn that they can't always do whatever they

feel like doing, many parents have an unfortunate tendency to confuse the *instrumental* and *expressive* functions of emotion. They try to regulate their children's actions by controlling their feelings. As a result, children learn to blunt their emotional experience to avoid making waves. Although this process is more or less universal, dysfunctional families tend to be less tolerant of the emotions that signal individuality than most. As a result, children in such families often grow up estranged from themselves and feeling only the residues of repressed affect: boredom, apathy, and anxiety.

While systemic therapists see the roots of symptomatic behavior in the dance of family interactions, experientialists view those interactions as the result of family members shadow dancing with the projections of each other's defenses. From this perspective, attempts to bring about positive change in families are more likely to be successful if family members first get in touch with their real feelings—their hopes and desires as well as their fears and anxieties. Thus experiential family therapy works from the inside out, helping individuals uncover their honest emotions and then forging more genuine family ties out of this enhanced authenticity.

Theoretical Concepts

Carl Whitaker summed up the experiential position on theory in a paper entitled, "The Hindrance of Theory in Clinical Work" (Whitaker, 1976a). Theory may be useful for beginners, Whitaker said, but his advice was to give up calculation as soon as possible in favor of just being yourself.

Being antitheoretical is, of course, itself a theoretical position. To say that therapy shouldn't be constrained by theories is to say that it should be spontaneous. Despite Whitaker's disdain for theory, however, experiential family therapy is very much a product of the existential–humanistic tradition.

Much of the theorizing of existential psychologists (e.g., Binswanger, 1967; Boss, 1963) was in reaction to perceived shortcomings of psychoanalysis and behaviorism. In place of *determinism*, existentialists emphasized freedom and the immediacy of experience. Where psychoanalysts posited a structuralized model of the mind, existentialists treated individuals as whole persons, and offered a positive model of humanity in place of what they saw as a pessimistic psychoanalytic model. Instead of settling for a reduction of their neuroses, existentialists believed that people should aim for fulfillment.

Despite their disinclination to theorize, certain basic premises define the experiential position. Whitaker emphasized that self-fulfillment depends on family cohesiveness, and Satir stressed the importance of good communication among family members, but the basic commitment was to *individual self-expression*. While there was some talk about family systems (e.g., Satir, 1972), the experiential model of families was more like a democratic group than a structured organization. Great emphasis is placed on *flexibility* and *freedom*. Treatment is designed to help individual family members find fulfilling roles for themselves, with less concern for the family as a whole. This is not to say that the needs of the family are denigrated, but that they are thought to follow on the heels of individual enhancement.[1]

After reading the previous paragraph, David Keith (in a personal letter) helped put into perspective the experiential position on the claims of the individual versus the claims of the family:

> There is a dialectical tension between the individual and the family—between dependence and independence. To overemphasize either individuality or family connectedness is to distort the human condition.

Theories of families as systems are translated into techniques that promote communication and interaction. The emphasis on altering interactions implies an acceptance of whatever level of individual experience is already present. This is where experiential theory differs from most systems approaches. Here the emphasis is on expanding experience. The assumption is that opening up individuals to their experience is a prerequisite to breaking new ground for the family group.

The underlying premise of experiential family therapy is that the way to promote individual growth and family cohesion is to liberate affects and impulses. Efforts to reduce defensiveness and unlock deeper levels of experiencing rest on an assumption of the basic goodness of human nature.

The exception to the experiential deemphasis on theory is Greenberg and Johnson's emotionally focused couples therapy, which draws on attachment theory (Bowlby, 1969). According to Greenberg and Johnson, emotion organizes attachment responses and serves a communicative function in relationships. When people express their vulnerability directly they're likely to elicit a compassionate response from their partners. But when an insecurely attached person fears vulnerability and shows anger instead, the response is more likely to be withdrawal. Thus, the person most in need of attachment may, by being afraid

---

1. Though, at one time, the family was portrayed as the enemy of freedom and authenticity (Laing & Esterson, 1970).

to expose that need, push away the loved ones he or she longs to get close to. The antidote for this dilemma is what experiential therapy is all about: helping people relax defensive fears so that deeper and more genuine emotions can emerge.

Normal Family Development

Experiential therapists subscribe to the humanistic faith in the natural wisdom of honest emotion. According to this point of view, if they are left alone, people tend to flourish. Problems arise because this innate tendency toward **self-actualization** (Rogers, 1951) runs afoul of social pressures. Society enforces repression to tame people's instincts and make them fit for group living. Unhappily, self-control is achieved at the cost of "surplus repression" (Marcuse, 1955). Families add their own controls to achieve peace and quiet, perpetuating outmoded **family myths** (Gehrke & Kirschenbaum, 1967) and using **mystification** (Laing, 1967) to alienate children from their experience.

In the ideal situation, parental control isn't excessive, and children grow up in an atmosphere of support for their feelings and creative impulses. Parents listen to their children, accept their feelings, and validate their experience. Affect is valued and nurtured; children are encouraged to experience life fully and to express the full range of human emotions.

Experiential therapists describe the family as a place of sharing experience (Satir, 1972). Functional families are secure enough to support and encourage a wide range of experiencing; dysfunctional families are frightened and bloodless. Neither problem-solving skills nor particular family structures are considered as important as nurturing open, natural, and spontaneous experiencing. In short, the healthy family offers its members the freedom to be themselves.

Development of Behavior Disorders

From an experiential perspective, denial of impulses and suppression of feeling are the root of family problems. Dysfunctional families are

locked into self-protection and avoidance (Kaplan & Kaplan, 1978). In Harry Stack Sullivan's (1953) terms, they seek *security*, rather than *satisfaction*. Their presenting complaints are many, but the basic problem is that they smother emotion and desire.

According to Whitaker (Whitaker & Keith, 1981), there's no such thing as a marriage—only two scapegoats sent out by their families to perpetuate themselves. Together they must work out the inherent conflict in this situation. Couples who remain together eventually reach some kind of accommodation. Whether based on compromise or resignation, reconciling themselves to each other lessens the previous friction. Dysfunctional families, terrified of conflict, adhere rigidly to the rituals that they establish. Having experienced the anxiety of uncertainty, they now cling to their routines.

In her portrayal of troubled families, Satir (1972) emphasized the atmosphere of emotional deadness. Such families are cold; they seem to stay together out of habit or duty. The adults don't enjoy their children, and the children learn not to respect themselves or care about their parents. In consequence of the lack of warmth in the family, these people avoid each other, and preoccupy themselves with work and other distractions.

It is important to notice that the "dysfunction" Satir described isn't the kind found in diagnostic manuals. Like others in the experiential camp, Satir was as concerned with normal people who lead lives of quiet desperation as with the officially recognized patients families usually focus on. As she (Satir, 1972) put it,

> It is a sad experience for me to be with these families. I see the hopelessness, the helplessness, the loneliness. I see the bravery of people trying to cover up—a bravery that can still bellow or nag or whine at each other. Others no longer care. These people go on year after year, enduring misery themselves or in their desperation, inflicting it on others. (p. 12)

Satir stressed the role of destructive communication in smothering feeling and said that there were four dishonest ways people communicate: *blaming, placating,* being *irrelevant,* and being *super reasonable.* What's behind these patterns of inauthentic communication? *Low self-esteem.* If people feel bad about themselves, it's hard to tell the truth about their feelings, and it is threatening to let others tell them honestly what they feel.

A healthy relationship, according to Susan Johnson, is a secure attachment bond—that is, one characterized by emotional accessibility and responsiveness (Johnson & Denton, 2002). Secure attachment refers both to having grown up with a sense of being lovable and worthwhile and to the confidence that comes from having a secure and rewarding intimate relationship. But when attachment security is threatened people typically respond with anger—a protest that, unfortunately, may drive the other person away rather than evoke the desired responsiveness. Recently, Johnson has introduced the notion of "attachment injuries," traumatic occurrences that damage the bond between partners and, if not resolved, maintain negative cycles and attachment insecurities.

How Therapy Works

In common with others in the humanistic tradition, experiential therapists believe that the way to emotional health is to uncover deeper levels of experiencing. Virginia Satir (1972) put it this way:

> We attempt to make three changes in the family system. First, each member of the family should be able to report congruently, completely, and honestly on what he sees and hears, feels, and thinks, about himself and others, in the presence of others. Second, each person should be addressed and related to in terms of his uniqueness, so that decisions are made in terms of exploration and negotiation rather than in terms of power. Third, differentness must be openly acknowledged and used for growth. (p. 120)

Experientialists emphasize the feeling side of human nature—creativity, spontaneity, and the ability to play—and, in therapy, the value of experience for its own sake.

Gus Napier (Napier & Whitaker, 1978) wrote, in *The Family Crucible,* a nice description of what experiential therapists think causes change. Breakthroughs occur when family members risk being "more separate, divergent, even angrier" as well as "when they risk being closer and more intimate." To help clients dare to take those risks, experiential therapists are alternately provocative and warmly supportive. This permits family members to drop their protective defenses and open up to each other.

Existential encounter is believed to be the essential force in the psychotherapeutic process (Kempler, 1973; Whitaker, 1976a). These encounters must be reciprocal; instead of hiding behind a professional role, the therapist must be a genuine person who catalyzes change using his or her personal impact on families. As Kempler (1968) said:

> In this approach the therapist becomes a family member during the interviews, participating as fully as he is able, hopefully available for appreciation and criticism as well as he is able to dispense it. He laughs, cries and rages. He feels and shares his embarrassments, confusions and helplessness. (p. 97)

For Satir, caring and acceptance were the keys to helping people open up to experience, and open up to each other:

> Some therapists think people come into therapy not wanting to be changed; I don't think that's true. They don't think they *can* change. Going into some new, unfamiliar place is a scary thing. When I first begin to work with someone, I am not interested in changing them. I am interested in finding their rhythms, being able to join with them, and helping them go inside to those scary places. Resistance is mainly the fear of going somewhere you have not been. (Quoted in Simon, 1989, pp. 38–39)

Therapy

Experiential family therapists share the humanistic belief that people are naturally resourceful and if left to their own devices will be energetic, creative, loving, and productive (Rogers, 1951). The task of therapy is therefore seen as unblocking defenses and releasing people's innate vitality.

Assessment

Because experientialists are less interested in solving problems than in enhancing family functioning, they pay limited attention to the specifics of the presenting problem. Moreover, because they focus on individuals and their experience, they have little interest in assessing the structure of family organization.

The following quotation illustrates the experientialist disdain for evaluation. "Diagnoses are the tombstones of the therapist's frustration, and accusations such as defensive, resistant, and secondary gain are the flowers placed on the grave of his buried dissatisfaction" (Kempler, 1973, p. 11). The point seems to be that the objective distance necessary for formal assessment fosters a judgmental attitude and isolates therapists from emotional contact with families.

For most experientialists, assessment takes place informally as the therapist gets to know a family. In the process of developing a relationship, the therapist learns what kind of people he or she is dealing with. Whitaker began by asking each family member to describe the family and how it works. In this way, he got a composite picture of individual family members and their perceptions of the family group. This kind of inquiry is about as formal as most experiential therapists get in sizing up families. The majority of what serves as assessment in this approach is an attempt to decode the defenses that emerge in the ongoing course of trying to help family members open up to each other.

Therapeutic Techniques

In experiential therapy, according to Walter Kempler (1968), there are no techniques, only people. This epigram neatly summarizes the faith in the curative power of the therapist's personality. It isn't so much what therapists do that matters, it's who they are.

To foster openness in their patients, therapists must themselves be open. However, this point is at least partly rhetorical. Whoever they are, therapists must also *do* something. Even if what they do isn't planned, it can nevertheless be described. Moreover, experiential therapists tend to do a lot; they're highly active and some (including Kempler) use a number of evocative techniques.

Some use structured devices such as *family sculpting* and *choreography*; others like Virginia Satir and Carl Whitaker rely on the spontaneity of just being themselves.

Virginia Satir had a remarkable ability to communicate. Like many great therapists, she was a dynamic personality. But she didn't rely merely on personal warmth. Rather, she worked to clarify communication, turned people away from complaining toward finding solutions, supported the self-esteem of every member of the family, pointed out positive intentions (long before "positive connotation" became a strategic device), and showed by example how to be affectionate (Satir & Baldwin, 1983). She was a loving but forceful healer.

One of Satir's hallmarks was the use of touch. Hers was the language of tenderness. She often began by making physical contact with children, as evidenced in her case "Of Rocks and Flowers." Bob, a recovering alcoholic, was the father of two boys, Aaron (four) and Robbie (two), whose mother had abused them repeatedly—pushing them down stairs, burning them with cigarettes, and tying them up under the sink. At the time of the interview, the mother was under psychiatric care and didn't see the children. Bob's new wife, Betty, had been abused by her previous husband, also an alcoholic. She was pregnant and afraid that the boys would abuse the baby. The boys had already been expressing the violence they'd been exposed to—slapping and choking other children. Bob and Betty, acting out of frustration and fear, responded roughly to the boys, which only increased their aggressiveness.

Throughout the session, Satir showed the parents how to touch the children tenderly and how to hold them firmly to stop them from misbehaving. When Bob started to tell Aaron something from a distance, Satir insisted on proximity and touch. She sat Aaron down in front of his father and asked Bob to take the little boy's hands and speak directly to him.

The following fragments from the session are taken from Andreas (1991).

Those little hands know a lot of things; they need to be reeducated. OK. Now, there is a lot of energy in both these youngsters, like there is in both of you. And I am going to talk to your therapist about making some room for you to have some respite (from the children). But use every opportunity you can to get this kind of physical contact. And what I would also recommend that you do is that the two of you are clear about what you expect.

And if you (Bob) could learn from Betty how to pay attention (to the kids) more quickly. I would like you to be able to get your message across without a "don't" in it, without a "don't"—and that your strength of your arms when you pick them up—I don't know if I can illustrate it to you, but let me have your arm for a minute (reaching for Bob's forearm). Let me show you the difference. Pick up my arm like you were going to grab me. (Bob grabs her arm.) All right. Now when you do that, my muscles all start to tighten, and I want to hit back. (Bob nods.) Now pick up my arm like you wanted to protect me. (Bob holds her arm.) All right. I feel your strength now, but I don't feel like I want to pull back like this. (Bob says, "yeah.")

And what I'd like you to do is to do *lots* and lots of touching of both of these children. And when things start (to get out of hand), then you go over—don't say anything—go over to them and just take them (demonstrating the protective holding on both of Robbie's forearms) but you have to know in your inside that you're not pulling them (Aaron briefly puts his hands on top of Virginia's and Robbie's arms) like this (demonstrating), but you are taking them in a strong way (stroking Bob's arm with both hands), like you saw the difference. I'll demonstrate it to you (Bob), too. First of all I am go-

ing to grab you (demonstrating) like that. (Bob says, "yeah.") You see you want to pull back. All right. Now, at this time what I am going to do is give you some strength (demonstrating holding his arm with both hands. Robbie pats Virginia's hand). But I am not going to ask you to retaliate. Now this is the most important thing for you to start with.

(Virginia turns to Betty and offers her forearm.) OK. Now I'd like to do the same with you. So, take my arm really tight, just (Betty grabs Virginia's arm, and Aaron does, too). Yeah, that's right, like you really wanted to give me "what for." OK. All right. Now give it to me like you want to give me support, but you also want to give me a boundary. (Aaron reaches toward Betty's hand and Virginia takes Aaron's free hand in her free hand.) It's a little bit tight, a little bit tight.

So the next time you see anything coming, what you do is you go and make that contact (Virginia demonstrates by holding Aaron's upper arm) and then let it go soft. (Virginia takes Aaron's hands and begins to draw him out of Betty's lap.) Now, Aaron, I'd like you to come up here so I could demonstrate something to your mother for a minute. (Aaron says, "OK.") Now, let's suppose some moment I'm not thinking and I take you like that (grabbing Betty's arms suddenly with both hands). You see what you want to do? (Betty nods.) All right. Now I am going to do it another way. I am giving you the same message (Virginia holds Betty's arm firmly with both hands, looking directly into her eyes, and starts to stand up), but I am doing it like this. And I am looking at you, and I'm giving you a straight message. OK. Now your body at that point is not going to respond negatively to me. It is going to feel stopped, but not negative. And then I will take you like this. (Virginia puts one arm around Betty's back and the other under her upper arm.) Just like this (Virginia puts both arms around Betty and draws her close) and now I will hold you. I will hold you like that for a little bit.

Following this session, Satir commented on her technique:

There had been so many things happening, and the fear was so strong in relation to these children that if you thought of one image it was like they were monsters. So one of the things that I wanted to do was also to see that they had the capacity to respond with a touch, using myself in that regard by having them put their hands on my face—that was a kind of mirror for the family itself, the people in the family. And then allowing them, and encouraging them to do that with their own parents. See, touch, that comes out of the kind of ambience which was there at the time, says things no words can say.

To encourage empathy and bring family members closer together, Satir often used the following exercise with parents (adapted from Satir & Baldwin, 1983):

1. Think of a difficult situation with your child. Perhaps your child has been doing something that you haven't known how to handle or that drives you up the wall.
2. Run your movie of this situation from your own point of view. Imagine you are going through this situation with your child again. Notice how you feel, what you see, what you hear.
3. Re-experience this situation, but this time as your child. Visualize the entire situation slowly and in detail, as you would imagine seeing it through the eyes of your child. Let yourself feel what your child must be feeling. Do you notice any feelings that you weren't aware your child might be having? Do you notice something that your child might need or want that you hadn't been aware of?
4. Re-experience the same situation, this time as an observer. Watch and listen to what's happening, and allow yourself to observe both your child and yourself. Do you notice anything about the way you and your child respond to each other? What do you see more clearly about yourself and your child?

Because he favored a personal encounter over a calculated approach, it's not surprising that Whitaker's style was the same with individuals, couples, or groups (Whitaker, 1958). He assidu-

ously avoided directing real-life decisions, preferring instead to open family members up to their feelings and join them in their uncertainty. This may sound trite, but it's an important point. As long as a therapist (or anyone else for that matter) is anxious to change people, it's hard, very hard, to help them feel understood—and even harder to really empathize with them.

A comparison between Whitaker's early work (Whitaker, Warkentin, & Malone, 1959; Whitaker, 1967) and his later work (Napier & Whitaker, 1978) shows how he changed over the years. He started out as deliberately outlandish. He might fall asleep in sessions and then report his dreams; he wrestled with patients; he talked about his own sexual fantasies. In later years he was less provocative. This seems to be what happens to therapists as they mature; they have less need to impose themselves and more willingness to listen.

Because Whitaker's treatment was so intense and personal, he believed it essential that two therapists work together. Having a cotherapist to share the burden keeps therapists from being absorbed in the emotional field of the family. Family therapy tends to activate therapists' own feelings toward certain types of family members. A detached, analytic stance minimizes such feelings; emotional involvement maximizes them.

The trouble with **countertransference** is that it tends to be unconscious. Therapists are more likely to become aware of such feelings after a session is over. Easier still is to observe countertransference in others. Consider the example of Dr. Fox, a married man who specializes in individual therapy, but occasionally sees married couples. In 75 percent of such cases, Dr. Fox encourages the couple to seek a divorce, and his patients have a high rate of following his advice. Perhaps if Dr. Fox were happier in his own marriage or had the courage to change it, he'd be less impelled to guide his patients where he fears to go.

To minimize countertransference, Whitaker recommended sharing feelings openly with the family. If feelings are openly expressed they're less likely to be acted out. At times, however, most therapists are unaware of their own feelings. This is where a cotherapist can be useful. A cotherapist often can recognize reactive feelings in a colleague. A strong investment in the cotherapy relationship (or treatment team) helps keep therapists from being **inducted** (drawn into families). Therapists who see families without a cotherapist may seek out supervision to help achieve the objectivity necessary to stay balanced.

Whitaker's first sessions (Napier & Whitaker, 1978) were fairly structured, and they included taking a family history. For him, the first contacts with families were opening salvos in "the battle for structure" (Whitaker & Keith, 1981). He wanted the family to know that the therapist was in charge.[2] This began with the first telephone call. Whitaker (1976b) insisted that the largest possible number of family members attend; he believed that three generations were necessary to ensure that grandparents would support, not oppose, therapy, and that their presence would help correct distortions. If significant family members wouldn't attend, Whitaker generally refused to see the family. Why begin with the cards stacked against you?

Along with Virginia Satir, Whitaker was among the foremost exponents of the therapist's use of self as a catalyst for change. But whereas Satir offered a warm, supportive presence, Whitaker was at times blunt, even confrontational. Actually, the provocative interventions of someone like Whitaker only become acceptable to families after the therapist has proven to be an understanding and caring person. Before challenging people, it is first necessary to win their trust.

Regardless of whether they are provocative or supportive, experiential therapists are usually extremely active. Instead of leaving them to work out their own issues with each other, family members are told, "Tell him (or her) what you feel!" or asked, "What are you feeling right now?"

Just as the best way to get a school teacher's attention is to misbehave, the best way to get an experiential therapist's attention is to show signs of emotion without actually expressing it.

Therapist: I see you looking over at Dad whenever you ask Mom a question. What's that about?

Kendra: Oh, nothing. . . .

Therapist: It must mean *something*. Come on, what were you feeling?

Kendra: Nothing!

Therapist: You must have been feeling something. What was it?

Kendra: Well, sometimes when Mom lets me do something, Dad gets mad. But instead of yelling at her, he yells at *me* (crying softly).

Therapist: Tell him.

Kendra: (Angrily, to the therapist) Leave me alone!

Therapist: No, it's important. Tell your Dad how you feel.

Kendra: (Sobbing hard) You're always picking on me! You never let me do anything!

Experiential therapists use a number of expressive techniques, including *family sculpting* (Duhl, Kantor, & Duhl, 1973), *family puppet interviews* (Irwin & Malloy, 1975), *family art therapy* (Geddes & Medway, 1977), *conjoint family drawings* (Bing, 1970), and *Gestalt therapy techniques* (Kempler, 1973). Among the accoutrements of experiential therapists' offices are toys, doll houses, clay, teddy bears, drawing pens and paper, and batacca bats.

In **family sculpting** the therapist asks one member of a family to arrange the others in a tableau. This is a graphic means of portraying each person's perceptions of the family and his or her place in it. This was a favorite device of Virginia Satir, who frequently used ropes and blindfolds to dramatize the constricting roles family members get trapped into (Satir & Baldwin, 1983).

The following example of sculpting occurred when a therapist asked Mr. N. to arrange the

---

2. We might add that there is a big difference between trying to control the structure of sessions and trying to control people's lives.

members of his family into a scene typical of the time when he comes home from work.

> *Mr. N.:* When I come home from work, eh? Okay (to his wife) honey, you'd be by the stove, wouldn't you?
>
> *Therapist:* No, don't talk. Just move people where you want them to be.
>
> *Mr. N.:* Okay.

He guided his wife to stand at a spot where the kitchen stove might be and placed his children on the kitchen floor, drawing and playing.

> *Therapist:* Fine, now, still without any dialogue, put them into action.

Mr. N. then instructed his wife to pretend to cook but to turn frequently to see what the kids were up to. He told the children to pretend to play for a while, but then to start fighting and complaining to Mommy.

> *Therapist:* And what happens, when you come home?
>
> *Mr. N.:* Nothing. I try to talk to my wife, but the kids keep pestering her, and she gets mad and says to leave her alone.
>
> *Therapist:* Okay, act it out.

Mrs. N. acted out trying to cook and referee the children's fights. The children, who thought this a great game, tried to outdo each other getting Mommy's attention. When Mr. N. "came home," he reached out for his wife, but the children came between them, until Mrs. N. finally pushed all of them away.

Afterward, Mrs. N. said that she hadn't realized her husband felt ignored. She just thought of him as coming home, saying hello, and then withdrawing into the den with his newspaper and bottle of beer.

Family sculpting is also used to illuminate scenes from the past. A typical instruction is, "Remember standing in front of your childhood home. Walk in and describe what typically happened." The idea is to make a tableau portraying

one's perceptions of family life. It's a device to focus awareness and heighten sensitivity.

Another expressive exercise is *family art therapy*. Kwiatkowska (1967) instructs families to produce a series of drawings, including a "joint family scribble," in which each person makes a quick scribble and then the whole family incorporates the scribble into a unified picture. Elizabeth Bing (1970) describes the *conjoint family drawing* as a means to warm families up and free them to express themselves. In this procedure families are told to "Draw a picture as you see yourselves as a family." The resulting portraits may disclose perceptions that haven't previously been discussed or may stimulate the person drawing the picture to realize something that he or she had never thought of before.

> A father drew a picture of the family that showed him off to one side, while his wife and children stood holding hands. Although he was portraying a fact well known to his wife and himself, they hadn't spoken openly of it. Once he showed his drawing to the therapist, there was no avoiding discussion.
>
> In another case, when the therapist asked each of the family members to draw the family, the teenage daughter was uncertain what to do. She had never thought much about the family or her role in it. When she started to work, her drawing just seemed to emerge. She was surprised to discover that she'd drawn herself closer to her father and sisters than to her mother. This provoked a lively discussion between her and her mother about their relationship. Although the two of them spent time together, the daughter didn't feel close because she thought her mother treated her like a child, never talking about her own concerns, and showing only superficial interest in the daughter's life. For her part, the mother was surprised, and not at all displeased, that her daughter felt ready to establish a relationship on a more mutual, caring basis.

In *family puppet interviews*, Irwin and Malloy (1975) ask one of the family members to make up a story using puppets. This technique, originally used in play therapy, is designed to highlight conflicts and alliances. In fact, its usefulness is probably limited to working with children. Most adults resist expressing anything really personal through such a childlike medium. Even an eight-year-old knows what's up when a therapist says, "Tell me a story."

Role-playing is another favorite device. Its use is based on the premise that experience, to be real, must be brought to life in the present. Recollection of past events and consideration of hoped-for or feared future events can be made more immediate by role-playing them in the immediacy of the session. Kempler (1968) encourages parents to fantasize and role-play scenes from childhood. A mother might be asked to role-play what it was like when she was a little girl, or a father might be asked to imagine himself as a boy caught in the same dilemma as his son.

When someone who isn't present is mentioned, therapists may introduce the Gestalt *empty chair technique* (Kempler, 1973). If a child talks about her grandfather, she might be asked to speak to a chair, which is supposed to personify grandfather. Whitaker (1975) used a similar role-playing technique, which he called "psychotherapy of the absurd." This consists of augmenting the unreasonable quality of a patient's response to the point of absurdity. It often amounts to calling a person's bluff, as the following example illustrates:

> *Patient:* I can't stand my husband!
>
> *Therapist:* Why don't you get rid of him, or take up a boyfriend?

At times this takes the form of sarcastic teasing, such as mock fussing in response to a fussy child. The hope is that patients will get objective distance by participating in the therapist's distancing; the danger is that patients will feel hurt at being made fun of.

These techniques have proven useful in individual therapy (Nichols & Zax, 1977) to intensify emotional experiencing by bringing memories into focus and acting out suppressed reactions. Whether such devices are necessary in family therapy is open to question. In individual treatment patients are isolated from the significant figures in their lives, and role-playing may be useful to approximate being with those people.

But because family therapy is conducted with significant people present, it seems doubtful that role-playing or other means of fantasy are necessary. If emotional action is wanted, plenty is available simply by opening dialogue between family members.

Two recent emotive approaches to family therapy that represent a more sophisticated understanding of family dynamics are emotionally focused couples therapy and the internal family systems model.

Emotionally Focused Couples Therapy. *Emotionally focused couples therapy* works on two levels in succession—uncovering the hurt and longing beneath defensive expressions of anger and withdrawal, and then helping couples understand how these feelings are played out in their relationship. Getting in touch with their underlying attachment longings helps partners to express themselves more genuinely and to see each other in a more sympathetic light. This more accurate and sympathetic view helps them have a new experience of each other and to change their interaction.

To begin with, the therapist acknowledges each client's immediate feelings—hurt and anger, say—to make them feel understood (Johnson, 1998). Having their feelings validated in this way helps couples deescalate their anxiety and the cycle of their arguing (Greenberg & Johnson, 1988).

> "You're getting angrier and angrier. It's upsetting for you to hear Will picture himself as innocent, isn't it?"

By interrupting a couple's quarrel and reflecting what each of them is feeling, the therapist defuses hostility and helps them focus on their experience rather than on each other's crimes. Then, to explore the perceptions that underlie the partners' emotional responses to each other, the therapist asks for a description of what happens at home.

> "Oh, so part of you believes him, but part of you is suspicious?

"Part of you is watching and expecting that he'll hurt you?

"Can you tell me about the part that believes him, that he's being honest?"

Next the therapist points out how the couple's emotions are driving them into cycles of escalating polarization.

> The cycle was formulated in terms of Will's protecting himself by staying distant and avoiding Nancy's anger, and Nancy's being vigilant and fighting to avoid being betrayed again. As she became more insecure and distrustful, Will then felt more helpless and distanced himself further. As he distanced, she felt betrayed and became more enraged. Both were framed as victims of the cycle, which I continually framed as a common problem that the partners need to help each other with. (Johnson, 1998, pp. 457–458)

The couple's growing awareness of how their emotional reactivity frustrates their longings sets the stage for uncovering and expressing the emotions that lie beneath their sparring. The resulting expression makes it possible for the couple to deepen their understanding of their destructive pattern with each other, and this circular process continues to be explored in the process of working through.

The value of this more genuine, softer expression of feeling lies not so much in catharsis as in creating a shift in the partners' perceptions of each other. No longer are partners seen as blaming, rejecting, or withdrawn, but as lonely, anxious, and afraid. It is seeing the other partner in a new way, not cathartic expression, that leads to change (Greenberg, James, & Conry, 1988).

Attachment theory helps the emotionally focused couples therapist pinpoint the issues that get stirred up when couples talk about their hurts and longings.

"Maybe you feel like no one really loves you?"

"You feel helpless and alone, don't you?"

The impact of this emotional evocation is enhanced by the fact that the partner is present to be addressed in this new and more feelingful way.

"So, can you tell her that?"

The ultimate aim of this work is to enable partners to risk being vulnerable with each other by acknowledging and expressing their attachment needs.

"Only you can face your fear and decide to risk depending on Will. He can't do it, can he? The only one who can drop your defenses and risk trusting him is you isn't it?"

"What's the worst thing that could happen?"

Again, working together with the couple means that once the partners risk expressing their needs and fears, their mates can be encouraged to respond.

"What happens to you, Will, when you hear this?"

The response to this question will of course be very different once the partners let down their guard and begin to talk about what they're afraid of and what they really want from each other.

The emotionally focused therapist frames couples' experiences in terms of deprivation, isolation, and loss of secure connectedness. This perspective, from attachment theory, helps individuals focus on their own longings rather than on each other's faults and failings.

The process of therapeutic intervention has been described in nine treatment steps (Johnson, Hunsley, Greenberg, & Schindler, 1999).

1. Assessment—creating an alliance and explicating the core issues in the couple's conflict using attachment theory.
2. Identifying the problematic interaction cycle that maintains attachment insecurity and relationship distress.
3. Uncovering the unacknowledged emotions underlying interactional positions.
4. Reframing the problem in terms of a problematic cycle with underlying emotions and attachment needs.
5. Encouraging acceptance and expression of disowned needs and aspects of the self.
6. Encouraging acceptance of the partner's new openness.

7. Encouraging the expression of specific needs and wants and creating an intimate, emotional engagement.
8. Facilitating new solutions to unresolved relationship issues.
9. Consolidating new positions and more honest expression of attachment needs.

In all of these steps the therapist moves between helping partners uncover and express their emotional experience and helping them reorganize the pattern of their interactions. For example:

The therapist might, then, first help a withdrawn, guarded spouse formulate his sense of paralyzed helplessness that primes his withdrawal. The therapist will validate this sense of helplessness by placing it within the context of the destructive cycle that has taken over the relationship. The therapist will heighten this experience in the session and then help his partner to hear and accept it, even though it is very different from the way she usually experiences her spouse. Finally, the therapist moves to structuring an interaction around this helplessness, as in, "So can you turn to her and can you tell her, 'I feel so helpless and defeated. I just want to run away and hide.'" This kind of statement, in and of itself, represents a move away from passive withdrawal and is the beginning of active emotional engagement. (Johnson, Hunsley, Greenberg, & Schindler, 1999, p. 70)

Internal Family Systems Therapy. In the *internal family systems model* (Schwartz, 1995), conflicting inner voices are personified as subpersonalities or **parts.** What makes this device powerful is that even when client family members are at odds with each other, their conflicts are often based on polarizations of part of what they feel. The truth is that people in conflict with each other are also often in conflict within themselves.

The adolescent's defiance and her parents' distrust are only one aspect of the complex feelings they have for each other. Or, to choose a different example, the couple caught in a pursuer–distancer pattern may be acting out only those parts of them that are terrified of abandonment and engulfment. By dramatizing the elements of their inner conflicts, internal family systems therapy helps family members sort out their feelings and reconnect with each other in less polarized ways.

To help clients begin to distinguish among their conflicting inner voices, Schwartz begins by introducing the language of parts.

"So there's a part of you that gets upset and angry when your son gets down on himself. Do you think that if that part didn't get so stirred up, it would be easier for you to help him?"

"It sounds like part of you agrees with your husband about getting stricter with the kids, but there's another part that says he's being too harsh. What is that second part? What does it say to you? What is it afraid of?"

By listening carefully to what clients are feeling and then construing their reactions as coming from a part of them, the therapist initiates a shift in family polarizations. It's easier for people to acknowledge that "a part of them" feels—angry, helpless, or whatever—than that "they" (as in all of them) feel that way. A parent who has trouble admitting that he's angry at his son for not doing well in school may find it easier to acknowledge that a part of him gets angry at his son's failures—and, moreover, that the angry part gets in the way of his sympathetic part.

Once the idea is introduced that various parts of family members are reacting to each other, instead of seeing themselves intrinsically at odds, they can begin to see that parts of one are triggering parts of another. The obvious implication is that if their aggravating emotions are contained in only parts of them, they have other feelings and other possibilities for interaction.

Thus: "So that angry part of your father seems to trigger a sad and helpless part of you, is that right?"

And, because many such polarizations become triangles, it might be that the father's angry part also triggers a protective part in his wife.

"So when you see your husband's angry part responding to your son, that triggers a protective part in you? A part of you feels that you need to fight your husband to protect your son?"

So instead of having a son who is a failure, a father who is unsympathetic, and parents who can't agree, the family discovers that each of them is having trouble with some of their parts. The father is transformed from a tyrant to a parent struggling with a frustrated and angry part of himself. His wife ceases to be basically at odds with him and instead is seen as having a protective part that gets triggered by his angry part. Instead of being a failure, the son becomes a boy with a part of him that feels helpless in the face of his father's angry part and his parents' conflict.

Like all experiential models, internal family systems therapy is founded on the belief that underneath people's emotionally reactive parts lies a healthy self at the core of the personality. When the therapist notices various parts taking over, he or she asks the person first to visualize them and then help them to calm down. If, for example, an angry part were seen as a snarling dog, that person might find that she could calm her anger by approaching the dog and petting it until it felt reassured and settled down. Or, to use another example (cited by Schwartz, 1998), if a frightened part were imagined as a rag doll, the client might relax her fears by imagining holding and comforting that doll.

Thus, by personifying people's polarizing emotional reactions as parts and then helping them visualize and reassure these reactive parts, internal family systems therapy releases people from the domination of fear and anger, which in turn allows them to work together more effectively to solve personal and family problems.

Current Status of the Model

Experiential therapy helps family members get beneath the surface of their interactions to explore the feelings that drive them. At its best this approach helps people drop their defenses and come together with more immediacy and au-

thenticity. Given family therapy's emphasis on behavior and cognition, the effort to help clients uncover the feeling side of their experience is surely a welcome idea.

Regardless of what approach to family therapy one takes, shifting to individuals and their experience is a good way to break through defensive squabbling. When family members argue, they usually lead with their defenses. Instead of saying, "*I'm* hurt " they say, "*You* make me mad"; instead of admitting they're afraid, they criticize each other. An effective way to interrupt the unproductive escalation of arguments is to explore the affect of the participants, one at a time. By talking to individuals about what they're feeling—and the roots of such feelings—family members can be helped to get past the defensiveness that keeps them apart and to reconnect on a more genuine level.

But just as approaches that focus entirely on families and their interactions leave something out, so too does an approach that concentrates too narrowly on individuals and their emotional experience. At the peak of their popularity in the 1970s, experiential therapists approached family therapy as if it were an encounter group for relatives. They put great faith in the value of individual emotional experiencing and had limited appreciation of the role family structure plays in regulating that experience. Not surprisingly, therefore, as family therapy focused more on organization, interaction, and narrative in the 1980s and 1990s, the experiential model fell out of favor.

As we have already suggested, a therapy designed primarily to elicit feelings may be more suited to encounter groups than to family therapy. However, the prevailing behavioral and cognitive models of family therapy could do with a little more attention to people's feelings. If "more attention to people's feelings" sounds vague, allow us to make it more concrete. Helping family members get in touch with their feelings accomplishes two things: It helps them as individuals to discover what they really think and feel—what they want and what they're afraid of—and it helps them as a family get beyond defensiveness and begin to relate to each other in a more honest and immediate way.

Two particularly creative approaches to helping individuals get in touch with their inner experience are emotionally focused couples therapy and internal family systems therapy. What sets Johnson and Greenberg's therapy apart is its combination of emotional expressiveness and attention to the dynamics of interaction between couples. Emotionally focused couples therapy begins, as all emotive approaches do, by eliciting and acknowledging the feelings clients come in with—even, or especially, if those feelings are defensive. You don't get beneath the surface of what people are feeling by ignoring it.

The combination of uncovering deeper and more vulnerable emotions and teaching couples about the reactive patterns their feelings drive them through creates a meaningful cognitive experience. As Lieberman, Yalom, and Miles (1973) demonstrated with encounter groups, an emotionally intense therapeutic experience only brings lasting value when paired with an intellectual understanding of the significance of those emotions. The only caveat we might offer is that explanations are most useful following an emotionally significant process of uncovering—which is what distinguishes psychotherapy from a conversation with your Aunt Harriet.

Emotionally focused couples therapy maintains that relationship difficulties generally stem from the disowning of attachment needs, creating defensive interactional cycles and ineffective communication patterns. The model identifies these issues and destructive cycles, helps clients acknowledge the feelings underlying these cycles, encourages empathy for the partner's position, and encourages couples to communicate needs and emotions more effectively in the spirit of generating solutions and solidifying new relationship positions to increase intimacy.

Schwartz's internal family systems approach helps family members come together with more understanding by helping individuals sort out their own conflicted experience. Personifying unruly emotions as "parts" is a powerful device for helping people achieve a clarifying distance from their conflicts. Unlike emotionally focused therapy, internal family systems therapy does not lean heavily on didactic explanations. In this approach, emotional experiencing is clarified but by learning to differentiate among one's own feelings rather than by explanations offered by the therapist.

In addition to anecdotal reports of successful outcome (Napier & Whitaker, 1978; Duhl & Duhl, 1981) and descriptions of techniques that are effective in catalyzing emotional expression within sessions (Kempler, 1981), emotionally focused couples therapy has received a good deal of empirical support (e.g., Johnson & Greenberg, 1985, 1988; Johnson, Maddeaux, & Blouin, 1998; Johnson, Hunsley, Greenberg, & Schindler, 1999).

Recently, researchers seeking to study the effectiveness of experiential techniques have followed Mahrer's (1982) suggestion to focus on the process, rather than the outcome, of therapy. Because he believed that studies of outcome have little impact on practitioners (who already "know" that what they do works), Mahrer recommended studying "in-therapy outcomes"—that is, what kinds of interventions produce desired results (emotional expression, more open communication) within sessions. Following Mahrer (1982) and others (Pierce, Nichols, & DuBrin, 1983) who looked at such in-therapy outcomes in individual treatment, Leslie Greenberg and Susan Johnson have found that helping an angry and attacking partner to reveal his or her softer feelings characterizes the best sessions of successful cases (Johnson & Greenberg, 1988) and that intimate self-disclosure leads to more productive sessions (Greenberg, Ford, Alden, & Johnson, 1993).

Once feeling–expression occupied center stage in psychological therapies; today that place is held by behavior and cognition. Psychotherapists have discovered that people think and act; but that doesn't mean we should ignore the immediate emotional experience that is the main concern of experiential family therapy.

—Summary———————————————————

1. Experiential therapy works from the inside out—strengthening families by encouraging individual self-expression, reversing the usual direction of effect in family therapy. Experiential family therapy is also distinguished by a commitment to emotional well-being as opposed to problem solving. Personal integrity and self-fulfillment are seen as innate human capacities that will emerge spontaneously once defensiveness is overcome. To challenge the familiar and enhance experiencing, therapists use their own lively personalities as well as a host of expressive techniques.

2. Although the experiential model lost popularity in the 1980s, it is now enjoying something of a resurgence, especially in the innovative work of emotionally focused couples therapy and the internal family systems approach. Once, the idea that families were systems was both novel and controversial; today it is the new orthodoxy. Now that the pendulum has swung so far in the direction of systems thinking, individuals and their private joys and pains are rarely mentioned. Surely one of the major contributions of experiential family therapy is to remind us not to lose sight of the self in the system.

—Questions to Consider———————————

1. Can you imagine how "the value of emotional expression" might be used by someone to justify defensive or abusive onslaughts or other forms of emotional dumping?
2. To what extent do you think the basic premise of experiential therapy—that getting in touch with and expressing one's feelings is therapeutic—is primarily relevant for an educated, middle-class clientele?
3. To what extent is it possible for a family therapist to work with the intrapsychic

experience of individual family members without detracting from a focus on their systemic interactions?
4. Can you think of an example where it might be helpful to analyze some conflict or indecision of your own as due to different "parts" of you having different agendas?
5. What does attachment theory offer a therapist beyond the generalization that people sometimes cover their real feelings with defensive responses?

—Key Concepts———————————————

countertransference Emotional reactivity on the part of the therapist.

emotionally focused couples therapy A model of therapy based on attachment theory, in which the emotional longings beneath a couple's defensive reactions are uncovered as they are taught to see the reactive nature of their struggles with each other, developed by Leslie Greenberg and Susan Johnson.

existential encounter A relationship based on direct, personal contact, rather than artificial professional roles.

family drawing An experiential therapy technique whereby family members are asked to draw their ideas about how the family is organized.

family myths A set of beliefs based on a distortion of historical reality and shared by all family members that help shape the rules governing family functioning.

family sculpting A nonverbal experiential technique in which family members position themselves in a tableau that reveals significant aspects of their perceptions and feelings.

induction   A countertransference reaction by which the therapist is drawn into playing a missing role in the family.

internal family systems therapy   A model of family therapy that uses systemic principles and techniques to understand and change intrapsychic processes, developed by Richard Schwartz.

mystification   R. D. Laing's concept that many families distort their children's experience by denying or relabeling it.

parts   Richard Schwartz's term for the various reactive elements that make up a person's subpersonalities.

role-playing   Acting out the parts of important characters to dramatize feelings and practice new ways of relating.

self-actualization   Carl Rogers's term for the innate human tendency for each of us to seek what is best for us. A tendency that gets subverted by the need to please but can be released again in the presence of unconditional positive regard.

—Recommended Readings

Duhl, B. S., and Duhl, F. J. 1981. Integrative family therapy. In *Handbook of family therapy*, A. S. Gurman and D. P. Kniskern, eds. New York: Brunner/Mazel.

Duhl, F. J., Kantor, D., and Duhl, B. S. 1973. Learning, space and action in family therapy: A primer of sculpture. In *Techniques in family therapy*, D. A. Bloch, ed. New York: Grune & Stratton.

Greenberg, L. S., and Johnson, S. M. 1988. *Emotionally focused therapy for couples*. New York: Guilford Press.

Keith, D. V., and Whitaker, C. A. 1977. The divorce labyrinth. In *Family therapy: Full length case studies*, P. Papp, ed. New York: Gardner Press.

Laing, R. D., and Esterson, A. 1970. *Sanity, madness and the family*. Baltimore: Penguin Books.

Napier, A. Y., and Whitaker, C. A. 1978. *The family crucible*. New York: Harper & Row.

Neill, J. R., and Kniskern, D. P., eds. 1982. *From psyche to system: The evolving therapy of Carl Whitaker*. New York: Guilford Press.

Satir, V. M. 1988. *The new peoplemaking*. Palo Alto, CA: Science and Behavior Books.

Satir, V. M., and Baldwin, M. 1983. *Satir step by step: A guide to creating change in families*. Palo Alto, CA: Science and Behavior Books.

Schwartz, R. C. 1995. *Internal family systems therapy*. New York: Guilford Press.

Schwartz, R. C. 1998. Internal family systems therapy. In *Case studies in couple and family therapy*, F. M. Dattilio, ed. New York: Guilford Press.

Whitaker, C. A., and Bumberry, W. M. 1988. *Dancing with the family: A symbolic experiential approach*. New York: Brunner/Mazel.

Whitaker, C. A., and Keith, D. V. 1981. Symbolic–experiential family therapy. In *Handbook of family therapy*, A. S. Gurman and D. P. Kniskern, eds. New York: Brunner/Mazel.

—References

Andreas, S. 1991. *Virginia Satir: The patterns of her magic*. Palo Alto: Science and Behavior Books.

Bing, E. 1970. The conjoint family drawing. *Family Process*. 9: 173–194.

Binswanger, L. 1967. Being-in-the-world. In *Selected papers of Ludwig Binswanger*, J. Needleman, ed. New York: Harper Torchbooks.

Boss, M. 1963. *Psychoanalysis and daseinanalysts*. New York: Basic Books.

Bowlby, J. 1969. *Attachment and loss: Vol. 1. Attachment*. New York: Basic Books.

Duhl, B. S., and Duhl, F. J. 1981. Integrative family therapy. In *Handbook of family therapy*, A. S. Gurman and D. P. Kniskern, eds. New York: Brunner/Mazel.

Duhl, F. J., Kantor D., and Duhl, B. S. 1973. Learning, space and action in family therapy: A primer of sculpture. In *Techniques of family psychotherapy*, D. A. Bloch, ed. New York: Grune & Stratton.

Geddes, M., and Medway, J. 1977. The symbolic drawing of family life space. *Family Process. 16:* 219–228.

Gehrke, S., and Kirschenbaum, M. 1967. Survival patterns in conjoint family therapy. *Family Process. 6:* 67–80.

Greenberg, L. S., Ford, C. L., Alden, L., and Johnson, S. M. 1993. In-session change in emotionally focused therapy. *Journal of Consulting and Clinical Psychology. 61:* 78–84.

Greenberg, L. S., James, P., and Conry, R. 1988. Perceived change processes in emotionally focused couples therapy. *Journal of Family Psychology. 2:* 1–12.

Greenberg, L. S., and Johnson, S. M. 1985. Emotionally focused couple therapy: An affective systemic approach. In *Handbook of family and marital therapy*, N. S. Jacobson and A. S. Gurman, eds. New York: Guilford Press.

Greenberg, L. S., and Johnson, S. M. 1986. Affect in marital therapy. *Journal of Marital and Family Therapy. 12:* 1–10.

Greenberg, L. S., and Johnson, S. M. 1988. *Emotionally focused therapy for couples*. New York: Guilford Press.

Irwin, E., and Malloy, E. 1975. Family puppet interview. *Family Process. 14:* 179–191.

Johnson, S. M. 1998. Emotionally focused couple therapy. In *Case studies in couple and family therapy*, F. M. Dattilio, ed. New York: Guilford Press.

Johnson, S. M., and Denton, W. 2002. Emotionally focused couple therapy: Creating secure connections. In *Clinical handbook of couple therapy*, 3rd ed., A. S. Gurman and N. S. Jacobson, eds. New York: Guilford Press.

Johnson, S. M., and Greenberg, L. S. 1985. Emotionally focused couples therapy: An outcome study. *Journal of Marital and Family Therapy. 11:* 313–317.

Johnson, S. M., and Greenberg, L. S. 1988. Relating process to outcome in marital therapy. *Journal of Marital and Family Therapy. 14:* 175–183.

Johnson, S. M., Hunsley, J., Greenberg, L., and Schindler, D. 1999. Emotionally focused couples therapy: Status and challenges. *Clinical Psychology: Science and Practice. 6:* 67–79.

Johnson, S. M., Maddeaux, C., and Blouin, J. 1998. Emotionally focused therapy for bulimia: Changing attachment patterns. *Psychotherapy. 35:* 238–247.

Kaplan, M. L., and Kaplan, N. R. 1978. Individual and family growth: A Gestalt approach. *Family Process. 17:* 195–205.

Kempler, W. 1968. Experiential psychotherapy with families. *Family Process. 7:* 88–89.

Kempler, W. 1973. *Principles of Gestalt family therapy*. Oslo, Norway: Nordahls.

Kempler, W. 1981. *Experiential psychotherapy with families*. New York: Brunner/Mazel.

Kwiatkowska, H. Y. 1967. Family art therapy. *Family Process. 6:* 37–55.

Laing, R. D. 1967. *The politics of experience*. New York: Ballantine.

Lieberman, M. A., Yalom, I. D., and Miles, M. B. 1973. *Encounter groups: First facts*. New York: Basic Books.

Mahrer, A. R. 1982. *Experiential psychotherapy: Basic practices*. New York: Brunner/Mazel.

Marcuse, H. 1955. *Eros and civilization*. New York: Beacon Press.

Napier, A. Y., and Whitaker, C. A. 1978. *The family crucible*. New York: Harper & Row.

Nichols, M. P., and Zax, M. 1977. *Catharsis in psychotherapy*. New York: Gardner Press.

Pierce, R., Nichols, M. P., and DuBrin, J. 1983. *Emotional expression in psychotherapy*. New York: Gardner Press.

Rogers, C. R. 1951. *Client-centered therapy*. Boston: Houghton Mifflin.

Satir, V. M. 1972. *Peoplemaking*. Palo Alto: Science and Behavior Books.

Satir, V. M., and Baldwin M. 1983. *Satir step by step: A guide to creating change in families*. Palo Alto: Science and Behavior Books.

Schwartz, R. C. 1995. *Internal family systems therapy*. New York: Guilford Press.

Schwartz, R. C. 1998. Internal family systems therapy. In *Case studies in couple and family therapy*, F. M. Dattilio, ed. New York: Guilford Press.

Simon, R. 1989. Reaching out to life: An interview with Virginia Satir. *The Family Therapy Networker. 13*(1): 36–43.

Sullivan, H. S. 1953. *The interpersonal theory of psychiatry*. New York: Norton.

Whitaker, C. A. 1958. Psychotherapy with couples. *American Journal of Psychotherapy. 12:* 18–23.

Whitaker, C. A. 1967. The growing edge. In *Techniques of family therapy*, J. Haley and L. Hoffman, eds. New York: Basic Books.

Whitaker, C. A. 1975. Psychotherapy of the absurd: With a special emphasis on the psychotherapy of aggression. *Family Process.* 14: 1–16.

Whitaker, C. A. 1976a. The hindrance of theory in clinical work. In *Family therapy: Theory and practice*, P. J. Guerin, ed. New York: Gardner Press.

Whitaker, C. A. 1976b. A family is a four-dimensional relationship. In *Family therapy: Theory and practice*, P. J. Guerin, ed. New York: Gardner Press.

Whitaker, C. A., and Keith, D. V. 1981. Symbolic-experiential family therapy. In *Handbook of family therapy*, A. S. Gurman and D. P. Kniskern, eds. New York: Brunner/Mazel.

Whitaker, C. A., and Malone, T. P. 1953. *The roots of psychotherapy*. New York: Blakiston.

Whitaker, C. A., Warkentin, J., and Malone, T. P. 1959. The involvement of the professional therapist. In *Case studies in counseling and psychotherapy*, A. Burton, ed. Englewood Cliffs, NJ: Prentice Hall.

Psychoanalytic Family Therapy

9

Many of the pioneers of family therapy, including Nathan Ackerman, Murray Bowen, Ivan Boszormenyi-Nagy, Carl Whitaker, Don Jackson, and Salvador Minuchin, were psychoanalytically trained. But with the eager enthusiasm of converts they turned away from the old—psychodynamics—and toward the new—systems dynamics. Some, like Jackson and Minuchin, moved far indeed from their psychoanalytic roots. Others, like Bowen and Boszormenyi-Nagy retained a distinctly analytic influence in their work.

In the 1960s and 1970s, family therapy followed Jackson and Minuchin in not only ignoring psychoanalytic thinking but denigrating it. Jackson (1967) went so far as to declare the death of the individual, and Minuchin (1989) proclaimed that, "We understood that the decontexted individual was a mythical monster, an illusion created by psychodynamic blinders."

Then in the 1980s a surprising shift occurred: Family therapists took a renewed interest in the psychology of the individual. This revival of interest reflected changes in psychoanalysis—from the individualism of Freudian theory to the more relationship-oriented object relations theories and self-psychology, as well as changes in family therapy itself, especially dissatisfaction with the mechanistic elements of the cybernetic model. Among the books calling for a rapprochement with psychoanalysis were *Object Relations: A Dynamic Bridge between Individual and Family Treatment* (Slipp, 1984); *Object Relations Family Therapy* (Scharff & Scharff, 1987); and *The Self in the System* (Nichols, 1987).

The reason these psychodynamic voices found a receptive audience was that, whereas family therapists discovered profound truths about systemic interactions, many believed they were wrong to turn their backs on depth psychology. Anyone who does not flee from self-awareness knows that the inner life is awash in conflict and confusion, most of it never expressed. While systemic therapists focused on the outward expression of this inner life—family interaction and communication—psychoanalytic therapists probed beneath family dialogues to explore individual family members' private fears and longings.

Evolution of the Model

Freud was interested in the family but saw it as old business—the place where people learned neurotic fears, rather than the contemporary context in which such fears were maintained. Faced with a phobic Little Hans, Freud (1909)

167

was more interested in analyzing the boy's Oedipus complex than trying to understand what was going on in his family.

Major advances were achieved in the understanding of family dynamics by child psychiatrists who began to analyze mothers and children concurrently (Burlingham, 1951). One example of the fruits of these studies was Adelaide Johnson's (Johnson & Szurek, 1952) explanation of the transmission of *superego lacunae,* gaps in personal morality passed on by parents who do things like tell their children to lie about their age to save a couple of bucks at the movies.

Subsequently, the concurrent analysis of married couples revealed the family as a group of interlocking, intrapsychic systems (Oberndorf, 1938; Mittlemann, 1948). From the 1930s to the 1950s, psychoanalytic researchers became more interested in the contemporary family. Erik Erikson explored the sociologic dimensions of ego psychology. Erich Fromm's observations about the struggle for individuality foreshadowed Bowen's work on differentiation of the self. Harry Stack Sullivan's interpersonal theory emphasized the mother's role in transmitting anxiety to her children.

In the 1950s, American psychoanalysis was dominated by ego psychology (which focuses on intrapsychic structures), whereas object relations theory (which lends itself to interpersonal analysis) flourished an ocean away in Britain. In the 1940s Henry Dicks (1963) established the Family Psychiatric Unit at the Tavistock Clinic in England, where teams of social workers attempted to reconcile couples referred by the divorce courts. By the 1960s Dicks (1967) was applying object relations theory to the understanding and treatment of marital conflict.

Meanwhile, the psychoanalysts who helped create family therapy were moving away from psychodynamics, and the analytic influence in their work was deliberately muted. The exception was Nathan Ackerman, the leading family therapist on the East Coast, who of all the pioneers retained the strongest allegiance to psychoanalysis. Students, among them Salvador Minuchin, flocked to New York to observe this master therapist at

work. His book, *The Psychodynamics of Family Life,* published in 1958, was the first devoted to diagnosis and treatment of families.

Edith Jacobson (1954) and Harry Stack Sullivan (1953) helped bring American psychiatry to an interpersonal point of view. Less well known, but more important to the development of family therapy, was the work carried out at the National Institute of Mental Health (NIMH). When NIMH opened in 1953, Irving Ryckoff moved from Chestnut Lodge, where he'd been working with schizophrenic patients, to develop a research project on families of schizophrenics under the leadership of Robert Cohen. He was joined by Juliana Day and Lyman Wynne and later by Roger Shapiro and John Zinner. This group produced a series of thoughtful papers introducing such concepts as *pseudomutuality* (Wynne, Ryckoff, Day, & Hirsch, 1958), *trading of dissociations* (Wynne, 1965), and *delineations* (Shapiro, 1968). But perhaps their most important contribution was the application of the concept of *projective identification* (from Melanie Klein) to family relationships. This group also introduced to psychoanalytic researchers the idea of seeing the family as a unit for study and to clinicians, the analytic group-interpretive approach to families (Shapiro, 1979).

In the 1960s, Ryckoff and Wynne inaugurated a course in family dynamics at the Washington School of Psychiatry, which led to a family therapy training program. They were joined by Shapiro and Zinner and Robert Winer. In 1975 they recruited Jill Savege (now Scharff) and David Scharff. By the mid-1980s, the Washington School of Psychiatry, under the directorship of David Scharff, had become a leading center of psychoanalytic family therapy. The Scharffs left in 1994 to form their own institute.

Among others who have incorporated psychoanalytic theory into family therapy are Helm Stierlin (1977), Robin Skynner (1976), William Meissner (1978), Arnon Bentovim and Warren Kinston (1991), Fred Sander (1979, 1989), Samuel Slipp (1984, 1988), Michael Nichols (1987), Nathan Epstein, Henry Grunebaum, and Clifford Sager.

The Basic Model

The essence of psychoanalytic treatment is uncovering and interpreting **unconscious** impulses and defenses against them. It isn't a question of analyzing individuals instead of family interactions: It's knowing where to look to discover some of the basic wants and fears that keep those individuals from interacting in a mature way. Consider the case of Carl and Peggy.[1]

—Case Study—

Whenever Peggy talked to Carl about their relationship, she got upset and started criticizing. The more upset Peggy got, the quieter Carl became. Only after enduring her tirades for several minutes did Carl get good and mad and start to shout back at her. As a result, Peggy got exactly the opposite of what she was looking for. Instead of understanding her concerns, Carl felt threatened and withdrew. When that didn't work, he lost his temper. At home, when the same scenario got out of hand, he sometimes slapped her.

The therapist concentrated on interrupting this cycle and then helping the two of them see the pattern so that they could prevent its recurrence. Unfortunately, while Carl and Peggy learned to relate more effectively in the therapist's office, at home they forgot. Week after week it was the same story. They would manage to listen to each other in their sessions, but at least once a month they would lose it at home. Eventually, when they got discouraged enough to stop coming, the therapist decided that they just weren't motivated enough to make the necessary changes.

As actors, perhaps we take ourselves too seriously; as observers, we take other selves not seriously enough. As family therapists, we see the actions of our clients as a product of their interactions. Yes, people are connected, but that connectedness should not obscure the fact that the nature of their interactions is partly dictated by psychic organization of unsuspected depth and complexity.

Consider again the case of Carl and Peggy, the combative couple who drifted away from therapy. Their pattern was relatively simple, and completely impervious to the therapist's efforts to change it. Why couldn't (wouldn't) Carl stop hitting his wife? The fact that she provoked him doesn't really explain anything. Not every husband who is provoked hits his wife.

Looking back, the therapist remembered how Carl used to say with a concern that seemed somewhat affected, "I *must* control my temper!" She also remembered how dramatically he described his intimidating outbursts and his wife's cowering. And she remembered that when Peggy talked about Carl's brutality, a smile played around the corners of his mouth. These hints of a willful, motivated quality to Carl's abuse could be described in the jargon of psychodynamics, which, because it is alien, might lead some people to dismiss it as a relic of outmoded thinking. Psychodynamic language might imply that Carl's unconscious was responsible for his abusing his wife; he was helpless in the face of inner conflicts.

Psychodynamic theory may be useful to understand the self in the system, but it isn't necessary to be highly technical. If we were to write a dramatic narrative about Carl, we could say that he was misrepresenting, even to himself, his feelings and intentions. He fooled his wife, he fooled himself, and he fooled his therapist (perhaps in part because she kept such a tight rein on her own aggression). Carl, who thinks himself concerned with his "temper" (his version of nonhuman agency), is actually pleased with his power to intimidate his wife and with the "manliness" it implies. This explanation does not replace the interactional one, only complicates it. Carl's attacks were triggered by the couple's interactions, but they were propelled by his own unrecognized insecurities. Knowing the motives behind his behavior enables us to help

---

1. This case is taken from *The Self in the System* (Nichols, 1987).

Carl understand that he hits his wife to make up for feeling weak and to help him find some other way to feel more powerful. As long as therapists stay at the simple behavioral level of interaction, with a certain number of their cases, they will make little headway.

Recognizing that people are more complicated than billiard balls means that we sometimes have to delve into their experience and the psychology of the self. Psychoanalytic theory gets so complex when you get into the specifics that it's easy to get lost. Here are the basics.

Freudian Drive Psychology

At the heart of human nature are the drives—sexual and aggressive. Mental conflict arises when children learn, and mislearn, that expressing these impulses directly may lead to punishment. The resulting conflict is signaled by unpleasant affect: Anxiety is unpleasure associated with the idea (often unconscious) that one will be punished for acting on a particular wish—for example, the anger you're tempted to express might make your partner stop loving you. Depression is unpleasure plus the idea (often unconscious) that the feared calamity *has already occurred*—for example, your anger at your mother long ago made her stop loving you; in fact, nobody loves you.

The balance of conflict can be shifted in one of two ways: by strengthening the defenses against one's impulses or by relaxing defenses to permit some gratification.

Self Psychology

The essence of **self psychology** (Kohut, 1971, 1977) is that every human being longs to be appreciated. If, when we're young, our parents are enthusiastically responsive and appreciative, we internalize this acceptance in the form of strong and self-confident personalities. But to the extent that our parents are unresponsive, flat, or withdrawn, then our craving for appreciation is retained in an archaic manner. As adults we alternately suppress the desire for attention and

then allow it to break through whenever we're in the presence of a receptive audience.

The child lucky enough to grow up with appreciative parents will be secure, able to stand alone as a center of initiative, and able to love. The unhappy child, cheated out of loving affirmation, will move through life forever craving the attention he or she was denied.

Object Relations Theory

Psychoanalysis is the study of individuals and their deepest motives (drives and the need for attachment); family therapy is the study of social relationships. The bridge between the two is **object relations theory.** Although the details of object relations theory can be quite complicated, its essence is simple: We relate to others on the basis of expectations formed by early experience. The residue of these early relationships leaves **internal objects**—mental images of self and others built up from experience and expectation. Those internalized objects form the core of the personality—an open system developing and maintaining its identity through social-relatedness, present *and* past.

In their observations of infants and young children, Rene Spitz and John Bowlby emphasized the child's profound need for *attachment* to a single and constant object. If this need is denied, the result is *anaclitic depression* (Spitz & Wolf, 1946), a turning away from the world and withdrawal into apathy. According to Bowlby (1969), attachment isn't simply a secondary phenomenon, resulting from being fed, but a basic need in all creatures. Those who don't have this experience are vulnerable to even the slightest lack of support and may become chronically dependent or isolated. This, in psychoanalytic terms, explains the genesis of *enmeshed* and *disengaged* relationships.

Margaret Mahler observed young children and described a process of **separation–individuation.** After an initial period of total merger, the child begins a gradual process of separation from the mother, progressively renouncing symbiotic fusion with her. The result of successful separation and individuation is a well-differentiated self (Mahler, Pine, & Bergman, 1975). Failure to achieve individuation undermines the development of a cohesive self and a differentiated identity, resulting in overly intense emotional attachments. Depending on the severity of the failure to separate, crises are liable to develop when a child reaches school age, enters adolescence, or prepares to leave home as an adult.

The shift from drives to object relations can also be seen in the interpersonal psychiatry of Harry Stack Sullivan (1953), who emphasized the importance of early mother–child interactions. When a mother is warm and nurturing, her child feels good; when a mother rebuffs or frustrates her child's need for tenderness, the child feels bad; and when the child is exposed to extreme pain or frustration he dissociates to escape anxiety that would otherwise be intolerable. These experiences create the self-dynamisms *good me, bad me,* and *not me,* which then become part of the person's response to future interpersonal situations.

The internal world of **object relations** never corresponds to the actual world of real people. It's an approximation, strongly influenced by the earliest object images, **introjections,** and **identifications.** This inner world gradually matures and develops, becoming progressively synthesized and closer to reality. The individual's internal capacity for dealing with conflict and failure is related to the depth and maturity of the internal world of object relations. Trust in one's self and in the goodness of others is based on the confirmation of love from internalized good objects.

Normal Family Development

A child doesn't mature in sublime indifference to the interpersonal world. The infant needs a facilitating environment in order to thrive. This environment doesn't have to be ideal; an *average expectable environment* featuring **good-enough mothering** (Winnicott, 1965a) is sufficient. The parents' capacity to provide security for the

baby's developing ego depends on whether they themselves feel secure. To begin with, the mother must be secure enough to channel her energy into caring for her infant. She withdraws interest from herself and her marriage and focuses it on the baby. As the baby comes to need less, the mother gradually recovers her self-interest, which allows her to permit the child to become independent (Winnicott, 1965b).

To the very young child, parents aren't quite separate individuals; they are, in Kohut's (1971, 1977) term, **selfobjects,** experienced as part of the self. As a selfobject, the mother transmits her love by touch, tone of voice, and gentle words, as though they were the child's own feelings. When she whispers, "Mommy loves you," the baby learns that he or she is (a) a person and (b) lovable.

In self psychology, two qualities of parenting are deemed essential for the development of a secure and cohesive self. The first is **mirroring**—understanding plus acceptance. Attentive parents convey a deep appreciation of how their children feel. Their implicit "I see how you feel" validates the child's inner experience. Parents also offer models for **idealization.** The little child who can believe "My mother (or father) is terrific, and I am part of her (or him)" has a firm base of self-esteem. In the best of circumstances, the child, already basically secure in his or her self, draws additional strength from identifying with the power and strength of the parents.

From a psychoanalytic perspective, the fate of the family is largely determined by the early development of individual personalities that make up the family. If the parents are mature and healthy adults, the family will be happy and harmonious.

Some of the most interesting and productive psychoanalytic ideas are contained in descriptions of the psychodynamics of marriage. In the 1950s, the marital bond was described as a result of unconscious fantasy (Stein, 1956). We marry a blurry blend of real and hoped-for mates. More recently, and more interestingly, however, psychoanalysts have described the

Ivan Boszormenyi-Nagy

Ivan Boszormenyi-Nagy's emphasis on loyalty, trust, and relational ethics—both within the family and between the family and society—made major contributions to the field of family therapy. An accomplished scholar and clinician, Boszormenyi-Nagy was trained as a psychoanalyst and his work has encouraged many family therapists to incorporate psychoanalytic ideas into family therapy.

Boszormenyi-Nagy is perhaps best known for developing the contextual approach to family therapy, which emphasizes the ethical dimension of family relationships.

overlapping and interlocking of fantasies and projections (Blum, 1987; Sander, 1989). Some authors have described this as *mutual projective identification* (Zinner, 1976; Dicks, 1967), others as *neurotic complementarity* (Ackerman, 1966), *marital collusion* (Dicks, 1967), *mutual adaptation* (Giovacchini, 1958), and *conscious and unconscious contracts* (Sager, 1981).

Among psychodynamic family therapists, few have made more important contributions than Ivan Boszormenyi-Nagy's **contextual therapy,** which emphasizes the ethical dimension of family development. Boszormenyi-Nagy considers relational ethics to be a fundamental force holding families and communities together. In a field that often seeks refuge in the illusion of neutrality, Boszormenyi-Nagy reminds us of the importance of decency and fairness.

For marital partners, Boszormenyi-Nagy's criterion of health is a balance between rights and responsibilities. Depending on their integrity and the complementarity of their needs, partners can develop a trustworthy give and take (Boszormenyi-Nagy, Grunebaum, & Ulrich, 1991). When needs clash, negotiation and compromise are essential.

Development of Behavior Disorders

According to classical psychoanalytic theory, symptoms are attempts to cope with uncon-scious conflicts and the anxiety that signals the emergence of repressed impulses. As psychoanalytic emphasis shifted from instincts to object relations, infantile dependence and incomplete ego development replaced the oedipal complex and repressed instincts as the core problems in development. Fear-dictated flight from object relations, which begins in early childhood, is now considered the deepest root of psychological problems.

One important reason for relationship problems is that children develop distorted perceptions by attributing qualities belonging to one person to someone else. Freud (1905) discovered this phenomenon and called it **transference** when his patient Dora displaced feelings for her father onto him and terminated treatment abruptly just as it was on the threshold of success. Others have observed similar phenomena and called them *scapegoating* (Vogel & Bell, 1960), *trading of dissociations* (Wynne, 1965), *merging* (Boszormenyi-Nagy, 1967), *irrational role assignments* (Framo, 1970), *delineations* (Shapiro, 1968), *symbiosis* (Mahler, 1952), and *family projection process* (Bowen, 1965). Regardless of name, all are variants of Melanie Klein's (1946) concept, *projective identification*.

Projective identification is a process whereby the subject perceives an object as if it contained unwelcome elements of the subject's personality *and* evokes responses from the object that conform to those perceptions. Unlike projection, projective identification is a truly interactional process. Not only do parents project anxiety-arousing aspects of themselves onto their children, the children collude by behaving in a way that confirms their parents' fears. By doing so, they may be stigmatized or scapegoated, but they also gratify aggressive impulses, as, for instance, in delinquent behavior (Jacobson, 1954), realize their own omnipotent fantasies, receive subtle reinforcement from their families, and avoid the terrible fear of rejection for not conforming (Zinner & Shapiro, 1972). Meanwhile the parents are able to avoid the anxiety associated with certain impulses, experience vicarious gratification, and still punish the children for expressing these impulses. In this way, intrapsychic conflict becomes externalized, with the parent acting as a superego, punishing the child for acting on the dictates of the parental id. That's one reason parents overreact: They're afraid of their own impulses.

> The J. family sought help controlling 15-year-old Paul's delinquent behavior. Arrested several times for vandalism, Paul seemed neither ashamed nor able to understand his compulsion to strike out against authority. As therapy progressed, it became clear that Paul's father harbored a deep but unexpressed resentment of the social conditions that made him work long hours for low wages in a factory, while the "fat cats didn't do shit, but still drove around in Cadillacs." Once the therapist became aware of Mr. J.'s suppressed hatred of authority, she also began to notice that he smiled slightly whenever Mrs. J. described Paul's latest exploits.

Parents' failure to accept that their children are separate beings can take extreme forms, leading to the most severe psychopathology. Lidz (Lidz, Cornelison, & Fleck, 1965) described a mother of identical twins who, when she was constipated, would give her two sons an enema.

Poorly differentiated children face a crisis in adolescence, when developmental pressures for independence conflict with infantile attachments. The outcome may be continued dependence or violent rebellion. But the teenager who rebels as a reaction to unresolved dependency needs is ill-equipped for mature relationships. Behind their facade of proud self-reliance, such individuals harbor deep longings for dependence. When they marry, they may seek constant approval, or automatically reject any influence, or both.

> Mr. and Mrs. B.'s complaints were mirror images. He claimed she was "bossy and demanding"; she said that he "had to have everything his own way." Mr. B was the youngest in a close-knit family of five. He described his mother as warm and loving, but said she tried to smother him, and that she discouraged all his efforts to be independent. Subjected to these same pressures, his two older sisters knuckled under and still remain unmarried, living with their parents. Mr. B., however, rebelled against his mother's domination and left home to join the Marines at 17. As he related his experience in the Marine Corps and successful business ventures, it was clear that he was fiercely proud of his independence.
>
> Once the story of Mr. B.'s success in breaking away from his domineering mother was brought into the open, both Mr. and Mrs. B. had a clearer understanding of his tendency to overreact to anything he perceived as controlling. Further analysis revealed that while Mr. B. staunchly rejected what he called "bossiness," he nevertheless craved approval. He had learned to fear his deep-seated dependency needs and protect himself with a facade of "not needing anything from anybody"; nevertheless, the needs were still there and had in fact been a powerful determinant of his choice of wife.

When it comes to choosing a romantic partner, psychoanalysts assure us, love is blind. Freud (1921) wrote that the overvaluation of the loved object when we fall in love leads us to make poor judgments based on **idealization.** The "fall" of falling in love reflects an overflow of narcissistic libido, so that the object of our love is elevated as a substitute for our own unattained ideals. Our own identity glows in the reflected radiance of an idealized companion.

Further complicating romantic relationships is that we hide some of our own needs and feelings in order to win approval. Children tend to suppress feelings they fear may lead to rejection. Winnicott (1965a) dubbed this phenomenon the **false self**—children behave as if they were perfect angels, pretending to be what they are not. In its most extreme form, a false self leads to schizoid behavior (Guntrip, 1969); even in less severe manifestations it affects the choice of a mate. During courtship both partners are eager to please and therefore present themselves in the best possible light. Powerful dependency needs, **narcissism,** and unruly impulses may be submerged before marriage. Once married, however, spouses relax into themselves, warts and all.

Families as well as individuals experience **fixation** and **regression.** Most families function adequately until they're overtaxed, at which time they become stuck in rigid and dysfunctional patterns (Barnhill & Longo, 1978). When faced with too much stress, families tend to revert to earlier levels of development. The amount of stress a family can tolerate depends on its level of development and the types of fixations its members have.

●

Psychiatrists, and especially psychoanalysts, have been criticized (Szasz, 1961) for absolving people of responsibility for their actions. To say that someone has "acted-out" "repressed" sexual urges through an extramarital affair is to suggest that he is not accountable. However, Ivan Boszormenyi-Nagy stresses the idea of ethical accountability in families. Good family relationships include behaving ethically with other family members and considering each member's welfare and interests. Boszormenyi-Nagy believes that family members owe one another *loyalty,* and that they acquire *merit* by supporting each other. To the degree that parents are fair and responsible, they engender loyalty in their children; however, parents create loyalty conflicts when they ask their children to be loyal to one parent at the expense of the other (Boszormenyi-Nagy & Ulrich, 1981).

Pathologic reactions may develop from **invisible loyalties**—unconscious commitments children take on to help their families to the det-riment of their own well-being. For example, a child may get sick to unite parents in concern. Invisible loyalties are problematic because they're not subject to rational scrutiny.

How Therapy Works

Analytic therapists foster insight by looking beyond behavior to the hidden motives below. Naturally, families defend against baring their innermost feelings. After all, it's a great deal to ask of anyone to expose old wounds and deep longings. Psychoanalysts deal with this problem by creating a climate of trust and by proceeding slowly. Once an atmosphere of security is established, the analytic therapist can begin to identify projective mechanisms and bring them back into the marital relationship. Once they no longer need to rely on projective identification, partners can acknowledge and accept previously split-off parts of their own egos. The therapist helps couples begin to recognize how their present difficulties emerged from unconscious perpetuation of conflicts from their own families. This work is painful and cannot proceed without the security offered by a supportive therapist. Nichols (1987) emphasizes the need for *empathy* to create a "holding environment" for the whole family.

—Case Study———

Three months after he went away to college, Barry J. had his first psychotic break. A brief hospital stay made it clear that Barry was unable to withstand separation from his family without decompensating; therefore, the hospital staff recommended that he should live apart from his parents in order to help him become an independent adult. Accordingly, he was discharged to a group home for young adults and seen twice weekly in individual therapy. Unfortunately, he suffered a second breakdown and within two months was rehospitalized.

As the time for discharge from this second hospitalization approached, the ward psychiatrist decided to convene the entire family in order to discuss plans for Barry's post-hospital adjustment. During this meeting it became painfully obvious that powerful forces within the family were impeding any chance for genuine separation. Barry's parents were pleasant people who separately were most engaging and helpful. Toward each other, however, they displayed an icy hatred. During those few moments in the interview when they spoke to each other, their hostility was palpable. Only their concern for Barry prevented their relationship from becoming a battleground—a battleground on which Barry feared one or both of them might be destroyed.

At the staff conference following this interview, two plans for disposition were advanced. One group, recognizing the destructive influence of the family, recommended that Barry be removed as far as possible from his parents and treated in individual psychotherapy. Only by isolating Barry from the family, they argued, was there hope that he could mature into an independent person. Others disagreed, arguing that only by treating them conjointly could the collusive bond between Barry and his parents be resolved. After lengthy discussion the group decided to try the latter approach.

Most of the early family meetings were dominated by the parents' anxious concern about Barry: about the apartment complex where he lived, his job, his friends, how he was spending his leisure time, his clothes, his grooming—in short, about every detail of his life. Gradually, with the therapist's support, Barry was able to limit how much of his life was open to his parents' scrutiny. As they were less able to preoccupy themselves with him, they began to focus on their own relationship. As Barry became more successful at handling his own affairs, his parents became openly combative.

Following a session during which the parents' marital relationship was the primary focus, the therapist recommended that the parents come for a few couples sessions. Unable to divert their attention to Barry, the J.s fought viciously, leaving no doubt that theirs was a seriously destructive relationship.

After two months of internecine warfare—during which time Barry continued to improve—Mr. and Mrs. J. sought a legal separation. Once they were separated, both parents seemed to become happier, more involved with their friends and careers, and less worried about Barry. As they released their stranglehold on their son, both parents began to develop a warmer and more genuine relationship with him. Even after the parents divorced they continued to attend family sessions with Barry.

Rather than isolate individuals from their families, psychoanalytic therapists convene families to help them learn to be independent as well as related. The case study of Barry J. illustrates how the goals of psychoanalytic family therapy were implemented with a particular family.

In Boszormenyi-Nagy's contextual therapy, the goal is a balance of fairness in the burdens and benefits of adult life. The fulfillment of the individual is seen to include giving as well as taking. Family members are helped to face and overcome irrational, unproductive guilt and to claim their **entitlements.** However, facing realistic guilt—based on actual harm done to others, even inadvertently—is seen as essential to expanding accountability within families. Thus, each person works toward self-fulfillment by asserting his or her rights and by living up to his or her obligations.

Therapy

Assessment

Analysts don't postpone treatment until they've made an exhaustive study of their cases; on the contrary, they may not even arrive at a final formulation until the end of treatment. However, although analytic clinicians may continue to refine their understanding over the course of treatment, effective therapy cannot proceed without some dynamic formulation. Beginning therapists—who lack theory as well as experience—sometimes proceed on the assumption that if they merely sit back and listen, understanding will emerge. This rarely works in family therapy. The following is an abbreviated sketch of an initial psychoanalytic evaluation of a family.

—Case Study—

After two sessions with the family of Sally G., who was suffering from school phobia, the therapist made a preliminary formulation of the family's dynamics. In addition to the usual descriptions of family members, the presenting problem, and their history, the formulation included assessments of the parents' object relations and the collusive, unconscious interaction of their marital relationship.

Mr. G. had been initially attracted to his wife as a libidinal object who would fulfill his sexual fantasies, including his voyeuristic propensities. Counterbalancing this was a tendency to idealize his wife. Thus he was deeply conflicted and intensely ambivalent in his sexual relations with her.

At another level, Mr. G. had unconscious expectations that she would be the same long-suffering, self-sacrificing kind of person as his mother. Thus he longed for motherly consolation. However, these dependent longings were threatening to his sense of masculinity, so he behaved outwardly as though he were self-sufficient and needed no one. That he had a dependent inner object inside himself was shown by his tender solicitude toward his wife and children when they were ill. But they had to be in a position of weakness and vulnerability to enable him to overcome his defenses enough for him to gratify his own dependency needs vicariously.

Mrs. G. expected marriage to provide her with an ideal father. Given this unconscious expectation, the very sexuality that attracted men to her was a threat to her wish to be cherished like a little girl. Like her husband, she was highly conflicted about sexual relations. Raised as an only child, she expected to come first. She was even jealous of her husband's warmth toward Sally and attempted to maintain distance between father and daughter by her own intense attachment to Sally.

At the level of her early selfobject images, she was a greedy, demanding little girl. Her introjection of her mother provided her with a model of how to treat a father figure. Unfortunately, what worked for her mother didn't work for her.

Thus, at an object-relations level, both spouses felt themselves to be deprived children, each wanting to be taken care of without having to ask. When these magical wishes weren't granted, both seethed with resentment. Eventually they reacted to trivial provocations with the underlying rage, and horrible quarrels erupted.

When Sally witnessed her parents' violent altercations, she became terrified that her own murderous fantasies might come true. Although her parents hated their own internalized bad-parent figures, they seemed to act them out with each other. Further enmeshing Sally in their conflict was the fact that the ego boundaries between herself and her mother were blurred—almost as though mother and daughter shared one joint personality.

Dynamically, Sally's staying home from school could be seen as a desperate attempt to protect her mother herself from her father's attacks and to defend both parents against her own, projected, murderous fantasies.

An excellent model for developing a psychodynamic focus is the work of Arnon Bentovim and Warren Kinston in Great Britain (Bentovim & Kinston, 1991), who offer a five-step strategy for formulating a focal hypothesis:

1. How does the family interact around the symptom, and how does the family interaction affect the symptom?
2. What is the function of the current symptom? (In the L. family they suspected that if the parents didn't draw together and exclude their son, the result would be severe conflict between the parents.)
3. What disaster is feared in the family that keeps them from facing their conflicts

more squarely? (Why, for example, in the L. family is marital conflict avoided?)

4. How is the current situation linked to past trauma?

5. How would the therapist summarize the focal conflict in a short, memorable statement? (The L. family is excluding the child so as to overcome a marital breakup, which occurred in the family of origin due to a competing parent–child relationship.)

Among the metaphors used to describe psychoanalytic treatment, "depth" and "uncovering" feature prominently. All therapies aim to uncover something. Even behaviorists look to uncover unnoticed contingencies of reinforcement before switching to a directive stance. What sets analytic therapy apart is that the process of discovery is protracted and directed not only at conscious thoughts and feelings, but also at fantasies and dreams. David Scharff (1992) related the following example of the use of dreams in couples treatment.

*J*ill and David Scharff are leading exponents of object-relations family therapy.

—Case Study—————

Lila and Clive played the all-too-familiar complementary roles whereby the more she sought closeness, the more he retreated. Unlike a systemic therapist, however, Scharff was interested not merely in the synchronicity of their behavior but in the inner experience underlying it. Because Clive had little awareness of his internal life and few memories of his early years, the therapist was frustrated in his attempts to understand what pushed Clive into retreat. The following dream proved instructive.

Clive dreamed about a baby with a wound on its behind. A woman was supposed to take care of the baby, but because she wasn't doing much, Clive stepped in and took the baby from her. When asked for his thoughts—"Does anything come to mind in connection with the dream?"— Clive's association was to the prospect of having

children and his concern that he might have to take all the responsibility. After acknowledging this worry, Dr. Scharff pointed out that the dream also suggested a fear of something being terribly wrong, so bad that Clive wouldn't be able to fix it. This triggered a memory of a time when Lila was upset and crying. Clive held her and tried to comfort her, but when her crying didn't subside, he got upset and went into the other room. Thus the dream could also symbolize Clive's fear of taking care of his wife. When she's upset, he may overestimate the depth of her hurt and, because he feels he's the only one who can take care of her, the responsibility feels overwhelming.

Now Lila spoke up, saying that when she gets upset and Clive tries to comfort her, she ends up having to reassure him that she's okay, that what he's doing *is* enough. Thus, even when she's in need of comfort, she has to take care of him. (As Lila's response demonstrates, dreams in couples therapy suggest how the dreamer experiences self and object, and the way dreams are told and related to in the session provides additional information about the partners' dynamics.)

When asked if she had any other thoughts about Clive's dream, Lila hesitated, then said she wondered if Clive thinks of her as the baby. This led to the interpretation that, in addition to Clive's thinking of Lila in some ways as a baby, he also thought of himself as a baby, deeply wounded by childhood hurts. This insight—that Clive's lifelong fear of female engulfment was superimposed on his own sense of infantile neediness and childhood losses—turned out to be pivotal. Lila began to see Clive's withdrawing less as a rejection of her than as a sign of his own vulnerability. She therefore felt less threatened by abandonment, which she now saw more as her own deep worry than as any real possibility. Clive, meanwhile, began to understand his anxiety in the face of his wife's emotional needs not so much as her doing, but as something in him, his own vulnerability. As a result of this understanding, he felt less urgency to withdraw from moments of intimacy and emotion.

Therapeutic Techniques

For all the complexity of psychoanalytic theory, psychoanalytic technique is relatively simple—not easy, but simple. There are four basic techniques: *listening, empathy, interpretations,* and *analytic neutrality.* Two of these—listening and analytic neutrality—may not sound terribly different from what other therapists do, but they are.

Listening is a strenuous but silent activity, rare in our culture. Most of the time we're too busy waiting to get a word in edgewise to listen more than perfunctorily. This is especially true in family therapy, where therapists feel a tremendous pressure to *do* something to help troubled and troubling families. This is where the importance of *analytic neutrality* comes in. To establish an analytic atmosphere, it's essential to concentrate on understanding without worrying about solving problems. Change may come about as a by-product of understanding, but the analytic therapist suspends anxious involvement with outcomes. It's impossible to overestimate the importance of this frame of mind in establishing a climate of analytic exploration.

The analytic therapist resists the temptation to be drawn in to reassure, advise, or confront families in favor of a sustained, but silent, immersion in their experience. When analytic therapists do intervene, they express *empathy* in order to help family members open up, and they make *interpretations* to clarify hidden aspects of experience.

Most psychoanalytic family therapy is done with couples; conflict between partners is taken as the starting point for exploring interpersonal psychodynamics. Take, for example, a couple who reported having an argument over the breakfast table. A systemic therapist might ask them to talk with each other about what happened, hoping to observe what they do to keep the argument from getting settled. The focus would be on behavior and interaction. A psychoanalytic therapist would be more interested in helping the partners explore their emotional reactions. Why did they get so angry? What do they want from each other? What did they expect? Where did these feelings come from? Rather than trying to resolve the argument, the analytic therapist would delve into the fears and longings that lay underneath it.

The signal of intrapsychic conflict is affect. Instead of focusing on who did what to whom, analytic therapists key in on strong feeling and use it as a starting point for detailed inquiry into its origins. "What were you feeling?" "When have you felt that way before?" "And before that?" "What do you remember?" Rather than staying on the horizontal plane of the couple's behavior, the therapist looks for openings into the vertical dimension of their internal experience.

To summarize, psychoanalytic couples therapists organize their explorations along four channels: (1) internal experience, (2) the history of that experience, (3) how the partner triggers that experience, and, finally, (4) how the context of the session and the therapist's input might contribute to what's going on between the partners. Here's a brief example.

—Case Study—

Having made great strides over the course of their first few couples sessions, Andrew and Gwen were all the more upset by their inability to discuss, much less settle, a heated disagreement about buying a new car. It wasn't the car but how to pay for it that set them so angrily at odds. Andrew wanted to take money out of savings for the down payment, to keep the monthly payments low. This made Gwen furious. How could he even consider cutting into their savings! Didn't he understand that their mutual fund paid twice as much interest as they'd have to pay on a car loan?

Unfortunately, they were both too bent on changing the other's mind to make any real effort to understand what was going on inside it. The therapist interrupted their arguing to ask each of them what they were feeling and what they were worried about. He wasn't primarily interested in settling the disagreement—although asking about the feelings underlying an altercation is often an effective opening to understanding and compromise; rather, he felt that the intensity of their reactions indicated that this issue touched key concerns.

Andrew was worried about the burden of monthly expenses. *"Don't you see,"* he implored, "if we don't take out enough to make a substantial downpayment, we'll have to worry every month about making the payments?" Gwen was ready to dispute this, but the therapist cut her off. He was more interested in the roots of Andrew's worry than in the couple's trying to convince each other of anything.

It turned out that Andrew had a lifelong fear of not having enough money. Having enough turned out to mean, not a big house and a fancy car, but enough to spend on things that might be considered indulgent—nice clothes, going out to dinner, flowers, presents. Andrew connected his urge to reward himself with modest material luxuries to memories of growing up in a spartan household. His parents were children of the Depression who thought that things like going out to dinner and buying clothes except when absolutely necessary were frivolous and wasteful. At a deeper level, Andrew's memories of austerity were a screen for his never having gotten the attention and affection he craved from his rather reserved mother.[2] And so he'd learned to soothe himself with a new shirt or fancy dinner at times when he was feeling low. One of Gwen's chief attractions was

her giving and expressive nature. She was openly affectionate and almost always happy to indulge Andrew's wish to buy something for himself.

Gwen connected her anxiety about having a cushion against the unexpected to memories of her father as an unreliable breadwinner. Unlike Andrew's parents, hers spent freely. They went out to dinner three or four times a week and took expensive vacations, and everyone in the family wore nice clothes. But, although he was a free spender, Gwen remembered her father as lacking the foresight to invest wisely or to expand his business beyond its modest success. Although it had never been part of her conscious memories, it seemed that, although her father lavished attention and affection on her, he never really took her seriously as a person. He treated her, in the familiar phrase, like "Daddy's little girl," as adorable—and insubstantial—as a kitten. That's why she was so attracted to what she saw as Andrew's serious and self-disciplined nature—and his high regard for her.

How did these two trigger such virulent reactions in each other? Not only did Gwen's anxious need to have money in the bank conflict with Andrew's need to have money to spend, but they each felt betrayed by the other. Part of Gwen's unconscious bargain with Andrew was that she could count on him to be a secure, steady pillar and to build for the future. Part of his unconscious expectations of her were that she would indulge him. No wonder they were so reactive to each other on this issue.

And the therapist's role in all this? On reflection, he realized that he'd been a little too anxious to smooth things over with this couple. Out of his own desire to see marital happiness he'd controlled the level of conflict in the sessions, intervening actively as a peacemaker. As a result, the couple's progress had come at a price. Deep longings and resentments had been pushed aside rather than explored and resolved. Perhaps, the therapist thought, he'd picked up the couple's fears of facing their own anger.

What use should a therapist make of such countertransferential reactions? Should he disclose his feelings? To say that countertransference may contain useful information isn't to say that

---

2. In Kohut's terms, Andrew's mother provided an inadequate *mirroring* selfobject function.

it's oracular. Perhaps the most useful thing to do is look to countertransference for hypotheses that need confirming evidence from the patients' side of the experience. In this case, the therapist acknowledged his sense that he'd been trying too hard to smooth things over, and he asked Gwen and Andrew whether they, too, were a little afraid to open up their anger.

Like many descriptions of clinical work, this one may seem a little pat. How did we get so quickly from arguing about buying a car to hunger for a mirroring selfobject and someone to idealize? Part of the explanation lies in the inevitably condensed account. But it's also important to recognize that one of the things that enables psychoanalysts to see beneath the surface of things is knowing where to look.

Sessions begin with the therapist inviting family members to discuss current concerns, thoughts, and feelings. In subsequent meetings, the therapist might begin by saying nothing or perhaps, "Where would you like to begin today?" The therapist then leans back and lets the family talk. Questions are limited to requests for amplification and clarification. "Could you tell me more about that?" "Have the two of you discussed how you feel about this?"

When initial associations and spontaneous interactions dry up, the therapist probes gently, eliciting history, people's thoughts and feelings, and their ideas about family members' perspectives. "What does your father think about your problems? How would he explain them?" This technique underscores the analytic therapist's interest in assumptions and projections. Particular interest is paid to childhood memories and associations to parents. The following vignette shows how transitions are made from the present to the past.

─Case Study────────

Among their major disappointments in each other, Mr. and Mrs. S. both complained that

the other one "doesn't take care of me when I'm sick, or listen to my complaints at the end of the day." Not only did they share the perception of the other's lack of "mothering," they both steadfastly maintained that they *were* supportive and understanding. Mrs. S.'s complaint was typical: "Yesterday was an absolute nightmare. The baby was sick and fussy, and I had a miserable cold. Everything was twice as hard and I had twice as much to do. All day long I was looking forward to John's coming home. But when he finally did, he didn't seem to care how I felt. He only listened to me for a minute before starting to tell me some dumb story about his office." Mr. S. responded with a similar account, but with the roles reversed.

At this point the therapist intervened to ask both spouses to describe their relationships with their mothers. What emerged were two very different but revealing histories.

Mr. S.'s mother was a taciturn woman, for whom self-reliance, personal sacrifice, and unremitting struggle were supreme virtues. Though she loved her children, she withheld indulgence and affection, lest they become "spoiled." Nevertheless, Mr. S. craved his mother's attention and constantly sought it. Naturally, he was often rebuffed. A particularly painful memory was of a time he came home in tears after getting beaten up by a bully at school. Instead of the consoling he hoped for, his mother scolded him for "acting like a baby." Over the years he learned to protect himself from these rebuffs by developing a facade of independence and strength.

With the second significant woman in his life, his wife, Mr. S. maintained his rigid defensiveness. He never talked about his problems, but because he continued to yearn for compassionate understanding, he resented his wife for not drawing him out. His own failure to risk rejection by asking for support served as a self-fulfilling prophecy, confirming his expectation, "She doesn't care about me."

Mrs. S.'s background was quite different. Her parents were indulgent and demonstrative. They doted on their only child, communicating their love by expressing constant, anxious concern for her well-being. When she was a little girl, the slightest bump or bruise was an occasion for lavish expressions of concern. She came to marriage used to talking about herself and her problems. At first Mr. S. was enchanted. *Here is someone who really cares about feelings,* he thought. But when he discovered that she didn't ask him to talk about his own concerns, he became resentful and progressively less sympathetic. This convinced her, *He doesn't care about me.*

After the roots of current family conflicts have been uncovered, interpretations are made about how family members continue to reenact past, and often distorted, images from childhood. The data for such interpretations come from transference reactions to the therapist or to other family members, as well as from childhood memories. Psychoanalytic therapists deal less with recollections of the past than with reenactments of the past's influence in the present.

Don Catherall (1992) described a very useful process for interpreting projective identification in couples therapy. First, it's important to understand that projective identification isn't some mysterious process in which quantities of one person's experience are passed to the other completely outside of awareness. Rather, the feelings are communicated and provoked by subtle but recognizable signals—though they are usually not focused on. You may have experienced projective identification yourself if you've ever been around someone who was behaving seductively but then acted shocked when you made an advance.

The first step in working with projective identification in couples therapy is to interrupt repetitive squabbling, which is likely to mask any expression of the partners' real feelings. Couples caught up in recurring patterns of conflict and misunderstanding are colluding to avoid feelings of vulnerability. Once a couple's quarreling is blocked, the therapist can explore what the individuals are feeling. Catherall recommends focusing first on what the *recipient* of the projection is feeling. Once that person's feelings are clarified, he or she can be helped to communicate those

feelings to the partner. To avoid provoking defensiveness, the recipient describing the formerly disavowed feelings is coached to describe only the feelings themselves, not what the projecting partner did to provoke them. Meanwhile, the *projecting partner* is told just to listen and not comment. When the recipient has finished, the projector is directed to feed back what he or she understood the partner to be saying. This encourages the projecting partner to assume the recipient's point of view and therefore makes it difficult to block identification with those feelings

The projecting partner is encouraged to empathize with the recipient. Hopefully at this point, the couple can stop trading accusations and start trying to understand how each other feels. Ideally, this sharing of feelings will help bring the partners closer—to understanding, and to each other. To illustrate, Catherall cites the example of "David" and "Sheila." The more anxious David was to have sex with Sheila, the more sensitive he was to any hint of rejection. He would respond to her disinterest by withdrawing, and they would remain distant until Sheila reached out. Sheila ended up feeling the same unloved feelings that David had felt when his mother shut him out. Meanwhile David felt powerless with Sheila, just as she had felt with an uncle who had molested her. Each, in other words, was experiencing concordant identifications stimulated through a mutual process of projective identification.

The therapist pursued Sheila's feelings by inquiring what it was like for her when David was so distant. Her initial answer was that it made her angry, but the therapist asked what did it make her angry about, and what was she feeling prior to getting angry? Sheila was then able to identify feelings of being unloved, uncared for, and generally lonely. These were the feelings that had been stimulated by David's projective identification, and they were feelings that Sheila would normally disavow by becoming angry and then cold.

Then the therapist asked Sheila to talk with David about what it was like for her to feel lonely and unloved. The therapist was careful to keep

Sheila focused on herself and what she was feeling, not on David and what he may have done to cause those feelings. Now that he was not being blamed, David was able to empathize and identify with the feelings of loneliness that Sheila was describing. When the therapist asked him if he knew what it was like to feel that way, David was finally able to talk more directly about the painful feelings that he had been warding off by projecting them onto Sheila.

Psychoanalytic family therapists are aware that their influence isn't confined to rational analysis but also includes a kind of reparenting. Thus therapists may act in a more controlling or permissive fashion, depending on their assessment of the particular needs of a family. One therapist who was acutely aware of his personal influence on families was Nathan Ackerman. His interventions (Ackerman, 1966) were designed to penetrate family defenses in order to surface hidden conflicts over sex and aggression. Unlike the traditionally reserved analyst, Ackerman related to families in a very personal manner. In this regard he wrote (1961):

> It is very important at the outset to establish a meaningful emotional contact with all members of the family, to create a climate in which one really touches them and they feel they touch back. (p. 242)

Ackerman encouraged honest expression of feeling by being honest himself. His spontaneous disclosure of his own thoughts and feelings made it hard for family members to resist doing likewise. Ackerman made full use of his charisma, but he did more than simply "be himself." He made deliberate use of confrontive techniques to bring out family conflicts. His memorable phrase to describe this was "tickling the defenses."

Psychoanalytic family therapists emphasize that much of what is hidden in family dialogues is not consciously withheld but rather repressed into unconsciousness. The approach to this material is guarded by resistance often manifested in the form of transference. This case study illustrates the interpretation of resistance.

—Case Study———

Mr. and Mrs. Z. had endured ten years of a loveless relationship in order to preserve the fragile security that marriage offered them. Mrs. Z.'s unexpected and uncharacteristic affair forced the couple to acknowledge the problems in their relationship, and so they consulted a family therapist.

Although they could no longer deny the existence of conflict, both spouses exhibited major resistance to confronting their problems openly. In the first session, both partners said that married life had been "more or less okay"; that Mrs. Z. had some kind of "midlife crisis"; and that it was she who needed therapy. This request for individual therapy was seen as a resistance to avoid the painful examination of the marriage, and the therapist said so. "It seems, Mr. Z., that you'd rather blame your wife than consider how the two of you might both be contributing to your difficulties. And you, Mrs. Z., seem to prefer accepting all the guilt in order to avoid confronting your husband with your dissatisfaction."

Accepting the therapist's interpretation and agreeing to examine their relationship deprived the couple of one form of resistance, as though an escape hatch had been closed. In the next few sessions both partners attacked each other vituperatively, but they talked only about her affair rather than about problems in the relationship. These arguments weren't productive because whenever Mr. Z. felt anxious he attacked his wife, and whenever she felt angry she became guilty and depressed.

Sensing that their fighting was unproductive, the therapist said, "It's clear that you've put each other through a lot of unhappiness and you're both quite bitter. But unless you get down to talking about specific problems in your marriage, there's little chance that you'll get anywhere."

Thus focused, Mrs. Z. timidly ventured that she'd never enjoyed sex with her husband and wished that he would take more time with foreplay. He snapped back, "Okay, so sex wasn't so great, is that any reason to throw away ten years of marriage and start whoring around!" At this, Mrs. Z. buried her face in her hands and sobbed uncontrollably. After she regained her composure, the therapist intervened, again confronting the couple with their resistance: "It seems, Mr. Z., that when you get upset, you attack. What makes you so anxious about discussing sex?" Following this the couple was able to talk about their feelings about sex in their marriage until near the end of the session. At this point, Mr. Z. again lashed out at his wife calling her a whore and a bitch.

Mrs. Z. began the following session by saying that she'd been depressed and upset, crying off and on all week. "I feel so guilty," she sobbed. "You *should* feel guilty!" retorted her husband. Once again, the therapist intervened. "You use your wife's affair as a club. Are you still afraid to discuss problems in your marriage? And you, Mrs. Z., cover your anger with depression. What is it that you're angry about? What was missing in the marriage? What did you want?"

This pattern continued for several more sessions. The spouses who had avoided discussing or even thinking about their problems for ten years used a variety of resistances to veer away from them in therapy. The therapist persisted in pointing out their resistance and urging them to talk about specific complaints.

Psychoanalytic family therapists endeavor to foster insight and understanding; they also urge families to consider what they're going to do about the problems they discuss. This effort—part of the process of working through—is more prominent in family therapy than in individual therapy. Boszormenyi-Nagy, for example, believes that family members must not only be made aware of their motivations but must also be held accountable for their behavior. In contextual therapy, Boszormenyi-Nagy (1987) points out that the therapist must help people face the stifling expectations involved in invisible loyalties and then help them find more positive ways of making loyalty payments in the family ledger. What this boils down to is developing a balance of fairness.

Ackerman, too, stressed an active working through of insights by encouraging families to constructively express the aggressive and libidinal impulses uncovered in therapy. To alleviate symptoms, impulses must become conscious, but, for lives to change, an emotional experience must be associated with increased self-awareness. To modify thinking and feeling is the essential task of psychoanalytic therapy, but family therapists are also concerned with supervising and analyzing changes in behavior.

Current Status of the Model

Too many family therapists neglect psychology in general and psychoanalytic theory specifically. Regardless of what other approach a therapist uses, the writings of psychoanalytically informed clinicians are a rich resource.

Having said this, we also wish to make a cautionary point. Doctrinaire psychoanalytic family therapies are powerful in the hands of trained psychoanalysts. However, many therapists who get discouraged with the usual contentious family dialogues gravitate to psychoanalytic methods as a way to cut through the defensive wrangling. Interrupting a family's arguments to explore the individuals' feelings is an excellent way to block arguments. If, however, therapists make themselves overly central (by directing all conversation through themselves), or if they overemphasize individuals and neglect family interactions, then the power of family therapy—addressing relationship problems directly—may be lost. Interrupting defensive sparring to get to the hopes and fears that lie beneath is all to the good. But, unless these interrogatories are followed by unstructured interchanges among family members themselves, these explorations may only produce the illusion of change as long as the therapist is present to act as detective and referee.

Psychoanalytic therapists have generally resisted attempts to evaluate their work using empirical standards. Because symptom reduction isn't the goal, it can't serve as the measure of success. And since the presence or absence of unconscious conflict isn't apparent to outside observers, whether an analysis is successful depends on subjective judgment. Psychoanalytic clinicians consider the therapist's observations a valid means of evaluating theory and treatment. The following quotation from the Blancks (1972) illustrates this point. Speaking of Margaret Mahler's ideas, they wrote,

> Clinicians who employ her theories technically question neither the methodology nor the findings, for they can confirm them clinically, a form of validation that meets as closely as possible the experimentalist's insistence upon replication as criterion of the scientific method. (p. 675)

Another example of this point of view can be found in the writing of Robert Langs. "The ultimate test of a therapist's formulation," says Langs (1982), "lies in the use of the therapist's impressions as a basis for intervention" (p. 186). What then determines the validity and effectiveness of these interventions? Langs doesn't hesitate; the patient's reactions, conscious and unconscious, constitute the ultimate litmus test. "True validation involves responses from the patient in both the cognitive and interpersonal spheres."

Is the ultimate test of therapy then the patient's reactions? Yes and no. First, patients' reactions are open to interpretation—especially because validation is sought not only in manifest responses but also in unconsciously encoded derivatives. Moreover, this point of view doesn't take into account the changes in patients' lives that occur outside the consulting room. Therapists occasionally report on the outcome of psychoanalytic family therapy, but mostly in uncontrolled case studies. One such report is Dicks's (1967) survey of the outcome of psychoanalytic couples therapy at the Tavistock Clinic, in which he rated as having been successfully treated 72.8 percent of a random sample of cases.

Summary

1. Psychoanalytically trained clinicians were among the first to practice family therapy, but when they began treating families most of them traded in their ideas about depth psychology for systems theory. Since the mid-1980s, there's been a resurgence of interest in psychodynamics among family therapists, an interest dominated by object relations theory and self psychology. In this chapter we've sketched the main points of these theories and shown how they're relevant to a psychoanalytic family therapy, integrating depth psychology and systems theory. A few practitioners (e.g., Kirschner & Kirschner, 1986; Nichols, 1987; Slipp, 1984) have combined elements of both; some have developed more frankly psychoanalytic approaches (notably Scharff & Scharff, 1987; Sander, 1989); none has achieved a true synthesis.

2. The essential aim of psychoanalytic therapy is to help people understand their basic motives and resolve conflicts over expressing those yearnings in a healthy fashion. Freudians emphasize sexual and aggressive impulses, self psychologists focus on the longing for appreciation, and object relations therapists concentrate on the need for secure attachment relationships. But all are united in the belief that couples and families can be helped to get along better if their individual members understand and begin to resolve their own personal conflicts.

3. In practice, psychoanalytic family therapists focus less on the group and their interactions and more on individuals and their feelings. Exploring these feelings is aided by psychoanalytic theory (or theories) that helps clinicians understand the basic underlying issues that all people struggle with.

—Questions to Consider————————————

1. To get an idea of how difficult it is to maintain a neutral, analytic attitude, the next time a friend tells you a story or a problem, try to listen with as few questions and as few of your own comments as possible. What distractions from what the other person was saying did you find yourself tempted to pursue?

2. Can you describe some situations in which resistance might not be just an impediment but a clue to important vulnerabilities and past unhappy experiences?

3. In a sample of clinical material that includes details, analyze the therapist's interventions to find examples of where the therapist might be trying to distract the client(s) from anxiety or pulling for some reassuring response from the client(s). For example, when some therapists make "reflections" they seem to be looking for the clients to appreciate that the therapist is being understanding.

4. Can you make sense of the notion that there is such a thing as two-person psychology? Psychoanalytic family therapists claim, for example, that projective identification is an example of two-person psychology. Do you think there is such a thing, or just two separate personalities interacting?

5. For a few days, keep track of the extent to which your mood varies with the quality of positive selfobject experiences in your life.

—Key Concepts————————————

contextual therapy Boszormenyi-Nagy's model that includes an appreciation of relational ethics.

delineations Parental acts and statements that express the parents' image of their children; may be objective or distorted.

entitlement Boszormenyi-Nagy's term for the amount of merit a person accrues for behaving in an ethical manner toward others.

false self Winnicott's term for a defensive facade that comes to dominate some people's dealings with others.

fixation Partial arrest of attachment or mode of behavior from an early stage of development.

good-enough mothering Winnicott's term for the average-expectable parenting, which is sufficient to nurture a reasonably healthy child.

idealization A tendency to exaggerate the virtues of someone, part of the normal developmental process in children's relationships to their parents and in intimate partnerships.

identification Not merely imitation but appropriation of traits of an admired other.

internal objects Mental images and fantasies of oneself and others, formed by early interactions with caregivers.

introjection A primitive form of identification; taking in aspects of other people, which then become part of the self-image.

invisible loyalties Boszormenyi-Nagy's term for unconscious commitments that children take on to help their families.

mirroring Kohut's term for the expression of understanding and appreciation—not praise but appreciation of what the other is feeling.

narcissism Self-regard. The exaggerated self-regard most people equate with narcissism is pathological narcissism.

object relations Internalized images of self and others based on early parent–child interactions that determine a person's mode of relationship to other people.

object relations theory Psychoanalytic theory derived from Melanie Klein and developed by the British School (Bion, Fairbairn, Guntrip, and Winnicott) that emphasizes relationships and attachment rather than libidinal and aggressive drives, as the key issues of human concern.

projective identification A defense mechanism whereby unwanted aspects of the self are attributed to another person and that person is induced to behave in accordance with these projected attributes.

regression Return to a less mature level of functioning in the face of stress.

selfobject Kohut's term for a person related to not as a separate individual but as an extension of the self.

self psychology Heinz Kohut's version of psychoanalysis that emphasizes the need for attachment and appreciation rather than sex and aggression.

separation–individuation Process whereby the infant begins, at about two months, to draw apart from the symbiotic bond with mother and develop his or her autonomous functioning.

transference Distorted emotional reactions to present relationships based on unresolved early family relations.

unconscious Memories, feelings, and impulses of which a person is unaware. Often used as a noun, but more appropriately limited to use as an adjective.

—Recommended Readings

Ackerman, N. W. 1966. *Treating the troubled family.* New York: Basic Books.

Boszormenyi-Nagy, I. 1972. Loyalty implications of the transference model in psychotherapy. *Archives of General Psychiatry. 27:* 374–380.

Boszormenyi-Nagy, I. 1987. *Foundations of contextual therapy.* New York: Brunner/Mazel.

Dicks, H. V. 1967. *Marital tensions.* New York: Basic Books.

Donovan, J. M. 2004. *Short-term object relations couples therapy: The five step model.* New York: Brunner-Routledge.

Meissner, W. W. 1978. The conceptualization of marriage and family dynamics from a psychoanalytic perspective. In *Marriage and marital therapy,* T. J. Paolino and B. S. McCrady, eds. New York: Brunner/Mazel.

Nadelson, C. C. 1978. Marital therapy from a psychoanalytic perspective. In *Marriage and marital therapy,* T. J. Paolino and B. S. McCrady, eds. New York: Brunner/Mazel.

Nichols, M. P. 1987. *The self in the system.* New York: Brunner/Mazel.

Sander, F. M. 1989. Marital conflict and psychoanalytic theory in the middle years. In *The middle years: New psychoanalytic perspectives,* J. Oldham and R. Liebert, eds. New Haven: Yale University Press.

Scharff, D., and Scharff, J. S. 1987. *Object relations family therapy.* New York: Jason Aronson.

Stern, M. 1985. *The interpersonal world of the infant.* New York: Basic Books.

Zinner, J., and Shapiro, R. 1976. Projective identification as a mode of perception of behavior in families of adolescents. *International Journal of Psychoanalysis. 53:* 523–530.

—References

Ackerman, N. W. 1958. *The psychodynamics of family life.* New York: Basic Books.

Ackerman, N. W. 1961. The emergence of family psychotherapy on the present scene. In *Contemporary psychotherapies,* M. I. Stein, ed. Glencoe, IL: The Free Press.

Ackerman, N. W. 1966. *Treating the troubled family.* New York: Basic Books.

Barnhill, L. R., and Longo, D. 1978. Fixation and regression in the family life cycle. *Family Process. 17:* 469–478.

Bentovim, A., and Kinston, W. 1991. Focal family therapy. In *Handbook of family therapy*. vol. II, A. S. Gurman and D. P. Kniskern, eds. New York: Brunner/Mazel.

Blanck, G., and Blanck, R. 1972. Toward a psychoanalytic developmental psychology. *Journal of the American Psychoanalytic Association. 20:* 668–710.

Blum, H. P. 1987. Shared fantasy and reciprocal identification: General considerations and gender–disorder. In *Unconscious fantasy: Myth and reality*, H. P. Blum et al., eds. New York: International Universities Press.

Boszormenyi-Nagy. I. 1967. Relational modes and meaning. In *Family therapy and disturbed families*, G. H. Zuk and I. Boszormenyi-Nagy, eds. Palo Alto: Science and Behavior Books.

Boszormenyi-Nagy, I. 1987. *Foundations of contextual therapy.* New York: Brunner/Mazel.

Boszormenyi-Nagy, I., Grunebaum, J., and Ulrich, D. 1991. Contextual therapy. In *Handbook of family therapy*. vol. II, A. S. Gurman and D. P. Kniskern, eds. New York: Brunner/Mazel.

Boszormenyi-Nagy, I., and Ulrich, D. N. 1981. Contextual family therapy. In *Handbook of family therapy*, A. S. Gurman and D. P. Kniskern, eds. New York: Brunner/Mazel.

Bowen, M. 1965. Family psychotherapy with schizophrenia in the hospital and in private practice. In *Intensive family therapy*, I. Boszormenyi-Nagy and J. L. Framo, eds. New York: Harper & Row.

Bowlby, J. 1969. *Attachment and loss.* vol. 1: *Attachment.* New York: Basic Books.

Burlingham, D. T. 1951. Present trends in handling the mother-child relationship during the therapeutic process. *Psychoanalytic study of the child.* New York: International Universities Press.

Catherall, D. R. 1992. Working with projective identification in couples. *Family Process. 31:* 355–367.

Dare, C. 1979. Psychoanalysis and systems in family therapy. *Journal of Family Therapy. 1:* 137–151.

Dicks, H. V. 1963. Object relations theory and marital studies. *British Journal of Medical Psychology. 36:* 125–129.

Dicks, H. V. 1967. *Marital tensions.* New York: Basic Books.

Framo, J. L. 1970. Symptoms from a family transactional viewpoint. In *Family therapy in transition*, N. W. Ackerman, ed. Boston: Little, Brown & Co.

Freud, S. 1905. Fragment of an analysis of a case of hysteria. *Collected papers.* New York: Basic Books, 1959.

Freud, S. 1909. Analysis of a phobia in a five-year-old boy. *Collected papers.* vol. III. New York: Basic Books, 1959.

Freud, S. 1921. Group psychology and the analysis of the ego. *Standard edition. 17:* 1–22. London: Hogarth Press, 1955.

Giovacchini, P. 1958. Mutual adaptation in various object relations. *International Journal of Psychoanalysis. 39:* 547–554.

Guntrip, H. 1969. *Schizoid phenomena, object relations theory and the self.* New York: International Universities Press.

Jackson, D. D. 1967. The individual and the larger context. *Family Process. 6:* 139–147.

Jacobson, E. 1954. *The self and the object world.* New York: International Universities Press.

Johnson, A., and Szurek, S. 1952. The genesis of antisocial acting out in children and adults. *Psychoanalytic Quarterly. 21:* 323–343.

Kirschner, D., and Kirschner, S. 1986. *Comprehensive family therapy: An integration of systemic and psychodynamic treatment models.* New York: Brunner/Mazel.

Klein, M. 1946. Notes on some schizoid mechanisms. *International Journal of Psycho-Analysis. 27:* 99–110.

Kohut, H. 1971. *The analysis of the self.* New York: International Universities Press.

Kohut, H. 1977. *The restoration of the self.* New York: International Universities Press.

Langs, R. 1982. *Psychotherapy: A basic text.* New York: Jason Aronson.

Lidz, T., Cornelison, A., Fleck, S. 1965. *Schizophrenia and the family.* New York: International Universities Press.

Mahler, M. S. 1952. On child psychosis and schizophrenia: Autistic and symbiotic infantile psychoses. *Psychoanalytic Study of the Child.* vol. 7.

Mahler, M., Pine, F., and Bergman, A. 1975. *The psychological birth of the human infant.* New York: Basic Books.

Meissner, W. W. 1978. The conceptualization of marriage and family dynamics from a psychoanalytic perspective. In *Marriage and marital therapy*, T. J. Paolino and B. S. McCrady, eds. New York: Brunner/Mazel.

Minuchin, S. 1989. Personal communication. Quoted from *Institutionalizing madness*, J. Elizur and S. Minuchin, eds. New York: Basic Books.

Mittlemann, B. 1948. The concurrent analysis of married couples. *Psychoanalytic Quarterly. 17:* 182–197.

Nichols, M. P. 1987. *The self in the system.* New York: Brunner/Mazel.

Oberndorf, C. P. 1938. Psychoanalysis of married couples. *Psychoanalytic Review. 25:* 453–475.

Sager, C. J. 1981. Couples therapy and marriage contracts. In *Handbook of family therapy,* A. S. Gurman and D. P. Kniskern, eds. New York: Brunner/Mazel.

Sander, F. M. 1979. *Individual and family therapy: Toward an integration.* New York: Jason Aronson.

Sander, F. M. 1989. Marital conflict and psychoanalytic therapy in the middle years. In *The middle years: New psychoanalytic perspectives,* J. Oldham and R. Liebert, eds. New Haven: Yale University Press.

Scharff, D. 1992. *Refining the object and reclaiming the self.* New York: Jason Aronson.

Scharff, D., and Scharff, J. 1987. *Object relations family therapy.* New York: Jason Aronson.

Shapiro, R. L. 1968. Action and family interaction in adolescence. In *Modern psychoanalysis,* J. Marmor, ed. New York: Basic Books.

Shapiro, R. L. 1979. Family dynamics and object relations theory. In *Adolescent psychiatry,* S. C. Feinstein and P. L. Giovacchini, eds. Chicago: University of Chicago Press.

Skynner, A. C. R. 1976. *Systems of family and marital psychotherapy.* New York: Brunner/Mazel.

Slipp, S. 1984. *Object relations: A dynamic bridge between individual and family treatment.* New York: Jason Aronson.

Slipp, S. 1988. *Technique and practice of object relations family therapy.* New York: Jason Aronson.

Spitz, R., and Wolf, K. 1946. Anaclitic depression: An inquiry into the genesis of psychiatric conditions early in childhood. *Psychoanalytic Study of the Child. 2:* 313–342.

Stein, M. 1956. The marriage bond. *Psychoanalytic Quarterly. 25:* 238–259.

Stierlin, H. 1977. *Psychoanalysis and family therapy.* New York: Jason Aronson.

Sullivan, H. S. 1953. *The interpersonal theory of psychiatry.* New York: Norton.

Szasz, T. S. 1961. *The myth of mental illness.* New York: Hoeber-Harper.

Vogel, E. F., and Bell, N. W. 1960. The emotionally disturbed as the family scapegoat. In *The family,* N. W. Bell and E. F. Vogel, eds. Glencoe, IL: Free Press.

Winnicott, D. W. 1965a. *The maturational process and the facilitating environment.* New York: International Universities Press.

Winnicott, D. W. 1965b. *The maturational process and the facilitating environment: Studies in the theory of emotional development.* New York: International Universities Press.

Wynne, L. C. 1965. Some indications and contradictions for exploratory family therapy. In *Intensive family therapy,* I. Boszormenyi-Nagy and J. L. Framo, eds. New York: Harper & Row.

Wynne, L., Ryckoff, I., Day, J., and Hirsch, S. 1958. Pseudomutuality in the family relations of schizophrenics. *Psychiatry. 21:* 205–220.

Zinner, J. 1976. The implications of projective identification for marital interaction. In *Contemporary marriage: Structure, dynamics, and therapy,* H. Grunebaum and J. Christ, eds. Boston: Little, Brown & Co.

Zinner, J., and Shapiro, R. 1972. Projective identification as a mode of perception and behavior in families of adolescents. *International Journal of Psychoanalysis. 53:* 523–530.

10

Cognitive-Behavior Family Therapy

When they first began working with families, behavior therapists applied learning theory to train parents in behavior modification and teach couples communication skills. These approaches proved effective with discrete, behavioral problems and well-motivated individuals. Anchored as they were in individual psychology, however, behavior therapists had little appreciation of the ways in which misbehavior and poor communication were embedded in family systems.

Behaviorists generally worked in academic settings and, despite developing an armamentarium of useful techniques, remained relatively isolated from mainstream family therapy. The past ten years, however, have seen sweeping changes in behavioral family therapy, with increasing sophistication about family dynamics and the incorporation of cognitive principles.

Evolution of the Model

Behavior therapy is a descendant of the investigations of Ivan Pavlov, the Russian physiologist whose work on conditioned reflexes led to the development of **classical conditioning.** In classical conditioning, an *unconditioned stimulus* (UCS), such as food, which leads to a reflex

unconditioned response (UCR), like salivation, is paired with a *conditioned stimulus* (CS), such as a bell. The result is that the conditioned stimulus begins to evoke the same response (Pavlov, 1932). Subsequently John B. Watson used classical conditioning to experimentally induce a phobia in "Little Albert" (Watson & Raynor, 1920), while Mary Cover Jones successfully resolved a similar phobia in the case of "Peter" (Jones, 1924).

In 1948, Joseph Wolpe introduced **systematic desensitization,** with which he achieved great success in the treatment of phobias. According to Wolpe (1948) anxiety is a persistent response of the autonomic nervous system acquired through classical conditioning. Systematic desensitization deconditions anxiety through *reciprocal inhibition,* by pairing responses incompatible with anxiety to the previously anxiety-arousing stimuli. For example, if Indiana Jones were frightened of snakes, Wolpe would teach Dr. Jones deep muscle relaxation and then have him imagine approaching a snake in a graded hierarchy of stages. Each time Indy became anxious, he would be told to relax. In this way the anxiety evoked by imagining snakes would be systematically extinguished.

Systematic desensitization proved to be even more effective when it included actual practice

189

in approaching the feared object or situation (*in vivo desensitization*).

Classical conditioning was applied to family problems primarily through the treatment of anxiety-based disorders, including agoraphobia and sexual dysfunction, pioneered by Wolpe (1958) and later elaborated by Masters and Johnson (1970). Effective behavioral treatments for enuresis were also developed using classical conditioning (Lovibond, 1963).

By far the greatest influence on behavioral family therapy came from B. F. Skinner's **operant conditioning.** The term *operant* refers to voluntary responses, as opposed to reflexes. The frequency of operant responses is determined by their consequences. Responses that are *positively reinforced* will repeat more frequently; those that are *punished* or ignored are *extinguished.*

The operant conditioner carefully observes target behavior and quantifies its frequency and rate. Then, to complete a **functional analysis of behavior,** the consequences of the behavior are noted to determine the **contingencies of reinforcement.** For example, someone interested in a child's temper tantrums would begin by observing when they occurred and what the consequences were. A typical finding might be that the child throws a tantrum whenever his parents deny his requests, and that the parents give in if the tantrums are prolonged. Thus the parents would be reinforcing the very behavior they least wanted. To eliminate the tantrums, they would be taught to ignore them. Moreover, they would be told that giving in, even occasionally, would maintain the tantrums, because behavior that is *intermittently reinforced* is the most difficult to extinguish. If the child were aware of the contingencies, he might think, "They're not giving in now, but if I keep fussing they eventually will; if not this time, then the next."

Operant conditioning is particularly effective with children because parents have considerable control over reinforcers and punishments. Boardman (1962) trained parents in effective use of punishment to deal with the aggressive antisocial behavior of their five-year-old. Wolpe (1958) described how to use parents as cotherapists in anxiety management. Risley and Wolf (1967) trained parents in the operant reinforcement of speech in their autistic children. In technical terms, these parents were trained to eliminate the contingencies that maintained deviant behavior and to reinforce behavior patterns that were incompatible with the deviant behavior (Falloon, 1991). In plain English, they were taught to ignore inappropriate behavior and reward good behavior.

Although no single figure was responsible for the development of behavioral family therapy, three leaders played a dominant role: a psychologist, Gerald Patterson; a psychiatrist, Robert Liberman; and a social worker, Richard Stuart.

Gerald Patterson, at the University of Oregon, was the most influential figure in developing behavioral parent training. Patterson and his colleagues developed methods for sampling family interactions in the home, trained parents in social learning theory, developed programmed workbooks (e.g., Patterson, 1971), and worked out strategies for eliminating undesirable behavior and substituting desirable behavior. Among others prominent in this field are Anthony Graziano, Rex Forehand, Daniel and Susan O'Leary, and Roger McAuley.

The second major figure in the development of behavioral family therapy was Robert Liberman. In his 1970 paper, "Behavioral Approaches to Family and Couple Therapy," he outlined an operant approach to the family problems of four adult patients with depression, intractable headaches, social inadequacy, and marital discord. In addition to using contingency management of mutual reinforcers, Liberman introduced the use of **role rehearsal** and **modeling** (Bandura & Walters, 1963) to family therapy.

The third major influence on behavioral family therapy was the **contingency contracting** of Richard Stuart (1969). Rather than focus on how the undesired behavior of one family member could be reduced, Stuart focused on how the exchange of positive behavior could be maximized using **reinforcement reciprocity.**

During the 1970s, behavioral family therapy evolved into three major packages: parent training, behavioral couples therapy, and sex therapy. At present the leading figures in behavioral couples therapy include Robert Weiss, Richard Stuart, Michael Crowe, Ian Falloon, and Gayola Margolin.

Recently, there has been a rapprochement between stimulus-response models and cognitive theories (e.g., Epstein, Schlesinger, & Dryden, 1988; Dattilio, 1998). **Cognitive-behavior therapy** refers to those approaches inspired by the work of Albert Ellis (1962) and Aaron Beck (1976) that emphasize the need for attitude change to promote and maintain behavioral modification. Among the leaders in cognitive-behavioral family therapy are Donald Baucom at the University of North Carolina, Norman Epstein at the University of Maryland, and Frank Dattilio, who is affiliated with Harvard and the University of Pennsylvania.

The Basic Model

The central premise of behavior therapy is that *behavior is maintained by its consequences.* Consequences that accelerate behavior are called *reinforcers;* those that decelerate behavior are known as *punishers.*

Some responses may not be recognized as operants—something done to get something— because people aren't aware of the reinforcing payoffs. For example, whining is usually reinforced by attention, although the people doing the reinforcing may not realize it. In fact, a variety of undesired behaviors, including nagging and temper tantrums, are often reinforced by attention. Thus, family problems are frequently maintained under conditions that are counterintuitive.

Extinction occurs when no reinforcement follows a response. Ignoring it is, of course, often the best response to behavior you don't like. The reason some people fail to credit this is that withholding a response rarely leads to *immediate*

cessation of unwanted behavior because most behavior problems have been intermittently reinforced and therefore take time to extinguish.

Despite the mechanistic sound of "schedules of reinforcement" and "controlling behavior," behavior therapists have increasingly become aware that people not only act but also think and feel. This recognition has taken the form of efforts to integrate stimulus–response behaviorism (Skinner, 1953) with cognitive theories (Mahoney, 1977). The central tenet of the cognitive approach is that our interpretation of other people's behavior affects the way we respond to them. Among the most troublesome of *automatic thoughts* are those based on "arbitrary inference," distorted conclusions, shaped by a person's **schemas,** or core beliefs about the world and how it functions. What makes these underlying beliefs problematic is that, although they are generally not conscious, they bias how we approach and respond to everything and everyone.

As behavior therapists shifted their attention from individuals to family relationships, they came to rely on Thibaut and Kelley's (1959) **theory of social exchange,** according to which people strive to maximize "rewards" and minimize "costs" in relationships. In a successful relationship, both partners work to maximize mutual rewards. By contrast, in unsuccessful relationships, the partners are too busy trying to protect themselves from getting hurt to consider ways to make each other happy. According to Thibaut and Kelley, behavior exchanges follow a norm of reciprocity over time, so that aversive or positive stimulation from one person tends to produce reciprocal behavior from the other. Kindness begets kindness; and the opposite is also true.

Normal Family Development

According to the behavior exchange model (Thibaut & Kelley, 1959), a good relationship is one in which giving and getting are balanced— or, in the model's terms, there is a high ratio of benefits to costs. Put as generally as this, little is added to commonsense notions of family satisfaction. But behaviorists have begun to spell out some of the details of what makes for relationship satisfaction. For example, Weiss and Isaac (1978) found that affection, communication, and child care are the most important elements in marital satisfaction. Earlier, Wills, Weiss, and Patterson (1974) found that unpleasant behavior reduced marital satisfaction more than pleasant behavior increased it. A good relationship, then, is one in which there is an exchange of positive responses and, even more important, minimal unpleasantness. Another way of putting this is that good relationships are under *positive reinforcement control.*

Communication skills—the ability to talk, especially about problems—is considered by behaviorists to be the most important feature of good relationships (Gottman, Markman, & Notarius, 1977; Jacobson, Waldron, & Moore, 1980). (It's also the most easily observed feature of relationships.)

In time all couples run into conflict and, therefore, a critical skill in maintaining family harmony is skill in conflict resolution (Gottman & Krokoff, 1989). Healthy families aren't problem-free but have the ability to cope with problems when they arise.

In a good relationship, partners are able to speak openly about conflicts. They focus on issues and keep them in perspective, and they discuss specific behaviors of concern to them. They describe their own feelings and request changes in the behavior of others, rather than just criticizing and complaining. "I've been kind of lonely and I wish you and I could go out more often" is more likely to get a positive response than, "You never care what I want! All you care about is yourself!"

Some people assume that good relationships will evolve naturally if people are well matched and they love each other. Behaviorists, on the other hand, emphasize the need to develop relationship skills. Good marriages, they believe, aren't made in heaven but are a product of learning effective coping behavior. The late Neil Jacobson (1981) described a good relationship

as one in which the partners maintain a high rate of rewards.

> Successful couples . . . expand their reinforcement power by frequently acquiring new domains for positive exchange. Spouses who depend on a limited quantity and variety of reinforcers are bound to suffer the ill effects of satiation. As a result, over time their interaction becomes depleted of its prior reinforcement value. Successful couples cope with this inevitable reinforcement erosion by varying their shared activities, developing new common interests, expanding their sexual repertoires, and developing their communication to the point where they continue to interest one another. (p. 561)

Development of Behavior Disorders

Behaviorists view symptoms as learned responses. They don't look for underlying motives, nor do they posit marital conflict as leading to children's problems. Instead they concentrate on the symptoms themselves and look for responses that reinforce problem behavior.

At first glance it would seem puzzling that family members reinforce undesirable behavior. Why would parents reward temper tantrums? Why would a wife reinforce her husband's distance? The answer lies not in some kind of convoluted motive for suffering but in the simple fact that people often inadvertently reinforce precisely those responses that cause them the most distress.

Parents usually respond to problem misbehavior in their children by scolding and lecturing. These reactions may seem like punishment, but they may in fact be reinforcing, because attention—even from a critical parent—is a powerful *social reinforcer* (Skinner, 1953). The truth of this is reflected in the sound advice to "Ignore it, and it will go away." The problem is, most parents have trouble ignoring misbehavior. Notice, for example, how quickly children learn that certain words get a big reaction. Moreover, even when parents do resolve to ignore misbehavior, they usually don't do so consistently.

This can make things even worse, because *intermittent reinforcement* is the most resistant to extinction (Ferster, 1963). This is why compulsive gambling is so difficult to extinguish.

In addition to behavior problems unwittingly maintained by parental attention, others persist because parents don't know how to make effective use of punishment. They make threats they don't follow through on; they punish too long after the fact; they use punishments so mild as to have no effect; or they use punishments so severe as to generate more anxiety than learning.

Learning, moreover, is not just a one-way street. Consider the behavior of a mother and daughter in the supermarket.

> The little girl asks her mother for a candy bar. The mother says, "No." The child begins crying and complaining. The mother says, "If you think I'm going to buy you candy when you make such a fuss, you have another think coming, young lady!" But the child escalates her tantrum, getting louder and louder. Finally, exasperated and embarrassed, the mother gives in: "All right, if you'll quiet down, I'll buy you some cookies."

Obviously, the child has been reinforced for throwing a temper tantrum. Not so obviously, but also true, the mother has been reinforced for giving in—by the child's calming down after being promised cookies. Thus a spiral of undesirable behavior is maintained by *reciprocal reinforcement*.

The use of **aversive control**—nagging, crying, withdrawing—is often cited as a major determinant of marital unhappiness (Stuart, 1975). Spouses typically reciprocate their partners' use of aversive behavior, and a vicious circle develops (Patterson & Reid, 1970). People in distressed relationships also show *poor problem-solving skills* (Vincent, Weiss, & Birchler, 1975; Weiss, Hops, & Patterson, 1973). When discussing a problem, they frequently change the subject; they phrase wishes and complaints in vague and critical ways; and they respond to complaints with countercomplaints. The following exchange demonstrates sidetracking, cross-complaining, and name-calling, all typical of distressed marriages.

> "I'd like to talk about all the sweets you've been giving the kids lately." "What sweets! Talk about *me*, you're always stuffing your face. And what do you ever do for the kids? You just come home and complain. Why don't you just stay at the office! The kids and I get along better without you."

Most behavioral analyses point to a lack of reinforcement for positive behavior in distressed families. The old adage, "The squeaky wheel gets the grease," seems to apply. Depressions, headaches, and temper tantrums tend to elicit concern and therefore more attention than pleasant behavior. Because this process is unwitting, family members are often mystified about their role in reinforcing annoying behavior.

According to cognitive-behaviorists, the schemas that plague relationships are learned in the process of growing up. Some of these dysfunctional beliefs are assumptions about specific family roles whereas others are about family life in general. These schemas are the underlying basis of the "shoulds," self-fulfilling prophesies, mind reading, jealousy, and bad faith that poison relationships by distorting family members' responses to each other's actual behavior.

How Therapy Works

The basic premise of behavior therapy is that behavior will change when the contingencies of reinforcement are altered. Behavioral family therapy aims to resolve specific targeted family problems through identifying behavioral goals, learning theory techniques for achieving these goals, and using social reinforcers to facilitate this process.

The hallmarks of behavioral family therapy are (1) careful and detailed assessment, to determine the baseline frequency of problem behavior, to guide therapy, and to provide accurate feedback about the success of treatment; and (2) strategies designed to modify the contingencies of reinforcement in each unique client family.

Although behavior change remains the primary focus, more and more therapists are recognizing the role of cognitive factors in resolving relationship problems. The cognitive approach first gained attention as a supplement to behavioral couples therapy (Margolin, Christensen, & Weiss, 1975). Interest in cognitive-behavioral approaches to couples eventually led to the recognition that cognition plays a significant role in all family interactions (Alexander & Parsons, 1982).

Therapy

Behavioral Parent Training

Most family therapists begin with the assumption that the family, not the individual, is the problem, so that the whole family should be convened to solve it. Behavior therapists, on the other hand, accept the parents' view that the child is the problem and generally meet with only one parent (guess which one) and the child, although some behaviorists (Gordon & Davidson, 1981) recommend that both parents and even siblings be included.

The most commonly used approach is operant conditioning, in which the reinforcers used may

be tangible or social. In fact, praise and attention have been found to be as effective as money or candy (Bandura, 1969). Operant techniques may be further divided into *shaping, token economies, contingency contracting, contingency management,* and *time-out.*

Shaping (Schwitzgebel & Kolb, 1964) consists of reinforcing change in small steps. **Token economies** (Baer & Sherman, 1969) use points or stars to reward children for successful behavior. **Contingency contracting** (Stuart, 1971) involves agreements by parents to make certain changes following changes made by their children. **Contingency management** (Schwitzgebel, 1967) consists of giving and taking away rewards based on the children's behavior. **Time-out** (Rimm & Masters, 1974) is a punishment whereby children are made to sit in the corner or are sent to their rooms.

Assessment.   In common with other forms of behavior therapy, parent training begins with a thorough assessment. Although the procedure varies from clinic to clinic, most assessments are based upon Kanfer and Phillips's (1970) *SORKC* model of behavior: *S* for stimulus, *O* for the state of the organism, *R* for the target response, and *KC* for the nature and contingency of conse-

Behavior therapists teach parents to use positive reinforcement rather than aversive control.

quences. The following example illustrates how this assessment model is applied.

> In the case of parents who complain that their son pesters them for cookies between meals and throws tantrums if they don't give him any, the tantrums would be considered the target behavior, *R. O*, the state of the organism, might turn out to be hunger or, more likely, boredom. The stimulus, *S*, might be the sight of cookies in the cookie jar; and the contingency of consequences, *KC*, might be that the parents give in by feeding the boy cookies occasionally, especially if he makes enough of a fuss.

In simple cases, such as the one above, applying the *SORKC* model is straightforward, but it quickly becomes more complex with families, in which there are long chains of interrelated behavior. Consider the following.

> Mr. and Mrs. J. complain that their two small children whine and fuss at the dinner table. A home observation reveals that when Mr. J. yells at the children for misbehaving they start to whine and stand by their mother's chair.

Given this sequence, it's not difficult to apply the *SORKC* model. Imagine, however, that the preceding sequence is only part of a more complex picture.

> In the morning, Mr. J. makes a sexual overture to his wife, but she, tired from taking care of the children, rolls over and goes back to sleep. Mr. J. is hurt and leaves for work after making some unkind remarks to his wife. She, feeling rejected by her husband, spends the entire day playing with the children for solace. By the time she has to cook dinner, Mrs. J. is exasperated with the children. Mr. J. comes home after a hard day at the office and tries to make up with his wife by hugging her. She responds but only perfunctorily because she's busy trying to cook. While she's at the stove, the children and Mr. J. vie for her attention, each wanting to tell her something. Finally, she blows up—at her husband—"Can't you see I'm busy!" He goes into the den and sulks until dinner is ready. Just as his wife finds it difficult to express anger at the children and takes it out on him, Mr. J. has trouble directing anger at his wife and so tends to divert it onto the chil-

dren. At the dinner table he yells at them for the slightest infraction, at which point they whine and turn to their mother. She lets one sit on her lap while she strokes the other's hair.

In this longer, but not atypical sequence, what is stimulus and what response? Obviously these definitions become circular, and their application depends on the perspective of the observer.

Assessment in behavioral parent training entails defining, observing, and recording the frequency of the behavior to be changed, as well as the events that precede it and those that follow. Interviews, usually with the mother, are designed to provide a definition of the problem and a list of potential reinforcers. Observations may be conducted behind a one-way mirror or during a home visit. Baseline data, collected prior to the initiation of therapy, may be recorded by therapists or family members. Typically, parents are trained to pinpoint problem behavior, observe and record its occurrence, and note the occurrence and frequency of various events that might serve as stimuli and reinforcers. Checklists and questionnaires provide information that may have been overlooked in interviews. The final product of this stage of the assessment is the selection of target behaviors for modification.

The measurement and functional analysis stage consists of actually observing and recording the target behavior as well as its antecedents and consequences. This may be done by the parents at home or by therapists in the clinic—and, now, more and more, by therapists in the natural setting (Arrington, Sullaway, & Christensen, 1988).

Therapeutic Techniques. Once the assessment is complete, the therapist decides which behaviors should be increased and which decreased. To accelerate behavior, the **Premack principle** (Premack, 1965) is applied; that is, high probability behavior (particularly pleasant activities) is chosen to reinforce behavior with a low probability of occurrence. Where once it was thought that reinforcers must satisfy some basic drive, such as hunger or thirst, it's now known that any behavior chosen more frequently (given a wide variety of choices) can serve as a reinforcer for those chosen less frequently.

Mrs. G. complained that she couldn't get her five-year-old son Adam to clean up his room in the morning. She went on to say that she tried rewarding him with candy, money, and toys, but "Nothing works!" A functional analysis of Adam's behavior revealed that, given his choice of things to do, the most probable behaviors were watching television, riding his bicycle, and playing in the mud behind his house. Once these activities were made contingent on tidying his room, he quickly learned to do so.

A variety of material and social reinforcers have been used to accelerate desired behaviors but, as the Premack principle demonstrates, to be effective, reinforcers must be popular with the child. Although money and candy seem like powerful rewards, they may not be as effective for some children as a chance to play in the mud.

Once effective rewards are chosen, parents are taught to *shape* the desired behavior by reinforcing successive approximation to the final goal. They are taught to raise the criteria for reinforcement gradually and to present reinforcement immediately contingent on the desired behavior.[1] Once the child is regularly performing the desired response, reinforcement becomes intermittent to increase the durability of the new behavior.

The most common technique for decelerating behavior is *time-out*. This means ignoring or isolating the child after he or she misbehaves. Studies have shown that about five minutes is most effective (Pendergrass, 1971). Children are first warned, to give them a chance to control their own behavior, before they are put into time-out. Other techniques used to decelerate behavior include verbal reprimand, ignoring, and isolation. Simply repeating commands to children has been shown to be the most ineffective way to change their behavior (Forehand et al., 1976).

---

1. The importance of immediate proximity is what makes time-out such an effective punishment and grounding second only to lecturing as an ineffective one.

Because of the inconvenience of reinforcing behavior immediately after it occurs, token systems have been popular with parent trainers. Points are earned for desirable behavior and lost for undesirable behavior (Christophersen, Arnold, Hill, & Quilitch, 1972).

Case Study

Mrs. F. is a mother of two small children; she came to the clinic complaining of headaches and crying spells. The intake interviewer found her to be mildly depressed and concluded that the depression was a reaction to difficulty coping with the children. Suzie, age five, was a shy child who had frequent temper tantrums. Robert, who was eight, was more sociable but did poorly in school. The children were a handful, and Mrs. F. felt helpless in dealing with them.

A functional analysis of behavior revealed that Suzie's shyness resulted in extra attention from her anxious mother. Whenever Suzie declined an invitation to play with other children, her mother spent time doing things to make her feel better. The therapist selected social behavior (not shyness) as the first target response and instructed Mrs. F. to reinforce all efforts at socializing and to ignore Suzie when she avoided social contact. Thereafter, whenever Suzie made any attempt to socialize with other children, Mrs. F. would immediately reinforce her with attention and praise. When Suzie chose to stay home rather than play with other children, her mother ignored her, instead busying herself with her own activities. In three weeks, Mrs. F. reported that Suzie "seemed to have gotten over her shyness."

Following this initial success the therapist felt it was time to help Mrs. F. tackle the more difficult problem of Suzie's tantrums. Because the tantrums were unlikely to occur while the family was at the clinic, the therapist instructed Mrs. F. to make observational notes for a week. These notes revealed that Suzie generally had tantrums when her parents denied her requests for a treat or some special indulgence, such as staying up to watch television. Tantrums were especially likely to occur at the end of the day when Suzie (and her parents) were tired. As to how the parents responded to these maddening outbursts, Mrs. F. reported that "We've tried everything. Sometimes we try to ignore her, but that's impossible; she just screams and shrieks until we can't stand it anymore. Then sometimes we spank her—or give her what she wants, just to shut her up. Sometimes after we spank her she cries so much that we let her watch television until she calms down. That usually works."

After listening to this description, the therapist explained how Mr. and Mrs. F. had inadvertently been reinforcing the tantrums and told them what they would have to do to stop them. For the next week, the F.s were instructed to ignore fits of temper whenever they occurred. If they occurred at bedtime, Suzie was to be put in bed; if she continued to cry and fuss, she was to be left alone until she stopped. Only when she stopped were her parents to talk with her about what was on her mind. The following week Mrs. F. reported that the tantrums had indeed decreased, except for one night when they took on a new and more troubling form. When Suzie was told that she wouldn't be able to stay up late to watch television she began to yell and cry as usual. Instead of relenting, Mrs. F. put Suzie in her room and told her to get ready for bed. However, realizing that her parents were going to ignore her, as they had earlier in the week, Suzie began to scream and smash things in her room. "She was completely out of control. She even smashed the little dog-shaped lamp I bought her. We didn't know what to do, so just that once we let her stay up." Again the therapist described the consequences of such behavior and explained to Mrs. F. how, should Suzie again become destructive, both parents should hold her until the tantrum subsided.

At the next session, Mrs. F. described how Suzie did "get out of control again." This time, however, instead of giving in, the parents held her as they had been told. Mrs. F. was amazed at the fury of the resulting tantrum. "But we remembered what you said—there was no way we were going to give in!" It took twenty minutes, but Suzie finally calmed down. This, it turned out, was the last time Suzie ever became violent during a temper tantrum. Nevertheless she did continue to have occasional flare-ups during the next few weeks. According to Mrs. F., the few tantrums that did occur seemed to take place in different settings or under different conditions than the usual episodes at home (which Suzie had now learned would not be reinforced). For example, one episode took place in the supermarket, when Suzie was told she couldn't have a candy bar. By this time, however, Mrs. F. was thoroughly convinced of the necessity of not reinforcing the tantrums, and so she didn't. Because she was embarrassed at all the noise her daughter was making in public, she did find it necessary to take her out of the store. But she made Suzie sit in the car and took pains not to let it be a pleasant experience. Very few tantrums followed this one.

Next the therapist turned her attention to Robert's poor school performance. A careful assessment revealed that Robert usually denied that he had any homework. After checking with Robert's teacher, the therapist discovered that the children generally did have homework and that they were expected to work between thirty minutes and an hour a night. Mrs. F. selected a high probability behavior, watching television, and made it contingent on Robert's having completed his homework. For the first two weeks of this regimen, Mrs. F. found it necessary to call the teacher every night to verify the assignments. But soon this was no longer necessary. Doing homework fairly quickly became a habit for Robert, and his grades increased from Ds and Cs to Bs and As. At this point, everyone was happier, and Mrs. F. felt the family no longer needed help.

A follow-up session in the fall found things continuing to go well. Suzie was now much more sociable and hadn't had any temper tantrums in months. Robert was doing well in school, although he had begun to neglect some of his more difficult assignments. To address this, the therapist explained to Mrs. F. how to institute a token system, and she was able to use it with excellent results.

The preceding example illustrates a form of behavioral parent training in which the therapist meets with the mother and instructs her in the use of operant conditioning principles. Another format is to observe parent and child interacting behind a one-way mirror in the clinic. In this way, the therapist can get a first-hand look at what actually transpires. With this approach, parents can be taught how to play with their children as well as how to discipline and negotiate with them. Sometimes the observing therapist may communicate to the parents through a remote microphone, or "bug in the ear."

The techniques that have been described are particularly effective with young children. With teenagers, the use of *contingency contracting* (Alexander & Parsons, 1973; Rinn, 1978) is more widely used. Contracting is introduced as a way for everybody in the family to get something by compromising. Parents and teenagers are asked to specify what behavior they'd like each other to change. These requests form the nucleus of the initial contract. To help family members arrive at contracts, the therapist encourages (1) clear communication of content and feelings; (2) clear presentation of requests; leading to (3) negotiation, with each person receiving something in exchange for some concession.

Alexander and Parsons (1973) recommend starting with easy issues while the family is learning the principles of contingency contracting. Success in dealing with minor issues increases a family's willingness to tackle more difficult problems. Some parents are reluctant to negotiate with their children to do things "that they *should do anyway, without being bribed.*" In fact, these parents have a legitimate point, and they should be helped to understand the difference between rules (which are nonnegotiable) and privileges (which can be negotiated).

Behavioral parent training is also conducted in packaged training programs, designed for preventive education. The content of these programs varies from general principles of operant behavior to specific techniques for dealing with particular problems. Many of these programs include instruction in charting the target behavior. Parents are also taught how to state and enforce rules and the importance of consistency. Training in the use of positive reinforcement includes helping parents increase the frequency and range of reinforcers that they apply. In addition to increasing behavior that their children are already engaging in, parents are taught to develop new behaviors through shaping, modeling, instruction, and prompting.

Behavioral Couples Therapy

Assessment.   As with parent training, behavioral couples therapy begins with an elaborate, structured assessment. This process usually includes clinical interviews, ratings of specific target behaviors, and marital questionnaires. The most widely used is the Locke-Wallace Marital Adjustment Scale (Locke & Wallace, 1959), a twenty-three-item questionnaire covering various aspects of marital satisfaction, including communication, sex, affection, social activities, and values.

Assessments are designed to reveal strengths and weaknesses in a couple's relationship and the manner in which rewards and punishments are exchanged. Interviews are used to specify and elaborate target behaviors. Some attempt is also made during interviews to understand the etiology of the problems couples describe as well as to observe problems other than those noted by the spouses themselves. In general, however, behavior therapists deemphasize interviews (Jacobson & Margolin, 1979) in favor of written questionnaires and direct observation of couples' interactions. Jacobson (1981) offers an outline for pretreatment assessment (Table 10.1).

Therapeutic Techniques.   After completing an assessment, the behavioral clinician presents the couple with an analysis of their relationship in social learning terms. In doing so, therapists take pains to accentuate the positive, striving to maintain optimistic expectancies and a collaborative set (Jacobson, 1981). Married partners

TABLE 10.1 Jacobson's Pretreatment Assessment for Marital Therapy

A. Strengths and skills of the relationship

What are the major strengths of this relationship?
What is each spouse's current capacity to reinforce the other?
What behaviors on the part of each spouse are highly valued by the other?
What shared activities do the couple currently engage in?
What common interests do they share?

B. Presenting problems

What are the major complaints, and how do these complaints translate into explicit behavioral terms?
What behaviors occur too frequently or at inappropriate times from the standpoint of each spouse?
What are the reinforcers that are maintaining these behaviors?
What behaviors occur at less than the desired frequency or fail to occur at appropriate times from the standpoint of each spouse?
What are the consequences of these behaviors currently, when they occur?
How did the current problems develop over time?
Is there a consensus on who makes important decisions in regard to various areas of the relationship?
What kinds of decisions are made collectively as opposed to unilaterally?

C. Sex and affection

Is either currently dissatisfied with rate, quality, or diversity of sex life together?
If sex is currently a problem, was there a time when it was mutually satisfying?
What are the sexual behaviors that seem to be associated with current dissatisfaction?
Are either or both partners dissatisfied with the amount or quality of nonsexual physical affection?
What is the couple's history regarding extramarital affairs?

D. Future prospects

Are the partners seeking therapy to improve their relationship, to separate, or to decide whether the relationship is worth working on?
What are each spouse's reasons for continuing the relationship despite current problems?

E. Assessment of social environment

What are each person's alternatives to the present relationship?
How attractive are these alternatives to each person?
Is the environment (parents, relatives, friends, work associates, children) supportive of either continuance or dissolution of the present relationship?

F. Individual functioning of each spouse

Does either spouse exhibit any severe emotional or behavioral problems?
Does either spouse present a psychiatric history of his/her own? Specify.
Have they been in therapy before, either alone or together? What kind of therapy? Outcome?
What is each spouse's past experience with intimate relationships?
How is the present relationship different?

Adapted from: Jacobson, N. S. 1981. Behavioral marital therapy. In *Handbook of Family Therapy*, A. S. Gurman and D. P. Kniskern, eds. (pp. 565–566). New York: Brunner/Mazel.

tend to state their goals negatively: "I want less arguing from him"; or "She nags too much." Most have difficulty describing behavior that they want their mates to accelerate. To help them do so, some therapists (Azrin, Naster, & Jones, 1973) ask couples to make a list of pleasing things their partners do during the week. Reviewing these lists in the following session provides the opportunity to emphasize the importance of positive feedback.

Stuart (1975) lists five strategies that summarize the behavioral approach to troubled marriages. First, couples are taught to express themselves in clear, behavioral descriptions rather than in vague complaints. Second, couples are taught new behavior exchange procedures, emphasizing positive in place of aversive control. Third, couples are helped to improve their communication. Fourth, couples are encouraged to establish clear and effective means of sharing power and making decisions. Fifth, couples are taught strategies for solving future problems, as a means to maintain and extend gains initiated in therapy.

Behavior exchange procedures are taught to help couples increase the frequency of desired behavior. Couples are advised to express their wishes and complaints specifically and behaviorally. A typical device is to ask each partner to list three things he or she would like the other to do more often. While explicitly exchanging "strokes" in this way, couples are implicitly learning ways of influencing each other through positive reinforcement. An alternative tactic is to ask each partner to think of things the other might want, do them, and see what happens. Weiss and his associates direct couples to have "love days," where one partner doubles his or her pleasing behavior toward the other (Weiss & Birchler, 1978). Stuart (1976) has couples alternate "caring days," where one partner demonstrates caring in as many ways as possible.

The following vignette, taken from a video workshop series, illustrates how Richard Stuart concentrates on helping couples learn to make each other happy, rather than trying to solve the problems that bring them to therapy.

—Case Study—

Wesley and Adele are a middle-aged, working-class couple. This is her third marriage and his fourth. Wesley feels rejected because Adele frequently works late; at the same time, she feels that he isn't affectionate with her and that he pulls away whenever she makes a sexual overture. Dr. Stuart begins with a brief family history of each spouse and then explores the history of their relationship with each other. In the second half of the interview, Dr. Stuart offers suggestions for improving the couple's relationship by making an effort to act "as if" things were good and they cared for each other.

When Dr. Stuart tells the couple that they can *choose* to make their marriage work by acting in loving ways toward each other, they both seem a little skeptical. When Adele reveals that she doesn't know if Wesley is committed to staying in the relationship, Dr. Stuart suggests that she needs to feel safe in his commitment and, using the example of his own marriage, tells them again that they can accentuate the positive by making a point of expressing their caring for each other.

Later Stuart suggests that Wesley start acting "as if" he felt close to Adele and reassures him that if he acts affectionately, she will respond in kind. Again, Stuart uses his own marriage as an example of how two people can make themselves happy by making a point of acting lovingly toward each other. In fact, he guarantees Wesley that if he acts affectionately Adele will respond, and Stuart asks Wesley to agree to try doing so as an experiment. Though they still seem a little skeptical, both Wesley and Adele agree to try the idea of acting positively toward each other.

In a carefully designed longitudinal study, Gottman and Krokoff (1989) found that disagreement and angry exchanges, which have often been considered destructive to relationships, may not be harmful in the long run. These patterns were correlated with immediate dissatisfaction but were predictive of improved satisfaction after three years. Defensiveness, stubbornness, and withdrawal from conflict, on the other hand, *did* lead to long-term deterioration in marriages. Passive compliance may create a facade of harmony, but it doesn't work in the long run—as many dominating partners with compliant mates discover when their partners, who "used to be so agreeable," suddenly become "so critical."

Conflict engagement often makes couples uneasy, but it may be an essential prelude to facing and solving problems. The anger that accompanies direct expression of dissatisfaction may be painful, but it may also be healthy. Gottman and Krokoff (1989) conclude: "If the wife must introduce and elaborate disagreements in marriages, our data suggest that, for the sake of long-term improvement in marital satisfaction, she may need to do this by getting her husband to confront areas of disagreement and to openly vent disagreement and anger" (p. 51). In other words, confrontation is effective only if it doesn't make the partner defensive. It isn't just honesty that counts, but honesty expressed in a way the partner can tolerate.

Training in *communications skills* may be done in a group format (Hickman & Baldwin, 1971; Pierce, 1973) or with individual couples. The training includes instruction, modeling, role playing, structured exercises, behavior rehearsal, and feedback (Jacobson, 1977; Stuart, 1976). Couples are taught to be specific, phrase requests in positive terms, respond directly to criticism instead of cross-complaining, talk about the present and future rather than the past, listen without interruption, minimize punitive statements, and eliminate questions that sound like declarations.

Once a couple has been taught to communicate in ways that are conducive to problem solving, they are introduced to the principles of *contingency contracting*—agreeing to make changes contingent on the partner's making changes. In **quid pro quo** contracts (Knox, 1971), one partner agrees to make a change after a prior change by the other. Each partner specifies desired behavior changes and, with the

therapist's help, they negotiate agreements. At the end of the session a written list is made and both partners sign it. Such a contract might take the following form:

Date _____

This week I agree to:

(1) Come home from work by 6 p.m.

(2) Play with the children for half an hour after supper.

_____

Husband's signature

Contingent on the above changes, I agree to:

(1) Go bowling once a week with my husband.

(2) Not serve leftovers for supper on weeknights.

_____

Wife's signature

An alternative form of contracting is the *good faith* contract, in which both partners agree to make changes that aren't contingent on what the other does (Weiss, Hops, & Patterson, 1973). Each partner's independent changes are independently reinforced. In the example above, the husband who comes home each night by 6:00 p.m. and plays with the children after supper might reward himself by buying a new shirt at the end of the week or be rewarded by his wife with a back rub.

Problem-solving training is used in situations that are too complicated for simple exchange agreements. Negotiations are preceded by a careful and specific definition of problems. Discussions are limited to one problem at a time. Each begins by paraphrasing what the other has said, and they are taught to avoid inferences about motivation—especially inferences of malevolent intent. They're also encouraged to avoid aversive responses. When defining a problem it's most effective to begin with a positive statement; instead of saying, "You never . . . ," partners are taught to say, "I appreciate the way you . . . and, in addition I wish. . . ."

As we move into the twenty-first century, the most significant advance in behavioral treatment is the increasing use of cognitive-behavioral methods (Epstein, Schlesinger, & Dryden, 1988; Dattilio, 1998). The cognitive mediation model (Beck, 1976) posits that emotions and actions are mediated by specific cognitions. Understanding these cognitions (*beliefs, attributions,* and *expectancies*) makes it possible to identify factors that trigger and maintain dysfunctional emotional and behavioral patterns. In practice, this boils down to uncovering assumptions that keep people stuck.

The Cognitive-Behavior Approach to Family Therapy

Cognitive family therapy followed the same progression as cognitive couples therapy—first as a supplement to the behavioral approach and then as a more comprehensive system of intervention. Munson (1993) noted at least eighteen different types of cognitive therapies used by various practitioners, but the focus of this discussion is limited to those approaches proposed by the rational-emotive (Ellis, 1962) and cognitive-behavioral theories (Beck, 1988; Teichman, 1984).

The rational-emotive therapist helps family members see how illogical beliefs serve as the foundation for their emotional distress. The use of the "*A-B-C* theory" is introduced, according to which family members blame their problems (*C*) on certain events in the family (*A*) and are taught to look for irrational beliefs (*B*), which are then challenged. The goal is to modify beliefs and expectations by putting them on a more rational basis (Ellis, 1978). The therapist's role is to teach the family that emotional problems are caused by unrealistic beliefs and that by revising these self-defeating ideas they may improve the overall quality of family life.

With rational-emotive therapy, it's hard to separate the approach from its creator. Ellis didn't merely challenge people's assumptions, he punctured them with fierce and gleeful sarcasm. It isn't necessary to imitate Ellis's acerbic style to take advantage of his insights. It seems fair to say, however, that rational-emotive therapists generally content themselves with lecturing people about generic assumptions rather than probing for more personal and closely held beliefs.

The cognitive-behavior method, which balances the emphasis on cognition and behavior, takes a more expansive and inclusive approach by focusing in greater depth on patterns of family interaction (Epstein, Schlesinger, & Dryden, 1988; Leslie, 1988). Family relationships, cognitions, emotions, and behavior are viewed as exerting mutual influence on one another, so that a cognitive inference can evoke emotion and behavior, and emotion and behavior can influence cognition.

The cognitive-behavior approach to families is also compatible with systems theory and includes the premise that members of a family simultaneously influence and are influenced by each other. The behavior of one family member triggers behavior, cognitions, and emotions in other members, which, in turn, elicit reactive cognitions, behavior, and emotions in the original member. As this process plays out, the volatility of family dynamics escalates, rendering the family vulnerable to negative spirals of conflict. Epstein and Schlesinger (1996) cite four means by which family members' cognitions, behavior, and emotions may interact and build to a volatile climax:

1. The individual's own cognitions, behavior, and emotion regarding family interaction (e.g., the person who notices himself or herself withdrawing from the rest of the family);
2. The actions of individual family members toward him or her;
3. The combined (and not always consistent) reactions several family members have toward him or her;
4. The characteristics of the relationships among other family members (e.g., noticing that two other family members

usually are supportive of each other's opinions).

As the number of family members involved increases, so does the complexity of the dynamics, adding momentum to the escalation process (Dattilio, 2001).

Cognitive therapy, as set forth by Aaron Beck (1976), emphasizes *schemas* or what have otherwise been defined as "core beliefs" (DeRubeis & Beck, 1988). Therapeutic intervention is aimed at the assumptions whereby family members interpret and evaluate one another.

The late 1980s and early 1990s saw the cognitive-behavioral approach applied more widely in family therapy. Edited books by Epstein, Schlessinger, and Dryden (1988) and a short text produced by Huber and Baruth (1989) were among the first works to address the cognitive-behavioral approach to family therapy. This was elaborated in subsequent articles by Schwebel and Fine (1992), Dattilio (1993, 1997), and Teichman (1992). Most recently, Dattilio (1998) has produced a major casebook that discusses the integration of cognitive-behavioral strategies with various modalities of couples and family therapy. This important work discusses the compatibility of cognitive-behavior therapy with a wide array of modalities. The application of cognitive-behavior therapy to couples and families was also featured in the recent addition of *The Family Therapy Handbook* (Dattilio & Epstein, 2004).

Treatment of Sexual Dysfunction

Wolpe's (1958) introduction of *systematic desensitization* led to major advances in the treatment of sexual dysfunction. According to Wolpe most sexual problems are the result of conditioned anxiety. His therapy consists of instructing couples to engage in a series of progressively intimate encounters while avoiding thoughts about erection or orgasm. Another approach that often proved useful was *assertiveness training* (Lazarus, 1965; Wolpe, 1958). In assertiveness training, socially and sexually inhibited persons are encouraged to accept and express their needs and feelings.

Although these behavioral remedies were often helpful, the real breakthrough came with the publication of Masters and Johnson's (1970) approach. This was followed by others who applied and extended Masters and Johnson's basic procedure (Lobitz & LoPiccolo, 1972; Kaplan, 1974, 1979).

Although the details vary, most sex therapists follow a general approach. As with other behavioral methods, the first step is a thorough assessment, including a complete medical examination and extensive interviews to determine the nature of the dysfunction and establish goals for treatment. In the absence of organic problems, cases involving lack of information, poor technique, and poor communication are most amenable to sexual therapy.

Therapists following Masters and Johnson tended to lump sexual problems into one category—anxiety that interferes with couples' ability to relax into arousal and orgasm. Helen Singer Kaplan (1979) pointed out that there are three stages of the sexual response and, hence, three types of problems: disorders of desire, arousal disorders, and orgasm disorders. *Disorders of desire* range from "low sex drive" to sexual aversion. Treatment focuses on (1) deconditioning anxiety and (2) helping clients resist negative thoughts. *Arousal disorders* include decreased emotional arousal and difficulty achieving and maintaining an erection or dilating and lubricating. These problems are often helped with a combination of relaxation and teaching couples to focus on the physical sensations of touching and caressing, rather than worrying about what comes next. *Orgasm disorders* include the timing of orgasm (premature or delayed), the quality of the orgasm, or the requirements for orgasm (e.g., some people only have orgasm during masturbation). Premature ejaculation usually responds well to sex therapy; lack of orgasm in women may respond to sex therapy, usually involving teaching the woman to practice on her own and learning to fantasize (Weeks & Gambescia, 2000, 2002).

Although sex therapy must be tailored to specific problems, most treatments are initiated with *sensate focus,* in which couples are taught how to relax and enjoy touching and being touched. They're told to find a time when they're both reasonably relaxed and free from distraction and get in bed together naked. Then they take turns gently caressing each other. The person being touched is told to relax and concentrate on the feeling of being touched. Later, the one being touched will let the partner know which touch is most pleasing and which is less so. At first couples are told not to touch each other in the breast or genital areas in order to avoid undue anxiety.

After they learn to relax and exchange gentle, pleasant caressing, couples are encouraged to gradually become more intimate—but to slow down if either should feel anxious. Thus sensate focus is a form of *in vivo desensitization.* Couples who are highly anxious and fearful of "having sex" (which some people reduce to a hectic few minutes of poking and panting) learn to overcome their fears through a gentle experience of mutual caressing. As anxiety decreases and desire mounts, they're encouraged to engage in more intimate exchanges. In the process, couples are taught to communicate what they like and don't like. So, for example, instead of enduring something unpleasant until she finally gets so upset that she snaps at her partner or avoids sex altogether, a woman might be taught how to gently show him, "No, not like that, like this."

Once sensate focus exercises have gone smoothly, the therapist introduces techniques to deal with specific problems. Among women the most common sexual dysfunctions are difficulties with orgasm (Kaplan, 1979). Frequently these problems are rooted in lack of information. The woman and her partner may be expecting her to have orgasms reliably during intercourse without additional clitoral stimulation. In men, the most common problem is premature ejaculation, for which part of the treatment is the *squeeze technique* (Semans, 1956), in which the woman stimulates the man's penis until he feels the urge to ejaculate. At that point, she squeezes the frenulum (at the base of the head) firmly between her thumb and first two fingers until the urge to ejaculate subsides. Stimulation begins again until another squeeze is necessary.

Techniques to deal with erectile failure are designed to reduce performance anxiety and increase sexual arousal. These include desensitization of the man's anxiety; discussions in which the partners describe their expectations; increasing the variety and duration of foreplay; the *teasing technique* (Masters & Johnson, 1970), in which the woman alternately starts and stops stimulating the man; and beginning intercourse with the woman guiding the man's flaccid penis into her vagina.

Successful sex therapy usually ends with the couple's sex life much improved but not as fantastic as frustrated expectations had led them to imagine—expectations that were part of the problem in the first place. As in any form of directive therapy, it's important for sex therapists to gradually fade out their involvement and control. Therapeutic gains are consolidated and extended by reviewing the changes that have occurred, by anticipating future trouble spots, and by planning in advance to deal with problems according to principles learned in treatment.

Current Status of the Model

In the thirty years since its inception, the technology of behavioral family therapy has become increasingly sophisticated. Behavior therapists have developed a host of experimentally tested techniques for a variety of family problems, but most of the emphasis remains on parent training, behavioral couples therapy, and treatment of sexual dysfunction.

The distinctive methods of behavioral family therapy are derived from classical and operant conditioning and, increasingly, cognitive theory. Target behavior is precisely specified in operational terms; operant conditioning, classical conditioning, social learning theory, and cognitive strategies are then used to produce change. As behavior therapists have gained experience with family problems, they have begun to address such traditionally nonbehavioral concerns as the therapeutic alliance, the need for empathy, and the problem of resistance, as well as communication, and problem-solving skills. However, even when dealing with such mainstream issues, behaviorists are distinguished by their methodical approach. More than by any technique, behavior therapy is characterized by careful assessment and evaluation.

Behavior therapy was born and bred in a tradition of research, and so it's not surprising that behavioral family therapy is the most carefully studied form of family treatment. Two trends emerge from this substantial body of evidence. The first is that both behavioral parent training and behavioral couples therapy have repeatedly been demonstrated to be effective. Among the most well-supported versions of these approaches are Gerald Patterson's parent training therapy (e.g., Patterson, Dishion, & Chamberlain, 1993; Patterson & Forgatch, 1995) and Neil Jacobson's behavioral couples therapy (e.g., Crits-Christoph, Frank, Chambless, Brody, & Karp, 1995).

The second trend in research on behavioral family therapy is that the leading exponents of these approaches have begun to see the need to extend their approaches beyond the basic contingency contracting and operant learning procedures of traditional behavior therapy. As already noted, one form this has taken has been the incorporation of cognitive techniques into more traditional stimulus-response behaviorism (e.g., Baucom & Epstein, 1990; Dattilio & Padesky, 1990).

Cognitive-behavior therapy still begins with behavior change. There are two general categories of intervention: substituting positive for aversive control and skills training. An example of the former would be the institution of "love days" or "caring days," on which partners are encouraged to increase positive things they do for each other. For example, to counteract the selective attention to negativity that characterizes many distressed couples, a cognitive-behavior

therapist might ask each partner to write down one positive thing that the other person did each day, to compliment or express appreciation to that individual for these actions, and to bring the list to therapy for further discussion (Baucom, Epstein, & LaTaillade, 2002). The cognitive component of cognitive-behavior therapy usually comes into play when the clients' attitudes and assumptions seem to get in the way of positive behavior changes—when, for example, family members notice only negative things about each other. The cognitive-behavior therapist helps clients explore their assumptions in a process of Socratic questioning. Thus cognitive-behavior therapy still focuses on behavior; therapists are still active and directive; but there is more attention paid to unhappy emotions and the assumptions underlying them.

Another new direction being undertaken by practitioners of behavioral family therapy is the incorporation of principles from systemically oriented family therapies. Gerald Patterson, for example, has begun to use elements of strategic family therapy in his approach to parent training (Forgatch & Patterson, 1998). When parents appear to be unsuccessful using time-outs and the withholding of privileges, Patterson and his colleagues introduce such strategic devices as paradoxical assignments and pretend techniques to overcome parental resistance to what they still consider the core of their approach—changing the contingencies of reinforcement for children's behavior.

The late Neil Jacobson in partnership with Andrew Christensen went even further in modifying traditional behavioral couples therapy along the lines of more traditional family therapy approaches. They retained the behavioral change techniques and developed novel strategies to bring about increased emotional acceptance in clients. In other words, before they start working with couples to produce changes in the partners' behavior, they endeavor to help them learn to be more accepting of each other. So different, in fact, is the resulting approach that we will consider it more extensively in our chapter on integrative approaches (Chapter 14).

—Summary—————————————————————————

1. Although behavior therapists have been applying their techniques to family problems for more than thirty years, they have done so for the most part within a linear frame of reference. Family symptoms are treated as learned responses, involuntarily acquired and reinforced. Treatment is generally time limited and symptom focused.

2. Initially, the behavioral approach to families was based on social learning theory, according to which behavior is learned and maintained by its consequences, and could be modified by altering those consequences. This focus has been broadened considerably by the introduction of cognitive interventions to address unhelpful assumptions and distorted perceptions. An essential adjunct to social learning theory is Thibaut and Kelley's theory of social exchange, according to which people strive to maximize interpersonal "rewards" while minimizing "costs." Hence, the general goals of behavioral family therapy are to increase the rate of rewarding exchanges, decrease aversive exchanges, and teach communication and problem-solving skills.

3. More contemporary approaches to cognitive-behavior therapy have expanded this approach to include the examination and restructuring of thoughts and perceptions. So, while specific techniques are applied to target behaviors, families are also taught general principles of behavior management along with methods for reevaluating automatic thoughts with an attempt to identify distortions and address misconceptions.

4. The behaviorists' focus on modifying the consequences of problem behavior accounts for the strengths and weaknesses of this approach. By concentrating on presenting problems, behaviorists have been able to develop an impressive array of effective techniques. Even such relatively intractable problems as delinquent behavior in children and severe sexual dysfunctions have yielded to behavioral technology. Contemporary cognitive-behavior therapists take

the posture, however, that behavior is only part of the human condition, and the problem person is only part of the family. You can't simply teach people to change if unresolved conflict is keeping them stuck.

5. Unhappiness may center around a behavioral complaint, but resolution of the behavior may not resolve the unhappiness. Treatment may succeed with the symptom but fail the family. Attitudes and feelings *may* change along with changes in behavior, but not necessarily. And teaching communication skills may not be sufficient to resolve real conflict. Behavior change alone may not be enough for family members whose ultimate goal is to feel better. "Yes, he's doing his chores now," a parent may agree. "But I don't think he *feels* like helping out. He still isn't really part of our family." Behavior isn't all that family members in distress are concerned about, and to be responsive to all their needs therapists need to deal with cognitive and affective issues as well.

6. Behaviorists rarely treat whole families. Instead they see only those subsystems they consider central to the targeted behavior. Unfortunately, failure to include—or at least consider—the entire family in therapy may doom treatment to failure. A therapeutic program to reduce a son's aggressiveness toward his mother can hardly succeed if the father wants an aggressive son, or if the father's anger toward his wife isn't addressed. Moreover, if the whole family isn't involved in change, new behavior may not be reinforced and maintained.

7. Despite these shortcomings, cognitive-behavior family therapy offers impressive techniques for treating problems with children and troubled marriages. Furthermore, its weaknesses can be corrected by broadening the focus of conceptualization and the scope of treatment to include families as systems. Perhaps the greatest strength of behavior therapy is its insistence on observing what happens and then measuring change. Cognitive-behaviorists have developed a

wealth of reliable assessment methods and applied them to evaluation, treatment planning, and monitoring progress and outcome. A second important advance has been the gradual movement from eliminating or reinforcing discrete "marker" behaviors to the teaching of general problem-solving, cognitive, and communicational skills. A third major advance in current behavioral family therapy is modular treatment interventions organized to meet the specific and changing needs of the individual and the family. Finally, the shift to address distorted cognitions that may underlie problematic family interactions has added a powerful new dimension to the behavioral approach.

—Questions to Consider———————————

1. What are some instances in which a systemic family therapist might usefully incorporate some behavioral techniques?
2. What are some examples of when using certain behavioral or cognitive-behavior techniques might undermine the practice of systemic family therapy?
3. Can you think of examples of instances where a clinician has described a clichéd generalization (e.g., "you always expect the worst") as opposed to uncovering a specific cognitive schema that the person in question actually holds?
4. Try keeping track for a day or so of the number of times you positively reinforce other people's behavior that you want to encourage.
5. Try keeping track for a day or so of the number of times you inadvertently (positively or negatively) reinforce other people's behavior that you *don't* want to encourage.

—Key Concepts———————————

aversive control   Using punishment and criticism to eliminate undesirable responses; commonly used in dysfunctional families.

behavior exchange theory   Explanation of behavior in relationships as maintained by a ratio of costs to benefits.

classical conditioning   A form of respondent learning in which an unconditioned stimulus (UCS), such as food, which leads to an unconditioned response (UCR), such as salivation, is paired with a conditioned stimulus (CS), such as a bell, the result of which is that the CS begins to evoke the same response; used in the behavioral treatment of anxiety disorders.

cognitive-behavior therapy   Treatment that emphasizes attitude change as well as reinforcement of behavior.

contingencies of reinforcement   The specific pattern of reinforcing (or punishing) consequences of a behavioral sequence.

contingency contracting   A behavior therapy technique whereby agreements are made between family members to exchange rewards for desired behavior.

contingency management   Giving rewards and punishments based on children's behavior.

extinction   Eliminating behavior by not reinforcing it.

functional analysis of behavior   In operant behavior therapy, a study of a particular behavior, what elicits it, and what reinforces it.

modeling   Observational learning.

operant conditioning   A form of learning whereby a person or animal is rewarded for performing certain behaviors; the major approach in most forms of behavior therapy.

Premack principle   Using high-probability behavior (preferred activities) to reinforce low-probability behavior (nonpreferred activities).

quid pro quo   Literally, "something for something," an equal exchange or substitution.

reinforcement   An event, behavior, or object that increases the rate of a particular response. A positive reinforcer is an event whose contingent presentation increases the rate of responding; a negative reinforcer is an event whose contingent withdrawal increases the rate of responding. Intermittent, or irregular, reinforcement is the most resistant to extinction.

reinforcement reciprocity   Exchanging rewarding behaviors between family members.

role rehearsal   The use of role-playing, especially in couples therapy.

schemas   Cognitive constructions, or core beliefs, through which people filter their perceptions and structure their experience.

shaping   Reinforcing change in small steps.

social learning theory   Understanding and treating behavior using principles from social and developmental psychology as well as from learning theory.

systematic desensitization   Gradual exposure to feared situations paired with relaxation.

theory of social exchange   Thibaut and Kelley's theory according to which people strive to maximize rewards and minimize costs in relationships.

time-out   A behavioral technique for extinguishing undesirable behavior by removing the reinforcing consequences of that behavior. Typically, making the child sit in a corner or go to his or her room.

token economy   A system of rewards using points, which can be accumulated and exchanged for reinforcing items or behaviors.

─Recommended Readings────────

Barton, C., and Alexander, J. F. 1981. Functional family therapy. In *Handbook of family therapy*, A. S. Gurman and D. P. Kniskern, eds. New York: Brunner/Mazel.

Baucom, D. H., Epstein, N., and LaTaillade, J. 2002. Cognitive-behavioral couple therapy. In *Clinical handbook of couple therapy*, 3rd ed., A. S. Gurman and N. S. Jacobson, eds., New York: Guilford Press.

Bornstein, P., and Bornstein, M. 1986. *Marital therapy: A behavioral-communications approach.* New York: Pergamon.

Dattilio, F. M. 1998. *Case studies in couple and family therapy: Systemic and cognitive perspectives.* New York: Guilford Press.

Dattilio, F. M. 2005. The restructuring of family schemas: A cognitive-behavioral perspective. *Journal of Marital and Family Therapy, 31:* 15–30.

Dattilio, F. M., and Epstein, N. B. 2004. Cognitive-behavioral couple and family therapy. In *The family therapy handbook*, G. Weekes and T. Sexton, eds. New York: Routledge.

Dattilio, F. M., and Reinecke, M. 1996. *Casebook of cognitive-behavior therapy with children and adolescents.* New York: Guilford Press.

Epstein, N., Schlesinger, S. E., and Dryden, W. 1988. *Cognitive-behavioral therapy with families.* New York: Brunner/Mazel.

Falloon, I. R. H. 1988. *Handbook of behavioral family therapy.* New York: Guilford Press.

Falloon, I. R. H. 1991. Behavioral family therapy. In *Handbook of family therapy*, vol. II. A. S. Gurman and D. P. Kniskern, eds. New York, Brunner/Mazel.

Gordon, S. B., and Davidson, N. 1981. Behavioral parent training. In *Handbook of family therapy*, A. S. Gurman and D. P. Kniskern, eds. New York: Brunner/Mazel.

Jacobson, N. S., and Margolin, G. 1979. *Marital therapy: Strategies based on social learning and behavior exchange principles.* New York: Brunner/Mazel.

Kaplan, H. S. 1979. *The new sex therapy: Active treatment of sexual dysfunctions.* New York: Brunner/Mazel.

Masters, W. H., and Johnson, V. E. 1970. *Human sexual inadequacy.* Boston: Little, Brown.

Patterson, G. R. 1971. *Families: Application of social learning theory to family life.* Champaign, IL: Research Press.

Sanders, M. R., and Dadds, M. R. 1993. *Behavioral family intervention.* Boston: Allyn and Bacon.

Stuart, R. B. 1980. *Helping couples change: A social learning approach to marital therapy.* New York: Guilford Press.

Weiss, R. L. 1978. The conceptualization of marriage from a behavioral perspective. In *Marriage and marital therapy*, T. J. Paolino and B. S. McCrady, eds. New York: Brunner/Mazel.

—References—

Alexander, J. F., and Parsons, B. V. 1973. Short-term behavioral intervention with delinquent families: Impact on family process and recidivism. *Journal of Abnormal Psychology. 51:* 219–225.

Alexander, J. F., and Parsons, B. V. 1982. *Functional family therapy*. Pacific Grove, CA: Brooks/Cole.

Arrington, A., Sullaway, M., and Christensen, A. 1988. Behavioral family assessment. In *Handbook of behavioral family therapy*, I. R. H. Falloon, ed. New York: Guilford Press.

Azrin, N. H., Naster, J. B., and Jones, R. 1973. Reciprocity counseling: A rapid learning-based procedure for marital counseling. *Behavior Research and Therapy. 11:* 365–383.

Baer, D. M., and Sherman, J. A. 1969. Reinforcement control of generalized imitation in young children. *Journal of Experimental Child Psychology. 1:* 37–49.

Bandura, A. 1969. *Principles of behavior modification*. New York: Holt, Rinehart & Winston.

Bandura, A., and Walters, R. 1963. *Social learning and personality development*. New York: Holt, Rinehart & Winston.

Baucom, D. H., and Epstein, N. 1990. *Cognitive-behavioral marital therapy*. New York: Brunner/Mazel.

Baucom, D. H., Epstein, N., and LaTaillade, J. 2002. Cognitive-behavioral couple therapy. In *Clinical handbook of couple therapy*, 3rd ed., A. S. Gurman and N. S. Jacobson, eds., New York: Guilford Press.

Beck, A. T. 1976. *Cognitive therapy and the emotional disorders*. New York: International Universities Press.

Beck, A. T. 1988. *Love is never enough*. New York: Harper & Row.

Boardman, W. K. 1962. Rusty: A brief behavior disorder. *Journal of Consulting Psychology. 26:* 293–297.

Christophersen, E. R., Arnold, C. M., Hill, D. W., and Quilitch, H. R. 1972. The home point system: Token reinforcement procedures for application by parents of children with behavioral problems. *Journal of Applied Behavioral Analysis. 5:* 485–497.

Crits-Christoph, P., Frank, E., Chambless, D. L., Brody, C., and Karp, J. F. 1995. Training in empirically validated treatments: What are clinical psychol-

ogy students learning? *Professional Psychology: Research and Practice. 26:* 514–522.

Dattilio, F. M. 1993. Cognitive techniques with couples and families. *The Family Journal. 1:* 51–65.

Dattilio, F. M. 1997. Family therapy. In *Casebook of cognitive therapy*, R. Leahy, ed. Northvale, NJ: Jason Aronson.

Dattilio, F. M. 1998. *Case studies in couple and family therapy: Systemic and cognitive perspectives*. New York: Guilford Press.

Dattilio, F. M. 2001. Behavior family therapy: Contemporary myths and misconceptions. *Contemporary Family Therapy. 23* (1): 3–18.

Dattilio, F. M., and Epstein, N. B. 2004. Cognitive-behavioral couple and family therapy. In *The family therapy handbook*, G. Weekes and T. Sexton, eds. New York: Routledge.

Dattilio, F. M., and Padesky, C. A. 1990. *Cognitive therapy with couples*. Sarasota, FL: Professional Resource Exchange.

DeRubeis, R. J., and Beck A. T. 1988. Cognitive therapy. In *Handbook of cognitive-behavioral therapies*, K. S. Dobson, ed. New York: Guilford Press.

Ellis, A. 1962. *Reason and emotion in psychotherapy*. New York: Lyle Stuart.

Ellis, A. 1978. Family therapy: A phenomenological and active-directive approach. *Journal of Marriage and Family Counseling. 4:* 43–50.

Epstein, N., and Schlesinger, S. E. 1991. Marital and family problems. In *Adult clinical problems: A cognitive-behavioral approach*, W. Dryden and R. Rentoul, eds. London: Routledge.

Epstein, N., and Schlesinger, S. E. 1996. Cognitive-behavioral treatment of family problems. In *Casebook of cognitive-behavior therapy with children and adolescents*, M. Reinecke, F. M. Dattilio, and A. Freeman, eds. New York: Guilford Press.

Epstein, N., Schlesinger, S. E., and Dryden, W., eds. 1988. *Cognitive-behavioral therapy with families*. New York: Brunner/Mazel.

Falloon, I. R. H. 1991. Behavioral family therapy. In *Handbook of family therapy*, vol. II, A. S. Gurman and D. P. Kniskern, eds. New York: Brunner/Mazel.

Ferster, C. B. 1963. Essentials of a science of behavior. In *An introduction to the science of human behavior*,

J. I. Nurnberger, C. B. Ferster, and J. P. Brady, eds. New York: Appleton-Century-Crofts.

Forehand, R., Roberts, M. W., Doleys, D. M., Hobbs, S. A., and Resnick, P. A. 1976. An examination of disciplinary procedures with children. *Journal of Experimental Child Psychology. 21:* 109–120.

Forgatch, M. S., and Patterson, G. R. 1998. Behavioral family therapy. In *Case studies in couple and family therapy: Systemic and cognitive perspectives.* F. M. Dattilio, ed. New York: Guilford Press.

Gordon, S. B., and Davidson, N. 1981. Behavioral parent training. In *Handbook of family therapy,* A. S. Gurman and D. P. Kniskern, eds. New York: Brunner/Mazel.

Gottman, J., and Krokoff, L. 1989. Marital interaction and satisfaction: A longitudinal view. *Journal of Consulting and Clinical Psychology. 57:* 47–52.

Gottman, J., Markman, H., and Notarius, C. 1977. The topography of marital conflict: A sequential analysis of verbal and nonverbal behavior. *Journal of Marriage and the Family. 39:* 461–477.

Hickman, M. E., and Baldwin, B. A. 1971. Use of programmed instruction to improve communication in marriage. *The Family Coordinator. 20:* 121–125.

Huber, C. H., and Baruth, L. G. 1989. *Rational-emotive family therapy: A systems perspective.* New York: Springer.

Jacobson, N. S. 1977. Problem solving and contingency contracting in the treatment of marital discord. *Journal of Consulting and Clinical Psychology. 45:* 92–100.

Jacobson, N. S. 1981. Behavioral marital therapy. In *Handbook of family therapy,* A. S. Gurman and D. P. Kniskern, eds. New York: Brunner/Mazel.

Jacobson, N. S., and Margolin, G. 1979. *Marital therapy: Strategies based on social learning and behavior exchange principles.* New York: Brunner/Mazel.

Jacobson, N. S., Waldron, H., and Moore, D. 1980. Toward a behavioral profile of marital distress. *Journal of Consulting and Clinical Psychology. 48:* 696–703.

Jones, M. C. 1924. A laboratory study of fear: The case of Peter. *Journal of Geriatric Psychology. 31:* 308–315.

Kanfer, F. H., and Phillips, J. S. 1970. *Learning foundations of behavior therapy.* New York: Wiley.

Kaplan, H. S. 1974. *The new sex therapy: Active treatment of sexual dysfunctions.* New York: Brunner/Mazel.

Kaplan, H. S. 1979. *Disorders of sexual desire and other new concepts and techniques in sex therapy.* New York: Brunner/Mazel.

Knox, D. 1971. *Marriage happiness: A behavioral approach to counseling.* Champaign, IL: Research Press.

Lazarus, A. A. 1965. The treatment of a sexually inadequate male. In *Case studies in behavior modification,* L. P. Ullmann and L. Krasner, eds. New York: Holt, Rinehart & Winston.

Leslie, L. A. 1988. Cognitive-behavioral and systems models of family therapy: How compatible are they? In *Cognitive-behavioral therapy with families,* N. Epstein, S. E. Schlesinger, and W. Dryden, eds. New York: Brunner/Mazel.

Lobitz, N. C., and LoPiccolo, J. 1972. New methods in the behavioral treatment of sexual dysfunction. *Journal of Behavior Therapy and Experimental Psychiatry. 3:* 265–271.

Locke, H. J., and Wallace, K. M. 1959. Short-term marital adjustment and prediction tests: Their reliability and validity. *Journal of Marriage and Family Living. 21:* 251–255.

Lovibond, S. H. 1963. The mechanism of conditioning treatment of enuresis. *Behavior Research and Therapy. 1:* 17–21.

Mahoney, M. J. 1977. Reflections on the cognitive learning trend in psychotherapy. *American Psychologist. 32:* 5–13.

Margolin, G., Christensen, A., and Weiss, R. L. 1975. Contracts, cognition and change: A behavioral approach to marriage therapy. *Counseling Psychologist. 5:* 15–25.

Masters, W. H., and Johnson, V. E. 1970. *Human sexual inadequacy.* Boston: Little, Brown & Co.

Munson, C. E. 1993. Cognitive family therapy. In *Cognitive and behavioral treatment: Methods and applications,* D. K. Granvold, ed. Pacific Grove, CA: Brooks/Cole.

Patterson, G. R. 1971. *Families: Application of social learning theory to family life.* Champaign, IL: Research Press.

Patterson, G. R., Dishion, T. J., and Chamberlain, P. 1993. Outcomes and methodological issues relating to treatment of anti-social children. In *Effective psychotherapy: A handbook of comparative research,* T. R. Giles, ed. New York: Plenum Press.

Patterson, G. R., and Forgatch, M. S. 1995. Predicting future clinical adjustment from treatment outcomes and process variables. *Psychological Assessment. 7:* 275–285.

Patterson, G. R., and Reid, J. 1970. Reciprocity and coercion: two facets of social systems. In *Behavior modification in clinical psychology,*

C. Neuringer and J. Michael, eds. New York: Appleton-Century-Crofts.

Pavlov, I. P. 1932. Neuroses in man and animals. *Journal of the American Medical Association.* 99: 1012–1013.

Pendergrass, V. E. 1971. Effects of length of timeout from positive reinforcement and schedule of application in suppression of aggressive behavior. *Psychological Record.* 21: 75–80.

Pierce, R. M. 1973. Training in interpersonal communication skills with the partners of deteriorated marriages. *The Family Coordinator.* 22: 223–227.

Premack, D. 1965. Reinforcement theory. In *Nebraska symposium on motivation,* D. Levine, ed. Lincoln, NB: University of Nebraska Press.

Rimm, D.C., and Masters, J. C. 1974. *Behavior therapy: Techniques and empirical findings.* New York: Wiley.

Rinn, R. C. 1978. Children with behavior disorders. In *Behavior therapy in the psychiatric setting,* M. Hersen and A. S. Bellack, eds. Baltimore: Williams & Wilkins.

Risley, T. R., and Wolf, M. M. 1967. Experimental manipulation of autistic behaviors and generalization into the home. In *Child development: Readings in experimental analysis,* S. W. Bijou and D. M. Baer, eds. New York: Appleton.

Schwebel, A. I., and Fine, M. A. 1992. Cognitive-behavioral family therapy. *Journal of Family Psychotherapy.* 3: 73–91.

Schwitzgebel, R. 1967. Short-term operant conditioning of adolescent offenders on socially relevant variables. *Journal of Abnormal Psychology.* 72: 134–142.

Schwitzgebel, R., and Kolb, D. A. 1964. Inducing behavior change in adolescent delinquents. *Behaviour Research and Therapy.* 9: 233–238.

Semans, J. H. 1956. Premature ejaculation: A new approach. *Southern Medical Journal.* 49: 353–357.

Skinner, B. F. 1953. *Science and human behavior.* New York: Macmillan.

Stuart, R. B. 1969. An operant-interpersonal treatment for marital discord. *Journal of Consulting and Clinical Psychology.* 33: 675–682.

Stuart, R. B. 1971. Behavioral contracting within the families of delinquents. *Journal of Behavior Therapy and Experimental Psychiatry.* 2: 1–11.

Stuart, R. B. 1975. Behavioral remedies for marital ills: A guide to the use of operant-interpersonal techniques. In *International symposium on behavior modification,* T. Thompson and W. Docken, eds. New York: Appleton.

Stuart, R. B. 1976. An operant interpersonal program for couples. In *Treating relationships,* D. H. Olson, ed. Lake Mills, IA: Graphic Publishing.

Teichman, Y. 1984. Cognitive family therapy. *British Journal of Cognitive Psychotherapy.* 2: 1–10.

Teichman, Y. 1992. Family treatment with an acting-out adolescent. In *Comprehensive casebook of cognitive therapy,* A. Freeman and F. M. Dattilio, eds. New York: Plenum.

Thibaut, J., and Kelley, H. H. 1959. *The social psychology of groups.* New York: Wiley.

Vincent, J. P., Weiss, R. L., and Birchler, G. R. 1975. A behavioral analysis of problem solving in distressed and nondistressed married and stranger dyads. *Behavior Therapy.* 6: 475–487.

Watson, J. B., and Raynor, R. 1920. Conditioned emotional reactions. *Journal of Experimental Psychology.* 3: 1–14.

Weeks, G. R., and Gambescia, N. 2000. *Erectile dysfunction: Integrating couple therapy, sex therapy and medical treatment.* New York: Norton.

Weeks, G. R., and Gambescia, N. 2002. *Hypoactive sexual desire: Integrating sex and couple therapy.* New York: Norton.

Weiss, R. L., and Birchler, G. R. 1978. Adults with marital dysfunction. In *Behavior therapy in the psychiatric setting,* M. Hersen and A. S. Bellack, eds. Baltimore: Williams & Wilkins.

Weiss, R. L., Hops, H., and Patterson, G. R. 1973. A framework for conceptualizing marital conflict, a technology for altering it, some data for evaluating it. In *Behavior change: Methodology, concepts and practice,* L. A. Hamerlynch, L. C. Handy, and E. J. Marsh, eds. Champaign, IL: Research Press.

Weiss, R. L., and Isaac, J. 1978. Behavior vs. cognitive measures as predictors of marital satisfaction. Paper presented at the Western Psychological Association meeting, Los Angeles.

Wills, T. A., Weiss, R. L., and Patterson, G. R. 1974. A behavioral analysis of the determinants of marital satisfaction. *Journal of Consulting and Clinical Psychology.* 42: 802–811.

Wolpe, J. 1948. An approach to the problem of neurosis based on the conditioned response. Unpublished M. D. thesis. University of Witwatersrand, Johannesburg, South Africa.

Wolpe, J. 1958. *Psychotherapy by reciprocal inhibition.* Stanford, CA: Stanford University Press.

11

Family Therapy in the Twenty-First Century

From a radical new experiment in the 1960s, family therapy grew into an established force, complete with its own literature, organizations, and legions of practitioners. Unlike other fields organized around a single conceptual model (psychoanalysis, behavior therapy), family therapy was always a diverse enterprise, with competing schools and a multitude of theories. What they shared was a belief that problems run in families. Beyond that, however, each school was a well-defined and distinct enterprise, with its own leaders, texts, and ways of doing therapy.

Today, all of that has changed. The field is no longer neatly divided into separate schools, and its practitioners no longer share a universal adherence to systems theory. As family therapists have always been fond of metaphors, we might say that the field has grown up. No longer cliquish or cocksure, the family therapy movement has been shaken and transformed by a series of challenges—to the idea that any one approach has all the answers, about the nature of men and women, about the American family—indeed, about the possibility of knowing anything with certainty. In this chapter, we examine those challenges and see what family therapy looks like in the twenty-first century.

Erosion of Boundaries

The boundaries between schools of family therapy gradually blurred in the nineties to the point where now fewer and fewer therapists would characterize themselves as purely Bowenian, or structural, or strategic, or what have you. One reason for this decline in sectarianism was that, as they gained experience, practitioners found no reason not to borrow from each other's arsenal of techniques. Suppose, for example, that a card-carrying structural therapist were to read White and Epston's little gem of a book, *Narrative Means to Therapeutic Ends*, and start spending more time exploring the stories clients tell about their lives. Would this therapist still be a structuralist? A narrative therapist? Or perhaps a little of both?

Suppose that our hypothetical therapist were to hear Jim Keim at a conference describing his strategic approach to families with oppositional children and started using it in her own practice. What would we call this therapist now? Structural-narrative-strategic? Eclectic? Or maybe just "a family therapist"?

Another reason for the erosion of orthodoxy was the growing recognition of the need for individualized techniques to deal with specific problems and populations. Once family therapists cherished their models. If a particular family didn't quite fit the paradigm, maybe they just weren't "an appropriate treatment case." Today, one-size-fits-all therapies are no longer seen as viable.

Now therapists approach families less as experts confident of fixing them than as partners hoping to shore up their resources. These resources are constrained not only by a family's structure but also by political and economic forces beyond their control. Some of the change in status of the classic schools was due to the death or retirement of their pioneers and the absence of dominating figures to replace them. Our current era of questioning and uncertainty is also related to a growing recognition among clinicians that doctrinaire models aren't always relevant to the specific needs of their clients. Family therapy is one of many social sciences that has been turned upside down by the postmodern revolution.

Postmodernism

Advances in science at the beginning of the twentieth century gave us a sense that the truth of things could be uncovered through objective observation and measurement. The universe was conceived as a mechanism whose laws of operation awaited discovery. Once these universal laws were known, we could control our environment. This modernist perspective was also the way family therapy's pioneers approached their clients—as cybernetic systems to be decoded and reprogrammed. The therapist was the expert. Structural and strategic blueprints were used to search out flaws that needed repair, regardless of whether families saw things that way themselves.

Postmodernism was a reaction to this kind of hubris. Not only are we losing faith in the validity of scientific, political, and religious truths, but we're coming to doubt whether absolute truth can ever be known. As Walter Truett

Anderson (1990) writes in *Reality Isn't What It Used to Be,* "Most of the conflicts that tore the now-ending modern era were between different belief systems, each of which professed to have the truth: this faith against that one, capitalism against communism, science against religion. On all sides the assumption was that somebody possessed the real item, a truth fixed and beyond mere human conjecture" (p. 2). In family therapy it was structural truth versus psychodynamics, Bowen versus Satir.

Einstein's relativity undermined our faith in certainties. Marx challenged the right of one class to dominate another. In the 1960s we lost trust in the establishment and gained a sense that there were other realities besides those of ordinary consciousness. The feminist movement challenged assumptions about gender that had been considered laws of nature. As the world shrank and we were increasingly exposed to people of different cultures, we had to reexamine our assumptions about their "peculiar" beliefs.

This mounting skepticism became a major force in the 1980s and shook the pillars of every human endeavor. In literature, education, religion, political science, and psychology, accepted practices were **deconstructed**—that is, shown to be social conventions developed by people with their own agendas. Social philosopher Michel Foucault interpreted the accepted principles in many fields as stories perpetuated to protect power structures and silence alternative voices. The first and perhaps most influential of those voices to be raised in family therapy was the feminist critique.

The Feminist Critique

Feminism prompted family therapy's rudest awakening. In an eye-opening critique heralded by an article by Rachel Hare-Mustin in 1978, feminist family therapists not only exposed the gender bias inherent in existing models, they also advocated a style of therapy that called into question systems theory itself.

Cybernetics encouraged us to view a family system as a flawed machine. Judith Myers Avis (1988) described this family machine as one that

> ...functions according to special systemic rules and is divorced from its historical, social, economic, and political contexts. By viewing the family out of context, family therapists locate family dysfunction entirely within interpersonal relationships in the family, ignore broader patterns of dysfunction occurring across families, and fail to notice the relationship between social context and family dysfunction. (p. 17)

The Batesonian version of cybernetics had claimed that personal control in systems was impossible because all elements are continually influencing one another in repetitious feedback loops. If all parts of a system are equally involved in its problems, no one is to blame.

To feminists, however, the notion of equal responsibility for problems looked "suspiciously like a hypersophisticated version of blaming the victim and rationalizing the status quo" (Goldner, 1985, p. 33). This criticism was particularly germane in crimes against women, such as battering, incest, and rape, for which psychological theories have long been used to imply that women provoked their own abuse (James & MacKinnon, 1990).

The problematic family constellation most commonly cited by family therapists was the peripheral father, overinvolved mother, and symptomatic child. For years, psychoanalysts had blamed mothers for their children's symptoms. Family therapy's contribution was to show how a father's lack of involvement contributed to the mother's overinvolvement, and so therapists tried to pry the mother loose by inserting the father in her place. This wasn't the boon for women that it might have seemed because, in too many cases, mothers were viewed no less negatively. They were still "enmeshed," but now a new solution appeared—bringing in good old dad to the rescue.

What feminists contended that therapists failed to see was that "the archetypal 'family case' of the overinvolved mother and peripheral father is best understood not as a clinical problem, but as the product of an historical process two hundred years in the making" (Goldner, 1985, p. 31). Mothers were overinvolved and insecure not because of some personal flaw but because they were in emotionally isolated, economically dependent, overresponsible positions in families, positions that were crazy-making.

*P*eggy Papp, Olga Silverstein, Marianne Walters, and Betty Carter, founding members of the Women's Project in Family Therapy.

Gender-sensitive therapists sought to help families reorganize so that no one, man or woman, remained stuck in such positions. Thus, instead of undermining a mother's self-esteem by replacing her with a peripheral father (who was likely to have been critical of her parenting all along), a feminist family therapist might help the family reexamine the roles that kept mothers down and fathers out. Fathers might be encouraged to become more involved with parenting—not because mothers are incompetent, but because it's a father's responsibility (Goodrich, Rampage, Ellman, & Halstead, 1988; Walters, Carter, Papp, & Silverstein, 1988).

Feminists weren't just asking therapists to be more sensitive to gender issues. Rather, they asserted that issues of gender or, more specifically, patriarchy, permeated therapists' work, even though we had been conditioned not to notice them. They therefore believed that gender inequality should be a primary concern for family therapists (Goldner, 1988; Luepnitz, 1988).

Only when we become more gender sensitive will we stop blaming mothers and looking to them to do all of the changing. Only then will we be able to fully counter the unconscious bias toward seeing women as ultimately responsible for childrearing and housekeeping; as needing to support their husbands' careers by neglecting their own; as needing to be married or at least to have a man in their lives (Anderson, 1995). Only then can we stop relying on traditional male traits, such as rationality, independence, and competitiveness, as the standards of health and stop denigrating or ignoring traits traditionally encouraged in women, like emotionality, nurturance, and relationship focus.

As one might anticipate, the feminist critique wasn't exactly welcomed by the family therapy establishment. The early to mid-1980s was a period of polarization, as feminists tried to exceed the establishment's "threshold of deafness." By the 1990s that threshold had been exceeded. The major feminist points are no longer debated, and the field is evolving toward a more collaborative and socially enlightened form of therapy.

Lest we get too complacent about family therapy's acceptance of feminism, it's well to remember that women still face political, economic, and social problems on a daily basis. Women still earn less than men for their labor. Women are still assigned most domestic work. Women are still often blamed for family problems. Men's violence against women is still tolerated. Moreover, although some men reject the macho ideal, it still influences most men, who strive to be "manly" and reject less aggressive men as geeks, wimps, or wusses. Although many men don't experience themselves as powerful in their own families, men still benefit from and appropriate power of women in society. As Rachel Hare-Mustin says, "Although it is true that men can cry now, too, they still have less to cry about."[1]

Social Constructionism and the Narrative Revolution

Constructivism was the lever that pried family therapy away from its belief in objectivity—the assumption that what one sees in families is what *is* in families. Human experience is fundamentally ambiguous. Fragments of experience are understood only through a process that organizes it, selects what's salient, and assigns meaning and significance.

Instead of focusing on patterns of family interaction, constructivism shifted the emphasis to exploring and reevaluating the perspectives that people with problems have about them. Meaning itself became the primary target.

In the 1980s and 1990s Harlene Anderson and Harry Goolishian translated constructivism into an approach that democratized the therapist–client relationship. Along with Lynn Hoffman and others, these **collaborative** therapists were united in their opposition to the cybernetic model

---

1. Rachel Hare-Mustin. 2001. "Family therapy and the future—2001." Plenary Address, American Family Therapy Academy Conference of the Americas, Miami, FL, June 27, 2001.

and its mechanistic implications. Their version of postmodernism focused more on caring than curing, and they sought to move the therapist out of the position of expert into a more egalitarian partnership with clients.

Perhaps the most striking example of this democratization of therapy was introduced by the Norwegian psychiatrist Tom Andersen, who leveled the playing field by hiding nothing from his clients. He and his team openly discuss their reactions to what a family says. This **reflecting team** (Andersen, 1991) has become a widely used device in the collaborative model's therapy by consensus. Observers come out from behind the one-way mirror to discuss their impressions with the therapist and family. This process creates an open environment in which the family feels part of a team and the team feels more empathy for the family.

What these collaborative therapists shared was the conviction that too often clients aren't heard because therapists are doing therapy *to* them rather than *with* them. To redress this authoritarian attitude, Harlene Anderson (1993) recommended that therapists adopt a position of **not-knowing,** which leads to genuine conversations with clients in which "both the therapist's and the client's expertise are engaged to dissolve the problem" (p. 325).[2]

This new perspective was in the tradition of an approach to knowledge that emerged from biblical studies called **hermeneutics,** from the Greek word for *interpretation.* Before it surfaced in family therapy, hermeneutics had already shaken up psychoanalysis. In the 1980s, Donald Spence, Roy Schafer, and Paul Ricoeur challenged the Freudian notion that there was one correct and comprehensive interpretation of a patient's symptoms, dreams, and fantasies. The analytic method isn't, they argued, archaeological or reconstructive; it's constructive and synthetic, organizing whatever is there into patterns it imposes (Mitchell, 1993).

From a hermeneutic perspective, what a therapist knows is not simply discovered through a process of free association and analysis—or enactment and circular questioning—it's organized, constructed, and fitted together by the therapist alone, or collaboratively with the patient or family. Although there's nothing inherently democratic about hermeneutic exegesis, its challenge to essentialism went hand in hand with the challenge to authoritarianism. In family therapy, the hermeneutic tradition seemed a perfect partner to efforts to make treatment more collaborative.

It's hard to give up certainty. A lot is asked of a listener who, in order to be genuinely open to the speaker's story, must put aside his or her own beliefs and, at least temporarily, enter the other's world. In so doing, the listener may find those beliefs challenged and changed. This is more than some therapists are willing to risk.

Constructivism focused on how individuals create their own realities, but family therapy has always emphasized the power of interaction. As a result, another postmodern psychology called **social constructionism** now influences many family therapists. Social psychologist Kenneth Gergen (1985), its main proponent, emphasized the power of social interaction in generating meaning for people.

Gergen challenged the notion that we are autonomous individuals holding independent beliefs and argued instead that our beliefs are fluid and fluctuate with changes in our social context. Gergen (1991b) asks, "Are not all the fragments of identity the residues of relationships, and aren't we undergoing continuous transformation as we move from one relationship to another?" (p. 28).

This view has several implications. The first is that no one has a corner on the truth; all truths are social constructions. This idea invites therapists to help clients understand the origins of their beliefs, even those they assumed were laws of nature. The second implication is that therapy is a linguistic exercise; if therapists can

---

2. Collaborative therapists distinguish these conversations from the nondirective, empathic Rogerian style because they don't just reflect but also offer ideas and opinions, though always tentatively.

lead clients to new constructions about their problems, the problems may open up. Third, therapy should be collaborative. Because neither therapist nor client brings truth to the table, new realities emerge through conversations in which both sides share opinions and respect each other's perspective.

Social constructionism was welcomed with open arms by those who were trying to shift the focus of therapy from action to cognition, and it became the basis for an approach that took family therapy by storm in the 1990s, *narrative therapy* (Chapter 13). The narrative metaphor focuses on how experience creates expectations, and how expectations shape experience through the creation of organizing stories. Narrative therapists follow Gergen in considering the "self" a socially constructed phenomenon.

The question for the narrative therapist isn't one of truth but of which points of view are useful and lead to preferred outcomes. Problems aren't in persons (as psychoanalysis had it) or in relationships (as systems theory had it); rather, problems are embedded in points of view about individuals and their situations. Narrative therapy helps people reexamine these points of view.

Family Therapy's Answer to Managed Care: Solution-Focused Therapy

Solution-focused therapy was the other new model to rise to prominence in the nineties. Steve de Shazer and his colleagues (Chapter 12) took the ideas of constructivism in a different, more pragmatic, direction. The goal of this approach is to get clients to shift from "problem talk"—trying to understand their problems—to "solution talk"—trying to understand what works. The idea is that focusing on solutions, in and of itself, often eliminates problems.

The popularity of the solution-focused model exploded during a period in which agency budgets were slashed and managed care dictated the number of sessions for which practitioners

could be reimbursed. This produced a tremendous demand for a brief, easy-to-apply approach, to which solution-focused therapy seemed the perfect answer.

Family Violence

In the early 1990s family therapy took a hard look at the dark side of family life. For the first time, books and articles on wife battering and sexual abuse began appearing in the mainstream family therapy literature (e.g., Trepper & Barrett, 1989; Goldner, Penn, Sheinberg, & Walker, 1990; Sheinberg, 1992). The field was shaken out of its collective denial regarding the extent of male-to-female abuse in families.

Judith Myers Avis (1992) delivered a barrage of shocking statistics about the number of women who have experienced sexual abuse before the age of 18 (37 percent), the percent of abusers who are men (95 percent), the number of women abused each year by the men they live with (1 in 6), the percent of male college students who had coerced sex from an unwilling partner (25 percent), and those who said they would commit rape if guaranteed immunity from punishment (20 percent). After reiterating the indictment of theories that call for therapist neutrality and that treat the abused as partially responsible for their abuse, she concluded that:

> As long as we train therapists in systemic theories without balancing that training with an understanding of the non-neutrality of power dynamics, we will continue producing family therapists who collude in the maintenance of male power and are dangerous to the women and children with whom they work. (p. 231)

Michele Bograd (1992) summarized one of the central predicaments for family therapy in this decade.

> In working with family violence, how do we balance a relativistic world view with values about human safety and the rights of men and women to self-determination and protection? When is the clinical utility of neutrality limited

or counterproductive? When is conviction essential to the change process? (p. 248)

The systemic view, now under attack, was that family violence was the outcome of cycles of mutual provocation, an escalation, albeit unacceptable, of the emotionally destructive behavior that characterizes many marriages. Advocates for women rejected this point of view. From their perspective, violent men don't lose control, they *take* control—and will stop only when they are held accountable.

Although the claim made by some women's advocates that couples therapy has no place in the treatment of violent marriages was controversial, their warnings provided a wake-up call. Domestic violence—let's call it what it is, wife battering and child beating—is a major public health problem, right up there with alcoholism and depression.

Multiculturalism

Family therapy has always billed itself as a treatment of people in context. In the postwar America of family therapy's birth, this principle was translated into a pragmatic look at the influence of a family's relationships on its members. Now as we've become a more diverse country enriched by a flow of immigrants from Asia, Central and South America, Africa, and Eastern Europe, family therapy as a profession has shown its willingness to embrace the positiveness of others. Not only are we learning to respect that families from other cultures have their own valid ways of doing things but our journals and professional organizations are making an effort to become more diverse and inclusive.

Monica McGoldrick and her colleagues (McGoldrick, Pearce, & Giordano, 1982) dealt the first blow to our ethnocentricity with a book describing the characteristic values and structure of a host of different ethnic groups. Following this and a spate of related works (e.g., Falicov, 1983, 1998; Boyd-Franklin, 1989; Saba, Karrer, & Hardy, 1989; Mirkin, 1990; Ingoldsby & Smith, 1995; Okun, 1996; McGoldrick, 1998), we are now more sensitive to the need to know something about the ethnic background of our client families, so we don't assume they're sick just because they're different.

Multiculturalism has become a prevailing theme in family therapy, as reflected in conference agendas, journal articles, and graduate school curricula. The attention to these issues represents a welcome sensitizing to the influence of ethnicity.

Multiculturalism is certainly an advance over ethnocentrism. Yet in highlighting differences, there is a danger of emphasizing identity politics. Segregation, even in the name of ethnic pride, isolates people and breeds prejudice. Perhaps "pluralism" is a better term than "multiculturalism" because it implies a balance between ethnic identity and connection to the larger group.

As we suggested in Chapter 4, ethnic sensitivity does not require becoming an expert—or thinking you're an expert—on every culture you might conceivably work with. If you don't know how a rural Mexican family feels about their children leaving home or what Korean parents think about their teenage daughter dating American boys, you can always ask.

Race

In the early days of family therapy, African American families received some attention (e.g., Minuchin et al., 1967), but for many years it seemed that the field, like the rest of the country, tried to ignore this population and the racism they live with every day. Finally, however, African American family therapists such as Nancy Boyd-Franklin (1993) and Ken Hardy (1993) brought race out of the shadows and forced it on the field's consciousness.

White therapists still, of course, have the option to walk away from these issues. People of color don't have that luxury (Hardy, 1993):

To avoid being seen by whites as troublemakers, we suppress the part of ourselves that feels hurt and outraged by the racism around us, instead developing an "institutional self"—an accommodating facade of calm professionalism calculated to be nonthreatening to whites. . . . Familiar only with our institutional selves, white people don't appreciate the sense of immediate connection and unspoken loyalty that binds black people together. . . . We are united by being raised with the same messages most black families pass on to their children: "You were born into one of the most despised groups in the world. You can't trust white people. You are somebody. Be proud, and never for one minute think that white people are better than you." (pp. 52–53)

Laura Markowitz (1993) quotes a black woman's therapy experience:

I remember being in therapy years ago with a nice white woman who kept focusing me on why I was such an angry person and on my parents as inadequate individuals. . . . We never looked at my father as a poor black man, my mother as a poor black woman and the context in which they survived and raised us. . . . Years later, I saw a therapist of color and the first thing out of her mouth was, "Let's look at what was going on for your parents." It was a joyous moment to be able to see my dad not as a terrible person who hated us but as a survivor living under amazingly difficult conditions. I could embrace him, and I could understand my anger instead of blaming myself for feeling that way. (p. 29)

It's hard for whites to realize how many doors were open to them based on their skin color and

Nancy Boyd-Franklin's Black Families in Therapy *was one of the first— and best—books on treating ethnic minority families.*

to understand how burdened by racism nonwhites are. African American families not only have to overcome barriers to opportunity and achievement but also the frustration and despair that such obstacles create.

The task of therapists working with nonwhite families is to understand their reluctance to engage in treatment and distance or hostility (particularly if the therapist is white) in the context of their environment and their history of negative interaction with white people, including the many social service agents they encounter. In addition, the therapist must recognize the family's strengths and draw from their networks or (if the family is isolated) help them create networks of support.

Finally, therapists must look inside and face their own attitudes about race, class, and poverty. Toward this end, several authors recommend curricula that go beyond lectures to personal encounters—that is, confronting our own demons of racism (Pinderhughes, 1989; Boyd-Franklin, 1989 Green, 1998).

Poverty and Social Class

Money and social class are not subjects that most people like to discuss. The shame of economic disadvantage is related to the pervasive individualist ethic that people are responsible for their own success or lack of it. If you're poor it must be your own fault.

Despite decreasing fees due to managed care, most therapists are able to maintain a reasonably comfortable lifestyle. They have little appreciation of the obstacles their poor clients face and of the psychological impact of those conditions. When poor clients don't show up for appointments or don't comply with directives, some therapists are quick to see them as apathetic or irresponsible. In many cases, this is also the way poor people come to see themselves—and that negative self-image can be the biggest obstacle of all.

How can we counter this tendency to think that poor people just can't cut it? First, therapists need to educate themselves to the social and political realities of being poor in the United States. Journalist Barbara Ehrenreich (1999) spent a year trying to live like a welfare recipient coming into the workforce. Living in a trailer park and working as a waitress left her with virtually nothing after expenses.

> How former welfare recipients and single mothers will (and do) survive in the low-wage workforce, I cannot imagine. Maybe they will figure out how to condense their lives—including child-raising, laundry, romance and meals—into the couple of hours between full-time jobs. Maybe they will take up residence in their vehicles [as she found several fellow workers had done], if they have one. All I know is that I couldn't hold two jobs and I couldn't make enough money to live on with one. And I had advantages unthinkable to many of the long-term poor—health, stamina, a working car, and no children to care for or support . . . The thinking behind welfare reform was that even the humblest jobs are morally uplifting and psychologically buoying. In reality these are likely to be fraught with insult and stress. (p. 52)

The fact is, this isn't the land of equal opportunity. The economy has built-in disparities that make it extremely difficult for anyone to climb out of poverty and that keep nearly one in four children living in poverty (Walsh, 1998).

These days, it isn't just families of poverty who live with financial insecurity. As mortgages, car payments, and college tuitions mount up, and corporations frequently lay off employees suddenly and ruthlessly, family life at all but the wealthiest levels is increasingly dominated by economic anxiety. Median family income has declined in the past three decades to the point where young families can't hope to do as well as their parents, even with the two incomes needed to support a very modest standard of living.

Therapists can't pay their clients' rent, but they can help them appreciate that the burdens they live with are not all of their own making. Even when they don't bring it up, a sensitive therapist should be aware of the role financial pressures play in the lives of their client families. Asking about how they manage to get by not only puts this issue on the table, it can also lead to a greater appreciation of the effort and ingenuity it takes to make ends meet these days.

Gay and Lesbian Rights

Family therapy's consciousness was raised about gay and lesbian rights in the same way it was for race. After a long period of neglect and denial, family therapy in the late 1980s began to face the discrimination that a sizable percentage of the population lives with (Krestan, 1988; Roth & Murphy, 1986; Carl, 1990; Laird, 1993; Sanders, 1993). The release in 1996 of a major clinical handbook (Laird & Green, 1996) and the magazine *In the Family* (edited by Laura Markowitz) meant that gay and lesbian issues were finally out of family therapy's closet.

Despite gains in tolerance in some segments of our society, however, gays and lesbians continue to face humiliation, discrimination, and violence because of their sexuality. After a childhood of shame and confusion, many gays and lesbians are rejected by their families once they come out. Because of the lack of social support, the bonds in gay and lesbian relationships can be strained, generating stress, jealousy, and the pressures of isolation.

Parents often feel guilty, in part because they blame themselves for their children's sexual orientation. Parental reactions range from denial, self-reproach, and fear for their child's future, to hostility, violence, and disowning (LaSala, 1997). Therapists should remember that a gay or lesbian child may have struggled for years to come to grips with his or her identity, and their parents may need time to catch up after the initial shock.

When working with gay, lesbian, bisexual, or transgendered clients, we recommend that therapists get as much information as they can about the unique identity formation and relationship issues that these beleaguered groups face. Therapists who aren't well informed about gay and lesbian experience should seek supervision from someone who is, or refer these clients to a clinician with more experience. It simply isn't true that individuals and families, regardless of their cultural context, all struggle with the same issues.

We hope the day will arrive soon when gay and lesbian families, bisexual and transgendered persons, African Americans, and other marginalized groups are studied by family therapists to learn not only about the problems they face but also about how they survive and thrive against such great odds. For example, gays and lesbians often create "families of choice" out of their friendship networks (Johnson & Keren, 1998). As Joan Laird (1993) suggested, these families have much to teach us "about gender relationships, about parenting, about adaptation to tensions in this society, and especially about strength and resilience" (p. 284). The question is whether we are ready to learn.

Spirituality

Throughout the twentieth century, psychotherapists, wanting to avoid any association with what science considers irrational, avoided bringing religion into the consulting room. We've also tried to stay out of the moralizing business, striving to remain neutral so that clients could make up their own minds about their lives.

In the nineties, as increasing numbers of people found modern life isolating and empty, spirituality and religion emerged as antidotes to a widespread feeling of alienation—both in the popular press (making the covers of both *Time* and *Newsweek*) and in the family therapy literature (Brothers, 1992; Burton, 1992; Prest & Keller, 1993; Doherty, 1996; Walsh, 1999).

Some of a family's most powerful influences have to do with how they find meaning in their lives and their ideas about a higher power, yet most therapists never ask about such matters. Is it possible to explore a family's spiritual beliefs without proselytizing or scoffing? More and

more therapists believe that it's not only possible, it's crucial. They believe that people's answers to those larger questions are intimately related to their emotional and physical well-being.

Tailoring Treatment to Populations and Problems

As family therapists have come down from the ivory towers of their training institutes to grapple with the messy problems of the real world, they find it increasingly necessary to fit their approaches to the needs of their clients, rather than the other way around. The maturing of family therapy is reflected in its literature. Once most of the writing was about one of the classic models and how they applied to families in general (e.g., Haley, 1976; Minuchin & Fishman, 1981). In the 1980s, books no longer tied to any one school began to focus on how to do family therapy with a host of specific problems and family constellations.

Books are now available on working with families of people who abuse drugs (Stanton, Todd, & Associates, 1982; Barth, Pietrzak, & Ramier, 1993), alcohol (Steinglass, Bennett, Wolin, & Reiss, 1987; Treadway, 1989; Elkin, 1990), food (Root, Fallon, & Friedrich, 1986; Schwartz, 1995), and each other (Trepper & Barrett, 1989; Friedrich, 1990; Madanes, 1990).

There are books about treating single-parent families (Morawetz & Walker, 1984), stepparent families (Visher & Visher, 1979, 1988), divorcing families (Sprenkle, 1985; Wallerstein & Kelley, 1980; Ahrons & Rogers, 1989; Emery, 1994), blended families (Hansen, 1982; Sager et al., 1983), and families in transition among these states (Pittman, 1987; Falicov, 1988).

There are also books on treating families with young children (Combrinck-Graham, 1989; Wachtel, 1994; Gil, 1994; Freeman, Epston, & Lobovits, 1997; Selekman, 1997; Smith & Nyland, 1997; Bailey, 1999; Nichols, 2004); with troubled adolescents (Price, 1996; Micucci, 1998; Sells, 1998) and young adults (Haley,

1980); and with problems among siblings (Kahn & Lewis, 1988). There are even books on normal families (Walsh, 1982, 1993) and "successful families" (Beavers & Hampson, 1990).

There are books for working with schizophrenic families (Anderson, Reiss, & Hogarty, 1986); families with bipolar disorder (Miklowitz & Goldstein, 1997); families with AIDS (Walker, 1991; Boyd-Franklin, Steiner, & Boland, 1995); families who have suffered trauma (Figley, 1985), chronic illness, or disability (Rolland, 1994; McDaniel, Hepworth, & Doherty, 1992); families who are grieving a death (Walsh & McGoldrick, 1991), have a child with a disability (Seligman & Darling, 1996), or have an adopted child (Reitz & Watson, 1992); poor families (Minuchin, Colapinto, & Minuchin, 1998); and families of different ethnicities (Boyd-Franklin, 1989; Okun, 1996; McGoldrick, Giordano, & Pierce, 1996; Lee, 1997; Falicov, 1998). There are also several books about treating gay and lesbian families.

In addition to these specialized books, the field extended systems thinking beyond the family to include the impact of larger systems like other helping agents or social agencies and schools (Schwartzman, 1985; Imber-Black, 1988; Elizur & Minuchin, 1989), the importance of family rituals and their use in therapy (Imber-Black, Roberts, & Whiting, 1988), and the sociopolitical context in which families exist (Mirkin, 1990; McGoldrick, 1998).

There are practical guides to family therapy not connected to any one school (Taibbi, 1996; Patterson et al., 1998), and edited books that include contributions from all of the schools but that are focused on specific problems or cases (Dattilio, 1998; Donovan, 1999). Thus, as opposed to the earlier days of family therapy, when followers of a particular model read little outside of what came from that school, the trend toward specialization by content rather than by model has made the field more pluralistic in this postmodern age.

Among the most frequently encountered family constellations with unique challenges are single-parent families, African American families, and gay and lesbian families. The following recommendations are offered as introductions to some of the issues encountered in treating these groups.

Single-Parent Families

The most common structural problem in single-parent families is the same as in most two-parent families: an overburdened mother, enmeshed with her children and disengaged from adult relationships. From this perspective, the goal of therapy is to strengthen the mother's hierarchical position in relation to her children and help her become more fulfilled in her own life. However, it's important to keep in mind that single parents rarely have the resources to manage much of a social life on top of working all day and then coming home to take care of the kids, cook dinner, wash dishes, and do six loads of laundry.

Before going any further, we should acknowledge that single-parent families come in many varieties (U.S. Census Bureau, 2001). The children may be living with a teenage mother and her parents, a divorced college professor, or a father whose wife died of cancer. Such families may be rich or poor, and they may be isolated or part of a large family network. In the discussion that follows, we will concentrate on the most common variant encountered in clinical situations: a financially burdened mother with children who is going it alone.

In working with single-parent families, therapists should keep in mind that supporting the parent's care of her children and helping her find more satisfaction in her own life are reciprocal achievements. A therapist should enter the system by addressing the presenting complaint, but whether that problem is, say, a mother's depression or a child's poor school performance, it's important both to help the parent take more effective charge of her children and increase her sources of support.

Effective therapy with a single parent begins with an actively supportive relationship. An empathic therapeutic alliance helps shore up the single parent's confidence to make positive changes and, later, serves as a bridge to help her connect with other people in her environment. To begin with, it's well to recognize that single parents are often angry and disappointed over the loss of a relationship, financial hardship, and trying to cope with the demands of work and children.

Poverty may be the most overwhelming burden on single parents and their children (Duncan & Brooks-Gunn, 1997). Therapists should not underestimate the impact of poverty on a mother's depression, self-esteem, independence, and the decisions she makes about putting up with soul-draining jobs and abusive relationships. Many single-parent families live on the edge of crisis, managing most of the time but always aware that any unexpected emergency can push them over the edge. A supportive therapist recognizes the burdens of financial hardship, makes accommodations to the parent's work schedule, and in some cases helps the single parent consider options, like going back to school, that might help her to become more financially stable.

Often one of the most readily available sources of support for the single parent is her own family. Here, the therapeutic task is twofold: facilitating supportive connections and reducing conflicts. Sometimes, by the way, it's easier to develop dormant sources of support than to resolve contentious existing ones. The sister who lives twenty miles away may be more willing to look after her nieces and nephews from time to time than a depressed single mother thinks. A single parent's family can provide financial support, a place to stay, and help with the children. However, since most parents have trouble getting over treating their grown children as children—especially when they ask for help—a therapist may have to meet with the grandparents, develop an alliance, and then help them and their adult children negotiate effective working relationships.

Pointing out these potential sources of assistance for single parents should not be taken to suggest that a family therapist's only, or even primary, function should be supportive counseling. Most families, single-parent or otherwise,

seek clinical services because they are stuck in conflict—psychological, interpersonal, or both. In working with single parents, a therapist's most important job is to identify and help resolve the impediments holding clients back from taking advantage of their own personal and interpersonal resources.

Sometimes the most significant conflict for single-mother households isn't visible: it's the potential involvement of the children's father, who is not infrequently described as "out of the picture." He may be out of the picture, but in most cases he shouldn't be.[3]

Many families of young mothers find it particularly difficult to support the involvement of the baby's father (Johnson, 2001). They may even consider him an enemy. If their understandable feelings are treated with respect, they can often be helped to support the father's involvement.

Facilitating the continued involvement of teen fathers deserves special attention because it's so important, and so challenging (Lehr & MacMillan, 2001). Since it's relatively easy for teen fathers to be ignored and to abandon contact with their child, it's important to reach out to them, to establish rapport, and to encourage them in becoming responsible parents.

Some of these men are caring fathers who would like to be involved in the lives of their children. Even invisible or unavailable fathers may well desire more contact, and be willing to take on more responsibility for the sake of their children. The therapist should consider contacting the noncustodial father to assess his potential contribution to his children's emotional and financial support.

Here, too, triangles can complicate the picture. In an effort to be sympathetic to their mates (and sometimes from unconscious jealousy), new partners often fan the flames of conflict with the noncustodial parent, which only reinforces the cutoff.

---

3. Those cases where abusive fathers would have a destructive influence on their children's welfare are usually obvious.

Case Study

Elana Santos contacted the clinic because her ten-year-old son, Tony, was depressed. "He's having trouble getting over my divorce," she said. "I think he misses his father." After two sessions, the therapist determined that Tony was not depressed and, although he did miss his father, it was his mother who hadn't gotten over the divorce. Tony *had* stopped hanging out with his friends after school; however, it was worrying about his mother, who'd become bitter and withdrawn, rather than depression that was keeping him in the house.

The therapist's formulation was that Mrs. Santos was enmeshed with her son and both were disengaged from contacts outside the family. The therapist told Mrs. Santos that her son was sad because he worried about her. "Do you need Tony to be your protector?" the therapist asked.

"No," Mrs. Santos said.

"Then I think you need to fire him. Can you convince Tony that he doesn't need to take care of you, that he can spend time with friends and that you'll be all right?"

Mrs. Santos did "fire" her son from the job of being her guardian angel. The therapist then talked about getting Tony more involved in after-school activities where he could make friends. "Who knows," the therapist said, "maybe if Tony starts making friends, you'll have some time to do the same thing."

The only person Mrs. Santos could think of to help look after Tony was the boy's father, and he was "completely unavailable." Rather than accept this statement at face value, the therapist expressed surprise "that a father would care nothing about his son." When Mrs. Santos insisted that her ex wouldn't be willing to spend any time with Tony, the therapist asked permission to call him herself.

When the therapist told Mr. Santos that she was worried about his son and thought the boy needed his father's involvement in his life, Mr. Santos seemed responsive. But then the therapist heard someone talking in the background, and Mr. Santos started to back off.

What had begun as a problem firmly embedded in one person's head—"It's my son, he's depressed"—turned out to involve not just the interaction between the boy and his mother, but also a triangular complication in which the father's girlfriend objected to his involvement because she didn't want "that bitch of an ex-wife taking advantage of him." What followed were a series of meetings—with the father and his girlfriend, the father and mother, the father and son, and finally all four of them together—in which the therapist concentrated on helping them clear the air by voicing feelings of resentment that stood in the way of their working cooperatively together.

The father's girlfriend had made the same mistake that a lot of us make when someone we love complains about how someone else is treating them. In response to his complaints about his ex-wife's angry phone calls, she had urged him to have nothing to do with her. In response to these feelings and to Mrs. Santos's own anger and resentment, the therapist helped them to understand an important distinction between two subsystems in a divorce. The first (*the couple*) was dead and should be buried; the second (*the parents*) still needed to find a way to cooperate in the best interests of their child. "Burying" the divorced couple's relationship in this case was facilitated by Mrs. Santos's having an opportunity to ventilate her bitterness and anger at having been abandoned by the man she loved, though most of these discussions took place in individual sessions with the therapist.

Reducing a single parent's disengagement from adult relationships enhances her ability to strengthen the generational boundary between herself and her children. This involves delegating age-appropriate responsibilities to older children, enforcing discipline, and helping the children get involved in activities of their own. The primary structural goal for the single parent is to assume power as the chief executive in the family system. This may be difficult for a parent who is demoralized by loss or depression. Therefore some structural goals may make sense but may not be practical. Setting up charts and token economies to rein in out-of-control children, for example, may require an unrealistic amount of monitoring for an already overburdened single parent. When feeling overwhelmed, single parents often lose the ability to set effective limits. Some parents may permit more misbehavior than they think they should to make up for the loss their children have suffered from divorce or lack of father involvement. Chores should be delegated, not abdicated—mother is still in charge—and a boy is not "the man of the house" (which implies that a son has taken his father's place).

Live-in partners—who shouldn't be overlooked any more than noncustodial parents—provide additional sources of support, and conflict. Many compete with the children for the mother's attention. Some undermine the mother's authority and rule setting, while others try to enforce their own, often stricter rules, setting up a triangle in which the mother is forced to side either with her boyfriend or her children. Live-in partners' attempts to enforce discipline are frequently rebuffed, especially by adolescents. Their job isn't that of a parent, but that of a supporter and a backup for the mother as the primary authority over her children.

Children may benefit from increased social contacts to help balance the intensity of the single-parent-and-child connection. Resources to consider include teachers, coaches, Big Brothers and Big Sisters, activity group leaders, community groups ("Parents Without Partners," "Mother's Day Out"), religious congregations, craft classes, and workplace contacts.

Families take many forms; the single-parent family is one of them. Families don't get broken or destroyed, but they do change shapes. Unfortunately, the transition from being together to being apart is a road without maps. No wonder there is so much pain and confusion.

African American Families

Therapists working with African American families should be prepared to expand the definition of family to include an *extended kinship system.* The kinship network remains one of the keys to coping with the pressures of oppression (Billingsley, 1992; Staples, 1994). A clinician should be aware that there may be a number of aunts, uncles, "big mamas," boyfriends, older brothers and sisters, cousins, deacons, preachers, and others who operate in and out of the African American home (White, 1972, p. 45). However, many families who come to the attention of mental health workers have become isolated from their traditional support network. Part of a therapist's task is to search for persons in the family or kin network who represent islands of strength and enlist their support in helping the family. Asking "Who can you depend on when you need help?" is one way to locate such individuals.

A structural assessment should consider not only those people who are involved with the family but also those who might be called on for support. In the African American community, these potential connections include an extensive kinship network, made up of both family and friends (Billingsley, 1968; McAdoo, 2002). This network might include not only all those mentioned above but also grandparents and great-grandparents, as well as godparents, babysitters, neighbors, friends, church members, ministers, and so on.

These extended connections, real and potential, mean that family boundaries and lines of authority can become quite blurred, as the following example illustrates.

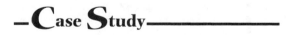

—Case Study—

When Juanita Williams entered a residential drug treatment program, she was lucky to have her friend, Nancy, willing to take in her three children. Six months later Juanita was ready to leave rehab and return home. By that time, the

Williams children had grown accustomed to living with "Aunt Nancy" and her two teenagers.

When the children's case worker arranged a meeting with Juanita and her children and "Aunt Nancy," Nancy praised Juanita for completing the rehab program and preparing to resume the responsibility for her children. "You know I love them, almost like they were my own," she said to Juanita, who nodded. "But now it's time for them to move back with their rightful mother." However, it appeared to the social worker that Nancy had effectively taken over the family and Juanita had lost her authority. Nancy did most of the talking while Juanita sat quietly, looking down. Martin (14), Jesse (12), and Coretta (11) said nothing.

The social worker concluded that Nancy and the Williams children were enmeshed while Juanita was disengaged; and the worker saw her job as helping Juanita and her children reconnect while Nancy stepped back into a supportive but less central role. Toward this end she said that Juanita was lucky to have such a good friend to act as foster mother to her children, but now it was time for her to reclaim her role as head of the family. She then set up an enactment in which she asked Juanita to talk with her children about her plans for the immediate future.

When Juanita began by telling the children how much she missed them, Nancy spoke up to say that the children missed her, too. Nancy's intentions were good, but her interruption was a sign of her overly central role. The therapist complimented Nancy for being helpful but said that it was time to show her support by letting Juanita speak for herself. Juanita resumed talking to her children, saying, "I know that I can't promise anything, but every day I will try my hardest to be the right kind of mother to you and not to give in to my disease. And," she went on with tears in her eyes, "I know that with God's help we can be the family that we used to be."

Martin looked down, Jesse and Coretta had tears in their eyes. Then Martin turned to the therapist and said, "Can I speak?" "Of course, Martin, you can say whatever you want."

"I love you, Mommy," he said. "And I hope to God that you don't go back to the drugs. But I

will never—*never*—live in a house where I have to watch my mother going into the streets again. When I don't know whether we're going to have any supper that night because you're out getting high. You will never put me through that again."

"Martin—" Once again Nancy started to interrupt, and once again the social worker blocked her.

Martin went on talking for fifteen minutes about the pain and rage of growing up with a mother who was a drug addict. He held nothing back. Juanita was crying hard. When Martin finished, there was a long, heavy silence.

Then Juanita spoke up. "I know what I put you through, Martin. What I put all my children through. And I know that I can never, ever make up for that. But, as God is my witness, I will do everything in my power never, ever again to let you down or make you ashamed of me. All I want is another chance."

It was a gut-wrenching exchange. Martin had spoken straight from the heart, and he and his mother had gotten through to each other—with no interference from well-meaning friends, or helpful professionals, anxious to put a good face on things.

The prominence of religion and spirituality in African American family life (Hines & Boyd-Franklin, 1982), like the extended kinship network, provides both a real and potential resource. Many African American families have gained strength from church membership and connection to their church community (Billingsley, 1994; Walsh, 1999). Therapists who work with black families can profit from developing a relationship with ministers in the African American community who have a great deal of influence and can often help mobilize support for an isolated single mother, an adolescent who is abusing drugs, or a mentally ill adult who is cut off from family support following the death of the main caregiver (Boyd-Franklin, 2003).

One reason father-absent households are so common among African Americans is that there are far fewer men than women in the black community. Among the reasons for the absence of black men are an epidemic of substance abuse, death related to hazardous jobs and to delays in seeking vital health care, military service, homicide, and, of course, the astonishingly high percentage of young black men in prison (U.S. Bureau of the Census, 2003). Not only are there fewer black men but their participation in family life is often undermined by limited job opportunities and a tendency on the part of mental health professionals to overlook men in the extended family system, including the father's kinship network and the mother's male friends, who may be involved in the children's lives.

Too many therapists resign themselves to the nonparticipation of fathers in family therapy. A father who is regarded as unavailable may agree to attend if contacted directly by the therapist. Even if the father has trouble getting away from work, he may agree to come to one or two sessions, if he's convinced that he's really needed. Therapists can also use phone calls and letters to keep fathers involved in their family's treatment. Respecting a father's family role decreases the likelihood of his sabotaging treatment (Hines & Boyd-Franklin, 1996), and even limited participation may lead to a structural shift in the family.

Partly as a consequence of absent fathers, many families in the African American community are three-generational systems, made up of a mother, her children, and a grandmother. Sometimes grandmothers are asked to take over the job of raising a second set of children. At other times, single mothers or fathers and their children move back in with the grandparents. In some cases, teenage mothers will turn their children over to their own mothers but later want to take back the responsibility of raising their children. While none of these family structures is inherently dysfunctional, they all create complications.

Grandmothers who take over may have trouble letting go. They see their young adult children behaving irresponsibly, and they treat them accordingly. Unfortunately, this perpetuates the classic control-and-rebel cycle that so many young people get caught up in with their parents. Therapists can't always remain neutral in this kind of impasse. It may be useful to support the young mother or father in the role of parent, while respecting the grandmother's contribution and availability for advice and support (Minuchin, Nichols, & Lee, 2007).

Within the past twenty years there has been an increase in the number of middle-class black families to where they now make up 25 percent of the African American community (Hill, 1999). However, the majority of African American clients encountered in clinical situations are likely to be dealing with the stigmas of race and class together. Although some black families have benefited from job and educational opportunities, most urban African American communities remain mired in multigenerational poverty (Boyd-Franklin, 2003).

Even the healthiest families have trouble functioning effectively under the crushing weight of financial hardship. When survival issues—like food, housing, and utilities—are involved, these take precedence over family conflicts. Therapists can usefully act as a resource to encourage family members to take effective steps and to work with available community and social agents in dealing with housing, job training, employment, and child care (Rojano, 2004).

The combination of discrimination and oppression, aggravated by racism and poverty, has produced a "fierce anger" in many African Americans (Cose, 1993). Service providers must realize that some of this anger may be directed against them. It's important not to get defensive. Nancy Boyd-Franklin (1989) recommends that mental health providers expect a certain amount of distrust and join with their black clients to build trust at the very outset of treatment. Communicating respect is key to successfully engaging families.

In working with poor, inner-city African American families, therapists must take into account that they may be enmeshed with a variety of organizations such as schools, hospitals, police courts, juvenile justice systems, welfare, child protective services, and mental health services (Henggeler & Borduin, 1990). Empowering families in this context can be accomplished by (1) setting up meetings with various agencies involved with the family, (2) writing letters in support of the family, and (3) setting up conferences with the supervisors of resistant workers (Boyd-Franklin, 2003). The point is to empower families by encouraging them to take charge of these issues themselves. Therapists can help but should not take over.

Therapy with Gay and Lesbian Families

Gay and lesbian partners struggle with the same sorrows of confusion and longing as any intimate partners. Every couple must find a way to balance time together with independent interests, choose whether and when to have children, and decide whose family to spend the holidays with. But same-sex couples also face unique challenges, including coping with homophobia in the larger society and their families; resolving relational ambiguities in the areas of commitment, boundaries, and gender-linked behavior; differences about being "out" professionally or socially; and developing networks of social support (Green & Mitchell, 2002). In order to work effectively with gay and lesbian clients, it's important neither to ignore nor exaggerate the unique nature of same-sex pairings.

While it may be reassuring for heterosexual therapists to dissociate themselves from the overt homophobia in our culture, it's a little more difficult to deal with internalized homophobia—in themselves and in their clients. Therapists who aren't comfortable with love and sex between two men or two women may have trouble talking frankly with gay couples, or may behave with patronizing deference. A therapist who is overly anxious to convey his or her progressive attitude may find it difficult to push for change or to ask the tough questions that may be necessary with couples who aren't getting along.

—Case Study————

Stephen and David sought therapy during a crisis induced by Stephen's wanting to open up their relationship to other partners and David refusing to even discuss this possibility. Their therapist, who was anxious to distance himself from the stereotype that gay men are promiscuous, got caught up in trying to solve the problem of Stephen's inability to commit, rather than exploring the broader problem of the couple's difficulty communicating and making decisions. Had the couple been a man and a wife disagreeing over whether to buy a house or rent an apartment, it's unlikely that the therapist would have so quickly taken sides and reduced therapy to an exercise in problem solving.

Homophobia may also manifest itself in subtle and not so subtle ways in lesbian and gay people themselves (Brown, 1994; Meyer & Dean, 1998). When you grow up in a society in which homosexuality is considered deviant, it's impossible not to absorb at least some of this attitude. Well-meaning heterosexual therapists who consciously affirm gays and lesbians may be especially blind to this dynamic.

In working with same-sex couples, it's important to probe for subtle manifestations of negative images of homosexuality and of same-sex relationships. One stereotype that can be particularly destructive is the cultural expectation that same-sex pairings are inherently unstable. Many people, gay as well as straight, believe that enduring relationships between same-sex partners (especially gay men) are impossible to achieve. As with many biases, it's probably more useful for therapists to examine and recognize their own attitudes and assumptions than to imagine themselves to be without bias. Identifying your assumptions makes it easier to hold them in check; pretending that you don't have assumptions allows them to act on you unsuspectingly.

The belief that same-sex couples are inherently unstable undermines many gay male couples, especially considering that leaving is often a knee-jerk response to conflict for men (Greenan & Tunnell, 2003). Given the frequency with which men threaten to end their relationships when they experience difficulty, it's wise to anticipate such threats and be prepared to confront them. Instead of accepting the threat at face value, a therapist can interpret it as a defense against feeling helpless. "Obviously you're upset, but if we can find a more constructive way to help you feel that your needs are being taken seriously, maybe you won't have to use tactics that potentially destroy the relationship when you have a disagreement."

Working with gay and lesbian couples requires sensitivity to the internalization of traditional gender norms, as well as the overt prejudice these couples continue to face in their current social environments. Heterosexual partners have typically been socialized for complementary roles. Women and men may no longer expect to be "Leave-It-to-Beaver" parents, but, like it or not, women are still taught to be more caring and to have a less distanced sense of self (Jordan et al., 1991), while men are brought up to be in control, to be territorial, to tolerate distance, and to thrive on competition. So what happens when same-sex partners get together? Who picks up the towels from the bathroom floor? Who initiates sexual activity?

Many gay and lesbian couples struggle as much as heterosexual couples over whether and when to have children. But, unlike their heterosexual counterparts, gays and lesbians have to resolve the issue of who (if either) will be the biological parent.

—Case Study—

Rachel and Jan had been together for ten years and were considering having a child. Both agreed that they would like to have a bio-

logical child. However, both women wanted to be the sperm recipient.

Seeing that Rachel and Jan were at an impasse, the therapist suggested that they consider adopting. Worn out and frustrated by their inability to decide which of them would give up the wish to carry their baby, the women jumped at this suggestion. However, their relief turned to anger when they discovered that the state they lived in (which starts with the letter V) did not allow gay and lesbian couples to adopt children. Their experience made them lose confidence in their therapist and they dropped out of treatment.

One of the issues in therapy with same-sex couples is likely to be the need to negotiate clear agreements about commitments and boundaries and roles. Among the questions a therapist might usefully ask are:

"What are the rules in your relationship about monogamy?"
"What are your agreements about finances, pooling of resources, and joint ownership of property?"
"Who does which tasks in the household, and how is this decided?"

These questions are offered as examples of how to explore issues once they are broached by clients. It's important, however, to strike a balance between helping couples address such issues and dictating that they should, especially when they may not be ready.

Some of the usual expectations that heterosexuals bring to marriage don't apply to same-sex couples unless they are discussed and explicitly agreed to (Green & Mitchell, 2002). Among these expectations are monogamy, pooled finances, caring for each other through serious illness, moving together for each other's career advancement, caring for each other's families in old age, and mutual inheritance, to name just a few. Because there are no familiar models for being a same-sex couple, partners may have discrepant visions about how these issues will be handled. We suggest that therapists be aware of these issues and prepared to help clients discuss them but not introduce these or any issues that clients don't yet seem ready to deal with.

Heterosexual therapists may underestimate the complexities involved in "coming out" to family and friends (LaSala, 1997). Here it may be well to remember that therapy isn't about pushing people to go where they're afraid to go, but is about helping them recognize and resolve the fears that hold them back.

Another difficulty that heterosexual therapists may overlook in same-sex relationships is the prevalence of extreme jealousy on the part of one of the partners (Green & Mitchell, 2002). This jealously is based on the belief that others are a threat because of lack of respect for the couple's commitment to each other. After all, how can a relationship be "real" if the partners aren't married?

—Case Study—————

Jim enjoyed the club scene as a way to socialize with his friends in the gay community. His partner Kyle preferred to avoid bars and clubs. According to Kyle, his objections weren't so much to Jim's having a good time, but that he believed other men in the clubs had little respect for the fact that Jim was part of a couple. "They don't care about us if they think they can get in your pants." Kyle was also concerned about the prevalence of drugs, like ecstasy, cocaine, crystal meth, and special K, that were part of the club atmosphere. Jim insisted that he wasn't interested in other men and didn't do drugs. He just wanted to hang out with his friends.

Although some therapists might see Jim's insistence on going to bars as a failure to accept that he was no longer single, the therapist in this case was aware that, in fact, *not* going to bars and clubs can result in a significant disconnect from much of the gay community. And so, rather than accept the Hobson's choice the couple presented—either Jim gave in and stayed home, or Kyle gave in and Jim continued to go clubbing—the therapist wondered out loud if there were alternative ways for the couple to socialize within the gay community.

———————————————

Therapists who fail to value gay and lesbian couples' commitment may, when they have serious problems, see them as insurmountable and support termination more quickly than they would for a married heterosexual couple. The opposite may also occur if a therapist, intent on overcoming the stereotype that same-sex relationships aren't permanent, acts as though staying together were the prime good rather than relationship satisfaction.

Anger can be a problem in any relationship, but it is particularly common in gay male couples who seek therapy (Greenan & Tunnell, 2003). It isn't just a failure to follow *Roberts Rules of Order* that makes people resort to anger as a defense mechanism. The goal of treatment for many couples is to create an atmosphere where the partners feel safe to explore any shame that they may have around their needs for affection and intimacy in their relationship (Bowlby, 1988). This level of work is essential in the treatment of gay men, who are often uncomfortable expressing their need for tenderness and understanding with another man (McWhirter & Mattison, 1984). This reticence may be exaggerated by a fear that tenderness is "effeminate." Most men—gay or straight—who equate their need for closeness with effeminacy want to avoid what Richard Isay (1989) calls "the sissy boy syndrome." Real men don't cry. One of the insidious things about prejudice is how minority groups often internalize the stereotypes attributed to them by the majority culture or imitate an exaggerated version of the majority image (Allport, 1958).

Maybe the best advice for therapists working with gay and lesbian couples is to ask themselves: "What messages am I communicating to this couple about the value of same-sex relationships?" It isn't just negative messages that therapists should be alert to but also the danger of glamorizing same-sex relationships.

Denigration and idealization have an equal potential for harm.

Home-Based Services

Home-based services are a descendent of the "friendly visitor movement," in which social workers, inspired by Mary Richmond, called on families in their own homes. In the past, social workers more often than not found themselves removing vulnerable children from harm's way. Unfortunately, this well-intentioned altruism often undermined the family unit. Beginning in the 1970s, influenced by the principles of deinstitutionalization and community care, there has been more of an effort to keep families together and to prevent placement of children (McGowen & Meezan, 1983). Like traditional family therapy, home-based services target the family as the primary recipient of mental health care (Friesen & Koroloff, 1990). Unlike conventional models, however, the home-based approach focuses more on expanding the network of a family's resources than on repairing family dysfunction (Henggeler & Borduin, 1990). While home-based services recognize and address problems in the family system, the primary emphasis is on building relationships between the family and various community resources.

Home-based services generally include four elements: family support services, therapeutic intervention, case management, and crisis intervention (Lindblad-Goldberg, Dore, & Stern, 1998). *Family support services* include respite care as well as assistance with food, clothing, and shelter. *Therapeutic intervention* may include individual, family, or couples treatment. The overriding therapeutic goal is strengthening and stabilizing the family unit. Families are empowered by helping them utilize their own strengths and resources for solving problems rather than relying on out-of-home placement of the child. *Case management* involves developing links to community resources, including medical care, welfare, education, job training, and legal services. *Crisis intervention* means making available 24-hour emergency services, either with the home-based agency or by contracting with an outside mental health emergency service.

Visiting a family at home gives a therapist an opportunity to show interest in the things that define their identity—such as children, pets, religious artifacts, mementos, awards, and so on. Looking through photo albums can be a valuable method in joining with a family and learning about their history and their hopes and dreams. Once a positive relationship has been established—but not before—the therapist can ask the family to reduce such distractions as smoking, loud television playing, or barking dogs. (Barking cats are less often a problem.) Roles and boundaries that are implicit in an office setting may need to be spelled out. Clarifying roles while in the home begins with defining what the process of treatment entails, the ground rules for sessions, and what the therapist's and family members' roles will be. The following comments illustrate the process of clarifying roles.

–Case Study–

"**B**efore we start, I want to say that I have no intention of coming here and telling you how to run your lives. My job is to help you figure out how you want to deal with your children. I can't solve your problems. Only you can do that.

In our meetings, it's important for you to say whatever you think and feel. We need to be honest. Tell me what you expect of me, and I'll tell you what I expect of you. I won't act like I have all the answers, because I don't.

Will Grandmother be coming tonight? If not, that's okay, but I would like her to attend future sessions, because I'm sure she has valuable ideas to contribute. Tonight, I'd like to get to know each of you a little bit. After that, I'd like to hear what concerns each of you has about your family life and what you'd like to change."[4]

---

4. Adapted from Lindblad-Goldberg, Dore, & Stern, 1998.

While family therapists tend to speak glibly about their "ecosystemic" orientation, home-based workers really must coordinate their efforts with other service systems. Rather than being critical of school personnel or juvenile justice workers who don't seem to support both the family and the child, home-based workers must learn to appreciate that these other agencies are equally concerned about the needs of their clients, even though their approaches may differ. A family served by multiple agencies who don't see eye to eye is no different from a child caught in a triangle between parents who can't function as a team.

While in-home therapy offers a unique opportunity to influence families in their natural environment, seeing people in their living rooms also increases the pressures of *induction* into a family's problematic patterns. Working with a cotherapist may help to minimize the tendency to be drawn unwittingly into a family's unproductive way of seeing things. Home-based therapists who don't work with cotherapists must make special efforts to maintain professional boundaries and to avoid being inducted into playing missing roles in the family. For example, if a child needs comforting, it's better to support the parents in providing it than to take over their function.

One of the most unfortunate things that happens in psychotherapy is that clients often recreate with their therapists the same unsatisfying kinds of relationships they have with most people. Perhaps the most important thing a therapist can do is to avoid being drawn in to the usual pattern. The most dangerous pattern for home-based workers to repeat is moving in too close and then pushing clients to go where they are afraid to go. Rather than start pushing for change right away, it's often more effective to begin by recognizing the obstacles to change.

Beleaguered families fear abandonment; insecure therapists fear not being helpful. The worker who feels pulled to do everything for a client may subsequently feel overwhelmed by the family's needs and back away by setting rigid limits and withholding support. The "rescuer" then becomes another "abandoner." This process reactivates the clients' anxiety and inevitably pushes them away. The lessons for the family are clear: Nothing will ever change—and don't trust anyone.

Psychoeducation and Medical Family Therapy

Over the past fifteen years a new conception of family therapy has emerged. Rather than solving problems, the goal of this approach is to help families cope with disabilities. This represents a shift from the idea that families cause problems to the idea that problems, like natural disasters, sometimes befall families. *Psychoeducational family therapy* emerged from working with schizophrenic patients and their families, whereas *medical family therapy* developed from helping families struggle with chronic illnesses such as cancer, diabetes, and heart disease.

Psychoeducation and Schizophrenia

The search for a cure for schizophrenia launched the field of family therapy in the 1950s. Ironically, when we now know that schizophrenia involves a biological vulnerability, family therapy, or at least the psychoeducational model, is once again considered part of the most effective treatment for this baffling disorder.

The psychoeducational model was born of dissatisfaction with both traditional family therapy and psychiatric approaches to schizophrenia. As Carol Anderson, Douglas Reiss, and Gerald Hogarty (1986) lamented,

> We have blamed each other, the patients themselves, their parents and grandparents, public authorities, and society for the cause and for the too often terrible course of these disorders. When hope and money become exhausted, we frequently tear schizophrenic patients from their families, consigning them to the existential terror of human warehouses, single room oc-

cupancy hotels, and more recently to the streets and alleys of American cities. (p. vii)

In their attempts to get at the function of the schizophrenic's symptoms, family therapists urged family members to express bottled-up feelings and thus created sessions of highly charged emotion, which often did little more than stir up tension. After noticing the frequent decline in functioning of patients and increased anxiety in their families after such sessions, Anderson and her colleagues (1986) "began to wonder if most 'real' family therapy was in fact antitherapeutic" (p. 2).

Meanwhile, studies began to show that the patients who fared best after hospitalization were those who returned to the least stressful households. A British group, including George Brown, John Wing, Julian Leff, and Christine Vaughn, focused on what they called "expressed emotion" (EE) in the families of schizophrenics—particularly criticism, hostility, and emotional overinvolvement—and found that patients returning to high EE households had higher rates of relapse (Brown et al., 1972; Vaughn & Leff, 1976; Vaughn et al., 1984).

Research on expressed emotion suggests that schizophrenia is a thought disorder that renders individuals particularly sensitive to the expression of criticism and hostility. The theory is that intense emotional input makes it difficult for patients to cope with the welter of chaotic thoughts that plague them. When recovering patients return to stressful family settings, where EE is high, intrusive overconcern and critical comments lead to increased emotional arousal, and it is this affective overload that triggers relapse. On the other hand (as Bowenian theory would suggest), patients returning to households with low EE and whose family members are not overly anxious are allowed more psychological space in which to recover (Leff & Vaughn, 1985).

Expressed emotion is now the most well-documented factor in the relapse of schizophrenia (Milkowitz, 1995):

> The family, then, is seen as a risk or protective factor that may augment or diminish the likelihood

that underlying genetic and/or biological vulnerabilities in a family member will be expressed as symptoms of mental disorder. (p. 194)

Moreover, the benefits of reducing EE in helping families cope with schizophrenia has been repeatedly demonstrated (Atkinson & Coia, 1995). Lowering EE has also been shown to contribute to reduced relapse rates for major depression and bipolar disorder (Muesser & Glynn, 1995).

With this in mind, three different groups in the late 1970s began experimenting with ways to reduce stress in the most common environments for schizophrenic patients, their parents' homes. Michael Goldstein led a group at UCLA (Goldstein et al., 1978) who designed a brief, structured model focused on anticipating the stresses a family was likely to face and reducing conflict around the patient. Following the Goldstein study, groups headed by Ian Falloon at the University of Southern California (whose model is primarily behavioral) and Carol Anderson at the Western Psychiatric Institute in Pittsburgh experimented with psychoeducational models.

Psychoeducators try not only to help families change their ideas about and interactions with patients but also to reverse the damage done by insensitive professionals. Instead of providing the information, support, and sense of control that these families need, many mental health professionals ignore family members except to gather information—information about what went wrong. The implications of this line of questioning add to the guilt and shame family members already feel. No wonder many families either give up or get into antagonistic battles with authoritarian professionals.

Psychoeducators seek to establish a collaborative partnership in which family members feel supported and empowered to deal with the patient. To achieve this kind of partnership, Anderson and her colleagues find that they must reeducate professionals to give up ideas that the family is somehow responsible for schizophrenia, reinforce family strengths, and share information with the family about this disease. It is this information-sharing that constitutes the educational element of psycho*education*. Information about the nature and course of schizophrenia helps family members develop a sense of mastery—a way to understand and anticipate the often chaotic and apparently uncontrollable process.

One of psychoeducation's key interventions is to lower expectations, to reduce pressure on the patient to perform normally. For example, the goals for the first year following an acute episode are primarily the avoidance of a relapse and the gradual taking on of some responsibilities in the home. Family members are to view the patient as someone who's had a serious illness and needs to recuperate. Patients may need a great deal of sleep, solitude, and limited activity for some time following an episode; they may also seem restless and have trouble concentrating. By predicting these developments, psychoeducators try to prevent conflict between the patient and the family.

Anderson's psychoeducational approach looks very much like structural family therapy, except that the family's organizational flaws are construed as the *result* of rather than *cause* of the presenting problem. Much of the therapy follows familiar themes: reinforcing generational boundaries, opening up the family to the outside world and developing support networks, urging parents to reinvest in their marriage, and getting family members to not speak or do for the patient.

Anderson and her colleagues begin with a day-long survival skills workshop in which they teach family members about the prevalence and course of schizophrenia, its biological etiology, current modes of pharmacologic and psychosocial treatment, common medications, and prognosis. The patient's needs and the family needs are discussed and family coping skills are introduced. Research findings on expressed emotion are presented and guidelines are offered for keeping EE in check. Families are encouraged not to pressure recovering patients or to urge them to hurry back to normal functioning. Families are also advised to respect boundaries and to allow the recovering family member to withdraw whenever necessary.

Bill McFarlane's multifamily approach typically includes five or six families and begins with lecture-and-discussion workshops. Following these workshops the patients and their families meet regularly for at least a year. The multifamily format is thought to offer increased social support. The goal for the patient is for symptoms to be reduced rather than cured. Families are encouraged to provide a quiet, stable milieu in which the recovering patient doesn't feel criticized or blamed, and not to expect too much of him or her during recuperation. The goal for the family is to learn coping techniques for the difficult and long-term task of living with a schizophrenic person and preventing or delaying his or her relapse and rehospitalization.

Table 11.1 presents a set of typical psychoeducational guidelines for managing rehabilitation following a schizophrenic episode.

Is the psychoeducational model effective? Yes. For example, in the study by Anderson and colleagues (1986),

> Among treatment takers (n = 90), 19% of those receiving family therapy alone experienced a psychotic relapse in the year following hospital discharge. Of those receiving the individual behavioral therapy, 20% relapsed, but *no* patient in the treatment cell that received both family therapy and social skills training experienced a relapse. These relapse rates constitute significant effects for both treatments when contrasted to a 41% relapse rate for those receiving only chemotherapy and support. (p. 24)

Other studies have shown equally impressive results (Falloon et al., 1982; Leff et al., 1982). There seems to be little question that psychoeducation can delay relapse and readmission to a hospital better than other approaches to schizophrenia.

Medical Family Therapy

If one considers schizophrenia a chronic disease, then psychoeducational family therapy can be

---

TABLE 11.1   Psychoeducational Guidelines for Families and Friends of Schizophrenics

---

Here is a list of things everyone can do to make things run more smoothly.

1. *Go slow.* Recovery takes time. Rest is important. Things will get better in their own time.
2. *Keep it cool.* Enthusiasm is normal. Tone it down. Disagreement is normal. Tone it down too.
3. *Give 'em space.* Time out is important for everyone. It's okay to offer. It's okay to refuse.
4. *Set limits.* Everyone needs to know what the rules are. A few good rules keep things calmer.
5. *Ignore what you can't change.* Let some things slide. Don't ignore violence or use of street drugs.
6. *Keep it simple.* Say what you have to say clearly, calmly, and positively.
7. *Follow doctor's orders.* Take medications as they are prescribed. Take only medications that are prescribed.
8. *Carry on business as usual.* Reestablish family routines as quickly as possible. Stay in touch with family and friends.
9. *No street drugs or alcohol.* They make symptoms worse.
10. *Pick up on early signs.* Note changes. Consult with your family physician.
11. *Solve problems step by step.* Make changes gradually. Work on one thing at a time.
12. *Lower expectations, temporarily.* Use a personal yardstick. Compare this month with last month rather than with last year or next year.

Source: Adapted from McFarlane, 1991, p. 375.

---

seen as a specialized form of medical family therapy. Medical family therapists work with families struggling with illness or disability in much the same way as described previously for families of schizophrenics.

Chronic illness often has a devastating impact. It can take over a family's life, ravaging health, hope, and peace of mind. As Peter Steinglass says, it can be like a robber, "who has appeared on the doorstep, barged inside the home and demanded everything the family has" (quoted in McDaniel, Hepworth, & Doherty, 1992, p. 21).

These demands of the illness interact with qualities of the family, such as the family's life-cycle stage and the role the stricken family member plays; the family's leadership resources and degree of isolation; and their beliefs about illness and who should help, derived from their ethnicity and history with illness. With an awareness of these factors, therapists can help families prepare to deal with an illness or, if the illness has been with them for years, gain perspective on their resulting polarizations and enmeshments.

In medical family therapy, the system isn't just the sick person's family; it's the family and the physicians and nurses involved in the sick person's care. The goal, therefore, is to foster communication and support not only within the family but also between the family and the medical personnel. Illness leaves people feeling helpless and confused. Medical family therapy is designed to combat such feelings by fostering communication and a sense of agency.

Medical family therapists work in collaboration with pediatricians, family practitioners, rehabilitation specialists, and nurses. They advocate that near the time of diagnosis, families should receive a routine consultation to explore their resources relative to the demands of the illness or disability. They cite the growing body of research suggesting a strong relationship between family dynamics and the clinical course of medical conditions (Campbell, 1986) and more recent research showing that family therapy has a positive effect on physical health and health-care usage (Law, Crane, & Russell, 2000).

In the early 1990s the field came of age, with three books setting the pace (McDaniel, Hepworth, & Doherty, 1992; Ramsey, 1989; Rolland, 1994). It has now mushroomed into a whole new paradigm called *collaborative family health care,* with a large annual conference that began in 1996 and now offers fourteen plenaries and more than fifty workshops. At the conference, well-known medical family therapists, such as John Rolland, Bill Doherty, Lorraine Wright, Susan McDaniel, and Thomas Campbell, present their work alongside experts in medicine, nursing, social work, and hospital administration. The hope and promise of this movement are to provide new careers for family therapists but also to become a new model for cost-effective and humane health care nationally.

In conclusion, psychoeducational and medical family therapy share many elements with the other models in this chapter that together represent a significant trend: a move toward a collaborative partnership with families. Therapists are now encouraged to look for a family's strengths rather than deficits and to find ways to lift families out of the guilt and blame that often accompany their problems.

Relationship Enrichment Programs

The psychoeducational method has also been applied to couples and families who wish to acquire skills for coping with everyday relationship problems. Some therapists are skeptical that self-help courses can substitute for the individual attention of a professionally trained therapist, yet these programs are enormously popular, not least because participants in *marital enrichment programs* feel little of the stigma that attaches to "being in therapy." One of the best known of these programs is the Relationship Enhancement system developed by Bernard Guerney, Jr. (1977). Facilitators teach participants to clarify their conflicts and to express what they are feeling, accept each other's feelings, negotiate and work through problems, and learn to achieve satisfaction by becoming emotional partners (Ginsberg, 2000). Both lectures and experiential training take place in each session, and homework assignments are given to practice and extend skills in participants' everyday lives.

Relationship Enhancement programs provide couples with training in three sets of core skills (Ginsberg, 2000):

- The *Expressive (Owning) Skill* (gaining awareness of one's own feelings, and taking responsibility for them without projecting them onto others)
- The *Empathic Responding (Receptive) Skill* (learning to listen the other person's feelings)
- The *Conversive (Discussion-Negotiation/Engagement) Skill* (learning to acknowledge the meaning of what was heard; partners may switch positions between listener and speaker)

To help couples assess their preparation for marriage, David Olson and his colleagues developed the Premarital Personal and Relationship Inventory (PREPARE). This 165-item questionnaire (Olson, 1996) is designed to help couples understand and discuss their backgrounds, expectations, and areas where they might encounter difficulties. Attitudes and expectations are explored in eleven areas, including marriage expectations, communication, sexual relationship, personality differences, financial management, conflict resolution, child rearing, leisure, family and friends, marital roles, and spiritual beliefs. PREPARE has proven useful for identifying potential conflicts and promoting discussions that may head off problems in the future (Stahmann & Hiebert, 1997).

By far the most popular and widespread of the relationship enhancement programs is the *marriage encounter* weekend, first introduced in Barcelona by a Jesuit priest, Father Gabriel Calvo (Chartier, 1986). These weekend retreats, which provide support and enrichment for Catholic couples, were imported into this country in the late 1960s and have since been widely adopted by a variety of church groups (Stahmann & Hiebert, 1997). Thousands of couples have taken advantage of these weekend enrichment programs to work on their communication, problem-solving skills, sexual intimacy, and spiritual issues. Some denominations even require couples to participate in such a program before they can be married in the church.

A more carefully researched relationship enrichment program is the Prevention and Relationship Enhancement Program (PREP), developed by Floyd, Markham, Kelly, Blumberg, and Stanley (1995) at the University of Denver. This social learning approach, developed in the 1980s, teaches communication and conflict-resolution skills, and explores attitudes and expectations about marriage. The primary goal is to help couples learn to face and resolve conflicts, and thus avoid incorporating unhealthy defensive patterns in their relationship.

PREP sessions come in two formats: weekly meetings over several weeks and marathon sessions held in a hotel over one weekend. Both versions include lectures and experiential exercises focusing on conflict management, communication, and forgiveness, as well as religious practices, recreation, and friendship. Couples learn such things as how and when to bring up conflictual subjects, how to identify hidden issues behind chronic arguments, a structured approach to problem solving, and making time for fun. Short-term gains in relationship satisfaction include improvement in communication, sexual satisfaction, and lower problem intensity. Long-term gains (at follow-up to four years) generally show sustained benefits, especially in communication (Silliman, Stanley, Coffin, Markman, & Jordan, 2002).

In Table 11.2 we offer some guidelines for making relationships work.

Managed Care

It seems ironic that with all the exciting developments in family therapy, the most powerful influence on the field today has nothing to do with clinical theory. Managed care companies increasingly control not only access to clients but also what kinds of therapies they receive, how long they can be treated, and how much therapists are paid.

In the first wave of **managed care,** therapists applied to be on panels to receive referrals. Once they received a referral, they had to ask permission from a case manager for a certain number of sessions and had to justify their treatment plans. Increasingly, managed care companies are finding this micromanagement too expensive; therefore the second wave involves incentives for therapists themselves to reduce costs. This involves giving "capitated" contracts in which therapists agree to provide mental health services for a specific group at a preset annual fee. Although the capitated system may discourage therapists from offering some services, at least therapists will be wrestling with their own consciences rather than with faceless strangers.

Therapists have reacted in a variety of ways. Some see managed care as a reasonable, or at least inevitable, correction to a situation that was out of control. They suggest that before managed care, psychotherapy was unaccountable and exploitative, with no incentive to contain runaway costs. These therapists learn how to please managed care companies and have plenty of business, even though they make less per hour. Others are trying to survive by increasing their marketing for clients who can pay out of pocket and by finding other ways to use their skills, such as divorce mediation; consulting to businesses, schools, and courts; teaching and leading workshops; and working in human resource departments. Still others are actively fighting the managed care tidal wave by organizing in groups that offer alternatives to managed care, by feeding the media a constant stream of managed care horror stories, and by pursuing antitrust suits.[5]

The final verdict on managed care isn't in yet. Although huge profits can be made by those who want to restrict services, dissatisfaction with those restrictions is growing. It's unlikely that we will return to the unrestricted days that some long for, and perhaps that's as it should be. It is likely, however, that as consumers realize they aren't getting the help they need, new alternatives will emerge to fill the demand and that these new alternatives will be more palatable to clients and therapists alike.

---

5. One such group is the National Coalition of Mental Health Professionals and Consumers (telephone: (516) 424-5232).

TABLE 11.2 Critical Skills for Effective Functioning as a Couple

A. Structure

1. Accommodation

   Learn to accept and adjust to each other's preferences and expectations, compromising on some issues, but not always giving in, so as not to build up resentment.

   She learned to accept his wish to eat supper early, while he agreed to join her for weekly religious services. But she didn't agree to put her career on a part-time basis; and he continued to take his yearly fishing trip with his brothers despite her hating to be left behind.

2. Boundary Making

   Create a protective boundary around your relationship that reduces but doesn't eliminate contact with outsiders.

   He stopped going out three nights a week with his buddies; she started asking him if it was okay before agreeing to let her parents come for the weekend.

   Demonstrating your commitment to your partner builds a secure base of attachment as well as confidence in the permanence of your relationship. Make sure your partner knows that you care, and that you are committed.

   He stopped defending himself by saying "If you don't like it, why don't you find someone else," because it only made her insecure and angry. She made a point of telling him who she had lunch with, because she knew his jealousy made him worry.

B. Communication

1. Listen to and acknowledge your partner's point of view.

   She discovered that making a sincere effort to say things like "So you like that one better because . . ." before countering with her own opinion made him feel that she respected his point of view. When it came to the most contentious issues, he discovered that asking first how she felt and then listening at length was essential. In some cases it was a good idea not even to express his side of the matter until a later time.

2. Short-circuit escalation in arguments by learning to back off before negative spirals get nasty. Call a time-out and agree to talk at a specific time later.

   "I'm getting upset; let's stop and talk about this tonight after supper, okay?"

3. Avoid invalidation and put-downs.

   "You're so irresponsible" may be an obvious put down, but equally invalidating is *"I think you're overreacting."* Don't criticize your partner's personality or deny what he or she is feeling.

C. Problem Solving

1. Make positive requests, such as *"Would you be willing . . . ?"* rather than criticisms, such as *"You never . . . !"*

2. If you ask for something, be prepared to give something in return.

   It was easier to get him to do things with her and the children if she also made a point of suggesting times when he could do some of the things he liked to do by himself. He learned that occasionally volunteering to do the shopping or cook dinner made her feel more like doing things for him—and that volunteering worked better than trying to make deals.

3. Wait until you're not angry before bringing up a problem to be solved. Raise concerns directly but gently.

   She was furious that he took her father's side against her in an argument. But she decided not to say anything until she calmed down. The following night after supper she began by saying "Honey, I want to talk about something I'm feeling but I'm afraid to because it might make you mad." Emphasizing that it was her feelings and saying that she was concerned about how he might react helped put him in a receptive mood.

4. Think of the two of you as a team working against the problem.

   Instead of battling over his "coldness" and her "dependency," they started talking about how they could adjust for their "different comfort levels." As a result they planned their next vacation so that they could play golf and tennis together, and she could visit friends while he took one day off for fishing.

5. Be sure you understand your partner's concerns before trying to work on a solution.

   He was upset that she wanted to make only a minimal down payment on their new house, because it would result in large mortgage payments. To him it made more sense to put down as much as they could in order to make the monthly payments as low as possible. But instead of continuing to argue he asked her what she was worried about. Her concern turned out to be that without a cushion of savings, they might be wiped out by some unforeseen emergency. Now at least he understood how she felt.

D. Consideration

---

1. Do pleasing things for your partner and the relationship.

   Spontaneous gestures—like compliments, hugs, little presents, calling in the middle of the day to say "I love you"—reassure your partner that you care and help to maintain a positive feeling about the relationship.

E. Fun

---

1. Make the effort to spend enjoyable time together, and don't use fun activities as a time to discuss difficult issues or conflicts.

   He got in the habit of inviting her to join him for a movie, a walk in the park, or a visit to the museum and then supper out on Saturdays. She learned that bringing up problems on these trips tended to spoil the mood.

Source: Adapted from Nichols, M. P. 1995.

—Summary——

1. During the past three decades, family therapy ran into a series of hard-hitting critiques—from feminists, postmodernists, social constructionists, multiculturalists, and those who work with violence and abuse, gays and lesbians, the poor, and the chronically ill. Therapists were challenged to become more collaborative; sensitive to differences in ethnicity, race, class, gender, and sexual orientation; and interested in beliefs and values rather than just actions and interactions. The clinical expert was dethroned by the compassionate conversationalist.

2. This new interest in collaboration is no accident—it reflects a maturing of the field. The pioneers first encountered the family as an adversary—"homeostatic," "resistant"—in part because they approached it with a built-in prejudice. Bent on rescuing "family" scapegoats," they saw mothers as enemies to be overcome and fathers as peripheral figures to be ignored. Systems do resist change, but one reason family therapists encountered so much resistance was that they were too eager to change people and too slow to understand them.

3. Family therapists taught us to see past individual personalities to the patterns that make them a family—an organization of interconnected lives governed by strict but unspoken rules. But in the process they created a mechanistic entity—the family system—and then set about

doing battle with it. Most of the challenges that have rocked and reshaped family therapy have been in reaction to this mechanism. But if the systemic revolution went too far in one direction, the same may be true of some of its critics.

4. The feminist critique was the first and perhaps most influential of the challenges to family therapy's traditions. In taking a stand against mother bashing, feminists challenged the essence of systems thinking by pointing out that concepts such as complementarity and circular causality can imply that subjugated women were as much to blame as their oppressors.

5. Family therapy's bridge to the twenty-first century was social constructionism. Much as was the case when the pioneers shifted their focus from individuals to families, this recent shift from behavior to cognition, and from challenging to collaborating, is opening up a new world of possibilities. We'll see just how exciting some of those possibilities are in the next few chapters.

6. Since Paul Watzlawick first brought out the constructivist implications of the MRI model in *The Invented Reality* (1984), family therapists have become increasingly aware of the power of the stories people tell themselves. As we shall see in Chapter 13, Michael White and his colleagues in the narrative movement have translated this insight into a powerful new approach to treatment. Helping clients construct new and more useful stories of their experience is surely an advance on the manipulative attempts to control them. But to the extent that narrative therapists merely substitute cognition for action and interaction, they risk ignoring all that we've learned about how family dynamics shape the lives of family members—regardless of what stories they tell themselves.

7. The two great values of postmodern skepticism are diversity and democracy. Surely, respecting multiple perspectives is a good thing. Two very positive expressions of this value are the rise of integrative models and a renewed respect for diverse forms of family organization. But it's not so good if we reject all norms and treat every individual as absolutely unique.

This means we have no need for knowledge and no room for guidelines. Family therapists have embraced democracy by advocating nonhierarchical approaches and opposing the imposition of influence. As Bateson pointed out, however, hierarchy is inherent in nature; certainly families in treatment, like other social systems, need some kind of executive decision-making team.

8. The headline story of family therapy's evolution from first- to second-order cybernetics, from MRI to solution-focused therapy, from Milan systemic to Hoffman and Goolishian, and from constructivism to social constructionism and now narrative is what's been in the forefront of intellectual discussion. While these front-page developments were taking place, family therapists practicing less trendy approaches (behavioral, psychoanalytic, structural, Bowenian, and experiential) have continued their work. So it can be a mistake to think that what's new and gets attention is the only or even major thing going on in the field.

9. The collaborative movement has raised new questions about the therapist's style of leadership. When Harlene Anderson and Harry Goolishian advocated a "collaborative approach," what was being rejected was the medical model—an authoritarian role model in which the clinician plays the expert to whom the patient looks for answers. But being an expert doesn't mean being an ogre. Here the advance is challenging the medical model, which, ironically, was perpetuated in such avant garde models of family therapy as the strategic and Milan systemic approaches. No longer do we see the therapist as a technocrat of change. But that doesn't mean therapists shouldn't be experts—leaders in the process of change.

10. Finally, it should be said that, just as family therapy hasn't stood still in recent years, neither has the family. Today's family is evolving and stressed. We've gone from the complementary model of the family in the 1950s to a symmetrical version—though we haven't come to terms with the new model yet. Perhaps it's time to ask the question: As the modern family

struggles through this stressful time of transition, what concepts does family therapy offer to help us understand and deal with the protean family forms of the twenty-first century?

—Questions to Consider——

1. How would you respond to the statement "family therapy is dead"? In what way is this true; in what way is it false?
2. Can you think of any advantages to entering the field of family therapy at a time when the excitement and enthusiasm for it as a revolutionary new approach have worn off?
3. How might you plan your education and training to maximize your potential to be a successful managed care provider?

4. Make a list of situations in which it might be difficult for a therapist to feel confident in challenging clients from other racial or ethnic groups or sexual orientations.
5. What are some advantages and disadvantages of offering to treat families in their own homes?

—Key Concepts——

collaborative model A more egalitarian view of the therapist's role; a stance advocated by critics of what they see as the authoritarianism in traditional approaches to family therapy.

constructivism A relativistic point of view that emphasizes the subjective construction of reality. It implies that what we see in families may be based as much on our preconceptions as on what's actually going on.

deconstruction A postmodern approach to exploring meaning by taking apart and examining taken-for-granted categories and assumptions, making possible newer and sounder constructions of meaning.

hermeneutics The art of analyzing literary texts or human experience, understood as fundamentally ambiguous, by interpreting levels of meaning.

managed care A system in which third-party companies manage insurance costs by regulating the terms of treatment. Managed care companies select providers, set fees, and control who receives treatment and how many sessions they are entitled to.

not-knowing Anderson and Goolishian's term for approaching families with as few preconceptions as possible.

postmodernism Contemporary antipositivism, viewing knowledge as relative and context dependent; questions assumptions of objectivity that characterize modern science. In family therapy, challenging the idea of scientific certainty, and linked to the method of deconstruction.

reflecting team Tom Andersen's technique of having the observing team share their reactions with the family at the end of a session.

second-order cybernetics The idea that anyone attempting to observe and change a system is therefore part of that system.

social constructionism Like constructivism, challenges the notion of an objective basis for knowledge. Knowledge and meaning are shaped by culturally shared assumptions.

solution-focused therapy Steve de Shazer's term for a style of therapy that emphasizes the solutions that families have already developed for their problems.

—Recommended Readings—

Andersen, T. 1991. *The reflecting team*. New York: Norton.

Anderson, C. M., Reiss, D., and Hogarty, B. 1986. *Schizophrenia and the family: A practitioner's guide to psychoeducation and management*. New York: Guilford Press.

Avis, J. M. 1992. Where are all the family therapists? Abuse and violence within families and family therapy's response. *Journal of Marital and Family Therapy. 18:* 225–232.

Fowers, B., and Richardson, F. 1996. Why is multiculturalism good? *American Psychologist. 51:* 609–621.

Gergen, K. 1985. The social constructionist movement in modern psychology. *American Psychologist. 40:* 266–275.

Goldner, V. 1985. Feminism and family therapy. *Family Process. 24:* 31–47.

Goodrich, T. J., ed. 1991. *Women and power: Perspectives for family therapy*. New York: Norton.

Greenan, D. E., and Tunnell, G. 2003. *Couple therapy with gay men*. New York: Guilford Press.

Hare-Mustin, R. T., and Marecek, J. 1988. The meaning of difference: Gender theory, postmodernism and psychology. *American Psychologist. 43:* 455–464.

Held, B. S. 1995. *Back to reality: A critique of post modern theory in psychotherapy*. New York: Norton.

Kellner, D. 1991. *Postmodern theory*. New York: Guilford Press.

Krestan, J., and Bepko, C. 1980. The problem of fusion in the lesbian relationship. *Family Process. 19:* 277–289.

Laird, J., and Green, R. J. 1996. *Lesbians and gays in couples and families: A handbook for therapists*. San Francisco: Jossey-Bass.

Luepnitz, D. 1988. *The family interpreted: Feminist theory in clinical practice*. New York: Basic Books.

McDaniel, S., Hepworth, J., and Doherty, W. 1992. *Medical family therapy*. New York: Basic Books.

McGoldrick, M., Giordano, J., and Pearce, J. 1996. *Ethnicity and family therapy*, 2nd ed. New York: Guilford Press.

Rolland, J. 1994. *Helping families with chronic and life-threatening disorders*. New York: Basic Books.

Walsh, F., ed. 1993. *Normal family processes*, 2nd ed. New York: Guilford Press.

—References—

Ahrons, C., and Rogers, R. 1989. *Divorced families: Meeting the challenges of divorce and remarriage*. New York: Norton.

Allport, G. 1958. *The nature of prejudice*. Garden City, NJ: Doubleday.

Andersen, T. 1991. *The reflecting team*. New York: Norton.

Anderson, C. M. 1995. *Flying solo*. New York: Norton.

Anderson, C. M., Reiss, D., and Hogarty, G. E. 1986. *Schizophrenia and the family: A practitioner's guide to psychoeducation and management*. New York: Guilford Press.

Anderson, H. 1993. On a roller coaster: A collaborative language systems approach to therapy. In *The new language of change*, S. Friedman, ed. New York: Guilford Press.

Anderson, W. T. 1990. *Reality isn't what it used to be*. San Francisco: Harper & Row.

Aponte, H. 1994. *Bread and spirit: Therapy with the new poor*. New York: Norton.

Atkinson, J. M., and Coia, D. A. 1995. *Families coping with schizophrenia: A practitioner's guide to family groups*. New York: Wiley.

Avis, J. M. 1988. Deepening awareness: A private study guide to feminism and family therapy. In *Women, feminism, and family therapy*, L. Braverman, ed. New York: Haworth Press.

Avis, J. M. 1992. Where are all the family therapists? Abuse and violence within families and family therapy's response. *Journal of Marital and Family Therapy. 18:* 223–230.

Bailey, E. 1999. *Children in therapy: Using the family as a resource*. New York: Norton.

Barth, R., Pietrzak, J., and Ramier, M. 1993. *Families living with drugs and HIV*. New York: Guilford Press.

Beavers, W., and Hampson, R. 1990. *Successful families: Assessment and intervention*. New York: Norton.

Billingsley, A. 1968. *Black families in White America*. Englewood Cliffs, NJ: Prentice-Hall.

Billingsley, A. 1992. *Climbing Jacob's ladder: The enduring legacy of African-American families.* New York: Simon & Schuster.

Billingsley, A. (ed.). 1994. The Black church. *National Journal of Sociology, 8:* (1–2) (double edition).

Bograd, M. 1992. Values in conflict: Challenges to family therapists' thinking. *Journal of Marital and Family Therapy. 18:* 243–253.

Bowlby, J. 1988. *A secure base: Parent–child attachment and healthy human development.* New York: Basic Books.

Boyd-Franklin, N. 1989. *Black families in therapy: A multisystems approach.* New York: Guilford Press.

Boyd-Franklin, N. 1993. Race, class, and poverty. In *Normal family processes,* F. Walsh, ed. New York: Guilford Press.

Boyd-Franklin, N. 2003. Race, class and poverty. In *Normal family processes: Growing diversity and complexity,* 3rd ed., F. Walsh, ed. New York: Guilford Press.

Boyd-Franklin, N., Steiner, G., and Boland, M. 1995. *Children, families, and HIV/AIDS.* New York: Guilford Press.

Brothers, B. J., ed. 1992. *Spirituality and couples: Heart and soul in the therapy process.* New York: Haworth Press.

Brown, L. S. 1994. *Subversive dialogues: Theory in feminist therapy.* New York: Basic Books.

Brown, G. W., Birley, J. L. T., and Wing, J. K. 1972. The influence of family life on the course of schizophrenic disorders: A replication. *British Journal of Psychology. 121:* 241–258.

Burton, L. A., ed. 1992. *Religion and the family.* New York: Haworth Press.

Campbell, T. 1986. Family's impact on health: A critical review and annotated bibliography. *Family Systems Medicine. 4:* 135–148.

Carl, D. 1990. *Counseling same-sex couples.* New York: Norton.

Carrington, C. 1999. *No place like home: Relationships and family life among lesbians and gay men.* Chicago: University of Chicago Press.

Chartier, M. R. 1986. Marriage enrichment. In *Psychoeducational approaches to family therapy and counseling,* R. F. Levant, ed. New York: Springer.

Combrinck-Graham, L. 1989. *Children in family contexts.* New York: Guilford Press.

Cose, E. 1993. *The rage of the privileged class.* New York: HarperCollins.

Dattilio, F., ed. 1998. *Case studies in couple and family therapy.* New York: Guilford Press.

Doherty, W. 1996. *The intentional family.* Reading, MA: Addison-Wesley.

Donovan, J. M., ed. 1999. *Short-term couple therapy.* New York: Guilford Press.

Duncan, G. J., and Brooks-Gunn, J. 1997. *Consequences of growing up poor.* New York: Russell Sage Foundation.

Ehrenreich, B. 1999. Nickel-and-dimed: On (not) getting by in America. *Harpers.* Jan. 37–52.

Elizur, J., and Minuchin, S. 1989. *Institutionalizing madness: Families, therapy and society.* New York: Basic Books.

Elkin, M. 1990. *Families under the influence.* New York: Norton.

Emery, R. 1994. *Renegotiating family relationships: Divorce, child custody, and mediation.* New York: Guilford Press.

Falicov, C. 1983. *Cultural perspectives in family therapy.* Rockville, MD: Aspen Systems.

Falicov, C. 1988. *Family transitions: Continuity and change over the life cycle.* New York: Guilford Press.

Falicov, C. 1998. *Latino families in therapy.* New York: Guilford Press.

Falloon, I. J. R., Boyd, J. L., McGill, C. W., Razani, J., Moss, H. B., and Gilderman, A. M. 1982. Family management in the prevention of exacerbations of schizophrenia. *New England Journal of Medicine. 306:* 1437–1440.

Figley, C. 1985. *Trauma and its wake: The study and treatment of post-traumatic stress disorder.* New York: Brunner/Mazel.

Floyd, F. J., Markham, H., Kelly, S., Blumberg, S. L., and Stanley, S. M. 1995. Preventive intervention and relationship enhancement. In *Clinical handbook of couples therapy,* N. S. Jacobson and A. S. Garman, eds. New York: Guilford Press.

Freeman, J., Epston, D., and Lobovits, D. 1997. *Playful approaches to serious problems.* New York: Norton.

Friedrich, W. 1990. *Psychotherapy of sexually abused children and their families.* New York: Norton.

Friesen, B. J., and Kroloff, N. M. 1990. Family-centered services: Implications for mental health administration and research. *Journal of Mental Health Administration. 17* (1): 13–25.

Gergen, K. 1985. The social constructionist movement in modern psychology. *American Psychologist. 40:* 266–275.

Gergen, K. 1991a. *The saturated self.* New York: Basic Books.

Gergen, K. 1991b. The saturated family. *Family Therapy Networker. 15:* 26–35.

Gil, E. 1994. *Play in family therapy.* New York: Guilford Press.

Ginsberg, B. G. 2000. Relationship enhancement couples therapy. In *Comparative treatments of relationship disorders,* F. M. Dattilio and L. J. Bevilacqua, eds. New York: Springer.

Goldner, V. 1985. Feminism and family therapy. *Family Process. 24:* 31–47.

Goldner, V. 1988. Generation and gender: Normative and covert hierarchies. *Family Process. 27:* 17–33.

Goldner, V., Penn, P., Sheinberg, M., and Walker, G. 1990. Love and violence: Gender paradoxes in volatile attachments. *Family Process. 29:* 343–364.

Goldstein, M. J., Rodnick, E. H., Evans, J. R., May, P. R., and Steinberg, M. 1978. Drug and family therapy in the aftercare treatment of acute schizophrenia. *Archives of General Psychiatry. 35:* 1169–1177.

Goodrich, T. J., Rampage, C., Ellman B., and Halstead K., 1988. *Feminist family therapy: A casebook.* New York: Norton.

Green, R. J. 1998. Training programs: Guidelines for multicultural transformations. In *Re-visioning family therapy,* M. McGoldrick, ed. New York: Guilford Press.

Green, R. J., and Mitchell, V. 2002. Gay and lesbian couples in therapy: Homophobia, relational ambiguity, and social support. In *Clinical handbook of couple therapy,* 3rd ed., A. S. Gurman and N. S. Jacobson, eds. New York: Guilford Press.

Greenan, D., and Tunnell, G. 2003. *Couple therapy with gay men.* New York: Guilford Press.

Grier, W., and Cobbs, P. 1968. *Black rage.* New York: Basic Books.

Guerney, B. G., Jr., ed. 1977. *Relationship enhancement: Skills training for therapy problem prevention and enrichment.* San Francisco: Jossey-Bass.

Haley, J. 1976. *Problem-solving therapy.* San Francisco: Jossey-Bass.

Haley, J. 1980. *Leaving home.* New York: McGraw-Hill.

Hansen, J. C. 1982. *Therapy with remarried families.* Rockville, MD: Aspen Systems.

Hardy, K. 1993. War of the worlds. *Family Therapy Networker. 17:* 50–57.

Hare-Mustin, R. T. 1978. A feminist approach to family therapy. *Family Process, 17:* 181–194.

Henggeler, S. W., and Borduin, C. M., ed. 1990. *Family therapy and beyond: A multisystemic approach to treating the behavior problems of children and adolescents.* Pacific Grove, CA: Brooks/Cole.

Hill, R. 1999. *The strengths of African American families: Twenty-five years later.* Lanham, MD: University Press of America.

Hines, P. M., and Boyd-Franklin, N. 1982. Black families. In *Ethnicity and family therapy,* M. McGoldrick, J. K. Pierce, & J. Giordano, eds. New York: Guilford Press.

Hines, P. M., and Boyd-Franklin, N. 1996. African American families. In *Ethnicity and family therapy,* 2nd ed., M. McGoldrick, J. K. Pierce, & J. Giordano, eds. New York: Guilford Press.

Imber-Black, E. 1988. *Families and larger systems: A family therapist's guide through the labyrinth.* New York: Guilford Press.

Imber-Black, E., Roberts, J., and Whiting, R. 1988. *Rituals in families and family therapy.* New York: Norton.

Ingoldsby, B., and Smith, S. 1995. *Families in multicultural perspective.* New York: Guilford Press.

Isay, R. A. 1989. *Being homosexual: Gay men and their development.* New York: Farrar Straus Giroux.

James, K., and MacKinnon, L. 1990. The "incestuous family" revisited: A critical analysis of family therapy myths. *Journal of Marital and Family Therapy. 16:* 71–88.

Johnson, W. E. 2001. Paternal involvement among unwed fathers. *Children and Youth Services Review, 23:* 513–536.

Johnson, T., and Keren, M. 1998. The families of lesbian women and gay men. In *Re-visioning family therapy,* M. McGoldrick, ed. New York: Guilford Press.

Jordan, J., Kaplan, A., Miller, J., Stiver, I., and Surrey J., eds. 1991. *Women's growth in connection: Writings from the Stone Center.* New York: Guilford Press.

Kahn, M., and Lewis, K. G. 1988. *Siblings in therapy.* New York: Norton.

Krestan, J. 1988. Lesbian daughters and lesbian mothers: The crisis of disclosure from a family systems perspective. *Journal of Psychotherapy and the Family. 3:* 113–130.

Laird, J. 1993. Lesbian and gay families. In *Normal family processes,* 2nd ed., F. Walsh, ed. New York: Guilford Press.

Laird, J., and Green, R. J. 1996. *Lesbians and gays in couples and families: A handbook for therapists.* San Francisco: Jossey-Bass.

LaSala, M. 1997. The need for thick skin: Coupled gay men and their relationships with their parents and in-laws. *Dissertation Abstracts International. 58:* 4444-A.

Law, D. D., Crane, D. R., and Russell, D. 2000. The influence of marital and family therapy on utilization of healthcare in a health maintenance organization. *Journal of Marital and Family Therapy.* 26: 281–291.

Lee, E. 1997. *Working with Asian Americans.* New York: Guilford Press.

Leff, J., Kuipers, L., Berkowitz, R. Eberlein-Vries, R., and Sturgeon, D. 1982. A controlled trial of social intervention in the families of schizophrenic patients. *British Journal of Psychiatry.* 141: 121–134.

Leff, J., and Vaughn, C. 1985. *Expressed emotion in families.* Thousand Oaks, CA: Sage.

Lehr, R., and MacMillan, P. 2001. The psychological and emotional impact of divorce: The noncustodial fathers' perspective. *Families in Society, 82:* 373–382.

Lindblad-Goldberg, M., Dore, M. M., and Stern, L. 1998. *Creating competence from chaos.* New York: Norton.

Luepnitz, D. 1988. *The family interpreted: Feminist theory in clinical practice.* New York: Basic Books.

Madanes, C. 1990. *Sex, love and violence.* New York: Norton.

Markowitz, L. 1993. Walking the walk. *Family Therapy Networker. 17:* 18–24, 27–31.

McAdoo, H., ed. 2002. *Black children: Social, educational and parental environments,* 2nd ed. Thousand Oaks, CA: Sage.

McDaniel, S., Hepworth, J., and Doherty, W. 1992. *Medical family therapy.* New York: Basic Books.

McFarlane, W. R. 1991. Family psychoeducational treatment. In *Handbook of family therapy (Vol II.),* A. S. Gurman and D. P. Kniskern, eds. New York: Brunner/Mazel.

McGoldrick, M. 1993. Ethnicity, cultural diversity, and normality. In *Normal family processes,* F. Walsh, ed. New York: Guilford Press.

McGoldrick, M., ed. 1998. *Re-visioning family therapy.* New York: Guilford Press.

McGoldrick, M., Giordano, J., and Pearce, J. 1996. *Ethnicity and family therapy,* 2nd ed. New York: Guilford Press.

McGoldrick, M., Pearce, J., and Giordano, J. 1982. *Ethnicity and family therapy.* New York: Guilford Press.

McGowen, B. G., and Meezan, W. 1983. *Child welfare: Current dilemmas, future directions.* Itasca, IL: Peacock.

McWhirter, D. P., and Mattison, A. M. 1984. *The male couple: How relationships develop.* New York: Norton.

Meyer, I. H., and Dean, L. 1998. Internalized homophobia, intimacy, and sexual behavior among gay and bisexual men. In *Stigma and sexual orientation: Understanding prejudice against lesbians, gay men, and bisexuals,* G. M. Herek, ed. Thousand Oaks, CA: Sage.

Micucci, J. 1998. *The adolescent in family therapy.* New York: Guilford Press.

Milkowitz, D. J. 1995. The evolution of family-based psychopathology. In *Integrating family therapy: Handbook of family psychology and systems theory,* R. H. Mikesell, D-D. Lusterman and S. H. McDaniels, eds. Washington, DC: American Psychological Association.

Miklowitz, D., and Goldstein, M. 1997. *Bipolar disorder; A family-focused treatment approach.* New York: Guilford Press.

Minuchin, P., Colapinto, J., and Minuchin, S. 1998. *Working with families of the poor.* New York: Guilford Press.

Minuchin, S., and Fishman, H. C. 1981. *Techniques of family therapy.* Cambridge, MA: Harvard University Press.

Minuchin, S., Montalvo, B., Guerney, B., Rosman, B., and Schumer, F. 1967. *Families of the slums.* New York: Basic Books.

Minuchin, S., Nichols, M. P., and Lee, W. Y. 2007. *Assessing families and couples: From symptom to system.* Boston: Allyn & Bacon.

Mirkin, M. P. 1990. *The social and political contexts of family therapy.* Boston: Allyn & Bacon.

Mitchell, S. 1993. *Hope and dread in psychoanalysis.* New York: Basic Books.

Morawetz, A., and Walter, G. 1984. *Brief therapy with single-parent families.* New York: Brunner/Mazel.

Muesser, K. T., and Glynn, S. M. 1995. *Behavioral family therapy for psychiatric disorders.* Boston: Allyn & Bacon.

Nichols, M. P. 2004. *Stop arguing with your kids.* New York: Guilford Press.

Nichols, M. P. 1995. *The lost art of listening.* New York: Guilford Press.

Okun, B. 1996. *Understanding diverse families.* New York: Guilford Press.

Olson, D. H. 1996. *PREPARE/ENRICH counselor's manual.* Minneapolis, MN: Life Innovations.

Patterson, J., Williams, L. Graul-Grounds, C., and Chamow, L. 1998. *Essential skills in family therapy.* New York: Guilford Press.

Pinderhughes, E. 1989. *Understanding race, ethnicity and power: The key to efficacy in clinical practice.* New York: The Free Press.

Pittman, F. 1987. *Turning points: Treating families in transition and crisis.* New York: Norton.

Prest, L., and Keller, J. 1993. Spirituality in family therapy. *Journal of Marital and Family Therapy.* 19: 137–148.

Price, J. 1996. *Power and compassion: Working with difficult adolescents and abused parents.* New York: Guilford Press.

Ramsey, R. N., ed. 1989. *Family systems in medicine.* New York: Guilford Press.

Reitz, M., and Watson, K. 1992. *Adoption and the family system.* New York: Guilford Press.

Rojano, R. 2004. The practice of community family therapy. *Family Process, 43:* 59–77.

Rolland, J. 1994. *Helping families with chronic and life-threatening disorders.* New York: Basic Books.

Root, M., Fallon, P., and Friedrich, W. 1986. *Bulimia: A systems approach to treatment.* New York: Norton.

Roth, S., and Murphy, B. 1986. Therapeutic work with lesbian clients: A systemic therapy view. In *Women and family therapy,* M. Ault-Riche and J. Hansen, eds. Rockville, MD: Aspen Systems.

Saba, G., Karrer, B., and Hardy, K. 1989. *Minorities and family therapy.* New York: Haworth.

Sager, C., Brown, H. S., Crohn, H., Engel, T., Rodstein, E., and Walker, L. 1983. *Treating the remarried family.* New York: Brunner/Mazel.

Sanders, G. 1993. The love that dares not speak its name: From secrecy to openness in gay and lesbian affiliations. In *Secrets in families and family therapy,* E. Imber-Black, ed. New York: Norton.

Schwartz, R. C. 1995. *Internal family systems therapy.* New York: Guilford Press.

Schwartzman, J. 1985. *Families and other systems: The macrosystemic context of family therapy.* New York: Guilford Press.

Selekman, M. 1997. *Solution-focused therapy with children.* New York: Guilford Press.

Seligman, M., and Darling, R. B. 1996. *Ordinary families, special children: A systems approach to childhood disability,* 2nd ed. New York: Guilford Press.

Sells, S. 1998. *Treating the tough adolescent.* New York: Guilford Press.

Sheinberg, M. 1992. Navigating treatment impasses at the disclosure of incest: Combining ideas from feminism and social constructionism. *Family Process.* 31: 201–216.

Silliman, B., Stanley, S. M., Coffin, W., Markman, H. J., and Jordan, P. L. 2002. Preventive intervention for couples. In *Family psychology: Science-based inter-* ventions, H. A. Liddle, D. A. Santisban, R. F. Levant, and J. H. Bray, eds. Washington, DC: American Psychological Association.

Smith, C., and Nylund, D. 1997. *Narrative therapies with children and adolescents.* New York: Guilford Press.

Sprenkle, D. 1985. *Divorce therapy.* New York: Haworth Press.

Stahlmann, R. F., and Hiebert, W. J. 1997. *Premarital and remarital counseling.* San Francisco: Jossey-Bass.

Stanton, M. D., Todd, T., and Associates. 1982. *The family therapy of drug abuse and addiction.* New York: Guilford Press.

Staples, R. 1994. *Black family: Essays and studies,* 5th ed. New York: Van Nostrand Reinhold.

Steinglass, P., Bennett, L., Wolin, S. J., and Reiss, D. 1987. *The alcoholic family.* New York: Basic Books.

Taibbi, R. 1996. *Doing family therapy.* New York: Guilford Press.

Treadway, D. 1989. *Before it's too late: Working with substance abuse in the family.* New York: Norton.

Trepper, T. S., and Barrett, M. J. 1989. *Systemic treatment of incest: A therapeutic handbook.* New York: Brunner/Mazel.

U.S. Bureau of the Census. 2001. *Statistical abstract of the United States.* 121st ed. Washington, DC: U.S. Gov't Printing Office.

U.S. Bureau of the Census. 2003. *Statistical abstract of the United States.* 123rd ed. Washington, DC: U.S. Gov't Printing Office.

Vaughn, C., and Leff, J. 1976. The measurement of expressed emotion in the families of psychiatric patients. *British Journal of Psychology.* 15: 157–165.

Vaughn, C. E., Snyder, K. S., Jones, S., Freeman, W. B., and Falloon, I. R. H. 1984. Family factors in schizophrenic relapse: Replication in California of British research on expressed emotion. *Archives of General Psychiatry.* 41: 1169–1177.

Visher, E., and Visher, J. 1979. *Stepfamilies: A guide to working with stepparents and stepchildren.* New York: Brunner/Mazel.

Visher, E., and Visher, J. 1988. *Old loyalties, new ties: Therapeutic strategies with stepfamilies.* New York: Brunner/Mazel.

Wachtel, E. 1994. *Treating troubled children and their families.* New York: Guilford Press.

Walker, G. 1991. *In the midst of winter: Systemic therapy with families, couples, and individuals with AIDS infection.* New York: Norton.

Wallerstein, J., and Kelly, J. 1980. *Surviving the breakup: How children and parents cope with divorce.* New York: Basic Books.

Walsh, F. 1982. *Normal family processes.* New York: Guilford Press.

Walsh, F. 1993. *Normal family processes,* 2nd ed. New York: Guilford Press.

Walsh, F. 1998. *Strengthening family resistance.* New York: Guilford Press.

Walsh, F., ed. 1999. *Spirituality in families and family therapy.* New York: Guilford Press.

Walsh, F., and McGoldrick. M., eds. 1991. *Living beyond loss: Death in the family.* New York: Norton.

Walters, M., Carter, B., Papp, P., and Silverstein, O. 1988. *The invisible web: Gender patterns in family relationships.* New York: Guilford Press.

Watzlawick, P., ed. 1984. *The invented reality.* New York: Norton.

White, J. 1972. Towards a Black psychology. In *Black psychology,* R. Jones, ed. New York: Harper & Row.

White, M., and Epston, D. 1990. *Narrative means to therapeutic ends.* New York: Norton.

12

Solution-Focused Therapy

Judging by its popularity, solution-focused therapy may be the treatment for our times. Its pragmatic minimalism, cognitive emphasis, and easily teachable techniques have combined to make it the hottest thing on the workshop circuit—and its promise of quick solutions has endeared it to the managed care industry. Indeed, when asked to indicate their therapeutic orientation, many applicants for provider status call themselves "solution-focused" regardless of whether or not they have any training in this approach. The spate of books on the model is further evidence of its popularity (de Shazer, 1988, 1991, 1994; O'Hanlon & Weiner-Davis, 1989; Walter & Peller, 1992; Furman & Ahola, 1992; Cade & O'Hanlon, 1993; O'Hanlon & Martin, 1992; Miller, Hubble, & Duncan, 1996), as well as to the model's application to couples (Weiner-Davis, 1992; Hudson & O'Hanlon, 1992), and alcoholism (Berg & Miller, 1992).

What is it—besides its remarkably appealing name—that has made this approach so popular? Its inspiration sprang from the MRI model, but it moves away from the focus on problems. Where strategic therapists explore the interactions around problems, looking for solutions that don't work, solution-focused therapists look for solutions that *have* worked.

The key ingredients in this approach are the conversational process by which therapists help clients shift their thinking from negative to positive and the creative use of tasks to engage clients in actions that lead to new perspectives and behavior (Friedman & Lipchik, 1999).

Accentuating the Positive

Solution-focused therapy takes the elegance of the MRI model and turns it on its head. While the one aims to help clients do less of what doesn't work, the other promotes more of what does. Both of these deliberately pragmatic approaches focus on the presenting complaint and aim to resolve it as parsimoniously as possible. The MRI model does so by looking for failed attempts to solve the presenting problem, whereas the solution-focused approach focuses on **exceptions**—times when the problem wasn't a problem.

The real difference between these two approaches, however, isn't merely a matter of where they punctuate problem sequences but that, while the MRI model focuses on behavior, the solution-focused model emphasizes cognition. It's assumed that people who come to therapy are already capable of behaving effectively but that their effectiveness has been blocked by a negative mind-set. Drawing their attention to times when they were doing well helps clients to see things differently:

> Problems are seen to maintain themselves simply because they maintain themselves and because clients depict the problem as *always happening*. Therefore, times when the complaint is absent are dismissed as trivial by the client or even remain completely unseen, hidden from the client's view. Nothing is actually hidden, but although these exceptions are open to view, they are not seen by the clients as differences that make a difference. For the client, the problem is seen as primary (and the exceptions, if seen at all, are seen as secondary), while for the therapists the exceptions are seen as primary; interventions are meant to help clients make a similar inversion, which will lead to the development of a solution. (de Shazer, 1991, p. 58)

The art of solution-focused therapy then becomes a matter of helping clients not only to see that their problems have exceptions, but also to realize that these exceptions are solutions that they still have in their repertoires. To get past the idea that exceptions just happen, the solution-focused therapist asks questions like, "How did you do that?"

Evolution of the Model

Solution-focused therapy grew from the work of Steve de Shazer, Insoo Berg, and their colleagues at the Brief Family Therapy Center (BFTC) in Milwaukee. This private training institute was started in 1979 when some of the staff at a community agency who were drawn to the MRI model became dissatisfied with the agency's constraints and broke off to form the BFTC. The initial group included married partners Steve de Shazer and Insoo Berg. De Shazer is considered the primary developer of solution-focused theory, though, sadly, he died in 2005. De Shazer had worked in Palo Alto and was strongly influenced by the MRI group.

Steve de Shazer, founder of solution-focused therapy.

Berg is known primarily as a clinician but has also contributed substantially to theory. She has trained therapists all over the world and has applied the model to alcoholism (Berg & Miller, 1992), marital therapy (Berg, 1994a), and family-based services to the poor (Berg, 1994b).

Other notable figures associated with the BFTC include Eve Lipchik, who worked there for eight years. She pioneered in applying the solution-focused model to wife battering (Lipchik & Kubicki, 1996). After training with de Shazer, Michele Weiner-Davis converted an agency in Woodstock, Illinois, to the solution-focused model. Weiner-Davis (1992) applied the model to marital problems in her popular book, *Divorce-Busting*. Scott Miller, now based in Chicago, was with the BFTC for three years, directing the alcohol and drug treatment services, and has written widely about the model.

Insoo Kim Berg, a leading practitioner of the solution-focused model.

John Walter and Jane Peller are in private practice in Chicago and are also popular presenters on the workshop circuit. They trained at the BFTC and wrote a book laying out the steps of the approach (Walter & Peller, 1992).

Bill O'Hanlon was never formally associated with the BFTC. After training with Milton Erickson and becoming a prominent translator of Erickson's ideas, the step toward the solution-focused approach was an easy one for O'Hanlon. He and Weiner-Davis (O'Hanlon & Weiner-Davis, 1989) have collaborated to expand on the groundwork laid by de Shazer.

The Basic Model

The assumptions that form the basis of solution-focused therapy are straightforward and uncomplicated. As Insoo Berg said, "We are very proud of our simplicity" (Wylie, 1990, p. 27).

Theoretical Concepts

One of the defining characteristics of family therapy has always been looking at the present, where problems are maintained, rather than searching the past to discover what "caused" them. Solution-focused therapists prefer to look to the future, where problems can be solved.

Like the MRI group, solution-focused therapists believe that people are constrained by narrow views of their problems into perpetuating rigid patterns of false solutions. As O'Hanlon and Weiner- Davis (1989) put it:

> So, the meanings people attribute to behavior limit the range of alternatives they will use to deal with a situation. If the methods used do not produce a satisfactory outcome, the original assumption about the meaning of the behavior is generally not questioned. If it were, new meanings might be considered, which in turn might prompt a different, perhaps more effective, approach. Instead, people often redouble their efforts to solve the problem in an ineffective way, thinking that by doing it more, harder or

better (e.g., more punishments, more heart-to-heart talks, and so on) they will finally solve it. (p. 48)

Solution-oriented therapists reject the notion that problems serve ulterior motives or that people are ambivalent about their problems. They assume that clients *really do* want to change. De Shazer (1984), in fact, has declared the death of resistance, suggesting that when clients don't follow directives, "it's their way of cooperating" by teaching the therapist the best way to help them.

The MRI model was strongly influenced by Milton Erickson's view of people as containing untapped and often unconscious resources. According to this view, people may only need a slight shift of perspective to release their potential. Early solution-focused theory showed more evidence of this Ericksonian view of people as resourceful. Since the postmodern revolution, the theorizing has moved increasingly from releasing unused capabilities to changing the way people talk about their problems.

Constructivists believe that language shapes reality. Through the influence of the analytic philosopher Ludwig Wittgenstein (1958), de Shazer has gradually moved toward a more radical position—namely, that language *creates* reality. "Language constitutes 'the human world and the human world constitutes the whole world'" (de Shazer & Berg, 1992, p. 73). Nothing exists outside of language. Thus de Shazer (1993) asserts that "There are no wet beds, no voices without people, no depressions. There is only *talk* about wet beds, *talk* about voices without people, *talk* about depression" (p. 89). If one accepts that language is reality, therapy becomes a relatively simple procedure. All that's needed is to change the way people talk. From this idea flows the solution-focused goal to steer clients from *problem-talk* to *solution-talk*.

Normal Family Development

Solution-focused therapists adhere to the constructivist idea that there are no absolutes; therefore, therapists shouldn't impose their view of normality. The search for structural flaws that characterize other forms of therapy is rejected. As de Shazer (1991) writes, "Structuralist thought points to the idea that symptoms are the result of some underlying problem, a psychic or structural problem such as incongruent hierarchies, covert parental conflicts, low self-esteem, deviant communication, repressed feelings, 'dirty games,' etc." The solution-focused therapist dispenses with such speculations and instead is interested only in language—the way people describe themselves and their problems.

Therapy, then, is highly relativistic. The therapist should be concerned only with the complaints that clients present and shouldn't impose values by suggesting that they address other, unpresented, problems.

> Solution-oriented therapists don't believe that there is any single "correct" or "valid" way to live one's life. We have come to understand that what is unacceptable behavior in one family or for one person is desirable behavior in another. Therefore, clients, not therapists, identify the goals to be accomplished in treatment. (O'Hanlon & Weiner-Davis, 1989, p. 44)

Development of Behavior Disorders

In the solution-focused world, this subject is closed. Just as they steer clients away from speculating about problem formation, solution-focused therapists also dissuade therapists from such conjecture. Their conviction is that solutions to problems are often unrelated to the way the problems developed and that tracking etiologic factors is engaging in "problem talk"—exactly what they seek to avoid.

Problem talk and the related preoccupation with the problem are the furthest solution-focused therapists go in identifying etiologic factors. They believe that problem-focused thinking keeps people from recognizing the effective solutions they've already used or could come up with in the future.

How Therapy Works

Solution-focused therapists assume that people already have the skills to solve their problems but have lost sight of these abilities because their problems loom so large to them that their strengths are crowded out of the picture. Sometimes a simple shift in focus from what's not going well to what they're already doing that works can remind clients of these resources. Other times, people may have to search for abilities that they aren't currently using and bring those dormant skills to bear on their problems.

At another level, the goal is simply to help clients begin to shift their language from talking about problems to talking about solutions. Once people begin speaking about what they *can* do effectively, what resources they have, what they've done in the past that worked, solution-focused therapists have achieved their primary aim. From that point on, the work is to build on the solutions that emerge from those more optimistic conversations.

Because solution-focused therapists aren't out to reorganize personalities or family structures, they're willing to settle for modest goals. A homeless woman may simply need to find a place to live, a single man may just need the courage to ask someone for a date. If a client's goal is vague—"I'd like to feel happier"—or utopian—"I never want to be sad again"—therapists ask questions designed to make the goal clear and specific. Helping clients set concrete and reachable goals is a major intervention in itself, and the process of thinking about the future and what one wants to be different is a large part of what solution-focused therapists do (Walter & Peller, 1996).

Solution-focused therapy works by helping clients amplify **exceptions** to their problems—effective solutions of which they are already in possession. From Berg and de Shazer's (1993) point of view, what's needed for change is a shift in the way the problem is "languaged."

> Rather than looking behind and beneath the language that clients and therapists use, we

think that the language they use is all that we have to go on. . . . What we talk about and how we talk about it makes a difference, and it is these differences that can be used to make a difference (to the client) . . . we have come to see that the meanings arrived at in a therapeutic conversation are developed through a process more like negotiation than the development of understanding or an uncovering of what it is that is "really" going on. (p. 7)

Thus, changing the way people talk about their problems is all one needs to accomplish, because "as the client and therapist talk more and more about the solution they want to construct together, they come to believe in the truth or reality of what they are talking about. This is the way language works, naturally" (Berg & de Shazer, 1993, p. 9). This is why solution-focused therapy can be so brief—it's a lot easier to get clients to talk differently about their problems than it is to get them to change their behavior. The assumption is, of course, that getting people to talk positively will help them think positively—and, ultimately, to act positively to solve their problems.

Therapy

Assessment

Therapists using this model studiously avoid any assessment of how problems develop. Nor are they interested in evaluating patterns of behavior that might be perpetuating those problems. What they are concerned with identifying are those patterns of behavior that existed when the problem *wasn't* operative.

Instead of dwelling on past problems, solution-focused therapists concentrate on assessing future goals. Clarifying goals is a proactive process that begins in the first session and continues throughout therapy, which might take the form of some of the following questions (adapted from Lipchik, 2002).

1. "What do you think the problem is now?"
2. "How will you know when the problem is solved?"

3. "How will you know you don't have to come here anymore? What will the signs be?"
4. "What will have to be different for that to happen in terms of your behavior, thoughts, and feelings?"
5. "What will you notice that is different about others involved in the situation?"
6. "What is your wildest fantasy about what you want to have happen?"

Because they aren't interested in assessing family dynamics, solution-focused therapists don't feel the need to convene any particular grouping of people, like whole families. Instead, they say that anyone who's concerned about the problem should come. They also need little intake information because they want to hear clients' constructions of their problems firsthand and without preconceptions.

Following de Shazer (1988), practitioners of this approach distinguish between "customers," "complainants," and "visitors." A **complainant** is someone who describes a complaint but isn't willing to work on solving it. A **customer** is someone motivated to change. These categories aren't qualities of character but qualities of the therapeutic relationship and therefore fluid. With a complainant the therapist's job is to engage in a solution-focused conversation, compliment the client, and possibly give an assignment to observe exceptions to the problem. By not pushing for change but shifting attention away from problems and toward solutions, the relationship may evolve into one in which the client becomes a customer. A therapist can take a more active role in helping the client look for exceptions if the client is a customer rather than just a **visitor,** someone with no motivation to change.

Therapeutic Techniques

In the early 1980s, de Shazer's team began experimenting with this orientation toward solutions by giving all clients the same assignments, which they called "formula tasks." Some of these assignments seemed to be universally effective regardless of the problem. One of these tasks, given in the first session, was to ask clients to observe what happens in their life or relationships that they want to continue (de Shazer, 1985). This assignment helped reorient people from dwelling on the bad things in their lives to thinking about the good. This shift in perspective seemed to build on itself—to create a more positive outlook that led to better interactions, which in turn reinforced and expanded that positive outlook.

This has become known as the **formula first-session task** and is the standard assignment given at the end of the first meeting. "Between now and the next time we meet, I would like you to observe, so you can describe to me next time, what happens in your (family, life, marriage, relationship) that you want to continue to have happen" (de Shazer, 1985, p. 137).

With the success of these formula tasks, it began to dawn on the team that the process of change could be initiated without much knowledge of the problem or the personalities of those suffering from it. They began to focus on ways to foster this problem-solving faculty in people, which they believed was inhibited by a focus on faults and foilings. This thinking led to the development of the "miracle question" and the "exception question," two mainstays of the solution-focused approach (de Shazer, 1985, 1988).

The **miracle question** is: "Suppose one night, while you were asleep, there was a miracle and this problem was solved. How would you know? What would be different?" This question activates a problem-solving mind-set by giving people a vision of their goal, perhaps in the same way that visualizing the perfect serve helps a tennis player. It also helps clients look beyond the problem to see that what they really want may not be the elimination of the problem per se, but instead to be able to do the things that the problem has been obstructing. If the therapist can encourage them to begin doing those things despite the problem, suddenly the problem may not loom as large.

For example, Mary says that if not for her bulimia, she'd get closer to people and have more

fun. If, with her therapist's encouragement, Mary begins to take interpersonal risks and has more fun, then her bulimia may become less of a problem, less of an obstacle in her life, which might also increase her ability to control it.

The miracle question is most effectively introduced when clients complain in vague terms.[1]

A therapist working with a couple tried to shift them away from complaining and toward solutions by asking a series of constructive questions, such as: "How do you usually solve problems like this?" "When you're feeling more appreciated by your partner, what is he doing differently?" Although the couple had plenty of complaints about each other, the husband was able to respond positively to the therapist's question, "So you both agree, the other feels as bad as you do; any ideas what the solution might be?"

> *Husband:* "Yeah, the solution would be more acceptance."
> *Therapist:* "On her part? On your part?"
> *Husband:* "Well, for both of us."
> *Wife:* "Well, the only solution I see is similar, but I've lost trust in him."

When the therapist asked her to elaborate on what a solution might look like, the wife kept coming back to her complaints. And so the therapist asked a modified form of the miracle question in hopes of shifting her toward a more specific vision of a direction for positive change. "And if by some miracle that trust would be there tomorrow, how would you know? What would be the signs be?"

The **exception question** ignores the picture of the problem clients present and, instead, directs their attention to the negative of that image—to times when they didn't have the problem. Exception questions (adapted from Hoyt, 2002) take the following forms:

- "When in the past might the problem have happened but didn't?"

---

1. This vignette is paraphrased from Friedman and Lipchik, 1999.

- "What is different about those times when the problem does not happen?"
- "How have you let your partner know when he (or she) does something that makes a positive difference to you?"

By exploring these times and what was different about them, clients find clues to what they can do to expand those exceptions. In addition, clients may find that in light of the fact that they were able to change or eliminate the problem, their outlook toward it may change. It seems less insurmountable.

Mary remembers several times during the previous week when she had the urge to binge and purge but didn't. She discovers that at those times she was away from her parents and didn't feel like she was disappointing them. She decides that it's time to become more independent. "Thus, a solution is a joint product of therapist and client talking together about whatever it is that the problem/complaint is not" (Berg & de Shazer, 1993, p. 21).

More recently, **scaling questions** have become prominent in the solution-focused literature. Scaling questions were first introduced to help therapists and clients talk about vague topics such as depression and communication, where it's difficult to identify concrete behavioral changes and goals (Berg & de Shazer, 1993).

> The therapist asks the depressed client, for example, "On a scale of one to ten, with one being how depressed you felt when you called me and ten being how you feel the day after the miracle, how do you feel right now?"
>
> The client might say two and the therapist might say, "So you feel a little better than when you called. How did you achieve this improvement?" Or the therapist might ask, "What do you think you need to do to achieve a three?" In this way, the therapist and client can recognize and nurture small changes toward the goal rather than being stuck in the "I'm either depressed or I'm not" kind of thinking that typifies such problems.

Scaling questions are also used to get clients to quantify their confidence that they can maintain their resolve. "On a scale of one to ten, how confident are you that you will be able to avoid losing your temper this week?" In practice this device has a kind of "prove it" implication. The response is followed up by asking clients what they might do to increase the odds of success. "What do you have to do to stick to your guns this time?" Scaling questions are a clever way of anticipating and disarming resistance and backsliding and of encouraging commitment to change.

Scaling questions can also be used to reduce goals that might seem dauntingly far off to more manageable small steps. "On a scale of one to one hundred, with one being never and one hundred being always, what percentage of the time would you say you are experiencing the problem?" Then, in response to the answer, "How many points would it have to go down for you to feel slightly better?" "What would a step from seventy-five to seventy look like?" "What would you be doing differently?" "What would others be doing differently?"

A Woman Who Was Stronger Than She Thought.   To illustrate the process of solution-focused therapy we will summarize a session reported by Insoo Berg and Peter De Jong (1996). The client, Lucinda, is a nineteen-year-old African American mother of two children, ages three and four, who had been removed from Lucinda and placed with foster parents eighteen months earlier. Lucinda had also been physically abused by a former partner. This is all the information the therapist chose to know before seeing Lucinda.

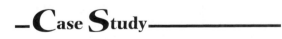

—Case Study——

Rather than inquiring about her problems, the therapist begins by asking "What can I do that would be helpful to you?" Lucinda says that she is depressed and wants someone to talk to because her kids aren't with her. She also alludes to the abusive relationship with a man she no longer sees.

Without any further discussion of Lucinda's predicament, the therapist asks a series of questions about how Lucinda was able to break off from the abusive relationship. Lucinda says it was hard because the man, Marvin, didn't want to leave and was threatening to kill her. The therapist said, "So that's when most women sort of become weak and they take him back. How come you didn't?" Lucinda replied, "A couple of times I did because I was scared. And the more I kept getting back with him, it got worse and worse." She goes on to describe how Marvin broke her son's leg, which is why she lost custody of her children, and that's when she drew the line and wouldn't take him back. The therapist punctuates her story with comments highlighting Lucinda's competence in protecting her kids, "But some women . . . would either get scared of him or, you know, somehow think that he's gonna change and take him back," and "Wow, I'm amazed by this. How did you do this?"

After letting Lucinda know she's impressed with her competence, the therapist turns to goal-setting questions. Lucinda says she wants her kids back and doesn't want to be afraid anymore. She wants advice on how to be strong with Marvin. The therapist says, "Sounds like you already are, though."

To clarify Lucinda's goal, the therapist asks her to imagine that after she goes to bed that night a miracle will happen and her problems—that she wants her kids back and wants to be stronger—will be solved. How would Lucinda be able to tell that the miracle has happened? Lucinda responds that her kids would be home and she would be very excited. The therapist asks her to elaborate on that miracle picture and Lucinda spends much of the session happily describing what she'd do with her children and how she and they would feel, with the therapist interjecting questions like, "Where did you learn to be such a good, loving mother?"

The therapist asks a scaling question, ". . . on a scale of one to ten, ten stands for how you will be when you finally get your kids back and one is what you were like when your children were taken away from you. . . . Where would you say things are today?" Lucinda says between eight

and nine. The therapist asks how she was able to climb that high. Lucinda says it's because she's sure her kids are coming back soon.

After giving more compliments, the therapist takes a break and returns to summarize her feedback. She says that it makes sense that Lucinda would be depressed given what she's lost and what she's experienced in her life, but the therapist is amazed at how Lucinda's used what she's learned. "And that's really absolutely amazing to me. For someone as young as you are . . . you are very wise already." The therapist also compliments her again on breaking up with Marvin. Lucinda agrees with all this, so the therapist says, "At this point I'm not sure if we ever need to get together again. What do you think?" Lucinda agrees that she doesn't need any more help and they end the session. She never called for another appointment and her children were returned to her.

Berg and De Jong (1996) believe that during the solution-focused conversation Lucinda's perceptions of herself as depressed and her passive demeanor shifted. They think she left with a clearer sense of what she wanted and how to make it happen.

Solution-focused therapists hold that if both client and therapist can reorient themselves in the direction of strengths—exceptions to the problem, clarified goals, and strategies to achieve them—then therapy can be quite brief. Two assumptions justify this belief. The first draws again from **constructivism** and the power of suggestion. As O'Hanlon and Weiner-Davis (1989) explain,

> Since what you expect influences what you get, solution-oriented therapists maintain those presuppositions that enhance client–therapist cooperation, empower clients, and make our work more effective and enjoyable. We hold assumptions which focus on strengths and possibilities; fortunately, these assumptions also help create self-fulfilling prophecies. (p. 34)

If one perspective is as valid as the next, why not assume that solutions can be found easily and quickly?

The second assumption is borrowed from the MRI model—that a small change is usually all that's needed because it can snowball into bigger changes. As O'Hanlon and Weiner-Davis (1989) put it, "Once a small positive change is made, people feel optimistic and a bit more confident about tackling further changes" (p. 42).

With these two assumptions about change, the solution-focused theorists have fashioned a set of pivotal questions and tasks designed to create an optimistic perspective and start the snowball rolling. In Lucinda's case, the therapist used the miracle question, exception questions, coping questions ("How did you do that?"), in-session compliments, and end-of-session feedback that emphasized her competencies. Lucinda left with the sense that the therapist thought she could achieve her goals.

Compliments, which are an important part of solution-focused therapy, are conveyed with questions that take the general form of "How did you do *that?*" or, to be more accurate, "Wow! How did you do *that?*" Notice that this phrasing calls attention to the fact that the person has already done something. Rather than asking questions like "Have you ever had a job before?" asking "What kinds of jobs have you had before?" invites clients to describe their successes and thus helps foster self-confidence (Berg & Dolan, 2001).

To be effective, compliments should point toward what to do more, not what to eliminate. Most clients know what's wrong but have run out of ideas about what to do to avoid repeating the same old ineffective solutions. Compliments, both direct and indirect, can be used to highlight successful strategies and keep clients focused on those that work (Berg & Dolan, 2001).

Solution-focused therapy is often practiced in a team approach, with one or more colleagues observing behind a one-way mirror. Whether working with a team or alone, the interviewing therapist usually takes a five-minute break near the end of the session. During this time the therapist (with the team or alone) composes a summary message to the clients.

The summary message consists of (1) feedback on what the therapist has heard during the session, (2) compliments on positive steps already taken, (3) a framework in which to place the client's predicament (usually emphasizing the normality of the situation), and (4) the suggestion of a task to be carried out between sessions.

The overall goal of the summary message is to provide a new and more hopeful perspective on the problem and to engender confidence and positive expectations.

> So, for example, the therapist might begin by saying, "What I heard you say today is. . . ." This statement includes what the therapist heard the clients say (using the clients' language as much as possible), their goals, progress, and comments about their feelings or emotions. Next, the therapist offers compliments, reinforces positive changes, normalizes, reframes, or presents information from a developmental perspective. Finally, a suggestion is made. This can be as simple as "Continue doing what you're already doing" or one more specifically designed to guide the clients toward doing something different. (Friedman & Lipchik, 1999, p. 332)

The summary message begins with a summary of what the therapist heard the clients say during the interview, including the problem, its background, the clients' goals, and pre-session progress and strengths: "What I heard you tell me today, Mr. and Mrs. X. is that. . . ." "Did I hear both of you correctly?" "Is there anything of importance that I omitted or that you want to add?" This summary is followed by a statement reflecting the therapist's reaction, including an expression of empathy ("I'm not surprised you're so depressed!"), a reflection of the emotional impact on the client ("My sense is that you must really be hurting a lot"), compliments on pre-session changes or strengths ("I was impressed by how many things you've tried to make better"), and some comments on the clients' shared goals. Finally, the therapist makes a suggestion about noticing or building on positives. "I would suggest that you notice what Patrick is doing at school that you want him to continue doing." "Patrick, I would suggest that you try to notice what's happening at school with the kids and your teacher that you like and want to continue to have happen."

Among the suggestions used commonly in solution-focused therapy are:

1. The formula first-session task (de Shazer, 1985). "Between now and next time we meet, I would like you to observe what happens in your family that you want to continue to have happen."
2. Do more of what works. "Since you said that you usually can talk together when you go for a walk, maybe you should try that once or twice and see what happens."
3. Do something different. "You mentioned that when you rely on Janine to be responsible for her own homework, she often fails to do it. Maybe you should try something different." If a client says, "I've said the same thing over and over again until I'm blue in the face," the suggestion to try something different invites the client to discover his or her own solution. The suggestion to do something different can be given as an experiment, as illustrated by Insoo Berg's example of parents, exasperated by their son's encopresis, who when given the suggestion to try something different, started filling the boy's potty seat with water and a toy boat, telling him that his job was to sink the boat (Berg & Dolan, 2001). It worked!
4. Go slowly. This suggestion, taken from the MRI model, is designed to help clients overcome fear and resistance to change by asking about possible negative consequences of changing and warning against trying to change too rapidly. "I have what may seem like a strange question: Could there possibly be any advantages to things staying the way they are?"
5. Do the opposite. This suggestion, also taken from the MRI model, is based on the notion that many problems are maintained by the attempted solution. Suggesting that clients try the opposite of

what they have been doing is especially useful for problems that exist between just two people (one member of a couple or one parent who's having trouble with a child). If scolding a child for being bad isn't working, parents can be encouraged to start praising her for being good. If a husband's attempt to avoid conversations with his wife about The Relationship aren't working, he could try initiating them when he's in the mood.

6. The prediction task (de Shazer, 1988). "Before you go to bed tonight predict whether the problem will be better or the same tomorrow. Tomorrow night rate the day and compare it with your prediction. Think about what may have accounted for the right or wrong prediction. Repeat this every night until we meet again."

As you can see, the compliments and suggestions of the summary message continue the basic thrust of the solution-focused approach, drawing attention to the family's resources and encouraging them to capitalize on their strengths in order to focus on solutions rather than problems.

Current Status of the Model

Although some have criticized solution-focused therapy as being simplistic, the approach contains useful ingredients that can help clients step out of their pessimism and move toward constructive action. Like any model in the early stages of evolution, it has been presented at times in a cookbook style that has led therapists with limited experience to use it as a set of formulaic techniques. More recently, some solution-focused therapists have recognized this problem and have stressed the importance of the overall philosophy and the relationship with clients.

Eve Lipchik, for example, points out that "The speed and success of solution construction depend on the therapist's ability to stay connected with the clients' reality throughout the course of therapy. This is the underpinning for the whole collaborative process, the grease that keeps the axles turning" (Lipchik, 1999, p. 329). Like any other therapy, the solution-focused approach isn't likely to be particularly effective if therapists, in a rush to get to their own agenda, fail to listen to clients and make them feel understood.

To their credit, solution-focused therapists have done research and reported results that weren't necessarily what they expected. One study of the process of solution-focused therapy stirred things up a bit. Linda Metcalf (1993; Metcalf et al., 1996) interviewed six couples who were considered to have achieved good outcome at the BFTC. She also interviewed their therapists. She found that in several ways what the therapists said happened (and what solution-focused theory says should happen) didn't match the clients' experience.

For example, in discussing what was helpful, therapists focused primarily on the techniques they used, whereas clients were more likely to point to their relationship with the therapist. In addition, whereas all the therapists believed that the decision to terminate therapy had been reached collaboratively, four of the six couples thought their therapist had made the decision unilaterally, and some of them felt pushed out prematurely. The study also found that the therapists generally took a more directive role than is suggested in the solution-focused literature.

In reviewing Lucinda's experience, described earlier, a case could be made that the therapist steered the interview in a certain upbeat direction and that the decision to stop after one session was less than mutual. After the therapist said, "At this point I'm not even sure if we need to get together again. What do you think?" It would have taken a very assertive client to say "No, I need more sessions."

The issue of whether solution-focused therapy is genuinely collaborative or directive has been raised frequently (Wylie, 1990; Storm, 1991; Lipchik, 1992, 1993, 1996; Efron & Veendendaal, 1993; Efran & Schenker, 1993; Miller, 1994; Nylund & Corsiglia, 1994; O'Hanlon, 1996). It has even been called "solution-forced" therapy by some people because of the perceived

tendency for therapists to pressure clients into discussing only the positive and aggressively disregarding anything negative. As Efran and Schenker (1993) ask, "What assurance is there that clients of solution-focused therapists haven't simply learned to keep their complaints to themselves in the presence of the therapist?" Acknowledging this concern, Eve Lipchik (1997, p. 167) writes "I have occasionally worked with clients who describe their experience with their past solution-focused professional as he or she having been too positive and not providing opportunity for talking about things that really bothered them."

Solution-focused therapists themselves have expressed reservations about the model's injunction to remain constantly upbeat (Storm, 1991; Lipchik, 1992, 1993; Efron & Veenendaal, 1993). As Cheryl Storm (1991) reported, "I have found that being relentlessly solution-focused is a mismatch for some clients. These individuals insist on talking about the problem in detail and, if ignored, fire the therapist. I thought I was misapplying the approach but now believe I . . . overemphasized change." Others (e.g., Efron & Veenendaal, 1993) echo these sentiments: "When we attempt to use these models and stances exclusively, we build up a sense of wrongness and futility, as if we were somehow pulling the wool over the eyes of clients and ourselves" (p. 17).

Like Lipchik, some solution-focused therapists are reading the feedback. According to Bill O'Hanlon (1996), "Carl Rogers taught us years ago that listening respectfully to clients and letting them know we can hear their perceptions and feelings and that we accept them as they currently are is a prerequisite for most people to cooperate in the change process" (p. 85).

Similarly, William Butler and Keith Powers (1996) stress the importance of validating the client's experience of the problem and note the absence of such validation in the solution-focused literature.

During the first interview the client complained about feeling increasingly depressed due to recent losses. . . . The therapist listened intently, reflected her feelings, and made many empathic comments. The most important thing the therapist did, however, was to *not ask* a series of future-oriented questions. . . . In the second interview, one week later, the client again told details of her long history of depression and loss. The therapist picked up on the theme of multiple losses and the many years of struggle. (p. 230)

It was only after going over in detail and empathizing with the large number of losses over the past ten years that the therapist introduced a solution-focused question: "But when I look over this long list [of losses] and consider what you've been through, I can't help but wonder—how do you keep it from getting worse?" (p. 230). The authors conclude that it was crucial to allow the client to fully express her struggles and have her experience validated before shifting the conversation to her strengths.

The problem some solution-focused therapists may have with this line of thinking is that the model could lose its claim to being distinctively brief. It may take several sessions before some clients feel fully understood and acknowledged. If they added an acknowledgment stage to the current model, wouldn't solution-focused therapy begin to resemble the usual supportive therapy, both in duration and in practice?

In other words, the refusal to talk about problems, which is what makes solution-focused therapy unique, turns out to be problematic. Reassuring someone who's worried that there's nothing to worry about isn't very reassuring. It can make you believe that your feelings aren't valid, because you wouldn't have them if you would only look at the bright side of things. Most people aren't eager to be changed by someone they feel doesn't understand them.

We hope that this debate helps solution-focused therapists continue to move away from the formulaic way the model was originally packaged. Many of the techniques are no doubt valuable to clients if properly timed and flexibly applied. But techniques can obscure a therapist's intuitive humanity. We hope students will remember Michele Weiner-Davis's (1993) candid confession that she doesn't always practice what she preaches: ". . . my clients cry and express pain, anger, disappointment and fears just as they might in any other therapist's office. And I respond with compassion . . . my therapy story [what she presents in workshops] is not the total picture of how I do therapy" (p. 157).

Summary

1. Solution-focused therapy is a direct descendant of the MRI approach, though it turns the problem-centered focus on its head. Where the MRI approach is focused on problems, solution-focused therapy is focused on solutions. The idea is that people often get stuck in their problems because by trying to get to the bottom of them they overlook solutions that are right under their noses.

2. This notion has led to the development of a set of techniques for changing "problem talk" into "solution talk." These techniques include *exception questions* (e.g., "Can you think of a time when you didn't have the problem? What were you doing then?"); the *miracle question* (e.g.,

"Suppose you went to sleep and a miracle happened such that when you awoke, your problem was solved. What would be different?"); *scaling questions* (e.g., "On a scale from one to ten, how do you feel now compared to when you called?"); *coping questions* (e.g., "Given how bad that was, how were you able to cope?"); the *formula first-session task* (e.g., "After you leave today, observe what happens that you want to continue during the next week."); and *giving compliments* ("Wow, you must be very smart to have thought of that!"). These techniques are put into practice as soon as possible to keep the work brief and to discourage clients from dwelling on the negative side of their experience.

3. More recently, therapists have questioned the model's emphasis on technique and speculated that qualities of the therapist–client relationship may be at the heart of the model's effectiveness. This has led to a call for greater collaboration with clients such that their feelings are acknowledged and validated before introducing solution-focused techniques.

4. Solution-focused therapy continues to have enormous appeal in the world of psychotherapy. Some of its popularity relates to the number of therapists who are struggling to find ways to feel effective while living with managed care's limited number of sessions. In addition, its techniques are relatively easy to learn—the basics can be picked up in a few workshops—and its upbeat nature makes it more enjoyable for many therapists. Yet its easy-to-learn formula leads some therapists to dismiss it as superficial once they get stuck. They don't understand that the techniques only work within the context of the solution-oriented philosophy, which takes time to assimilate.

5. Among the questions asked by critics are: Is the therapist really having a respectful conversation with a client when the therapist only praises, searches for exceptions, and coaxes optimism? Do such insistently upbeat dialogues have the effect of silencing people's doubts and their pain? Can the solution-focused therapist find a way to honor client perceptions that don't fit into the formula? Can clients trust the feedback of someone who constantly strives to find things to praise and never challenges or questions them? Can clients be honest regarding the outcome of their therapy with someone who seems to want so much for them to feel better all the time?

6. Other questions highlight the model's strengths: for example, Isn't it important for therapists to have clear, concrete guidelines so therapy doesn't become vague and directionless? Isn't it more empowering to help people envision their goals and focus on their strengths than on their problems and deficits? If people's experience of pain is tied to the way they think or talk about it, then isn't it better to use language to lead people out of pain than to dwell on it?

7. Solution-focused therapy is struggling to answer these questions and thereby find a coherent identity for the twenty-first century. We hope that this evolution won't be dictated entirely by the constraints of managed care or adherence to doctrine. Instead, we imagine that the maturing of solution-focused therapy will reflect a growing appreciation that whereas focusing on solutions can be helpful, people need acknowledgment for their lived experience, which isn't always upbeat.

─Questions to Consider─────────

1. When might it be important to understand *why* problems develop? When might this not be important?
2. See if you can find a time to inquire about exceptions when a friend tells you a problem. What did this experiment teach you?
3. What are some practical differences between accepting negative goals (i.e., to get rid of something undesirable) versus trying to come up with a positive goal (i.e., make something good happen or happen more often)?

─Key Concepts─────────

complainant   De Shazer's term for a relationship with a client who describes a complaint but is at present unwilling to work on solving it.

constructivism   A relativistic point of view that emphasizes the subjective construction of reality. Implies that what we see in families may be based as much on our preconceptions as on what's actually going on.

customer   De Shazer's term for a relationship to a client who describes a problem and is motivated to work on solving it.

exception   De Shazer's term for times when a client is temporarily free of his or her problem. Solution-focused therapists focus on exceptions to help clients build on successful problem-solving skills.

formula first-session task   Solution-focused therapists routinely ask clients at the end of the first session to think about what they *do not want to change* about their lives as a result of therapy. This focuses them on strengths in their lives and begins the solution-generating process.

miracle question   Asking clients to imagine how things would be if they woke up tomorrow and their problem was solved. Solution-focused therapists use the miracle question to help clients identify goals and potential solutions.

scaling questions   Solution-focused therapists use scaling questions to identify exceptions and to build a positive mind-set. Clients are asked on a one to ten scale, how much they want to resolve their problems, how bad the problem is, how much better it is than it was at the time of the last session, and so on. If the problem is a four the therapist can ask why it isn't a one or how the client can move it to a five.

solution-focused therapy   Steve de Shazer's term for a style of therapy that emphasizes the solutions that families have already developed for their problems.

visitor   De Shazer's term for a client who does not wish to be part of therapy, does not have a complaint, and does not wish to work on anything.

—Recommended Readings

de Shazer, S. 1988. *Clues: Investigating solutions in brief therapy.* New York: Norton.

de Shazer, S. 1991. *Putting difference to work.* New York: Norton.

Lipchik, E. 2002. *Beyond technique in solution-focused therapy.* New York: Guilford Press.

Miller, S., Hubble, M., and Duncan, B. 1995. *Handbook of solution-focused brief therapy.* San Francisco: Jossey-Bass.

Walter, J., and Peller, J. 1992. *Becoming solution-focused in brief therapy.* New York: Brunner/Mazel.

—References

Berg, I. K. 1994a. *Irreconcilable differences: A solution-focused approach to marital therapy* [Videotape]. New York: Norton.

Berg, I. K. 1994b. *Family-based services: A solution-focused approach.* New York: Norton.

Berg, I. K., and De Jong, P. 1996. Solution-building conversations: Co-constructing a sense of competence with clients. *Families in Society: The Journal of Contemporary Human Services.* June: 376–391.

Berg, I. K., and de Shazer, S. 1993. Making numbers talk: Language in therapy. In *The new language of change,* S. Friedman, ed. New York: Guilford Press.

Berg, I. K., and Dolan, Y. 2001. *Tales of solutions: A collection of hope-inspiring stories.* New York: Norton.

Berg, I. K., and Miller, S. 1992. *Working with the problem drinker: A solution-focused approach.* New York: Norton.

Butler, W., and Powers, K. 1996. Solution-focused grief therapy. In *Handbook of solution-focused brief therapy,* S. Miller, M. Hubble, and B. Duncan, eds. San Francisco: Jossey-Bass.

Cade, B., and O'Hanlon, W. 1993. *A brief guide to brief therapy.* New York: Norton.

de Shazer, S. 1984. The death of resistance. *Family Process.* 23: 11–21.

de Shazer, S. 1985. *Keys to solutions in brief therapy.* New York: Norton.

de Shazer, S. 1988. *Clues: Investigating solutions in brief therapy.* New York: Norton.

de Shazer, S. 1991. *Putting difference to work.* New York: Norton.

de Shazer, S. 1993. Creative misunderstanding: There is no escape from language. In *Therapeutic conversations,* S. Gilligan and R. Price, eds. New York: Norton.

de Shazer, S. 1994. *Words were originally magic.* New York: Norton.

de Shazer, S., and Berg, I. K. 1992. Doing therapy: A post-structural re-vision. *Journal of Marital and Family Therapy. 18:* 71–81.

Efran, J., and Schenker, M. 1993. A potpourri of solutions: How new and different is solution-focused therapy? *Family Therapy Networker. 17* (3): 71–74.

Efron, D., and Veenendaal, K. 1993. Suppose a miracle doesn't happen: The non-miracle option. *Journal of Systemic Therapies. 12:* 11–18.

Friedman, S., and Lipchik, E. 1999. A time-effective, solution-focused approach to couple therapy. In *Short-term couple therapy,* J. M. Donovan, ed. New York: Guilford Press.

Furman, B., and Ahola, T. 1992. *Solution talk: Hosting therapeutic conversations.* New York: Norton.

Hoyt, M. F. 2002. Solution-focused couple therapy. In *Clinical handbook of couple therapy.* 3rd ed., A. S. Gurman and N. S. Jacobson, eds. New York: Guilford Press.

Hudson, P., and O'Hanlon, W. H. 1992. *Rewriting love stories: Brief marital therapy.* New York: Norton.

Lipchik, E. 1992. Interview. *Journal of Strategic and Systemic Therapies. 11* (4): 22–26.

Lipchik, E. 1993. "Both/and" solutions. In *The new language of change,* S. Friedman, ed. New York: Guilford Press.

Lipchik, E. 1996. Mr. Spock goes to therapy. *Family Therapy Networker.* Jan/Feb: 79–84.

Lipchik, E. 1997. My story about solution-focused brief therapist/client relationships. *Journal of Systemic Therapies. 16:* 159–172.

Lipchik, E. 2002. *Beyond technique in solution-focused therapy.* New York: Guilford Press.

Lipchik, E., and Kubicki, A. 1996. Solution-focused domestic violence views: Bridges toward a new reality in couples therapy. In *Handbook of solution-focused brief therapy,* S. Miller, M. Hubble, and B. Duncan, eds. San Francisco: Jossey-Bass.

Metcalf, L. 1993. The pragmatics of change in solution-focused brief therapy. Unpublished doctoral dissertation, Texas Women's University, Denton, Texas.

Metcalf, L., Thomas, F., Duncan, B., Miller, S., and Hubble, M. 1996. What works in solution-focused brief therapy: A qualitative analysis of client and therapist's perceptions. In *Handbook of solution-focused brief therapy,* S. Miller, M. Hubble, and B. Duncan, eds. San Francisco: Jossey-Bass.

Miller, S. 1994. The solution-conspiracy: A mystery in three installments. *Journal of Systemic Therapies. 13:* 18–37.

Miller, S., Hubble, M., and Duncan, B. 1996. *Handbook of solution-focused brief therapy.* San Francisco: Jossey-Bass.

Nylund, D., and Corsiglia, V. 1994. Becoming solution-focused in brief therapy: Remembering something important we already knew. *Journal of Systemic Therapies. 13:* 5–12.

O'Hanlon, W. 1996. Case commentary. *Family Therapy Networker.* Jan/Feb: 84–85.

O'Hanlon, W., and Martin, M. 1992. *Solution oriented hypnosis: An Ericksonian approach.* New York: Norton.

O'Hanlon, W. H., and Weiner-Davis, M. 1989. *In search of solutions: A new direction in psycho therapy.* New York: Norton.

Storm, C. 1991. The remaining thread: Matching change and stability signals. *Journal of Strategic and Systemic Therapies. 10:* 114–117.

Walter, J., and Peller, J. 1992. *Becoming solution-focused in brief therapy.* New York: Brunner/Mazel.

Walter, J., and Peller, J. 1996. Rethinking our assumptions: Assuming anew in a postmodern world. In *Handbook of solution-focused brief therapy,* S. Miller, M. Hubble, and B. Duncan, eds. San Francisco: Jossey-Bass.

Weiner-Davis, M. 1992. *Divorce-busting.* New York: Summit Books.

Weiner-Davis, M. 1993. Pro-constructed realities. In *Therapeutic conversations,* S. Gilligan and R. Price, eds. New York: Norton.

Wittgenstein, L. 1958. *The blue and brown books.* New York: Harper & Row.

Wylie, M. S. 1990. Brief therapy on the couch. *Family Therapy Networker. 14:* 26–34, 66.

Narrative Therapy

The narrative model is a perfect expression of the postmodern revolution. When all knowledge is regarded as constructed rather than discovered, it's fitting that one leading approach to family therapy is concerned with the way people construct meanings rather than the way they behave.

The underlying premise of the narrative approach is that personal experience is fundamentally ambiguous. This doesn't mean that experience isn't real but rather that understanding human experience, including one's own, is never simply a process of seeing it. The elements of experience are understood only through a process that organizes those elements, puts them together, assigns meaning, and prioritizes them. To say that experience is fundamentally ambiguous is to say that its meaning isn't given but that it lends itself to multiple interpretations.

To illustrate how experience is shaped by the language we use to describe it, consider the difference between calling the heart-racing tension most people feel before speaking in public "stage fright" or "excitement." The first description makes this agitation a problem, something to overcome. The second suggests it's natural, an almost inevitable response to standing up in front of people whose approval you hope to win.

Whether people experience stage fright or excitement depends on how they interpret their arousal. Strategic therapists gave clients reframes—new interpretations—for their experience. "The next time you're speaking, just think of yourself as excited rather than nervous." Narrative therapists recognize that such interpretations don't take unless they fit the stories people construct about themselves. A man whose life story is that he's boring will have trouble seeing his trembling hands as due to excitement, no matter how hard someone tries to convince him. If the same man were helped to construct a new, more positive story about himself, the reframe becomes unnecessary. Once he starts to think well of himself, he'll expect people to appreciate what he has to say.

Unlike the cybernetic metaphor, which focused on self-defeating patterns of *behavior*, the narrative metaphor focuses on self-defeating *cognitions*—the stories people tell themselves about their problems. With the cybernetic metaphor, therapy meant blocking maladaptive interactions. The narrative metaphor, on the other hand, focuses on expanding clients' thinking to allow them to consider alternative ways of looking at themselves and their problems.

Stories don't just mirror life, they shape it. That's why people have the interesting habit of becoming the stories they tell about their experience. It's also why therapists in too much of a hurry to impose their own perspectives often fail—and why, by delving into people's stories, narrative therapists are able to understand and influence what makes them act as they do.

Evolution of the Model

Michael White, founder of the narrative movement, lives in Adelaide, Australia. He and his wife, Cheryl White, are based at the Dulwich Centre, out of which comes training, clinical work, and publications related to White's approach.

White initially worked as a mechanical draftsman before realizing that he preferred working with people to analyzing machines. Not surprisingly, he became staunchly anti-mechanistic and now rejects systems thinking and cybernetics.

In the late 1970s, White was drawn to the work of Gregory Bateson but found himself more interested in what Bateson said about how people map the world than in the behavioral patterns of systems-based models. Under the influence of Bateson and Michel Foucault—who criticized the dehumanizing aspects of institutions—White developed his novel ideas about how problems afflict people (regarding them as something operating on persons rather than as something they're doing).

David Epston, a family therapist from Auckland, New Zealand, is the second most influential leader of the narrative movement. Through his interest in anthropology, Epston encountered the narrative metaphor and convinced White that it was more useful for clients than cybernetics. He'd long had an interest in literature and for years was known as a storyteller, writing the "Story Corner" for the *Australian and New Zealand Journal of Family Therapy*.

Epston has contributed to most aspects of narrative theory and practice, but in particular has emphasized that to maintain their new narratives, clients need supportive communities. He fostered the development of self-help "leagues"—groups of clients battling similar problems, such as the Anti-Anorexia/Anti-Bulimia League of New Zealand. He also advocates writing letters to clients, pointing out that long after the influence of the therapist's presence has faded, clients can reread letters that bolster their new stories and resolve.

Jill Freedman and Gene Combs direct a small training center in Evanston, Illinois. Before joining the narrative camp, they were strategic therapists and social activists, drawn to White's approach in large part by its political emphasis. This combination—strategic therapy and political activism—characterizes the backgrounds of many prominent narrative therapists. Their book, *Narrative Therapy* (Freedman & Combs, 1996), is an excellent guide to narrative therapy.

Jeffrey Zimmerman and Vicki Dickerson are codirectors of the Bay Area Family Therapy Training Associates and together with John Neal conduct training in narrative therapy for the Mental Research Institute in Palo Alto. These two creative therapists pioneered the use of narrative therapy with difficult adolescents and with couples (Dickerson & Zimmerman, 1992; Zimmerman & Dickerson, 1993).

Stephan Madigan (1994; Madigan & Epston, 1995), in Vancouver, Canada, has contributed to narrative theory and is the founder of the Vancouver Anti-Anorexia/Anti-Bulimia League, a grass-roots organization that provides support and encouragement to resist media images that promote "body-guilt." Other prominent narrative therapists include Kathy Weingarten and Sallyann Roth at the Family Institute of Cambridge, and Janet Adams-Wescott in Tulsa, Oklahoma.

Harlene Anderson and the late Harry Goolishian, who developed a collaborative, conversational approach to family therapy (described in Chapter 11), can be seen as forerunners of the narrative model. Their work was based on the premise that problems are maintained in language and are subsequently dissolved through conversation. By adopting a "not-knowing" stance, Goolishian and Anderson subsumed their own expertise to allow clients to become

Michael White

Michael White began his professional life as a mechanical draftsman, but soon realized that he preferred people to machines. Following an initial attraction to the cybernetic thinking of Gregory Bateson, White became more interested in the ways people construct meaning in their lives than just with the ways they behaved.

White's innovative thinking helped shape the basic tenets of narrative therapy, which considers the broader historical, cultural, and political framework of the family. In the narrative approach, therapists try to understand how clients' personal beliefs and perceptions, or narratives, shape their self-concept and personal relationships.

the experts on their own lives. The link between this work and the narrative school was the belief that conversation generates meaning and that therapy should be a collaborative enterprise.

The Basic Model

The narrative approach first found its way into psychotherapy in the **hermeneutic** tradition in psychoanalysis. Following Freud, classical analysts believed that there was one correct way to interpret experience. Patients might not understand their dreams or symptoms because their motives were unconscious, but an analyst possessed of the truth of psychoanalytic theory could discover unconscious meaning much like an archaeologist uncovers the buried remains of the past. Then in the 1980s, revisionists such as Donald Spence, Roy Schafer, and Paul Ricoeur began to argue against this positivistic conception of psychoanalytic reality.

The truth of experience, they said, isn't discovered; it's created. The goal of therapy shifted from historical truth to narrative intelligibility.

The challenge was to construct truths in the service of self-coherence—not a true picture of the past. The therapist became more of a novelist than an archaeologist.

Family therapists found this narrative metaphor extremely useful. As they began to ask clients about their lives, therapists came to recognize how much narrative accounts affected perceptions and interpretations of those perceptions. Life stories function as filters that screen out experiences that don't fit the plot line or, if they can't be screened out, distort events until they somehow do fit. Consider the following example:

According to Tim, Kayla was never satisfied. All she did was complain. Their apartment, the furniture, her wardrobe—nothing was ever good enough. No matter what they had, she wanted more.

Kayla had no idea what Tim was talking about. She was, in fact, perfectly content. Well, except maybe for one thing. Every time she'd see a picture in a magazine of a beautiful sofa or a pretty dress, she'd point it out to Tim. "Wow, look at that," she'd say, "maybe we should get one of those." She was just dreaming out loud. But to Tim, who was brought up never to ask for anything, Kayla's fantasies felt like complaints. Notice, however, that it wasn't so much what Kayla said that hurt Tim, but how he interpreted it.

Looking deeper, it turned out that Tim was never satisfied with his own accomplishments. Growing up with a mother who wasn't given to praise, Tim dreamt of someday doing great things. Unfortunately, his own very real achievements never lived up to his expectations. Sure, other people praised him, but he still secretly dreamed the grand and glorious dreams of childhood.

Until he could begin to accept himself, it was hard for Tim to believe that anyone else could truly appreciate him. Trying to get such a man to change his behavior without addressing his controlling life story is futile, because no matter how many successes he has, he'll still find ways to dismiss them and continue to dwell on his failures—and his partner's (presumed) dissatisfaction.

Narrative theory is put into practice by therapists who (1) take a keen interest in their clients' stories; (2) search for times in their histories when they were strong or resourceful; (3) use questions to take a nonimposing, respectful approach to any new story put forth; (4) never label people but treat them as human beings with unique personal histories; and (5) help people separate from the dominant cultural narratives they have internalized so as to open space for alternative life stories (White, 1995; Freedman & Combs, 1996).

Narrative therapists oppose the functionalist elements in family systems and psychoanalytic models, which imply that problems are inherent in individuals (as psychoanalysis would have it) or families (as family systems would have it). Instead, they believe that problems arise because people are indoctrinated into narrow and self-defeating views of themselves and the world.

To counter the way society convinces people that they are their problems, narrative therapists **externalize** problems. Instead of *having* a problem or *being* a problem, they encourage clients to think of themselves as struggling *against* their problems. Neither the patient nor the family is the problem; the problem is the problem. Accordingly, narrative therapists aren't interested in problem-maintaining interactions or structural flaws. They aren't interested in the family's impact on the problem but rather in the problem's impact on the family.

As narrative therapists shifted their attention from families as the source of problems to cultural beliefs and practices, they turned to the writings of Michel Foucault (1965, 1980), the

Family arguments are often fueled by negative story lines about other family members.

French social philosopher, who devoted his life to exposing how various social discourses objectified and dehumanized various marginalized groups. Foucault not only believed that those constructing the dominant narratives in a society (those deemed to have expert knowledge) had the power to subjugate, but that the narratives themselves become internalized truths, such that people come to judge their bodies, achievements, and personalities on the basis of standards set by society's judges (doctors, educators, clergy, psychotherapists, politicians, celebrities). Thus, Foucault influenced White to take the **social constructionist** axiom that there are no absolute truths in the world in a political direction, toward deconstructing (reexamining) established truths that oppress people's lives.

Narrative therapists applied Foucault's political analysis to understand how individuals and families are dominated by oppressive narratives from which they need liberation. They drew from the work of Jerome Bruner (1986, 1991) to understand how personal narratives are constructed and can be deconstructed.[1]

Normal Family Development

Narrative therapists not only avoid judgments about what is normal, they reject the very idea of categorizing people. Recall how Foucault criticized the way theories of normality have been used to perpetuate patterns of privilege and oppression. Too often in human history the judgments made by people in power regarding normality and abnormality have been used to subjugate those with no voice in the matter.

While it's easy to see the dangers of reducing people to DSM-IV diagnoses, family therapists may have trouble seeing their own concepts, such as *rigid boundaries, cross-generational coali-*

tions, or *differentiation of self,* as dehumanizing. But becoming a postmodern narrative therapist means giving up all such categories. Not only do they avoid pigeonholing people by diagnosis or normality and abnormality, they also avoid general principles about what causes problems or what resolves them. They try not to stand over people in judgment—in any way—but instead strive to help them make sense of their own experience.

In the spirit of collaboration, narrative therapists endeavor to "situate" themselves with clients—that is, disclose the beliefs that inform their therapy so that clients can know what they're getting into. Clients are also encouraged to educate therapists regarding their cultural predicaments and to correct them when they make assumptions that don't fit their experience (Freedman & Combs, 1996).

Although narrative therapists try not to make judgments, it may be impossible not to have some assumptions about people and how they change. From the ideas described in the previous section we can distill certain basic assumptions narrative therapists make about normal families. People (1) have good intentions—they don't need or want problems; (2) are profoundly influenced by the discourses around them: (3) are not their problems; and (4) can develop alternative, empowering stories once separated from their problems and from the common wisdom they have internalized.

Development of Behavior Disorders

When the stories people tell themselves lead them to construe their experience in unhelpful ways, they tend to get bogged down with problems. Such problems are likely to persist as long as these unhelpful stories remain fixed, obscuring more optimistic versions of events.

Thus, for example, a single mother whose life narrative is that she can't trust that anyone loves her reacts furiously whenever her daughter breaks curfew. This narrative makes the mother notice all the times her daughter stays out late or leaves cigarette butts on the

---

1. The term *deconstructionism* is most closely associated with Jacques Derida (1992), who analyzed literary texts to show that they had no one true meaning. Narrative therapists use the term in a political way, as subverting dominant discourses, whereas Derida's intent was more relativistic.

porch and not notice the times when she gets her homework done or volunteers to wash the dishes. Each of the daughter's transgressions confirms the mother's story line that, like everyone else in her life, her daughter doesn't really love her. The daughter, in turn, is keenly aware of how often her mother criticizes her friends or explodes over small mistakes, but doesn't remember the times her mother showed respect for her opinion or praised her achievements. The daughter gradually develops a narrative around never being able to satisfy people and becomes increasingly controlled by "rebelliousness," which makes her not care what her mother thinks, and instead indulge in whatever makes her feel better, like partying late into the night. In short, both sides remain stuck not simply in a pattern of control and rebellion but, more specifically, of noticing only incidents of control or rebellion.

This analysis might not sound all that different from one which other schools of family therapy might make of an escalating cycle of antagonism between a mother and a daughter. The difference is that the narrative approach doesn't focus on behavior. Narrative therapists reject the cybernetic notion that the mother and daughter are stuck in a dysfunctional feedback loop—acting and reacting to each other in unhelpful ways. Instead, they concentrate on the way mother and daughter narrate their exchange. It's their stories (being unloved, being picked on) that affect not only what they notice (lateness, scolding) but also how they interpret it.

Narrative therapists refer to these patterns of tunnel vision as **problem-saturated stories,** which, once they take hold, encourage people to respond to each other in ways that perpetuate the problem story. As long as they focus on their children's misbehavior, parents will concentrate on criticizing and controlling them. As long as they think of their parents as hassling them, youngsters are likely to remain reactive and rebellious. Their responses to each other become invitations to more of the same and support further hardening of problem stories.

Such closed and rigid narratives make people vulnerable to being overtaken by destructive emotional states that narrative therapists like to portray as alien invaders. Narrative therapists don't really see problematic feelings or beliefs as external entities, but they do believe that such emotional responses *are* external in the sense that they are socially constructed. Externalizing problems cuts down on guilt and blame. The daughter isn't the problem, "rebelliousness" is. Mother isn't the problem, "oversensitivity" is. Mother and daughter can unite to combat rebelliousness and oversensitivity rather than each other.

Instead of looking inside families for the source of their problems, narrative therapists look outside to the toxic effects of the cultural narratives that govern our lives. In Michael White's (1995) words,

> The discourses of pathology make it possible for us to ignore the extent to which the problems for which people seek therapy are the outcome of certain practices of relationship and practices of the self, many of which are actually informed by modern notions of "individualism" . . . [and] are so often mired in the structures of inequality of our culture, including those pertaining to gender, race, ethnicity, class, economics, age, and so on. (p. 115)

Anorexia nervosa, for example, can be viewed as an internalization of our obsession with thinness and the worship of self-discipline. By seeing women who starve themselves as having a disease or a dysfunctional family, we not only ignore the bigger picture but also avoid having to confront our own participation in these cultural stereotypes.

How Therapy Works

Narrative therapists aren't problem solvers. Instead, they help people separate themselves from problem-saturated stories (and destructive cultural assumptions) to open space for new and more constructive views of themselves. Narrative therapy transforms identities from flawed to heroic, not by getting family members to confront their conflicts but by separating persons from problems and then uniting the family to fight a common enemy. It's also done by combing the family's history for **unique outcomes** or "sparkling events"—times when they resisted the problem or behaved in ways that contradicted the problem story.

If Alice sees herself as "codependent" because of the way she relates to men, a narrative therapist wouldn't explore the reasons for this condition or offer suggestions for altering this pattern. Instead, she would ask questions about the effect of *"Self-blame"* on her life, ask family members to help her defeat *Self-blame*, and highlight times in her life when she related to men in ways she prefers. She might also invite Alice to explore how our society's view of women contributed to *Self-blame's* grip on her life.

Thus, narrative therapists see their work as a political enterprise—freeing people from oppressive cultural assumptions and empowering them to become active authors of their own lives. Once liberated from problem-saturated stories, family members can unite with one another and with communities of support to deal with their problems with more optimism and persistence.

Therapy

Assessment

Narrative therapy works by helping clients **deconstruct** unproductive stories in order to **reconstruct** new and more productive ones. *Deconstruction,* a term borrowed from literary criticism, means questioning assumptions. Narrative therapists externalize problems from persons as one way to deconstruct disempowering assumptions. Rather than discuss "Sally's laziness," for example, they'll inquire about times when *"Procrastination* takes hold of her." Once a problem is externalized and redefined in more experience-near terms, the person can begin to resist it. By viewing the problem as an external entity, narrative therapists free families to challenge its influence on their lives.

After externalizing the problem narrative therapists ask about "unique outcomes"—times when clients resisted the problem's influence. Unique outcomes open room for counterplots, new and more empowering ways of constructing events. A man who identifies himself as depressed sees his life through a glass darkly. Depression becomes a career, a lifestyle. But if the man begins to think of, say, *"Self-doubt* getting the best of him,*"* then he may be able to remember times when he didn't let *Self-doubt* get him down. These newly attended-to times of effectiveness provide openings around which to weave a new and more optimistic story.

Just as externalization is used to shift clients' perceptions of themselves, narrative therapists also endeavor to shift family members' perceptions of each other from "totalizing views" (reducing them to one set of frustrating responses) that lead to antagonism and polarization. Thus parents who see their teenagers as "irresponsible"—as though that were the sum total of their being—are likely to be seen in return as "too critical." Likewise, parents who totalize their children as "lazy" may be seen as "bossy" or "demanding." As long as both sides remain fixed in such polarized perspectives, they may be too preoccupied to think about their own preferences. In unhappy families, people may be so busy *not* being what others expect that they have no time to figure out how they themselves want to be.

Michael White sets an inspiring example of seeing the best in people even when they've lost faith in themselves. He's famous for his persistence in questioning negative stories. He just won't allow people to slip away into their misery. You can tell that he is absolutely convinced that people are not their problems. His voice, his posture, his whole being radiates possibility and hope.

The tenacious confidence in people that narrative therapists convey with genuine respect and caring is contagious. As clients come to trust their therapist, they can borrow that confidence and use it in dealing with their problems.

Therapeutic Techniques

Narrative interventions are delivered in the form of questions. They almost never assert anything or make interpretations. They just ask question after question, often repeating the answers and writing them down.

In the first session, narrative therapists begin by finding out how people spend their time. This gives the therapist a chance to appreciate how clients see themselves, without getting into a lengthy history, and the attributions of blame so frequently a part of such histories. They pay special attention to people's talents and competencies. As a further means of establishing a collaborative atmosphere, Zimmerman and Dickerson (1996) encourage clients to ask any questions they might have about the therapists. They also invite clients to read their notes if they wish. And they take notes as each person talks, which not only helps them retain important points, but also gives clients a sense that their point of view is respected.

Externalizing: The Person Is Not the Problem.   Narrative therapists begin by asking clients to tell their problem-saturated story, and they listen long enough to convey their appreciation for what the family has been going through. After a sense of trust has been established, the therapist begins asking questions that externalize the problem and make its destructive effects apparent.

From the outset, the problem is seen as separate from people and as influencing them—"*It* brought them there"—and each person is asked for his or her own perspective on *It*. Externalizing language is used from the beginning. One way of doing this is to ask about the problem's effects rather than its causes (causative questions usually lead to attributions of blame), or "mapping the influence of the problem." "How does *Guilt* affect you?" "What other effects does it have?" "What does *Guilt* 'tell' you?"

The therapist's questions about the identified problem imply that it isn't possessed by anyone but instead is trying to possess them. For exam-

ple, in a case where parents describe the problem as a lack of trust in their daughter because of her sneakiness, the therapist doesn't reflect back, "So your daughter's sneakiness bothers you." Instead the therapist might say, "So *Sneakiness* made your daughter act in ways that caused a rift between you, is that right?"

Sometimes whole patterns of interaction are externalized. For example, in the case in which a teenager's parents were responding to her sneakiness with increasing control, Vicki Dickerson chose to highlight the rift that was encouraging this pattern—because one thing they could all agree on was that they didn't like the breach that was splitting them apart. Thus, instead of identifying the daughter's sneakiness or the parents' distrust as the problem, the *Rift* became the enemy that encouraged sneakiness and control. The *Rift* told the parents that their daughter couldn't be trusted; the *Rift* made the daughter more secretive and told her to pull away from her parents. The *Rift* was something they could join forces against (Zimmerman & Dickerson, 1996).

Problems are always personified—portrayed as unwelcome invaders that try to dominate people's lives. For example, while discussing her eating problems, a woman is asked how *Anorexia* convinces her to starve herself. A phobic child is asked how often *Fear* is able to make him do what it wants and how often he is able to stand up to it. A guilt-ridden mother is asked how *Self-hate* is making her feel bad about her parenting.

The following are examples of externalizing questions (adapted from Freedman & Combs, 2002):

"What feeds the problem?"
"What starves it?"
"Who benefits from it?"
"Who would justify or defend the problem?"
"Who would definitely be opposed to the problem and its intentions?"

This line of questioning can be disconcerting, unaccustomed as most people are to talking about imaginary entities in their households. Therapists who treat externalization merely as a gimmick may lack the conviction necessary to overcome the awkwardness of talking this way. On the other hand, therapists will find that externalizing questions flow naturally if they actually learn to think of problems as enemies that feed on polarizations and misunderstanding. White suggests that problems are dependent on their effects for their survival, so by standing up to a problem and not allowing it to affect them, clients cut off the problem's "life-support system."

Sallyann Roth and David Epston (1996) developed an exercise to help therapists grasp what it's like to think of problems as external. They have a group of trainees take turns being a problem—such as *Self-hatred*—while others interview them. The interviewers might ask the person playing *Self-hatred* such questions as: "Under what circumstances do you manage to get into X's world?" "How are you intervening in the lives of X's family and friends?"

Externalizing, by itself, can have a powerful impact. Over time, people become identified with their problems. They believe that the problem's existence is proof of their flawed character. This way of thinking poisons confidence. When the problem is externalized, it's as if the person can peek out from behind it; family members can see the healthier person that the problem has been hiding from them.

Bill no longer *is* a depressed person; instead, he is overcome at times by *Depression*, an antagonist he dislikes as much as his family does. As the therapist queries him about *Depression's* tactics and effects, Bill becomes motivated to fight back.

Who's In Charge, the Person or the Problem? Therapists ask a multitude of questions over many sessions that explore how the problem has managed to disrupt or dominate the family versus how much they have been able to control it. These are called **relative influence questions.** By including all family members in the discussion it usually becomes clear that the problem has succeeded in disturbing their relationships with each other—dividing and conquering them.

"How much has the *Bulimia* that's taken over Jenny kept you from being the way you want to be with her?" "When *Depression* gets the better of Dad, how does that affect family life?" "When *Tantrums* convince Joey to yell and scream, do you think your response gives *Tantrums* more or less fuel?"

Reading between the Lines of the Problem Story. While asking relative influence questions, the therapist listens for "sparkling events" or unique outcomes when clients were able to avoid the problem's effects and then asks for elaboration on how that was done:

"Can you remember a time when *Anger* tried to take you over, but you didn't let it? How did you do that?" "Have there been times when your daughter didn't believe the lies *Anorexia* tells her about her body?" "When Jenny has withstood the tremendous pressure she feels from *Alcoholism*, have you appreciated the magnitude of that accomplishment?" These unique outcomes become the building blocks of new, more heroic stories.

Reauthoring the Whole Story. Evidence of competence relative to the problem, gathered from sifting through the client's history, can serve as the start of new narratives regarding what kind of person he or she is. To make this connection, the therapist begins by asking about what the series of past and present victories over the problem say about the client. For example: "What does it say about you as a person that you were able to defeat *Depression* on those occasions?" "What qualities of character must your son possess to be able to do that?" The therapist can also expand the historical purview beyond episodes relating to the problem to find more evidence to bolster the new self-narrative. "What else can you tell me about your past that helps me understand how you were able to handle *Anger* so well?" "Who knew you as a child who wouldn't be surprised that you have been able to stand up to *Fear* on these occasions?"

As the new self-narrative begins to take shape, the therapist can shift the focus to the future, inviting the client or family to envision the upcoming changes that will fit the new story. "Now that you've discovered these things about yourself, how do you think these discoveries will affect your relationship with *Self-hate?*" The self-story now has a past, present, and future—it's a complete narrative.

Reinforcing the New Story.   Because they believe that the self is constituted in social interaction and, therefore, that people are susceptible to having their new stories undermined by the same contexts that bred the old ones, narrative therapists make a point of helping clients find an audience to support their progress in constructing new stories for themselves.

Clients might be asked to contact people from their past who can authenticate their new story—who can confirm and add to examples of the person's acting capably. Clients are also encouraged to recruit people in their lives who can serve as supportive witnesses to their new story. Sometimes "leagues" are formed, support groups of people with similar problems to reinforce one another's efforts to resist the problem. For example, the Vancouver Anti-Anorexia/Anti-Bulimia League (Madigan, 1994) has a newsletter and monitors the media, writing letters to company presidents, newspapers, and magazines that portray an emaciated ideal for women and encourage them to diet.

David Epston has pioneered the use of letter writing to extend the therapeutic conversation beyond the consultation room. These letters often convey a deep appreciation of what the client has endured, the outline of a new story, and the therapist's confidence in the client's ability to continue to progress. The advantage of this form of communication is that the words in a letter don't vanish the way words do after a conversation. Clients have reported to Epston that they regularly reread letters he sent them years earlier to remind themselves what they went through and how far they have come (Epston, 1994).

All of these efforts—recruiting authenticators and audiences, forming teams and leagues,

writing letters and making certificates—are in keeping with the social constructionist emphasis on interaction in creating and maintaining change. For people to solidify new identities, they need communities that confirm and reinforce re-visioned narratives and counter cultural and family messages to the contrary. What happens in a session is just a beginning, because the goal isn't merely to solve a problem; it's to change a whole way of thinking and living.

At the end of each session, narrative therapists summarize what happened, making sure to use externalizing language and emphasizing any unique outcomes that were mentioned. These summaries are what Epston often puts into his letters to clients. The effect of these reviews is to convey to clients that the therapist is with them and celebrates their blossoming new identity. This sense of being cheered on by the therapist can be extremely encouraging.

Deconstructing Destructive Cultural Assumptions.   At times, narrative therapists make the connection to cultural narratives more explicit. For example, an anorexic woman might be asked how she was recruited into the belief that her worth depended on her appearance. This would lead to other questions regarding the position of women in our society. Similarly, a violent man might be asked how he came to believe that men should never be weak or tender, and a deconstructing of the messages men receive would ensue.

To clarify what this deconstructing of cultural attitudes might look like, we present one of White's cases as described by Mary Sikes Wylie (1994):

John . . . came to see White because, says White, "he was a man who never cried"—he had never been able to express his emotions—and he felt isolated and cut off from his own family. As a child, John had been taught, both at home and at his Australian grammar school, that any show of gentleness or "softness" was unmanly and would be met with harsh punishment and brutal public humiliation. White asks John a series of questions that are at once political and personal, eliciting information about the man's "private" psychological suffering and linking it to the "public" cultural practices, rigidly sexist and aggressively macho, that dominated his youth. "How were you recruited into these thoughts and habits [of feeling inadequate, not sufficiently masculine, etc.]? What was the training ground for these feelings? Do you think the rituals of humiliation [public caning by school authorities, ridicule by teachers and students for not being good at sports or sufficiently hard and tough] alienated you from your own life? Were they disqualifications of you? Did these practices help or hinder you in recognizing a different way of being a male?" (p. 43)

After deconstructing the masculine image in this way, White helped John to remember times when he resisted it and to recognize the nobility of his efforts to remain gentle and loving despite his socialization.

A Case of Sneaky Poo. White's therapy comes to life in his case descriptions, as in the following excerpt from his description of a family with an encopretic child (White, 1989).

—Case Study—

When mapping the influence of family members in the life of what we came to call "Sneaky Poo," we discovered that:

1. Although Sneaky Poo always tried to trick Nick into being his playmate, Nick could recall a number of occasions during which he had not allowed Sneaky Poo to "outsmart" him. These were occasions during which Nick could have cooperated by "smearing," "streaking," or "plastering," but he declined to do so. He had not allowed himself to be tricked into this.
2. There was a recent occasion during which Sneaky Poo could have driven Sue into a heightened sense of misery, but she resisted and turned on the stereo instead. Also, on this occasion, she refused to question her competence as a parent and as a person.

3. Ron could not recall an occasion during which he had not allowed the embarrassment caused by Sneaky Poo to isolate him from others. However, after Sneaky Poo's requirements of him were identified, he did seem interested in the idea of defying these requirements....
4. ... It was established that there was an aspect to Sue's relationship with Nick that she thought she could still enjoy, that Ron was still making some attempts to persevere in his relationship with Nick, and that Nick had an idea that Sneaky Poo had not destroyed all of the love in his relationship with his parents.

After identifying Nick's, Sue's, and Ron's influence in the life of Sneaky Poo, I introduced questions that encouraged them to perform meaning in relation to these examples, so that they might "re-author" their lives and relationships.

How had they managed to be effective against the problem in this way? How did this reflect on them as people and on their relationships?... Did this success give them any ideas about further steps that they might take to reclaim their lives from the problem?... In response to these questions, Nick thought that he was ready to stop Sneaky Poo from outsmarting him so much, and decided that he would not be tricked into being its playmate anymore.... (pp. 10–11)

Two weeks later White found that Nick had fought Sneaky Poo valiantly, having only one minor episode, and he seemed happier and stronger. Sue and Ron had also done their parts in the battle. In her effort to not cooperate with Sneaky Poo's requirements for her to feel guilty, Sue had begun to "treat herself" when Sneaky Poo was getting her down, and Ron had fought Sneaky Poo's attempts to keep him isolated by talking to friends about the problem.

I encouraged the family to reflect on and to speculate about what this success said about the qualities that they possessed as people and about the attributes of their relationships. I also encouraged them to review what these facts suggested about their current relationship with Sneaky Poo. In this discussion, family members identified further measures that they could take to decline Sneaky Poo's invitations to them to support it. (p. 11)

White reports that the family expanded these efforts in the interim, and by the third session they felt confident that Sneaky Poo had been defeated. At a six-month follow-up they were still doing well.

Current Status of the Model

By externalizing problems, deconstructing pessimistic life stories, and conveying unswerving confidence in their clients, narrative therapists have constructed a powerful recipe for change. Packaging interventions in the form of questions makes their input less like advice to be resisted and fosters a sense of partnership with clients.

The two most powerful ingredients in narrative therapy are the narrative metaphor itself and the technique of externalizing problems. The strength and weakness of the narrative approach is its cognitive focus. In rejecting the cybernetic model—families stuck in dysfunctional feedback loops—narrative therapists repudiated the idea that families with problems have something wrong with them. Unfortunately, they also turned their backs on the three defining innovations of family therapy: (1) recognizing that psychological symptoms are often related to family conflict; (2) thinking about human problems as interactional, which means thinking in terms of twos (complementarity, reciprocity) and threes (triangles); and (3) treating the family as a unit.

Treating problems as stories to be deconstructed overlooks the fact that some families have real conflicts that don't disappear because they join together temporarily to fight an externalized problem. For example, parents whose lives are empty may have trouble letting their children grow up. Does that emptiness evaporate after they help their children battle *Rebelliousness*?

In the process of helping people restory their experience, narrative therapists often subscribe to a view of unhappy emotions—anger, fear, anxiety, depression—as annoyances to avoid rather than explore. They ask how anger or fear "defeats" clients but rarely why clients are angry or what they are afraid of.

Early versions of family therapy *did* cast families in a bad light and blamed them for maintaining problems. The narrative movement has helped shift the field toward more respect and collaboration with families. In the process of rejecting the patronizing consciousness of that earlier age, however, narrative therapists have rejected systems thinking, emphasizing its mechanistic elements while ignoring more humanistic versions. One of family therapy's greatest contributions was to bring a contextual understanding of people and their problems to psychotherapy. Nonsystemic therapists, influenced by the disease model, had encouraged people to fight problems (with medication, support groups, education) rather than explore the network of relationships in which their problems were embedded. Although opposed to the disease model, narrative therapists return to a similarly acontextual view of problems as things to be fought, and they eschew efforts to understand their ecological contexts.

In looking beyond families to the cultural assumptions in which they are embedded, narrative therapists have given a political cast to their work. Most narrative therapists would agree with Vicki Dickerson's statement that narrative therapy is "primarily about situating problems in their cultural context" (Freedman, 1996). That is, it's about helping clients identify and challenge the ubiquitous, but commonly unexamined, prescriptions that permeate society and make self-worth and harmonious relating difficult at best. But how does one do that without imposing one's own political biases?

Although some therapists still make a case for strict therapeutic neutrality, many now agree that it is sometimes necessary to question invidious cultural assumptions. It's true that popular culture promotes many unhelpful values. The question is, what is the best way to help people free themselves from those influences without imposing one's own values? This is a complex problem, and narrative therapy answers it one way. We hope that example inspires all family therapists to grapple with this issue.

—Summary—

1. The narrative approach is built around two organizing metaphors: personal narrative and social construction. When memory speaks it tells a "narrative truth," which comes to have more influence than "historical truth." The "facts" presented to a therapist are partly historical and partly constructions. The constructions that make up the shared reality of a family represent mutual understandings and shared prejudices, some of which are useful, some of which are not.

2. Narrative therapists seek to break the grip of unhelpful stories by *externalizing* problems. By challenging pessimistic versions of events, therapists make room for flexibility and hope. Uncovering *unique outcomes* provides an opening through which new and more optimistic stories can be envisioned. Finally, clients are encouraged to create audiences of support to witness and promote their progress in restorying their lives along preferred lines.

3. The strategies of narrative therapy fall into three stages: (1) the problem narrative stage: recasting the problem as an affliction (*externalizing*) by focusing on its effects rather than its causes; (2) finding exceptions: partial triumphs over the problem and instances of effective action; and (3) the recruitment of support. Encouraging some kind of public ritual to reinforce new and preferred interpretations moves cognitive constructions past private insight into socially supported action.

4. The tactics by which these strategies are put into practice involve an elaborate series of questions:

5. *Deconstruction Questions*—Externalizing the problem. "What does *Depression* whisper in your ear?" "What conclusions about your relationship have you drawn because of this problem?"

6. *Opening Space Questions*—Uncovering unique outcomes. "Has there ever been a time when *Arguing* could have taken control of your relationship but didn't?"

7. *Preference Questions*—Making sure unique outcomes represent preferred experiences. "Was this way of handling things better or worse?" "Was that a positive or a negative development?"

8. *Story Development Questions*—To develop a new story from the seeds of (preferred) unique outcomes. "How is this different from what you would have done before?" "Who played a part in this way of doing things?" "Who will be the first to notice these positive changes in you?"

9. *Meaning Questions*—Designed to challenge negative images of self and to emphasize positive agency. "What does it say about you that you were able to do that?"

10. *Questions to Extend the Story into the Future*—To support changes and reinforce positive developments. "What do you predict for the coming year?"

11. The social constructionist foundation of narrative therapy gives the approach its political cast and deemphasizes family dynamics and conflict. Instead of looking within families for dysfunctional interactions, narrative therapists look outside for destructive influences of various cultural values and institutions. They invite family members to pull together to oppose these values and practices. Instead of neutrality, they offer advocacy.

Questions to Consider

1. Re-read the cases in this chapter to see when you think narrative therapists do too much leading and not enough following of the client's narrative.
2. How relevant are social and political concerns to the practice of therapy?
3. How might it be possible to incorporate systems thinking into the practice of narrative therapy?
4. How might "externalizing" problems detract from a client's personal responsibility? And how can you avoid this happening?
5. In what, if any, ways do the actual interventions of narrative therapy differ from other cognitive approaches?

Key Concepts

deconstruction   A postmodern approach to exploring meaning by taking apart and examining taken-for-granted categories and assumptions, making possible newer and sounder constructions of meaning.

externalization   Michael White's technique of personifying problems as external to persons.

hermeneutics   The art of analyzing literary texts or human experience, understood as fundamentally ambiguous, by interpreting levels of meaning.

problem-saturated stories   The usual pessimistic and blaming accounts that clients bring to therapy, which are seen as helping keep them stuck.

reconstruction   The creation of new and more optimistic accounts of experience.

relative influence questions   Questions designed to explore the extent to which the problem has dominated the client versus how much he or she has been able to control it.

social constructionism   Like constructivism, challenges the notion of an objective basis for knowledge. Knowledge and meaning are shaped by culturally shared assumptions.

unique outcomes   Michael White's term for times when clients acted free of their problems, even if they were unaware of doing so. Narrative therapists identify unique outcomes as a way to help clients challenge negative views of themselves.

Recommended Readings

Bruner, J. S. 1986. *Actual minds, possible worlds.* Cambridge, MA: Harvard University Press.

Diamond, J. 2002. *Narrative means to sober ends: Treating addiction and its aftermath.* New York: Guilford Press.

Dickerson, V. C., and Zimmerman, J. 1992. Families with adolescents: Escaping problem lifestyles. *Family Process.* 31: 341–353.

Eron, J., and Lund, T. 1996. *Narrative solutions in brief therapy.* New York: Guilford Press.

Freedman, J. H., and Combs, G. 1996. *Narrative therapy: The social construction of preferred realities.* New York: Norton.

Gilligan, S., and Price, R. 1993. *Therapeutic conversations.* New York: Norton.

Minuchin, S. 1998. Where is the family in narrative family therapy? *Journal of Marital and Family Therapy.* 24: 397–403.

White, M. 1989. *Selected papers.* Adelaide, Australia: Dulwich Centre Publications.

White, M. 1995. *Re-authoring lives: Interviews and essays.* Adelaide, South Australia: Dulwich Centre Publications.

White, M., and Epston, D. 1990. *Narrative means to therapeutic ends.* New York: Norton.

Zimmerman, J., and Dickerson, V. 1996. *If problems talked: Adventures in narrative therapy.* New York: Guilford Press.

—References————————

Bruner, J. S. 1986. *Actual minds, possible worlds.* Cambridge, MA: Harvard University Press.

Bruner, J. S. 1991. The narrative construction of reality. *Critical Inquiry. 18:* 1–21.

Derida, J. 1992. In *Derrida: A critical reader,* D. Wood, ed. Oxford: Blackwell.

Dickerson, V., and Zimmerman, J. 1992. Families with adolescents: Escaping problem lifestyles. *Family Process. 31:* 341–353.

Epston, D. 1994. Extending the conversation. *Family Therapy Networker. 18:* 30–37, 62.

Foucault, M. 1965. *Madness and civilization: A history of insanity in the age of reason.* New York: Random House.

Foucault, M. 1980. *Power/knowledge: Selected interviews and other writings.* New York: Pantheon.

Freedman, J. H., 1996. AFTA voices on the annual meeting. *AFTA Newsletter.* Fall: 30–32.

Freedman, J. H., and Combs, G. 1996. *Narrative therapy: The social construction of preferred realities.* New York: Norton.

Freedman, J. H., and Combs, G. 2002. Narrative couple therapy. In *Clinical handbook of couple therapy,* 3rd ed., A. S. Gurman and N. S. Jacobson, eds. New York: Guilford Press.

Madigan, S. 1994. Body politics. *Family Therapy Networker. 18:* 27.

Madigan, S., and Epston, D. 1995. From "psy-chiatric gaze" to communities of concern: From professional monologue to dialogue. In *The reflecting team in action,* S. Friedman, ed. New York: Guilford Press.

Roth, S. A., and Epston, D. 1996. Developing externalizing conversations: An introductory exercise. *Journal of Systemic Therapies. 15:* 5–12.

White, M. 1989. *Selected papers.* Adelaide, Australia: Dulwich Centre Publications.

White, M. 1995. *Re-authoring lives: Interviews and essays.* Adelaide, Australia: Dulwich Centre Publications.

Wylie, M. S. 1994. Panning for gold. *Family Therapy Networker. 18:* 40–48.

Zimmerman, J., and Dickerson, V. 1993. Bringing forth the restraining influence of pattern in couples therapy. In *Therapeutic conversations,* S. Gilligan and R. Price, eds. New York: Norton.

Zimmerman, J., and Dickerson, V. 1996. *If problems talked: Adventures in narrative therapy.* New York: Guilford Press.

Integrative Models

In breaking with the dominant paradigm of the time, the first family therapists defined themselves in opposition to all things psychoanalytic. Did psychoanalysis maintain that behavior was an artifact of unconscious forces, that family relationships were a function of individual psychodynamics, and that only insight brought about lasting change? Then family therapists would insist that behavior could be understood without reference to "the ghost in the machine," that an individual's behavior was dictated by the structure of the family, and that "insight" was unnecessary to problem solving.

Similarly, as they worked out the implications of their own insights, the various schools of family therapy emphasized not only their own strengths but also their differences with each other. Bowen sought to reason with family members one at a time; Minuchin insisted that the way to get at relationships was to have people talk to each other. The new schools aren't immune from this us-against-them mentality; on the contrary, solution-focused and narrative therapists have made a point of rejecting some of the defining features of the traditional schools. They are anti-mechanistic, decidedly not behavioral, and they pretty much ignore conflict as a source of family problems.

For this very reason, radical revisionists often remain trapped within old categories. They represent an antithesis, not a synthesis; and they are condemned to the dispensability of all partial and polemical views. Just as it took systems therapists years to get over their denigration of psychodynamics, it will probably take time for these postmodernists to bring back what we've learned about family dynamics to their work.

In any field of endeavor, it seems that integration is only possible after a period of differentiation. It's no surprise then, that in the early years of family therapy, when the energies of the emerging schools were devoted to differentiating themselves, the idea of *integration* had a negative connotation—it was seen as a watering down, rather than an enrichment, of the classic models.

During the past decade, however, there has been a growing awareness that no single approach has a monopoly on clinical effectiveness. The time of distinct and competitive schools of family therapy has passed. As family therapy enters the twenty-first century, the dominant trend is integration.

When it's described as respect for the multiplicity of truth, integration seems like an unassailably good idea. The obvious argument for incorporating elements from different approaches is that human beings are complicated—thinking, feeling, and acting—creatures who exist in a complex system of biological, psychological, and social influences. No therapy can succeed without having an impact on all of these dimensions. There is, however, an equally valid argument that eclecticism can rob therapy of the intensity made possible by focusing on one or two elements of experience. There may be many ways to skin a cat, but it might not be advisable to try all of them at once.

As we see in this chapter, "integration" refers to three very different kinds of approaches. First there is **eclecticism,** which draws from a variety of models and methods. Second is **selective borrowing,** in which relative purists use a few techniques from other approaches. Third are **specially designed integrative models.** Of these there are theoretical models that draw on several influences, including, for example, the integrative approaches of William Nichols (1996) and Bill Pinsof (1995); pragmatic models that combine elements of two complementary approaches, such as Eron and Lund's (1996) narrative solutions therapy and Jacobson and Christensen's (1996) integrative couples therapy; and integrative models developed for specific clinical problems, such as Virginia Goldner and Gillian Walker's couples therapy for marital violence (Goldner, 1998).

Eclecticism

One of the advantages of graduate training is that students are exposed to a variety of approaches and taught to think critically about them. On the other hand, graduate schools sometimes produce better critics than clinicians.

What do you do in the first session? Try to make sure that everyone attends, greet each of them, and try to make them comfortable. Ask about the presenting problem, of course, but then what? Suppose a mother says that her fourteen-year-old has become rude and disrespectful. Do you focus on her feelings? Ask what her husband thinks? Set up an enactment in which she talks to her teenager? Inquire about exceptions? Any of these options might be useful. But trying to do all of them may lead to a lack of focus.

Effective integration involves more than taking a little of this and a little of that from various models. In creating a workable integration, there are two things to avoid. The first is sampling techniques from diverse approaches without conceptual focus. The problem here isn't so much theoretical inelegance as clinical inconsistency.

> A student who was being supervised in a psychodynamic approach asked to present at a case conference when, after some initial progress, the therapy bogged down. Most of the people at the case conference weren't familiar with the psychodynamic model, and they were impressed by what the student had accomplished. But when it came time for discussion, several of those present suggested that the way to get the case moving again might be to try a different approach—cognitive-behavioral, structural, narrative, or what have you, depending on who was doing the suggesting.

The second thing to avoid is switching horses in midstream. Almost every treatment runs into difficulty at some point. When this happens, beginners may be tempted to shift to a different model. If a structural approach isn't working, maybe a narrative one will. The problem here is that almost any strategy will work for a while—and then stall. Getting stuck isn't a reason to change models; rather it should be a signal that you and your clients are getting to what may be the heart of their problems. This is the time to sharpen your tools, not discard them.

Postgraduate training programs once provided an antidote to unfocused eclecticism through intensive instruction in one consistent approach. Unfortunately fewer and fewer therapists these days take the time and expense to get advanced training. Many recent graduates would like to get more training, but they have loans to pay off, they want to settle down, or they feel they already know enough to get started. Those who do make the sacrifice to get postdoctoral training are likely to consider it the best professional decision they ever made.

Selective Borrowing

When family therapy's elders were asked to discuss their careers in an issue of the *American Family Therapy Academy Newsletter* (Winter, 1999), many said that over the years they'd become less doctrinaire and had adopted ideas from other models—but they had held on to the core of their original theory as a base. For example, feminist family therapist Betty Carter was trained in Bowen's model and believed it to be substantial enough to evolve with her. "I never felt I had to trash the whole theory and start over again. Though, of course, Bowen's theory had the same blind spot that all the early theories had about power, so that all had to be added" (Mac Kune-Karrer, 1999, p. 24). Today there are few purists among seasoned therapists. Most, like Carter, become selective borrowers.

To borrow selectively, you need a solid foundation in one paradigm. Which one you choose will depend in part on what is available in your training program. It's a good idea to take advantage of what's offered by learning as much as you can from whomever you happen to be supervised by. However, the approach you eventually specialize in should also make sense to you. At some point you will be free to seek out training and supervision, and the approach you choose should be consistent with how you think about people and how you like to interact with them. If narrative therapy inspires you, seek out training in this approach. In graduate school you may not have a lot of choice about what your instructors offer. But after that it can be a mistake to settle for a particular kind of training merely because it's convenient.

Therapists who do eventually manage to combine approaches or successfully master more than one don't try to learn them all at once.

Using techniques from here and there without conceptual focus produces a muddled form of eclecticism. Effective borrowing doesn't mean a hodgepodge of techniques, and it doesn't mean switching from one approach to another whenever therapy reaches a temporary impasse. Borrowing techniques from other approaches is more likely to be effective if you do so in a way that fits into the basic paradigm within which you are operating.

> Consider, for example, a structural therapist treating a mother and daughter who are locked in a battle in which the mother constantly criticizes the daughter for being irresponsible, and the daughter constantly acts irresponsibly. If the mother would back off and stop criticizing, the girl might feel less browbeaten and begin to take more responsibility for herself—or if the daughter would start to take more responsibility, maybe the mother would back off. But as long as each of them remains preoccupied with the other one, and the awful things she's doing, neither is likely to break this cycle.
>
> Suppose the therapist were to try the narrative technique of externalizing the problem. Instead of "nagging" and "irresponsibility" polarizing the mother and daughter, perhaps they could be convinced to start thinking in terms of a "Breach" that's come between them. This shift might open space for them to recapture a more cooperative way of relating. But if the mother and daughter's quarreling is a product of enmeshment, attempting to bring them together in a more harmonious way might not solve the problem.

In fact, the case we've just described isn't hypothetical. Here's how the therapist actually did introduce the technique of externalizing in this situation.

> Because he saw the mother and daughter's quarreling as a result of their enmeshment, the therapist concentrated first on helping the mother address with her husband some of the conflicts that were keeping them apart. As they started to get closer, the mother began to spend less time worrying about what her daughter was or wasn't doing.
>
> Then, in separate sessions with the daughter, the therapist found a useful way to introduce the externalizing technique. As a result of her mother's nagging, the daughter had gotten into

the habit of shirking responsibility, and as a result her school performance had plummeted. It was as though when she had a homework assignment, she felt the same kind of oppression she felt from her mother's nagging.

The therapist pointed this out, but found that the girl had begun to internalize her mother's harsh characterizations. "I guess I'm just lazy," she'd say, in what was becoming a self-fulfilling prophecy. The therapist responded by asking her about times when "Procrastination" got the better of her, and times when "It" didn't. This device proved effective in helping the girl separate herself from the negative introject she'd adopted and, thus energized, she was able to start getting back on track with her school work.

Specially Designed Integrative Models

Although most practitioners eventually become selective borrowers, grafting ideas and practices onto their basic model, some therapists create a new synthesis out of complementary aspects of existing models. Some of these integrative efforts are comprehensive systems that include a whole range of approaches under one umbrella, whereas others simply combine elements of one approach with another, forming a hybrid model.

Comprehensive, Theoretically Inclusive Models

The maturing of the field has seen an erosion of sectarianism and a more pragmatic approach to practice. For some this has meant abandoning the idea of limiting one's practice to any one model in favor of drawing on a variety of approaches.

The advantage of these comprehensive approaches is that they bring a wider range of human experience into focus. They also offer more options for intervention. For example, rather than simply trying to pry apart an enmeshed mother and child, a therapist whose purview includes cultural issues might help the mother

reexamine the assumptions keeping her from getting more satisfaction out of her own life.

The disadvantage of comprehensive approaches is that they require a great deal of therapists. First, therapists can't just specialize in, say, untangling family triangles; they have to consider a variety of other issues—intrapsychic, transgenerational, even political—and a greater range of interventions. In addition, therapists who adopt a more comprehensive framework must guard against the tendency to switch haphazardly from one strategy to another.

Here we will present two examples of models designed to increase comprehensiveness. The first, *metaframeworks*, selects key ideas that run through the different schools of family therapy and connects them with superordinate principles. The second, *integrative problem-centered therapy*, links several different approaches in sequence and provides a decision tree for shifting from one to another when therapists get stuck.

The Metaframeworks Model. Metaframeworks grew out of the collaboration among three family therapy teachers who worked at the Institute for Juvenile Research in Chicago: Douglas Breunlin, Richard Schwartz, and Betty Mac Kune-Karrer. This approach offers a unifying theoretical framework operationalized with six core domains of human functioning, or *metaframeworks:* intrapsychic process, family organization, sequences of family interaction, development, culture, and gender (Breunlin, Schwartz, & Mac Kune-Karrer, 1992).

The application of metaframeworks is conceived in terms of releasing the constraints, at whatever level, keeping a family from solving its problems.

—Case Study—

For example, a depressed woman may be constrained on many fronts simultaneously. At the level of internal process, she may be burdened by guilt over wanting a little time for herself or because her children complain that they have no friends. (If children are unhappy, it must be their mother's fault, right?) At the level of family organization, she may be stuck in a stale second marriage to a man obsessed with his career while she's left to run the house and raise the kids. In addition, she may be preoccupied with her hyperactive son and polarized with her own mother over how to deal with him. This pattern may be part of a sequence in which her son's behavior gets worse after monthly visits with her ex-husband. Finally, the woman's situation may be part of a transgenerational pattern maintained by the family and cultural belief that women should be devoted to their families and never be "selfish."

As the therapist considers the network of constraints impeding this woman and her family, one framework often emerges as a point of departure, but the therapist is always aware of the others and can shift when necessary. Thus therapy may start in the gender metaframework by reexamining the woman's beliefs about selfishness and her husband's unbalanced expectations about the proper roles of men and women. At some point the focus might shift to the internal framework when the therapist asks about the parts of each partner that hold these beliefs and what they are related to from their pasts. This exploration might make the woman want to reorganize the family responsibilities and the shift is to the organizational metaframework. At another point the couple might discuss their son's oscillation between acting younger and older than his age, and they're in the developmental framework, and so on.

The metaframeworks model isn't simple. In an age when therapists often seek to fall back on formulaic techniques, it challenges clinicians to consider a wide range of possibilities. Yet, for many therapists who've felt boxed in by the narrow scope of the original models of family therapy, the metaframeworks model offers a more comprehensive view and a broader range of options.

Integrative Problem-Centered Therapy.
Whereas metaframeworks distills key elements from different theories into a new synthesis, *integrative problem-centered therapy* incorporates a variety of family and individual approaches in sequence, without trying to combine them. Integrative problem-centered therapy has been developed over the past twenty years by William Pinsof (1995, 1999) and his colleagues at the Family Institute at Northwestern University.

Like many therapists, Pinsof began his career convinced that the model he was trained in (strategic family therapy) could be effective with any and every sort of problem. Unlike selective borrowers, however, when he ran up against his theory's limitations, he didn't just add new techniques, he added whole new approaches. For example, if his strategic model didn't seem to be working, he might help family members explore and express their emotions à la Virginia Satir. In other cases, if problems persisted, he might recommend a psychopharmacological assessment. With continued failure, he might bring in grandparents or even offer individual therapy to some family members.

This sequencing made sense to Pinsof (1999) partly because it reflected his own personal development. It also makes sense, however, that some problems are deep-seated whereas others are not. Some families respond to behavioral interventions while others may need more of an in-depth focus. Why not consider the whole spectrum of psychotherapies if necessary rather than assume that all troubles should be treated with just one approach?

To illustrate Pinsof's approach, consider a couple in their sixties who have been caught up in picky but intense fights for the past year. They relate the fighting to the husband's increasing impotence. In exploring the meaning each attaches to these events, the therapist finds that the wife sees her husband's lack of sexual response as a reflection of her diminished attractiveness, whereas he considers it a sign of waning virility. These conclusions are painful to each of them, and so they avoid discussing, much less having, sex.

The therapist forms an alliance with each of them so they feel safe enough to disclose their private pain and clear up their misconceptions about each other's feelings. If at that point they respond well—fewer fights and more satisfactory sex—therapy can stop. If not, the therapist would explore possible physiological causes of the impotence—fatigue, depression, incipient diabetes. If improvements don't follow exploration at that level, the therapist might discuss with each partner unexamined assumptions about the aging process. If the problem still remains unsolved, the focus would shift to intrapsychic blocks, and either or both of them might be engaged in individual therapy.

By now the reader may be daunted at the prospect of having to master so many different therapeutic models. But Pinsof doesn't expect therapists to be competent in all these approaches. Integrative therapy often involves teamwork among a number of therapists, particularly when key family members are vulnerable and need their own therapists. Although separate therapists with differing orientations can be a nightmare, the integrative framework provides common ground for collaboration.

The metaframeworks and integrative approaches represent two possible reactions to the realization that all models have their limitations. One solution (metaframeworks) is alchemical—taking pieces from here and there to forge a new synthesis. The other (integrative) is additive—linking whole models together without trying to revise them or connect them theoretically.

Models that Combine Two Distinct Approaches

Some theorists who found one approach too limiting were satisfied to improve their model by combining it with just one other, believing that two heads were better than one—and probably also better than five or six.

The Narrative Solutions Approach. One of the things that troubles some seasoned practitioners is the tendency for solution-focused and narrative therapists to turn their backs on valuable elements of the older models. If it's true that a new broom sweeps clean, they're worried that some of what's being swept out might be worth keeping. That's why Joseph Eron and Thomas Lund's *narrative solutions model* (Eron & Lund, 1993, 1996), which combines the MRI model with narrative technique, is a welcome addition.

Among the reasons strategic therapy fell into disfavor were its mechanistic assumptions and manipulative techniques. The way some strategists applied the cybernetic model, families were seen as stubborn and couldn't be reasoned with. You can't talk sense to a machine. Family histories were dismissed as irrelevant. Therapy was ideological and therefore often impersonal. The meretriciousness of this kind of thinking, however, wasn't essential to the insight that families often get stuck applying solutions that don't work. Eron and Lund resuscitated that insight and incorporated it into a blend of strategic and narrative therapy.

Joseph Eron and Thomas Lund of the Catskill Family Institute in New York began collaborating in the early 1980s as brief, strategic therapists. Although they were attracted to the narrative movement, they didn't want to give up some aspects of the strategic approach. So they put the two together. The resulting narrative solutions approach revolves around the concept of the **preferred view.** Eron and Lund (1996) assume that people have strong preferences for how they like to see themselves and to be seen by others:

- Preferred views include the qualities people would like to possess and have noticed by others: for example, "determined," "caring," "responsible."
- Preferred views shape the *attributions* one makes about behavior. "I did that (got into that fight) because I am emotionally reactive, impulsive, cool, able to manage my own affairs."
- Preferred views also include people's hopes, dreams, and intentions for living their lives. "I want to be different from my mother who was a self-sacrificing martyr."

- Preferred views may or may not have anything to do with one's actual behavior. "I may not be doing well in school, but I like to think of myself as a hard-working and self-disciplined person. I expect to succeed in graduate school, even though, given how I'm doing now, it isn't likely."

Eron and Lund believe that problems arise when people aren't living according to their preferred views. To address this discrepancy, they use a combination of reframing from the MRI model and restorying from the narrative approach. They subscribe to the fundamental premise of the MRI model that problems develop innocently from the mishandling of life transitions. However, Eron and Lund are more specific. They propose that people begin to think and act in problematic ways when they experience a discrepancy between their preferred view of themselves and their perception of their actions or their impression of how others regard them.

Note that, whereas Eron and Lund (1996) follow the MRI model in looking for more-of-the-same cycles, they differ in focusing not just on behavior but also on what people think about their problems. Conflict, according to this model, is driven by disjunctions between individuals' preferred views of themselves and how they perceive others as responding to them. Thus, Eron and Lund have taken the MRI focus on altering problem-maintaining actions and added cognitive elements to take into account how people think about their lives and their futures.

The following questions may be asked to help clients get in touch with their preferred views:

- When are you at your best—at home, work, school, with friends?
- Who notices—family, colleagues, teachers, friends?
- What do they notice about you at these times?
- Who are your favorite relatives, friends, teachers, other adults?
- What do they like about you?

- What do they see in you?
- When you think back on your life, are there other times when you felt at your best?
- When you look into the future and you are the person you would like to be, what do you envision?

In *Narrative Solutions in Brief Therapy*, Eron and Lund (1996) offer the example of "Al," who became depressed in the wake of retirement and the onset of emphysema. Al preferred to think of himself as productive and useful. Yet he worried that he might not be able to remain as active as in the past and that his family would no longer view him as someone to rely on. The disjunction between Al's preferences and his perceptions led to his feeling sad and listless. The more depressed Al seemed, the more family members began to do for him, finishing projects he started and trying to cheer him up, which only deepened his despondency. The negative *frame* through which Al viewed his current circumstances affected the *stories* he recalled from the past. For example, he pictured himself following in the footsteps of his own father, who deteriorated rapidly after retiring. According to Eron and Lund, negative frames of the present shape the stories people recall from the past, which in turn influence their perspectives on the future.

Eron and Lund (1996) offer the following guidelines for managing helpful conversations. The therapist:

1. Maintains an interest in clients' preferences and hopes, paying attention to stories that reflect how they prefer to see themselves.
2. Explores how the problem keeps people from acting in line with their preferences.
3. Finds past and present stories that are in line with their preferences and contradict problem-maintaining views.
4. Discusses what the future will look like when the problem is resolved.
5. Asks **mystery questions**—for example, how did a person with X preferred attributes (hard working, productive) wind up

in *Y* situation (acting listless and feeling depressed)?

6. Coauthors with clients alternative explanations for the evolution of the problem that fit with how they prefer to be seen and inspires new actions.
7. Encourages clients to talk to significant others about their preferences, hopes, and intentions.

As they follow these guidelines, clients become aware that the therapist is seeing them in their preferred ways and they begin to notice their own strengths. They begin seeing the problem as a mystery to be explained rather than as truth that speaks to who they really are. They begin to restory how the problem evolved (a narrative practice) and to reframe (a strategic technique) their immediate situation. For example, Al felt empowered to talk to his doctor about his illness after he was able to recall preferred experiences indicating that he was a take-charge kind of guy. He also began reframing the motives of family members away from the belief that they saw him as useless to viewing them as bewildered, not knowing how to help him. Al's depression lifted after he met with his family and told them what was and wasn't helpful.

Integrative Couples Therapy. Neil Jacobson of the University of Washington, one of the preeminent behavioral family therapists, teamed with Andrew Christensen of UCLA to figure out how to improve the limited success rates they were finding with traditional couples therapy. They discovered that their results improved when they added a humanistic element to the standard behavioral mix of communication training, conflict resolution, and problem solving. The approach they developed is described in *Integrative Couple Therapy* (Jacobson & Christensen, 1996).

Traditional behavioral couples therapy is based on the behavior exchange model. After a "functional analysis" showing how partners in a relationship influence one another, they're taught to reinforce changes they wish to bring about in each other. Anyone who's been married for a long time can tell you what's missing from this formula. Therapy may be about change, but a successful relationship also involves a certain amount of acceptance of differences and disappointments. Some things in an unhappy marriage may need to change for the relationship to improve, but some things about our partners are part of the package, and couples who survive the break-in period learn to accept these things. It's this element, *acceptance,* that Jacobson and Christensen have added in their new approach.

In contrast to the teaching and preaching of traditional behavioral therapy, integrative couples therapy emphasizes support and empathy, the same qualities that therapists want couples to learn to show each other. To create a conducive atmosphere, they begin with a phase called the *formulation,* which is aimed at helping couples let go of blaming and open themselves to acceptance and personal change. The formulation consists of three components: a *theme* that defines the primary conflict; a *polarization process* that describes their destructive pattern of interaction; and the *mutual trap,* which is the impasse that prevents the couple from breaking the polarization cycle once it's triggered.

Common themes in couples' problems include conflicts around closeness and distance, a desire for control but unwillingness to take responsibility, and disagreements about sex. Whereas partners view these differences as indicating deficiencies in the other person and as problems to be solved, Jacobson and Christensen encourage couples to see that some differences are inevitable. This kind of acceptance can break the cycles that build up when each is constantly trying to change the other. Also, as the formulation phase continues, the partners begin to see that they are aren't victims of each other, but of the *pattern* they've both been trapped in. As with Michael White's externalizing, the couple can unite to fight a mutual enemy, the pattern. For example, when Jacobson asked a couple to describe their pattern,

The husband replied, "We fight over whether or not to be close. When she is not as close to me as she wants to be, she pressures me into being close, and I withdraw, which leads to more pressure. Of course, sometimes I withdraw before she has a chance to pressure me. In fact, that's how it usually starts." (Jacobson & Christensen, 1996, p. 100)

Notice how the formulation process helps this couple describe their fight as a pattern to which they both contribute, rather than in the accusatory language typical of distressed couples.

Strategies to produce change include the two basic ingredients of behavioral couples therapy: behavior exchange and communication skills training. Behavior exchange interventions involve "quid pro quo" and "good faith" contracts by which couples learn to exchange favors or to initiate pleasing behavior in the hope of getting the same in return. For example, each partner might be asked to generate a list of things he or she could do that would lead to greater satisfaction for the other. (Ask not what your partner can do for you; ask what you can do for your partner.) After each compiles a list, they're instructed to start doing some of the things they think will please their partner—and to observe the effect of this benevolence on the relationship.

The second ingredient—communication training—involves teaching couples to listen and to express themselves in direct but nonblaming ways. Learning to use "active listening" and to make "I-statements" is taught by assigned reading, instruction, and practice. As they learn to communicate less defensively, couples not only are better able to resolve conflicts but they are also more accepting of each other.

It's too soon to evaluate the effectiveness of integrative couples therapy, but it seems to be an improvement over traditional behavioral therapy. Its significance isn't only in improving a model, but in the shift it represents toward humanizing behavioral technology. In emphasizing acceptance and compassion, integrative couples therapy joins other family therapies of the twenty-first century—from solution-focused to strategic to narrative—in recognizing the im-

portance of nurturing relationships. Carl Rogers would be proud.

●

The narrative solutions model illustrates a principle that every good matchmaker knows: Make sure the partners aren't incompatible before pushing them together. Because MRI techniques are similar to narrative ones, and because both traditions emphasize changing cognitions rather than emotions and downplay psychic conflict and developmental history, they're fairly compatible. Had they tried to combine either with, say, psychoanalytic therapy, it might be like trying to mix oil and water.

Jacobson and Christensen's amalgamation also involved compatible marriage candidates—behavioral and experiential. Both models are concerned with communication; they just have different emphases. Behaviorists focus on contracts and reinforcement whereas experientialists are interested in emotions and empathy. Blending some of the latter into the former is not a huge stretch. Encouraging partners to show more compassion need not interfere with helping them learn to be better problem solvers.

Other Integrative Models.   Although we've singled out some of the most innovative examples, there are in fact so many integrative approaches that it's impossible to list them all. Although many of these models are new, some of them have been around so long they don't always get the attention they deserve. To cite just one example, Carol Anderson and Susan Stewart wrote one of the most useful integrative guides to family therapy back in 1983. Two other integrative approaches that have been around for a while are those designed by Larry Feldman (1990) and William Nichols (1996). The tradition of offering practical advice that transcends schools of family therapy is upheld in a splendid book by Robert Taibbi (1996) called *Doing Family Therapy*. Others have attempted to integrate structural and strategic therapies (Stanton, 1981; Liddle, 1984), strategic and behavioral (Alexander & Parsons, 1982), psychodynamic and systems theory (Sander, 1979; Kirschner & Kirschner, 1986;

Nichols, 1987; Scharff, 1989; Slipp, 1988), and experiential and systems theory (Duhl & Duhl, 1981; Greenberg & Johnson, 1988).

One particularly elegant model that's been around for a while (first described in 1981) is Alan Gurman's *brief integrative marital therapy,* which combines social learning theory and psychodynamics. As in behavior therapy marital problems are seen as due to poor communication and problem solving, but, as in object relations theory, these deficits are understood as having roots in unconscious conflicts. What might seem like simply a lack—poor relationship skills—may turn out to serve a protective function of limiting intimacy to a level that a couple can tolerate without undue anxiety and conflict.

Gurman's assessment begins with problematic themes in a couple's relationship. In a recent chapter on brief integrative marital therapy, Gurman (2002) describes a case in which Sue is angry and critical of Karl's emotional unavailability. This familiar demand-and-withdraw pattern is assumed to reflect not only the couple's interaction but also intrapsychic conflicts that motivate this interaction.

Like an analyst, Gurman sees Sue's attacking as serving the defensive function of avoiding dealing with her own fears of abandonment. Meanwhile Karl's distance helps him avoid his conflicts about intimacy. The partners' complaints about each other ("nagging," "withdrawing") allow them to maintain a consistent and tolerable sense of themselves, even if it limits the satisfaction they share in their relationship.

Like a behaviorist, Gurman also looks at the *consequences* of the couple's problematic interaction, noting what (positive and negative) reinforcements or punishments may be maintaining these patterns. Karl negatively reinforced Sue's criticism by apologizing and coming closer to her after her complaints reached the shouting stage. Sue inadvertently punished Karl's closeness by venting her anger and frustration whenever the couple did spend time together—thus violating the First Law of Social Learning Theory.[1]

In order to explore the impact of one or both partners' personal conflicts on the couple's relationship, Gurman may talk at some length to each partner individually while the other just listens. Talking separately to the partners (à la Murray Bowen) helps minimize anxiety and thus makes therapy a safer "holding environment."

Gurman's blocking of Sue's criticism allowed Karl to explore how he felt about trying to balance his commitments to career and family. As Karl opened up about his fears of failure, Sue softened enough to empathize with his struggles—and to share her own fears of being alone.

In addition to addressing couples' problematic interactions and the conflicts underlying them, Gurman's brief integrative marital therapy also includes practical problem-solving discussions, advice, teaching of self-control techniques, exploration of the past, modeling, coaching, bibliotherapy—in short, the wide and flexible variety of interventions that characterize the best kind of integration.

Other integrative approaches haven't received as much attention in mainstream family therapy as they have by federal funding agencies. These include Scott Henggeler's *multisystemic model* (Henggeler & Borduin, 1990) and Howard Liddle's *multidimensional family therapy* (Liddle, Dakoff, & Diamond, 1991). These approaches evolved out of research projects with difficult adolescents, a population that challenges theorists to expand their views beyond the limits of one school of therapy or one level of system.

Liddle developed his integrative approach while working with drug-abusing, inner-city adolescents. His multidimensional family therapy brings together the risk factor models of drug and problem behavior, developmental psychopathology, family systems theory, social support theory, peer cluster theory, and social learning theory. In practice, the model applies a combination of structural family therapy, parent training, skills training for adolescents, and cognitive-behavioral techniques.

One of the most useful aspects of Liddle's approach is the way he integrates individual and systems interventions. Although he makes

---

1. You catch more flies with honey than with vinegar.

liberal use of the structural technique of enact-ment, he frequently meets with individual family members to coach and prepare them to partici-pate more effectively in these family dialogues. Liddle also uses individual sessions to focus on teenagers' experiences outside the home. Here, sensitive subjects like drug use and sexual behav-ior can be explored more safely in private. The need to meet with teenagers to focus on their lives outside the family reflects a growing recog-nition of the limited influence families have in comparison with peers and culture.

Scott Henggeler of the University of South Carolina and a number of research-oriented col-leagues who work with "difficult-to-treat" chil-dren tried to improve on their systems-oriented family therapy by (1) more actively considering and intervening in the extrafamilial systems in which families are embedded, in particular their school and peer contexts; (2) including individ-ual developmental issues in assessments; and (3) incorporating cognitive-behavioral interven-tions (Henggeler & Borduin, 1990). This multi-systemic model has shown promising results in several well-designed outcome studies of juve-nile offenders and families referred for abuse or neglect (Henggeler et al., 1997, 1999). For that reason, it is highly regarded among governmen-tal funding agencies, and Henggeler has received a number of large grants.

Models Designed for Specific Clinical Problems

One sign that family therapy was maturing was when therapists began focusing on specific clinical problems rather than generic "families." Some groups applied preexisting models to the problems they were wrestling with; for example, structural family therapy was used with an-orexia nervosa and brittle diabetes (Minuchin, Rosman, & Baker, 1978). Other groups had to be more creative because they decided to tackle problems that weren't typically seen in the prac-tice of family therapy. Such problems often re-quire more than any single approach offers.

Working with Family Violence

One of the most impressive integrative efforts is the approach to treating spousal abuse devel-oped by Virginia Goldner and Gillian Walker at the Ackerman Institute in New York (Goldner, Penn, Sheinberg, & Walker, 1990; Walker & Goldner, 1995; Goldner, 1998). When Goldner and Walker began studying violence in couples, the standard approach involved separating the partners and treating the man in a group with other offenders and the abused woman in a sup-port group. This treatment was informed by the feminist critique of systems-based therapies that implied that both partners were responsible for the violence and, consequently, could be treated together like any other couple.

Goldner and Walker share the feminist convic-tion that regardless of the woman's role, the man is responsible for his violent behavior, no matter what provocation he might feel. But they also believe that there is value to treating the couple together and to attending to the woman's part in these couples' dangerous dramas. Instead of tak-ing sides in the systems theory versus feminism battles, they bridged the polarized thinking that pervaded the field of family violence. Could it be possible to take both positions simultaneously? Yes, the man is responsible for controlling his vi-olence; but both partners participate in a process of interaction that must change. As Goldner says, "A battered woman is not equally responsible for her broken nose, even if she acknowledges hav-ing been angry or 'provocative'; just as the vic-

Virginia Goldner's work with violent cou-ples combines a highly sophisticated clinical ap-proach with a passion-ate feminist sensitivity.

tim of sexual abuse is not equally responsible for what happened in the middle of the night, even if she felt aroused" (Goldner, 1988, p. 266). With this more nuanced position, it became possible to examine both partners' roles in their escalations of conflict without blaming the victim.

Rather than seeing each partner individually and insisting that they separate, Goldner and Walker work with the couple together, but insist that the violence must cease immediately and the man must take responsibility for making that happen. Here they combine the feminist emphasis on safety and responsibility with a systemic interest in the way the couple interacts. Goldner points out that separating violent couples rarely promotes safety because they are often so symbiotically attached that they quickly reunite, and those women who do manage to leave are the most likely to be attacked. On the other hand, if they are together in treatment, the victim can explain to the abuser how damaging his aggression is in the presence of a therapist who can emphasize the moral imperative to stop.

Goldner and Walker use the language of "parts" to help the partners detach from global labels like *abuser* and *victim* and to bring intrapsychic insights into the conversation. He can talk about the angry part of himself and she, the part that needs to protect him rather than look after herself. As they inquire into the origin of these parts, Goldner and Walker find themselves listening to painful stories from each partner's past. "Here we typically find ourselves back in a time when the man was a boy, subject to sadistic acts of violence, power and control" (Goldner, 1998, p. 275). This compassionate witnessing helps reduce the partners' antagonism toward each other.

Goldner and Walker also incorporate an active listening format so that not only are past traumas witnessed but also the man listens to the woman describe the pain and terror she suffered from his attacks. Here again there's a both/and message to the man: Yes, you suffered as a boy and that's related to your violent behavior; but you are still choosing to be violent, and that's unacceptable. Similarly, regardless of how passive

the woman has been in the past, she can choose to protect herself without feeling disloyal. This nondichotomous position is an advance over the either/or positions of both the feminist and psychoanalytic models. Feminist therapists believe that to explore a man's troubled childhood would imply excusing his violence, whereas psychoanalysts too often see violence as a symptom of an underlying pathologic condition for which they don't hold anyone accountable. Goldner writes that "From a both/and perspective, violence is best conceptualized as simultaneously willful and impulse-ridden, as both instrumental and dissociative" (Goldner, 1998, p. 279).

Although Goldner and Walker's approach was designed for violent couples, it offers important lessons for the integration of therapy models in general. It illustrates the value of stepping out of the dichotomies that dominate clinical work (especially around volatile issues like domestic violence) to see that more than one perspective has validity and can coexist with others. Too often, "Ideas that could mutually enrich one another have instead been set up as oppositional positions, creating a polarizing context of forced choices between adequate alternatives" (Goldner, 1998, p. 264). The depolarizing effect is a major virtue of integration.

Community Family Therapy

Many family therapists start out working in agencies with poor families, but as they realize how powerless therapy alone is to deal with many of the problems impoverished families face, they get discouraged and opt for private practice with middle-class clients. This recognition of family therapy's limits had the opposite effect on Ramon Rojano.

According to Rojano, the greatest obstacle poor people face is the sense of powerlessness that comes with being controlled by a multitude of dehumanizing bureaucracies and the futility of having no hope of achieving the dream of a decent job and a comfortable home. Rojano uses his knowledge of and personal connections with the helping systems to make clients feel reconnected to their communities and empowered to advocate for what they need. Not only does he help families find the resources to survive—child care, jobs, food stamps, housing—which is the essence of traditional casework, but he also begins encouraging aspirations beyond mere survival.

Laura Markowitz (1997) describes Rojano's work this way.

> Ramon Rojano is a professional nudge. Let's say you're a single mother on welfare who goes to him because your teenage son is skipping school and on the verge of being expelled. Leaning forward in his chair, the stocky, energetic Rojano will start prodding and poking with his questions in his Spanish accent, zeroing in on your son like he's herding a stray lamb back into the fold. After some minutes of this interrogation, you actually hear your boy admit what's going on with him and promise in a small, sincere voice you haven't heard come out of him in a long time, that he will go to school regularly if he can graduate. As your mouth opens in surprise, Rojano won't even pause. Now he'll urge the 15-year-old boy to apply for an after-school job he just heard about from someone who runs a program. . . . Rojano will write the phone number down and put it directly into the boy's hand, look him in the eye and use his name a few times to make sure he knows Rojano actually cares whether or not this kid ends up on the streets or in a gang. . . . You think the session is over, right? Not quite. He has plans for you too. Be prepared—he might ask you something outrageous, like whether you've thought about owning your own house. You may be a single mother barely getting by, but as he leans toward you it's like the force of his confidence in you pulls you in, and now he's pressing a piece of paper into your hand with the number of a woman he knows who runs a program that helps people with no money buy a home of their own. (Markowitz, 1997, pp. 25–26)

He'll ask clients about things that they, in their state of hopelessness and disconnection, never considered—running for the school board, going to college, starting a business or an advocacy program—in such a way that these things seem possible. This is partly because Rojano can see strengths that disheartened clients have forgotten and partly because he has the connections to get the ball rolling.

Rojano also recognizes that community empowerment is not enough. Without ongoing family therapy, it wouldn't be long before the single parent in the scenario above might start being late for work because of renewed conflicts with her son, and that dream of a house would evaporate.

So this is the integration: family therapy with community psychology and social work. Rojano has taken a version of structural family therapy and bolstered it with hands-on advocacy. Structural family therapy was developed in the Wiltwyck agency in Harlem in the late 1950s. But in retrospect Braulio Montalvo, one of its developers, said, "We couldn't get the resources around the family to uphold the changes they were able to make in family therapy" (quoted in Markowitz, 1997, p. 28). Forty years later, someone has taken the next step by incorporating those resources.

Once again we see that integration requires a new way of thinking. Rojano had to step out of the mind-set that said therapy takes place in an office, even though clients are often constrained by forces untouched in the office. Why not take it to the street so the whole system is addressed? It seems like an obvious question—but maybe not so obvious when you're trapped in your circumstances.

Summary

1. In the founding decades of family therapy, a number of clearly articulated models were developed, and most family therapists became disciples of one of these approaches. Each of the

major schools concentrated on a particular aspect of family life. Experientialists opened people up to feeling, behaviorists helped them reinforce more functional behavior, and Bowenians taught them to think for themselves. By concentrating their attention this way, practitioners of the classic models focused their power for change. If in the process they got a little parochial and competitive, what was the harm?

2. The harm was that by ignoring the insights of other approaches, orthodox disciples of the various schools limited their impact and applicability. But maybe this parochialism should be understood from a developmental perspective—as a necessary stage in the consolidation of the original insights of the founding models. Perhaps it was useful for the schools to pursue the truth as they knew it in order to mine the full potential of their ideas. If so, that time has passed.

3. Most of the schools of family therapy have been around long enough to have solidified their approach and proven their worth. That's why the time is ripe for integration.

4. Valuable as integrative efforts are, however, there remains a serious pitfall in mixing ingredients from different approaches. You don't want to end up with what happens when you blend several colors from a set of poster paints. The trick is to find a unifying conceptual thread. A successful integration draws on existing therapies in such a way that they can be practiced coherently within one consistent framework. Adding techniques willy-nilly from here and there just doesn't work.

5. A successful synthesizing effort must strike a balance between breadth and focus. Breadth may be particularly important when it comes to conceptualization. Contemporary family therapists are wisely adopting a broad, biopsychosocial perspective in which biological, psychological, relational, community, and even societal processes are viewed as relevant to understanding people's problems. When it comes to techniques, on the other hand, the most effective approaches don't overload therapists with scores of interventions.

6. Finally, an effective integration must have clear direction. The trouble with being too flexible is that families have a way of inducting therapists into their habits of avoidance. Good family therapy creates an environment where conversations that should happen at home, but don't, can take place. These dialogues won't happen, however, if therapists abruptly shift from one type of intervention to another in the face of resistance.

7. Family therapy is ultimately a clinical enterprise, its worth measured in results. The real reason to combine elements from various approaches is to maximize their usefulness, not merely their theoretical inclusiveness. To contradict Billy Crystal, it's better to be effective than to look marvelous.

—Questions to Consider—

1. What are the advantages of *not* integrating models of therapy?
2. List several pairs of family therapy models that might effectively be combined and say how. List models that probably should not be combined and say why.
3. In one column list several attributes of your preferred view of yourself; in a second column list a few important people in your life and how you think they view you in terms of these attributes; in a third column make guesses as to why these people see you in ways that you do or do not prefer to be seen.
4. Make a list of problems for which it's probably a good idea to develop specific treatment approaches (rather than simply applying one of the generic approaches).

—Key Concepts————————————————

eclecticism   A form of integration in which a large number of elements from different approaches are combined.

mystery questions   Questions designed to help clients begin to wonder how their problems got the best of them, which in turn helps to externalize the problems.

preferred view   Eron and Lund's term for the way people would like to think of themselves and be seen by others.

selective borrowing   A form of integration in which one follows a consistent model but makes occasional use of techniques from other approaches.

—Recommended Readings————————————

Anderson, C., and Stewart, S. 1983. *Mastering resistance: A practical guide to family therapy.* New York: Guilford Press.

Breunlin, D.C., Schwartz, R. C., and Mac Kune-Karrer, B. 1992. *Metaframeworks: Transcending the models of family therapy.* San Francisco: Jossey-Bass.

Eron, J., and Lund, T. 1996. *Narrative solutions in brief therapy.* New York: Guilford Press.

Goldner, V. 1998. The treatment of violence and victimization in intimate relationships. *Family Process. 37:* 263–286.

Gurman, A. S. 2002. Brief integrative marital therapy: A depth-behavioral approach. In *Clinical handbook of couples therapy.* 3rd ed. A. S. Gurman and N. S. Jacobson, eds., New York: Guilford Press.

Jacobson, N. S., and Christensen, A. 1996. *Integrative couple therapy.* New York: Norton.

Pinsof, W. M. 1995. *Integrative problem-centered therapy.* New York: Basic Books.

Taibbi, R. 1996. *Doing family therapy.* New York: Guilford Press.

—References————————————————————

Alexander, J., and Parsons, B. 1982. *Functional family therapy.* Pacific Grove, CA: Brooks/Cole.

Anderson, C., and Stewart, S. 1983. *Mastering resistance: A practical guide to family therapy.* New York: Guilford Press.

Breunlin, D., Schwartz, R., and Mac Kune-Karrer, B. 1992. *Metaframeworks: Transcending the models of family therapy.* San Francisco: Jossey-Bass.

Duhl, B. S., and Duhl, F. J. 1981. Integrative family therapy. In *Handbook of family therapy,* A. S. Gurman and O. P. Kniskern, eds. New York: Brunner/Mazel.

Eron, J., and Lund, T. 1993. An approach to how problems evolve and dissolve: Integrating narrative and strategic concepts. *Family Process. 32:* 291–309.

Eron, J., and Lund, T. 1996. *Narrative solutions in brief therapy.* New York: Guilford Press.

Feldman, L. 1990. *Multi-dimensional family therapy.* New York: Guilford Press.

Goldner, V. 1998. The treatment of violence and victimization in intimate relationships. *Family Process. 37:* 263–286.

Goldner, V., Penn, P., Sheinberg, M., and Walker, G. 1990. Love and violence: Gender paradoxes in volatile attachments. *Family Process. 29:* 343–364.

Greenberg, L. S., and Johnson, S. M. 1988. *Emotionally focused therapy for couples.* New York: Guilford Press.

Henggeler, S., and Borduin, C. 1990. *Family therapy and beyond: A multisystemic approach to treating the behavior problems of children and adolescents.* Pacific Grove, CA: Brooks/Cole.

Henggeler, S. W., Melton, G. B., Brondino, M. J., Scherer, D. G., & Hanley, J. H. (1997). Multisystemic therapy with violent and chronic juvenile offenders and their families. *Journal of Consulting and Clinical Psychology. 65:* 821–833.

Henggeler, S. W., Pickrel, S. G., & Brondino, M. J. (1999). Multisystemic treatment of substance abusing and dependent delinquents. *Mental Health Services Research. 1:* 171–184.

Jacobson, N., and Christensen, A. 1996. *Integrative couple therapy.* New York: Norton.

Kirschner, D., and Kirschner, S. 1986. *Comprehensive family therapy.* New York: Brunner/Mazel.

Liddle, H. A. 1984. Toward a dialectical-contextual-coevolutionary translation of structural-strategic family therapy. *Journal of Strategic and Systemic Therapies. 3:* 66–79.

Liddle, H. A., Dakoff, G. A., and Diamond, G. 1991. Adolescent substance abuse: Multidimensional family therapy in action. In *Family therapy with drug and alcohol abuse,* 2nd ed., E. Kaufman and P. Kaufman, eds. Boston: Allyn & Bacon.

Mac Kune-Karrer, B. 1999. A conversation with Betty Carter. *American Family Therapy Academy Newsletter.* Winter: 23–27.

Markowitz, L. 1997. Ramon Rojano won't take no for an answer. *Family Therapy Networker. 21:* 24–35.

Minuchin, S., Rosman, B., and Baker, L. 1978. *Psychosomatic families: Anorexia in context.* Cambridge, MA: Harvard University Press.

Nichols, M. P. 1987. *The self in the system.* New York: Brunner/Mazel.

Nichols, W. C. 1996. *Treating people in families: An integrative framework.* New York: Guilford Press.

Pinsof, W. 1995. *Integrative problem-centered therapy.* New York: Basic Books.

Pinsof, W. 1999. Choosing the right door. *Family Therapy Networker. 23:* 48–55.

Saunder, F. M. 1979. *Individual and family therapy: Toward an integration.* New York: Jason Aronson.

Scharff, J., ed. 1989. *The foundations of object relations family therapy.* New York: Jason Aronson.

Slipp, S. 1988. *Technique and practice of object relations family therapy.* New York: Jason Aronson.

Stanton, M. D. 1981. An integrated structural/strategic approach to marital and family therapy. *Journal of Marital and Family Therapy. 7:* 427–440.

Taibbi, R. 1996. *Doing family therapy.* New York: Guilford Press.

Walker, G., and Goldner, V. 1995. The wounded prince and the women who love him. In *Gender and power in relationships,* C. Burcke and B. Speed, eds. London: Routledge, Chapman and Hall.

15

Comparative Analysis

The exponential growth of family therapy crowded the field with competing models and produced a rich and varied literature, bearing witness to the vitality of the profession, while at the same time creating a confusing array of concepts and techniques. See Table 15.1 for a summary of these models. In this chapter we offer a comparative analysis of the various approaches. Each school proclaims a set of truths, yet despite some overlap there are notable conflicts among these truths.

Theoretical Formulations

Theories bring order out of chaos. They organize our awareness and help us make sense of what families are doing. Instead of seeing a "blooming, buzzing confusion," we begin to see patterns of pursuit and distance, enmeshment and disengagement, and problem-saturated stories. The minute you begin to see ineffectual attempts to settle arguments between children as enmeshment, your goal shifts from intervening more effectively to backing off and letting the children settle their own disputes. Here we evaluate theories in terms of their pragmatic function: understanding families in order to better help them.

Families as Systems

Communications therapists introduced the idea that families are systems. More than the sum of their parts, **systems** are the parts *plus* the way they function together. Once, not accepting systems theory was like not believing in apple pie and motherhood. Now the postmodern movement has challenged systems thinking as just another modernist framework, a metaphor taken too literally, and has shifted emphasis from action to meaning and from the organization of the family to the thinking of its members. It's easy to say that a good therapist takes into account both the self *and* the system. In practice, however, deciding when to delve into individual experience or focus on interactional patterns presents a host of hard choices.

Stability and Change

Communications theorists described families as rule-governed systems with a tendency toward stability or homeostasis (Jackson, 1965). But in order to adjust to changing circumstances, families must also be capable of revising their rules and modifying their structure.

The dual nature of families—*homeostatic* and *changing*—is best appreciated by the communi-

TABLE 15.1   Schools

	Bowenian	**Strategic**	**Structural**
Founder(s)	Murray Bowen	Don Jackson Jay Haley	Salvador Minuchin
Key Theoretical Constructs	Differentiation of self	Homeostasis Feedback loops	Subsystems Boundaries
Core Problem Dynamic	Triangles Emotional reactivity	More-of-the-same solutions	Enmeshment/ Disengagement
Key Techniques	Genogram Process questions	Reframing Directives	Enactments Boundary making

	Experiential	**Psychodynamic**	**Cognitive-Behavioral**
Founder(s)	Virginia Satir Carl Whitaker	Nathan Ackerman Henry Dicks Ivan Boszormenyi-Nagy	Gerald Patterson Robert Liberman Richard Stuart
Key Theoretical Constructs	Authenticity Self-actualization	Drives Selfobjects Internal objects	Reinforcement Extinction Schemas
Core Problem Dynamic	Emotional suppression Mystification	Conflict Projective identification Fixation and regression	Inadvertent reinforcement Aversive control
Key Techniques	Confrontation Structured exercises	Silence Interpretation	Functional analysis Teaching positive control

	Solution-Focused	**Narrative**
Founder(s)	Steve de Shazer Insoo Kim Berg	Michael White David Epston
Key Theoretical Constructs	Language creates reality	Narrative theory Social constructionism
Core Problem Dynamic	Problem talk	Problem-saturated stories
Key Techniques	Focusing on solutions Identifying exceptions	Externalization Identifying unique outcomes Creating audiences of support

cations, structural, and strategic schools. They don't presume that symptomatic families are inherently dysfunctional but rather that they have failed to adapt to changing circumstances.

Anyone who ignores this developmental principle runs the risk of placing undue emphasis on pathology. A therapist who sees a family having trouble, but fails to consider that they may be stuck at a transitional impasse, is apt to think they need an overhaul when a tuneup might do. Therapies that emphasize long-range goals are all susceptible to this therapeutic overkill. Psychoanalytic, experiential, and extended family practitioners are inclined to assume that families need fundamental reorganization. Because they have the equipment for major surgery—long-term therapy—they tend to see their clients as needing it.

The pioneers of family therapy (with the notable exception of Virginia Satir) tended to overestimate homeostatic forces in families and underestimate their flexibility and resourcefulness. This viewpoint encouraged therapists to act as provokers, controllers, and strategizers. The corollary of the family trapped by systemic forces they can't understand was the clever therapist who would do the understanding for them. Many of the newer approaches are designed to elicit families' resources rather than battle with their resistance. These models encourage therapists to collaborate with families to work out solutions rather than to assume that they won't change unless provoked. But when some of these "collaborative" approaches—like solution-focused therapy, for example—presume that change is easy, that seems as much naive as optimistic.

Process/Content

Most schools of family therapy emphasize the **process** of family interaction. Psychoanalysts and experientialists try to reduce defensiveness and foster open expression of thoughts and feelings; communications therapists increase the flow of interactions and help family members reduce the incongruence between levels of communication; Bowenians block triangulation and encourage "I-positions"; strategic therapists counter problem-maintaining interactions; behaviorists teach parents to use positive control and couples to eliminate coercive communication; structural therapists realign boundaries and strengthen hierarchical organization.

Despite their commitment to process, however, therapists often get distracted by content issues. Psychoanalysts lose sight of process when they concentrate on individual family members and their memories of the past. Experientialists often become overly central while working with individual family members to help them overcome emotional defensiveness. The danger is that by

so doing the therapist will neglect interactional processes that affect individual expression.

Behavior therapists neglect process in favor of content when they isolate behavior and ignore the interactional patterns surrounding it. They often interfere with the process of family interaction by assuming a directive, teaching role. (As long as a teacher stands in front of the class lecturing, there's little opportunity to find out what the students can do on their own.)

Process concepts are so central to Bowen systems therapy that there's little danger of forgetting them. Only naive misunderstanding of Bowen's theory would lead someone to think merely of reestablishing family ties, without also being aware of processes of triangulation, fusion, and differentiation. The same is true of structural family therapy and communications therapy; process issues are always at center stage.

The newer models, with their deemphasis on systems thinking, have moved away from process. Narrative constructivists are less interested in interactional patterns than in the ways family members understand their problems. They're less interested in changing behavior than in expanding stories. Similarly, because solution-focused therapists have no interest in how problems got started, they ignore the family processes that surround problems. The only processes they do attend to are interactions that constitute "exceptions"—times when the problem wasn't a problem.

Monadic, Dyadic, or Triadic Model

Some therapists (e.g., psychoeducational) continue to think of individuals as the patient and include the rest of the family as an adjunct to that person's treatment. Keep in mind that psychoeducational therapists work primarily with serious mental illness (schizophrenia, bipolar disorder), where the family's influence is almost certainly less than in the majority of cases treated by family therapists.

The same cannot, however, be said for narrative therapists, whose focus on cognition leads them to concentrate on individuals and largely ignore the three defining characteristics of family therapy: (1) that psychological symptoms are often the result of family conflict; (2) thinking about human problems as interactional, which means thinking in twos and threes (complementarity, triangles); and (3) treating the family as a unit. Although narrative therapists disregard family conflict in their formulations, their efforts to redefine problems as alien invaders have the effect of uniting families to overcome the problem's influence. It would be interesting to speculate on whether ignoring family conflict but rallying family members to unite in concern would be more effective in cases like anorexia, where problems take on a life of their own, than in others, like school refusal or misbehavior, where the problem is more likely to be a result of family conflicts.

Psychoanalysts tend to think about personality dynamics, whether they meet with individuals or families. They see family life as a product of internalized relationships from the past, and they're often more concerned with these mental ghosts than with the flesh-and-blood family of the present. Behavior therapists use a **monadic model** when they accept a family's definition of a symptomatic child as the problem and set about teaching parents to modify the child's behavior. Experiential therapists focus on individuals to help them uncover and express their feelings.

Actually, no living thing can adequately be understood in terms of the monadic model. A bird's egg may be the closest thing in nature to a self-contained unit. The fetus is locked away inside its shell with all the nutrients it needs to survive. Even this view is incomplete, however, for there is an exchange of heat between the egg and the surrounding environment. Without its mother's warmth, the baby bird will die.

Dyadic concepts are necessary to explain the fact that people act in relation to one another. Even the psychoanalytic patient, free-associating on the couch, filters memories and dreams through reactions to the analyst. Most of the time family therapists operate with dyadic concepts. Even with a large family in treatment, the focus is usually on various pairs or units of the family.

Helping two people learn to relate better doesn't always mean that the therapist thinks in dyadic terms. Behavior therapists work with couples but treat them as individuals, each deficient in the art of communicating. A true **dyadic model** is based on the recognition that two people in a relationship aren't independent entities interacting with each other; they each define the other. Using this model, a wife's agoraphobia would be understood as a reaction to her husband and as a means of influencing him. Likewise, his decision to send her for behavior modification reflects his reluctance to accept his role in her life.

Family therapists of all schools use some dyadic concepts: unconscious need complementarity, expressive/instrumental, projective identification, symbiosis, intimacy, quid pro quo, double bind, symmetrical/complementary, pursuer/distancer, and behavioral contract. Some terms are based on dyadic thinking even though they may involve more than two people: compliant (referring to a family's relationship to a therapist) or defiant. Some seem to involve only one: countertransference, dominant, and supercompetent. Still other concepts are capable of encompassing units of three or more but are often used to refer to units of two: boundary, coalition, fusion, and disengagement.

Too often family therapists neglect triadic complications. Murray Bowen did more than anyone to point out that human behavior is always a function of triangles. Structural therapists have consistently emphasized that enmeshment or disengagement between two people is a function of reciprocal relationships with third parties. Communications therapists wrote about triadic relationships but tended to think in units of two. The same is true of most strategic therapists, although Haley, Selvini Palazzoli, and Lynn Hoffman are consistently aware of triangles.

The advantage of the **triadic model** is that it permits a more complete understanding of behavior in context. If a child misbehaves when his mother doesn't use firm discipline, teaching her to be stricter won't work if her behavior reflects her relationship with her husband. Perhaps she allows her child to misbehave as a way of undermining her husband's authority, or she and her husband may have worked out a relationship where her ineffectiveness reassures him that he's the strong one.

The fact that triadic thinking permits a more complete understanding doesn't mean that family therapists must always include all parties in treatment. The issue isn't how many people are in the consulting room, but whether the therapist considers problems in their full context.

The Nuclear Family in Context

Just as most family therapists endorse the ideas of systems theory, most also describe families as **open systems.** The family is open in that its members interact not only with each other but also with extrafamilial systems. Indeed, a major emphasis in contemporary family therapy has been to expand the focus of attention to include how families are affected by race, gender, ethnicity, class, and sexual orientation. For today's therapist, talking about the social context of families is no longer an idle abstraction.

Members of the Palo Alto group introduced the concept of open systems but treated families as self-contained units. They paid little attention to stressors outside the family and rarely considered the impact of the community or extended family. The first to take the extrafamilial into account were Murray Bowen and Ross Speck. Bowen stressed the critical role of extended family relationships, and Speck mobilized networks of friends and neighbors to aid in treatment.

Bowen systems therapists and network therapists virtually always include people outside the nuclear family in treatment; psychoanalytic, solution-focused, behavioral, and narrative therapists rarely do. Among experientialists, Whitaker routinely included members of the extended family for one or two sessions. Including extended family members or friends in treatment is often useful, sometimes essential. It is not, however, the same as thinking of the family as an open system. An open system isn't a larger system; it's a system that interacts with its environment.

Nowhere is the idea of families as open systems better articulated than in Minuchin's (1974) *Families and Family Therapy.* Writing about "Man in His Context," Minuchin contrasts family therapy with psychodynamic theory. The latter, he says, draws on the concept of man as a hero, remaining himself despite the circumstances.[1] On the other hand, "The theory of family therapy is predicated on the fact that man is not an isolate. He is an acting and reacting member of social groups" (p. 2). Minuchin credits Gregory Bateson with erasing the boundary between inner and outer space and goes on to say that, just as the boundary separating the individual from the family is artificial, so is the boundary separating the family from the social environment.

One of the things that anyone who works with agency families quickly learns is that attempts to help them often get caught in a sticky web of competing influences from courts, probation departments, child protective agencies, family services, housing programs, group homes, domestic violence agencies, and so on. If middle-class families can be treated as organizationally closed units, with poor families that's impossible. Poor families live in homes without walls.

As services proliferate, fiefdoms multiply. The most obvious problem is lack of coordination. Take, for example, a recent case involving a fifteen-year-old boy who had sexually abused his two adolescent sisters and younger brother. There were agencies working with the female victims, one with the older girl, and another with the younger one. One agency worked with the younger boy, one worked with the perpetrator, and one worked with the mother of the victims. There was an art therapist in the public school working with the sexually abused children, and the fifteen-year-old was in a residential school where he had individual and group therapy. Is

---

1.   Although we recognize that it was until recently the rule, use of the masculine pronoun here may be particularly apt. The model of the hero is of a man who keeps his moral integrity hard and intact. He is an isolate, stoic and enduring, cut off from family, community, and faith—that is, the trivial, suffocating world of women.

It's impossible to understand relationships without taking into account the social and cultural forces impinging on the partners.

it any wonder that these helpers were pulling in different directions? A second, more invidious, problem is that most agencies are mandated to serve individuals—victims or victimizers, adults or children. By addressing themselves to the rights of persons in need of protection or correction, these agencies support individuals, not the family unit.

The usual reaction of therapists who run into these networks of unorganized altruism is to make an effort to coordinate the various inputs, and then, when they discover their lack of leverage with all these agencies and helpers, to give up and do the best they can with the family in the office. Among those who aren't willing to give up, Evan Imber-Black (1988) and Richard Kagan and Shirley Schlosberg (1989) have written practical books about working with families in "perpetual crisis." Patricia Minuchin, Jorge Colapinto, and Salvador Minuchin (1998)

published an inspiring account of their efforts to bring a family focus to agency social work with families of the poor.

Under the influence of social constructionism, the newer models of family therapy have become acutely aware of the social context of the families they treat. This awareness is, however, less likely to take the form of including people outside the family in treatment than being sensitive to social and political influences on the modern family.

The Personal as Political

At one time it was axiomatic that therapists should maintain therapeutic neutrality: They shouldn't make judgments, take sides, or tell people what to do. They should remain steadfastly objective, encouraging communication or making interpretations, but refrain from imposing their personal opinions and values. Today, however, many practitioners believe that therapists should stand for some things and against others.

Since feminist family therapists first challenged us to face up to gender inequality (e.g., Hare-Mustin, 1978; Goldner, 1985), a growing number of practitioners in the narrative tradition have begun to help family members identify the harmful influence of certain cultural values and practices on their lives and relationships (e.g., White & Epston, 1990; Freedman & Combs, 1996). Indeed, one of the most powerful ways they motivate people to become more active in their own destinies is to help them think of themselves as not flawed but oppressed. Once they start to make progress, the narrative therapist seeks to recruit other people as witnesses and a cheering squad to support the client's new and more positive sense of self.

There is certainly a case to be made for helping people question values that may be contributing to their problems. Who says women should be as thin as runway models? That adolescence must be a time of turmoil? That a man's first obligation is to his career? Moreover, by defining certain destructive assumptions as culturally imposed, narrative therapists invite family members to pull together in opposing those values. Questions can be raised, however, about how this political awareness is put into practice.

Sometimes a readiness to identify oppressive cultural attitudes can lead to ignoring a client's role in his or her own problems in favor of projecting blame outward. Take, for example, the case of a woman who starts to wonder if something about what she's doing might be responsible for her lack of success with men. What happens if the therapist redefines the woman's problem as "The Voice of Insecurity" and urges her to consider this doubt as part of a cultural pattern whereby women learn to conform to the expectations of men? It may be true that women do more accommodating than men, but what about *this* woman? If her consideration of how she might be contributing to the pattern of unsuccessful relationships in her life is blamed on society, does this empower her?

It's fine to be sympathetic, even to be the client's champion, but when therapists start assuming that their patients are victims of patriarchy, men, racism, or heterosexism, they may fall into the kind of linear, blaming mentality that family therapy was designed to combat in the first place.

At times the readiness to identify cultural influences as villains in the lives of clients seems like posturing, with the therapist as a knight in shining armor against the forces of oppression. On the other hand, ignoring racism, sexism, ethnocentrism, poverty, crime, and alienation—thinking of families as though they were living on a desert island—makes about as much sense as hiding your head in the sand.

Given the impact of social conditions on families, do family therapists have a unique role to play in politics and society, or are they, at least in their professional capacity, primarily clinicians, trained to treat psychological problems but having no special authority or expertise to right social wrongs? These are important questions without easy answers.

Boundaries

The most useful concepts of interpersonal boundaries are found in the works of Murray Bowen and Salvador Minuchin. Bowen is best at describing the boundary between the self and the family; Minuchin is best at identifying boundaries among various subsystems of the family. In Bowen's terms, individuals vary on a continuum from **fusion** to **differentiation,** whereas Minuchin describes boundaries as ranging from diffuse to rigid, with resultant **enmeshment** or **disengagement.**

Bowen's thinking reflects the psychoanalytic emphasis on *separation* and *individuation* (Mahler, Pine, & Bergman, 1975), with special attention to the resolution of oedipal attachments and leaving home. In this model, we become ourselves by learning to stand alone. Bowen paid less attention to the emotional isolation stemming from rigid boundaries, treating this as an artifact—a defense against a lack of psychological separateness. Bowen used a variety of terms—*togetherness, fusion, undifferentiation, emotional reactivity*—all referring to the danger of people losing themselves in relationships.

Minuchin offers a more balanced view, describing the problems that result when **boundaries** are either too weak *or* too strong. *Diffuse boundaries* allow too much interference into the functioning of a subsystem; *rigid boundaries* allow too little support between members of the family. Bowen described only one boundary problem—fusion—and only one goal—differentiation. Fusion is like a disease—you can have a bad case or a mild one. Minuchin speaks of two possibilities—enmeshment or disengagement—and his therapy is designed to fit the specific case.

Bowen's "fusion" and Minuchin's "enmeshment" both deal with blurred boundaries, but they aren't synonymous. **Fusion** is a psychological quality of individuals, the opposite of individuation. The dynamics of fusion have an impact on relationships (especially in the form of reactivity and triangulation), but fusion is *within* the person. Enmeshment is *between* people.

These conceptual differences also lead to differences in treatment. Bowenian therapists encourage relationships but emphasize autonomy. Success is measured by differentiation of self. Structuralists encourage authenticity but strive to restructure family relationships by strengthening *or* weakening boundaries. Success is measured by the harmonious functioning of the whole family.

Normal Family Development

As a rule, family therapists have had little to say about developmental issues.[2] One of the distinguishing characteristics of family therapy is its focus on problematic here-and-now interactions. Normal family development, which involves the past and what's healthy, has therefore been underemphasized.

Most therapists have assumptions about what's normal, and these ideas influence their work. The problem is that as long as these implicit models remain unarticulated, they may reflect personal bias as much as anything else. When it comes to setting goals for family treatment, the choice isn't between having or not having a model of what's healthy, but between using a model that's been spelled out and examined or operating on the basis of ill-defined, personal standards.

Family therapists concerned with the past, especially members of Bowenian and psychoanalytic schools, have had the most to say about normal development. Although most schools of family therapy aren't concerned with how families get started, Bowenians and psychoanalysts have a great deal to say about marital choice. Bowen talked about *differentiation, fusion,* and *triangles,* while psychoanalytic writers speak of *unconscious need complementarity, projective identification,* and *idealization;* however, they seem to be using different terms to describe similar phenomena. Psychoanalysts speak of marital choice as an object of *transference* from the family of origin and of people choosing partners to match their own level of maturity; Bowen said

that people pick partners who replicate familiar patterns of family interaction and select mates at the same level of differentiation.

These are descriptions of ways in which people marry their own alter egos. Both schools also discuss how people choose mates who appear to be different, at least on the surface, in ways that are exciting and seem to make up for deficiencies in the self. Obsessive individuals tend to marry hysterical individuals and, according to Bowen, togetherness-oriented people often marry distancers. This brings up another way in which the Bowenian and psychodynamic schools are similar to each other and different from others. Both recognize that personalities have layers. Both think that the success of a relationship depends not only on shared interests and values but also on the nature of the partners' internal, introjected object images.

Even if they don't emphasize the past, most of the other schools of family therapy have concepts for describing normal family development. For example, communications therapists speak of the *quid pro quos* (Jackson, 1965) exchanged in normal marriages, while behaviorists describe the same phenomenon in terms of *social exchange theory* (Thibaut & Kelley, 1959).

Virginia Satir described normal families as those in which communication is direct and honest, where differences are faced rather than hidden, and where emotions are openly expressed. Under these conditions, she believed, people develop healthy *self-esteem* that enables them to take the risks necessary for authentic relationships.

According to Minuchin (1974), clinicians should have some appreciation of the facts of ordinary family life to become effective therapists. Clinicians need to distinguish functional from dysfunctional structures, as well as pathological structures from structures that are simply transitional.

Because structural therapy begins by assessing the adequacy of a family's structure, it sometimes appears to impose a standard. In fact, however, normality is defined in terms of functionality, and structural therapists recognize that diverse patterns may be equally functional.

---

2.   This is true despite the current popularity of disavowing impositional models of normality. It's one thing to challenge universals in favor of the particular, but accusing traditional family therapists of operating with fixed views of normality is a straw man argument.

The clarity of subsystem boundaries is more important than the composition of the subsystem. For example, a parental subsystem made up of a single parent and oldest child can function effectively if the lines of authority are clearly drawn. Patterns of enmeshment and disengagement are viewed as preferred styles, not necessarily as indications of abnormality.

Most therapists don't think in terms of remaking families and therefore believe they have little need for models of what a family should be like. Instead, they intervene around specific problems—problem-maintaining interactions, problem-saturated stories, forgotten solutions—conceptualized in terms of function, not structure. The patterns they observe are dysfunctional; therefore, by implication, what's functional must be just the opposite.

While it may not be necessary to have a way of understanding a family's past in order to help them, it is useful to have a way of understanding the family's organization in the present, using a model of normal behavior to set goals for treatment. Such a model should include a design for the present and for change over time. Among the ideas presented in this book, the most useful for a basic model of normal family functioning include *structural hierarchy, effective communication,* and *family life-cycle development.*

Development of Behavior Disorders

In the early days of family therapy, patients were seen as innocents—"scapegoats"—whose deviance maintained family stability. Much of the literature was about dysfunctional ways of keeping the peace: for example *scapegoating, pseudomutuality, family projection process, double bind, mystification.* These malignant mechanisms may have driven young people crazy but they helped keep families together. It was a simple and satisfying tale of malevolence. No one exactly blamed the parents—their coercions weren't really deliberate—but these explanations did rest on parental faults and failings, and as such had

mythic force. The idea that schizophrenia was a sacrifice children made for their families was absolutely riveting—and absolutely untrue.

Today, family therapists think less about what causes problems than about how families unwittingly perpetuate them. Each of the schools of family therapy has unique ideas about how symptomatic families fit together, but the following themes are useful to define some of the differences of opinion.

Inflexible Systems

Early observers of schizophrenic families emphasized their inflexibility. Wynne coined the term *rubber fence* to dramatize how psychotic families resist outside influence and *pseudomutuality* to describe their facade of harmony. R. D. Laing showed how parents, unable to tolerate their children's individuality, used **mystification** to deny their experience. Communication theorists thought that the most striking disturbance in schizophrenic families was that they lacked mechanisms for changing their rules. They were programmed for negative feedback, treating novelty and change as deviations to be resisted.

This tradition of viewing families of mentally ill patients as rigidly homeostatic was taken into the 1980s by Selvini Palazzoli in the form of her concept of "dirty games." Carol Anderson and Michael White countered this negative perspective by suggesting that rigidity might be the result of living with serious problems and of being blamed for them by mental health professionals.

Explaining family problems in terms of homeostatic inflexibility became one of the cornerstones of the strategic school. Dysfunctional families respond to problems with a limited range of solutions. Even when the solutions don't work, these families stubbornly keep trying. Behaviorists use a similar idea when they explain symptoms as resulting from faulty efforts to control behavior. Often when parents think they're punishing misbehavior, they're actually reinforcing it with attention.

According to psychoanalytic and experiential theories, intrapsychic rigidities, in the forms of *conflict, developmental arrest,* and *emotional suppression,* are the individual's contribution to family inflexibility. Psychoanalysts consider unhealthy families as closed systems that resist change. When stressed, inflexible families regress to earlier levels of development, where unresolved conflicts left them fixated.

Experientialists describe dysfunctional families as emotionally stagnant. If it's true that you sometimes have to try something different just to know you're alive, families afraid of rocking the boat become timid and lifeless. The symptom-bearer is a victim of the family's opposition to the life force.

Structural therapists locate the inflexibility of families in the boundaries between subsystems. But structural problems are not necessarily the result of some flaw in the family. Otherwise normal families may develop problems if they are unable to modify a previously functional structure to cope with an environmental or developmental crisis. Family therapists should be extremely clear on this point: Symptomatic families are often basically sound; they may simply need help adjusting to a change in circumstances.

Solution-focused and narrative therapists avoid implicating family members in the development of their problems. Both camps prefer to focus on the strengths of individuals in the family and on times when they used their resources to triumph over their troubles. What these models identify as problematic are rigid habits of thought that lead people to consider themselves defeated. Solution-focused therapists leave it at that; they don't speculate about the origins of defeatist thinking. Narrative therapists point to what they consider toxic systems of belief in the culture that are internalized by family members. It's society, not the family, that's inflexible.

Pathologic Triangles

Pathologic triangles lie at the heart of several family therapy explanations of behavior disorder. Among these, Bowen's theory is the most elegant. Bowen explained how, when two people are in conflict, the one who experiences the most anxiety will triangle in a third person. This model not only provides an explanation of systems pathology but also serves as a warning: As long as a therapist remains tied to one party in an emotional conflict, he or she is part of the problem.

In psychoanalytic theory, oedipal conflicts are considered the root of neurosis. Here the triangle is triggered by family interactions but lodged in the individual psyche. Mother's tenderness may be seductive and father's jealousy threatening, but the wish to do away with the father and possess the mother is a product of fantasy. Pathological fixation of this conflict may be caused by developments in the outer space of the family, but the conflict is harbored in the inner space of the child's mind.

Structural family theory is based on triangular configurations in which a dysfunctional boundary between two subsystems is the reciprocal of a boundary with a third. Father and son's enmeshment reflects father and mother's disengagement; a single mother's disengagement from her children is the counterpart of her overinvolvement outside the family. Structural theory also uses the concept of pathologic triangles to explain *conflict-detouring triads,* whereby parents divert their conflict onto their child. Minuchin, Rosman, and Baker (1978) have even demonstrated that physiological changes occur when parents in conflict transmit their stress to a psychosomatic child.

Strategic therapists typically work with a dyadic model, in which one person's symptoms are maintained by others' efforts to resolve them. Haley and Selvini Palazzoli, however, used a triangular model in the form of **cross-generational coalitions.** These "perverse triangles," as Haley (1977) calls them, occur when a parent and child, or a grandparent and child, collude to form a bastion of covert opposition to the other parent.

Triangular functioning is less central to the newer models because they're not concerned with *how* families develop problems. It might even be argued that ignoring family dynamics is one of the strengths of narrative and solution-focused approaches, if doing so helps these therapists zero in on the constricting habits of thought they're interested in. It might also be said, however, that ignoring family dynamics is one of the weaknesses of these approaches, especially in cases in which conflict in a family isn't just going to dissapear because family members work together to solve a common problem.

●

When things go wrong it's tempting to look for someone to blame. Your partner never talks about his feelings? He must be from Mars. Families drop out after the first couple of sessions? They must be resistant. Before we get too judgmental, let's recognize that it's perfectly natural to attribute our problems to other people's influence. Because we look at life from inside our own skins, we're most aware of other people's contributions to our mutual problems. But therapists, we'd hope, aren't handicapped by this egocentric bias. No, they're handicapped by another bias.

Whenever we hear one side of an unhappy story, it's only natural to sympathize with the person doing the telling. If a friend tells you her boss is a jerk, your sympathy puts you automatically on her side. Experience suggests that most stories have two sides. But when your impulse is to show solidarity with someone who's telling you his or her troubles, the temptation is to look abroad for villains. Among professional helpers, this temptation is too often not resisted.

One reason for blaming family problems on easily vilified influences—men, racism, mothers—is that it's hard to see past individual personalities to the patterns of interaction that make them a family, unless you see the whole group and see them in action. That's why family therapy was invented in the first place.

Therapy

Comparing techniques by reading about them is difficult because clinicians often describe their interventions in abstract terms. When techniques are described in theoretical jargon— restructuring, unbalancing, externalizing, differentiating—it's not always clear precisely what's meant. In this section, we treat issues of technique as a series of practical questions about how to conduct therapy.

Assessment

Each school of family therapy has a theory about families that determines where they look for problems and what they see. Some consider the whole family (Milan, structural, Bowenian); some concentrate on individuals (psychoanalytic, experiential); some focus on sequences that maintain symptoms (strategic, behavioral); and some pay very little attention to what causes problems, preferring instead to mobilize people to work against them (solution-focused, narrative).

Behaviorists place the greatest value on assessment and use the most formal procedures. Assessment is the first order of business. The advantage of the behavioral emphasis on assessment is that it provides clear baseline data, definite goals, and a reliable way to determine whether therapy succeeds. The disadvantage is that, by using standardized interviews and questionnaires, you don't see families in natural interaction. By looking only at part of the family (mother and child, or marital couple), you miss the total context; by relying on questionnaires, you learn only what the family reports.

Structural therapists also emphasize assessment, but their evaluations are based on observation. Enactments give the therapist a chance to observe patterns of enmeshment and disengagement. The strengths of this school's assessment procedure are that it uses the family's patterns of interaction among themselves, it includes the entire family, and it's organized in simple terms that point directly to desired changes.

The Bowenian school also does an excellent job of considering the whole family in its assessment. Unlike structuralists, however, Bowenians rely on what they're told, and they're interested in the past as well as the present.

The breadth of psychoanalytic theory enables practitioners to speculate well ahead of their data; a little information suggests a great deal. The advantage is that the theory provides valuable leads to hidden meanings. The danger is that the theory may distort the data, leading clinicians to see only what they expect to see. Experientialists have neither these advantages nor disadvantages. Their evaluations are guided by a simple notion about feelings and how they are suppressed; they tend not to uncover much that's hidden, but they also tend not to see things that aren't there.

Two of the newer schools, narrative and solution-focused, eschew any form of assessment. Solution-focused therapists believe that dwelling on problems and their causes undermines the positive thinking they hope to generate. They also believe that solutions aren't necessarily related to the ways problems come about. Narrative therapists believe that looking within families for problems perpetuates the therapist-as-expert stance they want to get away from. By personifying problems and talking about their effects rather than their causes, they circumvent the finger pointing that often accompanies family discussions of how problems got started. The danger is that by disregarding how problems arise they may overlook real conflicts. And conflict, as you may have noticed, doesn't necessarily go away simply because you ignore it.

Decisive Interventions

Family therapists use a wide variety of techniques, some dictated by their model, others by the therapist's personality and experience. Even if we limited our attention to the techniques specific to each of the schools, the list would be long and confusing. Some techniques are used by virtually everyone who practices family therapy—asking questions, reflecting feelings, clarifying communication—and this list has been growing as the field has become more integrated. Each school, however, relies on one or two techniques that are unique and decisive.

In psychoanalytic therapy there are two definitive techniques. The first of these, *interpretation*, is well known but not well understood. Properly used, interpretation refers to elucidating unconscious meaning. It does not mean statements of opinion—"You need to express your feelings before you can really be close"; advice—"As long

as you continue writing to him, the affair isn't over"; theory—"Some of the reasons you were attracted to him were based on unconscious needs"; or confrontations—"You said you didn't care, but you were really angry." Interpretations are statements about unconscious meaning. "You've been complaining about your son's arguing with you all the time. Based on what you've said previously I think that some of your anger is deflected from your husband. He does the same thing, but you're afraid to tell him so, and that's why you get so mad at your son."

By refraining from asking questions or giving advice, psychoanalytic practitioners maintain a stance of listening and fostering understanding. By limiting interventions to interpretations, the therapist makes it clear that treatment is designed for learning; whether families take advantage of this atmosphere and change their behavior as a result of what they learn is up to them.

The second decisive technique in analytic treatment is *silence*. A therapist's silence permits him or her to discover what's on a patient's mind and to test the family's resources; it also lends force to eventual interpretations. When a therapist is silent, family members talk, following their own thoughts rather than responding to the therapist's. When they learn that the therapist won't interrupt, they react and respond to each other. This produces a wealth of information that might not otherwise emerge. If a father begins by saying, "The problem is my depression," and the therapist immediately asks, "How long have you been depressed?" he or she may not discover what thoughts are associated in the man's mind with his depression or how the man's wife responds to his complaint.

The decisive technique in experiential therapy is *confrontation*. Confrontations are designed to provoke emotional reactions and are often blunt. It isn't unusual for experiential therapists to tell clients to shut up or to mock them for being insincere. Confrontations are often combined with *personal disclosure*, the second signature technique of this school. Experientialists use themselves as emotionally expressive models. Finally, most experiential therapists also use *structured exercises.* These include role playing, psycho-drama, sculpting, and family drawings. The rationale for these techniques is that they stimulate emotional experiencing; their drawback is that, because they're artificial, the reactions they provoke may be divorced from ordinary experience. Family members may get something off their chests in a structured exercise but may not transfer this to their interactions at home.

Most people associate reinforcement with behavior therapy, but reinforcement isn't a technique used in behavioral family therapy; *observation* and *teaching* are the vehicles of this approach. Behavioralists begin by observing the contingencies of reinforcement in the families they work with. Their aim is to discover the antecedents and consequences of problem behavior. Once they've completed a *functional analysis of behavior,* they become instructors, teaching families how they inadvertently reinforce undesirable behavior. As teachers, their most useful lesson is the use of positive control. They teach parents that it's more effective to reward good behavior than to punish bad behavior; they teach married couples to substitute being nice to each other for their usual bickering.

Positive control—that is, rewarding desirable behavior—is one of the most useful principles in psychotherapy. It's a valuable lesson for families, and for therapists. Therapists, like parents, tend to chide their charges for mistakes; unfortunately, if you're told that you're suppressing your feelings, spoiling your children, or using coercive control, you're apt to feel picked on and put down. Although it may be necessary to point out people's mistakes, it's more effective to concentrate on praising the positive aspects of their behavior. Among practicing family therapists this point seems best understood by structuralists, who speak of working with the family's strengths; by strategists and Milan therapists, who use reframing and positive connotation to support efforts to do the right thing; and of course by solution-focused and narrative therapists, who have raised the power of positive thinking to an art form.

Bowen systems therapists are also teachers, but they follow a different curriculum. They *teach people to be responsible for themselves* and how by doing so they can transform their entire families. Being responsible for yourself means getting clear about what you think and feel—not what your mother says or what you read in The *New York Times* but what you really believe—and then being true to your beliefs in dealings with other people. You don't take responsibility by changing others or wishing they were different; you do so by speaking for yourself and maintaining your own values. The power of this position is tremendous. If a client can accept who he or she is and that other people are different from himself or herself, then he or she no longer has to approach relationships with the idea that someone has to change. This enables the client to be in contact with people without becoming unduly upset or emotionally reactive.

In addition to teaching differentiation, Bowenian therapists promote two corollary lessons: *avoiding triangulation* and *reopening cut-off family relationships.* Taken together, these three lessons enable one person to transform the whole network of his or her family system. Even if her spouse nags, if his children are disobedient, if her mother never comes to visit, the *client* can create a change. Other schools of therapy gain leverage by including the entire family in treatment; Bowenians teach individuals to be themselves, to make contact with others, and to deal directly with the people they have conflicts with. This gives a person a tool for change that's portable and lasting.

Communications family clinicians contributed so much to the theoretical base of family therapy that it's difficult to single out their interventions. Perhaps their greatest achievement was pointing out that communication is multilayered and that often the most important things being said are said covertly. Therapy was designed to make the covert overt. Initially this was done by *clarifying communication* and pointing out hidden messages. When this direct approach met with resistance, therapists began using directives to make the rules of family functioning explicit and to provoke changes in the rules.

Strategic therapy is an offshoot of communications theory, and the techniques used by strategists are refinements of those used by communicationists. Principal among these are *reframing*, *directives*, and *positive connotation*. Strategic practitioners begin by getting concrete descriptions of problems and attempts to solve them. In the process, they pay particular attention to the family's language and expectations. They try to grasp the family's point of view and acknowledge it—in a positive connotation; then they use reframing to shift the family's point of view and directives to interrupt problem-maintaining behavior.

Directives are designed to interrupt homeostatic patterns, they are assigned to be carried out when the family is at home, and they are often paradoxical. Although strategic therapists emphasize fitting the treatment to the patient, they often assume that indirect interventions are necessary to outwit resistance. This is sometimes but not always true. It's not so much that some families are resistant and others aren't, but that resistance isn't a property *in* families; it's a quality of interaction *between* therapist and family. A therapist who proceeds on the assumption that families are unable and unwilling to follow advice is likely to encounter the expected resistance.

Structural family therapy is also a therapy of action, but in this approach the action occurs in the session. The decisive techniques are *enactments* and *boundary making*. Rigid boundaries are softened when the therapist gets people to talk with each other and blocks attempts to interrupt them. Diffuse boundaries are strengthened when the therapist works to support autonomy of individuals and subsystems.

Several promising techniques emerged in the 1980s around which whole models of therapy were built. Steve de Shazer and his colleagues expanded the technique of focusing on successful *solutions* that family members had tried but abandoned. The result was solution-focused therapy. Michael White did the same with the technique of *externalization*—personifying problems and attributing oppressive intentions to them, which is a powerful device for getting family members to unite against a common enemy.

Actually, externalization is a concept, not a technique. The decisive technique of narrative therapy is a persistent and forceful series of *questions*—whereby the therapist begins by trying to understand the clients' experiences of suffering but then switches from understanding to prodding the clients to think about their problems as malevolent agents. Narrative therapists use a relentless series of questions to challenge negative images and convince clients that they have reason to be proud of themselves and that their fates are in their own hands.

In reaction to the sectarian techniquism that reached a peak in the early 1980s, family therapists today borrow freely from other approaches and deemphasize technique in favor of a less hierarchical and more respectful quality of therapist–family relationship. Both trends are healthy, but we would like to end this section with two questions: When is cross-fertilization enriching, and when does eclecticism rob approaches of their muscle by watering down their distinctive elements? How best can family therapists get away from a formulaic emphasis on technique without losing leverage altogether by practicing a more congenial but less effective form of treatment?

—**S**ummary

1. The theme of the early years in the development of family therapy was the proliferation of competing schools, each advertised as unique and uniquely effective. Now, as family therapy moves into the twenty-first century, the theme is integration. So many talented therapists have been working for so long that the field has accumulated a number of useful ways of looking at and treating families. In what follows, we offer some very subjective comments about a few of the concepts and methods that have proven themselves classics of family therapy.

2. Theories of family functioning have both a scientific and a practical purpose. The most useful theories treat families as systems; have concepts to describe forces of stability and change; notice the process underlying the content of family discussions; recognize the triadic nature of human relationships; remember to consider the context of the nuclear family rather than viewing it as a closed system; and appreciate the function of boundaries in protecting the cohesiveness of individuals, subgroups, and families.

3. Clinicians are more concerned with pathology and change than with normality, but it's useful to have some ideas about normal family functioning, both to mold treatment goals and to distinguish what's problematic and needs changing from what is normal and doesn't. Some of the most useful concepts of normal family functioning include the structural model of families as open systems in transformation; the communications model of direct, specific, and honest communication in a family, with rules clear enough to ensure stability and flexible enough to allow change; the behavioral model of equitable exchange of interpersonal costs and benefits, the use of positive control instead of coercion, and mutual reinforcement between partners; the strategic model of systemic flexibility, which allows adjustment to changing circumstances and the ability to find new solutions when old ones don't work; and the Bowenian model, which explains how differentiation of self enables people to be independent at times, intimate at others.

4. Most family therapy concepts of behavior disorder focus on systems and interactions, but the psychoanalytic, Bowenian, narrative, and experiential models add psychological depth to the interactional view, bridging the gap between inner experience and outward behavior. The fact that many divorced people repeat the mistakes of their first marriages supports the idea that some of what goes on in families is a product of individual character. Some of the most valuable concepts of personal dysfunction in families are Bowen's concept of fusion; the experiential concepts of repressed affect and fear of taking risks;

and the psychoanalytic concepts of developmental arrest, internal object relations, instinctual conflict, and hunger for appreciation.

5. These concepts of individual dynamics are useful adjuncts, but the major ideas in the field explain behavior disorder in terms of systems theory. The most influential of these are about inflexible systems, too rigid to accommodate individual strivings or to adjust to changing circumstances; symptomatic family members promoting cohesion by stabilizing the nuclear and extended families; inadequate hierarchical structure; families too tightly or too loosely structured; and pathologic triangles.

6. Some of the goals of family therapy are practically universal—clarifying communication, solving problems, promoting individual autonomy—and some are unique. Some of the schools take presenting problems at face value, whereas others treat them as metaphors and signs. In either case, goals shouldn't be so broad as to neglect symptom resolution, or too narrow to ensure the stability of symptom resolution. Incidentally, values are seldom discussed in the family therapy literature, the notable exception being Boszormenyi-Nagy. Too little consideration has been given to practicing therapists' ethical responsibilities, including the possibility of conflicting responsibilities to individuals, families, and the larger community.

7. If narrative therapists have tended to ignore family dynamics in order to emphasize the ills of the culture, perhaps this will turn out to be one of those swings of the pendulum that inevitably correct itself. There's surely no need to neglect systems theory to introduce an ethical dimension to working with people in context.

8. Some of the major differences among family therapists about how behavior is changed are focused on the following issues: action or insight; change in the session or change at home; duration of treatment; resistance; family–therapist relationship; paradox; and the extent to which it's important to work with the whole family system, part of it, or just motivated individuals. Even though consensus exists about

some issues—for example, once most family therapists believed that action was primary and insight was secondary—there have always been divergent opinions on every one of these points. Strategic therapists, for example, flatly denied that insight is useful.

9. We've looked at some of the major methodological issues and tried to separate out the decisive techniques of the different systems. As is always the case when a number of variables are involved in a final result, it's not easy to know how much each variable contributes to that re-

sult or how important each one is. Furthermore, the more we talk about techniques, the greater the danger of seeing family therapy as a purely technological enterprise. Studying families is like solving a riddle; the act of treating them is to relieve suffering and anguish. The job of the theoretician is to decode or decipher, which requires theory and ingenuity. The job of the therapist is healing, which requires theory but also conviction, perseverance, and caring. Treating families isn't only a matter of theory and technique; it's also an act of love.

—Questions to Consider

1. Can you think of examples of when a problem was understood in monadic or dyadic terms that ignored triangular complications to the detriment of solving the problem?
2. Can you think of unfortunate examples of ignoring the context of a nuclear family?
3. When might it be more useful to use Bowen's concept of *fusion?* When might it be more useful to use Minuchin's concept of *enmeshment?*
4. What therapeutic changes are more likely to happen at home; which are more likely

to happen in the consulting room? Which should a therapist focus on?
5. What are some useful consequences of the concept of *resistance?*
6. How important is it that you choose to practice an approach to therapy that fits your personality? Which approaches seem to fit your personality, and why?
7. In which models are interventions delivered primarily in the form of questions?

—Key Concepts

boundary Emotional and physical barriers that protect and enhance the integrity of individuals, subsystems, and families.

closed system A functionally related group of elements regarded as forming a collective entity that does not interact with the surrounding environment.

cross-generational coalition An inappropriate alliance between a parent and child, who side together against a third member of the family.

differentiation of self Psychological separation of intellect and emotions, and independence of self from others; opposite of fusion.

disengagement Minuchin's term for psychological isolation that results from overly rigid boundaries.

dyadic model Explanations based on the interactions between two persons or objects: Johnny shoplifts to get his mother's attention.

enmeshment Minuchin's term for loss of autonomy due to a blurring of psychological boundaries.

fusion A blurring of psychological boundaries between self and others and a contamination of emotional and intellectual functioning; opposite of differentiation.

monadic model Explanations based on properties of a single person or object: Johnny shoplifts because he is rebellious.

mystification R. D. Laing's concept that many families distort their children's experience by denying or relabeling it.

open system A set of interrelated elements that exchange information, energy, and material with the environment.

process/content Distinction between how members of a family or group relate and what they talk about.

social exchange theory Explanation of behavior in relationships as maintained by a ratio of costs to benefits.

system An organized group of parts plus the way they function together.

triadic model Explanations based on the interactions among three people or objects; Johnny shoplifts because his father covertly encourages him to defy his mother.

—Recommended Readings

Dattilio, F. M. 1998. *Case studies in couple and family therapy: Systemic and cognitive perspectives.* New York: Guilford Press.

Donovan, J. M., ed. 1999. *Short-term couple therapy.* New York: Guilford Press.

Gurman, A. S. 1978. Contemporary marital therapies: A critique and comparative analysis of psychoanalytic, behavioral and systems theory approaches. In *Marriage and marital therapy*, T. J. Paolino and B. S. McCrady, eds. New York: Brunner/Mazel.

Madanes, C., and Haley, J. 1977. Dimensions of family therapy. *Journal of Nervous and Mental Diseases. 165:* 88–98.

Piercy, F. P., Sprenkle, D. H., and Wetchler, J. L. 1996. *Family therapy sourcebook.* 2nd ed. New York: Guilford Press.

Simon, G. M. 2003. *Beyond technique in family therapy: Finding your therapeutic voice.* Boston: Allyn & Bacon.

Sluzki, C. E. 1983. Process, structure and world views: Toward an integrated view of systemic models in family therapy. *Family Process. 22:* 469–476.

Sluzki, C. E. 1987. Family process: Mapping the journey over 25 years. *Family Process. 26:* 149–153.

—References

Freedman, J., and Combs, G. 1996. *Narrative therapy: The social construction of preferred realities.* New York: Norton.

Goldner, V. 1985. Feminism and family therapy. *Family Process. 24:* 31–47.

Haley, J. 1977. Toward a theory of pathological systems. In *The interactional view*, P. Watzlawick and J. Weakland, eds. New York: Norton.

Hare-Mustin, R. T. 1978. A feminist approach to family therapy. *Family Process. 17:* 181–194.

Imber-Black, E. 1988. *Families and larger system: A family therapist's guide through the labyrinth.* New York: Guilford Press.

Jackson, D. D. 1965. Family rules: The marital quid pro quo. *Archives of General Psychiatry. 12:* 589–594.

Kagan, R., and Schlosberg, S. 1989. *Families in perpetual crisis.* New York: Norton.

Mahler, M. S., Pine, F., and Bergman, A. 1975. *The psychological birth of the human infant.* New York: Basic Books.

Minuchin, P., Colapinto, J., and Minuchin, S. 1998. *Working with families of the poor.* New York: Guilford Press.

Minuchin, S. 1974. *Families and family therapy.* Cambridge, MA: Harvard University Press.

Minuchin, S., Rosman, B., and Baker, L. 1978. *Psychosomatic families: Anorexia in context.* Cambridge, MA: Harvard University Press.

Thibaut, J. W., and Kelley, H. H. 1959. *The social psychology of groups.* New York: Wiley.

White, M., and Epston, D. 1990. *Narrative means to therapeutic ends.* New York: Norton.

Family Therapy Research: Empirical Foundations and Practice Implications

Cynthia Rowe, Ligia Gómez, and Howard Liddle

The foundations of family intervention science are now well established (Liddle, Bray, Levant, & Santisteban, 2001). Well-controlled studies have documented the effectiveness of family-based interventions for virtually every type of disorder and relational problem in children, adolescents, and adults (Pinsof & Wynne, 2000). Family-based interventions are now recognized as among the most effective treatments for several disorders, most notably childhood behavioral problems and adolescent drug abuse and delinquency (Northey, Well, Silverman, & Bailey, 2003; Rowe & Liddle, 2003). Treatments that target other family members and the family system as a whole not only reduce symptoms of the identified patient, but also enhance engagement and retention of clients (Stanton, 2004), decrease related problems (Lebow & Gurman, 1995), and have a positive impact on the functioning of other family members (Kelley & Fals-Stewart, 2002). **Meta-analyses,** which examine the magnitude of therapy's effects across many studies, reveal that family therapy generally demonstrates superior effects in comparison to alternative treatments (e.g., Stanton & Shadish, 1997; Shadish, Ragsdale, Glaser, & Montgomery, 1995).

The most positive sign of the field's development in recent years is the fact that these research activities are starting to affect clinical practice. Family therapy research is increasingly being conducted in real-world settings, addressing and examining some of the processes that maintained the research–practice disconnect for many years. Treatment developers are examining family-based models and attempting to minimize barriers to treatment adoption, such as the complexity of treatment packages tested in clinical trials (NIDA, 2002a). While practicing therapists often feel that research-based therapies are biased toward the interests of academics (e.g., heavy emphasis on behavioral techniques) and removed from the realities of clinical settings (Hawley, Bailey, & Pennick,

2000), the most recent studies in this specialty are beginning to demonstrate how providers in the community learn and integrate these empirically validated interventions in standard practice (NIDA, 2002b). Thus new research in this field is addressing the frequently cited criticism that family therapy research has historically failed to address realistic issues or practically outline the steps to implementing interventions into practice (Pinsof & Wynne, 2000).

Because the newest empirically supported family-based models are more systems-oriented and integrative (Kaslow & Lebow, 2002), incorporating components from traditions as diverse as individual psychotherapy (Josephson & Serrano, 2001), child and adolescent psychiatry (Malone, 2001), in-home therapy (Rowe, Liddle, McClintic, & Quille, 2002), and case management (Fishman, Andes, & Knowlton, 2001), they tend to have more ecological validity and appeal to therapists in the community. Professional practice guidelines for many disorders, such as attention-deficit hyperactivity disorder (ADHD), conduct disorder, and substance abuse, now prescribe family interventions as essential aspects of treatment (Bukstein et al., 1997; McCrady & Ziedonis, 2001; Steiner et al., 1997).

This chapter provides an update on the latest empirical findings on family-based interventions, with a focus on findings with the most clinical significance. New studies on the process, outcome, and implementation of these interventions in "real-world" practice settings are highlighted. Finally, we conclude with suggestions for further reducing the gap between family therapy research and practice.

Family Therapy Outcomes

Childhood and Adolescent Behavior Disorders

Family Risk and Protective Factors for Behavior Problems.   Childhood and adolescent behavior problems have been consistently linked to family factors such as conflict and aggression (Dadds, Sanders, Morrison, & Rebgetz, 1992; Lindahl, 1998). Evidence strongly suggests that antisocial behavior is learned at an early age in the home through negative reinforcement of coercive patterns (e.g., a child's aggressive behavior reinforced by the cessation of his parents' arguments), and then generalizes to the school and peer group environments (Patterson, 1995; Snyder & Patterson, 1995). Coercive parenting and poor parental monitoring at age four and a half each predict conduct problems among disadvantaged minority children as early as age six (Kilgore, Snyder, & Lentz, 2000). Longitudinal studies show that ineffective parenting practices in childhood maintain antisocial behavior into adolescence (Vuchinich, Bank, & Patterson, 1992) and young adulthood (Klein, Forehand, Armistead, & Long, 1997). Parental substance abuse and antisocial personality disorder, as well as conflict between parents, are also risk factors for oppositional defiant disorder (ODD) and conduct disorder (CD) (Marcus, Lindahl, & Malik, 2001). Positive family factors, including parental responsiveness, acceptance, and strong connections among parents and children serve as protective factors against ADHD, ODD, and CD (Lindahl, 1998).

Family-Based Interventions for Child Behavior Problems.   Given the primary role of the family in disruptive behavior problems, it's not surprising that treatments to alter these family risk factors are among the most potent treatments for childhood and adolescent conduct problems. Family interaction is accessible, as family therapists well know. This is fortunate because some contributors to dysfunction, such as deviant peer influence, are less available to therapeutic intervention. Family-based treatment specifically targets the coercive family patterns maintaining behavior problems while at the same time bolstering protective factors in the family and other systems affecting the child (Blechman & Vryan, 2000). In several reviews of treatments for child and adolescent behavior problems, family-based treatments have been highlighted as among the most promising interventions (Kazdin, 1991; Estrada & Pinsof, 1995; Hinton, Sheperis, & Sims, 2003; Northey et al., 2003).

Engagement and Retention in Therapy. Family-based approaches have the advantage of addressing many of the barriers that keep troubled children from getting the help they need (Coatsworth, Santisteban, McBride, & Szapocznik, 2001; Fishman et al., 2001), such as parental resistance to change (Stoolmiller, Duncan, Bank, & Patterson, 1993), family adversity (Prinz & Miller, 1994), perceived challenges of therapy itself, and a disconnected relationship with the therapist (Kazdin, Holland, & Crowley, 1997). In fact, one of family therapy's major contributions is an increased focus on engaging difficult youth and their families in treatment (Stanton, 2004; Henggeler, Pickrel, Brondino, & Crouch, 1996). For instance, in early studies using specialized engagement strategies within a structural family therapy model for Hispanic boys with behavior problems, Jose Szapocznik and colleagues demonstrated that their intervention was more successful than alternative treatments in retaining families (Szapocznik et al., 1988, 1989). They went on to refine these engagement techniques, successfully retaining families and reducing behavioral problems among more severe cases, and identifying cultural factors that influence engagement (Coatsworth et al., 2001; Santisteban et al., 1996).

Parent Management Training (PMT). Of the family-based interventions for child and adolescent behavior problems, **parent management training** has received the most empirical attention and support (Mabe, Turner, & Josephson, 2001; Northey et al., 2003). The basic approach, aimed at developing parents' skills and correcting parenting behaviors that contribute to negative coercive cycles (Wierson & Forehand, 1994), is characterized by:

Jose Szapocznik's studies demonstrate that making family treatment responsive to cultural context greatly increases its effectiveness with high-risk individuals and families.

1. Focusing on the parent in treatment;
2. Helping parents identify and react to the child's problem behavior in new ways;
3. Applying social learning principles to increase positive parenting skills (e.g., praise for good behavior, and effective use of mild punishment such as time out) to shape the child's behavior;
4. Providing opportunities to practice new parenting skills in the home (Kazdin 1991).

Gerald Patterson and his colleagues have produced significant support for the effects of PMT with a range of ages and samples, demonstrating impressive changes in children's behavior in comparison to standard family therapy, attention-placebo, peer group intervention, services as usual in the community, and no treatment (Bank, Marlowe, Reid, & Patterson, 1991; Dishion & Andrews, 1995). These investigators developed a prototype for the application of basic scientific findings about family functioning into an elegant and effective clinical model.

Most recently, Patterson and his colleagues have embarked on an ambitious international program of study that examines the processes by which providers learn and implement PMT in practice settings. For example, in response to a call for the implementation of empirically based interventions to reduce problem behavior and promote social competence among Norwegian youth, Marion Forgatch is currently involved in a project with the University of Oslo aimed at having trained PMT therapists available in every municipality to intervene at the early stages of deviant child behavior in an effort to prevent later substance use, child antisocial behavior, delinquency, and school failure (Ogden & Halliday-Boykins, 2004; Ogden et al., 2003).

PMT also shows promise as a treatment for children and teens with ADHD (Northey et al., 2003). For instance, Russell Barkley and his colleagues (1992) reported preliminary evidence supporting the use of PMT with adolescents suffering from ADHD, although the effects were not significantly greater than structural family therapy or a family problem-solving approach, nor did many adolescents in any of the treatments show clinically significant change. A second study by the same group with ADHD adolescents similarly showed few differences in either a combination of PMT (first stage of therapy) plus a family problem-solving approach (second stage of therapy) versus family problem solving alone, although PMT techniques appear to be important in the first stage of treatment to reduce drop out from family therapy (Barkley et al., 2001). However, other researchers report positive effects of parent training on child inattention and overactivity, noncompliance, and aggression, as well as parental stress and self-esteem with an ADHD sample (Sonuga-Barke et al., 2001). Another recent advance has been to expand parent training to address other family and school issues, helping parents deal with school problems directly with the teacher, as well as minimizing their own stress and angry outbursts (Wells et al., 2000).

PMT is also promising as a preventive approach with young children identified as at-risk for conduct problems (Nye, Zucker, & Fitzgerald, 1995; Sanders, Markie-Dadds, Tully, & Bor, 2000). Other groups have shown that a combination of parent and child management training appears to be superior to either approach alone in reducing child aggression and promoting positive functioning among both parents and children

(Kazdin, Siegel, & Bass, 1992; Webster-Stratton & Hammond, 1997). Carolyn Webster-Stratton has also developed and tested an innovative version of PMT using videotape review to provide feedback to parents (Webster-Stratton, 1994, 1996). Positive long-term effects of PMT have consistently been demonstrated from one year (Webster-Stratton, Hollinsworth, & Kolpacoff, 1989; Webster-Stratton & Hammond, 1997; Dishion & Andrews, 1995) up to fourteen years following treatment (Long, Forehand, Wierson, & Morgan, 1994).

Functional Family Therapy. Functional family therapy (FFT; Alexander & Parsons, 1982) is another promising family-based approach for the prevention and treatment of childhood and adolescent conduct problems. This model is based on the assumption that children's behavior problems serve a function within the family system, and are initiated and maintained by maladaptive interpersonal processes. Treatment therefore targets change in these destructive interactional patterns, and uses behavioral interventions to reinforce more positive ways of responding (Alexander & Sexton, 2002). Early research, among the first well-controlled trials of family therapy for adolescent behavior problems (Alexander & Parsons, 1973; Barton et al., 1985), established that functional family therapy improved family functioning and reduced recidivism among delinquent teens to a greater extent than juvenile court–based group therapy, group home therapy, psychodynamic therapy, or no treatment. The preventive impact of this model was revealed with younger siblings of the adolescents treated in the original trial, who were assessed two and a half years later and found to have significantly lower rates of juvenile justice involvement than siblings in alternative treatments (Klein, Alexander, & Parsons, 1977). A more recent study of FFT with an urban sample of violent offenders showed a lower reoffending rate in comparison to matched controls (20 percent versus 36 percent); FFT youth committed fewer crimes and engaged in less serious criminal activities (Sexton & Alexander, 2002).

Multisystemic Therapy (MST). Perhaps the most promising therapeutic approach for the treatment of juvenile delinquency is multisystemic therapy (MST; Henggeler et al., 1991, 1996). In a series of rigorously controlled trials with serious juvenile offenders, Scott Henggeler and his colleagues have demonstrated impressive results of the model's ability to engage families in treatment (Henggeler, Pickrel, Brondino, & Crouch, 1996) and to reduce recidivism up to four years post-treatment (Henggeler, Clingempeel, Brondino, & Pickrel, 2002). In comparison to juvenile court services as usual and individual therapy, MST has not only shown significantly lower recidivism rates and reduced time incarcerated, but has also demonstrated greater positive effects on family functioning and aggression with peers (Henggeler, Melton, & Smith, 1992). Finally, these investigators conducted one of the only cost-effectiveness studies of family-based interventions. In comparison to outpatient treatment, MST significantly reduced the youth's involvement with the legal system within six months after treatment, and this decrease was not offset by an increase in out-of-home placements (Schoenwald et al., 1996).

●

To summarize, the evidence supporting family interventions for child and adolescent behavior problems is quite strong. Several different models have demonstrated effectiveness in community-based studies. State-of-the-art, family interventions for child and adolescent behavioral disorders are increasingly focused on devising strategies for intervening in the many systems that influence these youth and their families (Blechman & Vryan, 2000; Fishman et al., 2001). These therapies promote positive outcomes such as prosocial peer relationships and family functioning, as well as reducing conduct problems. Because of the impressive effects of these interventions with the most severe clinical populations, they are gaining widespread

attention from providers and health service administrators.

Family Therapy for Depression and Anxiety

Family Risk and Protective Factors for Depression and Anxiety. There is evidence for particular family processes in the development and maintenance of anxiety and depression among children, adolescents, and adults. For instance, insecure attachment relationships (Sexson, Glanville, & Kaslow, 2001), dysfunctional communication patterns (Slesnick & Waldron, 1997), generally negative messages communicated by parents (Stark et al., 1993), and other family factors increase risk for child and adolescent depression (Kaslow & Racusin, 1994). Parent–adolescent conflict (Cole & McPherson, 1993; Forehand et al., 1988), parental rejection (Whitbeck et al., 1992), and parental depression (Downey & Coyne, 1990) have also been linked to depression in childhood and adolescence. Conversely, adolescents' perceptions of family cohesion and support serve as protective factors against depression (Cumsille & Epstein, 1994). Among adults, investigators have outlined characteristics of marital interactions that are linked to depressive symptoms, such as marital infidelity and separation (Cano & O'Leary, 2000), marital dissatisfaction and lack of intimacy (Basco et al., 1992), and poor communication and problem-solving skills (Goldman Sher & Baucom, 1993). Further, family dysfunction predicts poor prognosis and relapse of depressive illness (Miller et al., 1992), particularly perceived criticism from one's spouse (Hooley & Teasdale, 1989) and high expressed emotion among family members (Hinrichsen & Pollack, 1997; Miklowitz et al., 2004).

Although less research has focused on the role of the family in the development of anxiety disorders, there is evidence that maternal characteristics such as low warmth, negativity, catastrophizing, and low autonomy granting, as well as psychopathology (Fristad & Clayton, 1991) and alcoholism (Chassin, Pitts, DeLucia,

& Todd, 1999) may leave children vulnerable to anxiety (Whaley, Pinto, & Sigman, 1999). Anxious children's tendencies to interpret information as threatening and to develop avoidant responses have been shown to increase during problem-solving family interactions (Barrett, Rapee, Dadds, & Ryan, 1996). Anxiety has also been linked to marital negativity and dissatisfaction (Caughlin, Huston, & Houts, 2000).

Family-Based Treatment for Child and Adolescent Emotional Problems.   Despite the strong evidence for family influence on child and adolescent depression and anxiety, the potential of family-based treatments for these disorders has not been fully realized. Brent and colleagues (1997) tested systemic behavior family therapy (SBFT, which utilizes functional family therapy, communication, and problem-solving techniques) in a **randomized trial** for depressed adolescents in comparison to individual cognitive behavior therapy (CBT) and individual supportive therapy. Results favored individual CBT over the comparison interventions in the rate of recovery from depressive symptoms, although all three treatments were associated with similar reductions in suicidality and functional impairment. In one- and two-year follow-up analyses, however, all three treatments were equally effective in helping adolescents achieve remission from a depressive disorder (Birmaher et al., 2000). Further analyses revealed that SFBT was more effective in addressing parent–adolescent conflict than either of the other treatments (Kolko et al., 2000).

Attachment-based family therapy (ABFT; Diamond, Siqueland, & Diamond, 2003), a brief treatment model tailored to the specific needs of depressed adolescents and their families, has been tested in a randomized clinical trial (Diamond et al., 2002). ABFT relies on interpersonal models of depression, and its clinical procedures draw from structural therapy, multidimensional family therapy, and emotionally focused therapy. Eighty-one percent of the adolescents who participated in ABFT no longer met criteria for a di-

agnosis of depression post-treatment, compared to 56 percent of those in the wait-list condition. In addition, completion of ABFT was associated with significant reductions in family conflict and anxiety, and yielded nearly significant changes in attachment to mother, hopelessness, and suicidal ideation (Diamond et al., 2002).

Results of studies testing combination treatments for depression with parent components have been mixed. Lewinsohn, Clarke, Hops, & Andrews (1990) demonstrated no additional benefit from adding a parent psychoeducational and skills training module to a CBT group intervention for adolescent depression, yet Stark (1990) reported significantly greater reduction in children's depressive symptoms using a combination school-based CBT approach with family therapy sessions in comparison to traditional supportive counseling. Thus, the few studies that have been conducted on family-based interventions provide limited support for their efficacy with depressed children and adolescents.

New research on family-based interventions for pediatric bipolar disorder have yielded encouraging results. In fact, family psychoeducational approaches may be the most carefully studied psychosocial interventions for pediatric bipolar disorder (Pavuluri et al., 2004). Multifamily psychoeducational groups aim to educate families about the nature of mood disorders and provide support for families in managing the symptoms of mania and depression. Fristad, Goldberg-Arnold, and Gavazzi (2002) report positive effects of multifamily groups in changing parents' attitudes about the disorder, improving family climate, and increasing social support for children with mood disorders. Family-focused psychoeducational therapy, developed originally for adults with bipolar disorder, also shows promise with young bipolar patients (Miklowitz et al., 2004). Family-focused therapy (FFT) is similar in structure to behavioral family therapy, incorporating didactic information sessions, communication-enhancement training, and problem-solving skills training, as well as behavioral techniques designed to provide opportunities to practice and refine new skills. Preliminary results of FFT for adolescents with bipolar disorder show positive trajectories toward clinical improvement over the year following treatment (Miklowitz et al., 2004). Finally, a variant of FFT for younger children with bipolar disorder, called child and family-focused cognitive-behavioral therapy (CFF-CBT), addresses the unique symptoms associated with pediatric bipolar disorder. A pilot study of CFF-CBT demonstrated its feasibility in terms of treatment fidelity and consumer satisfaction (Pavuluri et al., 2004).

Family-based interventions for child anxiety disorders have used CBT and graded exposure techniques, teaching parents to support and reinforce children in their efforts to deal with stressful situations. These family-based interventions also aim to improve the parent–child relationship and increase parenting effectiveness. Combination CBT and family-based interventions have shown effectiveness with anxious children and their parents (Northey et al., 2003). For instance, Dadds and colleagues (1997) tested a ten-week school-based cognitive-behavioral and family-based group early intervention for children screened for anxiety problems in comparison to a monitoring condition. Both treatments reduced anxiety symptoms, yet only the CBT family-based intervention maintained treatment gains at six months and up to two years following the intervention (Dadds et al., 1999). Another investigation of this approach tested CBT-group, CBT-group plus family management (problem solving and skills training for parents in helping manage their child's anxiety), and a wait-list control group for children with anxiety disorders (Barrett, 1998). Both interventions were superior to the wait-list control. Further, the addition of the family management component demonstrated slightly better effects than the CBT-group alone (Barrett et al., 1996). Group-based CBT that involved both parents and children more effectively increased anxious children's coping skills than either group CBT for children or group CBT for parents (Mendlowitz et al., 1999). Finally, Spence, Donovan, and Brechman-Toussaint

(2000) demonstrated positive effects of group CBT with a family component for children with social phobia in comparison to a wait-list control condition. These results suggest that incorporating parenting skills training and family therapy techniques in the treatment of child and adolescent anxiety disorders can have important benefits over CBT alone.

Family-Based Treatment for Adult Depression and Anxiety. Due to the strong link between depression and marital problems (Jacobson, Holtzworth-Munroe, & Schmaling, 1989), family-based interventions for adult depression have focused mainly on the application of behavioral couples therapy. Behavioral marital therapy (BMT) for depression focuses on teaching couples to communicate and problem-solve more effectively, while increasing positive interactions and reducing aversive interchanges. Generally, these marital interventions have been shown to be as effective as state-of-the-art alternative treatments (e.g., interpersonal psychotherapy and cognitive therapy) in reducing depressive symptoms and are more effective than these other treatments in improving the quality of the marital relationship (Jacobson et al., 1989; O'Leary & Beach, 1990). Behavioral couples therapy appears to work equally well in decreasing marital dissatisfaction, eliminating negative communication, and improving psychological functioning for distressed couples and couples with a depressed partner (Goldman Sher, Baucom, & Larus, 1990). However, Jacobson and colleagues (1991) reported that BMT was less effective than cognitive therapy in reducing depressive symptoms among women who were not maritally distressed at intake. Further, there is no evidence to suggest that marital and couples therapy is superior to cognitive therapy in reducing relapse rates in the year following treatment (Jacobson et al., 1993). Generally, couples therapy has generated convincing empirical support in the treatment of depression, particularly among women whose depressive symptoms are related to marital distress.

Family-based psychoeducational treatment with adult bipolar patients is also gaining empirical support. Simoneau et al. (1999) randomly assigned patients to either nine months of family-focused therapy (FFT, described above) or crisis management (both conditions involving medication management). Results demonstrated the superiority of FFT in increasing positive nonverbal family exchanges and reducing patients' symptoms in the year following treatment entry. Longer follow-ups reveal that FFT patients have lower relapse rates, lower rates of hospital admissions, better medication compliance, greater improvement in communication and problem-solving skills, and significant reduction in mood symptoms in comparison to individually focused treatment up to fifteen months post-treatment (Miklowitz et al., 2004; Rea et al., 2003). These results suggest that psychoeducational family interventions offer promise in the treatment of bipolar patients.

Family-based interventions for adult anxiety disorders have been infrequently tested and have not demonstrated great success. For instance, behavioral family therapy as applied to post-traumatic stress disorder (PTSD) symptoms among combat veterans had no additional impact when delivered in combination with exposure therapy (Glynn et al., 1999). Involvement of the spouse in therapy for agoraphobia and obsessive-compulsive disorder (OCD) appears to have some beneficial effects, although the evidence for these interventions is inconsistent (Baucom et al., 1998; Jacobson et al., 1989).

●

In sum, family-based interventions for child and adolescent emotional disorders have lagged behind the progress seen in the application of family approaches for behavioral disorders. However, new studies of family interventions for pediatric bipolar disorder have yielded encouraging results. Certainly family-based interventions for both childhood depression and anxiety have promise, yet further study of these approaches is necessary.

In the treatment of adult emotional disturbances, significant support exists for the use of behavioral couples therapy with depressed patients and their partners, yet little evidence supports the use of family-based interventions for adults with anxiety disorders. Family therapy appears to be an effective approach for bipolar patients. Couples therapy may be a useful adjunct to exposure therapy for adult anxiety disorders. Overall, family-based interventions for depression and anxiety offer promise and warrant further study.

Family Therapy for Substance Use Disorders

Family Risk and Protective Factors for Substance Abuse. Family factors have been strongly linked to substance abuse problems. Further, substance abuse wreaks havoc on families (Rotunda, Scherer, & Imm, 1995). Relationship factors such as parent–adolescent attachment consistently predict adolescent drug use across cultures (Brook et al., 2001). Parenting practices such as low monitoring, ineffective discipline, and poor communication are also implicated in substance abuse problems among youth (McGillicuddy, Rychtarik, Duquette, & Morsheimer, 2001), although parenting clearly interacts with a host of other factors in predicting the onset of drug abuse and related problems (Dishion & Kavanagh, 2000). Other family factors have been shown to exert a strong protective influence against drug problems (Morojele & Brook, 2001). For instance, youth whose parents strongly disapprove of drug use were significantly less likely to report current use of an illicit drug (SAMHSA, 2001). Studies with adults show that couple and marital factors, such as the partners' poor coping strategies for dealing with the substance abuse (Barber, 1995) and generally negative communication patterns within the marriage (Fals-Stewart & Birchler, 1998) are associated with the substance abuser's more frequent use. Further, research shows that maintaining close relationships within healthy families-of-origin may buffer adult substance abusers from relapse (Lavee & Altus, 2001).

Family-Based Interventions for Adolescent Substance Abuse. Family-based treatments appear to be the treatment of choice for adolescent drug problems (Stanton & Shadish, 1997; Williams & Chang, 2000; Vaughn & Howard, 2004). Two decades of rigorously controlled trials have established the efficacy of family-based interventions for adolescent drug abuse (Joanning, Quinn, Thomas, & Mullen, 1992; Liddle et al., 2001, 2004). The most effective models are integrative approaches designed to alter the life ecology of the drug-abusing teen, as well as changing maladaptive family patterns and improving functioning in school, work, and legal involvement (Henggeler et al., 1991; Liddle, 2002a; Szapocznik & Williams, 2000).

Family-based interventions have been found to have superior treatment effects on levels of adolescent drug use compared to individual therapy (Henggeler et al., 1991; Liddle, 2002b; Waldron et al., 2001), adolescent group therapy (Joanning et al., 1992; Liddle et al., 2004), and family psychoeducational drug counseling (Joanning et al., 1992; Liddle et al., 2001). These reductions in drug use seen in family-oriented treatments have demonstrated long-term effects up to twelve months after termination (Liddle, 2002b). Further, family-based treatments exert positive effects on family functioning (Joanning et al., 1992; Liddle et al., 2001), school performance (Azrin et al., 2001; Liddle et al., 2001), comorbid symptomatology (Azrin et al., 2001; Liddle, 2002b), and delinquency (Henggeler, Pickrel, & Brondino, 1999). Integrative family-based approaches combining elements of CBT also show promise (Waldron et al., 2001). Finally, family-based prevention approaches that help parents institute effective practices against drug use are being implemented and tested in school (Dishion & Kavanagh, 2000) and community settings (Hogue, Liddle, Becker, & Johnson-Leckrone, 2002).

Brief strategic family therapy (BSFT) has a long clinical tradition, founded in earlier work treating Hispanic boys with behavior problems (Szapocznik et al., 1986). BSFT borrows from structural and strategic family therapy in its aim to change the problematic family patterns maintaining drug abuse and related symptoms, as well as intervening with the school and other systems to reduce risk and bolster protective factors. In a recent clinical trial with drug-abusing minority teens, BSFT more effectively reduced marijuana use and behavior problems and improved family functioning in comparison to group treatment (Santisteban et al., 2003).

The multidimensional family therapy (MDFT) approach has been recognized as one of the most effective interventions in a new generation of comprehensive and empirically supported adolescent drug abuse treatments (Brannigan, Schackman, Falco, & Millman, 2004; Lebow & Gurman, 1995; NIDA, 1999b). This multidimensional approach assumes that reductions in target symptoms and increases in prosocial behavior occur via multiple pathways. With the adolescent, the therapist seeks to transform the youth's drug-using lifestyle into a developmentally normative lifestyle and to improve peer relations, identity formation, bonding to school and other social institutions, and autonomy within the parent–adolescent relationship. Goals with parents include increasing parental commitment, improving communication with the adolescent, and increasing knowledge and skills in parenting (e.g., limit-setting, monitoring).

The MDFT model has been distinguished among the multisystemic family-based treatment programs based on evidence of its clinically significant impact on drug use over time, as well as its large effect sizes in comparison to other treatments (Austin, Macgowan, and Wagner, 2005). MDFT has demonstrated efficacy in comparison to alternative treatments in four controlled trials, including a prevention study, with mainly juvenile justice–involved and comorbid, drug-abusing youth (Hogue et al., 2002; Liddle et al., 2001, 2004; Liddle, 2002b). The clinical outcomes achieved in these randomized studies indicate that MDFT is effective in comparison to state-of-the-art treatments (individual CBT, peer group treatment, and family education models) in significantly reducing substance use and related problems up to one year following treatment completion. A recent study showed that MDFT was more effective than individual CBT in impacting drug use and comorbid symptoms with more severely impaired youth (Henderson et al., 2004).

Family-Based Interventions for Adult Substance Abuse. Family-based interventions for adult substance abusers have also made major strides in the past two decades (Edwards & Steinglass, 1995; Heath & Stanton, 1998; O'Farrell & Fals-Stewart, 2003). Empirical support for both behavioral family therapy and family systems approaches in treating adult substance abusers has accumulated. Several approaches effectively mobilize natural supports and utilize leverage within the family to motivate substance abusers into treatment (e.g., Dakof, Rowe, Liddle, & Henderson, 2003; Miller, Meyers, & Tonigan, 1999). Stanton and Shadish (1997) concluded from their meta-analysis of family therapy for drug abuse that family interventions work equally well for adults and adolescents, and that family therapy studies with adults and adolescents tend to be of good design quality, show better results than nonfamily approaches, and, with adult narcotic addicts, are a cost-effective component of methadone maintenance. In recent years, the application of effective family-based models for alcoholics has shown promise for the treatment of adult drug abusers (e.g., Fals-Stewart & O'Farrell, 2003).

Family therapy techniques have been successfully utilized to increase the engagement of substance abusers into treatment by mobilizing family supports. Azrin's (1976) "community reinforcement approach" serves as the foundation for much of this work. This model is based on behavioral principles, and targets specific interventions with the substance abuser and

family members to reinforce abstinence. Early studies revealed that community reinforcement techniques demonstrated greater efficacy than treatment-as-usual in engaging alcoholics into treatment (e.g., Sisson & Azrin, 1986). The Community Reinforcement and Family Training (CRAFT) program (Meyers & Smith, 1995), which incorporates skills-training strategies aimed at reducing significant others' distress, has shown promise in engaging substance abusers into treatment (Meyers, Miller, & Smith, 2001). For instance, in a rigorously controlled study comparing CRAFT with two commonly practiced interventions (Al-Anon facilitation therapy and Johnson Institute confrontation intervention), Miller, Meyers, and Tonigan (1999) found that CRAFT was more effective in engaging unmotivated alcoholic patients into treatment.

Gayle Dakof and her colleagues developed and tested the efficacy of a manualized, in-home drug abuse treatment that intervenes at the level of the individual and family. The Engaging Moms program has roots in the relational model of women's development, family systems models of drug abuse treatment, and family preservation models of service delivery. Results demonstrated that significantly more women assigned to the Engaging Moms program enrolled in drug abuse treatment than did women assigned to the community engagement as usual (control) condition (Dakof et al., 2003).

Significant advances have been made in applying behavioral couples therapy (BCT) to the treatment of adult alcoholics and drug abusers in recent years (O'Farrell & Fals-Stewart, 2003). The approach generally involves an initial agreement for the alcoholic to commit to sobriety and the partner to reinforce this commitment daily. BCT includes strategies to help the alcoholic cope with cravings and help the couple deal with crises concerning relapse, communicate more effectively, and increase enjoyable activities that don't involve substance use. BCT delivered in group and individual formats has been instrumental in helping alcoholics reduce their drinking as well as incidents of domestic violence, improve marital functioning, and shows significant savings in reduced hospitalizations and jail costs up to two years post-treatment (Epstein & McCrady, 1998; Jacobson et al., 1989; O'Farrell & Fals-Stewart, 1999). Couples alcohol-focused interventions have clear effects on drinking frequency and relapse rates over standard behaviorally oriented alcohol treatment (Walitzer & Dermen, 2004). The use of BCT with alcoholics has ignited significant interest due to its efficacy evidence and applicability to practice settings (Baucom et al., 1998).

Recent studies by William Fals-Stewart and his colleagues suggest that BCT has considerable potential in the treatment of drug abusers as well as alcoholic patients. Fals-Stewart, Birchler, and O'Farrell (1996) demonstrated the efficacy of BCT in a randomized trial versus individual therapy for male drug abusers.

Fals-Stewart and O'Farrell (2003) recently adapted the BCT approach as a component of naltrexone treatment with male opioid-dependent clients and demonstrated better naltrexone compliance, treatment attendance, abstinence rates, and fewer drug-related, legal, and family problems than individual therapy in the year following treatment. Taken together, these results lend solid support for the benefits of BCT with both male and female drug abusers, as well as their relationships with their partners and overall family functioning, and their children's adjustment.

●

To summarize, family-based approaches for both adolescent and adult substance abusers hold significant promise. New studies are focusing on the processes by which community-based providers successfully implement these approaches in practice.

Family Therapy for Schizophrenia

Family Risk and Protective Factors for Schizophrenia. Family researchers have been intrigued by the family dynamics of schizophrenia since the 1960s, when relational patterns known as "communication deviance" (Singer & Wynne, 1965) and "expressed emotion" (Vaughn & Leff, 1976) were posited as having unique explanatory power in the web of factors influencing the development of psychotic disorders. Subsequent research strongly supports the role of disturbed family dynamics as a contributing factor, perhaps secondary to biological processes, but contributing nonetheless, in the onset and chronicity of schizophrenia. For instance, a number of studies have linked family "communication deviance"—unclear, distorted, and vague interactions—to schizophrenia (Doane et al., 1989; Goldstein, 1987; Miklowitz et al., 1991).

Other studies have focused on the link between **expressed emotion** (EE), a pattern of emotional over-involvement and criticism, to schizophrenia. Relatives of schizophrenic patients have been shown to make more negative, intrusive statements than relatives of bipolar patients (Miklowitz, Goldstein, & Nuechterlein 1995). Further, relatives of schizophrenics characterized as high-EE tend to make causal attributions about the patient's illness to factors that are internal to and controllable by the patient (Brewin, MacCarthy, Duda, & Vaughn, 1991), and families' attributions and criticism of the patient are important in determining the course of illness (Lopez, Nelson, Snyder, & Mintz, 1999). High expressed emotion in the family has been consistently linked to greater risk for relapse after treatment (Parker & Hadzi-Pavlovic, 1990), thus interventions are increasingly devoted to helping families cope with the stress of taking care of their loved one and modifying their attitudes and interactions to support the patient's recovery (Backer & Richardson, 1989; Marsh & Johnson, 1997).

Family-Based Interventions for Schizophrenia. The advent of psychoactive medication in the 1960s, which revolutionized institutional treatment for mentally ill patients, also left communities and families with much of the burden of caring for schizophrenic patients.

Family interventions were subsequently developed based on the accumulating evidence of family risk factors noted above in schizophrenia onset and relapse and the significant stress of caring for mentally ill family members. These family-based treatments have been designed to augment pharmacological interventions, with the aim of improving the family environment (including reducing criticism and hostility and increasing stability and structure) and assisting families with management of the illness (Hahlweg & Wiedemann, 1999). The interventions generally consist of engagement strategies, psychoeducation, training in coping and problem-solving skills to lower family stress, and crisis intervention. Considerable support now exists for the use of these family-based interventions within a multi-modal treatment regimen for schizophrenic patients (Goldstein & Miklowitz, 1995).

Family-based interventions for schizophrenic patients can generally be classified in three categories: family consultation, family education, and family psychoeducation (Marsh & Lefley, 2003). Family consultation helps families identify and prioritize their needs, deal with their concerns and questions about mental illness, make informed decisions about appropriate services, and formulate a family service plan. Family education provides families with information about the illness, effective coping strategies, and community resources. While family education has shown positive effects on family members' understanding of the illness, more realistic expectations of the patient, better family relationships, and increased hope among patients (Marsh, 2001), its effects on schizophrenic symptoms have been limited.

Psychoeducational approaches, which combine education with training in family coping skills, have accumulated the most empirical support of the family-based treatments for schizophrenia. Early research supported the effectiveness of behavioral family management (incorporating psychoeducation with communication and problem-solving skills) in increas-ing the schizophrenic's social skills, decreasing family stress, and improving communication, as well as significantly reducing relapse rates in comparison to standard psychiatric care (Falloon, Boyd, & McGill, 1984). Mueser and colleagues (2001) compared supportive family management (consisting of two years of monthly support groups) and applied family management (involving one year of behavioral family therapy with support groups continuing for a second year), with all patients receiving medication management. Their results showed slight advantages of adding behavioral family therapy in terms of less rejection of the patient and reduced friction among family members, yet the interventions did not differ in relation to patients' social functioning or family burden at the two-year follow-up point. More intensive family intervention did not enable patients to be maintained on lower medication doses. Finally, William McFarlane and his colleagues developed a multiple-family supportive intervention with emphasis on improving family members' social support. The model demonstrated lower relapse rates than individual family therapy approaches up to four years post-treatment (McFarlane et al., 1995).

While the benefits of family psychoeducational approaches for schizophrenia are well established, there is concern that the time and resource burden placed on families, professionals, and health care systems may limit their adoption (McFarlane, Hornby, Dixon, & McNary, 2002). As in other specialties, recent studies in this area have focused on addressing these barriers to implementation in clinical practice. For instance, Kelly and Newstead (2004) describe strategies to overcoming barriers encountered in implementing a psychosocial family intervention. In fact, the family intervention decreases family burden as well as reducing relapse (NICE, 2002). Another group assessed the cost-effectiveness of three family interventions for schizophrenia: behavioral family management, behavioral intervention for families, and multiple family groups. All three interventions demonstrated favorable incremental cost-effectiveness ratios when introduced into standard mental health care in Australia (Mihalopoulos, Magnus, Carter, & Vos. 2004).

Thus there is clear evidence to support the use of family interventions as a component of multimodal strategies for the treatment of schizophrenics (McFarlane, Dixon, Lukens, & Luckstead, 2003). Certain family patterns, notably high criticism and rejection, complicate the recovery process. Further, the stress of managing a family member's illness necessitates social support and skill development for all involved family members. Interventions that increase understanding and acceptance of the family member's illness and provide support and skills training for caregivers appear to bolster protective mechanisms and reduce relapse. For instance, an innovative structured group counseling therapy approach that involves wives of male schizophrenics in treatment appears to help manage psychotic symptoms by increasing marital affection and satisfaction (Croake & Kelly, 2002). As these research avenues are pursued and advocacy for the families of chronically mentally ill patients increases, the utilization of empirically supported family-based models in the community will likely become more common in standard practice (Backer & Richardson, 1989; Baucom et al., 1998).

Family Therapy for Eating Disorders

Family Risk and Protective Factors for Disordered Eating. Salvador Minuchin's classic work with eating-disordered girls and their families (Minuchin, Rosman, & Baker, 1978) was inspired by the clinical observation that the families of these patients were deficient in providing nurturance and support. In fact, research supports these clinical observations. Parents of eating-disordered individuals have been characterized in empirical studies as overprotective (Wade, Treloar, & Martin, 2001), enmeshed and overly critical (Polivy & Herman, 2002), and as having diffuse boundaries with

their adolescents (Rowa, Kerig, & Geller, 2001). Interactional patterns in families of eating-disordered patients tend to constrain autonomy and intimacy (Maharaj et al., 2001), disrupt attachment relations (Ratti, Humphrey, & Lyons, 1996), and are characterized by destructive communication (Lattimore, Wagner, & Gowers, 2000). Parental substance abuse may also increase vulnerability for eating disorders (Lyon et al., 1997). However, some evidence suggests that the influence of family dysfunction on the development of eating disorders is indirect; high conflict, low cohesion, and childhood abuse may impact disordered eating through depressive symptoms (Mazzeo & Espelage, 2002). Yet there is little doubt that family problems not only affect the development of eating disorders, but that family factors such as high criticism also predict poorer treatment prognosis among both bulimics and anorexics (Reiss & Johnson-Sabine, 1995; van Furth et al., 1996).

Family-Based Interventions for Eating Disorders. Since Minuchin's groundbreaking application of structural family therapy to the treatment of anorexia (Minuchin et al., 1978), several controlled trials lend support to family-based interventions for both bulimic and anorexic patients (Lemmon & Josephson, 2001). A series of studies at the Maudsley Hospital in London have tested a multimodal family-based treatment that emphasizes collaboration with the family as a valuable resource in the patient's recovery and avoids blaming the parents. The model borrows heavily from Minuchin's structural family therapy techniques, using a family meal in the first stage of therapy and reorganizing parental coalitions in later therapeutic work, as well as aspects of the Milan approach in examining and addressing the intergenerational context of the patient's problems. The model has demonstrated impressive results in weight gain and maintenance up to five years post-treatment in comparison to individual supportive therapy, particularly for adolescents with more recent onset of problems (Russell,

Dare, Eisler, & LeGrange, 1994; Russell, Szmukler, Dare, & Eisler, 1987).

Behavioral family systems therapy, which emphasizes parental control over eating and incorporates cognitive restructuring and problem-solving training, has also been tested in comparison to individual therapy for anorexic patients. The model was more effective than an individual approach focused on building ego strength and facilitating autonomy in terms of increasing body weight from pre- to post-treatment (approximately sixteen months of therapy), although the treatments were equally effective in most of the outcomes measured, including eating attitudes, body shape dissatisfaction, and depressive symptoms (Robin et al., 1994). Further, a comparison of structural family therapy and a family psychoeducational group revealed no statistically significant differences in effectiveness for anorexic patients (Geist et al., 2000). A new integrative family-based approach for anorexic patients combining structural, strategic, and Bowenian techniques with CBT and narrative therapy interventions (Krautter & Lock, 2004a) demonstrated high satisfaction ratings from patients, particularly in terms of the positive changes perceived in their families (Krautter & Lock, 2004b).

Finally, multiple family therapy approaches have recently been pilot tested with encouraging results (Asen, 2002; Colahan & Robinson, 2002). This type of model treats families together in hospital settings using a multidisciplinary approach and actively involves family members in the treatment of the eating-disordered patient in intensive family work (Scholz & Asen, 2001). Further investigation of these approaches is certainly warranted, given their promising preliminary findings. Overall, about two thirds (65 percent) of anorexic patients are estimated to improve significantly in family therapy (Lock, le Grange, Agras, & Dare, 2001). Taken together, the support for family-based interventions with eating-disordered patients is growing, although questions remain about the most effective dosage of family work within the generally multimodal programs necessary to treat these patients. Family-based interventions for bulimic clients have yet to be developed and empirically validated.

Efficacy of Couples Therapy

As discussed earlier, couples therapy has demonstrated efficacy in the treatment of several disorders, including alcoholism, drug abuse, and depression (Baucom et al., 1998). A range of approaches, including behavioral, cognitive-behavioral, insight-oriented, systemic, and psychoeducational, have generated positive findings in improving couples' relationships (e.g., Goldman & Greenberg, 1992; Kaiser, Hahlweg, Fehm-Wolfsdorf, & Groth, 1998; Snyder, Wills, & Grady-Fletcher, 1991).

Behavioral couples therapy has been the most extensively studied of all couples therapy approaches (Jacobson et al., 2000). As previously noted, BCT involves behaviorally oriented interventions designed to reinforce effective communication, problem solving, and positive interactions, and to decrease negative exchanges between couples. Behavioral techniques include contracting for follow-through of specific tasks or activities, and homework assignments to generalize skills outside of therapy. Consensus has been reached that BCT effectively improves marital adjustment and satisfaction (Dunn & Schwebel, 1995; Jacobson & Addis, 1993; Lebow & Gurman, 1995; Shadish et al., 1993) and results in clinically significant change for most participants (Baucom et al., 1998). Followup results are somewhat disappointing, with treatment gains maintained in most studies up to one year (Hahlweg & Markman, 1988), although a significant percentage (38 percent) of couples divorce within four years of receiving BCT (Snyder et al., 1991).

A new approach, integrative behavioral couple therapy (Jacobson et al., 2000; see Chapter 14), addresses some of the limitations of BCT, including its reduced impact over time (Hahlweg & Markman, 1988). The integrative approach emphasizes acceptance of partners' characteristics that are most difficult to change and uses these obstacles as platforms for achieving greater intimacy. The integrative approach has demonstrated preliminary comparative efficacy in comparison to traditional BCT, using effect sizes and clinical significance ratings to measure marital satisfaction, and has also been adapted successfully into a group format (Jacobson et al., 2000). In addition, an enhanced version of BCT with cognitive restructuring and affect exploration was also tested in comparison to standard BCT and found to be equally effective as the more traditional behavioral approach in decreasing negative communications and cognitions in session and at home (Halford, Sanders, & Behrens, 1993). Similarly, a recent investigation of integrative BCT (emphasizing emotional acceptance of genuine incompatibilities) with significantly distressed married couples showed similar improvements in relationship satisfaction, stability, and communication to those in traditional BCT (Christensen et al., 2004).

Cognitive-behavioral marital therapy (CBMT) builds on the foundation of BCT but also seeks to change the unrealistic expectations and beliefs that interfere with adaptive relationships and intimacy. In Dunn and Schwebel's (1995) meta-analysis of fifteen methodologically sound randomized trials of marital therapy, CBMT was superior to both BCT and insight-oriented marital therapy in changing spouses' relationship-related cognitions from pre- to post-treatment. However, studies in which cognitive techniques were tested against standard BCT or used to augment standard behavioral marital therapy failed to provide any evidence that cognitive interventions are more effective than BCT (Fincham, Bradbury, & Beach, 1990). Baucom and colleagues (1998) describe CBMT as "possibly efficacious," given small sample sizes in the studies reviewed and the lack of evidence suggesting added benefits of cognitive techniques over traditional BCT.

Insight-oriented approaches, including insight-oriented couples therapy and emotion-ally focused couples therapy, have also been subjected to clinical trial investigations and found to be superior to no treatment (Jacobson & Addis, 1993), with some evidence for their superiority in comparison to other established approaches (Baucom et al., 1998). The insight-oriented marital therapy approach (IOMT; Snyder & Wills, 1989) has increased in popularity and focus in empirical investigations. IOMT blends Gestalt and systemic techniques to increase couples' insight into their intrapersonal and relationship dynamics, with focus on the affective nature of interactions and facilitation of partners' responses to the emotional needs expressed by their mates. Dunn and Schwebel's (1995) meta-analysis revealed that IOMT is more successful than BCT or CBMT in improving spouses' perceptions of general relationship quality. Snyder, Wills and Grady-Fletcher (1991) discovered few differences between IOMT and BCT in marital outcomes at post-test or at six-month followup, but a four-year follow-up study indicated that a significantly greater percentage of couples in BCT had subsequently divorced than those in IOMT (38 percent versus 3 percent).

Emotionally focused couples therapy (EFCT; Greenberg & Johnson, 1988; see Chapter 8) maintains that relationship difficulties generally stem from the disowning of feelings and attachment needs, creating negative interactional cycles and ineffective communication patterns. The model identifies these issues and negative cycles; helps clients to acknowledge the emotions underlying these cycles; assists in the acceptance of partners' positions; and encourages partners to communicate needs and emotions more effectively. EFCT has shown greater efficacy than wait-list controls (Goldman & Greenberg, 1992; Jacobson & Addis, 1993) and demonstrated superior efficacy to BCT in improving marital adjustment in one study with moderately distressed couples (Johnson & Greenberg, 1985). One study with parents of chronically ill children showed that EFCT more effectively reduced marital distress than a wait-list control condition (Walker, Johnson, Manion, & Cloutier, 1996).

Finally, evidence for the use of strategic therapy techniques in the context of couples therapy is provided by Goldman and Greenberg (1992) and Davidson and Horvath (1997). Goldman and Greenberg found that an integrated systemic therapy model was equally effective as EFCT and more effective than a wait-list control in alleviating relationship distress and improving target complaints and conflict resolution. Further, couples in integrated treatment showed greater maintenance of treatment gains at the four-month followup than couples in emotionally focused couple therapy. Davidson and Horvath developed and tested a brief (three-session) couple therapy approach based on the MRI model, incorporating reframing and restraining interventions as well as homework assignments. Brief strategic couples therapy was more effective in improving relationship adjustment, conflict resolution, and target complaints than a wait-list control condition from intake to six-week followup.

Recent methodological papers highlight potentially fruitful avenues for the next generation of couples therapy studies. For instance, Christensen, Baucom, Vu, and Stanton (2005) outline steps to address unexplored questions about the outcomes of multifaceted couples treatment packages, their components, the mechanisms by which they achieve outcomes, and their effects with diverse populations. These authors provide guidelines for research that would advance couples therapy by facilitating the integration of existing approaches for multiple-problem couples.

Family Therapy Process Research

Identifying Mechanisms of Therapeutic Change in Family Therapy

Although the findings reviewed above are valuable in establishing what types of family interventions have potential for alleviating psychological and interpersonal problems, they offer only limited information about the essential ingredients of family therapy. Questions about *why* certain therapies are effective, *how* families change, *what* specific techniques of treatment are most important, and *which* client and therapist variables affect change are not addressed in **outcome research.** These questions can only be answered by looking inside therapies and using different methodologies (e.g., task analysis; Heatherington & Friedlander, 1990a) and analytic tools (e.g., growth modeling; Willett, Ayoub, & Robinson, 1991) to link specific therapeutic factors to the "mini-outcomes" throughout treatment (Pinsof, 1989). **Process research** has the potential to lead to the development of more effective treatments and to bridge the gap between science and practice by increasing the relevance of empirical findings to practitioners (Pinsof & Wynne, 2000; Hogue, Liddle, Singer, & Leckrone, 2005). This section discusses some of the most important family therapy process research findings to date, although a complete presentation of this area would require at least an entire chapter. We suggest further reading in this area for a more comprehensive exploration of family therapy process research (e.g., Alexander, Holtzworth-Munroe, & Jameson, 1994; Friedlander, Wildman, Heatherington, & Skowron, 1994; Pinsof, 1989).

Process of Therapeutic Alliance Formation in Family Therapy

The process of building and negotiating therapeutic alliances is more complex in couples and family therapy than in individual therapy. Some family therapy models have emphasized the formation of multiple therapeutic alliances rather than a single therapeutic alliance (Liddle, 2002a). A recent study by Robbins, Turner, Alexander, and Perez (2003) provided evidence for understanding the alliance in family therapy as a function of systemic rather than individual processes. For thirty-four adolescents and their parents receiving functional family therapy for adolescent substance abuse and related behavior problems, individual parent and adolescent therapeutic alliances did not predict retention. However, dropout cases had significantly higher levels of unbalanced alliances, characterized by high levels of discrepancy between parent and adolescent alliances with the therapist, than did completer cases (Robbins et al., 2003). Several researchers have focused on how therapists establish and maintain the important therapeutic alliance with different family members. For instance, Heatherington and Friedlander (1990b) explored relational control communication patterns and their impact on the development of the therapeutic alliance in systemic family therapy. They found that therapists and family members tended to interact in complementary ways, rather than having symmetrical, or competitive, exchanges. However, neither pattern was related to family members' perceptions of the quality of the therapeutic relationship.

Garfield's recent review of research on alliance in couples therapy (e.g., Symonds & Horvath, 2004; Knobloch-Fedders, Pinsoff, & Mann, 2004) provides a number of helpful recommendations for working with partners with a variety of problems. Garfield (2004) reviews three dimensions of factors affecting the therapeutic alliance: the "loyalty dimension," the impact of partners' early family-of-origin experiences, and the impact of partners' gender concerns, and presents empirical rationales and clinical considerations related to each dimension.

In attachment-based family therapy (ABFT) with depressed adolescents, Diamond et al. (2003) have explored the contributions of general family therapy and ABFT-specific therapeutic alliance processes to outcome. For both adolescents and parents, therapist–client agreement on individual and family goals for treatment was related to stronger therapeutic alliance and improvement in adolescent depression. In an effort to understand the actual therapeutic processes that lead to strong alliances with parents, a task-analytic study was carried out. The analysis yielded a five-stage model for the development of strong parent–therapist alliance characterized by the therapist acknowledging the parents' strengths and accomplishments, exploring the parent–adolescent relationship and its impact on the adolescent's well being, defining and working on parental goals for treatment, and finally reinforcing the parents' contribution to the adolescent's improvement.

In family therapy with adolescent substance abusers, investigators have examined the impact of adolescent engagement interventions on improving therapist–adolescent alliances over the first three sessions of multidimensional family therapy (MDFT) (Diamond, Liddle, Hogue, & Dakof, 1999). Significant gains in working alliance were evident when therapists emphasized the following alliance-building interventions: attending to the adolescent's experience, formulating personally meaningful goals, and presenting oneself as the adolescent's ally. Lack of improvement or deterioration in alliance was associated with the therapist spending too much time explaining the nature of therapy, thus waiting too long to discuss how the therapy could be personally meaningful for the teenager. A more recent examination of the alliance building process in MDFT demonstrated that adolescents are more likely to complete treatment when therapists have stronger relationships with their parents. Additionally, stronger therapeutic relationships with adolescents were associated with greater decreases in their drug use, but only when the therapeutic alliance with the parent was of moderate or high strength (Shelef, Diamond, Diamond, & Liddle, 2005).

Jackson-Gilfort, Liddle, Tejeda, and Dakof (2001) showed that the therapeutic discussion of culturally specific themes enhanced treatment engagement of African American male substance-abusing youths. Exploration of particular themes—anger, alienation, and the journey from boyhood to manhood (i.e., what it means to become an African American man)—were associated with both increased participation and decreased negativity by adolescents in the very next treatment session. These and other studies of the alliance in family therapy have yielded clinically important findings; however, future research needs to examine the links between the therapeutic relationship and outcomes in family therapy.

Critical Change Events in Family Therapy

Process research also focuses on the nature and sequences that determine important change events in family therapy, or those interventions that lead to resolution of problems or relational shifts within the family. For example, Friedlander, Heatherington, Johnson, and Skowron (1994) studied the dynamics of structural family therapy cases in which families were able to successfully move from disengagement to engagement. Using a modified analytic induction method, successful sustaining engagement events were identified and examined, and found to involve both interpersonal and personal learning experiences by each family member. Although no consistent pattern characterized the resolution of each family's impasse, sustained engagement generally involved active solicitation by the therapist of each family member's thoughts and feelings about the impasse and the benefits of reengagement, and helping other family members to hear each other's point of view. Similarly, in process studies of emotionally focused couple therapy, Greenberg, Ford, Alden, and Johnson (1993) found that peak session events were more frequently associated with affiliative, self-focused positive (e.g., self-disclosing, expressing) statements and accepting, friendly statements by partners than were poor session events. Further, partners were significantly more likely to respond with an affiliative statement after therapists facilitated self-disclosure from the other partner.

Michael Nichols and his colleagues validated a rating scale to examine the process of successful enactments in family therapy (Allen-Eckert et al., 2001). Their research with highly trained and experienced family therapists suggests that breaking through family conflict and helping families shift their relational stance is a complex process that requires active, directive facilitation by the therapist (Nichols & Fellenberg, 2000). Essential ingredients of successful enactments include pre-enactment preparation with family members, specification of an agenda and explanation of the need for dialogue, direction about how the discussion should go, avoiding interrupting unless absolutely necessary, keeping the action going by pushing family members to work harder in the process of communicating, and closing by providing clients with clear direction in how to communicate with each other.

Diamond and colleagues (2003) focused on exploring the processes involved in shifting the treatment focus from "adolescent as the problem" to "strengthening family relations as the solution" in ABFT for depressed adolescents. The first part of this investigation involved assessing clients' views of responsibility for the problems that brought the family to treatment. Adolescents tended to rate both themselves and their parents as contributing to and being willing to solve the problem, while parents tended to rate themselves low in contributing to the problem and high in their willingness to solve it. Interviews with parents after the first sessions to review key therapeutic moments revealed that eliciting strong, often vulnerable, feelings associated with the conflicts that had brought the family to treatment helped change negative cognitions about these problems and the adolescents themselves. The greatest clinical influence occurred when parents came to realize how ruptures in the parent-adolescent relationship contributed to the adolescent's depression.

Diamond and Liddle (1996) used task analysis to identify the combination of clinical interventions and family interactions necessary to resolve in-session impasses in MDFT. Therapist behaviors that contributed to defusing negative interactions included: (a) actively blocking or addressing and working through negative affect; (b) evoking and amplifying thoughts and feelings that promote constructive dialogue; and (c) creating emotional treaties among family members by alternately working in session with parents alone and adolescents alone—a kind of shuttle diplomacy. In cases with successful resolution of the impasse, the therapist transformed the nature and tone of the conversation in the session, shifting the parent s blaming to a focus on their feelings of regret and loss, and eliciting the adolescent's thoughts and feelings about relationship roadblocks with parents and others.

In sum, process studies examining successful change events have illuminated some of the essential ingredients of effective family therapy. Taken together, the results of these investigations suggest that change events are facilitated in a range of family interventions by the therapist moving family members to a more vulnerable, self-disclosing, affective level, and helping other family members to listen and subsequently respond.

Gender in the Process of Family Therapy

Newberry, Alexander, and Turner (1991) examined microsequences of therapist–client exchanges in the first stage of functional family therapy to explore the effects of therapist and client sex roles on the behavior of each in therapy. They found that rates of supportive and structuring interventions did not differ between male and female therapists in training, nor did they differ in the frequency of utilization with male and female clients; however, the sequences of behavior between therapists and clients were affected by gender. Fathers responded more positively to structuring interventions than did mothers, and female therapists were more likely than male therapists to receive supportive responses from both male and female clients following their use of supportive interventions. Interestingly, female therapists subsequently responded with more structuring responses than males following client supportive responses.

In an investigation of gender in the first interview using a structural/strategic family therapy approach, Shields and McDaniel (1992) similarly uncovered no differences in the frequency of supportive statements by male and female therapists, but they did find differences in the ways that family members respond to therapists depending on the therapists' gender. For instance, family members made more conflictual statements to each other in the presence of female therapists, and made more structuring comments to therapists who were male. Finally, Werner-Wilson, Price, Zimmerman, and Murphy (1997) analyzed videotapes of family therapy sessions to explore the role of gender in conversational control and found that family therapists in training interrupt women three times more than male clients.

Process Investigations in Family Therapy with Child and Adolescent Behavior Problems

Patterson and Chamberlain's (1992) groundbreaking process study identified ways in which therapists contribute to parental resistance in therapy, and thus paved the way for advances in family interventions with problem children and adolescents. Schmidt, Liddle, and Dakof (1996) investigated the nature and extent of change in parenting behavior in MDFT, as well as the link between parental subsystem change and reduction in adolescent drug abuse and other symptomatology. Parents showed significant decreases in aversive parenting (e.g., negative affect, verbal aggression) and increases in positive parenting (e.g., monitoring and limit-setting, positive affect, and commitment) over the course of therapy. Moreover, these changes in parenting behavior were associated with reductions in adolescent drug use and problem behavior.

New findings linking session focus to outcomes with adolescent drug abusers in MDFT demonstrate that therapists' attention to family-related treatment themes predicted greater reduction of teens' substance use and comorbid symptoms (Hogue et al., 2004). These results support a basic tenet of family-based treatments:

change in a fundamental aspect of the family system (parenting practices) is related to a reduction of adolescent symptoms.

Mann, Borduin, Henggeler, and Blaske (1990) found that families with delinquent adolescents had more cross-generational coalitions and marital conflict than healthy control families. Further, over the course of multisystemic therapy, decreases in adolescents' and fathers' symptoms were linked to improvements in the marital relationship. Although the results did not support a link between reductions in adolescents' symptoms and improved parent–adolescent relationships, these findings did show the negative impact of unhealthy, unbalanced coalitions in family therapy. However, a subsequent investigation revealed a clear association between improved family functioning and reduced delinquency among adolescents, mediated by decreased affiliation with delinquent peers (Huey, Henggeler, Brondino, & Pickrel, 2000). This study was unique in that it investigated the extent to which therapeutic "dosage," or the extent of fidelity to the prescribed model, impacted the improvements of family functioning and adolescent symptoms. In fact, therapists' adherence to their model determined the extent of family change, which was associated with reduced affiliation with negative peers, and subsequently with decreased delinquency.

Finally, functional family therapy researchers have investigated the sequences of therapist and family behavior that lead to positive behavior from delinquent adolescents and their parents in session. Robbins, Alexander, Newell, and Turner (1996) found that therapist reframes were the only interventions that were met with positive responses from delinquent adolescents in first sessions of functional family therapy, suggesting that the reframe may have a particularly important role in engaging resistant adolescents during the early stage of therapy. Robbins, Alexander, and Turner (2000) subsequently studied the processes by which therapists were able to disrupt defensive interactions among delinquent adolescents and their parents. Similar to the first study, therapist reframes were the only interven-

tions that effectively reduced family members' defensive statements.

●

This is only a sample of process research conducted by family intervention scientists. Without doubt, the field is moving toward greater specification of the interventions necessary to produce changes among clients and family members. For instance, an adherence evaluation of the extent to which therapists delivered MDFT and CBT in a clinical trial with teenage drug abusers not only established that therapists achieved fidelity to their respective models, but also that the implementation of very specific interventions could be differentiated using a therapy rating instrument (Hogue et al., 1998). In a more recent study, Hogue and colleagues (2005) examined fidelity in a family-based intervention for at-risk adolescents, multidimensional family prevention (MDFP), in comparison to MDFT and CBT, in order to identify how specific model components were translated to actual practice by trained counselors. Results from this study demonstrated adherence to MDFP core principles, and clear differentiation from CBT across intervention parameters and techniques. Furthermore, the findings identified a lack of parental monitoring interventions, presenting a new and empirically supported platform for the ongoing development of MDFP. These and other coding systems are advancing the investigation of the sequencing and successful implementation of specific therapeutic interventions (Hogue, Liddle, & Rowe, 1996; Allen-Eckert et al., 2001). Yet while these process investigations have answered important questions about critical within-therapy patterns of change, the family therapy field has very limited knowledge about the ways in which interventions and therapy change processes are linked to long-term outcomes (Friedlander, 2001).

Myrna Friedlander and her colleagues (1994) suggest that process research can also be advanced by studying the experiences and perspectives of family members in therapy and afterward, as well as examining in greater detail how interventions affect change among family members in different ways. Process research clearly offers important opportunities to advance the field of family therapy and continue to lessen the research and practice divide.

Conclusions and Future Directions

While the research advances in family intervention science in recent years are substantial, the field remains limited by the gap that still separates family therapy research from clinical practice (Pinsof & Wynne, 2000). The significant strides made in family therapy research have yet to make a major impact on front-line clinicians (Fals-Stewart & Birchler, 2001). However, new research on therapy adaptation and dissemination is expanding the boundaries of traditional clinical trials and examining the real-world applications of these promising approaches. Early dissemination efforts have highlighted the need for flexibility and the necessity of adapting these models to the realities of community practice settings. Resources are scarce, providers have heavy demands and limited time, supervision structures do not always support the implementation of complicated protocols, and the typical therapist in community-based clinics has little training in family therapy. Family therapists and trainers are in a position to contribute new knowledge about how effective practices can be modified for real-world contexts while retaining their effects.

Some of this work to integrate family-based interventions in community settings and adapt family therapy to further its reach and relevance for practice has begun. For instance, suggestions for extending family interventions for medical settings have been made based on the strong link between medical problems and family stress, as well as associations between overall family functioning and service utilization and patients' recovery from a variety of illnesses (Johnson, Kent, & Leather, 2005). A relatively new family therapy approach called "community family therapy" has been proposed to address the need for broader systemic interventions for low-income, urban families (Rojano, 2004; see Chapter 14). The premise of this approach is that building community support and personal empowerment and competencies among disadvantaged families would alleviate many of the actual sources of risk for a range of mental health and relational problems. Another example of an innovative family-based approach aimed at overcoming barriers to traditional service delivery is "walk-in family therapy" (Miller & Slive, 2004). This approach places more responsibility on families to focus on what they need from treatment and to seek services when they feel ready or in need.

There are many contextual and implementation issues, having to do with training and professional development and lack of opportunities to institute effective models in clinical settings, that have limited the influence of research findings on the practice of family therapy. This is where professional associations come into play. Professional organizations can do a great deal to support the inclusion of science-based therapies in everyday practice. State administrations of mental health, substance abuse, and juvenile justice now routinely link funds for services to the capacity of service providers to implement treatments with proven efficacy. Combined with the positive reception to family therapy research in federal funding circles as well as in private foundation funding and policy-making groups, these developments suggest that family therapy research has made more of an impact outside of family therapy than within it. Not until family therapy research becomes integrated into the training programs in which clinical methods are taught will the culture of family therapy relative to its research values and beliefs change once and for all.

The popularity of family-based therapies has soared over the last decade or so, as therapists and researchers have confirmed that including parents and other family members in treatment is critical to successful engagement of clients and to overall effectiveness. Certain manual-guided, family-based therapies are experienced by therapists not as constraining, but as providing sufficient flexibility (Godley et al., 2001). Numerous practice guidelines and reports of influential private foundations and policy-making groups have endorsed the importance of working with the parents and families of clients,

representing a major shift from a decade ago. Research can, as we have seen in recent years, influence policy- and practice-level changes that support increased resources and opportunities for the dissemination of empirically supported family-based treatments into practice.

—Questions to Consider—

1. How can someone who reads psychotherapy research studies determine if the therapy was practiced by experienced and skillful therapists (as opposed to graduate students or therapists in training)?

2. Can you think of (or find) any research studies that have had a significant impact on the way therapy is practiced?

3. What are some things researchers do that lead practicing clinicians to ignore or mistrust research findings?

4. What are some questions of practical clinical interest to you that you think research is likely to be able to answer? Have you checked to see if studies have already been conducted on these questions?

5. What are the relative advantages and disadvantages of process and outcome studies?

6. What are the relative advantages and disadvantages of qualitative and quantitative studies?

—Key Concepts—

expressed emotion (EE)   A family member's expression of critical and hostile comments directed at a person with psychopathology, coupled with over involvement in that person's life.

meta-analyses   A quantitative approach to summarizing results across studies.

outcome research   Studies designed to evaluate the effectiveness of various treatments in producing desired changes as a result of therapy.

parent management training   A behavioral approach to children's problems that involves teaching their parents behavioral skills, such

as the effective use of reinforcement to increase desired behavior and time-outs and other punishments to decrease maladaptive behavior.

process research   Studies designed to explore events that occur within the therapy process, typically such things as what kinds of therapist interventions lead to what kinds of in-session responses from clients.

randomized trials   Studies of comparative effectiveness of various treatments in which patients are randomly assigned to competing models of therapy.

—Recommended Readings—

Alexander, J. F., Holtzworth-Munroe, A., and Jameson, P. B. 1994. Research on the process and outcome of marriage and family therapy. In *Handbook of psy-*

chotherapy and behavior change, 4th ed., A. E. Bergin and S. L. Garfield, eds. New York: John Wiley & Sons.

Baucom, D. H., Shoham, V., Mueser, K. T., Daiuto, A. D., and Stickle, T. R. 1998. Empirically supported couple and family interventions for marital distress and adult mental health problems. *Journal of Consulting and Clinical Psychology.* 66(1): 53–88.

Estrada, A. U., and Pinsof, W. M. 1995. The effectiveness of family therapies for selected behavioral disorders of childhood. *Journal of Marital and Family Therapy.* 21: 403–440.

Friedlander, M. L., Wildman, J., Heatherington, L., and Skowron, E. A. 1994. What we do and don't know about the process of family therapy. *Journal of Family Psychology.* 8(4): 390–416.

Gottman, J. M., Ryan, K. D., Carrere, S., and Erley, A. M. 2001. Toward a scientifically based marital therapy. In *Family psychology: Science-based interventions*, H. A. Liddle, D. A. Santisteban, R. F. Levant, and J. H. Bray, eds. Washington, DC: American Psychological Association.

Lebow, J. L., and Gurman, A. S. 1995. Research assessing couple and family therapy. *Annual Review of Psychology.* 46: 27–57.

Liddle, H. A., Bray, J. H., Levant, R. F., & Santisteban, D. A. 2001. Family psychology intervention science: An emerging area of science and practice. In *Family psychology: Science-based interventions*, H. A. Liddle, D. A. Santisteban, R. F. Levant, and J. H. Bray, eds. Washington, DC: American Psychological Association.

O'Farrell, T. J., and Fals-Stewart, W. 1999. Treatment models and methods: Family models. In *Addictions: A comprehensive guidebook*, B. S. McCrady & E. E. Epstein, eds. New York: Oxford University Press.

Patterson, G. R., and Chamberlain, P. 1992. A functional analysis of resistance (A neobehavioral perspective). In *Why don't people change? New perspectives on resistance and noncompliance*, H. Arkowitz, ed. New York: Guilford.

Pinsof, W. M., and Wynne, L. C. 1995. The efficacy of marital and family therapy: An empirical overview, conclusions and recommendations. *Journal of Marital and Family Therapy.* 21: 585–614.

Pinsof, W. M., and Wynne, L. C. 2000. Toward progress research: Closing the gap between family therapy practice and research. *Journal of Marital and Family Therapy.* 26(1): 1–8.

Shadish, W. R., Ragsdale, K., Glaser, R. R., and Montgomery, L. M. 1995. The efficacy and effectiveness of marital and family therapy: A perspective from meta-analysis. *Journal of Marital and Family Therapy.* 21: 345–360.

Snyder, D. K., Cozzi, J. J., and Mangrum, L. F. 2001. Conceptual issues in assessing couples and families. In *Family psychology: Science-based interventions*, H. A. Liddle, D. A. Santisteban, R. F. Levant, and J. H. Bray, eds. Washington, DC: American Psychological Association

—**R**eferences

Alexander, J. F., Holtzworth-Munroe, A., and Jameson, P. B. 1994. Research on the process and outcome of marriage and family therapy. In *Handbook of psychotherapy and behavior change*, 4th ed., A. E. Bergin and S. L. Garfield, eds. New York: John Wiley & Sons.

Alexander, J. F., and Parsons, B. V. 1973. Short-term behavioral intervention with delinquent families: Impact on family process and recidivism. *Journal of Abnormal Psychology.* 81: 219–225.

Alexander, J. F., and Parsons, B. V. 1982. *Functional family therapy.* Monterey, CA: Brooks/Cole.

Alexander, J. F., and Sexton, T. L. 2002. Functional Family Therapy (FFT) as an integrative, mature clinical model for treating high risk, acting out youth. In *Comprehensive handbook on psychotherapy,*

Volume IV: Integrative/eclectic, J. Lebow, ed. New York: John Wiley.

Allen-Eckert, H., Fong, E., Nichols, M. P., Watson, N., and Liddle, H. A. 2001. Development of the Family Therapy Enactment Rating Scale. *Family Process.* 40(4): 469–478.

Asen, E. 2002. Multiple family therapy: An overview. *Journal of Family Therapy.* 24(1): 3–16.

Austin, A. M., Macgowan, M. J. and Wagner, E. F. 2005. Effective family-based interventions for adolescents with substance use problems: A systematic review. *Research on Social Work Practice.* 15(2): 67–83.

Azrin, N. H. 1976. Improvements in the community-reinforcement approach to alcoholism. *Behavioral Research and Therapy.* 14: 339–348.

Azrin, N. H., Donohue, B., Teichner, G. A., Crum, T., Howell, J., and DeCato, L. A. 2001. A controlled evaluation and description of individual-cognitive problem solving and family-behavior therapies in dually-diagnosed conduct-disordered and substance-dependent youth. *Journal of Child and Adolescent Substance Abuse.* *11*(1): 1–43.

Backer, T. E., and Richardson, D. 1989. Building bridges: Psychologists and families of the mentally ill. *American Psychologist.* *44*(3): 546–550.

Bank, L., Marlowe, J. H., Reid, J. B., and Patterson, G. R. 1991. A comparative evaluation of parent-training interventions for families of chronic delinquents. *Journal of Abnormal Child Psychology.* *19*(1): 15–33.

Barber, J. G. 1995. Working with resistant drug abusers. *Social Work.* *40*(1): 17–23.

Barkley, R. A., Edwards, G., Laneri, M., Fletcher, K., and Metevia, L. 2001. The efficacy of problem-solving communication training alone, behavior management training alone, and their combination for parent-adolescent conflict in teenagers with ADHD and ODD. *Journal of Consulting and Clinical Psychology.* *69*(6): 926–941.

Barrett, P. M. 1998. Evaluation of cognitive-behavioral group treatments for childhood anxiety disorders. *Journal of Clinical Child Psychology.* *27*(4): 459–468.

Barrett, P. M., Rapee, R. M., Dadds, M. M., and Ryan, S. M. 1996. Family enhancement of cognitive style in anxious and aggressive children. *Journal of Abnormal Child Psychology.* *24*(2): 187–203.

Barton, C., Alexander, J. F., Waldron, H., Turner, C. W., and Warburton, J. 1985. Generalizing treatment effects of Functional Family Therapy: Three replications. *American Journal of Family Therapy.* *13*: 16–26.

Basco, M. R., Prager, K. J., Pita, J. M., Tamir, L. M., & Stephens, J. J. 1992. Communication and intimacy in the marriages of depressed patients. *Journal of Family Psychology.* *6*: 184–194.

Baucom, D. H., Shoham, V., Mueser, K. T., Daiuto, A.D., and Stickle, T. R. 1998. Empirically supported couple and family interventions for marital distress and adult mental health problems. *Journal of Consulting and Clinical Psychology.* *66*(1): 53–88.

Birmaher, B., Brent, D. A., Kolko, D. J., Baugher, M., Bridge, J., Iyengar, S., and Ulloa, R. E. 2000. Clinical outcome after short-term psychotherapy for adolescents with major depressive disorder. *Archives of General Psychiatry.* *57*: 29–36.

Blechman, E. A., and Vryan, K. D. 2000. Prosocial Family Therapy: A manualized preventive intervention for juvenile offenders. *Aggression and Violent Behavior.* *5*(4): 343–378.

Brannigan, R., Schackman, B. R., Falco, M., and Millman, R. B. 2004. The quality of highly regarded adolescent substance abuse treatment programs: Results of an in-depth national survey. *Archives of Pediatrics & Adolescent Medicine.* *158*: 904–909.

Brent, D. A., Holder, D., Kolko, D., Birmaher, B., Baugher, M., Roth, C., Iyengar, S., and Johnson, B. A. 1997. A clinical psychotherapy trial for adolescent depression comparing cognitive, family, and supportive therapy. *Archives of General Psychiatry.* *54*: 877–885.

Brewin, C. R., MacCarthy, B., Duda, K., and Vaughn, C. E. 1991. Attribution and expressed emotion in the relatives of patients with schizophrenia. *Journal of Abnormal Psychology.* *100*(4): 546–554.

Brook, J. S., Brook, D. W., Arencibia-Mireles, O., Richter, L., and Whiteman, M. 2001. Risk factors for adolescent marijuana use across cultures and time. *Journal of Genetic Psychology.* *162*(3): 357–374.

Bukstein, O. G., and The Work Group on Quality Issues (1997). Practice parameters for the assessment and treatment of children and adolescents with substance use disorders. *Journal of the American Academy of Child and Adolescent Psychiatry.* *36*(Sup. 10): 140S–156S.

Cano, A., and O'Leary, K. D. 2000. Infidelity and separations precipitate major depressive episodes and symptoms of nonspecific depression and anxiety. *Journal of Consulting and Clinical Psychology.* *68*(5): 774–781.

Caughlin, J. P., Huston, T. L., and Houts, R. M. 2000. How does personality matter in marriage? An examination of trait anxiety, interpersonal negativity, and marital satisfaction. *Journal of Personality and Social Psychology.* *78*(2): 326–336.

Chassin, L., Pitts, S. C., DeLucia, C., and Todd, M. 1999. A longitudinal study of children of alcoholics: Predicting young adult substance use disorders, anxiety, and depression. *Journal of Abnormal Psychology.* *108*(1): 106–119.

Christensen, A., Atkins, D.C., Berns, S., Wheeler, J., Baucom, D. H., and Simpson, L. E. 2004. Traditional versus integrative Behavioral Couples Therapy for significantly distressed married couples. *Journal of Consulting and Clinical Psychology.* *72*(2): 176–191.

Christensen, A., Baucom, D. H., Vu, C. T. A., and Stanton, S. 2005. Methodologically sound, cost-effective research on the outcome of couple therapy. *Journal of Family Psychology.* 19(1): 6–17.

Coatsworth, J. D., Santisteban, D. A., McBride, C. K., and Szapocznik, J. 2001. Brief Strategic Family Therapy versus community control: Engagement, retention, and an exploration of the moderating role of adolescent symptom severity. *Family Process.* 40(3): 313–332.

Colahan, M., and Robinson, P. H. 2002. Multi-family groups in the treatment of young adults with eating disorders. *Journal of Family Therapy.* 24(1): 17–30.

Cole, D. A., and McPherson, A. E. 1993. Relation of family subsystems to adolescent depression: Implementing a new family assessment strategy. *Journal of Family Psychology.* 7(1): 119–133.

Croake, J. W., and Kelly, F. D. 2002. Structured group couples therapy with schizophrenic and bipolar patients and their wives. *The Journal of Individual Psychology.* 58(1): 76–86.

Cumsille, P. E., and Epstein, N. 1994. Family cohesion, family adaptability, social support, and adolescent depressive symptoms in outpatient clinic families. *Journal of Family Psychology.* 8(2): 202–214.

Dadds, M. R., Holland, D. E., Laurens, K. R., Mullins, M., Barrett, P. M., and Spence, S. H. 1999. Early intervention and prevention of anxiety disorders in children: Results at 2-year follow-up. *Journal of Consulting and Clinical Psychology.* 67(1): 145–150.

Dadds, M. R., Sanders, M. R., Morrison, M., and Rebgetz, M. 1992. Childhood depression and conduct disorder II. An analysis of family interaction patterns in the home. *Journal of Abnormal Psychology.* 101(3): 505–513.

Dadds, M. R., Spence, S. H., Holland, D. E., Barrett, P. M., and Laurens, K. R. 1997. Prevention and early intervention for anxiety disorders: A controlled trial. *Journal of Consulting and Clinical Psychology.* 65(4): 627–635.

Dakof, G. A., Rowe, C. L., Liddle, H. A., and Henderson, C. 2003, March. *Engaging and retaining drug abusing youth in home-based Multidimensional Family Therapy.* Poster presented at the NIMH/NIDA/NIAAA Conference, "Beyond the Clinic Walls: Expanding Mental Health, Drug and Alcohol Services Research Outside the Specialty Care System." Washington, DC.

Davidson, G. N. S., and Horvath, A. O. 1997. Three sessions of brief couples therapy: A clinical trial. *Journal of Family Psychology.* 11(4): 422–435.

Diamond, G. M., Liddle, H. A., Hogue, A., and Dakof, G. A. 1999. Alliance building interventions with adolescents in family therapy: A process study. *Psychotherapy.* 36: 355–368.

Diamond, G. S., and Liddle, H. A. 1996. Resolving a therapeutic impasse between parents and adolescents in multidimensional family therapy. *Journal of Consulting and Clinical Psychology.* 64: 481–488.

Diamond, G. S., Reis, B. F., Diamond, G. M., Siqueland, L., and Isaacs, L. 2002. Attachment based family therapy for depressive adolescents: A treatment development study. *Journal of the American Academy of Child and Adolescent Psychiatry.* 41: 1190–1196.

Diamond, G. S., Siqueland, L., and Diamond, G. M. 2003. Attachment-based family therapy for depressed adolescents: Programmatic treatment development. *Clinical Child and Family Psychology Review.* 6(2): 107–127.

Dishion, T. J., and Andrews, D. W. 1995. Preventing escalation of problem behaviors with high-risk young adolescents: Immediate and 1-year outcomes. *Journal of Consulting and Clinical Psychology.* 63(4): 538–548.

Dishion, T. J., and Kavanagh, K. 2000. A multilevel approach to family-centered prevention in schools: Process and outcome. *Addictive Behaviors.* 25(6): 899–911.

Doane, J. A., Miklowitz, D. J. Oranchak, E., Flores de Apodaca, R., Karno, M., Strachan, A. M., and Jenkins, J. H. 1989. Parental communication deviance and schizophrenia: A cross-cultural comparison of Mexican- and Anglo-Americans. *Journal of Abnormal Psychology.* 98(4) 487–490.

Downey, G., and Coyne, J. C. 1990. Children of depressed parents: An integrative review. *Psychological Bulletin.* 108(1): 50–76.

Dunn, R. L., and Schwebel, A. I. 1995. Meta-analytic review of marital therapy outcome research. *Journal of Family Psychology.* 9(1): 58–68.

Edwards, M. E., and Steinglass, P. 1995. Family therapy treatment outcomes for alcoholism. *Journal of Marital and Family Therapy.* 21(4): 475–509.

Epstein, E. E., and McCrady, B. S. 1998. Behavioral couples treatment of alcohol and drug use disorders: Current status and innovations. *Clinical Psychology Review.* 18(6): 689–711.

Estrada, A. U., and Pinsof, W. M. 1995. The effectiveness of family therapies for selected behavioral disorders of childhood. *Journal of Marital and Family Therapy. 21:* 403–440.

Falloon, I. R. H., Boyd, J. L., and McGill, C. W. 1984. *Family care of schizophrenia.* New York: Guilford.

Fals-Stewart, W., and Birchler, G. R. 1998. Marital interactions of drug-abusing patients and their partners: Comparisons with distressed couples and relationship to drug-using behavior. *Psychology of Addictive Behaviors. 12*(1): 28–38.

Fals-Stewart, W., and Birchler, G. R. 2001. A national survey of the use of couples therapy in substance abuse treatment. *Journal of Substance Abuse Treatment. 20:* 277–283.

Fals-Stewart, W., Birchler, G. R., and O'Farrell, T. J. 1996. Behavioral couples therapy for male substance-abusing patients: Effects on relationship adjustment and drug-using behavior. *Journal of Consulting and Clinical Psychology. 64*(5): 959–972.

Fals-Stewart, W., and O'Farrell, T. J. 2003. Behavioral Family Counseling and naltrexone for male opioid-dependent patients. *Journal of Consulting and Clinical Psychology. 71*(3): 432–442.

Fincham, F. K., Bradbury, T. N., and Beach, S. R. H. 1990. To arrive where we began: A reappraisal of cognition in marriage and in marital therapy. *Journal of Family Psychology. 4*(2): 167–184.

Fishman, H. C., Andes, F., and Knowlton, R. 2001. Enhancing family therapy: The addition of a community resource specialist. *Journal of Marital and Family Therapy. 27*(1): 111–116.

Forehand, R., Brody, G., Slotkin, J., Fauber, R., McCombs, A., and Long, N. 1988. Young adolescent and maternal depression: Assessment, interrelations, and family predictors. *Journal of Consulting and Clinical Psychology. 56*(3): 422–426.

Friedlander, M. L. 2001. Family therapy research: Science into practice, practice into science. In *Family therapy: Concepts and methods*, M. Nichols and R. Schwartz. Boston, MA: Allyn and Bacon.

Friedlander, M. L., Heatherington, L., Johnson, B., and Skowron, E. A. 1994. Sustaining engagement: A change event in family therapy. *Journal of Counseling Psychology. 41*(4): 438–448.

Friedlander, M. L., Wildman, J., Heatherington, L., and Skowron, E. A. 1994. What we do and don't know about the process of family therapy. *Journal of Family Psychology. 8*(4): 390–416.

Fristad, M. A., and Clayton, T. L. 1991. Family dysfunction and family psychopathology in child psychiatry outpatients. *Journal of Family Psychology. 5*(1): 46–59.

Fristad, M., Goldberg-Arnold, J., and Gavazzi, S. (2002). Multifamily psychoeducation groups (MFPG) for families of children with bipolar disorder. *Bipolar Disorder. 4:* 254–262.

Garfield, R. 2004. The therapeutic alliance in couples therapy: Clinical considerations. *Family Process. 43*(4): 457–465.

Geist, R., Heinmaa, M., Stephens, D., Davis, R., and Katzman, D. K. 2000. Comparison of family therapy and family group psychoeducation in adolescents with anorexia nervosa. *Canadian Journal of Psychiatry. 45:* 173–178.

Glynn, S. M., Eth, S., Randolph, E. T., Foy, D. W., Urbaitis, M., Boxer, L., Paz, G. G., Leong, G. B., Firman, G., Salk, J. D., Katzman, J. W., and Crothers, J. 1999. A test of behavioral family therapy to augment exposure for combat-related posttraumatic stress disorder. *Journal of Consulting and Clinical Psychology. 67*(2): 243–251.

Godley, S. H., White, W. L., Diamond, G. S., Passetti, L., and Titus, J. C. 2001. Therapist reactions to manual-guided therapies for the treatment of adolescent marijuana users. *Clinical Psychology: Science and Practice. 8*(4): 405–417.

Goldman, A., and Greenberg, L. 1992. Comparison of integrated systemic and emotionally focused approaches to couples therapy. *Journal of Consulting and Clinical Psychology. 60*(6): 962–969.

Goldman Sher, T., and Baucom, D. H. 1993. Marital communication: Differences among maritally distressed, depressed, and nondistressed-nondepressed couples. *Journal of Family Psychology. 7*(1): 148–153.

Goldman Sher, T., Baucom, D. H., and Larus, J. M. 1990. Communication patterns and response to treatment among depressed and nondepressed maritally distressed couples. *Journal of Family Psychology. 4*(1): 63–79.

Goldstein, M. J. 1987. Family interaction patterns that antedate the onset of schizophrenia and related disorders: A further analysis of data from a longitudinal prospective study. In *Understanding major mental disorder: the contribution of family interaction research*, K. Hahlweg and M. J. Goldstein, eds. New York: Family Process Press.

Goldstein, M. J., and Miklowitz, D. J. 1995. The effectiveness of psychoeducational family therapy in the treatment of schizophrenic disorders. *Journal of Marital and Family Therapy. 21:* 361–376.

Greenberg, L. S., Ford, C. L., Alden, L. S., and Johnson, S. M. 1993. In-session change in emotionally focused therapy. *Journal of Consulting and Clinical Psychology.* 61(1): 78–84.

Greenberg, L. S., and Johnson, S. M. 1988. *Emotionally focused therapy for couples.* New York: Guilford.

Hahlweg, K., and Markman, H. J. 1988. Effectiveness of behavioral marital therapy: Empirical status of behavioral techniques in preventing and alleviating marital distress. *Journal of Consulting and Clinical Psychology.* 56: 440–447.

Hahlweg, K., and Wiedemann, G. 1999. Principles and results of family therapy in schizophrenia. *European Archives of Psychiatry and Clinical Neuroscience. 249(Sup. 4):* 108–115.

Halford, W. K., Sanders, M. R., and Behrens, B. C. 1993. A comparison of the generalization of behavioral marital therapy and enhanced behavioral marital therapy. *Journal of Consulting and Clinical Psychology.* 61(1): 51–60.

Hawley, D. R., Bailey, C. E., and Pennick, K. A. 2000. A content analysis of research in family therapy journals. *Journal of Marital and Family Therapy.* 26(1): 9–16.

Heath, A. W., and Stanton, M. D. 1998. Family-based treatment: Stages and outcomes. In *Clinical textbook of addictive disorders,* 2nd ed., R. J. Frances and S. I. Miller, eds. New York: Guilford.

Heatherington, L., and Friedlander, M. L. 1990a. Applying task analysis to structural family therapy. *Journal of Family Psychology.* 4(1): 36–48.

Heatherington, L., and Friedlander, M. L. 1990b. Complementarity and symmetry in family therapy communication. *Journal of Counseling Psychology.* 37(3): 261–268.

Henderson, C. E., Greenbaum, P., Dakof, G. A., Rowe, C. L., and Liddle, H. A. 2004, August. Subtypes of treatment responses among substance abusing adolescents. In *Family-based treatment for adolescent drug abuse: New findings,* H. Liddle, chair, Symposium conducted at the annual convention of the American Psychological Association, Honolulu, Hawaii.

Henggeler, S. W., Borduin, C. M., Melton, G. B., Mann, B. J., Smith, L. A., Hall, J. A., Cone, L., and Fucci, B. R. 1991. Effects of multisystemic therapy on drug use and abuse in serious juvenile offenders: A progress report from two outcome studies. *Family Dynamics of Addiction Quarterly.* 1: 40–51.

Henggeler, S. W., Clingempeel, W. G., Brondino, M. J., and Pickrel, S. G. 2002. Four-year follow-up of Multisystemic therapy with substance-abusing and substance-dependent juvenile offenders. *Jour-*

nal of the American Academy of Child and Adolescent Psychiatry. 41(7): 858–874.

Henggeler, S. W., Melton, G. B., and Smith, L. A. 1992. Family preservation using Multisystemic Therapy: An effective alternative to incarcerating serious juvenile offenders. *Journal of Consulting and Clinical Psychology.* 60(6): 953–961.

Henggeler, S. W., Pickrel, S. G., and Brondino, M. J. 1999. Multisystemic treatment of substance abusing and dependent delinquents: Outcomes, treatment fidelity, and transportability. *Mental Health Services Research.* 1: 171–184.

Henggeler, S. W., Pickrel, S. G., Brondino, M. J., and Crouch, J. L. 1996. Eliminating (almost) treatment dropout of substance abusing or dependent delinquents through home-based Multisystemic Therapy. *American Journal of Psychiatry.* 153: 427–428.

Henggeler, S. W., Rodick, J. D., Borduin, C. M., Hanson, C. L., Watson, S. M., and Urey, J. R. 1996. Multisystemic treatment of juvenile offenders: Effects on adolescent behavior and family interaction. *Developmental Psychology.* 22: 132–141.

Hinrichsen, G. A., and Pollack, S. 1997. Expressed emotion and the course of late-life depression. *Journal of Abnormal Psychology.* 106(2): 336–340.

Hinton, W. J., Sheperis, C., and Sims, P. 2003. Family-based approaches to juvenile delinquency: A review of the literature. *The Family Journal.* 11: 167–173.

Hogue, A., Liddle, H. A., Becker, D., and Johnson-Leckrone, J. 2002. Family-based prevention counseling for high-risk young adolescents: Immediate outcomes. *Journal of Community Psychology.* 30: 1–22.

Hogue, A., Liddle, H. A., and Rowe, C. 1996. Treatment adherence process research in family therapy: A rationale and some practical guidelines. *Psychotherapy: Theory, Research, Practice, & Training.* 33: 332–345.

Hogue, A., Liddle, H. A., Rowe, C., Turner, R. M., Dakof, G., and LaPann, K. 1998. Treatment adherence and differentiation in individual versus family therapy for adolescent substance abuse. *Journal of Consulting and Clinical Psychology.* 45: 104–114.

Hogue, A., Liddle, H. A., Singer, A., and Leckrone, J. 2005. Intervention fidelity in family-based prevention counseling for adolescent problem behaviors. *Journal of Community Psychology.* 33(2): 191–211.

Hooley, J. M., and Teasdale, J. D. 1989. Predictors of relapse in unipolar depressives: Expressed emotion, marital distress, and perceived criticism. *Journal of Abnormal Psychology. 98*(3): 229–235.

Huey, S. J., Henggeler, S. W., Brondino, M. J., and Pickrel, S. G. 2000. Mechanisms of change in multisystemic therapy: Reducing delinquent behavior through therapist adherence and improved family and peer functioning. *Journal of Consulting and Clinical Psychology. 68*(3): 451–467.

Jackson-Gilfort, A., Liddle, H. A., Tejeda, M., and Dakof, G. 2001. Facilitating engagement of African American male adolescents in family therapy: A cultural theme process study. *Journal of Black Psychology. 27:* 321–340.

Jacobson, N. S., and Addis, M. E. 1993. Research on couples and couple therapy: What do we know? Where are we going? *Journal of Consulting and Clinical Psychology. 61*(1): 85–93.

Jacobson, N. S., Christensen, A., Prince, S. E., Cordova, J., and Eldridge, K. 2000. Integrative behavioral couple therapy: An acceptance-based, promising new treatment for couple discord. *Journal of Consulting and Clinical Psychology. 68*(2): 351–355.

Jacobson, N. S., Dobson, K., Fruzzetti, A. E., Schmaling, D. B., and Salusky, S. 1991. Marital therapy as a treatment for depression. *Journal of Consulting and Clinical Psychology. 59:* 547–557.

Jacobson, N. S., Fruzzetti, A. E., Dobson, K., Whisman, M., and Hops, H. 1993. Couple therapy as a treatment for depression II. The effects of relationship quality and therapy on depressive relapse. *Journal of Consulting and Clinical Psychology. 61*(3): 516–519.

Jacobson, N. S., Holtzworth-Munroe, A., and Schmaling, K. B. 1989. Marital therapy and spouse involvement in the treatment of depression, agoraphobia, and alcoholism. *Journal of Consulting and Clinical Psychology. 57*(1): 5–10.

Joanning, H., Quinn, Q., Thomas, F., and Mullen, R. 1992. Treating adolescent drug abuse: A comparison of family systems therapy, group therapy, and family drug education. *Journal of Marital and Family Therapy. 18:* 345–356.

Johnson, G., Kent, G., and Leather, J. 2005. Strengthening the parent-child relationship: A review of family interventions and their use in medical settings. *Child: Care, Health & Development. 31*(1): 25–32.

Johnson, S. M., and Greenberg, L. S. 1985. Emotionally focused couples therapy: An outcome study. *Journal of Marital and Family Therapy. 11:* 313–317.

Josephson, A. M., and Serrano, A. 2001. The integration of individual therapy and family therapy in the treatment of child and adolescent psychiatric disorders. *Child and Adolescent Psychiatric Clinics of North America. 10*(3): 431–450.

Kaiser, A., Hahlweg, K., Fehm-Wolfsdorf, G., and Groth, T. 1998. The efficacy of a compact psychoeducational group training program for married couples. *Journal of Consulting and Clinical Psychology. 66*(5): 753–760.

Kaslow, F. W., and Lebow, J. 2002. *Comprehensive handbook of psychotherapy: Vol. 4. Integrative/eclectic.* New York: John Wiley & Sons.

Kaslow, F. W., and Racusin, G. R. 1994. Family therapy for depression in young people. In *Handbook of depression in children and adolescents. Issues in clinical child psychology,* W. M. Reynolds and H. F. Johnston, eds. New York: Kluwer Academic Publishers.

Kazdin, A. E. 1991. Effectiveness of psychotherapy with children and adolescents. *Journal of Consulting and Clinical Psychology. 59*(6): 785–798.

Kazdin, A. E., Holland, L., and Crowley, M. 1997. Family experience of barriers to treatment and premature termination from child therapy. *Journal of Consulting and Clinical Psychology. 65*(3): 453–463.

Kazdin, A. E., Siegel, T. C., and Bass, D. 1992. Cognitive problem-solving skills training and parent management training in the treatment of antisocial behavior in children. *Journal of Consulting and Clinical Psychology. 60*(5): 733–747.

Kelly, M., and Newstead, L. 2004. Family intervention in routine practice: It is possible! *Journal of Psychiatric and Mental Health Nursing. 11*(1): 64–72.

Kelley, M. L., and Fals-Stewart, W. 2002. Couples- versus individual-based therapy for alcohol and drug abuse: Effects on children's psychosocial functioning. *Journal of Consulting and Clinical Psychology. 70*(2): 417–427.

Kilgore, K., Snyder, J., and Lentz, C. 2000. The contribution of parental discipline, parental monitoring, and school risk to early-onset conduct problems in African American boys and girls. *Developmental Psychology. 36*(6): 835–845.

Klein, K., Forehand, R., Armistead, L., and Long, P. 1997. Delinquency during the transition into early adulthood: Family and parenting predictors from early adolescence. *Adolescence. 32*(125): 61–80.

Klein, N. C., Alexander, J. F., and Parsons, B. V. 1977. Impact of family systems intervention on recidivism and sibling delinquency: A model of primary prevention and program evaluation. *Journal of Consulting and Clinical Psychology.* 45: 469–474.

Knobloch-Fedders, L. M., Pinsof, W. M., and Mann, B. J. 2004. The formation of the therapeutic alliance in couple therapy. *Family Process.* 43(4): 425–442.

Kolko, D. J., Brent, D. A., Baugher, M., Bridge, J., and Birmaher, B. 2000. Cognitive and family therapies for adolescent depression: Treatment specificity mediation, and moderation. *Journal of Consulting and Clinical Psychology.* 68(4): 603–614.

Krautter, T. H., and Lock, J. 2004a. Treatment of adolescent anorexia nervosa using family-based manualized treatment. *Clinical case studies.* 3(2): 107–123.

Krautter, T. H., and Lock, J. 2004b. Is manualized family-based treatment for adolescent anorexia nervosa acceptable to patients? Patient satisfaction at the end of treatment. *Journal of Family Therapy.* 26: 66–82.

Lattimer, P. J., Wagner, H. L., and Gowers, S. 2000. Conflict avoidance in anorexia nervosa: An observational study of mothers and daughters. *European Eating Disorders Review.* 8(5): 355–368.

Lavee, Y., and Altus, D. 2001. Family relationships as a predictor of post-treatment drug abuse relapse: A follow-up study of drug addicts and their spouses. *Contemporary Family Therapy: An International Journal.* 23(4): 513–530.

Lebow, J. L., and Gurman, A. S. 1995. Research assessing couple and family therapy. *Annual Review of Psychology.* 46: 27–57.

Lemmon, C. R., and Josephson, A. M. 2001. Family therapy for eating disorders. *Child and Adolescent Psychiatric Clinics of North America.* 10(3): 519–542.

Liddle, H. A. 2002a. Advances in family-based therapy for adolescent substance abuse: Findings from the Multidimensional Family Therapy research program. In *Problems of Drug Dependence 2001: Proceedings of the 63rd Annual Scientific Meeting,* L. S. Harris, ed. NIDA Research Monograph No. 182, NIH Publication 02–5097. Bethesda, MD: National Institute on Drug Abuse.

Liddle, H. A. 2002b. *Multidimensional Family Therapy for Adolescent Cannabis Users, Cannabis Youth Treatment (CYT) Series, Volume 5.* Center for Substance Abuse Treatment (CSAT), Rockville, MD.

Liddle, H. A., Bray, J. H., Levant, R. F., and Santisteban, D. A. 2001. Family psychology intervention science: An emerging area of science and practice. In *Family psychology: Science-based interventions,* H. A. Liddle, D. A. Santisteban, R. F. Levant, and J. H. Bray, eds. Washington, DC: American Psychological Association.

Liddle, H. A., Dakof, G., and Diamond, G. 1991. Adolescent substance abuse: Multidimensional family therapy in action. In *Family therapy approaches with drug and alcohol problems,* 2nd ed., E. Kaufman and P. Kaufmann, eds. Boston, MA: Allyn and Bacon.

Liddle, H. A., Dakof, G. A. Parker, K., Diamond, G. S., Barrett, K., and Tejeda, M. 2001. Multidimensional family therapy for adolescent substance abuse: Results of a randomized clinical trial. *American Journal of Drug and Alcohol Abuse.* 27(4): 651–687.

Liddle, H. A., Rowe, C. L., Dakof, G. A., Ungaro, R. A., and Henderson, C. E. 2004. Early intervention for adolescent substance abuse: Pretreatment to post-treatment outcomes of a randomized controlled trial comparing Multidimensional Family Therapy and peer group treatment. *Journal of Psychoactive Drugs.* 36: 49–63.

Lindahl, K. M. 1998. Family process variables and children's disruptive behavior problems. *Journal of Family Psychology.* 12(3) 420–436.

Lock, J., le Grange, D., Agras, W. S., and Dare, C. 2001. *Treatment manual for anorexia nervosa: A family-based approach.* New York: Guilford.

Long, P., Forehand, R., Wierson, M., and Morgan, A. 1994. Does parent training with young noncompliant children have long-term effects? *Behaviour Research and Therapy.* 32(1): 101–107.

Lopez, S. R., Nelson, K. A., Snyder, K. S., and Mintz, J. 1999. Attributions and affective reactions of family members and course of schizophrenia. *Journal of Abnormal Psychology.* 108(2): 307–314.

Lyon, M., Chatoor, I., Atkins, L., Silber, T., Mosimann, J., and Gray, J. 1997. Testing the hypothesis of the multidimensional model of anorexia nervosa in adolescents. *Adolescence,* 32(125): 101–111.

Mabe, P. A., Turner, K., and Josephson, A. M. 2001. Parent management training. *Child and Adolescent Psychiatric Clinics of North America.* 10(3): 451–474.

Maharaj, S., Rodin, G., Connolly, J., Olmsted, M., and Daneman, D. 2001. Eating problems and the observed quality of mother-daughter interactions among girls with type I diabetes. *Journal of Consulting and Clinical Psychology.* 69(6): 950–958.

Malone, C. A. 2001. Child and adolescent psychiatry and family therapy. *Child and Adolescent Psychiatric Clinics of North America.* 10(3): 395–413.

Mann, B. J., Borduin, C. M., Henggeler, S. W., and Blaske, D. M. 1990. An investigation of systemic conceptualizations of parent-child coalitions and symptom change. *Journal of Consulting and Clinical Psychology.* 58(3): 336–344.

Marcus, N. E., Lindahl, K. M., and Malik, N. M. 2001. Interparental conflict, children's social cognitions, and child aggression: A test of a mediational model. *Journal of Family Psychology.* 15(2): 315–333.

Marsh, D. T. 2001. *A family-focuses approach to serious mental illness: Empirically supported interventions.* Sarasota, FL: Professional Resource Press.

Marsh, D. T., and Johnson, D. L. 1997. The family experience of mental illness: Implications for intervention. *Professional Psychology: Research and Practice.* 28(3): 229–237.

Marsh, D. T., and Lefley, H. P. 2003. Family interventions for schizophrenia. *Journal of Family Psychotherapy.* 14(2): 47–68.

Mazzeo, S. E., and Espelage, D. L. 2002. Association between childhood physical and emotional abuse and disordered eating behaviors in female undergraduates: An investigation of the mediating role of alexithymia and depression. *Journal of Counseling Psychology.* 49(1): 86–100.

McCrady, B. S., and Ziedonis, D. 2001. American Psychiatric Association practice guideline for substance use disorders. *Behavior Therapy.* 32: 309–336.

McFarlane, W. R., Dixon, L., Lukens, E., and Luckstead, A. 2003. Family psychoeducation and schizophrenia: A review of the literature. *Journal of Marital and Family Therapy.* 29(2): 223–245.

McFarlane, W. R., Hornby, H., Dixon, L., and McNary, S. 2002. Psychoeducational multifamily groups: Research and implementation in the United States. In *Family interventions in mental illness: International perspectives,* H. P. Lefley and D. L. Johnson, eds. Westport, CT: Praeger.

McFarlane, W. R., Link, B., Dushay, R., Marchal, J., and Crilly, J. 1995. Psychoeducational multiple family groups: Four-year relapse outcome in schizophrenia. *Family Process.* 34: 127–144.

McGillicuddy, N. B., Rychtarik, R. G., Duquette, J. A., and Morsheimer, E. T. 2001. Development of a skill training program for parents of substance-abusing adolescents. *Journal of Substance Abuse Treatment.* 20: 59–68.

Mendlowitz, S. L., Manassis, K., Bradley, S., Scapillato, D., Miezitis, S., and Shaw, B. F. 1999. Cognitive-behavioral group treatments in childhood and anxiety disorders: The role of parental involvement. *Journal of the American Academy of Child and Adolescent Psychiatry.* 38: 1223–1229.

Meyers, R. J., Miller, W., and Smith, J. E. 2001. Community reinforcement and family training (CRAFT). In *A community reinforcement approach to addiction treatment. International research monographs in the addictions,* R. J. Meyers and W. R. Miller, eds. New York: Cambridge University Press.

Meyers, R. J., and Smith, J. E. 1995. *Clinical guide to alcohol treatment: The community reinforcement approach.* New York: Guilford.

Mihalopoulos, C., Magnus, A., Carter, R., and Vos, T. 2004. Assessing cost-effectiveness in mental health: Family interventions for schizophrenia and related conditions. *Australian and New Zealand Journal of Psychiatry.* 38: 511–519.

Miklowitz, D. J., George, E. L., Axelson, D. A., Kim, E. Y., Birmaher, B., Schneck, C., Beresford, C., Craighead, W. E., and Brent, D. A. 2004. Family-focused treatment for adolescent with bipolar disorder. *Journal of Affective Disorders.* 82(Sup.): S113–S128.

Miklowitz, D. J., Goldstein, M. J., and Nuechterlein, K. H. 1995. Verbal interactions in the families of schizophrenic and bipolar affective patients. *Journal of Abnormal Psychology.* 104(2): 268–276.

Miklowitz, D. J., Velligan, D. I., Goldstein, M. J., Nuechterlein, K. H., Gitlin, M. J., Ranlett, G., and Doane, J. A. 1991. Communication deviance in families of schizophrenic and manic patients. *Journal of Abnormal Psychology.* 100(2): 163–173.

Miller, I. W., Keitner, G. I., Whisman, M. A., Ryan, C. E., Epstein, N. B., and Bishop, D. S. 1992. Depressed patients with dysfunctional families: Description and course of illness. *Journal of Abnormal Psychology.* 101(4): 637–646.

Miller, J. K., and Slive, A. 2004. Breaking down the barriers to clinical service delivery: Walk-in family therapy. *Journal of Marital and Family Therapy.* 30(1): 95–103.

Miller, W. R., Meyers, R. J., and Tonigan, J. S. 1999. Engaging the unmotivated in treatment for alcohol problems: A comparison of three strategies for intervention through family members. *Journal of Consulting and Clinical Psychology.* 67(5): 688–697.

Minuchin, S., Rosman, B. L., and Baker, L. 1978. *Psychosomatic families: Anorexia nervosa in context.* Cambridge, MA: Harvard University Press.

Morojele, N. K., and Brook, J. S. 2001. Adolescent precursors of intensity of marijuana and other illicit drug use among adult initiators. *Journal of Genetic Psychology. 162*(4): 430–450.

Mueser, K. T., Sengupta, A., Schooler, N. R., Bellack, A. S., Xie, H., Glick, I. D., and Keith, S. J. 2001. Family treatment and medication dosage reduction in schizophrenia: Effects on patient social functioning, family attitudes, and burden. *Journal of Consulting and Clinical Psychology. 69*(1): 3–12.

National Institute for Clinical Excellence (NICE). 2002. *Schizophrenia core interventions in the management of schizophrenia in primary and secondary care.* London: HMSO.

National Institute on Drug Abuse (NIDA). 1999a. *National drug abuse treatment Clinical Trials Network (CTN).* RFA-DA-00-002. Retrieved May 15, 2004, from http://grants.nih.gov/grnats/guide/rfa-files/FRA-DA-00-002.html.

National Institute on Drug Abuse (NIDA). 1999b. *Scientifically based approaches to drug addiction treatment. In Principles of Drug Addiction Treatment: A research-based guide.* Rep. No. NIH publication No. 99-4180, pp. 35–47. Rockville, MD: National Institute on Drug Abuse.

National Institute on Drug Abuse (NIDA). 2002a. *Modifying and testing efficacious behavioral therapies to make them more community friendly.* RFA-DA-02-006. National Institute on Drug Abuse (www.nida.nih.gov).

National Institute on Drug Abuse (NIDA). 2002b. *Guidance for behavioral treatment providers: Research on knowledge and skill enhancement.* RFA-DA-03-005. Retrieved May 15, 2004, from http://grants.nih.gov/grants/guide/rfa-files/RFA-DA-03-005.html

Newberry, A. M., Alexander, J. F., and Turner, C. W. 1991. Gender as a process variable in family therapy. *Journal of Family Psychology. 5*(2): 158–175.

Nichols, M. P., and Fellenberg, S. 2000. The effective use of enactments in family therapy: A discovery-oriented process study. *Journal of Marital and Family Therapy. 26*(2): 143–152.

Northey, W. F., Wells, K. C., Silverman, W. K., and Bailey, C. E. 2003. Childhood behavioral and emotional disorders. *Journal of Marital and Family Therapy. 29*(4): 523–545.

Nye, C. L., Zucker, R. A., and Fitzgerald, H. E. 1995. Early intervention in the path to alcohol problems through conduct problems: Treatment involvement and child behavior change. *Journal of Consulting and Clinical Psychology. 63*(5): 831–840.

O'Farrell, T. J., and Fals-Stewart, W. 1999. Treatment models and methods: Family models. In *Addictions: A comprehensive guidebook,* B. S. McCrady and E. E. Epstein, eds. New York: Oxford University Press.

O'Farrell, T. J., and Fals-Stewart, W. 2003. Alcohol abuse. *Journal of Marital and Family Therapy. 29*(1):121–146.

O'Leary, K. D., and Beach, S. R. H. 1990. Marital therapy: A viable treatment for depression and marital discord. *American Journal of Psychiatry. 147:* 183–186.

Ogden, T., Forgatch, M., Askeland, E., Bullock, A., and Patterson, G. 2003. *Large scale dissemination and implementation of the PMTO model: The case of Norway.* Manuscript submitted for publication.

Ogden, T., and Halliday-Boykins, C. A. 2004. Multisystemic treatment of antisocial youth in Norway: Replication of clinical outcomes outside of the US. *Child and Adolescent Mental Health. 9*(2): 77–83.

Parker, G., and Hadzi-Pavlovic, D. 1990. Expressed emotion as a predictor of schizophrenic relapse: An analysis of aggregated data. *Psychological Medicine. 20*(4): 961–965.

Patterson, G. R. 1995. Coercion as a basis for early age of onset for arrest. In *Coercion and punishment in long-term perspectives,* J. McCord, ed. New York: Cambridge University Press.

Patterson, G. R., and Chamberlain, P. 1992. A functional analysis of resistance (A neobehavioral perspective). In H. Arkowitz, ed. *Why don't people change? New perspectives on resistance and noncompliance,* New York: Guilford.

Pavuluri, M. N., Grazyk, P. A., Henry, D. B., Carbray, J. A., Heidenreich, J., and Mikowitz, D. J. 2004. Child- and family-focused cognitive behavioral therapy for pediatric bipolar disorder: Development and preliminary results. *Journal of the American Academy of Child and Adolescent Psychiatry. 43*(5): 528–537.

Pinscf, W. M. 1989. A conceptual framework and methodological criteria for family therapy process research. *Journal of Consulting and Clinical Psychology. 57*(1): 53–59.

Pinsof, W. M., and Wynne, L. C. 2000. Toward progress research: Closing the gap between family therapy practice and research. *Journal of Marital and Family Therapy.* 26(1): 1–8.

Polivy, J., and Herman, P. C. 2002. Causes of eating disorders. *Annual Review of Psychology.* 53(1): 187–213.

Prinz, R. J., and Miller, G. E. 1994. Family-based treatment for childhood antisocial behavior: Experimental influences on dropout and engagement. *Journal of Consulting and Clinical Psychology.* 62(3): 645–650.

Rait, D. S. 2000. The therapeutic alliance in couples and family therapy. *JCLP/In Session: Psychotherapy in Practice.* 56(2): 211–224.

Ratti, L. A., Humphrey, L. L., and Lyons, J. S. 1996. Structural analysis of families with a polydrug-dependent, bulimic, or normal adolescent daughter. *Journal of Consulting and Clinical Psychology.* 64(6): 1255–1262.

Rea, M., Tompson, M., Miklowitz, D., Goldstein, M., Hwang, S., and Mintz, J. 2003. Family-focused treatment vs. individual treatment for bipolar disorder: Results of a randomized clinical trial. *Journal of Consulting and Clinical Psychology.* 71: 482–492.

Reiss, D., and Johnson-Sabine, E. 1995. Bulimia nervosa: 5-year social outcome and relationship to eating pathology. *International Journal of Eating Disorders.* 18(2): 127–133.

Robbins, M. S., Alexander, J. F., Newell, R. M., and Turner, C. W. 1996. The immediate effect of reframing on client attitude in family therapy. *Journal of Family Psychology.* 10(1): 28–34.

Robbins, M. S., Turner, C. W., Alexander, J. F., and Perez, G. A. 2003. Alliance and dropout in family therapy for adolescents with behavior problems: Individual and systemic effects. *Journal of Family Psychology.* 17(4): 534–544.

Robin, A. L., Siegel, P. T., Koepke, T., Moye, A. W., and Tice, S. 1994. Family therapy versus individual therapy for adolescent females with anorexia nervosa. *Developmental and Behavioral Pediatrics.* 15(2): 111–116.

Rojano, R. 2004. The practice of Community Family Therapy. *Family Process.* 43(1): 59–77.

Rotunda, R. J., Scherer, D. G., and Imm, P. S. 1995. Family systems and alcohol misuse: Research on the effects of alcoholism on family functioning and effective family interventions. *Professional Psychology: Research and Practice.* 26(1): 95–104.

Rowa, K., Kerig, P. K., and Geller, J. 2001. The family and anorexia nervosa: Examining parent-child boundary problems. *European Eating Disorders Review.* 9(2): 97–114.

Rowe, C. L., and Liddle, H. A. 2003. Substance abuse. *Journal of Marital and Family Therapy,* 29(1): 97–120.

Rowe, C. L., Liddle, H. A., McClintic, K., and Quille, T. 2002. Integrative treatment development: Multidimensional family therapy for adolescent substance abuse. In *Comprehensive handbook of psychotherapy. Volume 4: Integrative/Eclectic therapies,* F. Kaslow and J. Lebow, eds. New York: John Wiley and Sons.

Russell, G. F. M., Dare, C., Eisler, I., and LeGrange, P. D. F. 1994. Controlled trials of family treatments in anorexia nervosa. In *Psychobiology and the treatment of anorexia nervosa and bulimia nervosa,* K. A. Halmi, ed. Washington, DC: American Psychiatric Press.

Russell, G. F. M., Szmukler, G. I., Dare, C., and Eisler, I. 1987. An evaluation of family therapy in anorexia nervosa and bulimia nervosa. *Archives of General Psychiatry.* 44: 1047–1056.

Sanders, M. R., Markie-Dadds, C., Tully, L. A., and Bor, W. 2000. The Triple P-Positive Parenting Program: A comparison of enhanced, standard, and self-directed behavioral family intervention for parents of children with early onset conduct problems. *Journal of Consulting and Clinical Psychology.* 68(4): 624–640.

Santisteban, D. A., Coatsworth, J. D., Perez-Vidal, A., Kurtines, W., Schwartz, S. J., LaPerriere, A., and Szapocznik, J. 2003. Efficacy of Brief Strategic Family Therapy in modifying Hispanic adolescent behavior problems and substance use. *Journal of Family Psychology.* 17(1): 121–133.

Santisteban, D. A., Szapocznik, J., Perez-Vidal, A., Kurtines, W. M., Murray, E., and LaPerriere, A. 1996. Efficacy of intervention for engaging youth and families into treatment and some variables that may contribute to differential effectiveness. *Journal of Family Psychology.* 10(1): 35–44.

Schmidt, S. E., Liddle, H. A., and Dakof, G. A. 1996. Changes in parenting practices and adolescent drug abuse during multidimensional family therapy. *Journal of Family Psychology.* 10: 12–27.

Schoenwald, S. K., Ward, D. M., Henggeler, S. W., Pickrel, S. G., and Patel, H. 1996. MST treatment of substance abusing or dependent adolescent offenders: Costs of reducing incarceration, inpatient, and residential placement. *Journal of Child and Family Studies.* 5: 431–444.

Scholz, M., & Asen, E. 2001. Multiple family therapy with eating disordered adolescents: Concepts and preliminary results. *European Eating Disorders Review. 9:* 33–42.

Sexson, S. B., Glanville, D. N., and Kaslow, N. J. 2001. Attachment and depression: Implications for family therapy. *Child and Adolescent Psychiatric Clinics of North America. 10*(3): 465–486.

Sexton, T. L., and Alexander, J. F. (2002). Functional Family Therapy: An empirically supported, family-based intervention model for at-risk adolescents and their families. In *Comprehensive handbook of psychotherapy, volume II: Cognitive, behavioral, and functional approaches,* T. Patterson, ed. New York: John Wiley.

Shadish, W. R., Montgomery, L. M., Wilson, P., Wilson, M. R., Bright, I., and Okwumabua, T. 1993. Effects of family and marital psychotherapies: A meta-analysis. *Journal of Consulting and Clinical Psychology. 61*(6): 992–1002.

Shadish, W. R., Ragsdale, K., Glaser, R. R., and Montgomery, L. M. 1995. The efficacy and effectiveness of marital and family therapy: A perspective from meta-analysis. *Journal of Marital and Family Therapy. 21:* 345–360.

Shelef, K., Diamond, G. M., Diamond, G. S., and Liddle, H. A. 2005. Adolescent and parent alliance and treatment outcome in Multidimensional Family Therapy. *Journal of Consulting and Clinical Psychology. 73*(4).

Shields, C. G., and McDaniel, S. H. 1992. Process differences between male and female therapists in a first family interview. *Journal of Family Psychology. 18:* 143–151.

Simoneau, T. L., Miklowitz, D. J., Richards, J. A., Saleem, R., and George, E. L. 1999. Bipolar disorder and family communication: Effects of a psychoeducational treatment program. *Journal of Abnormal Psychology. 108*(4): 588–597.

Singer, M., and Wynne, L. 1965. Thought disorder and family relations of schizophrenics: IV. Results and implications. *Archives of General Psychiatry. 12:* 201–212.

Sisson, R. W., and Azrin, N. H. 1986. Family-member involvement to initiate and promote treatment of problem drinkers. *Behavior Therapy and Experimental Psychiatry. 17:* 15–21.

Slesnick, N., and Waldron, H. B. 1997. Interpersonal problem-solving interactions of depressed adolescents and their parents. *Journal of Family Psychology. 11*(2): 234–245.

Snyder, D. K., and Wills, R. M. 1989. Behavioral versus insight-oriented marital therapy: Effects on individual and interspousal functioning. *Journal of Consulting and Clinical Psychology. 57:* 39–46.

Snyder, D. K., Wills, R. M., and Grady-Fletcher, A. 1991. Long-term effectiveness of behavioral versus insight-oriented marital therapy: A 4-year follow-up study. *Journal of Consulting and Clinical Psychology. 59*(1): 138–141.

Snyder, J. J., and Patterson, G. R. 1995. Individual differences in social aggression: A test of a reinforcement model of socialization in the natural environment. *Behavior Therapy. 26*(2): 371–391.

Sonuga-Barke, E. J. S., Daley, D., Thompson, M., Laver-Bradbury, C., and Weeks, A. 2001. Parent-based therapies for preschool attention-deficit/hyperactivity disorder: A randomized, controlled trial with a community sample. *Journal of the American Academy of Child and Adolescent Psychiatry. 40:* 402–408.

Spence, S. H., Donovan, C., and Brechman-Toussaint, M. 2000. The treatment of childhood social phobia: The effectiveness of social skills training-based, cognitive behavioural intervention with and without parent involvement. *Journal of Child Psychology and Psychiatry. 41*(6): 713–726.

Stanton, M. D. 2004. Getting reluctant substance abusers to engage in treatment/self-help: A review of outcomes and clinical options. *Journal of Marital and Family Therapy. 30*(2): 165–182.

Stanton, M. D., and Shadish, W. F. 1997. Outcome, attrition, and family-couples treatment for drug abuse: A meta-analysis and review of the controlled, comparative studies. *Psychological Bulletin. 122*(2): 170–191.

Stark, K. D. 1990. *Childhood depression school-based intervention.* New York: Guilford.

Stark, K. D., Humphrey, L. L., Laurent, J., Livingston, R., and Christopher, J. 1993. Cognitive, behavioral, and family factors in the differentiation of depressive and anxiety disorders during childhood. *Journal of Consulting and Clinical Psychology. 61*(5): 878–886.

Steiner, H., and the Work Group on Quality Issues 1997. Practice parameters for the assessment and treatment of children and adolescents with conduct disorder. *Journal of the American Academy of Child and Adolescent Psychiatry. 36*(Sup. 10): 122S–139S.

Stoolmiller, M., Duncan, T., Bank, L., and Patterson, G. R. 1993. Some problems and solutions in the study of change: Significant patterns in client resistance. *Journal of Consulting and Clinical Psychology. 61*(6): 920–928.

Substance Abuse and Mental Health Services Administration (SAMHSA). 2001. *Summary of findings from the 2000 National Household Survey on Drug Abuse.* Rockville, MD: Author.

Symonds, D., and Horvath, A. O. 2004. Optimizing the alliance in couples therapy. *Family Process. 43:* 443–455.

Szapocznik, J., Perez-Vidal, A., Brickman, A., Foote, F. H., Santisteban, D. A., Hervis, O., and Kurtines, W. M. 1988. Engaging adolescent drug abusers and their families in treatment: A strategic structural systems approach. *Journal of Consulting and Clinical Psychology. 56*(4): 552–557.

Szapocznik, J., Rio, A., Murray, E., Cohen, R., Scopetta, M., Rivas-Vazquez, A., Hervis, O., Posada, V., and Kurtines, W. M. 1989. Structural family versus psychodynamic child therapy for problematic Hispanic boys. *Journal of Consulting and Clinical Psychology. 57*(5): 571–578.

Szapocznik, J., Rio, A., Perez-Vidal, A., Kurtines, W., and Santisteban, D. 1986. Family effectiveness training (FET) for Hispanic families. In *Cross-cultural training for mental health professionals,* P. B. Pederson and H. Lefley, eds. Springfield, IL: Charles C. Turner.

Szapocznik, J., and Williams, R. A. 2000. Brief strategic family therapy: Twenty-five years of interplay among theory, research and practice in adolescent behavior problems and drug abuse. *Clinical Child and Family Psychology Review. 3*(2): 117–134.

van Furth, E. F., van Strien, D.C., Martina, L. M. L., van Son, M. J. M., Hendrickx, J. J. P., and van Engeland, H. 1996. Expressed emotion and the prediction of outcome in adolescent eating disorders. *International Journal of Eating Disorders. 20*(1): 19–31.

Vaughn, C. E., and Leff, J. P. 1976. The influence of family and social factors on the course of psychiatric illness. *British Journal of Psychiatry. 129:* 125–137.

Vaughn, M. G., and Howard, M. O. 2004. Adolescent substance abuse treatment: A synthesis of controlled evaluations. *Research on Social Work Practice. 14*(5): 325–335.

Vuchinich, S., Bank, L., and Patterson, G. R. 1992. Parenting, peers, and the stability of antisocial behavior in preadolescnt boys. *Developmental Psychology. 28*(3): 510–521.

Wade, T. D., Treloar, S. A., and Martin, N. G. 2001. A comparison of family functioning, temperament, and childhood conditions in monozygotic twin pairs discordant for lifetime bulimia nervosa. *American Journal of Psychiatry. 158*(7): 1155–1157.

Waldron, H. B., Slesnick, N., Brody, J. L., Turner, C. W., and Peterson, T. R. 2001. Treatment outcomes for adolescent substance abuse at 4- and 7-month assessments. *Journal of Consulting and Clinical Psychology. 69*(5): 802–813.

Walitzer, K. S., and Dermen, K. H. 2004. Alcohol-focused spouse involvement and Behavioral Couples Therapy: Evaluation of enhancements to drinking reduction treatment for male problem drinkers. *Journal of Consulting and Clinical Psychology. 72*(6): 944–955.

Walker, J. G., Johnson, S., Manion, I., and Cloutier, P. 1996. Emotionally focused marital intervention for couples with chronically ill children. *Journal of Consulting and Clinical Psychology. 64*(5): 1029–1036.

Webster-Stratton, C. 1994. Advancing videotape parent training: A comparison study. *Journal of Consulting and Clinical Psychology. 62*(3): 583–593.

Webster-Stratton, C. 1996. Early intervention with videotape modeling. Programs for families of children with oppositional defiant disorder or conduct disorder. In *Psychosocial treatments for child and adolescent disorders: Empirically based strategies for clinical practice,* E. D. Hibbs & P. S. Jensen, eds. Washington DC: American Psychological Association.

Webster-Stratton, C., and Hammond, M. 1997. Treating children with early-onset conduct problems: A comparison of child and parent training interventions. *Journal of Consulting and Clinical Psychology. 65*(1): 93–109.

Webster-Stratton, C., Hollinsworth, T., and Kolpacoff, M. 1989. The long-term effectiveness and clinical significance of three cost-effective training programs for families with conduct-problem children. *Journal of Consulting and Clinical Psychology. 57*(4): 550–553.

Wells, K. C., Pelham, W. E., Kotkin, R. A., Hoza, B., Abikoff, H. B., Abramowitz, A., et al. 2000. Psychosocial treatment strategies in the MTA study: Rationale, methods, and critical issues in design and implementation. *Journal of Abnormal Psychology. 28:* 483–505.

Werner-Wilson, R. J., Price, S. J., Zimmerman, T. S., and Murphy, M. J. 1997. Client gender as a process variable in marriage and family therapy: Are women clients interrupted more than men clients? *Journal of Family Psychology.* 11(3): 373–377.

Whaley, S. E., Pinto, A., and Sigman, M. 1999. Characterizing interactions between anxious mothers and their children. *Journal of Consulting and Clinical Psychology.* 67: 826–836.

Whitbeck, L. B., Hoyt, D. R., Simons, R. L., Conger, R. D., Elder, G. H., Lorenz, F. O., and Huck, S. 1992. Intergenerational continuity of parental rejection and depressed affect. *Journal of Personality and Social Psychology.* 63(6): 1036–1045.

Wierson, M., and Forehand, R. 1994. Parent behavioral training for child noncompliance: rationale, concepts, and effectiveness. *Current Directions in Psychological Science.* 3(5): 146–150.

Willett, J. B., Ayoub, C. C., and Robinson, D. 1991. Using growth modeling to examine systematic differences in growth: An example of change in the functioning of families at risk of maladaptive parenting, child abuse, or neglect. *Journal of Consulting and Clinical Psychology.* 59(1): 38–47.

Williams, R. J., and Chang, S. Y. 2000. A comprehensive and comparative review of adolescent substance abuse treatment outcome. *Clinical Psychology: Science and Practice.* 7: 138–166.

Selected Readings

General Principles of Family Systems

Carter, B., and McGoldrick, M. 1999. *The expanded family lifecycle: A framework for family therapy*, 3rd ed. Boston: Allyn and Bacon.

Guerin, P. J., Fogarty, T. F., Fay, L. F., and Kautto, J. G. 1996. *Working with relationship triangles: The one-two-three of psychotherapy*. New York: Guilford Press.

Hoffman, L. 1981. *The foundations of family therapy*. New York: Basic Books.

Imber-Black, E., ed. 1993. *Secrets in families and family therapy*. New York: Norton.

Kerr, M. E., and Bowen, M. 1988. *Family evaluation*. New York: Norton.

Minuchin, S. 1974. *Families and family therapy*. Cambridge, MA: Harvard University Press.

Nichols, M. P. 1999. *Inside family therapy*. Boston: Allyn and Bacon.

Paolino, T. J., and McCrady, B. S., eds. 1978. *Marriage and marital therapy*. New York: Brunner/Mazel.

Watzlawick, P., Beavin, J., and Jackson, D. 1967. *Pragmatics of human communication*. New York: Norton.

Culture and Family Therapy

Boyd-Franklin, N. 1989. *Black families in therapy: A multisystems approach*. New York: Guilford Press.

Davis, L., and Proctor, E. 1989. *Race, gender, and class: Guidelines for practice with individuals, families and groups*. Englewood Cliffs, NJ: Prentice-Hall.

Greenan, D. E., and Tunnell, G. 2003. *Couple therapy with gay men*. New York: Guilford Press.

Pedersen, P. 1987. The frequent assumptions of cultural bias in counseling. *Journal of Multicultural Counseling and Development*. 15: 16–24.

Pinderhughes, E. 1989. *Understanding race, ethnicity, power: The key to efficacy in clinical practice*. New York: The Free Press.

Sue, D. W., and Sue, D. 1990. *Counseling the culturally different: Theory and practice*, 2nd ed. New York: Wiley.

Walsh, F. 1998. *Re-visioning family therapy*. New York: Guilford Press.

Marriage

Dicks, H. V. 1967. *Marital tensions*. New York: Basic Books.

Guerin, P. J., Fay, L., Burden, S., and Kautto, J. 1987. *The evaluation and treatment of marital conflict: A four-stage approach*. New York: Basic Books.

Lederer, W., and Jackson, D. 1968. *The mirages of marriage*. New York: Norton.

Lerner, H. G. 1985. *The dance of anger: A woman's guide to changing patterns of intimate relationships*. New York: Harper & Row.

Scarf, M. 1987. *Intimate partners: Patterns in love and marriage.* New York: Random House.

Solot, D., and Miller, M. 2002. *Unmarried to each other: The essential guide to living together as an unmarried couple.* New York: Marlow & Company.

In-Laws and the Extended Family

Guerin, P. J., ed. 1976. *Family therapy: Theory and practice.* New York: Gardner Press.

Lerner, H. G. 1989. *The dance of intimacy: A woman's guide to courageous acts of change in key relationships.* New York: Harper & Row.

McGoldrick, M., and Gerson, R. 1985. *Genograms in family assessment.* New York: Norton.

Families with Babies and Small Children

Brazelton, T. B. 1983. *Infants and mothers: Differences in development.* Rev. ed. New York: Dell.

Combrinck-Graham, L., ed. 1988. *Children in family contexts: Perspectives on treatment.* New York: Guilford Press.

Faber, A., and Mazlish, E. 1974. *Liberated parents, liberated children.* New York: Grosset & Dunlap.

Ginott, H. 1969. *Between parent and child.* New York: Macmillan.

Nichols, M. P. 2004. *Stop arguing with your kids.* New York: Guilford Press.

Patterson, G. 1975. *Families: Application of social learning theory to family life.* Champaign, IL: Research Press.

Families with Older Children

Bank, S., and Kahn, M. 1982. *The sibling bond.* New York: Basic Books.

Blos, P. 1979. *The adolescent passage: Developmental issues.* New York: International Universities Press.

Faber, A., and Mazlish, E. 1987. *Siblings without rivalry.* New York: Norton.

Fishel, E. 1979. *Sisters: Love and rivalry inside the family and beyond.* New York: Quill/William Morrow.

Micucci, J. 1998. *The adolescent in family therapy.* New York: Guilford Press.

Schlaadt, R., and Shannon, P. 1986. *Drugs of choice,* 2nd ed. Englewood Cliffs, NJ: Prentice-Hall.

Sells, S. 1998. *Treating the tough adolescent.* New York: Guilford Press.

Divorce, Remarriage, and Stepparenting

Ahrons, C., and Rodgers, R. 1987. *Divorced families: A multidisciplinary developmental view.* New York: Norton.

Isaacs, M. B., Montalvo, B., and Abelsohn, D. 1986. *The difficult divorce.* New York: Basic Books.

Vaughan, D. 1986. *Uncoupling: Turning points in intimate relationships.* New York: Oxford University Press.

Visher, E., and Visher, J. 1988. *Old loyalties, new ties: Therapeutic strategies with stepfamilies.* New York: Brunner/Mazel.

Leaving Home and the Postchildrearing Years

Levinson, D. 1978. *The seasons of a man's life.* New York: Ballantine.

Nichols, M. P. 1987. *Turning forty in the eighties.* New York: Fireside/Simon & Schuster.

Viorst, J. 1986. *Necessary losses.* New York: Simon & Schuster.

Family Therapy Technique

Anderson, C., and Stewart, S. 1983. *Mastering resistance: A practical guide to family therapy.* New York: Guilford Press.

Gerson, M. J. 1996. *The embedded self: A psychoanalytic guide to family therapy.* New York: Analytic Press.

Guerin, P. J., Fay, L., Burden, S., and Kautto, J. 1987. *The evaluation and treatment of marital conflict: A four-stage approach.* New York: Basic Books.

Isaacs, M. B., Montalvo, B., and Abelsohn, D. 1986. *The difficult divorce: Therapy for children and families.* New York: Basic Books.

Minuchin, S., and Fishman, H. C. 1981. *Family therapy techniques.* Cambridge, MA: Harvard University Press.

Minuchin, S., and Nichols, M. P. 1994. *Family healing: Tales of hope and renewal from family therapy.* New York: Touchstone/Simon & Schuster.

Taibbi, R. 1996. *Doing family therapy: Craft and creativity in clinical practice.* New York: Guilford Press.

White, M., and Epston, D. 1990. *Narrative means to therapeutic ends.* New York: Norton.

Careers and Training

Becoming a Family Therapist

There are many paths to becoming a family therapist. Not all of them involve going through an academic program in marital and family therapy, although that's the most direct path. Many people who have a state marital and family therapy (MFT) license or certificate graduated with a traditional degree—master's or Ph.D. in clinical psychology, an MSW from a social work program, or a master's in counseling or nursing. Depending on their state's requirements, these therapists, after completing their non-MFT degree, have to take some additional MFT course work and receive extensive supervision in order to be able to call themselves marital and family therapists (see the section on licensing that follows).

Which path you choose should depend on what you want to do in your career. For example, if you hope to teach or do research in family therapy, you would do well to go through a Ph.D. program. If, on the other hand, you primarily want to do clinical practice, either in an agency or in private practice, you may not need a Ph.D. and could go to one of the many master's programs in MFT (for a list of approved MFT academic programs, contact the American Association for Marriage and Family Therapy, described later).

If you're interested in studying an aspect of mental health not thoroughly covered in MFT programs, for example, psychological testing, social policy, individual psychotherapy, or psychopharmacology, you could get a non-MFT degree and then pick up the required courses and supervision from one of the many nonacademic family therapy institutes described in the last section of this appendix.

Professional Organizations

The *American Association for Marriage and Family Therapy* (AAMFT), located in Alexandria, VA, was organized in 1942 by Lester Dearborn and Ernest Graves as a professional organization to set standards for marriage counselors. In 1970 it was expanded to include family therapists and has become the major credentialing body for the field. Through its requirements for membership, standards have been set for becoming a family therapist that are used by the various states that regulate the profession. The AAMFT also lobbies state and federal governments for the interests of family therapists, such as state licensing.

Membership in AAMFT has grown enormously, reflecting the growth of the field. The organization has more than doubled since 1982 and now represents 23,000 marital and family therapists. This kind of membership and the money generated from it have made AAMFT a powerful player in mental health politics and have aided in public and governmental recognition of family therapy as a distinct field.

The AAMFT has a code of ethics that covers the following issues: responsibility to clients; confidentiality; professional competence and integrity; responsibility to students, employees, supervisees, and research subjects; financial arrangements; and advertising. The AAMFT is located at 112 S. Alfred Street, Alexandria, VA 22314; telephone: 703-838-9808; website: http://www.aamft.org.

Although the AAMFT has a presence in California, the dominant organization for MFTs there is the California Association of Marriage and Family Therapists (CAMFT). With 29 regional chapters and 25,000 members, CAMFT's size has given it a strong voice in the state legislature. CAMFT sponsors an annual conference and publishes the *California Therapist*. For further information, contact CAMFT, 7901 Raytheon Road, San Diego, CA 92111; telephone: 858-292-2638; website: http://www.camft.org.

The *American Family Therapy Academy* (AFTA) was organized in 1977 to serve the needs of the field's senior researchers, clinicians, and trainers who wanted a smaller, more intimate context for sharing ideas and developing common interests. Despite high standards for membership regarding years of teaching and clinical experience and an interest in remaining small, AFTA's membership has doubled since 1983, from 500 to over 1,000. AFTA is a high-level think tank focused around its annual conference, described in the next section, and its newsletter. For more information, contact AFTA, 1608 20th Street, NW, 4th Floor, Washington, DC 20009; telephone: 202-483-8002; website: www.afta.org.

The *International Family Therapy Association* (IFTA) was begun in 1987 as a way for family therapists around the globe to connect. Each year IFTA sponsors the World Family Therapy Congress in a different country. So far the countries that have hosted the congress include Finland, Greece, Holland, Ireland, Israel, Hungary, Mexico, Poland, Germany, the United States, Norway, Brazil, and Slovenia. In addition, IFTA biannually publishes *The International Connec-*tion. The official journal of IFTA is the *Journal of Family Psychotherapy*. IFTA can be reached at the Family Studies Center, Purdue University Calumet, Hammond, IN 46323; telephone: 219-989-2541; website: www.ifta-familytherapy.org.

Conferences

Besides the multitude of workshops or conferences privately sponsored or put on by local chapters of AAMFT, there are four main national meetings. The largest is AAMFT's annual conference each October. With over 200 presentations on various family therapy topics to select from, there is usually something for everyone.

The second largest (over 2,000) is the Psychotherapy Network Symposium held each March in Washington, D.C. Sponsored by the *Family Therapy Networker* magazine (described later), all presenters are invited so that quality throughout the eighty workshops is ensured. Each year the symposium has a theme, and invited plenary speakers are often famous for work done outside the field of family therapy. For information, telephone: 202-829-2452.

AFTA's annual meeting deliberately has a flavor different from that of other conferences. Because of its small size (usually around 300—it's not open to nonmembers), it's the one place where leaders of the field can gather in a relatively informal setting to discuss ideas. Rather than workshops, the meeting is organized around interest groups and brief presentations designed to promote dialogue and debate.

The other conference where many family therapists can be found isn't devoted exclusively to family therapy. The American Orthopsychiatric Association is a multidisciplinary organization whose annual conference usually contains a sizable percentage of presentations devoted to family therapy and issues of interest to systems-oriented clinicians.

Publications

The first book devoted entirely to the diagnosis and treatment of families was Nathan Ackerman's *The Psychodynamics of Family Life*, published in 1958. The field's first journal, *Family Process*, was founded in 1961. Since these early publications, the family therapy literature has proliferated to the point where it is virtually impossible to stay on top of it. We count over twenty journals or newsletters devoted to some aspect of family therapy published in the United States, with many other countries publishing their own journals. The number of books is equally overwhelming, so we refer the reader to Appendix A, *Selected Readings*, for a selective guide to some of the most useful books and articles in the field. We describe some of the major periodicals in the following discussion.

Family Process continues to exert a powerful influence on the field. Many of the debates and developments described in earlier chapters of this book appeared first in its pages. Founded in 1961 by Don Jackson and Nathan Ackerman, its editors have included Jay Haley, Don Bloch, Carlos Sluzki, Peter Steinglass, and Carol Anderson. The *Journal of Marital and Family Therapy* is also quite influential and, as the official journal of AAMFT, has a large readership. Under the editorship of Alan Gurman during the 1980s and Douglas Sprenkle and Froma Walsh in the 1990s, it increased its focus on research and improved its standards. Current editor, Ronald J. Chenail, is balancing the research and clinical foci.

The *Psychotherapy Networker*, a magazine devoted to issues related to family therapy and psychotherapy in general, also has a strong influence. Its large readership (over 70,000) has been won through tackling provocative issues with high-quality writing. Rich Simon has turned what began as a small newsletter into the most widely read publication on psychotherapy and, in doing so, has introduced many of family therapy's ideas to therapists throughout the country. In 1993, the *Networker* won the American Magazine Award for feature writing, the highest honor possible for a magazine.

Like *Family Process* and the *Journal of Marital and Family Therapy*, a number of other well-established journals are devoted to general issues in the field. These include the *American Journal of Family Therapy*, *Journal of Family Psychotherapy*, *International Journal of Family Therapy*, *Contemporary Family Therapy*, and *Family Therapy Collections*. In addition, a number of specialized journals have emerged. For example, the *Journal of Systemic Therapies* (formerly the *Journal of Strategic and Systemic Therapies*) is widely read by therapists who use those adjectives to describe themselves, whereas Bowen systems therapists read *Family Systems* and those interested in Michael White's work subscribe to the *Dulwich Centre Review* and *Family Therapy Case Studies*.

The cross-fertilization of family therapy with other fields is represented by *Families, Systems, and Health*, a journal devoted to the collaboration between medicine and family therapy; by the *Journal of Family Psychology*, published by a division of the American Psychological Association; and by *Feminism and Family Therapy*, which reflects the growing influence of feminist thought on the field.

News within the field and digests of important developments are conveyed through the AAMFT's newsletter, *Family Therapy News*, and through the *Marriage and Family Review* and the *Brown University Family Therapy Newsletter*. Those interested in the branch of sociology called family studies have much in common with family therapists and read *Family Relations* and the *Journal of Marriage and the Family*.

Licensing

Forty-eight states currently regulate MFTs, and several other states are currently considering licensing bills. Most state requirements for licensure are comparable to the standards for Clinical Membership in AAMFT. Common requirements include graduation from an accredited marital and family therapy program, two years of post-degree supervised clinical experience, and passing the state exam (eighteen states require this) or the national exam for MFTs, which is conducted by the Association of Marital and Family Therapy Regulatory Board.

Training Centers

As discussed earlier, family therapy developed primarily outside academia. However, a handful of doctoral programs and a larger number of master's degree programs specialize in marital and family therapy in universities around the country. The American Association for Marriage and Family Therapy accredits seventy-five graduate and postgraduate programs. Because we are aware of no comparable list of the major nonacademic training centers, we describe some of the best-known centers in the United States here. Although other major centers exist throughout the world, our space is too limited to list them here. The reader may notice that the majority of the centers described are clustered in the Northeast where family therapy is most strongly rooted. We begin there and move west.

The *Family Institute of Cambridge* in Massachusetts was founded in 1976. Now located in Watertown, it is a nonprofit center of training and research in applied systems theory. Faculty members include such notable therapists as Michele Bograd, Laura Chasin, Richard Chasin, Terry Real, Kathy Weingarten, and Sallyann Roth. The institute offers four training sequences: (1) narrative approaches, (2) family systems theory, (3) couples therapy, and (4) women's group process. The institute also offers a wide variety of long- and short-term courses, group supervision, and conferences; it has some research stipends for its students. For more information, contact Suzanne Bourque, 51 Kondazian Street, Watertown, MA 02172.

The *Kantor Family Institute*, in Somerville, Massachusetts, was founded by David Kantor after he left the Family Institute of Cambridge in 1980. It is informed by his structural/analytic model of therapy, as well as by psychodynamic and other family therapy influences. This institute offers a sequence of three one-year training programs that build on each other but can be taken independently. They also offer a special-

ized program in couples treatment and in organizational consultation, as well as a variety of apprenticeships, internships, and courses. For more information, contact Ulrike Dettling, Kantor Family Institute, 7 Shepard Street, Cambridge, MA 02138.

The *Minuchin Center for the Family* is a nonprofit training and consultation institute in New York City, founded in 1981 by Salvador Minuchin. The faculty also includes David Greenan, Richard Holm, and Wai-Yung Lee. Special programs are designed for on-site training and consultation with agencies that work with poor families, foster care, substance abuse, the homeless, and children in psychiatric facilities. The extern training program is at three levels: beginning family therapists, more experienced therapists, and supervision for supervisors. The orientation emphasizes structural family therapy but has been influenced by feminism and multiculturalism. A summer intensive and one-day workshops offer clinicians with limited time opportunities to study at the Center. Inquiries may be directed to David Greenan, Executive Director, 114 East 32nd Street, New York, NY 10016 or to the website: www.minuchincenter.org.

The *Ackerman Institute for the Family* in New York City was founded as the Family Institute by Nathan Ackerman in 1960. Following Ackerman's death in 1971, the center was renamed in his honor and the directorship was assumed by Donald Bloch, who recently passed the baton to Peter Steinglass. In addition to Bloch and Steinglass, the institute has such noted family therapists and theorists as Peggy Penn, Peggy Papp, Jorge Colapinto, Olga Silverstein, Marcia Scheinberg, Virginia Goldner, Peter Fraenkel, and Gillian Walker. The institute offers training in systemic family therapy. It offers a two-year clinical externship program for more experienced family therapists and weekend workshops throughout the year. For further information contact Marcia Sheinberg, Director of Training and Clinical Services, 149 East 78th Street, New York, NY 10021.

The *Family Institute of Westchester* in Harrison, New York, is directed by Elliott Rosen. The institute teaches the multicontextual approach, which includes aspects of structural and strategic techniques, and is based on the Bowenian model. The institute has been in operation since 1977 and is primarily known for its training program, which usually takes three years to complete. There is also a two-year externship that meets weekly. Specialized training programs are offered in multicultural family therapy and therapy with gay and lesbian couples and families. Additional information is available from Pat Colucci-Coritt, Director of Training, Family Institute of Westchester, 600 Mamaroneck Ave., Suite 303, Harrison, NY 10528.

The *Center for Family Learning* in Rye Brook, New York, was founded in 1973 by Philip Guerin, who was trained by Murray Bowen. The center has maintained a threefold mission for thirty years: the development of family systems models of clinical intervention; postgraduate education in these models; and community education through the mechanism of public meetings and cable television. Postgraduate training is tailored to the specific educational needs of individuals, groups, or organizations. For additional information, contact Patricia Schmolling, Administrator, at 16 Rye Ridge Plaza, Suite 228, Rye Brook, NY 10573. Telephone: 914-253-9190 or e-mail at PJGuerinM.D.@aol.com.

The *Family Therapy Training Program at the University of Rochester* was established in 1983 by Judith Landau-Stanton and M. Duncan Stanton. This program teaches the Rochester model, an integration of structural, strategic, transgenerational, experiential, and ecosystemic approaches in a series of externships and seminars. Special areas of interest are cultural transition and medical family therapy. Cases are provided for trainees. The faculty includes Lyman Wynne, Susan McDaniel, David Seaburn, and the founders. For more information, contact Pieter le Roux, Director, Family Therapy Training Program, Department of Psychiatry, University of Rochester, 300 Crittenden Boulevard, Rochester, NY 14642-8409.

The *Multicultural Family Institute* was founded in 1991 by its directors, Monica McGoldrick and Nydia Garcia Preto. The institute is committed to training, research, and service in support of cultural diversity and the empowerment of those voices our society silences. In addition to a two-year certificate program and an annual cultural conference, the institute offers a variety of workshops, lectures to the community, and consultation to schools and other organizations. Minority scholarships are available. Other notable therapists participating on the faculty include Eliana Gil, Paulette Moore Hines, Rhea Almeida, and Charlesetta Sutton. For further information contact Monica McGoldrick, 328 Denison St., Highland Park, NJ 08904; telephone: 732-565-9010; website: www.multiculturalfamily.org.

The *International Institute of Object Relations Therapy* is led by codirectors David and Jill Scharff and is located in the suburbs of Washington, D.C. Formerly at the Washington School of Psychiatry, the Scharffs are the leading exponents of object relations family therapy. The institute has a variety of training programs, speakers, and workshops, including two-year courses in Object Relations Theory and Couple, Child, and Family Therapy. Both programs consist of weekly seminars and two-week summer institutes. In addition to the Scharffs, the faculty includes many distinguished clinicians from throughout the world (notably from the Tavistock Center). In addition to its headquarters in Washington, D.C., the institute has satellite programs in Burlington, VT; Charlottesville, VA; Long Island, NY; Manhattan, NY; New Orleans, LA; Omaha, NE; Philadelphia, PA; Salt Lake City, UT; San Diego, CA; and Panama City, the Republic of Panama. For more information, telephone: 301-215-7377; e-mail: iiort@mindspring.com; website: www.iiort.org; or write David Scharff, M.D. and Jill Savege Scharff, M.D., Codirectors, International Institute of Object Relations Therapy, 6612 Kennedy Drive, Chevy Chase, MD 20815-6504.

The *Georgetown Family Center*, located in Washington, DC, exists to refine, test, and extend, Bowen systems theory. Murray Bowen founded and directed this center until his death in 1990. Michael Kerr, Daniel V. Papero, and Ruth Riley

Sagar comprise the current Board of Directors. Training programs include a weekly postgraduate program and a special program for out-of-towners that meets for three consecutive days, four times a year. Other learning opportunities include the monthly Clinical Conference Series and the annual Main Symposium. Descriptions of these programs are available from Daniel Papero, Director of Training, Georgetown Family Center, 4400 MacArthur Boulevard NW, Suite 103, Washington, D.C. 20007.

The *Family Therapy Practice Center of Washington, DC*, was founded in 1980 by Marianne Walters, after she left the Philadelphia Child Guidance Clinic. The center has a structural family therapy base and offers a postgraduate externship. In addition, the center develops programs for dealing with at-risk populations and changing family structures such as their adolescent foster care project, family violence assistance project, and runaway youth/multiple family group project. For more information, contact Director of Training, 2153 Newport Place NW, Washington, D.C. 20037.

The *Philadelphia Child and Family Training Center, Inc.* was created in the late 1990s to continue the training programs previously conducted at the famous Philadelphia Child Guidance Center. Most of the center's faculty taught at the former institution and worked there with Salvador Minuchin as he developed structural family therapy. Faculty include notable structural therapists: Marion Lindblad-Goldberg, Ann Itzkowitz, Iolie Walbridge, and C. Wayne Jones. The center runs a two-year, COAMFTE-accredited postgraduate program, a three-week summer practicum, AAMFT-approved correspondence courses, and an AAMFT-approved supervision of supervision course. Traveling faculty conduct training in agencies and institutions nationally and abroad. The center is known for its development of mental health home-based services and training. For more information contact Marion Lindblad-Goldberg, Director, Philadelphia Child and Family Therapy Training Center, Inc., P. O. Box 4092, Philadelphia, PA 19118-8092.

The *Brief Family Therapy Center* (BFTC) of Milwaukee is known for its specialization in the research, training, and clinical practice of brief, solution-focused therapy. BFTC provides short- and long-term training in solution-focused therapy that attracts practitioners from across North America, Europe, and Asia. The staff includes Steve de Shazer and Insoo Kim Berg, who have presented workshops and seminars in more than thirty countries and have written extensively on solution-focused therapy. For further information, contact Brief Family Therapy Center, P.O. Box 13736, Milwaukee, WI 53213.

The *Family Institute at Northwestern University* (formerly of Chicago) was founded in 1968 by Charles Kramer to provide training, research, and clinical services. William Pinsof is the president of the institute, which probably has the largest full-time faculty in the country, including notable family therapists Douglas Breunlin, Cheryl Rampage, and Jay Lebow. They offer a variety of training programs grounded in a multilevel, integrative approach. Elements of the approach include integrative problem-centered therapy, the metaframeworks perspective, feminism, and multiculturalism. They offer a two-year certificate program that is accredited by AAMFT, a master's program in family therapy in affiliation with Northwestern University, a one-year clinical training practicum, a psychology internship, a postgraduate fellowship, and a variety of courses, consultation, continuing education workshops, and conferences. In 1994 the institute opened a spacious new facility in Evanston, Illinois. For more information, contact The Family Institute, Bette D. Harris Center, 618 Library Place, Evanston, IL 60201; telephone: 847-733-4300.

The *Chicago Center for Family Health* (CCFH) was begun in 1991 by codirectors John Rolland and Froma Walsh. Affiliated with the University of Chicago, the center's strengths-based family resilience orientation integrates systems theory with a multigenerational family life-cycle framework. In addition to general training in family therapy, CCFH offers specialized training in couples therapy, school-based partnerships, divorce mediation, and family-oriented health care. Training programs include a two-year certificate program, workshops and courses, and consultation groups. Faculty also includes other notable family therapists such as Gene Combs, Jill Freedman, and Tom Todd. For more information, contact CCFH, Suite 2700, 35 E. Wacker Drive, Chicago, IL 60601; telephone: 312-372-4731.

The *Houston Galveston Institute*, a private, nonprofit organization, was founded in 1977 by Harlene Anderson and the late Harry Goolishian. The orientation of the institute is a "collaborative language systems approach" that emphasizes openness, sharing of clinical experiences, live consultation, and observation of faculty work. Programs include (1) residential (fellowships, internships, and apprenticeships); (2) external programs (externships, seminars, supervision, and workshops); and (3) international visitor study programs. For more information, contact Susan Levin, 3316 Mount Vernon, Houston, TX 77006.

The *Mental Research Institute* (MRI) in Palo Alto, California, was founded in 1969 by the late Don Jackson and is considered one of the birthplaces of family therapy. The MRI is best known for its brief therapy approach to families. Its faculty includes such notable names as Paul Watzlawick, Richard Fisch, and Arthur Bodin. The MRI offers a wide variety of training programs, including workshops, continuing seminars, four- or six-week residency programs, and programs in brief therapy or in Michael White's approach. A program for on-site training has also begun recently. For further information, contact Director of Training, 555 Middlefield Road, Palo Alto, CA 94301.

Name Index

Subject Index

Photo Credits

p. 4, National Library of Medicine; p. 15, Photo courtesy of Lyman Wynne and used with his permission: p. 19, Photo courtesy of Wendel Ray. Used with permission of the Jackson Estate of the Don D. Jackson Archive, MRI; p. 73, Photo courtesy of the Psychotherapy Networker. Used with permission of Monica McGoldrick; p. 82, Photo courtesy of Andrea Mahoney Schara and used with her permission; p 83, Photo courtesy of the Psychotherapy Networker. Used with permission of Philip J. Guerin; p. 87, Photo courtesy of Betty Carter and used with her permission; p. 103, Photo courtesy of the Milton Erickson Foundation, www.erickson-foundation.org. Used with permission of Jeffrey K. Zeig; p. 104, Photo courtesy of Jay Haley and used with his permission; p. 114, Photo courtesy of Cloe Madanes and used with her permission; p. 127, Photo courtesy of the Psychotherapy Networker. Used with permission of Salvador Minuchin; p. 148, Photo courtesy of the Psychotherapy Networker. Used with permission of Muriel V. Whitaker; p. 149, Photo courtesy of the Psycho-

therapy Networker. Used with permission of Avanta, The Virginia Satir Network, 2104 SW 152nd Street #2 Burien, WA 98166. www.avanta.net. All rights reserved; p. 177, Photo courtesy of the Psychotherapy Networker. Used with permission of David and Jill Scharff; p. 194, Amy Etra/PhotoEdit; p. 214, Photo courtesy of the Psychotherapy Networker. Used with permission of Peggy Papp, Olga Silverstein. Marianne Walters, and Betty Carter; p. 219, Photo courtesy of the Psychotherapy Networker. Used with permission of Nancy Boyd-Franklin; p. 249 (top), Photo courtesy of Steve de Shazer and used with his permission; p. 249 (bottom), Photo courtesy of Insoo Kim Berg and used with her permission; p. 265, Photo courtesy of Michael White and used with his permission; p. 266, Robert Clay; p. 288, Photo courtesy of the Psychotherapy Networker. Used with permission of Virginia Goldner; p. 299, Richard Lord Enterprises, Inc./The Image Works; p. 313, Photo courtesy of Jose Szapocznik and used with his permission.

Text Credits

p. 154, From Steve Andreas, *Virginia Satir: The Patterns of Her Magic*. Reprinted by permission of Science and Behavior Books; p. 290, From Laura Markowitz, *Family Therapy Networker. 21*: 25–26. Reprinted by permission of the *Family Therapy Networker.*